THE  TIMES

GREAT WOMEN'S LIVES

THE TIMES

GREAT WOMEN'S LIVES

A CELEBRATION IN OBITUARIES

EDITED BY SUE CORBETT

The History Press

First published 2014
This paperback edition published 2019

The History Press
97 St George's Place, Cheltenham
Gloucestershire, GL50 3QB
www.thehistorypress.co.uk

British Library Cataloguing in Publication Data.
A catalogue record for this book is available from the British Library.

ISBN 978 0 7509 9255 8

Typesetting and origination by The History Press
Printed and bound in Great Britain by TJ International Ltd.

CONTENTS

FOREWORD

A GIRL'S GUIDE TO GREATNESS

by Lucy Worsley

What is it that makes a woman great? The answer, as revealed in these 125 obituaries from *The Times* newspaper, has changed over time in ways that can't fail to fascinate.

One of the encouraging themes of the collection is that scientists, writers, performers, politicians and campaigners are not born, nor are they made. They make themselves. And a soaring rise from a humble background certainly makes for a good obituary. We learn that Eva Perón, First Lady of Argentina, was a "Cinderella in real life" to the young people she inspired, and I was tickled to discover that the Labour politician Barbara Castle began her career selling crystallised fruit in a Manchester department store while dressed as "Little Nell". A tragic death cutting off early promise also makes for a striking story: aviator Amy Johnson at 37 in 1941; troubled singer Amy Winehouse at 27 in 2011; mountaineer Alison Hargreaves on K2 at only 33 in 1995.

It might not surprise the cynical to discover how important good looks have been to the greatness of women, or at least so it has been in the eyes of their obituarists. The suffragette Christabel Pankhurst, we hear, was "a most attractive young woman with fresh colouring, delicate features, and a mass of soft brown hair". Striking looks, constantly mentioned, sometimes had unusual consequences: the blue-eyed Swedish soprano Jenny Lind, for instance, gave her name to a breed of potatoes with blue specks on their skins. The only woman in the whole collection whose looks are disparaged seems to be George Eliot, notable for "her resemblance to Savonarola". With all this emphasis on appearance, I don't blame Joan Crawford in the slightest for keeping her birthdate so secret that *The Times* was only able to give her age at death as falling somewhere in the range between 69 and 76.

And being nice has been just as good as being skilled at what you do. It's a strain that persists surprisingly, and depressingly, far through the collection's chronology. Among the earlier subjects, Christina Rossetti produced writing that manifested "purity of thought", while it was the happy lot of Elizabeth Garrett Anderson, the first female doctor to qualify in England, to "emerge not only successful but still a 'womanly woman'". But when you reach obituaries from the late twentieth century, the convention of the lovely lady persists in ways that read almost like a parody: the crystallographer Dame Kathleen Lonsdale was described in 1971 as looking "in no way unfeminine", despite having "golliwog" hair, and is praised for having "made herself a neat hat for a few shillings" for a visit to Buckingham Palace. "The most successful princesses in history," claims the obituary of Diana, Princess of Wales, in 1997, "have been those who loved children and cared for the sick." Not exactly an uncontestable statement.

Because of the same convention of niceness, the early obituaries sometimes have difficulty in expressing what they're talking about. Philanthropist Baroness Burdett-Coutts founded a "Home" at Shepherd's Bush for single mothers, which was euphemistically described as "one of the earliest practical attempts to reclaim women who had lost their characters". It's actually quite hard to puzzle out exactly what Josephine Butler did, so obliquely is it described in her obituary. She's hailed as "a woman of extreme delicacy and refinement of mind, with a horror... of contact with vice". In fact she campaigned against the Contagious Diseases Act, which decreed that, on the mere say-so of a policeman, a woman could have her private parts inspected for venereal disease and be imprisoned if she refused.

If you can't be nice, however, be difficult. This theme emerges as the decades pass. Here Bette Davis excelled ("Nobody's as good as Bette when she's bad"), while the French actress Sarah Bernhardt slept in a coffin and killed her pet alligator by giving it too much champagne. And being angry works, too. Coco Chanel, inventor of the strappy sandal and the cardigan jacket, had a comeback in the 1950s inspired by the "irritation of seeing Paris fashion taken over by men designers". Pat Smythe, international showjumper, might have been equally chagrined at being given a silver cigar box for winning a competition with the words: "Sorry about this, we were not expecting a woman rider to be as good as you." Being uncommunicative seems an excellent means of finding the time to get on with being great. Elizabeth David, the cookery writer, instructed directory enquiries not to tell anyone her number, "under any circumstances, even in case of death", while Barbara McClintock, Nobel Prize-winning scientist, said that "anyone who wanted to talk to her... could write a letter".

Being on the left politically will definitely help you achieve greatness, because it puts you in the vanguard of struggle and change. We have "Red Ellen", the

Labour MP Ellen Wilkinson (following the rules about good looks above, she nevertheless had an "oddly picturesque person") and "the Red Dame", actress and CND supporter Peggy Ashcroft. Movingly, the former "Little Nell", Barbara Castle, gets a standing ovation at the Labour Party Conference at the age of 86 even before having reached the microphone.

Most of all, though, it's courage that's celebrated here. Courage is what links Emmeline Pankhurst, campaigner for votes for women, who was "of the stuff of which martyrs are made", to Odette Hallowes, who had her toenails pulled out during the war for her Resistance work. She shares it too with Marian Anderson, the first black singer to appear at the Metropolitan Opera in New York. Refused tuition at a Philadelphia music school on the grounds that "we don't take coloured", Anderson reportedly trembled when she first stood on the stage of the Met. In her own words, though, it was worth it: "My mission is to leave behind me a kind of impression that will make it easier for those who follow."

Well, all of these women have done this wonderfully well – even the ones with messy hair.

INTRODUCTION

by Sue Corbett

The 125 *Times* obituaries of great women in this volume had their genesis in the second issue of the paper, on Monday, January 3, 1785. *The Times* started life (as the *Daily Universal Register*) on Saturday, January 1, 1785, without any obituaries as the modern reader would understand the word. There were, instead, death notices, just two, very brief. By the following Monday, the number had doubled to four, with the addition, this time, of a dash of human interest. Two of the deceased were described as Mrs Alice Hermen, 93, a "native of Hanover and nurse to the late Prince Frederic", and Mrs Margaret Scurral, who had "retained all her faculties (sight only excepted) till within a fortnight of her death" at the even more astonishing age, for that time, of 108.

These two intriguing little Georgian snippets offered a small foretaste of the first golden age of *Times* obituaries, which still lay decades away in the Victorian era (at the conclusion of which the paper would devote a 49,741-word obituary to Queen Victoria and her epoch). Meanwhile, lengthier obituaries did begin to appear, but haphazardly, so that in 1802 a Lord Chief Justice would receive upwards of 300 words, but in 1822 the death of Percy Bysshe Shelley received no attention whatsoever. Again, in 1825 the Earl of Carlisle's death was deemed worthy of an obituary of 327 words, even though the piece itself acknowledged that his lordship "never attained any great distinction as a politician, a legislator, an author, or a man of talent", while the novelist Lady Caroline Lamb's death three years later was marked by just 125 words that defined her almost entirely in terms of the men whose daughter, sister, wife and daughter-in-law she had been.

A more orderly approach was imposed by John Thadeus Delane, *Times* editor from 1841 to 1877, who instituted the practice, which survives today, of preparing detailed, authoritative obituaries of the more important and influential personalities of the day while they are still alive. He oversaw the new regime himself because there would be no *Times* obituaries editor as such until the 1920s. And so, when the hero of Waterloo died on September 14, 1852, it was Delane who ordained that, in the paper the following day, "Wellington's death will be the only topic." Obituaries set in train by Delane were often very long, but none surpassed the wordage allotted the Iron Duke. Under the heading, "Death of the Duke of Wellington", the obituary ran to 30,674 words on September 15, and a further 16,013 the next day.

Delane's hand can also be seen in *The Times*'s lengthy tribute to Queen Victoria on January 23, 1901. Although her death the evening before occurred nearly a quarter of a century after he had retired, it is inconceivable, given the obituary's length and the myriad topics it covered, that Delane wouldn't, while still in office, have commissioned an obituary to be updated as necessary.

Delane was not, however, in the habit of handing out very many column inches to other female notables of the time (of whom there were comparatively very few, of course, most professions being closed to women). The composer Fanny Mendelssohn's death in May 1847, for example, passed completely unnoticed in *The Times*. Her name did not even feature in her beloved brother Felix's 989-word obituary in the paper when he died six months afterwards.

And the paper's only acknowledgment of Gothic novelist Mary Wollstonecraft Shelley, author of *Frankenstein*, when she died in February 1851, was to print a 21-word death notice, misspelling Wollstonecraft and simply describing her as "widow of the late Percy Bysshe Shelley, aged 53".

Charlotte Brontë's obituary in 1855, borrowed by *The Times* from the *Manchester Guardian*, amounted to just 86 words and Brontë's biographer, the novelist Elizabeth Gaskell, was given only 207 words when she died in 1865 – these, too, reprinted from another publication, this time *The Globe*. Delane's reforms were clearly not yet all they might have been.

It is the 1872 obituary of the scientist and mathematician Mary Somerville (pp. 16-18) that marks a new deal for women. The first of the obituaries of prominent women reproduced in this volume, it is detailed, authoritative and, at 1,240 words, remarkably long for a woman's obituary of that era. It does lack the human interest that a modern obituarist strives for – the "telling anecdotes" and domestic details – but this was provided two days later when a letter to the editor was published from a friend of the great woman (clearly a forerunner of contributors to the modern *Times*'s "Lives Remembered" postscripts to published obits). The anonymous obituarist may well have kicked himself for not having spoken to the friend, Sir Henry Holland, in the first place. "It is told, and I believe the anecdote to be well founded," Sir Henry wrote, "that Laplace himself [the French mathematician and astronomer], commenting on the English mathematical school of that period, said there were only two persons in England who thoroughly understood his work, and these two were women—Mrs Greig and Mrs Somerville. The two thus named were, in fact, one. Mrs Somerville [was] twice married." Unlike the obituarist, he also mentioned Mrs Somerville's children, something no *Times* obituarist would omit to do today.

At nearly 2,500 words, the sheer exhaustiveness of this volume's second obituary, that of Harriet Martineau (pp. 18-23), who died in 1876, may have denied readers the chance of adding a postscript – at any rate, none was published. But Miss Martineau's rare status as one of the comparatively few women of the time to be granted a *Times* obituary was emphasised when it appeared as the solitary woman's obituary alongside 54 obits of men in the 1870-1879 volume of *Eminent Persons: Biographies Reprinted from The Times*, a series of books covering obituaries from 1870 until 1894.

Matters improved for women's obituaries in the final 20 years of Victoria's reign. From George Eliot's (pp. 23-27) in 1880 to Rosa Bonheur's (pp. 42-44) in 1899, there were seven women's obits of a quality meriting inclusion in this anthology. They are substantial pieces, doing justice (or something very close to it) to women who had a major impact on their age – two novelists, an opera singer, a headmistress, a poet, a composer and an artist; four of them British, the rest Swedish, German or French.

Next, on January 23, 1901, came the big one: Queen Victoria's obituary – too long, alas, to be included here, where we have chosen to reproduce only complete obituaries. Partly because her obituary was almost as much a reflection on the Victorian era as on the monarch herself, "complete" in Queen Victoria's case means 49,741 words, enough to break the back of any anthology.

Instant coverage on so vast a scale has not been matched by obituaries since. At 14,218 words, Sir Winston Churchill's obituary was much more succinct. So were those of Baroness Thatcher (10,960 words) and Queen Elizabeth the Queen Mother (7,400 words), both included in this book (pp. 437-460 and 330-346).

As with Queen Victoria's obituary, all three of those later obituaries (and especially that of Queen Elizabeth the Queen Mother who died at 101) were long in the making. "*Times* notices may be elaborate composites, updated over many years, sometimes by more than one hand," says Ian Brunskill, the paper's obituaries editor from 1999 to 2013. "If it weren't for the tradition of *Times* obits being published anonymously, the obituary of Queen Elizabeth the Queen Mother, for instance, would have needed half a dozen bylines, some of them for writers who had predeceased their subject by several years."

Colin Watson, obituaries editor from 1956 to 1982, was as influential in his time as John Thadeus Delane had been in his. As Watson's own obituary in January 2001 had it: "He assumed his office at an opportune moment. The mid-1950s saw the beginning of a period of accelerating change in social attitudes… At a time when to be of the ruling establishment or the nobility might to some have seemed a prerequisite for getting one's obituary in *The Times*, Watson extended the frontiers of acceptability… An account of so lurid a life as that of the singer, Janis Joplin [pp. 166-167], little calculated to appeal to the traditional readership, was seen as having established the principle of treating the heroes of the new sub-culture on the merits of their impact on the age."

Seventy years on from Joplin's death, Ian Brunskill wouldn't have thought twice about commissioning the obituary of Amy Winehouse (pp. 424-428). A prime concern of Brunskill's, he says, was to avoid "the tendency to sentimentalise anyone reasonably prominent when they die". His obituarists, therefore, eschewed excesses of the sort to which Ellen Terry's 1928 obituary (pp. 96-101) succumbs from time to time – she was, it says, "an actress whose every movement was a poem, whose speech was music, and whose ebullient spirits were constantly caught and guided into a stream of beauty by some natural refinement".

They incline instead to the even-handed approach of Agatha Christie's obituary of 1976 (pp. 176-178): "She was not, in fact, a particularly good writer, certainly not the equal of Dorothy Sayers. But she had a real and subtle narrative gift." Or Sue Ryder's of 2000 (pp. 316-319): "Since she had a formidable appetite for work, and typically got up shortly before 4.30am, she was a difficult woman to work with; but it may be that a congenial woman would not have achieved so much." Or the Queen Mother's of 2002: "It may be argued that after 1945 her essential conservatism may have somewhat delayed the process of evolution and adaptation of the royal household that the times required. But her relatively old-fashioned views never cost her any popularity, partly because they were widely shared in the community, but also because her personal charm prevailed over any criticism."

Well-rounded characterisations have certainly come to the fore during the 140-plus years this anthology covers, as I hope readers will agree.

Sue Corbett
General Editor

Notes on Style

We have tried to present the obituaries in this volume as close to their original published form as possible. This has led to some inconsistencies of style; for example it has been *Times* style for many years to italicise the titles of books, newspapers, songs etc, but where this was not the case in the past we have left the text alone.

However, each article has been given a descriptive headline in the manner now familiar on the paper's obituary pages, and at the end a paragraph giving the dates of the life, again written as if the subject had just died, has been added where none was published.

Crossheads, single words picked out in bold which used to act as a visual break in long, grey sections of text, have been removed, as have the full stops which the Victorians used after each mention of Mr or Mrs.

In keeping with the long-standing *Times* tradition, obituary writers' anonymity has been preserved, except in the one or two cases where contributors' names were originally given.

—◦◦◦—

Photographs

All the photographs in this book were taken by *Times* photographers. It is not been possible to credit each picture but the work of the following is included: Jack Barker, David Bebber, John Bulmer, Stanley Devon, Chris Harris, Frank Hermann, David Hooley, Harry Kerr, Sidney Martin, Peter Nicholls, Sally Soames, John Trievnor, Bryan Wharton, Graham Wood.

MARY SOMERVILLE

SCOTTISH MATHEMATICIAN
AND ASTRONOMER WHO
PIONEERED THE ROLE OF
WOMEN IN SCIENCE

DECEMBER 2, 1872

Mary Somerville died on Friday in the neighbourhood of Naples, where she had of late years taken up her residence. Had she lived to the 26th of the present month she would have attained her 83rd year. Mary Somerville, or, to give her maiden name, Mary Fairfax, was a lady of good Scottish ancestry, being the daughter of the late Vice-Admiral Sir William George Fairfax, who was a cadet of the noble Scottish house of Lord Fairfax, and who commanded His Majesty's ship *Venerable* at the Battle of Camperdown. She was born on the 26th of December, 1789; her mother was Margaret, daughter of Mr Samuel Charters, Solicitor of Customs for Scotland. All that is known of her early life is that she was a great reader, even from childhood, and that she was brought up at a school at Musselburgh, in the vicinity of Edinburgh.

Before many of the most distinguished cultivators of physical science were born, Mrs Somerville had already taken her place among the original investigators of nature. In the year 1826 she presented to the Royal Society a paper on "The magnetizing power of the more refrangible solar rays," in which she detailed her repetitions of the experiments made by Morichini of Rome, and Bérard of Montpelier. The paper had for its object to prove whether solar light is a source of magnetic power. By means of a prism the component rays of a sunbeam were separated, and those which are now known as the chymical or actinic rays were allowed to fall upon delicately poised needles of various sizes which had been previously proved to be devoid of magnetism. In every instance the steel exhibited the true magnetic character after an exposure of several hours to the violet light. Experiments were then made by covering unmagnetic needles with blue glass shades and placing them in the sun, and in all cases they became magnetic. From these experiences Mrs Somerville concluded that the more refrangible rays of the solar spectrum, even in our latitude, have a strong magnetic influence. This communication was printed in the *Philosophical Transactions* at the time; it led to much discussion on a very difficult point of experimental inquiry, which was only set at rest some years later by the researches of two German electricians, Riess and Moser, who showed that the action upon the magnetic needle was not caused by the violet rays.

In 1831 or 1832 Mrs Somerville published her *Mechanism of the Heavens*. This book, her only strictly astronomical work, which is largely derived from Laplace's celebrated treatise, *La Mécanique Céleste*, and is understood to have been originally suggested by Lord Brougham, was originally proposed by its author as one of the publications of the Society for the Diffusion of Useful Knowledge; but, being moulded on too large a scale for their series, it was given to the world in an independent shape. A few years later her name became more widely known by her *Connexion of the Physical Sciences*, which obtained the praise of the *Quarterly Review* as "original in plan and perfect in execution," and, indeed, "a true 'Kosmos' in the nature of its design and in the multitude of materials collected and condensed into the history which it affords of the physical phenomena of the universe." This she followed up with her *Physical Geography*, which, as its name imports, comprises the history of the earth in its whole material organization. These two works, in addition to their popularity in this country, as testified by the many editions through which they have passed, have been translated into several foreign languages; and their author's services to geographical science were recognized in 1869 by the award of the Victoria medal of the Royal Geographical Society. In the same year she gave to the world her *Molecular and Microscopic Science*, a work which, to use the expression of a writer in the *Edinburgh Review*, "contains a complete conspectus of some of the most recent and most abstruse researches of modern science, and describes admirably not only the discoveries of our day in the field of physics and chymistry, but more especially the revelations of the microscope in the vegetable and animal worlds."

The publication of such a work as that last mentioned by a lady in, we believe, her eightieth year* is without a parallel in the annals of science. In it that which most forcibly strikes the reader is the extraordinary power of mental assimilation of scientific facts and theories which is displayed by its author. In it Mrs Somerville first gives us a clear account of the most recent discoveries in organic chymistry, in the elementary condition of matter, and tells us of the latest researches into the synthesis of organic carbon compounds. She next leads us on to the relations of polarization of light in crystalline form, and, quitting the subject of molecular physics with an account of the phenomena of spectrum analysis as applied to the stars and nebulae, she begins the consideration of the microscopic structure of the vegetable world; then passing in review the whole of the organisms from algae to exogenous plants, she lands us in her second volume among the functions of the animal frame in its lowest organizations, and describes the morphology of the various groups of animals from the protozoa to the mollusc. In thus traversing this immense field of modern scientific inquiry, Mrs Somerville does not attempt to generalize to any great extent, much less to bring forward any original observations of theories of her own; but, as she modestly hints in her preface, she has simply given in plain and clear language a résumé of some of the most interesting results of the recent investigations of men of science.

For some few years before her death Mrs Somerville was in the receipt of a literary pension, bestowed upon her in recognition of her services to science. This was the nation's tribute to her worth. But among men of science a far higher value than pecuniary grants can have is set upon those rewards which can be bestowed only by such as can appreciate the labours and aims of a toiler in the scientific field. And these Mrs Somerville received; the Geographical Society, as we have said, awarded her its medal; the Royal Astronomical Society elected her, in 1834, one of its honorary Fellows, the same honour being at the same time bestowed upon Miss Caroline Herschel — the only two ladies on whom such a distinction was ever conferred. The Fellows of the Royal Society also signified their appreciation of her works and their personal regard for their author by subscribing for a bust of Mrs Somerville, which Chantrey executed, and which the Duke of Sussex publicly presented to the Society in 1842, in his own name and in that of the subscribers. This monument adorns the Library of the Royal Society.

Mrs Somerville was twice married. Early in life she became the wife of Mr Samuel Greig, who is described in *Burke's Peerage* as "a Captain and Commissioner in the Russian Navy." Her union with him became the means of developing her latent scientific powers, as he took great pleasure in mathematical inquiry, and carefully initiated her in both the theory of mathematics and their practical application.

Her second husband was Dr William Somerville, a member of a good old family of Scottish extraction.

Mary Somerville, mathematician and scientist, was born on December 26, 1780. She died on November 29, 1872, aged 91

* *Editor's note*: Mrs Somerville's *Times* obituarist obviously did not have access to her *Personal Recollections, from Early Life to Old Age*, published in 1874. These give her year of birth as 1780, so she would have been nearly 90 when her *Molecular and Microscopic Science* was published.

—◦◦◦—

HARRIET MARTINEAU

PHILOSOPHER, CRITIC, BIOGRAPHER AND NOVELIST WHOSE LARGE LITERARY OUTPUT WAS ACHIEVED DESPITE ILL HEALTH AND HEARING LOSS

JUNE 29, 1876

So far back as the year 1832, Miss Lucy Aikin wrote to Dr Channing, "You must know that a great new light has arisen among English women," and a still greater authority, Lord Brougham, remarked to a friend about the same time: "There is at Norwich a deaf girl who is doing more good than any man in the country. You may have seen the name and some of the productions of Harriet Martineau in the 'Monthly Repository;' but what she is gaining glory by is a series of 'Illustrations of Political Economy' in some tales published periodically, of which nine or ten have appeared. Last year she called on me several times, and I was struck with marks of such an energy and resolution in her as, I thought, must command success in some line or other of life, though it did not then appear in what direction. She has a vast store of knowledge on many deep and difficult subjects — a wonderful store for a person scarcely 30 years old; and her observation of common things must have been extraordinarily correct as well as rapid. I dined yesterday in the company of Mr Malthus and Miss Martineau, who are great allies. She pursues her course steadily, and I hear much praise of her new tale on the Poor Laws. I fear, however, that it is the character of her mind to adopt extreme opinions upon most subjects, and without much examination. She has now had a full season of London 'lionizing,' and, as far as one can judge, it has done her nothing but good. She loves her neighbours the better for their good opinion of her; and, I believe, she thinks the more humbly of herself for what she has seen of other persons of talent and merit."

Harriet Martineau was born at Norwich on the 12th of June, 1802. In her biography of Mrs Opie she gives us a picture of life in this eastern cathedral city in the early part of the 19th century when its Bishop was the liberal and enlightened Dr Bathurst; and she tells us how the proclivities of the city, alike towards clerical exclusiveness and to intellectual stagnation, were largely corrected by the social gatherings of one or two highly-cultivated families, and by a large infusion of French and Flemish manufacturing industry, the result of the revocation of the Edict of Nantes. The Martineaus were among the families whom that measure drove to our shores; and at Norwich they had flourished for the best part of a century, part of the family devoting itself to silk weaving on a large scale, while other members were in practice as surgeons, enjoying a high reputation in the city of their adoption. Not much is known of Harriet's father, who died early, except that he had eight children, of whom she was the youngest. Her education was conducted under the supervision of her uncle, one of the most eminent surgeons in the east of England, and who took every means to give his nephews and nieces the best instruction Norwich could afford. Like most persons of a high order of intellect, however, young Harriet Martineau at an early age resolved to walk alone, and not in educational leading-strings, and practically taught herself history and politics while her brothers and sisters were reading their "Goldsmith" and "Mrs Markham." Not that she had any lack of teachers or instructors; but from a child she resolved to practise the virtue of self-reliance and to fit herself for life in earnest by such literary exertions as sooner or later, she felt, would at least make her independent.

She was barely of age when she appeared before the public as an author. Her first work, however, was not one which gave any great scope to literary talents, and must be regarded rather as a proof of her internal piety, on the model of the Unitarian school in which she had been brought up, than as a criterion of her intellectual ability. It was entitled "Devotional Exercises for the Use of Young Persons," and was published in 1823. It was, however, the harbinger of a long series of far more important works which were destined to appear thenceforth in rapid succession. In 1824 and the following year Miss Martineau came before the public as the authoress of two tales, entitled "Christmas Day," and a sequel to it, "The Friend;" these she followed up with several other stories all more or less dealing with social subjects, and more especially illustrating by argument and by example the rights and interests of the working classes. The best known of these are "Principle and Practice," "The Rioters," "The Turn Out," "Mary Campbell," and "My Servant Rachel." It is needless to add that in these the work of helping the weaker and poorer members of society is not only enforced upon the wealthier classes as a duty, but shown to be no less the common interest of both the one and the other. These publications carry down the story of the life of our author to about the year 1830 or 1831.

With this period we come to a new era in the literary career of Miss Martineau. This is shown by her choice of more elevated subjects, and possibly a more elevated tone is to be discovered in her treatment of them also. Her first publication after that date was a charming collection of "The Traditions of Palestine," and her next, if we remember right, her "Five Years of Youth." About the same time also she made her name known far more widely than before by gaining three prizes for as many separate Essays on subjects proposed by the Unitarian Association. The subjects were independent of each other, though mutually connected in their plan; and on opening the sealed envelopes, containing the names of the writers, it was found that on each of the three subjects the successful competitor was a young lady, just 30 years of age, named Harriet Martineau. The three subjects were respectively, The Faith as unfolded by many Prophets; Providence, as manifested through the dealings of God with Israel; and the Essential Faith of the Universal Church. These Essays were published, and thoroughly established the writer's claim to the credit of being a profound thinker and reasoner upon religious as well as on social questions.

The next subject to which she applied her fertile and versatile pen was a series of "Illustrations of Political Economy," in which she attempted to popularize, by familiar and practical illustrations and examples, the principles which — speaking generally — Adam Smith, Jeremy Bentham, and Romilly, and other men of original minds, had laid down in an abstract and strictly philosophical manner. These "Illustrations" extended to above 20 numbers; they were afterwards republished in a collective form, and, having since been translated into French and German, have helped perhaps more than any other work of modern times to spread abroad, in other countries as well as in our own, a knowledge of that science which till our own day had been so little known and studied. These she followed up by two similar series, on cognate subjects — "Illustrations of Taxation" and "Illustrations of Poor Laws and Paupers."

In the year 1834 Harriet Martineau paid a visit to the United States, whither she found that the fame of her social writings had travelled before her. There she met with a most cordial reception from the leaders of thought and action on the other side of the Atlantic; and on her return to Europe she published her comments on the social, political, and religious institutions in the United States, under the title of "Society in America," and her observations on the natural aspects of the Western World and its leading personages, under that of "A Retrospect of Western Travel." On returning to England she found awaiting her plenty of offers of literary engagements from the leading publishers; but she chose to throw in her lot mainly with Mr Charles Knight, who was then in the zenith of his high and well-earned reputation, as the publisher of the Society for the Diffusion of Useful Knowledge, under the auspices of such men as Lord Brougham, Grote, Thirlwall, and Lord John Russell. To

Charles Knight's series of cheap and popular publications she contributed a most useful little manual called "How to Observe," which she followed up by others, respectively intended as guides for the Housemaid, the Maid-of-all-Work, the Lady's-maid, and the Dressmaker. With the object of lightening her literary labours by variety, she next employed her pen on a series of tales for children, which she gave to the world under the title of "The Playfellow." Of these graphic tales the most popular were "The Crofton Boys," "The Settlers at Home," "The Peasant and the Prince," and "Feats on the Fiord." At the same time she addressed to children of a larger growth two novels of a very marked and distinctive character, called "Deerbrook" and "The Hour and the Man," the latter of which works passed through several editions.

About this time her health, which was never of the strongest, appears to have suffered so much from the continual strain of her literary exertions, that she was obliged to lay aside her pen, and Lord Melbourne offered and, we believe, even pressed upon her acceptance a literary pension. But she was either too proud or too independent to accept it; and possibly also even a higher motive came into play; at all events in declining it she was largely influenced by a feeling that "she could not conscientiously share in the proceeds of a system of taxation which she had reprobated in her published works." Her illness lasted several years; but she found means to turn even sickness to account by writing and publishing her "Life in a Sick-room," — a book suggested by her own experiences of suffering, and, therefore, appealing powerfully to the sympathies of many of her readers.

In 1844, soon after her restoration to health and strength, we find Miss Martineau once more at work upon her favourite themes — social subjects — and publishing three volumes of tales and sketches illustrative of the evil effects of our "Forest and Game Laws," which she followed up with a more fanciful work, "The Billow and the Rock." In 1846 she varied the monotony of her quiet and laborious life by a visit to the East; and she recorded her impressions of the scenes and countries through which she travelled in a book which she published in 1848, and which is still most justly popular — namely, "Eastern Life, its Past and Present."

In 1850 or 1851 appeared a work by Miss Martineau of a totally different character from all its predecessors — namely, a volume of "Letters on the Laws of Man's Nature and Development," which had passed between herself and a philosophic friend named Atkinson; and it was this work which first gave the public a hint that when she had reached something more than middle life she was inclined to adopt the teachings of the "Positive" school of philosophy, founded by Auguste Comte. Two or three years later she still more thoroughly identified herself with this school of thought and faith by giving to the world a condensed version of Comte's "Positive Philosophy." But while thus employed

in the study of scientific and semi-religious subjects, she found time to devote to her "History of England during the Thirty Years Peace," a book which is to be admired for its singular clearness and the studied impartiality of its views.

We next find the indefatigable pen of Miss Martineau employed in contributing to the "People's Journal," and her essays in that periodical soon came to be so widely in demand that they were subsequently republished under the title of "Household Education." About the same time she employed her leisure hours in compiling a work of less pretension — we mean her "Complete Guide to the Lakes," which appeared in 1854, and for which her long residence at the pretty cottage near Ambleside, which she made her home during her declining years, eminently qualified her. From and after this date it was mainly as a contributor of leading articles, and of biographical and other literary papers to the *Daily News*, and as a writer of social articles, "historiettes" and graphic personal reminiscences of the celebrities of the present century, in the early volumes of "Once a Week," that we must look mainly for evidence of Miss Martineau's literary activity; but the weight of increasing years began to tell heavily upon her, and after a long illness in or about the year 1865 she almost entirely withdrew from those engagements. Her biographical contributions to the *Daily News* and "Once a Week" were republished in a collected form in the early part of 1869.

In this brief sketch we have had no space to mention the other works, mostly of a more or less ephemeral character, which are identified with the name of Harriet Martineau. Of these the best known, perhaps, are her "Essay on British India" (1851); "The Factory Controversy; a Warning against Meddling Legislation" (1855); "Corporate Tradition" and "National Rights and Local Dues on Shipping" (1857); "Endowed Schools in Ireland" (1859); "England and her Soldiers" — a work on the vexed question of Army reform (1859) — and "Health, Husbandry, and Handicraft," a collection of stray papers contributed to some of the leading serials of the day.

At her charming home near Ambleside, so long as health and strength remained to her, Miss Martineau rejoiced to entertain a circle of attached literary and political friends, and to receive the visits of such strangers, both English and foreign, as cared to travel in order to gratify some higher interests than those of mere pleasure. From mere pleasure, apart from the business of life, and to mere pleasure-seekers and idlers and triflers, she had an unconquerable aversion; but if any one sought to benefit his fellow creatures, high or low, rich or poor, and to lead a useful life as a social being, and a member of the busy hive of English labour, or, indeed, of humanity at large, to him or to her the doors of Miss Martineau's house and of her heart were at once open. To the last, in spite of a painful chronic illness, she took the greatest interest in every

movement which had for its object the social, physical, and moral improvement of the world in which her lot was cast, and she corresponded largely with the various leaders of such movements, who seldom sought in vain for her counsel and advice. If any lady of the 19th century, in England or abroad, may be allowed to put in a claim for the credit of not having lived in vain, that woman, we honestly believe was Harriet Martineau.

Harriet Martineau, critic and novelist, was born on June 12, 1802. She died on June 27, 1876, aged 74

—⁓—

GEORGE ELIOT

NOVELIST WHO BECAME A HOUSEHOLD NAME WITH NOVELS SUCH AS *THE MILL ON THE FLOSS* AND *MIDDLEMARCH*

DECEMBER 24, 1880

A great English writer has suddenly passed away. "George Eliot," to give her the name by which Mrs Cross was known wherever the English language is spoken or English literature is prized, died on Wednesday evening, after only three days' illness. On Sunday evening last she received the visits of several old friends at the house in Cheyne-walk which she and her husband (to whom she was only married last May) had lately occupied, and when they left her she was apparently in good health and spirits. That night, however, she was seized with a sudden chill, which first attacked the larynx. On the following day, at Dr Andrew Clark's request, Dr G. W. Mackenzie, of Lowndes-square, saw Mrs Cross, that he might report on the case, and not until Wednesday evening, about 6 o'clock, when Dr Andrew Clark visited her for the first time with Dr Mackenzie, did the case appear to assume an alarming aspect. It was discovered in the course of their examination that since the morning inflammation had arisen in the pericardium and heart, and that death was not only inevitable, but near at hand. The heart rapidly losing power, Mrs Cross became insensible, and died about 10 o'clock, without either agitation or pain.

For the biography of George Eliot, to give her the name by which Mrs Cross was known wherever the English language is spoken or English literature is prized, few materials exist. Many apocryphal stories have been told, not the least remarkable of which is one concerning the authorship of "Adam Bede," to which we shall presently refer, and some few of these can be corrected; but the time has not yet come for that full record of her private life and literary history which, as we may hope, may some day be given to the world.

Marian Evans — whom all the world knew as "George Eliot" — was born, we believe, in Warwickshire, little short of sixty years ago. She was not, as has often been stated, the daughter of a poor clergyman, nor is it true that she was adopted in early life by another clergyman of greater wealth, who gave her a first-class education. Her father, Robert Evans, was a land agent and surveyor, who lived in the neighbourhood of Nuneaton, and served for many years as agent for the estates of more than one old Warwickshire family; he is still remembered as a man of rare worth and character by many neighbours in the Midlands. The father of George Eliot is the prototype of more than one character in the writings of his daughter. Of these "Caleb Garth" in "Middlemarch" will be recognized as the chief example; but the same note of character — the craftsman's keen delight in perfect work — is struck in "Adam Bede" and in the little poem on Stradivarius.

George Eliot's early years were spent in the country of Shakespeare. The sleepy life of the rural Midlands before the time of the Reform Bill, their rich and tranquil scenery, their homely and old-world inhabitants all left an indelible impress on her imagination — most strongly felt, perhaps, in "Adam Bede" and "The Mill on the Floss," but reappearing with a difference in "Middlemarch," and inspiring one or two passages as tender and graceful as anything she ever wrote in "Theophrastus Such." It is not very clear when she left her father's home, nor where her education was acquired, but she seems to have come to London almost as a girl, and to have devoted herself to serious literature in a manner far more common among women of the present day than it was nearly 40 years ago. She became associated with many of the writers in the

Westminster Review, with John Stuart Mill, Mr Herbert Spencer, George Henry Lewes, Mr John Chapman, and others. She was a frequent contributor to the *Review*, and at one time, we believe, she edited the section devoted to "Contemporary Literature" in that periodical. Her first serious work was a translation of the celebrated Strauss's "Life of Jesus," published in 1846, when she must have been barely 25 years of age. Of this almost forgotten effort it was said at the time that it exhibited an equal knowledge and mastery of the German and English languages. Seven years afterwards, in 1853, Miss Evans published a translation of Feuerbach's "Essence of Christianity," the intervening period being that of her greatest activity as a contributor to the *Westminster Review*.

Soon after this Miss Evans began to turn her attention to fiction. It is said that the manuscript of "Scenes of Clerical Life," her first imaginative work, was sent anonymously to *Blackwood's Magazine* by George Henry Lewes, and was eagerly accepted by the editor, who discerned in it the promise, since abundantly fulfilled, of rare and pre-eminent genius. It was not, however, until "Adam Bede" was published in 1859 that the world at large discerned that a new novelist of the first rank had appeared. "Adam Bede" made the name of George Eliot a household word throughout England, and set curiosity at work to discover the real name and sex of the author. Those who had studied "Scenes of Clerical Life" at all

closely felt sure that the writer was a woman, notwithstanding the masculine tone and breadth conspicuous in "Adam Bede." A singular controversy arose in our columns on the subject. On April 15, 1859, a few days after we had reviewed "Adam Bede," and conjectured that the author, whether man or woman, could neither be young nor inexperienced, we received and published the following letter:—

"Sir,—The author of 'Scenes of Clerical Life' and 'Adam Bede' is Mr Joseph Liggins, of Nuneaton, Warwickshire. You may easily satisfy yourself of my correctness by inquiring of any one in that neighbourhood. Mr Liggins himself and the characters whom he paints are as familiar there as the twin spires of Coventry. Yours obediently H. ANDERS, Rector of Kirkby."

This produced on the next day the following rejoinder from the real George Eliot:—

"Sir,—The Rev. H. Anders has with questionable delicacy and unquestionable inaccuracy assured the world through your columns that the author of 'Scenes of Clerical Life' and 'Adam Bede' is Mr Joseph Liggins, of Nuneaton. I beg distinctly to deny that statement. I declare on my honour that that gentleman never saw a line of those works until they were printed, nor had he any knowledge of them whatever. Allow me to ask whether the act of publishing a book deprives a man of all claim to the courtesies usual among gentlemen? If not, the attempt to pry into what is obviously meant to be withheld — my name — and to publish the rumours which such prying may give rise to, seems to me quite indefensible, still more so to state these rumours as ascertained truths. — I am, Sir, yours, &c., GEORGE ELIOT."

Notwithstanding this protest, the secret soon leaked out. Long before "The Mill on the Floss," the second great novel of the series which has immortalized the name of George Eliot, was published in 1860, it was well known, in literary circles at least, that George Eliot was none other than Marian Evans, the Westminster Reviewer and translator of Strauss, better known to her intimates as Mrs Lewes; for by this time was established that close association and literary friendship with the gifted George Henry Lewes, which terminated only with the death of the latter a little more than two years ago. "The Mill on the Floss," in which some critics discerned a falling-off from "Adam Bede," and others the richer maturity of a splendid genius, was followed, in 1861, by "Silas Marner," the shortest, but as many think, the most perfect, of all George Eliot's novels. "Romola" — that marvellous tale of Florence in the time of Savonarola, in which the author essayed a task harder by far than that of Thackeray in "Esmond," and accomplished it triumphantly — followed in 1863. In "Felix Holt," published in 1866, George Eliot returned to English life, but somehow failed to recover that sureness of touch and blitheness of humour which gave Mrs Poyser and Mrs Tulliver to the world.

After a silence of five years, broken only by several poems, not, indeed, unworthy of her genius, but still deriving more repute from her name than they conferred upon it, George Eliot returned to fiction with "Middlemarch," which was published in numbers during 1871 and 1872. "Middlemarch" carried the reader back once more to the Midlands, and gave us the family portrait of Caleb Garth, and perhaps a sketch in his daughter of the early life of the author herself; but the satire was more copious and less kindly than in the earlier novels, and the humour, though still abundant, was not so genial as it had been. "The Legend of Jubal," with other poems, followed in 1874, and "Daniel Deronda," the author's last novel, was published in 1876. "Daniel Deronda" was "caviare to the general;" none but George Eliot could have written it, perhaps, but we almost may hazard the conjecture that if any other had written it few would have read it. It is the great work of a great writer, very instructive and profound, but regarded as a novel it commits the unpardonable sin of failing to entertain. The last work of George Eliot was "Theophrastus Such," published in the course of last year. Fiction, in its ordinary sense, is here abandoned for the heavier and less attractive style of the essayist and thinker. Here and there occurs a gem of humour or of thought worthy of the author of "Adam Bede," but the imagination is cold and no longer attempts to fuse the mass of thought into a luminous and consistent creation.

The life of George Eliot is, as we have said, little more than the history of her literary activity. A mere catalogue of her writings will stir many memories, and far better than a critical estimate of their value will remind her innumerable readers of the keen and innocent pleasure she has afforded them, of the stirring and elevated thoughts she has lavished on their entertainment. Those who only knew her books will deplore an irreparable loss to English letters, while those who also knew the writer will feel that a great and noble spirit, supreme in intellect as in culture, as tender as it was strong, has passed away from the world. The friends of George Eliot have long recognized her rare and commanding gifts both of intellect and character, and it was impossible even for casual acquaintances to pass a few minutes in her society without falling under the spell of a strangely fascinating and sympathetic personality. Her gracious manner, condescending as became her genius, but never either patronizing or indifferent, overcame at once the diffidence of any who approached her, and her winning smile irradiated and softened features that were too strongly marked for feminine beauty. Those who have seen her either in private or in public, as at the Popular Concerts, at which she was a constant attendant, cannot but have been struck with her resemblance to Savonarola as he appears in the portrait by Fra Bartolommeo at Florence. She is gone, and the pen which drew Savonarola with all the strength of a man, and Romola with all the tenderness of a woman, which has produced a gallery of English portraits almost unrivalled in fiction, is laid aside for ever. But her memory lives in the gratitude of countless thousands of readers, and the thought of the life of a great and noble woman suddenly cut off in the promise of renewed happiness will sadden many a household in the midst of Christmas rejoicings.

George Eliot, novelist, was born on November 22, 1819. She died on December 22, 1880, aged 61

———

JENNY LIND

OPERA SINGER WHO WAS KNOWN AS "THE SWEDISH NIGHTINGALE"

NOVEMBER 3, 1887

We regret to announce the death, early yesterday morning, at Malvern, of Madame Lind-Goldschmidt, who is better known and will be remembered in history by the name of Jenny Lind. Her health had been failing for some time, and she was compelled not long ago to resign her post as professor of singing at the Royal College of Music — the last link still connecting her with the practice of an art which she had loved from girlhood and in which her successes had been equalled by few. From the stage she had retired at a comparatively early age and while still in the zenith of her power, and her last important appearance on the concert platform abroad took place in 1870, when she sang the soprano part in her husband's oratorio, *Ruth*, at Düsseldorf. Since then she was occasionally heard at charitable concerts and in private; but to the present generation of amateurs she had become a stranger and an honoured name. Seventeen years of retirement are apt to dim the brightest fame of an executive artist in the minds of living men. If Madame Goldschmidt had died 30 or 40 years ago, when the "Jenny Lind fever" was at its highest, the news would have sent a thrill through musical Europe. As it is, the loss will be felt chiefly by the large circle of friends who loved and esteemed her in private life.

Jenny Lind was born on October 6, 1820 at Stockholm, and is said to have evinced musical talent and a beautiful voice in her fourth year. Mdlle Lundberg, the famous dancer, heard the child in her ninth year, and induced her parents to send her as a pupil to the school of singing attached to the Court Theatre of her native city. Berg and Crölius were her first masters, and she made her debut as Agatha in *Der Freischütz* at Stockholm in 1838, playing also Euryanthe, Alice in *Robert le Diable*, and Spontini's *La Vestale* with signal success. But although she pleased the public she failed to satisfy herself, and in 1841, when her engagement at Stockholm had expired, she went to Paris, to place herself under Manuel Garcia, with whom she studied for several months, and appeared once at the Grand Opéra in 1842, but

without success. It is said that this disappointment induced her to make a vow never to sing in Paris again, and this she strictly kept, although tempting offers were not wanting at a later period when her fame had become European. In another sense, however, her stay in Paris was to have important consequences. Meyerbeer heard her, and discovered the rich promise which the Parisian public had failed to see, and it was through his means that she obtained the engagement at the Berlin Opera, from which her international celebrity may be said to date. This was in 1844, when Jenny Lind appeared in Meyerbeer's *The Camp of Silesia*, the principal soprano part of which had been specially written for her. Here her success was instantaneous. The public greeted her as the "Swedish Nightingale" and Moscheles, who happened to be in Berlin, and later on in London became one of her warmest friends, speaks of her in a letter to his wife:—"Jenny Lind has truly enchanted me. She is unique of her kind, and the air with two *obbligato* flutes is perhaps the most incredible thing in the way of *bravura* that can be heard anywhere." This testimony from a highly competent musician may be supplemented by that of a still greater one, Mendelssohn, who wrote:—

"In my whole life I have not seen an artistic nature so noble, so genuine, so true as is that of Jenny Lind. Natural gifts, study, and depth of feeling I have never seen united in the same degree; and although one of these qualities may have been more prominent in other persons, the combination of all three has never existed before."

The posthumous fame of a singer could not rest on a safer basis than such words from such men. It is true that other contemporary critics are not always equally favourable. The author of "Musical Recollections of the Last Half Century," who witnessed Jenny Lind's debut in London, declares that "to my ear she invariably sang somewhat sharp, and I could by no means consider any *prima donna* to be a great artist who was only positively successful in four operas — *Roberto, La Sonnambula, La Figlia del Reggimento*, and *Le Nozze di Figaro*, her Norma having been a complete failure." The charge of the lady's continually singing sharp may be safely dismissed in the face of ample evidence to the contrary, but the fact of her *répertoire* being somewhat limited cannot altogether be denied. Jenny Lind as a stage singer was a vocal artist rather than the interpreter of great dramatic emotions. It is true that her acting as Alice in the scene at the Cross is spoken of as a carefully-studied performance, but some competent witnesses whom we have consulted agree in saying that Jenny Lind belonged to the class of *soprani leggieri* who sing first and act afterwards. It is quite true that her and the public's favourite operas required more singing than acting; at the same time it is an interesting subject for speculation how Jenny Lind and some of her famous contemporaries would have acquitted themselves in the more dramatic style which has since come into vogue. That her own bias was not really for the stage is sufficiently proved by the fact that she left the opera as early as 1849, her last appearance "on any stage" as Alice in *Robert le Diable* taking place on March 18 of that year.

Henceforth she confined herself exclusively to the concert platform, and there she gained laurels even greener and more lucrative than those of the earlier stages of her career. Her singing of Swedish songs was in its way unequalled; these simple ditties became the rage of the town, and Moscheles and other fashionable composers of the day transferred them to the piano. But still greater triumphs were in store for the artist in oratorio. Her singing in Mendelssohn's *Elijah* still lives in the memory of those who heard it. The first performance in England of Schumann's *Paradise and the Peri*, with Jenny Lind as the principal soprano, which was given at the Hanover-square Rooms in the presence of the Queen (July, 1856), was also a memorable incident in the great artist's career.

Jenny Lind's first appearance on the London stage took place at Her Majesty's Theatre on May 4, 1847, and was preluded by every art of *réclame* then in fashion. Two rival managers, Lumley and Bunn, went to law over her, and one of them recovered heavy damages, afterwards reduced, in the Court of Queen's Bench. The lady's Continental successes and her private virtues, her charity, and her childlike innocence, were canvassed by the newspapers with a fullness of detail which would do credit to modern journalism of a certain class. No wonder that on the eventful evening the house was crowded, and the tickets were retailed by the agents at fabulous prices. The "Jenny Lind fever," already alluded to, raged during that and the following season with unabated violence, taking the form of portraits printed on handkerchiefs, fans, and similar objects. One chronicler even mentions "Jenny Lind potatoes," called so from the blue specks on their skins, because the *prima donna* had blue eyes. Mr Chorley, the well-remembered critic, says:—

"From the first moment till the end of that season (1847) nothing else was thought about, nothing else talked about, but the new Alice, the new Sonnambula, the new Maria in Donizetti's charming comic opera — his best. Pages could be filled by describing the excesses of the public. Since the days when the world fought for hours at the pit door to see the seventh farewell of Siddons nothing had been seen in the least approaching the scenes at the entrance of the theatre where Mdlle Lind sang. Prices rose to a fabulous height. In short, the town, sacred and profane, went mad about 'the Swedish Nightingale.'"

The fame of Sweden as the home of operatic songbirds has, it may be parenthetically stated, been fully sustained since then by such artists as Madame Nilsson and Mdlle Arnoldson, the promising *débutante* of last season. In 1850 Jenny Lind went to America under the auspices of Mr Barnum, and accompanied by Mr, afterwards Sir, Julius Benedict. Here she remained for two years giving concerts under Mr Barnum's management, and later on on her own account, and the profits realized by her were fabulous, being variously stated as £20,000 and $3,000,000. It was at Boston, on February 5, 1852, that she married Mr Otto Goldschmidt, the well-known composer, whom she had previously known at Hamburg, and who assisted her at her concerts. Readers of Mr Bayard Taylor's autobiography will remember the amusing incident of the ode written in connexion with Mdlle Lind's triumphs and conferring upon the poet a celebrity the reverse of agreeable. Returned to Europe, the young couple settled first at Dresden and afterwards at Wiesbaden and Hamburg. In 1856, however, Jenny Lind once more appeared on the English concert platform; and England she finally made her home. Living in comparative retirement from society, the great artist gathered round her a circle of admiring friends, and never lost her interest in the two chief objects of her life, music and charity. A writer in "Grove's Dictionary" states that —

"The whole of her American earnings was devoted to founding and endowing art scholarships and other charities in her native Sweden; while in England, the country of her adoption, among other charities she has given a whole hospital to Liverpool and a wing of another to London. The scholarship founded in memory of her friend Felix Mendelssohn also benefited largely by her help and countenance; and it may be said with truth that her generosity and sympathy were never appealed to in vain by those who had any just claims upon them."

Of late years Madame Lind-Goldschmidt was actively interested in the Bach Choir, as long as it was conducted by her husband, and she was seen at the head of the *soprani* at each of the concerts given by that institution. She also held, as already mentioned, a professorship of singing at the Royal College of Music. Her holidays she loved to spend at a house bought by her on the slope of the Malvern Hills, and it was here that she died, surrounded by her husband and her family.

Jenny Lind, opera singer, was born on October 6, 1820. She died on November 2, 1887, aged 67

—◦◦◦—

FRANCES MARY BUSS

HEADMISTRESS AND PIONEER OF WOMEN'S EDUCATION

DECEMBER 25, 1894

We regret to announce the death of Miss Frances Mary Buss, which took place yesterday, at the age of 67. She was the eldest child and only surviving daughter of the late Mr R. W. Buss, painter-etcher, and one of the illustrators of the "Pickwick Papers." She received her education in a private school, which was attended by the daughters of many artists who lived in the neighbourhood of Camden-town. When she left school as a pupil she continued as a teacher, but after a time joined her mother in a school which had been opened in Kentish-town, and secured a good number of pupils. During this time she availed herself of certain classes which were formed in Queen's College. She received certificates of proficiency in several subjects, this being at the time the only channel through which such testimonials could be given. The present headmistress of Cheltenham Ladies' College was also a student at these classes. It was in the year 1850 that the school in Kentish-town was moved to a larger house in Camden-street, and under the auspices of the Rev David Laing, who secured for it the interest of Canon Dale, assumed the name of the North London Collegiate School for Ladies. The increase of pupils was rapid, and soon another house was required to accommodate them.

When the Cambridge University local examinations were opened to girls in 1863, and offered an outside test by which the education of girls could be proved, Miss Buss was foremost among those who availed themselves of this advantage, and her pupils commenced that series of successes which has been continued to the present time. In 1864 an application was made by Miss Davies and Miss Bostock to the Schools Inquiry Commission that girls' schools should be included in the inquiry, with the view of obtaining endowments for the education of girls. This application being granted, Miss Buss was summoned as a witness, and gave much striking evidence. The Commission reported in 1868, and stated that, with but few exceptions, of which the North London Collegiate School for Ladies was one, the provision for the education of girls was quite inadequate.

About this time the Brewers' Company were contemplating the foundation of a school for girls in St Pancras, as in that parish they had large estates. When the matter came before the Charity Commissioners, it was suggested that it would be better to help an established school than to create a rival, and to this the members of the Court cordially assented. The North London Collegiate School for Ladies had been removed from Camden-street to more spacious premises in the Camden-road, and in the houses thus vacated the Camden School for Girls recently founded by Miss Buss was located. A trust was formed for carrying on the schools as the North London Collegiate and Camden Schools for Girls, and it was these schools that were chosen as the recipient of the Brewers' bounty. Subsequently a scheme was framed which received the sanction of her Majesty in Council. By means of the endowment provided by the Brewers' Company, supplemented by the Clothworkers', the governing body constituted under this scheme were able to secure a suitable freehold site for the two schools, and on them to erect suitable buildings. Besides this

a provision was made for scholarships and other purposes. With this equipment the two schools were able to offer a liberal education for girls such as had hitherto not been attainable.

But the influence of Miss Buss's work in education stretched far beyond the boundaries of her own two schools, even in these earlier days. When the Girls' Public Day School Company began its excellent work of establishing first-grade girls' schools throughout the country the North London Collegiate School was taken as the model to be visited and studied at the outset by newly-appointed head mistresses. Among the first to take advantage of the women's colleges at Cambridge was a contingent of pupils from Miss Buss's school. In the earlier years this contingent sometimes formed as much as one-third of the total number of Girton College, and scholarship winners from North London have always been conspicuously present on the College roll and in the Tripos lists. Miss Buss, with Miss Davies, Miss Clough, and Miss Beale, are known to this generation as the veteran leaders in the movement for the higher education of women.

In 1870 the University of London provided special examinations for women, and it was a pupil of the school over which Miss Buss so ably presided who took the first certificate that was obtained. In 1879 the University in the most complete sense was opened to women, and since then North London scholars have taken a full share of the honours made available for women.

Miss Buss has taken an active part in all movements for the development both of the profession of teachers and of the art of teaching. The Head Mistresses Association was one of the earliest organizations of the kind, and its formation was largely due to her energy and her insight into the needs of her time. She was also one of the most active promoters of the Teachers' Guild, to which she gave much of her time and labours, and she was a zealous worker on the council of the College of Preceptors, of which she held the diploma of Fellow. She was ardent in her aspirations for the development of scientific educational principles, and the "Maria Grey" and still more the Cambridge Training Colleges for Women owed much to her support and assistance in their initial stages. Moreover, she maintained the principle that the teacher should be trained for her work in the most effective of all effective ways, by requiring that all her more recently appointed assistants should be trained.

But the effect of the work and influence of Frances Mary Buss was much more than can be sketched in a summary of the facts of her life's work. It can only be gauged by the devoted admiration of her co-workers in every field, the colleagues of her own school who shared daily her inspiration, the mistresses of other schools who gladly came to her for counsel, and the great multitude of girls and young women who have enjoyed the inestimable benefits of an education under the stimulus of her great personality.

The funeral will take place on Monday next; the first part of the service will be at Holy Trinity Church, Clarence-road, Kentish-town, at 10 o'clock, and the interment at Theydon Bois at 2 o'clock.

Frances Mary Buss, educationist, was born on August 16, 1827. She died on December 24, 1894, aged 67

—◦◦◦—

CHRISTINA ROSSETTI

POET OF GRACE AND DELICACY AND SISTER OF DANTE GABRIEL ROSSETTI

JANUARY 1, 1895

We regret to record the death of Miss Christina Georgina Rossetti, the poet, who passed quietly away at her residence in Torrington-square on Saturday. The cause of death was cancer. Two years ago Miss Rossetti underwent an operation, and during the past five months she had been a great sufferer. Her nurse was the only person present when she died. The funeral will take place to-morrow. There will be a memorial service at Christ Church, Woburn-square, at 11 a.m., and the interment will take place at Highgate Cemetery later in the day.

Miss Rossetti was the youngest of a family all of whose members attained distinction in literature. Her father, Gabriele Rossetti, an Italian poet, critic, and man of letters, was born at Vasto, in the Abruzzi — then forming part of the kingdom of Naples — in 1783, and died in London in 1854. He had escaped to England after the constitutional struggle with Ferdinand in 1821. Settling down in London, he published various original works as well as critical dissertations on Dante, and he also taught the Italian language and literature. His wife (who died in 1886) was Frances Mary Lavinia Polidori, sister of Byron's travelling physician. The Rossettis had four children — namely, Maria Francesca, author of "A Shadow of Dante," &c., who was born in 1827 and died in 1876; Gabriel Charles Dante, usually known as Dante Gabriel, the famous poet and artist, who was born in 1828 and died in 1882; William Michael, the critical writer and editor of Shelley, who was born in 1829, and who still survives; and Christina Georgina, whose death we announce to-day.

Miss Rossetti was born in Charlotte-street, Portland-place, London, on December 5, 1830. She was educated at home, under her accomplished mother's tuition, and early became a member of the Church of England. In her opening years she furnished evidence of inherited genius; and it is stated that while still quite a child she wrote verses, "remarkable not only for sweetness and purity of feeling, but also for genuine singing impulse and a keen sense of fitness in the means of expression." Before she was 17 a little

volume of her poetry, entitled "Verses by Christina G. Rossetti, dedicated to her Mother," was privately printed by her maternal grandfather, Gaetano Polidori, who kept a printing press for his own convenience at his residence in London. In 1830, under the *nom de plume* of "Ellen Alleyne," she contributed to the *Germ*, the well-known but short-lived organ of the Pre-Raphaelites, Dante Rossetti, Holman Hunt, Thomas Woolner, and others. She also contributed fugitive poems to various other magazines. Her first published work in book form, "Goblin Market and other Poems," appeared in 1862, and it immediately established her reputation as one of the most promising poets of the day. It was followed in 1866 by "The Prince's Progress and other Poems." The poem which gave the title to this volume was, perhaps, the most important and ambitious of her lengthier efforts, but it lacked the spontaneity of her shorter pieces.

Her next venture was in prose. It appeared in 1870, and was entitled "Commonplace, and other Short Stories." While not possessing the remarkable beauty and originality of her verse, this work still manifested real elevation and purity of thought and diction. "Sing-Song, a Nursery Rhyme Book," was published in 1872, and "Speaking Likenesses" — couched in *quasi*-allegorical prose — in 1874. Both these volumes were illustrated by Mr Arthur Hughes, and were specially written for children. The devotional element had been conspicuous in Miss Rossetti's earliest poetical works, and it was further exemplified in 1874 by a work exclusively devotional, "*Annus Domini*; a Prayer for each day of the year, founded on a text of Holy Scripture." A collected edition of her poems, which included besides a considerable number of new compositions, was brought out in 1875. Then came two religious works in prose — "Seek and Find," and a double series of "Short Studies of the Benedicite" — issued in 1879. In 1881 appeared "A Pageant and other Poems," and the same year also witnessed the production of another prose work, "Called to the Saints: the Minor Festivals Devotionally Studied." In 1883 appeared "Notes on the Commandments," and two years later a work of a similar kind, but in alternate prose and verse, entitled, "Time Flies: a Reading Diary." A new edition of the "Goblin Market, the Prince's Progress, and other Poems," was published in 1884; and again in 1890 the majority of Miss Rossetti's poems were re-issued in a collected form. Several of her lyrics were set to music, and cantatas for two of her longer poems — "Goblin Market" and "Songs in a Cornfield" — were composed by Mr Aguilar and Professor Macfarren.

For many years before her death Miss Rossetti led a very secluded life, partly due to her natural shrinking from the outer world and society, and partly to her enfeebled health. Her devotion to her aged mother — who survived her husband for the long period of 32 years — was touching and beautiful. The earnest religious convictions of the deceased poetess were ever translated into daily thought and action, and her life may well be described as saintly in character. It may here be mentioned that she sat for the face and figure of the Virgin in her brother's striking early Pre-Raphaelite picture, "The Girlhood of Mary Virgin." He afterwards painted several other portraits of his sister.

Miss Rossetti had much of the richness of style and beauty of imagery of her still more eminent brother, though she was not capable of his sustained flights. Some of her lyrics, such as the one beginning, "Does the road wind up-hill all the way?" produce a very vivid and lasting impression. In all that she did she was the finished artist, while her poems were able to stimulate and to elevate as well as to delight. In the sphere of the religious emotions few writers have given the world thoughts so full of beauty and pathos. While Dante Rossetti excelled in masculine vigour and artistic excellence, Christina Rossetti's qualities were rather those of grace and delicacy combined with a clear and pellucid style and a singular tenderness and sensitiveness of feeling. Her death leaves a distinct gap in the poetic literature of the time.

Christina Rossetti, poet, was born on December 5, 1830. She died of cancer on December 29, 1894, aged 64

CLARA SCHUMANN

GERMAN PIANIST AND
COMPOSER WHO WAS ALSO
THE INSPIRATION OF HER
HUSBAND, ROBERT

MAY 22, 1896

By the death of Mme Schumann, which occurred at Frankfurt on the Main, on Wednesday, from paralysis, the musical world has lost, not only the ablest exponent of Robert Schumann's pianoforte music, but also perhaps the most richly gifted of all female musicians. Mme Schumann, who had attained to a recognized position under her maiden name of Clara Wieck, was born at Leipzig, September 13, 1819, and, having studied the pianoforte under her father, the illustrious teacher, Friedrich Wieck, she made her first appearance in public just nine years later, and rapidly made her mark as a pianist of the first rank.

Schumann's romantic attachment to her was the directly inspiring cause of many of his most beautiful and individual compositions. So little smoothly did the course of their love run that an action at law was one of the incidents of their story.

Married on the eve of her birthday, September 12, 1840, she was not only a most devoted wife until the time of his tragic death in July, 1856, but a fellow-artist worthy in every way to help him in the interpretation of his best creations. From a period shortly before the composer's death until comparatively recently she devoted her life mainly to the work of obtaining wide recognition for his compositions. In England, where she appeared at a Philharmonic Concert for the first time but three months before Schumann's death, the task was a particularly heavy one; but in the course of years she was most amply rewarded, not so much by the heartfelt enthusiasm with which her later appearances were always greeted as by the high place ultimately accorded to Schumann's compositions in the musical world of London. Although these were peculiarly and in a special sense her own, yet she was not less remarkable as a player of the classics, and, indeed, as a distinguished critic has truly said, "She was one of the greatest pianoforte players that the world has ever heard." The sonatas of Beethoven received new meaning at her hands, and in works of lighter calibre, such as the harpsichord pieces of Scarlatti, her success was complete. In the expression of the deepest and most refined emotion, in dignity of style and breadth and variety of tone, she was without rival, and her compositions, though extending only to opus 23 or thereabouts, reach a very high degree of excellence and show real poetic insight.

No doubt the excessive smallness of the list of her works is due to an artistic fastidiousness and a power of self-criticism which prevented her from publishing anything not entirely representative of the power that was in her. Gradually increasing deafness caused her latterly to shun the concert platform, but her work as a teacher was almost phenomenally successful. Among her English pupils Mr Franklin Taylor (as a teacher), Miss Fanny Davies, Miss Adeline de Lara, and Mr Leonard Borwick (as players) are the most distinguished, and the Hoch Conservatorium became famous mainly through the co-operation of Mme Schumann and her daughters.

Clara Schumann, pianist and composer, was born on September 13, 1819. She died on May 20, 1896, aged 76

—∿—

HARRIET BEECHER STOWE

AMERICAN WRITER WHOSE ANTI-SLAVERY NOVEL "UNCLE TOM'S CABIN" WAS AN INTERNATIONAL BESTSELLER

JULY 2, 1896

NEW YORK, July 1: Mrs Harriet Beecher Stowe died at noon to-day at her home in Hartford, Connecticut, in her 85th year. She had had three successive attacks of paralysis since Monday. It is the breaking of almost the last link between the America of to-day and that America which Mrs Stowe found dead to the sin of slavery and woke to life. The three great names in connexion with that period of transition before the Civil War are Garrison, Wendell Phillips, and the author of "Uncle Tom's Cabin." That is the judgment of those Americans who know that period best, and Mrs Stowe is not the least of the three. — *Our Own Correspondent.*

Mrs Harriet Beecher Stowe, one of the most popular and versatile of American writers, was the daughter of Dr. Lyman Beecher, a Presbyterian minister. She was born at Litchfield, Connecticut, in June, 1812, one year before her distinguished brother, Henry Ward Beecher, who died in 1887, thus predeceasing her by eight years. Harriet Beecher lost her mother early in youth, and in one of the best of her many pathetic stories she has retold the incidents of the daily life of her motherless brothers and sisters. At the age of 13 she entered the Female Seminary at Hartford, of which her sister Catherine was the principal, and two years afterwards became a teacher in that institution. In 1832 she went with her family to Cincinnati, and in 1836 married the Rev Calvin E. Stowe, D. D., sometime Professor of Natural and Revealed Religion in Bowdoin College, Brunswick, Maine.

The literary career of the deceased did not really begin until after her marriage, though a few years before she had written for the Semi-colon Club sketches and papers exhibiting much promise. One of these was afterwards published, with additions, in 1849, under the title of "The Mayflower" — a series of sketches of incident and character drawn from the descendants of the Pilgrim Fathers. In 1850 Mrs Beecher Stowe accompanied her husband to Brunswick, in order to take up their residence at Bowdoin College. It was at this juncture that the Fugitive Slave Law of the United States was passed, and Mrs Stowe, who had always taken a profound interest in the slavery question, and had, indeed, frequently concealed runaway slaves in her own house, was moved to the quick by the sufferings of the negro race.

In June, 1851, she began in the *National Era*, an anti-slavery newspaper published in Washington, her celebrated story, "Uncle Tom's Cabin." It was written for the express purpose of exposing the system of slavery, and with no expectation of reward. It exhibited the system in its most degraded and also in its most refined aspects, and from both points of view was equally severe in its condemnation. The success of the novel was without precedent in the history of fiction. Nearly half a million copies were soon disposed of in the United States alone. Long afterwards, when the author was questioned respecting her work, she said:—"I did not write it. God wrote it. I merely did His dictation." "Uncle Tom's Cabin" was one of those spontaneous literary productions written under the sway of an overpowering emotion; and its moving pathos made its way at once to the heart of every reader. Its characters

also were vigorously and boldly drawn, and its pictures of slave life were startling in their vividness and irresistible because of their truth. Of course, Mrs Stowe was violently attacked by the friends of slavery; but to prove the accuracy of her representations she published a "Key to Uncle Tom's Cabin," giving the original facts upon which the story was founded, together with corroborative statements in verification and justification of the work.

Just before the issue of "Uncle Tom's Cabin" Mrs Stowe had been much troubled by the fact that slavery was pursuing its victims more relentlessly than ever into the free States, and that Canada even was threatened. To avert the possible contingency of the closing of Canada as a haven of refuge for the oppressed, she wrote earnest letters to Prince Albert, to the Duke of Argyll, the Earls of Carlisle and Shaftesbury, Macaulay, Dickens, and others whom she knew to be friendly to the cause of the slaves. With these letters were despatched early copies of her forthcoming story. The replies she received were most sympathetic; the work was commended for its graphic power and its righteous mission; and that which its writer apprehended — the closing of Canada to the fugitive slave — happily never came to pass.

In April, 1852, "Uncle Tom's Cabin" was first brought out in England, and edition followed edition with great rapidity. From April to December 12 different editions were published, and within twelve months from its first appearance 18 different London publishing houses were engaged in supplying the immense demand that had set in, the total number of editions being 40. The aggregate number of copies circulated in a short time in Great Britain and the colonies exceeded one-and-a-half million. The Library of the British Museum contains some 40 different editions in English. In the course of a few years the story was translated into 22 languages.

During the summer of 1853 Mrs Stowe visited Europe, and met with a most enthusiastic reception throughout England. She and her husband and her brother, Charles Beecher, arrived at Liverpool in April. Glasgow was the first point of their tour, and from that city they proceeded to Edinburgh, where the "National Penny Anti-Slavery Offering" was presented to Mrs Stowe, consisting of 1,000 sovereigns on a magnificent silver salver. The money was all subscribed by the poorer classes. On the 8th of May a grand reception was given to her at Stafford-house. Here she met Lord Palmerston, of whom she wrote:— "There is something peculiarly alert and vivacious about all his movements; in short, his appearance perfectly answers to what we know of him from his public life. While talking with him I could not but remember how often I had heard father and Mr Stowe exulting over his foreign despatches by our own fireside. There were present, also, Lord John Russell, Mr Gladstone, and Lord Granville. The latter we all thought very strikingly resembled in his appearance the poet Longfellow."

Lord Shaftesbury read an address from the ladies of England, cordially welcoming Mrs Stowe to the mother country. A superb gold bracelet, formed as a slave's shackle, and presented by the Duchess of Sutherland to Mrs Stowe, bore the inscription, "We trust it is a memorial of a chain that is soon to be broken." On two of the links were inscribed the dates of the abolition of the slave trade and of slavery in English territory; and years after the presentation Mrs Stowe was able to have engraved on the clasp of the bracelet, "Constitutional amendment for ever abolishing slavery in the United States." Mrs Stowe afterwards made a tour on the Continent.

Early in 1854 she published an account of her European experiences, in the form of letters written to her friends at home, under the title of "Sunny Memories of Foreign Lands." Both before and after her return to the United States Mrs Stowe added to the literature connected with "Uncle Tom's Cabin" by the publication — in addition to the "Key" — of "A Peep into Uncle Tom's Cabin for Children" and "The Christian Slave, a Drama founded on Uncle Tom's Cabin." In 1856 she produced a second anti-slavery novel, entitled "Dred, a Tale of the Dismal Swamp." It was a powerful work, and attained considerable popularity, but its unrelieved gloom, and the absence of the genial humour which had marked its predecessor, prevented it from taking the same intense hold upon the masses.

Mrs Stowe paid a second visit to England and Europe in 1856. She was accompanied by her husband, her two eldest daughters, her son Henry, and her sister. The party spent some time at Inverary Castle, and afterwards at Dunrobin Castle. They were informally received at one of the Scotch railway stations by her Majesty the Queen, who was then travelling in Scotland. Professor Stowe, in describing this incident, said:— "The Queen seemed really delighted to see my wife, and remarkably glad to see me for her sake. She pointed us out to Prince Albert, who made two most gracious bows to my wife and two to me, while the four Royal children stared their big blue eyes almost out looking at the authoress of 'Uncle Tom's Cabin.' Colonel Grey handed the Queen, with my wife's compliments, two copies of the new book 'Dred.' She took one volume herself, and handed the other to Prince Albert, and they were soon both very busy reading."

In the summer of 1859 Mrs Stowe paid her last visit to Europe, accompanied by all her family except her youngest son. At Rome she saw a good deal of the Brownings, with whom she formed a warm friendship.

Before her final European tour, Mrs Stowe had been closely engaged in literary work, and in 1858 she began the publication of "The Minister's Wooing" in the *Atlantic Monthly*, and "The Pearl of Orr's Island" simultaneously in the *Independent*.

The American Civil War broke out in 1861, and one of the first volunteers was Mrs Stowe's son Frederick, who was severely, though not fatally, wounded at the Battle of Gettysburg. In 1863

Mrs Stowe published her Italian story, "Agnes of Sorrento," which was suggested to her on her last tour in Italy. But the most important event of this time was the publication in the *Atlantic Monthly* of Mrs Stowe's reply to "The Affectionate and Christian Address of many thousands of Women of Great Britain and Ireland, to their Sisters, the Women of the United States of America." The address had been presented to Mrs Stowe eight years before, accompanied by 26 folio volumes, containing considerably more than half a million signatures of British women. These signatures formed the most remarkable part of the address. Beginning at the very steps of the Throne, they went down to the names of women in the very humblest conditions of life. Mrs Stowe's reply took the form of an eloquent and most powerful appeal to her sisters in Great Britain to stand true to the cause of the North and of human freedom. The fratricidal strife in the United States happily came to an end in 1865, and the cause of the union and of emancipation triumphed.

In 1866 Mrs Stowe removed with her family to the South. In addition to other reasons, she was anxious to do her share towards educating and leading to a higher life those coloured people whom she had so largely helped to set free. Florida was selected as the best field, and she bought a place at Mandarin. She had now joined the Episcopal Church, in which her daughters were already communicants, and with the aid of the Bishop of Florida she established a number of churches along the St John's River. In 1869 Mrs

Stowe published her "Old Town Folks," a story of New England life; and during this and the next few years, while her husband preached in a little church on the Florida property, she conducted Sunday schools, sewing classes, singing classes, &c., which were well attended by both the white and coloured residents of the neighbourhood.

Mrs Stowe's reputation was seriously overshadowed in 1870 by her attack upon Lord Byron. We cannot avoid all mention of this regrettable incident, seeing that the fame of one of the greatest of modern English poets was involved in the terrible charges advanced by Mrs Stowe. While in Europe Mrs Stowe had contracted a friendship with Lady Byron, upon whose authority the allegations were understood to be based. The Countess Guiccioli having published in 1868 her "Recollections of Lord Byron," which contained some severe reflections on the character of Lady Byron, Mrs Stowe wrote a paper in reply, entitled "The True Story of Lady Byron's Life," which appeared in the *Atlantic Monthly* for September, 1869, and also in *Macmillan's Magazine*. This article, which excited much comment, was extended into a volume called "Lady Byron Vindicated," issued in 1870. It was felt that the grounds for the attack were of an altogether inadequate character, and there was a strong revulsion of feeling against the calumniator.

Among Mrs Stowe's best and most attractive works in later life were:— "The Chimney Corner," issued in 1869; "My Wife and I," published in 1871; and "Palmetto Leaves," a series of Florida sketches, which appeared in 1873. Then she wrote "Poganue People: their Loves and Lives," her last undertaking of any length in volume form. It consisted of a series of delightful reminiscences of New England life. In addition to the works already cited she also produced a great number of minor stories and sketches.

In 1872 Mrs Stowe carried through a successful campaign for the American Literary Lecture Bureau of Boston, when she delivered a course of 40 readings from her own works in the principal cities of the New England States. She made another reading tour in the West the following year, but she would never undertake a third, although she frequently read on behalf of charitable objects. Mrs Stowe had now left Florida and returned to the North, where she permanently resided. For some years before her death Mrs Stowe's mind was more or less clouded, but her physical health remained strong and vigorous almost to the very last.

In all the relations of private life Mrs Stowe was widely beloved. Her writings are conceived in a high and elevated vein, and had it not been for the unfortunate controversy she provoked on the subject of Lord Byron there would have been no female American writer who would have been held in such high and general esteem in England and Europe. Mrs Stowe took a deep interest in the religious, temperance, and philanthropic questions of the time, as well as in all movements for raising the social, intellectual, and moral status of the less fortunate members of her own sex.

Harriet Beecher Stowe, writer and abolitionist, was born on June 14, 1811. She died on July 1, 1896, aged 85

ROSA BONHEUR

FRENCH ARTIST WHO RANKED WITH ENGLAND'S LANDSEER AS A PAINTER OF ANIMALS

MAY 27, 1899

We learn with regret from our Paris correspondent of the death of Mlle Rosa Bonheur, which took place at the village of By, on the border of the Forest of Fontainebleau, late on Thursday night. The whole world of art is thus the poorer for the loss of a great painter. It is somewhat strange that, though pictorial art is a profession, open to all, in which one would expect women to excel, the great female artists may almost be counted on the fingers of one hand. Mlle Bonheur was an exception, and a notable one, to the rule which gives her sex a great deal of facility in art but no great degree of distinction. Nor had she any very exceptional advantages, though she belonged to a family of painters. Her father, Raymond Bonheur, was a painter, and so were his two sons, François Auguste and Isidore Jules, as well as his other daughter, Juliette, Mme Peyrol. At the Salon of 1847 the father, the two sons, and Rosa were all exhibitors.

Rosalie Bonheur was born at Bordeaux in 1822, and is said to have shown at a very early age the direction in which her tastes lay. Her delight as a child was to cut out animals in paper. She was hardly seven years old when her family removed to Paris, where she was sent to a boys' school. She lost her mother while she was still a mere child, and was then apprenticed to the uncongenial business of a dressmaker, an occupation which she disliked and did not long pursue. She preferred to frequent the Louvre, making copies of the pictures there, and selling them to advantage. She achieved her first triumph when she was only 19 years old, two of her pictures, "Chèvres et Moutons" and "Deux Lapins," being hung at the Salon. Further successes followed so soon that she is said to have sold one of her works for £600 at the early age of 24. Her father married a second time in 1845, and she was then enabled to pursue her own special studies of animal life in the country. She learned animal anatomy at the *abattoirs*, and made many sketches for a picture, "Boeufs Rouges du Cantal," which was awarded the third medal at the Salon of 1846. It should be noted, however, that she did not entirely confine herself to animal painting, but also produced, both in the earlier and later parts of her career, several landscapes of considerable merit. But undoubtedly it is as a painter of animals, and especially of cattle and horses, that she was now becoming famous.

The most marked of her early successes was in 1848 — namely, her "Labourage Nivernais," which is now at the Luxembourg and will by and by, now that she is no more, be transferred to the Louvre. A medal was awarded her for it. In the following year she lost her father, who was very proud of his promising daughter, and she felt this bereavement so keenly that she did not again exhibit till 1853, when her "Marché aux Chevaux" was one of the chief attractions of the Salon. It is probably her best known work. A replica of it is in the National Gallery, and engravings of it have been popular in this country. The original has been exhibited in America, and has since been sold for £12,000. Certainly it shows her art at its best, and combines excellent composition and texture with a power, not always fully possessed by animal painters, of drawing horses in motion. It would be superfluous to name all the many works that have come from her studio since the "Horse Fair." All the Salons during the Second Empire exhibited her pictures, and brought not only money, but the honourable recognition of the Emperor and Empress. "Sheep at the Seaside" was bought by the Empress in 1867. But long before that, in 1855, Mlle Bonheur had bought an estate in the Forest of Fontainebleau, where the Emperor was an occasional visitor, and the Empress, in 1865, personally invested her with the Cross of the Legion of Honour. Many years later she received from President Carnot the insignia of an officer of the Legion. She was the only Frenchwoman in that grade.

Happily, none of the events of 1870 either drove her from Fontainebleau or even caused her to interrupt her work. Fontainebleau, during the siege of Paris, cannot have been a convenient residence, but the Crown Prince of Prussia, following classical precedent, "bade spare" the artist's house and estate, and paid her a visit, which, though he was accompanied by Uhlans, she stoutly refused to receive. Here, at least, the invader was repulsed. The story goes that he was invited to see the pictures in the studio, but was refused admission to the presence of the lady herself. So, both in war and peace, Rosa Bonheur continued to paint, perhaps without greatly adding to the great reputation won by her in the fifties and sixties, but always in such a manner as to command the applause and attention of the artistic public. One of her later achievements was a large landscape, "Haymaking in Auvergne," which was sent to the Paris International Exhibition of 1885.

She was, however, as we have said, *par excellence* an animal painter, and one of the very best. This is by no means the kind of art which lady artists usually regard with favour; but, having discovered her particular gift, she cultivated it with great industry and zeal. She adopted a masculine costume in order that she might more conveniently attend horse fairs, and visited them regularly in search of subjects. Her portraits, in a costume that was rational enough when it was worn for a good reason, must be familiar to many of our readers. She even kept a species of menagerie of her own, and her "Lion at Home," exhibited in London in 1882, was painted from one of its temporary inhabitants. Part of her studio, too, was boarded off so as to serve as a stable for her more ordinary models. In short, genius, force of character, and singleness of purpose made her, within her chosen range, a great artist. She may rank worthily with Landseer, and possibly in some respects above him. Her technical knowledge, both of painting and of animals, was not inferior to his. Sentiment and humour — the sentiment, for example, of Landseer's wounded swans, and the humour of "High Life and Low Life" — she did not aim at; but in thorough knowledge of such animals as horses, cattle, and sheep she was wholly unsurpassed. Her powers were recognized not only in France, but in England, America, Germany, and Belgium. On the Imperial Russian visit to Paris their Majesties expressed a wish to see her, and she was one of those who escorted them through the Louvre. This, however, was a solitary exception to the secluded habits of her later years, and she was almost inaccessible to strangers, not even answering the letters of proposed visitors. She was made a member of the Institute of Antwerp in 1868, and in 1880 the King of the Belgians gave her the Cross of the Order of Leopold, and the King of Spain the Cross of the Order of Isabella the Catholic. In both cases she was the first lady to be thus distinguished.

Rosa Bonheur, artist, was born on March 16, 1822. She died on May 25, 1899, aged 77

DOROTHEA BEALE

EDUCATIONAL PIONEER AND PRINCIPAL OF CHELTENHAM LADIES' COLLEGE

NOVEMBER 10, 1906

We announce with much regret that Miss Dorothea Beale, principal of the Ladies' College, Cheltenham, died about noon yesterday. Last week she underwent a slight operation, which was successful, and a rapid recovery was expected. On Monday, however, there was a change for the worse, and she was found to be suffering from nervous prostration.

Miss Dorothea Beale was a pioneer, in the strictest dictionary meaning of the term — one who goes before to prepare the way. The "way" which she prepared was that of a rational education for her own sex. She once said of herself, "I was born in the dark ages and have witnessed the Renaissance." Modesty forbade her to add, what a great host of contemporaries and followers will add for her, that she was foremost among those who made the Renaissance possible.

The surroundings of her birth and childhood were favourable to the development of her character and capacity, and formed a suitable environment, fitting her for her life's work. Her father,

Mr Miles Beale, M.R.C.S., took an active interest in the improvement of the social and educational conditions of his time. He prompted the establishment of literary institutes, was a shareholder in the London Institution and one of the first members of the Society of Arts, and was himself a not infrequent lecturer on literary and scientific subjects. His daughter, Dorothea, was born in 1831, and among the influences moulding her character and aspirations she never failed to mention the name of her mother's aunt, Mrs Cornwallis, and that of her cousin, Miss Caroline Cornwallis, a very remarkable woman, who, from early childhood, devoted herself to scholarship of all kinds, studied Greek, Latin, Hebrew, and German, philosophy, law and criminal procedure, and was the author of a number of books, well known in their day, called "Small Books on Great Subjects." The influence of these relatives, though very helpful to Miss Beale at a later period of her intellectual development, was not sufficient to protect her from the pernicious pretence of education which was all that was available in the boarding school for young ladies of the early forties. She learnt by heart useless epitomes, and went through the usual course of Mangnall's questions, and Pinnock's catechisms. She referred in after life with some bitterness to the "noxious brood of catechisms" which impart information on such points as the number of prepositions which begin with "u," the number of people who died of the Plague, the number of houses burnt in the Fire of London, and other entirely disconnected fragments of fact, or supposed fact, which then did duty as "education," but bear as much resemblance to the real thing as a heap of loose pebbles does to a building.

Whatever the demerits of her early education, it had at least one saving quality — it did not quench her desire for knowledge. She left school conscious that there was such a thing as learning, that there were vast tracts to be explored, and that her education, if begun, was only just begun. She read voraciously, taught herself Euclid, attended classes and lectures, and was especially influenced by the Gresham Professor of Astronomy, Mr Pullen, of Cambridge, who awakened in her a passion for mathematics. She was also early in her adolescence brought under the influence of deep religious feeling, and this remained a motive power guiding her thoughts and conduct to the end of her life. She has written of this herself, "Religion quickened the intellectual life, for sacramental teaching was, to the leaders of that movement, no narrow dogmatism, but the discovery of the river of the water of life, flowing through the whole desert of human existence, and making it rejoice and blossom as the rose."

Throughout her subsequent career as the creator and organizer of the largest and most successful of girls' schools, the most intensely vital part of her work was rooted in her religion. It was a revelation of a spirit finely touched to fine issues to hear her read the Bible, and offer the prayers with which the school day at Cheltenham invariably begins.

A strong Churchwoman, and a member of the council of the Church of England High Schools Company, she had no touch of the fanatic. The normal religious instruction of the Ladies' College, Cheltenham, was according to the Church of England, but any parent was at liberty to withdraw a girl from it, and no teaching of the Catechism or any distinctively Church doctrine was ever suggested if Miss Beale knew a child to belong to a Dissenting family or to the Scotch Church. Her endeavour was to make the religious teaching practical as regards the daily duties of life, on which there is general agreement, rather than to dwell on points of doctrine on which differences arise.

An epoch in the history of women's education was the opening of Queen's College, Harley-street, in 1846, mainly through the instrumentality of Dr (afterwards Archbishop) Trench, Professor Plumptre, and the Rev Frederic Denison Maurice. Miss Beale attended its opening lecture, and she and her sisters were among the first recipients of its certificates. The classes thus opened enabled her to read Sophocles and Plato with Dr Plumptre, Literature and Philosophy with Mr Maurice, and other subjects with equally eminent teachers. She now found the mental food which her earlier training had failed to give, and devoted herself to study with something which can only be described as rapture. She was appointed mathematical, and later also classical, tutor at Queen's College, and soon showed herself as enthusiastic a teacher as she had been a learner. Her vacations, both at this time and afterwards, were frequently spent in Switzerland or Germany, visiting colleges, hearing lessons given, and profiting, and enabling her pupils later to profit, by improved methods which she then saw in practice. Her plan of teaching Euclid without a book, which she explained in her evidence given before the Schools Inquiry Commission in 1866, was largely based on what she had seen in Professor Weileman's class in the Canton Schule at Zurich.

She was always learning, always preserving the open mind, and ever ready to consider new and improved methods. Long before its now general adoption, she had given practical approval to the rational method of teaching foreign languages. Her plan was to begin with facts, names of things, short sentences, and so forth, and proceed thence to grammatical principles. She quoted with great approval a description by Dr Bryce, of Glasgow, of the way in which a teacher imparted to a class of boys a knowledge of Newton's great discovery of gravitation. He did not tell them the result of Newton's investigations, but "he enumerated the phenomena by which Newton arrived at it, taking care to present them in the order most likely to suggest it. As fact after fact was marshalled before them they became eager and excited more and more, for they saw that something new and great was coming; and when at last the array of phenomena was complete and the magnificent conclusion burst upon their sight, the whole class started from their seats with a scream of delight."

This sort of teaching, as Miss Beale was never weary of insisting, was real education. What a contrast did it not present to "the noxious breed of catechisms" of her youth!

She held her posts at Queen's College for seven years and then resigned because she was dissatisfied with the management. The professors of King's College, to whom the credit of starting Queen's was due, were too absolute in its management; some were unpunctual in their attendances; some were too much engaged in other work to give the time required for the correction of exercises and so forth; and Miss Beale felt particularly that there was a great want at Queen's, as then constituted, arising from the absence of a strong womanly influence over the students. She next accepted the post of head teacher of the Clergy Daughters' School at Casterton, Charlotte Brontë's "Lowood." If there was too little supervision at Queen's, there was too much at Casterton. The life was absolutely conventual and absolutely monotonous. The children were all dressed alike, and individual property in books or in clothes was discouraged. Books were in common and dresses were passed on from one to another. The children seldom went home; there was almost nothing to break the monotony of their lives; the Sundays were one continual round of lessons and services. Miss Beale was an unusually well-equipped teacher, but her acquirements failed to come up to the encyclopaedic knowledge which the managing committee of Casterton demanded. She was prepared to teach Scripture, classics, mathematics, arithmetic, and French and German; but she was expected also to teach ancient and modern history, Church history, English literature, English composition and political and physical geography. When teaching meant nothing but hearing pupils repeat passages out of a book, it was possible to combine all the 'ologies in the person of one unfortunate governess, but that was not what Miss Beale understood by education. She only remained at Casterton a year, and resigned wearied in mind and body.

Six months later, in 1858, a vacancy occurred in the post of headmistress of the Ladies' College, Cheltenham, and Miss Beale entered upon the work with which her name will always be associated. Cheltenham was the only proprietary college for girls then in existence. In 1858 it was in its fourth year from its commencement. It had opened with 80 pupils, a number which a little later increased to over 100. But after this a period of decline set in, and when Miss Beale took the command the numbers had fallen to 69. She found at Cheltenham a school framed, as regards classes and removes, on the experience of the best boys' schools, but a great part of the teaching required remodelling. No science was taught, no mathematics, no ancient languages. Miss Beale proceeded with caution in the reforms she desired to introduce. Notwithstanding Sydney Smith's argument in 1810 that the great institutions of nature do not depend on teaching women a little more or a little less, that learning Latin would not dry up the fountain of a woman's affections, and that no female mathematician had been known to forsake her infant for a quadratic equation, she found in full force the old superstition that girls would be turned into boys if they studied the same subjects. She felt that geometry would be particularly useful to girls in helping them to form clear ideas and to set their thoughts in order, but she also felt that the mere name of geometry might have been the death of the college; so she walked delicately, and under the name of "physical geography" she was able to do a good deal. This was thought an eminently safe feminine subject, as few boys learnt any geography at all.

It would be impossible within the necessarily narrow limits of this notice to follow step by step the various means by which Miss Beale raised the Ladies' College, Cheltenham, to the almost unique position it soon occupied under her able guidance. The council, or governing body, felt complete confidence in her aims and methods of pursuing them, and very wisely left her almost entirely a free hand. The introduction of a University examiner from Oxford in 1863 to test the educational work done in the college caused a considerable stir. Some parents refused to allow their girls to take part in the examination. Other parents, however, fully sympathized with what Miss Beale was doing, and appreciated the thoroughness of the education she was offering their children.

One main difficulty at the outset, long as it was before the opening of University education to women, was the scarcity of well-trained and well-educated teachers. Miss Beale grappled with this in a characteristic fashion by training her teachers herself; and the training department has for close upon half a century been an important part of the educational institutions of Cheltenham. In 1877 Miss Beale started in Cheltenham St Hilda's College. This is a hall of residence for elder girls, for teachers in course of training, and other ladies preparing for University degrees. In 1900 St Hilda's College was amalgamated with St Hilda's Hall, Oxford, another of Miss Beale's creations. Therefore, besides the great school over which she was called to preside in 1858, Miss Beale called into existence two colleges for women where work of University standard is done.

The jubilee of Cheltenham Ladies' College was spread over two years, 1904 and 1905. At this time the number of pupils under instruction was 1,000, divided between four departments — (1) the kindergarten; (2) the junior school (for children from eight to 12); (3) the middle school (for children from 13 to 15); (4) the college proper, for elder girls. Buildings, including art and technical schools, a first-rate scientific laboratory, and a library, had been erected at a cost of more than £100,000, besides boarding-houses, sanatorium, playgrounds, &c., which had cost an additional £60,000. These figures are sufficiently eloquent when it is remembered that the college was founded with a total capital of only £2,000. In 1905 its annual income was £60,000.

Among the visitors assembled to do honour to Miss Beale at the jubilee gathering in 1905 were the Marquis of Londonderry, President of the Board of Education, the Bishop of Bristol and the Dean of Durham, representing the older Universities, heads of women's colleges in Oxford, Cambridge, and London, the borough member, a representative of the Corporation of Cheltenham, and last, but by no means least in interest, the Dean of the Women's University of Japan.

The high value of Miss Beale's services to education received a large and well-deserved measure of public recognition. In 1889 she was made Officier de l'Académie de Paris; in 1895 she became tutor in letters of Durham University; in 1901 she was placed on the advisory board of London University for arranging the matriculation examination; in the same year the freedom of the borough of Cheltenham was conferred upon her; and in 1902 she received the honorary LL.D. degree of the University of Edinburgh. Her advice was sought by educationists far and wide. The late Master of Balliol, Dr Jowett, after a visit to Cheltenham, wrote to her with much cordiality of the "great institution" which she had cre-ated; he sought her advice as to how Oxford could best help to raise the standard of education in girls' schools.

She was keenly alive to the importance of family and domestic claims on women, and advocated for them better education, a wider sphere of activity, and a share in public life, including women's suffrage, because she believed the reflex action of these changes upon the family and upon domestic life would be beneficial.

Some of her critics, among educational reformers, have said that Cheltenham was the be-all and end-all of her existence, that her horizon in educational matters was bounded by its requirements. This may in part be true; even if wholly true it is not inexcusable. To have created so great an institution is no mean accomplishment, no unworthy life's work. To see it a little out of its true proportion may be forgiven to its creator. She sometimes quoted the saying, "Usefulness is the rent we pay for room upon the earth." No one can say of her that her rent was in arrear.

Dorothea Beale, educational pioneer and principal of Cheltenham Ladies' College, was born on March 21, 1831. She died on November 9, 1906, aged 75

BARONESS BURDETT-COUTTS

PHILANTHROPIST WHOSE
ENDOWMENTS RANGED FROM
CHURCHES AND HOUSING
PROJECTS TO A FISHERY
SCHOOL IN IRELAND

DECEMBER 31, 1906

We announce with deep regret the death of the Baroness Burdett-Coutts, which occurred yesterday morning, at her residence in Stratton-street, Piccadilly, at the age of 92. Her ladyship had been in Stratton-street with Mr Burdett-Coutts, MP, since October. She was seized, as we announced on Saturday, with acute bronchitis. Late on Friday night she made somewhat of a rally, and her wonderful vitality, which had saved her several times in recent years, gave some hope that her life might be prolonged. After a consultation at noon on Saturday, her doctors stated that her condition showed no improvement and that, if anything, she was rather weaker. During the latter part of the day she grew worse, but was able to recognize the older members of her household, giving her hand to each in turn. She was always conscious to the very end, and Mr Burdett-Coutts, who was with her throughout, remained at her bedside during the last 12 hours.

About 5 o'clock yesterday morning it seemed apparent that the end had come, but she partially rallied again and again during the next five hours until she passed peacefully away at 10.30am.

The Queen and the Princess of Wales sent telegrams of sympathy and inquiry to Mr Burdett-Coutts on Saturday. Her Majesty's telegram contained a gracious personal message to the Baroness, which the latter was able to understand and appreciate. The King and other members of the Royal Family were informed by telegraph when Lady Burdett-Coutts died, and many distinguished personages who had made sympathetic inquiries in the course of Saturday were similarly informed.

The following telegram from Lord Knollys, at Sandringham, was sent to Mr Burdett-Coutts:—"I am commanded by the King and Queen to express their great regret to hear of the death of Lady Burdett-Coutts. They sincerely sympathize with you in your loss."

Throughout yesterday Mr Burdett-Coutts was in almost constant receipt of telegrams from all parts of the country and of written communications from sympathizers who are out of town. The Lord Mayor sent the following telegram:—"Very sorry. Deeply sympathize with you. The City of London has lost one of its noblest and best beloved honorary freemen." The Rev Dr. Sheppard, the Sub-Dean of the Chapels Royal and Sub-Almoner to the King, announced the death at the service held at the Chapel Royal yesterday morning.

The Right Hon Angela Georgina, Baroness Burdett-Coutts, was born on April 21, 1814, and was the youngest daughter of Sir Francis Burdett, the well-known Radical Member for Westminster. Her mother was one of the three daughters of Thomas Coutts, the founder of the famous banking house — three daughters who, thanks to their beauty and wealth, and in spite of the humble origin of their Scotch mother, all made great marriages. Susan, the eldest, became Countess of Guilford; Frances, the second, became Marchioness of Bute; and Sophia, the youngest, married Sir Francis Burdett, who, though he professed opinions which were at that time generally ostracised by "society," was the head of an old and distinguished English family.

Thomas Coutts himself was an interesting character, to whose great business capacity, shrewd insight into things, and kindness of heart, combined with extreme frugality of habits, reference is often made in the current literature of his time, and who was brought back to notice a few years ago by his letters, printed in the Whitefoord Papers. He and his brothers were bankers in Edinburgh, who in the third quarter of the eighteenth century set up a branch in London, and who rose into importance after the crash caused by the failure of their swindling countryman Fordyce. Late in life, having survived all his brothers, and being by that time very rich, Thomas Coutts married as his second wife the fascinating actress Harriet Mellon, to whom on his death in 1821 he bequeathed

his great fortune. His widow presently became Duchess of St Albans; but when she died, in 1837, she restored her wealth to the family from which it came, leaving practically the whole of it to Thomas Coutts's grand-daughter, Miss Burdett, then a young woman of three-and-twenty. Miss Burdett thus became the owner of a half-share of the profits of the bank, of the well-known house at the corner of Stratton-street, and of a large quantity of plate, jewellery, and other valuable property; and in recognition of the source of all this wealth she took the surname of Coutts in addition to her own. At any time such wealth would have marked out its owner for notice, especially if she happened to be a young and attractive woman; but in those days, when international finance was in its infancy, when there were no American railway kings, and when the Transvaal had not been heard of, the owner of a million of money — and Miss Burdett-Coutts's fortune was probably more — naturally filled a greater position than would be the case at the present day. Miss Burdett-Coutts at once became an excessively interesting personage.

"The faymale heiress, Miss Anjaley Coutts," as Barham called her in his ballad on the Coronation, attracted all eyes, and became the object of the curiosity of all the world and of the cupidity of a good part of it. If she kept the letters containing offers of marriage, they must fill chests of drawers, and of course the more avowedly begging letters which she received from this time till the end of her life were annually to be numbered by many thousands. But all through her early and middle life she remained resolutely single, finding enough to occupy her mind and her heart in the great schemes of charity and practical beneficence to which she henceforth devoted herself. The record of her life is, in fact, a record of attempts consistently made to alleviate the lot of the suffering and to further schemes which she believed to be of public advantage. It must be remembered that in 1837 the true theory of giving was far less understood than it is now; the common notion of "doing good" was more or less the old notion of Lady Bountiful and of somewhat indiscriminate almsgiving. It will always be reckoned to the credit of Miss Burdett-Coutts that, young as she was, and without any guidance except her own good sense, she saw the unsatisfactoriness of such a system; and she endeavoured from the first so to arrange her great charities that they should be of real service to those who received them. From the modern point of view, indeed, it would be possible to find fault with many of her proposals and actions. Sometimes, as in the case of one of her favourite foundations, Columbia Market, she fought against economical conditions and trade combinations which were too strong for her, and naturally she was defeated; but, on the whole, a survey of her life only leads to the conclusion that the popular admiration felt towards her by the masses of London was well founded, and that she consistently maintained a noble view, rare

among millionaires of every epoch, of the responsibilities of wealth.

Any attempt to specify the schemes of public benevolence which were founded or encouraged by Miss Burdett-Coutts must be very imperfect; but we may mention a few, which will show how wide were her sympathies and how far-reaching her ideas of social improvement. If any single principle is to be discovered in her purely charitable benefactions, it is that she desired, not to keep unfortunate people in conditions of life which had been proved to lead to failure, but, by providing them with new conditions, to give them a fresh start. For example, her "Home" at Shepherd's-bush was one of the earliest practical attempts to reclaim women who had lost their characters; and its method was first to get them back into habits of honest work, and secondly to send them out to the colonies under kindly supervision, where a large number of them found happiness and a new life. Similarly, when the Spitalfields silk trade began to fail, Miss Burdett-Coutts founded sewing schools in that district, and thus qualified large numbers of women and girls for a change of work. Again, she was largely instrumental in founding the Shoeblack Brigade; and, when the cruel winter of 1860-61 revealed the unsatisfactory condition of the weaving and tanning trades in East and South-East London, she took a decisive part in organizing an aid association which enabled many families to emigrate to Queensland. These, with the less successful Columbia Market scheme, are notable instances of the efforts made by Miss Burdett-Coutts to help the poor of London; but many more might be added to them in this department alone. For example, three drinking fountains in London bear her name — one in Victoria Park, one at the entrance to the Zoological Gardens, and one near Columbia Market. Again, she founded and supported more than one institute in London, especially the St Stephen's Technical Institute in Vincent-square, Westminster; while she was chiefly responsible for the admirable public library and swimming bath in Great Smith-street, which she opened in 1893. The former of these, the St Stephen's Institute, was founded by Miss Burdett-Coutts in 1846 and maintained by her down to her death — a leading instance of the manner in which she sometimes anticipated the ideas of a later generation on matters of public utility.

London alone, however, did not by any means exhaust the charitable energies of Miss Burdett-Coutts. She very early recognized, as we have indicated, the great fact of the unity of the British Empire and of the general good that may be effected by well-managed emigration. But she was not wedded to this idea; she did not find in emigration a cure for every social ill. If, for example, she did much to help certain districts of Ireland and of the west coast of Scotland by assisting some of the inhabitants to emigrate, she did still more by her long and consistent efforts to improve the fisheries of Ireland, especially near Skibbereen, and by her

industrial fishing school at Baltimore, on the coast of Cork. The reception which was given her at this place in 1887 was extremely enthusiastic; and it is certain that no little good, if not quite as much as she and others had hoped for, has resulted from these well-meant efforts. And if these are proofs that her charity extended from London to the Kingdom and the Empire, it could at times be cosmopolitan as well.

One instance, which occurred a few years ago, showed the touch of sentimentalism which existed in her, as it must, we suppose, in all philanthropists. This was her visit, in 1896, when she was already more than eighty years of age, to the island of Corsica, in order that she might restore to the inhabitants the mortal remains of their great patriot, General Paoli, which for more than a century had rested in the churchyard of Old St Pancras. The idea was the Baroness' s own, and she bore the whole expense of the transfer. Naturally the warm-hearted Southern people, mindful of the old friendship between their island and ourselves, were deeply touched, and there was great enthusiasm throughout Corsica. Another of these examples of what we have called cosmopolitan charity was the institution of the Turkish Compassionate Fund during the war of 1877-78, through which some £30,000 were distributed among the starving peasantry and the fugitives. Political feeling ran high in this country at that moment; and possibly the Baroness may have been partly influenced by it in wishing that, while the Russian and Servian wounded were being comforted through other funds, the Turkish side should not be neglected; but we may be sure that the dominant motive on her part was one of pure human compassion, which must be counted to her for righteousness.

Although in her charities properly so-called Lady Burdett-Coutts knew no distinction of creed or sect, she was herself a loyal and very beneficent daughter of the Church of England. Her contributions to churches and church schools throughout the country were large and numerous, while some of her benefactions of this kind demand special notice. With a far-sighted care for the interests of the Empire at large which was less common sixty years ago than it is to-day, she devoted one of the earliest and greatest of her benefactions to strengthening the position of the Church in the Colonies. It was in 1847, when she was a young woman of 33, that she endowed out of her own purse the Bishoprics of Cape Town and Adelaide; and ten years later, at the cost of no less than £50,000, she founded the Bishopric of British Columbia, and provided a fund for endowing churches and clergy in that colony. At home, Miss Burdett-Coutts's first considerable work was to build and endow, in one of the poorest districts of Westminster, a church in memory of her father; and not only a church but schools and buildings which presently developed into a great technical institute and the home of innumerable guilds and benefit clubs. The work began in 1846, and on June 24, 1850, the large Gothic church of St Stephen, the work of

Mr Ferry, a Manchester architect, was consecrated by the Bishop of London. It used to be said that for this work Miss Burdett-Coutts had signed a cheque for £30,000. So in fact she did; but before the site had been paid for, the tenants compensated, the buildings completed, and the large endowment fund provided, the total cost had amounted not to £30,000 but to £90,000. In 1864, at the request of Bishop Waldegrave, prompted by Dr Tait, then Bishop of London — Miss Coutts's constant friend and adviser — she built another church dedicated to St Stephen in one of the poorest districts of Carlisle; and here again she was not content with half-measures, but built and endowed what a high authority has called "a model church." Later she largely contributed to the restoration of the churches of Ramsbury and Baydon, in Wiltshire, her father's county, and gave £15,000 to the Bishop of London as a contribution to the building of three churches in the metropolitan area.

The help she gave to elementary education, in the dark days before 1870, was scarcely less considerable. We have spoken of the schools of St Stephen's, Westminster; and, though these were her first care, she constantly interested herself in helping forward education elsewhere. For example, she was one of the first trustees of the Townshend Schools (founded out of the bequest of the Rev. Chauncey Hare Townshend) for the benefit of the children of the very poor, who could not afford to pay the fees that until 1890 were required in almost all schools; she placed at her own expense hundreds of East-end boys in training-ships; and she showed her practical sympathy with the night-school movement by maintaining a large school of that type in Cooper's-gardens in the East-end. She was the first, also, to establish cooking and sewing schools in London. At the same time she was quite alive to the importance of helping the claims of a somewhat more advanced education; for she was a constant supporter of the Birkbeck Literary and Scientific Institute, she established the first Art Students' Home for Ladies, and she cordially aided the development of the St Stephen's Institute into the Westminster Institute of Technical Training.

No subject lay closer to the Baroness's heart than the protection of animals and the prevention of cruelty. It need scarcely be said that she was a very active member of the SPCA; and in these columns she often uttered some indignant protest against the ill-treatment of dogs, the trapping of singing birds, and the like. Those who remember the extraordinary story of "Greyfriars Bobby" — the little dog which followed his master to the grave in Edinburgh, and who constantly revisited that spot from the year 1858 to the time of his own death in 1872 — may like to be reminded that the Baroness erected a monument and drinking-fountain in the dog's honour at the corner of George IV Bridge. She made effective protests against the cruelties of the over-sea cattle trade; and improved cattle trucks were planned and carried out at her expense for the home railway traffic. Probably nothing contributed more to her popularity with the working classes in London than her efforts, not only on behalf of the costermongers, but on behalf of their donkeys. She built large stables for them on the Columbia estate, and the costers' donkey shows, in which prizes were given for the best-kept animals, were, and we believe still are, a great feature in the life of East London. The Baroness was also one of the founders of the Whit Monday Cart-horse Parade, now one of the most popular and useful of annual institutions; and one of the most memorable days in her life was that on which, in May, 1882, she attended a parade at Newcastle and distributed the prizes not only to the owners of cart-horses, but to the colliers who brought their pit-ponies, harnessed to the little trollies with which they work underground. A local paper at the time said that "a hundred-thousand people came into town to see the Baroness," and their enthusiasm was extraordinary.

Special mention should be made of the Baroness's efforts in practical beneficence made in the cause of Ireland. Neither she nor her friends imagined that she was going to solve the Irish question by helping a single fishery centre; but here as elsewhere she believed that she might not only be of direct service to a number of individuals, but that she might lead other private benefactors and public authorities in the right way. Long afterwards the Duchess of Teck, writing to the committee of the Chicago Exhibition

on the subject of the Baroness's philanthropic work, said with truth that,
"great as have been the intrinsic benefits that the Baroness has conferred on
others, the most signal of all has been
the power of example — an incalculable quantity, which no record of events
can measure." The Duchess meant
primarily the example of character,
but we may extend the phrase to the
definite example set by her good works.
The success of her efforts in the then
miserable district of Skibbereen and
Baltimore in Co Cork, which began
so long ago as 1862, to start a fishing
industry and a lads' training-school
in fishery, was considerable enough to
have encouraged many similar efforts
round the coast of Ireland; and if the
example has not been largely followed,
it is not the Baroness's fault. In the
evil days of 1880, when a failure of the
crops combined with the new agrarian
agitation to make the Irish question
more acute than ever, the Baroness
proposed to the Government a scheme
more splendidly munificent than any
of her previous benefactions — nothing less than the advance of £250,000
for providing seed to impoverished
peasantry. In a word, her desire to help
the poor of Ireland was just as keen as
her desire to help forward the material and moral interests of the poor of
London. But in this matter, as in others,
she carefully kept herself clear of any
sort of political partisanship. She never
took any step in favour of a Liberal or a
Conservative Government as such; she
never appeared on a political platform,
even in her husband's constituency of
Westminster; and we believe it to be
a fact that she carried the principle of
non-intervention so far that some time
before each Westminster election she
left London, lest she should be supposed to influence the votes of the poor
people whom she had benefited.

The definite events in the life of Lady
Burdett-Coutts which afford matter
to the chronicler are not many; perhaps, indeed, only three emerge from
the constant series of benefactions,
unobtrusively performed, of which we
have mentioned some of the chief. The
first of these events took place in May,
1871, when Queen Victoria, in the
Premiership of Mr Gladstone, offered
Miss Burdett-Coutts a peerage, and
she became Baroness Burdett-Coutts of
Highgate and Brookfield, in the county
of Middlesex. The second was the
interesting and as yet unique ceremony
in the Guildhall on July 18, 1872, when
the freedom of the City was conferred
upon the Baroness Burdett-Coutts, the
only lady, as the City Chamberlain
remarked, who had ever been admitted to that distinguished fellowship. It
may be added that similar distinctions
were conferred about this time upon
Lady Burdett-Coutts by the Turners'
Company, by the Haberdashers'
Company, and by the city of Edinburgh.
The last and most important of the
three events took place in 1881, when,
to the surprise of the whole world, it
was announced that her ladyship, who
was then nearly 67 years of age and
who was thought to be as much vowed
to celibacy as the Virgin Queen herself,
was about to be married. Her choice fell

upon Mr William Lehmann Ashmead-Bartlett, her private secretary and the administrator of her charities in Bulgaria, who was born in 1851. The marriage took place in February, the bridegroom took the name of Burdett-Coutts, and four years later the electors of Westminster elected him their representative in Parliament, a position which he still holds.

At the time of her death Lady Burdett-Coutts had reached so great an age that to a certain extent she experienced the fate of all those who outlive their contemporaries. Such people necessarily find that the details of their work are forgotten and that a new age has brought new conditions and new ideals, superseding those with which they were familiar. But, none the less, history will always regard her as one of the striking figures of the Victorian age in England; as one of those who, having become possessed of great opportunities, did all that in her lay to make use of them for the benefit of her fellow-citizens. She was a queen in her own circle; and it is not fanciful to say that in her realm of beneficence she modelled herself so far as was possible on the great Queen of whom she was one of the most devoted subjects. That is to say, she felt herself born to high responsibilities, and she fulfilled them with complete self-abnegation, with conscientious thoughtfulness, and with the help of the best advice that she could command. The task of dealing with the immense problems of London poverty as a whole was beyond her power, as it is beyond the power of any private person or group of persons. But she did much, and she showed the way in which others might do more. Let it be remembered that in the days of her greatest activity there was no Elementary Education Act, and that Mr Torrens, Lord Cross, and other reformers had not begun to make even the first attempts to solve the housing problem. Local government was extremely imperfect; the sanitary laws more imperfect still, there was no Charity Organization Society, and Mr Charles Booth had not laid out the ground for future reformers by writing his great book on the London poor. That, in the face of so much general ignorance and disorganization one woman, furnished with nothing but wealth, a warm heart, and a clear head, should have accomplished so much is an astonishing fact; and, however the details of her achievements may be open to the criticism of a later age, nothing can deprive the Baroness Burdett-Coutts of her claim to lasting public gratitude.

In Westminster Abbey yesterday the "Dead March" in *Saul* was played at the conclusion of the service, and the Archdeacon of Westminster in the course of his sermon alluded to Lady Burdett-Coutts in the following terms:—"Now and again the Divine nature immanent in humanity provides us with a sample pattern of a life lived for others. Such a life pre-eminently was that which, after 92 years in the body, passed out of the body this morning. The life of the Baroness Burdett-Coutts stands next to that of Queen Victoria herself in the Victorian era. It would not be possible here and now to enumerate her countless services to humanity, the Bishoprics she has endowed, the churches she has built, the charities she has helped to initiate. She is the only woman upon whom a peerage of the United Kingdom has been conferred in recognition of personal merit and public service. Her great philanthropic work in Ireland will never be forgotten. She was the first to erect model dwellings for the artisan class. She inaugurated the Royal Society for the Prevention of Cruelty to Children. She contributed more than any individual of her time to the furtherance of education. Unflinching devotion to duty, ceaseless recognition of responsibility for the public welfare, fidelity to the lofty demands of freedom, justice, and purity — these were the motive forces of her whole being and it would be difficult to imagine a life more deserving of the epitaph pronounced upon King David, majestic in its simplicity, exhaustive in its comprehensiveness:—"After she had, in her own generation, served the counsel of God, she fell asleep and was laid unto her fathers."

Baroness Burdett-Coutts, philanthropist, was born on April 21, 1814. She died on December 30, 1906, aged 92

JOSEPHINE BUTLER

CAMPAIGNER FOR WOMEN'S RIGHTS AND HEALTH

JANUARY 2, 1907

We regret to announce the death of Mrs Josephine Butler, which occurred on Sunday night at Wooler, in Northumberland.

A correspondent writes:— Josephine Grey was a Northumbrian, the daughter of John Grey, of Dilston, where she was born on April 13, 1828. In 1851 she met George Butler, then a tutor at Durham University, whom his intimate Froude described as "the most variously gifted man in body and mind that I ever knew"; and the marriage took place at Dilston early in 1852. The first five years of her married life were spent at Oxford, where she proved a most capable and sympathetic helpmate to her husband, drawing maps for his lectures, or puzzling out old Chaucers in the Bodleian. It was here in Oxford that her indignation was first aroused against "certain accepted theories in society" — as "that a moral lapse in a woman was immensely worse than in a man," and that the social evil was to be passed over in silence. "There echoed in my heart," she says, "the terrible prophetic words of the painter-poet Blake:—

'The harlot's curse, from street to street,
Shall weave old England's winding-
sheet.'"

It was here too that the Butlers, who were absolutely at one on the moral question, took from Newgate into their service a young betrayed mother who had been sentenced for the murder of her infant; "the first of the world of unhappy women" who were thus welcomed. In 1857 came a double trial; her father's heavy losses by a bank failure, and her own ill-health, which made removal from Oxford imperative. Her husband now accepted the vice-principalship of Cheltenham College. At Cheltenham her health greatly improved, but a still greater trial was in store — the death of her only daughter by falling over a banister. From 1866 till 1882 her husband was principal of Liverpool College; and in that great city she was, as she says, "possessed with an irresistible desire to go forth and find some pain keener than my own." The result of her visits to the hospital and oakum-picking sheds of the Liverpool workhouse, and to the quays, drew down upon her "an avalanche of miserable but grateful womanhood." Into the garrets of their house the Butlers "crowded as many as possible of the most friendless girls who were anxious to make a fresh start." In time the pair of good Samaritans established a House of Rest for such cases — which long afterwards became a municipal institution — and also an industrial home for healthy and active but friendless girls.

It was in 1869 that a group of medical men, who had been strenuously opposing the introduction into England of "the principle of regulation by the State of the social evil,"* became convinced that some far stronger force than scientific argument was needed to ensure success, and that women, "insulted by the Napoleonic system," must find champions among their own sex. Appeals for Mrs Butler's help poured in, and the call seemed clear to her mind; but at first she shrank back. A woman of extreme delicacy and refinement of mind, with a horror not only of contact with vice, but of publicity and agitation, she was only driven to action by passionate love of purity and justice, and boundless love of her unhappy sister-women. She entered the arena in the spirit of a martyr going to the lions. "The toils and conflicts of the years that followed," she says, "were light in comparison with the anguish of that first plunge." Her husband, foreseeing what it meant for her and for himself, loving peace and hating strife, his happiness (like hers) centring in domestic life, nevertheless recognized "the call of God to conflict." Mr Butler — Canon Butler, as he became, of Winchester — took an active and by no means perfunctory part in the movement; and on one occasion, at the Church Congress of 1872 in Nottingham, when he began to read a paper on "The Duty of the Church of England in Moral Questions," he was shouted down; but he was necessarily fettered by his work at Liverpool, and one of the many trials with which they paid for their devotion to public duty was the frequent separation of husband and wife. Together or apart, as Mrs Butler says, they had to endure "the cold looks of friends, the scorn of persons in office and high life, the silence of some from whom one hoped for encouragement, the calumnies of the Press, and occasionally the violence of hired mobs." But, she adds, "the working classes were always with us"; and the forces of organized religion by degrees ranged themselves largely, and in many cases enthusiastically, on the same side.

One of her earliest helpers in the movement was Mrs Butler's cousin, the Rev Charles Birrell, a gifted Baptist minister at Liverpool — Mr Augustine Birrell's father. Among the distinguished women who supported the movement were Florence Nightingale, Harriet Martineau, and Mary Carpenter. The agitation spread to the Continent; international congresses were held, and a central office for the propaganda was established in Switzerland. In France Mgr Dupanloup and M Yves Guyot were among those who welcomed the Butlers' aid. In England a Royal Commission was appointed in 1871, but reported against the object of the agitation, though Mr Cowper-Temple and Mr Applegarth dissented from the view of their fellow Commissioners. The first debate and division on the subject in the House of Commons took place in 1873, when the attack on the Contagious Diseases Acts was repelled by 265 to 128 votes. Ten years more of persistent agitation led to a practical victory; the enforcement of the obnoxious laws was suspended in consequence of a vote of the House of Commons. In 1886 the House resolved,

nemine contradicente, that the Acts ought to be repealed — an amendment, declaring that repeal should be accompanied with the provision of hospital accommodation for women voluntarily seeking admission, having been defeated by 245 to 131. The repeal actually came in April of the same year.

Canon Butler died in 1890, and it is from Mrs Butler's published "Recollections" of him that I have drawn the quotations in this article. Mrs Butler also wrote a life of Catharine of Siena; a biography of Oberlin; and a sketch of her sister, Mme Meuricoffre; besides such controversial books and pamphlets as "Government by Police" and "Personal Reminiscences of a Great Crusade." She did not consider the crusade ended with the legislation of 1886; and in 1898, in a prefatory note to a pamphlet attacking the continuance in India of the system abolished in England, she wrote:— "I love my country. It is because of my great love for her... that I will not cease to denounce the crimes committed in her name so long as I have life and breath." Mrs Butler's father had been an active worker with Clarkson for the abolition of the slave trade; and she herself published in 1900 a book, "Native Races and the War," controverting the pro-Boer views of many of her friends.

Mrs Butler is described by one of her fellow-workers as "an almost ideal woman; a devoted wife, exquisitely human and feminine, with no touch in her of the 'woman of the platform,' though with a great gift of pleading speech; with a powerful mind, and a soul purged through fire."

Josephine Butler, social reformer, was born on April 13, 1828. She died on December 30, 1906, aged 78

* *Editor's note*: The "principle of regulation by the State of the social evil", which *The Times* of 1906 was too fastidious to spell out, is a reference to the Contagious Diseases Acts, which controlled the spread of venereal disease by empowering magistrates to order humiliating genital examinations of prostitutes and to detain in hospital those found to be infected.

———

FLORENCE NIGHTINGALE

A "MINISTERING ANGEL" IN THE MILITARY HOSPITALS OF THE CRIMEA AND A DETERMINED REFORMER OF HOSPITAL NURSING AT HOME AND ABROAD

AUGUST 15, 1910

We deeply regret to state that Miss Florence Nightingale, OM, the organizer of the Crimean War Nursing Service, died at her residence, 10, South-street, Park-lane, on Saturday afternoon. She had been unwell about a week ago, but had recovered her usual cheerfulness on Friday. On Saturday morning, however, she became seriously ill and she gradually sank until death occurred about 2 o'clock. The cause of death was heart failure. Two members of her family were present at the time.

Miss Nightingale, who had for some time been an invalid and had been under the constant care of Sir Thomas Barlow, was in her 91st year. She celebrated her 90th birthday on May 12 last, and one of the first acts of the present King since coming to the throne — King Edward had died on May 6 — was to send her a telegram of congratulation. The message was worded as follows:—

"On the occasion of your 90th birthday I offer you my heartfelt congratulation, and trust that you are in good health.—George R. & I."

The funeral will take place in the course of the next few days, and will be of the quietest possible character in accordance with the strongly expressed wish of Miss Nightingale. In Miss Florence Nightingale there has passed away one of the heroines of British history. The news of her death will be received to-day with feelings of profound regret throughout not merely the land of her birth, but in all lands where her name has been spoken among men.

Florence Nightingale was born on May 12, 1820, at Florence, from which city she took her name. She was the younger of the two daughters and co-heiresses of Mr William Shore Nightingale, of Embley Park, Hampshire, and Lea Hall, Derbyshire, a descendant of the old Derbyshire family of Shore, and himself the possessor of large estates and considerable wealth. Her mother was a daughter of William Smith, the friend of Wilberforce and his supporter in the House of Commons in the abolitionist and other movements. From Lea Hall the family removed, about 1826, to Lea Hurst, a house about a mile distant, and the one with which the name of Florence Nightingale has been more especially associated. Florence, who even in her young days was a child of extremely strong sympathies, quick apprehension, and excellent judgment, was carefully trained, acquiring, among other accomplishments, under the direction of her father, a knowledge of the classics, mathematics, and also of modern languages. But while applying herself to the culture of her mind she was, at the same time, the consoler and benefactress of all the villagers to whom her help or her kindly words might be of service, displaying even thus early in life that bent of her mind and disposition which afterwards spread her fame throughout the world.

Seeking for wider experience than her position as a squire's daughter in a small Derbyshire village could give her, she visited all the hospitals in London, Dublin, and Edinburgh, many country hospitals, and some of the naval and military hospitals in England; all the hospitals in Paris, studying with the Soeurs de Charité; the Institute of Protestant Deaconesses at Kaiserswerth, on the Rhine, where she was twice in training as a nurse; the hospitals at Berlin, and many others in Germany; while she also visited Lyons, Rome, Alexandria, Constantinople, and Brussels. On her return to Derbyshire, where she hoped to have the rest of which she stood in need after her travels, she was appealed to, in 1850, on behalf of the Home for Sick Governesses, 90, Harley-street, London, which was languishing from lack, not only of proper support, but also of proper management. She responded to the appeal by herself taking over the entire control of the institution, and devoting alike time, energy, and fortune to re-establishing it (with the help of Lady Canning, the original founder) on a sound basis. She also took an active interest in the ragged schools and other similar institutions in London. Altogether something like ten years had been spent by her in preparing, unconsciously, for the great events of her life, and these came with the Russian war.

On September 20, 1854, the battle of Alma was fought, and it is not too much to say that the accounts published in the columns of *The Times* from our Correspondent, the late Dr (afterwards Sir William Howard) Russell, as to the condition of the sick and wounded sent a feeling of horror throughout the length and breadth of the land. There is no necessity to dwell here in detail on the harrowing stories he related. Suffice it to say that he showed how the commonest accessories of a hospital were wanting; how the sick appeared to be tended by the sick, and the dying by the dying; how, indeed, the manner in which the sick and wounded were being treated was "worthy only of the savages of Dahomey"; and how, while our own medical system was "shamefully bad," that of the French was exceedingly good, and was, too, rendered still more efficient because of the sisters of charity who had followed the French troops in incredible numbers.

On October 12, 1854, a leading article appeared in *The Times* in which it was pointed out that while "we are sitting by our firesides devouring the morning paper in luxurious solitude... these poor fellows are going through innumerable hardships"; and the article went on to suggest that the British public should subscribe to send them "a few creature comforts." On the following day we published an extremely sympathetic letter from Sir Robert Peel, starting a fund with a cheque for £200, and so generally and so liberally was his example followed that £781 was received by us within two days, £7,000 within seven days, and £11,614 by the end of the month, when the fund was closed. But, in the meantime, the terrible cry from the East had met with a response which was of even more effectual service to the suffering soldiers than the thousands of pounds thus promptly and generously contributed. On October 15, Miss Nightingale wrote to Mr Sidney (afterwards Lord) Herbert, Secretary at War, offering to go to Scutari, and, as it happened, her own letter was crossed by one to herself from Mr Sidney Herbert. Medical stores, he said, had been sent out by the ton weight, but the deficiency of female nurses was undoubted. Lady Maria Forrester had proposed to go with or to send out trained nurses, "but there is," Mr Herbert went on to

say, "only one person in England that I know of who would be capable of organizing and superintending such a scheme... A number of sentimental and enthusiastic ladies turned loose in the hospital at Scutari would probably, after a few days, be *mises à la porte* by those whose business they would interrupt and whose authority they would dispute. My question simply is, Would you listen to the request to go out and supervise the whole thing?" Miss Nightingale, as we have seen, had already answered this question, and preparations could thus be set on foot without a moment's delay. But, as showing how little she was known to fame at that time, we may mention as a curious fact that in *The Times* of October 19, 1854, there appeared the announcement — "We are authorized to state that Mrs (*sic*) Nightingale" had undertaken to organize a staff of female nurses, who would proceed with her to Scutari at the cost of the Government. Not, indeed, until several days had elapsed does it seem to have been realized that "Mrs" Nightingale was really "Miss" Nightingale, and even then the *Examiner* found it necessary to publish an article, headed "Who is Miss Nightingale?" setting forth who she really was, and bearing eloquent testimony to her accomplishments, her experience, and the nobility of her character.

Within a week Miss Nightingale had selected from hundreds of offers, received from all parts of the country, a staff of 38 nurses, including 14 Anglican sisters, ten Roman Catholic sisters of mercy, and three nurses selected by Lady Maria Forrester. It may be interesting to recall that among the ladies forming the gallant little band was Miss Erskine, eldest daughter of the Dowager Lady Erskine, of Pwll-y-crochan, North Wales. Miss Nightingale and her nurses left London on October 21, passing through Boulogne on October 23 on their way to Marseilles; and a letter which appeared in *The Times* some days afterwards, written by a correspondent who had been staying at Boulogne, related how the arrival of the party there caused so much enthusiasm that the sturdy fisherwomen seized their bags and carried them to the hotel, refusing to accept the slightest gratuity; how the landlord of the hotel gave them dinner, and told them to order what they liked, adding that they would not he allowed to pay for anything; and how waiters and chambermaids were equally firm in refusing any acknowledgment for the attentions they pressed upon them.

From Marseilles the party proceeded to Constantinople, where they arrived on November 4, the eve of the battle of Inkerman. They found there were two hospitals at Scutari, of which one, the Barrack Hospital, already contained 1,500 sick and wounded, and the other, the General Hospital, 800, making a total of 2,300; but on the 5th of November there arrived 500 more who had been wounded in the course of that day's fighting, so that there were close on 3,000 sufferers claiming the immediate attention of Miss Nightingale and her companions.

In the best of circumstances the task which the nurses thus found before them would have been enormous; but the circumstances themselves were as bad as the imagination can conceive, if indeed imagination, unaided by fact, could call up so appalling a picture. Neglect, mismanagement, and disease had "united to render the scene one of unparalleled hideousness." The wounded, lying on beds placed on the pavement itself, were bereft of all comforts; there was a scarcity alike of food and medical aid; fever and cholera were rampant, and even those who were only comparatively slightly wounded, and should have recovered with proper treatment, were dying from sheer exhaustion brought about by lack of the nourishment they required.

Miss Nightingale, as "Lady-in-Chief," at once set to work to restore something like order out of the chaos that prevailed. Within ten days of her arrival she had had an impromptu kitchen fitted up, capable of supplying 800 men every day with well-cooked food, and a house near to the Barrack Hospital was converted into a laundry, which was also sorely needed. In all this work she was most cordially supported by Mr MacDonald, the almoner of *The Times* Fund, the resources of which were, of course, freely placed at her disposal. But in other directions Miss Nightingale had serious difficulties to encounter. The official routine which had sat as a curse over the whole condition of things continued as active, or, rather, as inefficient, as ever. Miss Nightingale was at first scarcely tolerated by those who should have co-operated with her. She had, at times, the greatest possible difficulty in obtaining sufficient Government stores for the sick and wounded; for though, as Mr Sidney Herbert had written, medical stores had been sent out by the ton weight, they were mostly rotting at Varna instead of having been forwarded to Scutari. On one occasion, when she was especially in need of some that had arrived but were not to be given out until they had been officially "inspected," she took upon herself to have the doors opened by force and to remove what her patients needed.

But her zeal, her devotion, and her perseverance would yield to no rebuff and to no difficulty. She went steadily and unwearyingly about her work with a judgment, a self-sacrifice, a courage, a tender sympathy, and withal a quiet and unostentatious demeanour that won the hearts of all who were not prevented by official prejudices from appreciating the nobility of her work and character. One poor fellow wrote home:—"She would speak to one and nod and smile to a many more; but she could not do it to all, you know. We lay there by hundreds; but we could kiss her shadow as it fell, and lay our heads on the pillow again, content." Mr MacDonald, too, wrote in February, 1855:—

"Wherever there is disease in its most dangerous form and the hand of the despoiler distressingly nigh, there is that incomparable woman sure to be seen. Her benignant presence is an influence for good comfort, even amid the struggles of expiring nature.

She is a 'ministering angel' without any exaggeration in these hospitals, and as her slender form glides quietly alone each corridor, every poor fellow's face softens with gratitude at the sight of her. When all the medical officers have retired for the night and silence and darkness have settled down upon those miles of prostrate sick, she may be observed alone, with a little lamp in her hand, making her solitary rounds. The popular instinct was not mistaken which, when she set out from England on her mission of mercy, hailed her as a heroine. I trust she may not earn her title to a still higher though sadder appellation. No one who has observed her fragile figure and delicate health can avoid misgivings lest those should fail. With the heart of a true woman, and the manners of a lady, accomplished and refined beyond most of her sex, she combines a surprising calmness of judgment and promptitude and decision of character."

It was also written of her:—

"She has frequently been known to stand 20 hours on the arrival of fresh detachments of sick, apportioning quarters, distributing stores, directing the labours of her corps, assisting at the painful operations where her presence might soothe or support, and spending hours over men dying of cholera or fever. Indeed, the more awful to every sense any particular case might be the more certainly might be seen her light form bending over him, administering to his case by every means in her power, and seldom quitting his side till death released him."

Meanwhile the reports which Miss Nightingale made both to Lord Raglan, the Commander-in-Chief, and to the War Minister at home were of invaluable service in enabling them to put their finger on the weak spots of the administration. On the other hand, it is painful to recall the fact that while, in all these various ways, Miss Nightingale was doing such admirable work in the East, sectarian prejudices at home had led to unscrupulous attacks being made alike on her religious views and on her motives in going out. "It is melancholy to think," as Mrs Herbert wrote to a lady correspondent, "that in Christian England no one can undertake anything without these most uncharitable and sectarian attacks... Miss Nightingale is a member of the Established Church of England, and what is called rather Low Church; but ever since she went to Scutari her religious opinions and character have been assailed on all points. It is a cruel return to make towards one to whom all England owes so much." Happily a check was put to this campaign of slander and uncharitableness by a letter written by Queen Victoria from Windsor Castle, dated December 6, 1854, to Mr Sidney Herbert, asking that accounts received from Miss Nightingale as to the condition of the wounded should be forwarded to her, and saying:—

"I wish Miss Nightingale and the ladies would tell these poor noble wounded and sick men that no one takes a warmer interest, or feels more for their sufferings, or admires their courage and heroism more, than their Queen. Day and night she thinks of her beloved troops. So does the Prince. Beg Mrs Herbert to communicate these my words to those ladies, as I know that our sympathy is much valued by these noble fellows." The eminently tactful indication conveyed in this letter of her Majesty's complete confidence in Florence Nightingale did much not only towards silencing the ungenerous critics at home, but also towards strengthening the position of the Lady-in-Chief in meeting the difficulties due to excessive officialism in the East.

In January, 1855, Miss Nightingale's totally inadequate staff was increased by the arrival of Miss Stanley with 50 more nurses; and how greatly they were needed is shown by the fact that there were then 5,000 sick and wounded in the various hospitals on the Bosporus and the Dardanelles, 1,000 more being on their way down. By February there was a great increase of fever, which in the course of three or four weeks swept away seven surgeons, while eight more were ill, twenty-one wards in the Barrack Hospital being in charge of a single medical attendant. Two of the nurses also died from fever. Miss Nightingale told subsequently how for the first seven months of her stay in the Crimea the mortality was at the rate of 60 per cent per annum from disease alone, a rate in excess, she added, of that which prevailed among the population of London during the Great Plague.

By May, however, the position of affairs had so far improved at Scutari, thanks mainly to the untiring energies and devotion of Miss Nightingale, that she was able to proceed to Balaclava to inspect the hospitals there. Her work at Balaclava was interrupted by an attack of Crimea fever, and she was afterwards urged to return home; but she would go no further than Scutari, remaining there until her health had been re-established. Thereupon she again left for the Crimea, where she established a staff of nurses at some new camp hospitals put up on the heights above Balaclava, and took over the superintendence of the nursing department, herself living in a hut not far away. She also interested herself in organizing reading and recreation huts for the army of occupation, securing books and periodicals from sympathizers at home. Among the donors were Queen Victoria and the Duchess of Kent. Another institution she set up was a café at Inkerman, as a counter-attraction to the ordinary canteens. Then she started classes, supported the lectures and school-rooms which had been established by officers or chaplains, and encouraged the men to write home to their families. Already at Scutari she had opened a money-order office of her own, through which the soldiers could send home their pay. She thus set an example which the Government followed by establishing official money-order offices at Scutari, Balaclava, Constantinople, and elsewhere. Some £70,000 passed through these offices in the first six months of 1856.

Florence Nightingale remained in the Crimea until the final evacuation in July, 1856, her last act before leaving being the erection of a memorial to the fallen soldiers on a mountain peak above Balaclava. The memorial consisted of a marble cross 20ft high, bearing the inscription, in English and Russian—

"LORD, HAVE MERCY UPON US,
"GOSPODI POMILORI NASS."

Calling at Scutari on her way home, Miss Nightingale left that place in a French vessel for Marseilles, declining the offer made by the British Government of a passage in a man-of-war, and reached Lea Hurst on August 8, 1856, having succeeded in avoiding any demonstration on the way.

Before returning to England Florence Nightingale had received from Queen Victoria an autograph letter with a beautiful jewel, designed by Prince Albert; the Sultan had sent her a diamond bracelet; and a fund for a national commemoration of her services had been started, the income from the proceeds, £45,400, being eventually devoted partly to the setting up at St Thomas's Hospital of a training school for hospital and infirmary nurses and partly to the maintenance and instruction at King's College Hospital of midwifery nurses. For herself she would have neither public testimonial nor public welcome. She was honoured by an invitation to visit the Queen and Prince Consort at Balmoral in September, and addresses and gifts from working men and others were sent or presented privately to her. But though her fame was on every one's lips, and her name has ever since been a household word among the peoples of the world, her life from the time of her return home was little better than that of a recluse and confirmed invalid. Her health, never robust, broke down under the strain of her arduous labours, and she spent most of her time on a couch, while in the closing years of her life she was entirely confined to bed.

But, though her physical powers failed her, there was no falling off either in her mental strength or in her intense devotion to the cause of humanity. She was still the "Lady-in-Chief" in the organization of the various phases of nursing which, thanks to the example she had set and the new spirit with which she had imbued the civilized world, now began to establish themselves; she was the general adviser on nursing organization not only of our own but of foreign Governments, and was consulted by British Ministers and generals at the outbreak of each one of our wars, great or small; she expanded important schemes of sanitary and other reforms, though compelled to leave others to carry them out, while at all times her experience and practical advice were at the command of those who needed them.

Almost the entire range of nursing seems to have been embraced by that revolution therein which Florence Nightingale was the chief means of bringing about. Following up the personal services she had already rendered in the East in regard to Army nursing, she prepared, at the request of the War Office, an exhaustive and confidential report on the working of the Army Medical Department in the Crimea as the precursor to complete

reorganization at home; she was the means of inspiring more humane and more efficient treatment of the wounded both in the American Civil War and the Franco-German War; and it was the stirring record of her deeds that led to the founding of the Red Cross Society, now established in every civilized land. By the Indian Government also she was almost ceaselessly consulted on questions affecting the health of the Indian Army. On the outbreak of the Indian Mutiny she even offered to go out and organize a nursing staff for the troops in India. The state of her health did not warrant the acceptance of this offer; but no one can doubt that, if campaigns are fought under more humane conditions today as regards the care of wounded soldiers, the result is very largely due to the example and also to the counsels of Florence Nightingale.

But advance no less striking is to be found in other branches of the nursing art as well. In regard to general hospitals, the pronounced success of the nursing school established at St Thomas's as the outcome of the Nightingale Fund led to the opening of similar schools elsewhere, so that to-day hospital nursing in general occupies a far higher position in the land than it has ever done before, while this, in turn, advanced the whole range of private nursing in the country. Then, again, the system of district nursing, which is now in operation in almost every large centre of population, has had an enormous influence alike in bringing skilled nurses within the reach of sufferers outside the hospitals, and of still further raising the *status* of nursing as a profession. "Missionary nurses," Florence Nightingale once wrote, "are the end and aim of all our work. Hospitals are, after all, but an intermediate stage of civilization. While devoting my life to hospital work, to this conclusion have I always come — viz., that hospitals were not the best place for the sick poor except for severe surgical cases."

District nursing was really set on foot in this country by the late Mr William Rathbone, who, in compliance with the dying request of his first wife, started a single nurse in Liverpool in 1859 as an experiment, The demand for district nurses soon became so great that more were clearly necessary, and Miss Nightingale was consulted as to what should be done. She replied that all the nurses then in training at St Thomas's were wanted for hospital work, and she recommended that a training school for nurses should be started in Liverpool. The suggestion was adopted, and in November, 1861, on being consulted about the plans, she wrote to the chairman of the training school committee:—

"God bless you and be with you in the effort, for it is one which meets one of our greatest national wants. Nearly every nation is before England in this matter — viz., in providing for nursing the sick at home; and one of the chief uses of a hospital (though almost entirely neglected up to the present time) is this — to train nurses for nursing the sick at home."

By about 1863 there was a trained nurse at work among the poor in each of the 18 districts into which Liverpool had been divided for the purposes of the scheme. The example of Liverpool was speedily followed by Manchester, where a district nursing association was formed in 1864; the East London Nursing Society was established in 1868, and the Metropolitan and National Association followed in 1874. In the organization of the last-mentioned society Florence Nightingale took the deepest interest, sending to *The Times* a long letter, in which she expressed her gratification at the idea of the nurses having a central home, set forth in considerable detail the nature and importance of the duties the district nurses were called upon to perform, and appealed strongly — and successfully — for donations towards the cost of a home. After these pioneer societies had been successfully started many others followed; but the greatest development of all was afforded by Queen Victoria's Jubilee Institute for Nurses, the operations of which have been of the highest importance in spreading the movement throughout the United Kingdom. When, in December, 1896, a meeting was held at Grosvenor House for the purpose of organizing a Commemoration Fund in support of the Institute, a letter from Florence Nightingale was read, in which she expressed the heartiest sympathy with the proposal.

Great and most beneficent changes, again, have followed the substitution in workhouse infirmaries of trained nurses for the pauper women to whose tender mercies the care of the sick in those institutions was formerly left. It was a "Nightingale probationer," the late Agnes Jones, and 12 of her fellow-nurses from the Nightingale School at St Thomas's who were the pioneers of this reform at the Brownlow-hill Infirmary, Liverpool; and it was undoubtedly the spirit and the teaching of Florence Nightingale that inspired them in a task which, difficult enough under the conditions then existing, was to create a precedent for Poor Law authorities all the land over.

Midwifery was another branch of the nursing art which Florence Nightingale sought to reform. She published in 1871 "Introductory Notes on Lying-in Hospital"; and, in 1881, writing on this subject to the late Miss Louisa M. Hubbard, who was then projecting the formation of the Matrons' Aid Society, afterwards the Midwives' Institute, she said, referring to these "Introductory Notes":—

"The main object of the 'Notes' was (after dealing with the sanitary question) to point out the utter absence of any means of training in any existing institutions in Great Britain. Since the 'Notes' were written next to nothing has been done to remedy this defect... The prospectus is most excellent... I wish you success from the bottom of my heart if, as I cannot doubt, your wisdom and energy work out a scheme by which to supply the deadly want of training among women practising midwifery in England. (It is a farce and a mockery to call them midwives or even midwifery nurses, and no certificate now given makes them so.) France, Germany, and even Russia would consider it woman-slaughter to 'practise' as we do."

No less keen was her interest in rural hygiene. The need of observing the laws of health should, she thought, be directly impressed on the minds of the people, and to this end she organized a health crusade in Buckinghamshire in 1892, employing — with the aid of the County Council Technical Instruction Committee — three trained and competent women missioners, who were to give public addresses on health questions, following up these by visiting cottagers in their own homes and giving them practical advice.

Further evidence of Florence Nightingale's activity and beneficent efforts is afforded by the series of books, pamphlets, and papers that came from her pen. In 1858 appeared her "Notes on Matters affecting the Health, Efficiency, and Hospital Administration of the British Army," a volume of 560 pages, in which, "so far as the state of my health," she writes, "has permitted me," she makes an exhaustive review of the defects that led to the "disaster" at Scutari, and discusses in the most thorough and lucid manner the various points calling for consideration in regard to the management and efficiency of army hospitals. The value of this work, still great, was simply incalculable at the time it was first issued. In October, 1858, Miss Nightingale contributed two papers to the Liverpool meeting of the National Association for the Promotion of Social Science on "The Health of Hospitals" and "Hospital Construction." In 1860 she published "Notes on Nursing." So popular has this work become by reason of its thoroughly practical hints, given in the clearest possible language, that some 100,000 copies of it are said to have been sold. For the Edinburgh meeting of the National Association for the Promotion of Social Science, held in 1863, Miss Nightingale contributed a paper on "How People may Live and not Die in India"; and she followed up the same subject, when the association met at Norwich, in 1873, with a paper on "Life or Death in India," this paper being subsequently reprinted with an appendix on "Life or Death by Irrigation," in which considerations arising out of the Bengal famine are discussed more especially from the point of view of the paramount necessity of combining drainage with irrigation.

In these various ways one sees how Florence Nightingale, though a bedridden invalid and well advanced in years, was still ever ready, as she had been throughout life, to devote her energies to promoting the practical well-being of her fellow-creatures. What with writing papers, pamphlets, and letters, receiving reports concerning the many movements in which she was interested, and dealing with communications from Governments, authorities, and others all the world over, she was, even in the closing years of her life, essentially a hard-working woman. How great, indeed, were the demands made upon her time is well shown by a letter addressed by her on October 21, 1895, to the Rev T. G. Clarke, curate of St Philip's Birmingham, and local secretary of the Balaclava Anniversary Commemoration. In the course of this letter she said:—"I could not resist your appeal, though it is an effort to me, who know not what it is to have a leisure hour, to write a few words"; and she added:—"I generally resist all temptations to write, except on ever-pressing business. I am often speaking to your Balaclava veterans in my heart, but I am much overworked."

Yet, among all these manifold claims upon her attention, she never forgot that unpretending "Home" in Harley-street, W., over which she was still presiding when she went out to the Crimea. In *The Times* of November 12, 1901, she appealed for further support for this institution, declaring that it was "Doing good work — work after my own heart, and I trust, God's work. There is [she continued] no other institution exactly like this. In it our governesses (who are primarily eligible), the wives and daughters of the clergy, of our naval, military, and other professional men, receive every possible care, comfort, and first-rate advice at the most moderate cost... Every one connected with this home and haven for the suffering is doing their utmost for it and it is always full. It is conducted on the same lines as from its beginning, by a committee of ladies, of which Mrs Walter is the president, and she will be glad to receive contributions at 90, Harley-street, W. I ask and pray my friends who still remember me not to let this truly sacred work languish and die for want of a little more money."

On the occasion of her 84th birthday, in May, 1904, Miss Nightingale (who had already received the Red Cross from Queen Victoria) had conferred upon her by King Edward the dignity of a Lady of Grace of the Order of St John of Jerusalem. October 21, 1904, was the jubilee of the memorable expedition on which she set forth in 1854; to few great reformers had the mercy been vouchsafed of seeing within their own lifetime results so striking and so beneficial as those that had followed the noble efforts of "The Lady with the Lamp"; and the congratulations she received on the occasion of her jubilee were but a sample of that universal veneration she had won.

Further recognition of the value of her life's labours came to Miss Nightingale with the announcement in the *London Gazette* of November 29, 1907, that the King had been graciously pleased to confer upon her the Order of Merit, she being the only woman upon whom this exceptionally distinguished mark of Royal favour has been conferred. On March 16, 1908, Miss Nightingale received the honorary freedom of the City of London, an honour which had been conferred upon only one woman before — namely, the late Baroness Burdett-Coutts. Owing to her advanced age, Miss Nightingale was unable to be present at the Guildhall to receive this mark of distinction, and her place was taken by a relative. At her own request the money which would have been spent on a gold casket was devoted to charity, the sum of 100 guineas being given instead to the Hospital for Invalid Gentlewomen; and the casket presented to Miss Nightingale was of oak.

Florence Nightingale, OM, nursing reformer, was born on May 12, 1820. She died on August 13, 1910, aged 90

—⁓—

OCTAVIA HILL

PIONEER OF AFFORDABLE HOUSING

AUGUST 15, 1912

Widespread regret will be felt at the announcement of the death, on Tuesday, at her house in Marylebone-road, of Miss Octavia Hill, who deserves to be remembered as one of the most practical and most energetic of women philanthropists of her day.

Born about 1838, she was the daughter of Mr James Hill, and a granddaughter of Dr Southwood Smith, an earnest promoter of sanitary science. Quite early in life she showed leanings in the same direction, and when still young she was one of the band of workers who laboured among the London poor under the leadership of Frederick Denison Maurice. The experiences she thus gained convinced her that people are greatly influenced in their habits and ways of thought by their domestic surroundings, and that sanitary science should be followed up in the case of the poor for the purpose of improving not only their dwellings, but the people themselves. In this way, she thought, the work of bringing about their social and spiritual elevation was to be advanced by enabling people to live in conditions of cleanliness, comfort, and decency, and she argued that an important educational reform could be effected by developing in their minds an actual taste in these directions. But she found it hopeless to think of all this as long as tenants were left to the tender mercies of a low-class type of landlord or landlady, whose only idea was to make as much money out of them as possible; and Miss Hill conceived the then novel idea of herself obtaining possession of some squalid house property, of collecting her own weekly rents, and of exercising what influence she could in securing the transformation alike of dwellings and of tenants. She laid her proposals before Mr Ruskin, who not only entered heartily into the scheme, but himself advanced altogether £3,000 for the carrying out of what was avowedly an experiment. It is true that the experiment proved a financial success, the £3,000 being duly returned, but it was none the less creditable to Mr Ruskin that he should have risked so large a sum when, as Miss Hill herself confessed, "not many men would have trusted that the undertaking would succeed."

Having secured the necessary means, Miss Hill began operations by purchasing, for £750, the unexpired term of the lease of three houses near to her own home in Marylebone. They were well-built houses, but in a deplorable condition of dirt and neglect. As her own rent-collector, Miss Hill entirely did away with a middleman; but in the interests of the people themselves she was extremely strict in enforcing punctual payment of rent. On the other hand, she encouraged the tenants to keep the houses in the cleanly condition to which she had them put, and she set aside a certain amount per year for repairs for each house, the surplus, after breakages and other damage had been made good, being expended in such improvements as the tenants themselves desired. Any suggestion of charity, however, was absolutely discarded. The scheme was organized on a business footing, and it worked so well that, though tenants got two rooms for the amount they had previously paid for one, Miss Hill secured, in a year and a half, 5 per cent interest on the capital, and had repaid out of the rents £48 of the money she had borrowed from Mr Ruskin.

The next purchase was one of six houses, which were also in a most squalid condition, but crowded with inmates. The houses faced a bit of desolate ground occupied by dilapidated cowsheds and manure heaps. The needful repairs and cleaning were carried out, the waste land was turned into a playground, where Mr Ruskin had some trees planted (in addition to creepers against the houses), and Miss Hill, with a strong idea of the moral effects of the playground, arranged with lady friends to go there and teach the children games. For the boys she started a drum and fife band, and for the parents she built at the back of her own house a large room where she could meet them from time to time for the purposes of talk or entertainment. Her weekly call for the rent was, however, the great hold which she kept over her tenants, though her treatment of them was the very reverse of that of merely a sympathetic and easy-going philanthropist. "The main tone of action," she wrote, "must be severe. There is much of rebuke and repression needed, although a deep and silent under-current of sympathy may flow beneath. If the rent is not ready notice to quit must be served. The money is then almost always paid, when the notice is, of course, withdrawn. Besides this inexorable demand for rent (never to be relaxed without entailing cumulative evil on the defaulter, and setting a bad example, too readily to be followed by others) there must be a perpetual crusade carried on against small evils." Happily, too, this crusade was completely successful. Not only did the tenants acquire the habit of being punctual in their payments, but they learned the blessings of cleanliness and of an abundance of air, light, and water, while the lady-crusader herself, strict as she was in all these things, became the family counsellor for each household and the peacemaker in the settlement of neighbours' quarrels.

Towards the end of 1869 six ten-roomed houses in a court in Marylebone were bought by the Countess of Ducie, and five more by another lady, and placed under the care of Miss Hill. The inhabitants of the houses were mainly costermongers and small hawkers who were supposed to have sunk to the lowest depths of degradation, and the houses themselves were in an indescribable condition of filthiness and neglect. Even so brave-hearted a woman as Miss Hill might have hesitated to go to these dwellings at night to collect the rents, for the people could only be seen at the end of their day's toil. But she did not shrink from her task. She had a few improvements done at once — though, for the most part, these were done only gradually, as the people became more capable of valuing them. Then she paid the elder girls to scrub regularly and preserve as models of cleanliness the stairs and passages for which the landlady was responsible, with the result that the girls acquired cleanly habits, and the lesson taught by the stairs soon spread to the rooms. In the same way the tenants, when out of work, were employed to do repairs to the premises, so that "little by little the houses were renovated, the grates reset, the holes in the floor were repaired, the cracking, dirty plaster replaced by a clean smooth surface, the heaps of rubbish removed," and a general progress made towards order. There was, too, a corresponding moral improvement in the people, and though the new landlady never unduly interfered, never entered a room unless invited, and never offered any gift of money or necessaries of life, she came to be regarded as the best friend of the tenants, and not only "got hold of their hearts," but was often able to help them at some important crisis or other in their lives.

Altogether Miss Hill secured a distinct success in the working out of the principle on which she had started. As time went on many more blocks of dwellings came under her management in different parts of London in addition to those mentioned, and a number of ladies assisted her in her self-imposed labours. In 1887 a very practical step in this direction was made by the formation of the Women's University Settlement in Blackfriars-road, whose members have co-operated with Miss Hill in working some dozen or more courts or streets of cottages in Southwark. In addition to this a number of blocks erected by the Ecclesiastical Commissioners were put at once under Miss Hill's care. Recognizing, however, the comparatively limited scope of such efforts as her own — inasmuch as they depended so much on individual workers — and the necessity for providing increased accommodation for the working classes generally, Miss Hill gave an active support to the Artizans' Dwellings Act of 1874, and in 1884 she was one of the witnesses examined by the Special Commission which inquired into the question of the housing of the poor.

Of late years this question, in its wider development as the housing of the artisan classes, has assumed proportions far greater than either Miss Octavia Hill or Mr Ruskin could have contemplated when they started joint operations as social reformers, and the action taken alike by private companies, wealthy philanthropists, and the London County Council in the provision of improved dwellings for the working classes seems to put entirely in the shade Miss Hill's modest efforts. On the other hand, she was undoubtedly one of the first, if not actually the first, to start the general movement, and on this movement her example and her writings have had a most powerful effect, notwithstanding the fact that it has been continued along broader, more comprehensive, and much more costly lines than were within the limits of her own resources. In 1905 she was appointed a member of the Royal Commission on the Poor Laws and signed the Majority Report in 1909.

Miss Hill also took part in the foundation and development of the Charity Organization Society, whose principles are so well in accord with her life-long contention that an ill-advised almsgiving merely undermines the providence of the poor. She also became an active supporter of the Commons Preservation Society as the result of an effort of her own — though an unsuccessful one — to save from the builder certain fields in the Finchley-road, which she was anxious to preserve as an open space for the enjoyment of the poorer residents of Swiss Cottage. At the instance of Miss Hill a second society, known as the Kyrle Society, was formed for the purpose of brightening in every practical way the homes of the poor, while from the Kyrle Society there was developed Lord Meath's Metropolitan Gardens Association, which has done, and is still doing, invaluable work in the protection, provision, and improvement of open spaces. Still another organization with which Miss Hill had been actively connected from the first was the National Trust for Places of Historical Interest.

A Correspondent writes:—If Miss Octavia Hill had cared for any appraisement of her character she would have wished it to be sought in the record of her work. But those who had the privilege of being associated with her will find the secret of her usefulness in the personality of the worker. Qualities which are commonly supposed to be distinct or incompatible were in her harmonious parts of a consistent whole. Her enthusiasm was always directed by calm inflexible reason; her sympathies were keen and many-sided, but found expression in efforts to effect the practicable good. No ideal was too high to lie beyond her range of thought; no detail was too dull or too exacting to be neglected, if it were a means to the appointed end. She threw herself with equal zeal into the long labour of providing decent accommodation for the Southwark poor and into the effort to save a fine view point in Surrey or some stretch of mountain side in the Lake Country. Her reason was in each case the same — the abiding faith that the enjoyment of beauty and the command of physical comfort were alike essential elements in happy human life.

Her methods formed a notable contrast to much of the fashionable philanthropy of the day. She believed in quiet ways. The collection of her "Annual Letters to Fellow Workers" is a wonderful chronicle of the good that was done without any appeal to public benevolence. But her influence was even wider and more fruitful than the immediate results of her activity. At Red Cross Hall and in other departments she gathered round her a band of devoted disciples, and it was the consolation of her declining years that her work would be maintained.

Unflinching sincerity, earnestness, and concentration were factors in her success. She steadfastly refused to give her name to movements in which she could exercise no personal control, and on points of principle she was not easily led to consent to compromise. Her sense of responsibility was acute. During the time that the Royal Commission on the Poor Law was sitting and the report was being framed, her labours were of a painfully exacting kind, and it was not without hesitation that she adopted the recommendations of the majority of her colleagues.

A musical voice and a fine gift of literary expression rendered her a most persuasive advocate on public occasions. Few women of her time were more fortunate in the range of their friendships. But her tastes were simple. In recent years, a cottage at Toy's Hill — commanding a beautiful view — furnished a pleasant retreat from the work-a-day cares of London. The death of her sister Miranda was a keen sorrow to one in whom family affection was the very soul of life.

Octavia Hill, housing and social reformer, was born on December 3, 1838. She died on August 13, 1912, aged 73

—◇—

ELIZABETH GARRETT ANDERSON

THE FIRST WOMAN TO QUALIFY AS A DOCTOR IN ENGLAND

DECEMBER 18, 1917

We regret to announce that Mrs Elizabeth Garrett Anderson, MD, died at Alde House, Aldeburgh, Suffolk, yesterday. She was 81 years of age.

Mrs Garrett Anderson was one of the pioneers of that phase of the movement for the "emancipation" of women which aimed at throwing open to them the profession of medicine, and was herself the first woman to secure a medical diploma in this country. The world has, by this time, become familiar with the idea of women doctors, alike as private practitioners and as the holders of public appointments, and the war has made them as necessary at home as they have been for years in India, where the Countess of Dufferin's Fund has conferred an incalculable boon on native women. Yet when Miss Elizabeth Garrett and a few others endeavoured to devote their lives to this work, and sought to obtain the necessary qualifications for so doing, they had to endure for many years an amount not only of prejudice, but of direct and sometimes violent hostility, which would have broken down the courage of persons of less determined spirit and less convinced than they were that their cause was the cause both of justice and of humanity.

Elizabeth Garrett, known after her marriage as Mrs Garrett Anderson, was the daughter of Mr Newson Garrett, of Aldeburgh, Suffolk, and was born in London in 1836. Her attention was attracted to medicine by Miss Elizabeth Blackwell, an English woman who had emigrated with her parents to the United States, and, after many fruitless attempts to enter various medical schools there, was permitted to graduate MD of the University of Geneva, USA, in 1849. Ten years afterwards, on the strength of this foreign qualification, and of her having prescribed for friends during a visit to England, she was put on the British Medical Register; so that, while, as already stated, Miss Garrett was the first woman to secure an English diploma, Miss Blackwell had precedence of her as regards registration. Miss Garrett made Miss Blackwell's acquaintance in 1858, and resolved to follow in her friend's footsteps, but to get an English qualification instead of a foreign one. She began her medical studies in earnest in 1860. There were, however, two great difficulties before her. In the first place, there was no school where she could be received, and, in the next place, there was no examining body willing to admit her to its examinations. At Middlesex Hospital the male students presented a memorial against the admission of women, and though she made repeated attempts elsewhere, she met for some years with effectual repulse in every direction. In these attempts she had the cordial support of her father, to whose sympathy and courage she afterwards attributed the success she secured.

After a time the Society of Apothecaries was advised by its counsel, Mr (afterwards Lord) Hannen, that as the purpose of its charter was to enable it to sell drugs, and as there was no legal ground for refusing to allow a woman to sell drugs, the society could not refuse to admit a woman to the examination imposed on candidates for its licence. Thereupon the society authorized Miss Garrett to get her education privately from teachers of recognized medical schools, and finally gave her, in 1865, the desired qualification of LSA. In 1866 she opened a dispensary near Lissongrove, Marylebone, for the benefit of poor women and children, and for some years she was the only medical officer there. The Society of Apothecaries had adopted a new rule which refused recognition of certificates granted for private studies; there was no medical school in England that would admit women, and the struggle carried on by the late Miss Jex-Blake and others at Edinburgh University had been in vain. But medical degrees were to be had abroad; Miss Garrett herself passed the examinations, and took the MD of Paris in 1870; and, others taking similar steps, she secured assistants at her dispensary, which was subsequently converted into a small hospital, and after various changes developed into the "New Hospital for Women" in the

Euston-road. It was during the period of these early struggles that a woman pamphleteer, writing in opposition to "women's rights" in general, said of Miss Garrett:—

"Miss Garrett possesses a superior mind as well as superior attainments, and her character appears to correspond to her intellectual qualities. She has great calmness of demeanour, a large amount of firmness, usually a good deal of fairness and coolness in argument, a pleasant countenance, a decided but perfectly feminine manner, and attire at once apart from prevalent extravagance and affected eccentricity."

In November, 1970, Miss Garrett became a candidate at the London School Board election, and was returned at the head of the poll for Marylebone with no fewer than 47,858 votes. In 1871 she married Mr J. G. S. Anderson, of the Orient line of steamships to Australia, but she lost none of her zeal for the profession she had adopted, and continued it as actively as before, devoting herself especially to the diseases of women and children. In October, 1874, Miss Jex-Blake returned from Edinburgh vanquished in her attempts to secure admission to the medical schools in that city, the male students having carried their opposition so far as to mob her and her friends. Mrs Garrett Anderson thereupon joined with Miss Jex-Blake and other ladies in establishing the London School of Medicine for Women. But the General Medical Council of England stipulated that only a general hospital having 150 beds could be recognized as adequate for the purposes of teaching, and the hospital which Mrs Garrett Anderson was carrying on had then only 26 beds. The larger hospitals were appealed to, but in vain, until at last, in 1877, an alliance was formed between the Women's School and the Royal Free Hospital, Gray's-inn-road, which met all requirements in respect to teaching.

In the meantime there had been proceedings in the Law Courts and attempts at legislation in the House of Commons in the interests of the would-be women doctors; and at last, thanks to a more enlightened public opinion and to the abundant proofs of the excellent work which Mrs Garrett Anderson and her sister practitioners were doing, a Bill introduced in the House of Commons in 1876 by Mr Russell Gurney was passed "enabling" the British examining bodies to extend their examinations to women as well as men. The King and Queen's College of Physicians in Ireland was the first to take advantage of this enactment, and a number of other bodies afterwards adopted the same course. But in 1878 the feeling in the medical profession against women doctors was still strong, and Mrs Garrett Anderson remained the only female member of the British Medical Association until 1892, when the Nottingham meeting, on the proposal of Dr S. H. Galton, carried by a large majority the repeal of a rule which he described as "a blot on the association's fair fame, a stain left from the high tide of prejudice." Mrs Garrett Anderson, who was present at this meeting, had thus the satisfaction of seeing the victorious end of the campaign on which she had started in 1860.

For 23 years Mrs Garrett Anderson was Lecturer on Medicine at the London School of Medicine for Women, and for 10 years its Dean. For 24 years she was Senior Physician of the New Hospital for Women. In 1896-97 she was President of the East Anglian branch of the British Medical Association, and in 1908 she was elected Mayor of Aldeburgh, where she had her home, being the first woman made a Mayor in England. Her interest in sanitation and housing here made itself felt to good practical effect. In the following year she was re-elected. Of such a woman as Dr Garrett Anderson it need scarcely be said that she believed that women ought to have Parliamentary votes, and that she worked to that end in the years preceding the war. Recently her powers were failing; but she was fond of going to London stations to bid Godspeed to soldiers starting for the front.

Mrs Garrett Anderson's sister is Dr Millicent Garrett Fawcett, to whose husband, the blind Postmaster-General, she acted as medical adviser. Her son, Sir Alan Garrett Anderson, last August succeeded Sir Eric Geddes as Controller of the Navy; and the first list of appointments to the new Order of the British Empire, which we published last August, contained not only his name among the Knight Commanders, but that of his sister, Dr Garrett Anderson, among the Commanders, as "organizer of the first hospital run by women at the front." Dr Garrett Anderson is now head of the military hospital in Endell-street.

The entrance of women into the medical profession was one of those events that would certainly, in any case, have been brought about sooner or later, but it was none the less to the credit of Mrs Garrett Anderson that she recognized the desirability and the justice of this step at a time when few other persons did, and that she herself fought so valiantly against prejudices so strong and interests so powerful as those confronting her in that "fiery ordeal" from which it was her happy lot to emerge not only successful but still a "womanly woman."

The funeral will be at Aldeburgh on Friday, at 2.30pm, and there will be a memorial service at Christ Church, Endell-street (Military Hospital) on Saturday, at 11am.

Elizabeth Garrett Anderson, pioneering physician, was born on June 9, 1836. She died on December 17, 1917, aged 81

—ᨒ—

LADY RANDOLPH CHURCHILL

DAZZLING SOCIAL FIGURE, WRITER AND MOTHER OF WINSTON CHURCHILL

JUNE 30, 1921

The sudden death yesterday morning of Lady Randolph Churchill is announced on another page.

Those who have known London life for three or four decades will realize that in Lady Randolph Churchill a once brilliant and high-stepping figure has passed away. Jeannette, daughter of Leonard Jerome, of New York, had all the dash and her full share of the various talent for which American young womanhood is remarkable. She flung herself ardently into many occupations and amusements: Literature, hunting, drama, politics, marriage. And sometimes she combined two or more of them, as when, after reading Renan, she named her black mare (by Trappist out of Festive) L'Abbesse de Jouarre.

She was 19 when, in 1873, at a dance given by the officers of the cruiser Ariadne in honour of the Cesarevitch, she first met Lord Randolph Churchill. Three days later he proposed to her. In the following year they were married. She was already a woman of the world. Some of her childhood had been spent in Trieste, where her father was American Consul; some of her girlhood in Paris, whence she escaped in the last train that left before the siege of 1870 began. Lord Randolph was a man of many interests, and she shared most of them. She hunted with him; she entertained with him, the charm of her society, her wit, and her French cook making her dinner-table grateful to King Edward (then Prince of Wales) and many another good judge. On Lord Randolph's visits to Russia and to Germany she "went down" notably well at the Imperial Courts. At electioneering she shone. In 1885 she helped her husband so dashingly that Lord James of Hereford wrote to her:—

"But my gratification is slightly impaired by feeling I must introduce a new Corrupt Practices Act. Tandems must be put down, and certainly some alteration, a correspondent informs me, must be made in the means of ascent and descent therefrom; then arch looks have to be scheduled, and nothing must be said 'from my heart.' The graceful wave of a pocket-handkerchief will have to be dealt with in committee."

And in later years, while canvassing for Mr Burdett-Coutts, she made a famous repartee. When a waverer observed slyly, "If I could get the same price as was once paid by the Duchess of Devonshire for a vote, I think I could promise." "Thank you very much," she replied, "I'll let the Baroness Burdett-Coutts know at once."

Behind all this brilliance lay a power of hard and steady work. Lady Randolph was a woman of solid ability as well as of dash and daring. In his meteoric political career, and especially, perhaps, in the Primrose League, she helped her husband "like a man"; and history, perhaps, will never have the chance of revealing how much the early career of her son, Mr Winston Churchill, owed to his mother's intellect and energy.

Outside the field of strict politics, the dearest wish of this American wife of one Cabinet Minister and mother of another was to render the United States and Great Britain intelligible to each other. During the Boer War she equipped the *Maine* as a hospital ship with American money, sailed in it to South Africa, and headed the executive committee which controlled it.

The dashing Lady Randolph Churchill

And the same purpose underlay her most solid contribution to literature — the *Anglo-Saxon Review*, which she founded, owned, and edited. The idea was permanence. "Articles full of solid thought and acute criticism, of wit and learning, are read one day and cast into the waste-paper basket the next." To issue them in a more costly form would be to lengthen their existence; buyers would preserve a book they had paid highly for, and contributors would write the better for that expectation. No pains were spared in the production; a new cover was to be designed for each issue; and each was to be a facsimile of some celebrated binding of the 16th, 17th, and 18th centuries. The price was fixed at a guinea for each quarterly number. Among the contributors were Swinburne, Henry James, Mr Max Beerbohm, and Mrs Craigie (John Oliver Hobbes). But permanence cannot be guaranteed; and the *Anglo-Saxon Review*'s career was brief.

Lady Randolph could write, as well as edit. Her "Reminiscences" (1908) were discreet, but interesting. Her book of essays, "Small Talks on Great Subjects" (1916), was readable. Her love of the drama was expressed not only in her passion for attending first nights, but in the authorship of two plays, *His Borrowed Plumes* (1909) and *The Bill* (1914). The latter was a political play, and proved rather too discreet to be entertaining. The men in it, wrote a critic, were humdrum, but she was far more successful with her women, the naughty little roguey-poguey and the elderly cats. These say and do amusing things, because Lady Randolph knows her sex, and does not hesitate to let her lively sense of humour play freely over it.

She had been beautiful; she had been brilliant; she filled her life with work and play. She had her worldly rewards — the Order of the Crown of India, the Order of the Royal Red Cross, the Ladyship of Grace of the Order of St John of Jerusalem; not to mention great social success. It came to her to be called upon to fit her vigorous, daring personality to a narrower mould than that which it had once filled. But to the last no illness nor social change could dim her courage and her kindliness.

To Lord Randolph Churchill (who died in 1895) she bore two sons, Mr Winston Leonard Spencer Churchill and Mr John Spencer Churchill. In 1900 she married Mr George Cornwallis West, whom she divorced in 1913. In 1918 she married Mr Montagu Porch, who survives her.

Lady Randolph Churchill, writer and social figure, was born on January 9, 1854. She died on June 29, 1921, aged 67

—◆◆◆—

EMILY DAVIES

CAMPAIGNER FOR UNIVERSITY EDUCATION FOR WOMEN, AND FOUNDER OF GIRTON COLLEGE, CAMBRIDGE

JULY 14, 1921

We regret to announce that Miss (Sarah) Emily Davies, a pioneer in women's causes, especially education, died yesterday at her home in Belsize Park, Hampstead, in her 92nd year.

Miss Emily Davies was the daughter of the Rev J. Davies, DD, at one time rector of Gateshead, and was born on April 22, 1830. Her education was completed at home, according to the custom of the time. Girls' public day schools were not in existence, and in middle-class families boarding schools formed the only alternative to the private governess. A change, however, was at hand. The disclosures of the Schools

Inquiry Commission of 1864 aroused an agitation for the reform of girls' secondary education. A committee was formed to obtain the opening of the Cambridge (boys) Local Examinations to girls, and Miss Davies, who had taken up her residence in London, became honorary secretary. Cambridge yielded in 1865, after an experimental examination in which only six out of 40 senior girls from different parts of the country passed, the remainder failing in elementary arithmetic. By 1870 Edinburgh, Dublin, and Oxford had all thrown open their local examinations.

If Miss Davies had accomplished nothing else she would have deserved well of her sex. Her task, however, was only begun. She next took part in the attempts made to obtain admission for women to the University of London degrees. Special interest attached to the application, for Miss Elizabeth Garrett (Mrs Garrett Anderson, MD) was working her way into the medical profession and knocking in vain at the doors of examining bodies for a qualifying diploma. For a time the attack on the University failed, but Miss Davies and her friends persisted, and the London degrees were thrown open to women in 1874.

Meanwhile University lectures to ladies had been started in several large towns in the north of England, and their success had stimulated the desire for systematic instruction of the same type. Queen's College (over which Miss Davies's brother, the Rev Llewelyn Davies, presided) and Bedford College, excellent though they were, hardly fulfilled the new ideal. In 1867 a committee was formed with Miss Davies as honorary secretary, and a scheme drawn up for a college "designed to hold in relation to girls' schools and home teaching a position analogous to that occupied by the Universities towards the public schools for boys." Hitchin was chosen as the locality, since lecturers could thus be obtained from both London and Cambridge, but the share of Cambridge predominated.

When in October, 1869, six students assembled in the private house at Hitchin which was leased for the college the promoters of women's education throughout the country told each other with jubilation that a new era had begun. In 1870 five of the Hitchin students passed the previous examination by private arrangement with the examiners, and two years later, under the same conditions, Miss Woodhead obtained a second class in the Mathematical Tripos, and Miss Cook a second and Miss Lumsden a third in the Classical Tripos. The results were remarkable when we consider that to most of the students the subjects were new and to all the methods of study were unaccustomed. Their success established the reputation of the college and assured its future; if women could pass honour examinations it was clearly worthwhile providing facilities for study.

The college committee, however, had made up their minds some time before. "It is decided," wrote Miss Davies in August, 1870, "that as soon as we can raise £7,000, including what has been already promised, we shall begin to build for 30 students on a plan to which additions can be made hereafter. It is to be either at Hitchin, or at some place within three or four miles of Cambridge, but not in Cambridge itself." The "three or four miles" were diminished to two, but from the decision to keep outside the boundaries of Cambridge the committee declined to swerve. Miss Davies had thoroughly made up her mind as to the form the new institution should take, and she never faltered. Convinced that a high standard of attainment was only possible by adopting University methods, she decided that the model should be followed in small matters as well as great.

In 1873 the college entered into possession of its new buildings at Girton, Miss Davies herself residing as mistress during the first three or four years. As a working head she was perhaps hardly so successful as an organizer, but by her presence on the spot she was enabled to impress the desired form upon the college institutions during their early growth. For long after this close connexion had ceased Miss Davies continued to watch closely over the fortunes of Girton.

Miss Davies was a member of the first London School Board, a life governor of University College, and a governor of the Hitchin Grammar School. Her interest in educational matters was maintained till her death, and she was a warm advocate of extension of the Parliamentary vote to women. In the various demonstrations and processions her aged figure, small but alert,

formed a striking and justly honoured feature. She lived to record her vote at a Parliamentary election.

An address and a cheque for 700 guineas were presented to Miss Davies in 1912 by members of the various groups of women who had profited by her labours. She offered the money at once to the Council of Girton College towards the extension of the buildings. *Emily Davies, campaigner for women's right to university education, was born on April 22, 1830. She died on July 13, 1921, aged 91*

—◆—

SARAH BERNHARDT

FRENCH TRAGIC ACTRESS
WHOSE STAGE CAREER
SPANNED 60 YEARS

MARCH 27, 1923

No temperament more histrionic than Mme Bernhardt's has, perhaps, ever existed. To read her memoirs or her biographies is to live in a whirl of passions and adventures — floods of tears, tornadoes of rage, deathly sickness and incomparable health and energy, deeds of reckless bravado, caprices indescribable and enormous. Her determination and independence of character were always strong; and when they, with her energy, became concentrated on her principal art they established a supremacy which would have been unmistakable even without the aid of her eccentricities. The marvellous voice of gold, that wide range of beautiful movement, queenly, sinuous, terrible, alluring, that intensity of passion and that bewitching sweetness have brought men and women of all degrees — from professional critics to ranchers, from anarchists to kings, from men of pleasure to Puritan ladies — in homage to her feet.

In spite of their common training, her theory of her art was the opposite of Coquelin's. She was all for the "artist," the creator, as opposed to the "comedian," the exponent of science and rule. She loved "the limelight," and time was when she kept it pretty constantly upon her off the stage, whether in her wonderful house (or museum) in the Boulevard Péreire in Paris, on tour over the habitable globe, or in her holiday home at Belle-Ile-en-mer, near Morbihan, in Brittany. But all the fierce battles which raged about her life and conduct never obscured the fact of her greatness, by temperament and by accomplishment alike.

Sarah Bernhardt was born at No 265, Rue Saint Honoré, Paris, on October 23, 1845. She was the eleventh of a family of fourteen children. Her mother was a Dutch Jewess, but Sarah was baptized at the age of 12 and sent to school at the Augustinian Convent at Grandchamp, Versailles. At the age of 16, on the advice of her mother's friend, the Duc de Morny, she was put to the stage as a profession. She had no inclination to it, but won a couple of second prizes at the Conservatoire. She never won a first prize. When she made her début at the Français in *Iphigénie*, her fellow-student Coquelin *aîné* being in the cast, the only genuine emotion that she felt was fear, and the audience laughed at her long, thin arms.

Less than a year had passed when the gawky young Jewess gave a taste of her elemental fury. Mme Nathalie, a well-known old actress, was rough with Mlle Bernhardt's younger sister. Sarah flew at her and boxed her ears. An apology was demanded by the Comédie Française — and refused. Very soon afterwards Mme Nathalie found means to render Mlle Bernhardt's life at the theatre intolerable. She gave in her resignation and left the Français for the first time. For the next two or three years her career was chequered. She played in burlesque at the Porte Saint-Martin (the scene of some of her later triumphs), and at the Gymnase in vaudeville. In 1864, disgusted with a poor part at the latter house, she ran away, with characteristic impulsiveness, for a totally unauthorized holiday in Spain.

In 1867 brighter days dawned. She joined the company at the Odéon. Here, as Zacharie in *Athalie*, Mlle Bernhardt made her first success; here, too, she won great favour in M. Coppée's *Le Passant*; and here she boxed the ears of Taillade because he asked her, in a play, to kiss the hem of his robe. In 1869, shortly after the production of George Sand's *L'Autre*, the Franco-Prussian War brought about the closing of the theatre. Mlle Bernhardt was patriotic to the core. Few things made the

Dutch-French Jewess more angry than to be taken for a German Jewess; some years later she reduced to confusion the German Minister at Copenhagen and all the other guests present at a public banquet by remarking aloud, as he proposed the toast of "France," "I presume, Baron, that you mean the whole of France?" During the war her patriotism found vent in equipping and managing a hospital for wounded soldiers in the Odéon, one of the first patients being M. Porel, later the husband of Mme Réjane and manager of the Vaudeville.

When the war and the Commune were over the Odéon became a theatre again, and Mlle Bernhardt improved her position. She owed a great deal to the consistency with which Sarcey championed her in the *Temps*, while other critics were complaining of her thin voice and still thinner figure, her monotony and her languor. In 1872 there came a turning-point in her career. Victor Hugo had returned to Paris, and in the production of his *Ruy Blas* at the Odéon Mlle Sarah made so great a success as the Queen that Perrin, the manager of the Français, was practically compelled by the newspapers and by public opinion to re-engage her for the national theatre.

Her membership lasted for eight years, and little by little — certainly not all at once — she forged her way to eminence. Her enemies on the Press were active, and even Sarcey seemed for a while to turn against her. But she worked with her characteristic energy and did her best to overcome her disabilities. In December, 1874, she played

Phèdre for the first time. During the first act nervousness drove her into a fault which she had, apparently, picked up from her mother — that of speaking nasally through clenched teeth. As the performance went on she warmed to her work, and played so well that her audience raised no protest when she made nonsense of a line which, of course, they knew, with the rest of the play, by heart. Sarcey declared her superior to Rachel, and thenceforward she was one of the lions of Paris. The exhibition of two specimens of her sculpture in the Salon of the following year made her still more notorious.

This was the period when the Sarah legend began to grow — the legend of the coffin in which she slept (a white satin-lined coffin with the softest of mattresses and the richest of perfumes, and love-letters, bouquets, and so forth stitched into the lining); the legend of wild animals kept for pleasure and decapitated or tortured from curiosity; the legend of retirement to a convent after one of her frequent attacks of apparently grave, but very momentary, illness — legends which at least suffice to show that Mlle Sarah was one of the most talked-of persons in Paris. Meanwhile she went on working hard at the Français, and found in Zola a sturdy and generous champion, who did his best to dissipate the clouds of gossip which gathered round her exploits in ballooning, animal training, and the rest of it.

In 1879 came the well-remembered visit of the members of the Comédie Française — Got, Coquelin, Delaunay,

Mounet-Sully, and others — to London and the Gaiety Theatre. Their repertory included *Phèdre*, *L'Etrangère*, *Le Sphinx*, *Hernani*, *Andromaque*, *Zaïre*, and other great pieces, and Mlle Bernhardt was a very important person in the troupe. Even during her absence Paris was full of gossip about her: she was exhibiting her works of art in London, and hanging about at the gallery to show herself off; she was going about in man's clothes, and so forth; and Mlle Sarah felt herself compelled to write to the French Press to state that she was not going about in man's clothes because she had left her suits at home.

Meanwhile, in spite of several little *contretemps*, she was being loudly acclaimed by the English Press and public. But the engagement in London was not over before her friends and foes were provided with a real scandal to quarrel over. Mlle Bernhardt was due, on a certain Saturday, to play in *L'Etrangère* in the afternoon and in *Hernani* in the evening. She sent a message that she was too tired to appear. But she had not been too tired to give, the evening before, a performance at a private house; and the right to give these private performances was a bone of contention between her and the Français. There was an uproar. When the news reached Paris, Paris was furious. The company had been insulted. But Mlle Sarah was too valuable to be lost. When she hurled her resignation at the head of Got, the Français replied by making her a *sociétaire*, with a full share in the profits.

After all, the breach was only healed for a time, and a short time. Less than a year later she failed notably in a revival of Augier's *L'Aventurière*. She complained of insufficient rehearsal, resigned on the spot, and was off to Havre before they could stop her. So, for the second time, she left the Comédie Française, and this time never to return. An interviewer flew north to Sainte-Adresse and found Mlle Sarah wielding brush and chisel and determined never to return to the stage.

A month later she was acting in London with her sister Jeanne and others, playing in *Adrienne Lecouvreur* and *Froufrou*. Then the news reached her that the Courts had fined her 100,000f and deprived her of her share in the reserve fund; and she realized that great measures must be taken. And so began that long series of tours — royal progresses, triumphal processions, theatrical hurricanes sweeping over the habitable globe — which lasted till not so long ago.

Her first tour was in 1880; it embraced Sweden, Norway, and Denmark, and was followed by a run through the south of France and Switzerland. That autumn, she whirled herself, her company, her servants, agents, animals, and her 28 trunks full of dresses across the Atlantic for her first tour in America. Here, amid incredible adventures, she added an alligator to her menagerie (but it died in the flower of its youth — of champagne), a very large sum to her fortune, and thousands to her admirers. When she landed at Havre in May, 1881, she was welcomed by a crowd reckoned at 50,000 persons. There followed almost immediately a tour which embraced practically the whole of Europe except the hated Germany (although on one occasion in her career she did act in Berlin). While St Petersburg paid £20 for a box to see her, Kieff insulted her and Odessa stoned her in the streets for a Jewess; at Genoa she all but died one night, and started next morning for Basel; in London, on April 4, she committed "the only eccentricity she had not yet perpetrated" by getting married at the Greek Consulate to a member of her company, M. Damala, and whisking him off the same morning to Marseilles, en route for Spain. Almost before Paris had got over the shock the pair had separated.

In 1886 came one of her greatest undertakings, the tour which began in London and ran through South America, the United States, and Canada for 13 months. Adulation reached its limits. Jules Lemaître has described how "already rich men, wearing black whiskers, and covered with jewels, like idols, used to wait outside the stage door and lay their handkerchiefs on the ground so that dust should not soil the feet of Phèdre or Théodora." The Argentines gave Mme Bernhardt an estate of 13,000 acres; and Mme Bernhardt gave a lady in her company a horse-whipping, which brought them both before the law. The profits of the whole tour were one million dollars, and her own share amounted to £60,000.

She rarely failed once a year to visit London, a place which she grew to love, and one in which her admirers were as hearty, if not so fiery, as the whiskered gentlemen of Buenos Aires. In 1882 London first saw her in *Fédora*; in 1888 she played *Françillon* at the Lyceum; in 1889 she brought us *La Tosca*. In 1891 she started on another immense tour through the Americas and Australia (the trunks now numbered 80), which lasted for 17 months; and in 1900 came yet another American tour, her company then including Coquelin *aîné*.

Meanwhile, when Paris had been sufficiently punished, she consented to forgive it. In the winter of 1882 she took a regular engagement at the Vaudeville in M. Sardou's new play of *Fédora*. Nearly every year from 1883 to 1893 she spent her winters at the Porte Saint-Martin, and it was here that she produced some of her greatest modern successes, many of them written by M. Sardou. In 1884 came *Théodora*, in 1887 *La Tosca*, in 1890 *Jeanne d'Arc* and *Cléopâtre*; and here too she appeared as Lady Macbeth in Richepin's version, and as Ophelia in a subsequently discarded version of *Hamlet*. Year by year she fortified her position of eminence. In 1893 she bought the Théâtre de la Renaissance, her temple of dramatic art, and opened it with M. Jules Lemaître's *Les Rois*; it was here that she was joined for a short time by Coquelin in 1895, and here she produced in the same year M. Rostand's *La Princesse Lointaine*, and in 1897 his great religious drama, *La Samaritaine*,

Musset's *Lorenzaccio*, and d'Annunzio's *La Ville Morte*. In 1896 Paris indulged itself in a great festival in her honour, with banquets, speeches, performances, and a sonnet from M. Rostand.

In 1899 she moved to a larger theatre, now the Théâtre Sarah Bernhardt; and here she produced the version of *Hamlet* by MM. Morand and Schwab in which she gave Paris, and, later, London, the chance of seeing her as Hamlet himself — a weak and violent prince, whose character she thought "perfectly simple." What is there to add? There is *Magda*, which she played in a French version in London in the eighteen-nineties, giving an opportunity for hot little disputes between the worshippers of Bernhardt and Druse; there is *L'Aiglon*; there are one or two huge spectacular dramas, and the performance of that repertory in which her *Phèdre* has won its way to recognition as the masterpiece. And there is the fact that years after she had passed her prime, Mme Bernhardt became an idol of the English music-hall public. Her annual visit to play snippets at the Coliseum was an "event of the vaudeville year"; and in 1921 the great Mme Sarah, now 75 years old, was acting in *Daniel* by Louis Verneuil at the Princes Theatre. An address from the actresses of England was presented to her as "the greatest artist of our time."

During the year 1914 an old injury condemned her to lie for eight months on her back with her right leg in plaster of paris. By February, 1915, the indomitable woman could endure it no longer, and demanded an operation. "Operation," in this case, meant nothing less than amputation, and amputated the leg was. It is no exaggeration to say that the event turned the thoughts of many aside from the Great War. Crowned heads sent telegrams of inquiry and condolence; and Mme Bernhardt, then a woman of 70, was no sooner safely relieved of the offending limb than she began to make plans for future tours and the adaptation of old plays to the new needs.

By the autumn she was back in her own theatre in Paris, playing M. Morand's dramatic war poem, *Les Cathédrales*; and when she brought the piece to the London Coliseum in December London found that, though she must sit in a chair throughout the performance, her power, her fury of energy, and her incomparable charm were undiminished. So it went on throughout the war. She went to the United States in 1916, when she played Shylock in *The Merchant of Venice* (her caprices were indeed violent), and again the following year. She even played Phèdre, though she could no longer move about the stage. She believed that French drama was to be ennobled by the great trials of the French nation; and to the last she was full of plans. In the autumn of 1921 she achieved a fresh triumph in Maurice Rostand's drama, *La Gloire*, and last summer she produced *Régine Armand*, a play written for her by M. Verneuil. In November she toured in Italy, and in December was taken ill in Paris while rehearsing a new play by Sacha Guitry.

Sarah Bernhardt, actress, was born on October 22, 1844. She died on March 26, 1923, aged 78

———~~~———

GERTRUDE BELL

EXPLORER AND
ARCHAEOLOGIST WHOSE
DEEP KNOWLEDGE OF ARABIA
WAS USED BY BRITISH
INTELLIGENCE DURING
THE FIRST WORLD WAR

JULY 13, 1926

Miss Gertrude Bell was perhaps the most distinguished woman of our day in the field of Oriental exploration, archaeology, and literature, and in the service of the Empire in Iraq. Her life has been in some ways quite unique, for she is the only Englishwoman who has travelled right across the wild deserts of Arabia, winning for herself thereby the gold medal of the Royal Geographical Society, and who, having placed her rare knowledge of the East at the disposal of the British authorities during the Great War, and been sent to Baghdad soon after the British occupation, has held a high position in the Political Department of the Government of India, originally in charge of Mesopotamian affairs. Her premature death must be ascribed to the deep interest in her work and to the

unflinching sense of duty which, except for two very short holidays at home, kept her for nearly ten years almost continuously at Baghdad, even during the torrid heat of the Mesopotamian summers, when the thermometer stands for weeks together about and above 120deg in the shade.

Her career was entirely of her own choosing and making, though in its early stages she could naturally not, in the least, foresee the shape it would ultimately take. The eldest daughter of Sir Hugh Bell, the great Yorkshire iron-master, she studied at Queen's College, London, and at Oxford University, where she took a first class in history in 1887. Not long afterwards she went out to Persia, where her uncle, the late Sir Frank Lascelles, was then British Minister, and it was at Teheran that she first heard the East a'calling.

But though Persia and the Persians first captured her imagination, it was the Arab countries and Arab life and Arabic literature that soon acquired a far stronger and more enduring hold upon her. She began to travel on her own account and to watch from year to year, while the Arab lands still formed part of the old Ottoman Empire, the stirrings of a new Arab sense of nationhood during the last period of Abdul Hamid's reign and under the Committee of Union and Progress after the Turkish Revolution. She was a keen observer of the political changes which were taking place all over the Near East under the powerful impact of the West, but her chief interest and delight was in the life of the East, the picturesque habits and customs of the humbler folk, the intellectual outlook of the ruling classes, whether they still stood firm and stubborn in the ancient ways or were taking on a veneer of modern civilization. Doughty's masterpiece of Arab travel, then almost unnoticed in England, exerted a potent influence upon her, and she learnt from him to seek out the black tents of the Beduin tribesmen, whose confidence she captured by reciting to them favourite passages from the old desert poets as familiar to them as the Old Testament stories to our Roundheads.

At the end of 1906 she revealed herself to her fellow-countrymen in a volume entitled "The Desert and the Sown," perhaps the most brilliant one she ever wrote, with the breath of the desert still upon her, and yet with the restraint of one whose mind was already trained to sober judgment. It was followed at the end of 1910 by "Amurath to Amurath," in which archaeological and topographical research in the silent Mesopotamian borderland plays as important a part as her shrewd speculations in the more tumultuous field of Near Eastern politics, then ripening for the bloody harvest of war.

It was in 1913 that her adventurous spirit compassed and carried out a bold scheme for crossing the Arabian peninsula from west to east and visiting the Shammar stronghold at Hayil, to which no European had penetrated for 20 years, and it is worth noting to-day that the large store of information she brought back with her included an estimate of Ibn Saud of Al Riadh as "the chief figure in Central Arabia," though very little was then known about him, which the events of the last few years have signally borne out. All these exhausting and often dangerous journeys she accomplished without any European companion and attended only by her one devoted Syrian servant, Fattuh, to whose resourcefulness and loyalty she has paid many warm tributes. She never attempted to disguise her nationality or her sex, and, indeed, she rightly believed that her sex was her best safeguard among the fierce but proud children of the desert who respect the reliance placed in their good faith, whether they are inclined to look upon the strange traveller as a mad woman, and therefore under the special protection of Allah, or as one who comes of a great and honoured race whose customs are inviolable. The real secret of her success in conquering the desert, which she sometimes loved and sometimes hated, was that with a splendid constitution and great powers of endurance she combined absolute fearlessness and quick sympathy and understanding, whatever the particular type of humanity with which she happened to be thrown into contact.

The war changed her life, and not merely "for the duration." She had hitherto been her own mistress and had done as she listed. She realized at once the magnitude of the issues involved in the East as well as in the West and she threw herself into the service of her country where she knew she would be most needed. After some valuable work in France and in the Intelligence

Department in Egypt, she went out at the request of the then Viceroy, Lord Hardinge, to Mesopotamia, where her almost unrivalled knowledge of Arab tribal politics and of many of the most influential tribesmen was invaluable in the critical stages of the Mesopotamian campaign and still more in the work of administrative reconstruction which followed the expulsion of the Turk. She had not perhaps in the first years, when British policy in Mesopotamia was being shaped largely by Indian military administrators, the influence which she acquired afterwards when Sir Percy Cox and more lately Sir Henry Dobbs as High Commissioners had settled down to lay the foundations of a more stable order of things in transition to a constitutional State of Iraq under a British mandate, and ultimately with full rights of sovereignty as soon as the people shall have been proved capable of governing and protecting themselves without foreign help and support.

If Iraq has already made some progress towards that goal, if King Feisal already sits on a less uneasy throne, it is in no small measure due to the indefatigable spade work done by Miss Bell. The close friendship between her and the Sovereign of Iraq dated back to the Paris Peace Conference, which he attended as the son and representative of King Hussein of the Hedjaz, and she as an acknowledged expert on all questions connected with Arabia. But since he was chosen to be King of Iraq and came to reign at Baghdad, no one has enjoyed his confidence more completely or used her influence with him

more tactfully and beneficially than the English lady whom he delighted to call his "sister." In many moments of crisis she was the unobtrusive channel for confidential and delicate communications between the Residency and the Palace, and equally trusted by both. In ordinary times her work was chiefly connected with tribal affairs, but there were few administrative questions on which her ripe knowledge of the country and the people was not consulted or failed to carry weight, and it is to her exhaustive survey of the civil administration, laid before Parliament four years ago, that the British public owes the fullest information yet given to it on the condition of Iraq.

With the conclusion and ratification of last year's Treaty between Great Britain and Iraq, which formally consecrated the new *régime*, Miss Bell began to feel that the consummation for which she had always worked in the interests of both countries had been as fully assured as the condition of a still storm-tossed world allowed, and during her last short visit home, barely a year ago, she confessed to her friends that the strain of so many arduous years in so pitiless a climate was beginning to tell even upon her iron constitution. There seemed then some hope that she would return before long, perhaps even this year, to enjoy a much needed rest before turning to the no less valuable work she still hoped to do on the vast materials she had collected and had not yet had time to utilize. But a compelling interest arose for her as soon as she got back to Baghdad in connexion with the development of an archaeological department on which she had long set her heart, and the last piece of work she sent home was a catalogue of the small Iraq Museum of which she was bent on securing the future. The results of the recent excavations at Ur of the Chaldees strengthened her conviction that there lie still buried under the sands of Iraq innumerable remains of a great antiquity equally precious from the point of view of history and of art, and it is a pathetic coincidence that the news of her death should have reached London on the very day on which Mr Woolley was displaying at the British Museum some of the remarkable finds made during the last winter season at Ur to which her private letters have frequently referred with all her old enthusiasm.

Her death is a grievous loss to her country, whom she served in many fields, lending distinction to all; to Iraq, who has had no better friend; to the personal friends who learnt to know her fine character as well as her fine intellect; and to the large circle of those whose admiration she won through her books and her work, and won abundantly. With all the qualities which are usually described as virile she combined in a high degree the charm of feminine refinement, and though only revealed to few, even amongst her intimates, great depths of tender and even passionate affection.

Gertrude Bell, CBE, traveller and archaeologist, was born on July 14, 1868. She died on July 12, 1926, aged 57

EMMELINE PANKHURST

CO-FOUNDER OF THE WOMEN'S SOCIAL AND POLITICAL UNION, WHICH CAMPAIGNED MILITANTLY FOR WOMEN'S RIGHT TO VOTE

JUNE 15, 1928

Mrs Emmeline Pankhurst was born in Manchester on July 14, 1858. In her early childhood she was brought into close touch with those who had inherited the spirit of the Manchester reformers. Her father, Mr Robert Goulden, a calico-printer, was keenly interested in the reform question and the dawn of the movement for woman suffrage; her grandfather nearly lost his life in the Peterloo franchise riots in 1819. At the age of 13, soon after she had been taken to her first woman suffrage meeting by her mother, she went to school in Paris, where she found a girl-friend of her own way of thinking in the daughter of Henri Rochefort. In 1879 she married Dr R. M. Pankhurst, a man many years older than herself. An intimate friend of John Stuart Mill and an able lawyer, he shared and helped to mould his wife's political views. She served with him on the committee which promoted the Married Women's Property Act, and was at the same time a member of the Manchester Women's Suffrage Committee.

In 1889 she helped in forming the Women's Franchise League, which, however, was discontinued after a few years. She remained a Liberal until 1892, when she joined the Independent Labour Party. After being defeated for the Manchester School Board, she was elected at the head of the poll for the board of guardians and served for five years. When her husband died, in 1898, she was left not well off, and with three girls and a boy to bring up. Accordingly she found work as registrar of births and deaths at Chorlton-on-Medlock, but her propaganda activities were considered inconsistent with this official position, and she resigned.

In 1903 her interest in the cause of woman suffrage was reawakened by the enthusiasm of her daughter Christabel, and she formed the Women's Social and Political Union, the first meeting of which was held in her house in Manchester in October of that year. Two years later the militant movement was started as the immediate result of the treatment received by Miss Christabel Pankhurst and Miss Annie Kenney, two members of the union who endeavoured to question Sir Edward Grey on the prospects of woman suffrage at a political meeting held in Manchester. In 1906 Mrs Pankhurst and her union began a series of pilgrimages to the House of Commons, which resulted in conflicts with the police and the imprisonment of large numbers of the members. In October, 1906, she was present at the first of these demonstrations, when 11 women were arrested. In January, 1908, she was pelted with eggs and rolled in the mud during the Mid-Devon election at Newton Abbot, and a month later she was arrested when carrying a petition to the Prime Minister at the House of Commons, but was released after undergoing five of the six weeks' imprisonment to which she was sentenced.

Some months later, in October, a warrant was issued for her arrest, together with Miss Pankhurst and Mrs Drummond, for inciting the public to "rush" the House of Commons. During her three months' imprisonment in Holloway Gaol she led a revolt of her followers against the rules of prison discipline, demanding that they should be treated as political prisoners. In 1909, the year in which the "hunger strike" and "forcible feeding" were first practised in connection with these cases, she was once more arrested at the door of the House of Commons, and after her trial, and pending an appeal founded on the Bill of Rights and a statute of Charles II, dealing with petitions to the Crown, she went to America and Canada on a lecturing tour; two days before her return her fine was paid by some unknown person, so that she did not go to prison.

As soon, however, as she was back in England, she again devoted her energies to the encouragement of the campaign of pin-pricks and violence to which she was committed and by which she hoped to further the cause which she had at heart. In 1912, for her own share in these lawless acts, she was twice imprisoned, but in each case served only five weeks of the periods of two months and nine months — for conspiracy to break windows — to which she was sentenced. A year later she was arrested on the more serious charge of inciting to commit a felony, in connexion with the blowing-up of Mr Lloyd George's country house at Walton. In spite of the ability with which she conducted her own defence, the jury found her guilty — though with a strong recommendation to mercy — and she was sentenced by Mr Justice Lush to three years' penal servitude.

On the tenth day of the hunger strike which she at once began (to be followed later on by a thirst strike) she was temporarily released, under the terms of the measure introduced by Mr McKenna commonly known as the Cat and Mouse Act, because of the condition of extreme weakness to which she was reduced. At the end of five months, during which she was several times released and rearrested, she went to Paris, and then to America (after a detention of two and a half days on Ellis Island), having served not quite three weeks of her three years' sentence. On her return to England the same cat-and-mouse policy was resumed by the authorities — and accompanied by more and more violent outbreaks on the part of Mrs Pankhurst's militant followers — until at last, in the summer of 1914, after she had been arrested and released nine or ten times on the one charge, it was finally abandoned, and the remainder of her term of three years' penal servitude allowed to lapse.

Whether, but for the outbreak of the Great War, the militant move-

Emmeline Pankhurst

ment would have resulted in the establishment of woman suffrage is a point on which opinions will probably always differ. But there is no question that the coming of the vote, which Mrs Pankhurst claimed as the right of her sex, was sensibly hastened by the general feeling that after the extraordinary courage and devotion shown by women of all classes in the nation's emergency there must be no risk of a renewal of the feminist strife of the days of militancy. When the War was over it was remembered that on its outbreak Mrs Pankhurst, with her daughter Christabel and the rest of the militant leaders, declared an immediate suffrage truce, and gave herself up to the claims of national service and devoted her talents as a speaker to the encouragement of recruiting, first in this country and then in the United States. A visit to Russia in 1917, where she formed strong opinions on the evils of Bolshevism, was followed by a residence of some years in Canada and afterwards in Bermuda for the benefit of her health. Since she came home, at the end of 1925, she had taken a deep interest in public life and politics, and had some thoughts of standing for Parliament, though she declined Lady Astor's offer to give up to her her seat in Plymouth.

Whatever views may be held as to the righteousness of the cause to which she gave her life and the methods by which she tried to bring about its achievement, there can be no doubt about the singleness of her aim and the remarkable strength and nobility of her character. She was inclined to be autocratic and liked to go her own way. But that was because she was honestly convinced that her own way was the only way. The end that she had in view was the emancipation of women from what she believed, with passionate sincerity, to be a condition of harmful subjection. She was convinced that she was working for the salvation of the world, as well as of her sex. She was a public speaker of very remarkable force and ability, with a power of stimulating and swaying her audience possessed by no other woman of her generation, and was regarded with devoted admiration by many people outside the members of her union. With all her autocracy, and her grievous mistakes, she was a humble-minded, large-hearted, unselfish woman, of the stuff of which martyrs are made. Quite deliberately, and having counted the cost, she undertook a warfare against the forces of law and order the strain of which her slight and fragile body was unable to bear. It will be remembered of her that whatever peril and suffering she called upon her followers to endure, up to the extreme indignity of forcible feeding, she herself was ready to face, and did face, with unfailing courage and endurance of body and mind.

Emmeline Pankhurst, campaigner for women's suffrage, was born on July 14, 1858. She died on June 14, 1928, aged 69

—◦◦◦—

DAME ELLEN TERRY

COMPELLING SHAKESPEAREAN ACTRESS OF GREAT VITALITY AND CHARM

JULY 23, 1928

The death of Dame Ellen Terry has been received with universal sorrow. In the history of the English stage no other actress has ever made for herself so abiding a place in the affections of the nation.

Ellen Alice Terry was born at Coventry on February 27, 1848, and was the second in age of three sisters, Kate (Mrs Arthur Lewis), Ellen, and Marion, who, with their brother, Mr Fred Terry, made up a famous theatrical family. Their parents, Mr and Mrs Benjamin Terry, were well-known provincial actors in the days of stock companies, and Miss Ellen Terry took early to their calling. At the age of eight she was engaged by Charles Kean to play Mamillius in *The Winter's Tale* at the Princess's Theatre, and she remained in his company for some years, acting, among other parts, Puck in *A Midsummer Night's Dream* and Arthur in *King John*. Even in those early days she appears to have shown the characteristics that made her irresistible in her prime; roguish comedy in Mamillius and Puck, pathos in Arthur, and personal charm in all three.

Kean gave up the Princess's Theatre in 1860, and Ellen Terry went to the provinces in search of experience. For some time she was in the old-established stock company of the Chutes at Bristol, of which her sister Kate, Madge Robertson (now Dame Madge Kendal), and Henrietta Hodson were also members. She returned to London in 1863, to play the part of Gertrude in *A Little Treasure* at the Haymarket to the Captain Maydenblush of Sothern; here, too, she first played Beatrice in *Much Ado About Nothing* before a London audience. Another performance in London was that of Desdemona to the Othello of Walter Montgomery. That was in 1863, and soon after it there came a break in Miss Terry's theatrical career. In February, 1864, she was married to G. F. Watts, the great painter,

who was nearly 30 years her senior. In June, 1865, they parted.

In 1867 occurred an event pregnant with interest. Having left the stage for two years, Miss Terry accepted an engagement at the now extinct Queen's Theatre in Long Acre; and here she first acted with Henry Irving. He and she played Petruchio and Katherine in *The Taming of the Shrew*, or rather in *Katherine and Petruchio*, Garrick's version of that play. Her elder sister, Kate, had married at the height of her career, and retired from the stage. Ellen Terry was looked upon as her worthy successor, but only the next year she retired once more from the stage, and she remained in private life till 1874. Even then she was only 26 years old, and an actress of her talent had little difficulty in making up lost ground. It even seemed that the interval had done her service by ripening the individual characteristics on which the great part of her success depended.

Returning to the Queen's Theatre for a time, she found her first great opportunity in April, 1875, when Mr and Mrs Bancroft put on *The Merchant of Venice* at the old Prince of Wales's Theatre, and, being unable to secure Mrs Kendal for Portia, turned to Miss Terry. A better move could not have been made. Ellen Terry was always the ideal Portia. More than 20 years later, when she was hampered by a distressing lack of memory and some slight loss of vitality, her beauty (she was well compared to a portrait by Veronese), her dignity, and her graciousness were unimpaired, and the bubbling spring of her mirth seemed as fresh as ever; it would be well worth while to be old to have seen her play the part at 27. The revival, admirable though it was, was short-lived, chiefly owing, it is said, to Coghlan's Shylock; but Miss Terry's reputation was doubled. She remained with the same management for more than a year, playing Clara Douglas in *Money*, Mabel Vane in *Masks and Faces*, and Blanche Haye in *Ours*. On leaving the Prince of Wales's Theatre she joined John Hare's management at the old Court, where, among other parts, she appeared for the first time as Olivia in Wills's adaptation of "The Vicar of Wakefield."

When Henry Irving took over the Lyceum, at the close of the Bateman management in 1878, one of his first steps was to engage Ellen Terry as his leading lady, and for the next 13 years they acted together, almost without a break. Her first part under the new management was Ophelia, and the influence of Irving was apparent at the outset. The part had been thought out as a whole, and one result was that the "mad scene" had a meaning. The phrases no longer appeared to be ungoverned spurts of lunacy; each proved to have been born of that character in those circumstances; and the effect of all was not only to intensify the devotion, the tenderness, and the innocence of Ophelia herself, but to point the tragedy of the whole story. No doubt Irving had found good material to work on; beauty (as Ophelia, said M. Jules Claretie in *La Presse*, Miss Terry looked like a "living model

of Giovanni Bellini's"), rare personal charm, intense vitality, and no lack of intelligence; but it says much for Irving's own power, and for the loyalty of one who might practically be called his pupil, that at her very first appearance under his management a born comedian should achieve a triumph in the part of Ophelia.

Her first season at the Lyceum was typical of the years of hard work that were to follow; besides Ophelia it included her appearance as Pauline, Lady Anne, Ruth Meadows, and Henrietta Maria. One of the most remarkable features of her career, indeed, is the loyal and patient manner in which she subordinated her own bias to fulfil the demands of her manager and his theatre. She played a great variety of parts, and though she played them not all equally well, she was always able to present a reasoned and consistent interpretation, while her irresistible personal charm went far to conceal the fact that she was frequently out of her depth. Lady Macbeth, for instance, was a part to which her special gifts were totally unsuited; but to recall her rendering of it is to recall far more than the regally beautiful woman who appears in Sargent's picture. It fell short of the magnificent, perverted nature which Shakespeare conceived, but it displayed a firmness that was an admirable foil to the moral cowardice of Macbeth, and something of the tragedy of a great love unworthily bestowed.

To chronicle all Miss Terry's appearances between 1878 and 1901 would be to chronicle the history of the

Lyceum Theatre. In only two plays — *Nance Oldfield* and *The Amber Heart* — did she appear without Sir Henry Irving; and to these might be added *Olivia*, as distinctly her triumph rather than his. In consecrating her best years to the Lyceum Miss Terry no doubt sacrificed many chances of appearing in plays, new or old, which might have exploited her personal bent; on the other hand, she was freed from the dangers of an ever-narrowing range and a faulty judgment which too often beset leading actors and actresses; she gained breadth and knowledge by playing whatever part Sir Henry Irving wished her to play, and she had the satisfaction of knowing herself a member of one of the greatest histrionic partnerships the English stage has seen.

Still on stage at the age of 80: Dame Ellen Terry

Like Irving, she commanded the attention; it was impossible to take one's eyes off her — until he appeared on the stage; unlike him, she commanded by appealing, by charming, rather than by interesting. Womanly, tender, mirthful, witty, graceful, musical, with a clear and melodious enunciation and rhythmical, flowing movements, she made the most perfect foil to her partner that could be imagined.

And once or twice, where Irving was least successful, it happened that Miss Terry was most in her element. Her matchless Portia we have referred to; Irving's Shylock was long unacceptable to the town; Miss Terry's Viola (a performance unfortunately cut short by illness) was inimitable, one of her finest achievements, while Irving's

Malvolio was all in the wrong key. In *Romeo and Juliet* they failed together, and in *Hamlet* they succeeded together. As Beatrice (which was perhaps the very finest of all the adorable performances she gave) she was so enchanting that the memory of her wit and charm leaves Irving's Benedick somewhat dim.

Of all Miss Terry's failures probably her Madame Sans-Gêne was the most outright, and the best deserved. The incarnation of all that was gracious and graceful, an actress whose every movement was a poem, whose speech was music, and whose ebullient spirits were constantly caught and guided into a stream of beauty by some natural refinement, she turned in that part to try to be vulgar. That she failed was only a new proof of the distance that separated her from the realistic school represented by Mme Réjane, a new illustration of the rare quality of her gifts. Though she lacked great tragic power, in scenes of simple pathos and affection, like those of Olivia or Cordelia, the emotions of her audience were utterly at her command; her highest moments came in the high-bred raillery of Portia and Beatrice.

Miss Terry left the Lyceum company in 1901, after the end of the run of *Coriolanus*, but appeared as Portia in the performance of *The Merchant of Venice* which closed the history of the theatre in July, 1902. A short season at the Imperial Theatre in 1903 under her own management brought no success. The name of her son, Edward Gordon Craig, was not then so well known in England as it is now, and his theories of scenery and of stage-lighting were even more puzzling to London then than they would be to-day. And so the interesting — it might be called the prophetic — production of Ibsen's *The Vikings at Helgeland* fell flat. In subsequent years Miss Terry appeared as Mistress Page in *The Merry Wives of Windsor* at His Majesty's Theatre; she played with indescribable fascination Lady Cecily Waynflete in Shaw's *Captain Brassbound's Conversion*; she appeared in *Alice Sit-by-the Fire* and in *Pinkie and the Fairies*, and she delivered in many towns of England and the United States two series of wilful, witty, very "feminist," and very perspicacious, lectures on Shakespeare's heroines.

In June, 1906, the 50th anniversary of Miss Terry's first appearance on the stage was celebrated at the Theatre Royal, Drury Lane, amid fervent enthusiasm. She had always been idolized by the public; and even the shrewdest critics found their judgment seduced by her supreme vitality and personal charm. At that "Jubilee", public, critics, and the theatrical profession (to whose memories she had endeared herself by her unfailing kindness, consideration, and unselfishness) joined to show her how much she was loved and admired. In spite of advancing years, failing memory, and increasing restlessness, she was always welcome on the stage; and she preserved her gaiety and verve to the end.

In May, 1922, Miss Terry received the hon. degree of LL.D. at St Andrews. In the New Year honours of 1925, to the delight of her countless admirers, she received the Grand Cross of the Order of the British Empire. In celebration of this event she and her sister Dames created at the same time — namely, Dame Millicent Fawcett and the late Dame Louisa Aldrich-Blake — were presented with wreaths of laurel at a reception held by a number of distinguished women. Her 80th birthday was celebrated last February with messages and tributes from her countless admirers, headed by the King and Queen, and it drew from old playgoers an interesting correspondence in *The Times* containing reminiscences of her triumphs. Some day, perhaps, a full and authoritative biography will fill the gaps inevitably left by her modesty and consideration for others in the fascinating book of memories which was her chief contribution to literature. She was a woman of genius; but her genius was not that of the brain so much as of the spirit, and of the heart. She was a poem in herself — a being of an exquisite and mobile beauty. On the stage or off she was like the daffodils that set the poet's heart dancing.

Dame Ellen Terry, GBE, Shakespearean actress, was born on February 27, 1848. She died on July 21, 1928, aged 80

—⌇⌇—

DAME MILLICENT FAWCETT

MODERATE BUT DETERMINED PRESIDENT OF THE NATIONAL UNION OF WOMEN SUFFRAGE SOCIETIES

AUGUST 6, 1929

The death of Dame Millicent Garrett Fawcett, which occurred early yesterday morning, recalls a long and important chapter in the story of the political emancipation of women.

The seventh child of Newson Garrett, of Aldeburgh, Suffolk, she was born there on June 11, 1847. Before she was 20 she was married to Henry Fawcett. A few years earlier he had become Professor of Political Economy at Cambridge, an office which he held till his death. His political career was still to come. His wife shared his interests in economics, and herself published various works on that subject, including "Political Economy for Beginners," 1870, "Tales in Political Economy, 1875, and, with her husband, a book of "Essays and Lectures," 1872.

After her widowhood she published biographies of Queen Victoria and of Sir William Molesworth, one of the old "philosophical Radicals," and biographical studies of "Some Eminent Women of our Time," 1889, and "Five Famous Frenchwomen," 1906. In old age she published a volume of reminiscences, "What I Remember," 1924, and an account of a visit to Palestine, "Easter in Palestine," 1926, a country which she visited three times in her old age. But probably those of her books which will last longest are the two in which she describes the movement to which her life work was mainly devoted — "Women's Suffrage: a Short History of a Great Movement," 1911, and "The Women's Victory — and After," 1919. It happens that her public life was exactly co-extensive with this movement. It began with her first platform speech in March, 1870, on behalf of the first Women's Suffrage Bill to be introduced into the House of Commons. Its active stages ended shortly after the Representation of the People Act, 1918, which granted the first great instalment of women's suffrage, and it has finally terminated not long after the first woman MP has achieved Cabinet rank — an event which may be said to have rounded off the achievement of political equality between men and women.

During her married life she could give only a divided allegiance to the women's cause. Her blind husband, who never saw her with his bodily eyes, was very closely dependent on her. Without the aid which the entire community of opinion and sympathy between them enabled her to give, he could scarcely have so succeeded in his political life as to earn the title of "Member for India" and become a remarkably successful Postmaster-General. A portrait of Mrs Fawcett and her husband, painted by Ford Madox Brown a few years before this appointment to office, is to be seen in the National Portrait Gallery. For years after his death it was noted by one of her intimates that any allusion to him in her presence caused a pallor and rigidity which showed that the wound was still too deep for even the gentlest handling. She did not, however, even at the first, allow herself to fall into a selfish lethargy.

During her residence at Cambridge, in her husband's lifetime, they both worked hard for the extension of University education to women. Through her sister, Dr Elizabeth Garrett Anderson, she was also associated with the movement to open the medical profession to women, and her own passionate conviction enlisted her under the banner of Mrs Josephine Butler in the campaign against the Contagious Diseases Acts. But her special task — said to have been assigned to her by her elder sisters while she was still a schoolgirl — was that of political enfranchisement. The atmosphere of hopefulness with which it began is shown by the assurance given by a prominent supporter, Mr Davenport Hill, to a meeting in 1868, that "He was asking them to help a great cause which, unlike all other great causes, would only require their support for a very short time. The claim was so clear and reasonable; it had but to be brought before Parliament to be granted."

Yet a few years later the mere appearance of Mrs Fawcett on a public platform to speak for "votes for women" caused her and a fellow speaker, also an MP's wife, to be described in the House as "Two ladies, wives of members of this House, who have disgraced themselves." The speaker added that he would not further disgrace them by mentioning their names. Shortly afterwards Mrs Fawcett found herself being taken into dinner by this gentleman and amused herself by offering to get their hostess to find him a partner who had not disgraced herself. After this exchange of amenities they got on very well. After all, commented Mrs Fawcett, what he had said was mild compared to Horace Walpole's description of Mary Wollstonecraft Godwin as "a hyena in petticoats."

It was lucky for her that she was always able to find entertainment in the excesses of her opponents. For some forty years after its hopeful beginnings the movement to which she had dedicated herself made but a slow upward progress, broken by many successive disappointments. After the death of Lydia Becker she became its recognized leader until the invention of militant tactics by the Pankhursts divided it into two (later three) independent forces. Thanks to the good sense of all concerned, they never turned their arms against each other, even when, as happened in 1912, Mrs Fawcett and her followers believed that the renewal of militant tactics, in a more violent and dangerous form than before, had helped to turn the tide of public feeling and led to the defeat of the Conciliation Bill. Even then she maintained her belief that the responsibility rested, not on the women infuriated by what they believed deliberate treachery, but upon the politicians whose levity and contempt were more galling than open hostility.

Mrs Fawcett herself was never goaded into losing either her balance, her courage, her faith, her temper, or her sense of humour. But, as she often said of herself, she was "not a forgiving person." She never forgave Mr Gladstone for his vacillations and inconsistencies on the subject of women's suffrage, nor Mr Asquith for the determined hostility which for some years was the chief impediment to the progress of the cause. She has described with humour and malice his gradual change of front, from contemptuous to respectful hostility, and so to a support which, though she never quite admitted it, became really understanding and helpful. On her last meeting with him she "could not resist saying to him that she had never seen a man so improved."

During the years of militant suffragism it seemed to many a spiritless leadership that kept Mrs Fawcett's followers to the long, uphill stretches of constitutional propaganda. But it is questionable which is the greater — the courage which braves ridicule, odium, and imprisonment, or that which plants seeds which require a generation to grow to maturity and then spends a life-time in fostering them. It requires perhaps something better than courage to resist all temptation to quicken the pace by succumbing to the dangerous doctrine that the end justifies the means, and to hold fast to the Kantian maxim of statesmanship: "Act so that the maxim of thy actions might become law universal." One of Mrs Fawcett's favourite quotations was the message said to have been sent by General Foch to General Joffre at a critical moment in the battle of the Marne:—

"My centre is giving way; my right is falling back; situation excellent; I attack."

It was that spirit which she inculcated on her followers when one Suffrage Bill after another during a campaign of 50 years was talked out, laughed out, read a second time (always a second time, never a third), till even *Punch* put into the mouth of the woman suffragist the saying, "Don't talk to me of Sisyphus; he wasn't a woman." She was rewarded by ultimate success and by a devotion which, to the very end of her life, brought every woman's meeting to its feet the moment that little figure, crowned by its coils of abundant russet hair, appeared on the platform.

No account of her would be complete which did not note two other characteristic traits. One was her thoughtful kindness, especially to obscure people. An office typist who had scarcely realized that Mrs Fawcett knew her by sight, and the lift man of some buildings she occasionally visited, have recorded how, when taken ill, they found themselves recipients of a steady stream of little kindnesses — visits, letters, books which showed her knowledge of their special tastes. The other trait was her inarticulate but passionate patriotism. The instant the South African War broke out she insisted on the abandonment of suffragist agitation, and probably no public honour ever shown her gratified her so much as being chosen with her daughter to investigate the charges against the administration of the concentration camps for Boer women and children. She has recorded that the day when the Great War broke out was perhaps the blackest of her life. The still-running deep waters of her devotion to individuals, to the cause of women, and to her country were, indeed, the springs which fed all her manifold activities.

In 1919 Mrs Fawcett retired from the presidency of the National Union of Women Suffrage Societies, which then became the National Union of Societies for Equal Citizenship. Since then she lived a quiet but far from inactive life, writing, occasionally speaking at meetings, and actually undertaking a journey to Ceylon in the spring of the present year. She was created a Dame of the Order of the British Empire in 1925.

For many years she had lived with her elder sister, Miss Agnes Garrett, and with her only child, Miss Philippa Fawcett, now principal assistant in the Education Department of the LCC, whose success at Newnham, where she achieved the honour of being placed "above the Senior Wrangler," had been so great a joy to her. Her death took place at 2, Gower-street, which had been her home for many years.

The funeral will be at Golders Green Crematorium on Thursday at 11.30. An announcement will be made later of a memorial service to be held in the autumn.

Dame Millicent Fawcett, GBE, campaigner for women's suffrage, was born on June 11, 1847. She died on August 5, 1929, aged 82

—∾—

ANNA PAVLOVA

RUSSIAN PRIMA BALLERINA WHO CREATED THE ROLE OF THE DYING SWAN FOR FOKINE

JANUARY 23, 1931
Mme Pavlova appeared first on the London stage on April 18, 1910. All adored, and rightly, the memory of Mme Adeline Genée, who had not long ceased dancing at the Empire. Isadora Duncan, with a fine artistic severity, had lately brought some hint of ancient Greece back to the art of the dance; and Miss Maud Allan, with

no artistic severity at all, had made a public for her "impressionist" gestures and postures. And now before a London which was still prone to think of high kicking as proof of accomplishment in dancing, there came two unknown Russians, Anna Pavlova and Michael Mordkin, who (with a little company of eight to support them) seemed to do all that Mme Genée had done, all that Isadora Duncan had done, all that Miss Maud Allan had done well, and a great deal that none of them had done, and that none of the audience had ever seen done before. Mme Pavlova danced as Columbine, and she and M. Mordkin did pirouettes that equalled Mme Genée's for technical accuracy and bewildering speed. They danced to Rubinstein's "Valse Caprice"; and we got a new idea of rhythm and grace and the play of light and shade over the face and the whole body of the dancer. They danced an "Automne Bacchanale" by Glazounov and infected the whole house with the mad gaiety, the luxurious ecstasy, of that passionate poem in movement.

This was not actually the first time that Mme Pavlova had danced in London: two summers before she had come over from Paris to dance at a private house before King Edward and Queen Alexandra. But this was the first time that any section of the London public had seen the strictest technique of the Imperial Russian Ballet flowering into individual expression, and "impressionism" beaten hollow at its own game through the mastery of the traditional forms.

Mme Pavlova had been through the school of the Imperial Russian Ballet, that "cloister," as she called it, "where inflexible rule obtains," had left it at 16 with the official title of *première danseuse*, and had since become one of the five officially entitled ballerinas. Daughter of a poor widow and born in St Petersburg in 1885, she had determined to be a dancer on that day in her childhood when her mother took her to see Tchaikovsky's *Sleeping Beauty*. She would dance the Sleeping Beauty — nothing less; and in years to come she often did. From 10 to 16 she worked in the school of the Imperial Ballet; and after a few years at the Marinsky Theatre, which was the ballet's home, she started in 1907 on the first of those many tours which have made her famous all over the civilized world.

She had joined Diaghilev's company in 1908. In 1911 the full glory of the Russian Ballet broke upon London, when Pavlova, Nijinsky, and many another came to Covent Garden, and we saw *Pavillon d'Armide* and *Les Sylphides* and *The Spectre of the Rose* and much else that was a revelation of beauty. But the story of Mme Pavlova belongs rather to her special visits, with M. Novikoff or M. Volinine, or both, and a small *corps de ballet*, mostly of her own training. At ballet on large lines she was not supreme. Whoever designed them for her, her bigger productions lacked certainty and cohesion of movement; and audiences would resign themselves to wait patiently till Pavlova came on again to dance a solo or a duet. She was inventive and adventurous in her subjects. She made a ballet of Don Quixote, and as time went on she turned more and more to the East, to India, Japan, China, for her plots and scenes. But it was in dancing that she was unmatched; and in the little *divertissements* — the *Dying Swan*, the *Blue Danube*, a waltz by Chopin, and, most wonderful of all, the *Papillons* — she showed the purity and power of her genius.

To say that she founded her individual expression on her mastery of the traditional technique, uniting the old and the new, is to explain some of her art; and a little more may be explained by saying that she knew how to dance not only with her face and her head and every part of her body, but with all at once and in tune with each other, so as to reveal new wonders of significant movement, making the dance a revelation of the body through the spirit, and the body seem somehow a medium for the play of light and shade, an instrument of music, a field of colour, a thing to be apprehended and enjoyed with every sense at once. But in the end there is no explaining a beauty which was made up of knowledge, accomplishment, imagination, grace — so many elements combined in a particular person and personality. There can never be another Pavlova.

Mme Pavlova may be said to have lived for her art, although after her marriage to M. Victor Dandré she loved her home in Hampstead. A law suit brought against her last year showed her to be a strict disciplinarian where her company was concerned; and the best of

her many pupils caught from her the old spirit of the school in St Petersburg, where they knew better than to suppose that dancing was easy and the dancer's life a soft one.

Anna Pavlova, Russian prima ballerina, was born on February 12, 1881. She died on January 23, 1931, aged 49

———✍———

DAME NELLIE MELBA

AUSTRALIAN OPERATIC SOPRANO WHO STUDIED ROLES WITH VERDI AND PUCCINI

FEBRUARY 24, 1931

Melba, to use the name by which she was universally known until the prefix of Dame Nellie was attached to it, was born near Melbourne in 1859, and began her career as Helen Porter Mitchell. Her Scottish parents, who had settled in Australia, had themselves some musical proclivities. But it was not until after her early marriage to Mr Charles Armstrong that it became clear that her gifts must be taken seriously.

It was largely by her own efforts that she came to England in 1886 with the intention of cultivating her voice. When she arrived the experts to whom she appealed in London did not realize her possibilities. It is amusing to record that she was refused work in the Savoy

Opera Company by Sullivan, though probably he did her and the world at large the greatest service by his refusal. She went to Paris, and to Mme Mathilde Marchesi belongs the credit of having instantly recognized that, to quote her own phrase, she "had found a star."

A year of study and of close companionship with this great teacher was all that was needed to give Nellie Armstrong a brilliant *début* at "La Monnaie" in Brussels as Mme Melba. She made her first appearance there on October 13, 1887, in the part of Gilda in *Rigoletto*. Her second part was Violetta in *La Traviata*, so that from the first she was identified with the earlier phases of Verdi, in which she has been pre-eminent ever since. Although, contrary to the traditions of the Brussels theatre, she sang in Italian, she aroused such enthusiasm that when a little later she was to sing *Lakmé*, and the question arose as to whether her French accent was sufficiently secure, the composer, Delibes, is said to have exclaimed, "Qu'elle chante *Lakmé* en français, en italien, en allemand, en anglais, ou en chinois, cela m'est égal, mais qu'elle la chante."

Her first appearance at Covent Garden on May 24, 1888, in *Lucia di Lammermoor*, was a more qualified success. Curiously enough, she was more commended at first for some supposed dramatic power than for the only two things which have ever really mattered in her case — the exquisite voice and the perfect use of it. From London she returned to the more congenial atmosphere of Brussels, and in the following year, 1889, proceeded to the conquest of Paris, where she triumphed as Ophélie in Ambroise Thomas's *Hamlet*. In Paris Mme Melba had the advantage of studying the parts of Marguerite in *Faust* and of Juliette with Gounod, and she took part in the first performance of *Roméo et Juliette* in French at Covent Garden in 1889.

From this time onward Mme Melba had only to visit one country after another to be acclaimed. From St Petersburg, where she sang before the Tsar in 1891, to Chicago, where in 1893 her singing with the de Reszkes was one of the features of the "World's Fair," the tale of her triumphs was virtually the same. But from the musical point of view a more important episode was her prolonged visit to Italy between these two events. Here she met the veteran Verdi and the young Puccini. Verdi helped her in the study of Aïda and of Desdemona (*Otello*). She made the acquaintance of Puccini's *Manon*, but *La Bohème*, the only one of his operas with which she was to be identified, was not yet written. Another young composer who begged leave to be presented was Leoncavallo. She sang Nedda in the first London performance of *I Pagliacci* a little later.

Mme Melba's early American appearances recall her few experiments with Wagner. She sang Elisabeth in *Tannhäuser* at the Metropolitan Opera House, New York, during her first season there, and it was later in America that she made her single appearance as Brünnhilde. She had previously sung Elsa (*Lohengrin*) at

Covent Garden, but she quite rightly realized that Wagner's music was not for her. The only pity, when one recalls her repertory, is that either lack of opportunity or of inclination prevented her from turning to Mozart instead.

Her actual repertory amounted to 25 operas, of which, however, only some 10 parts are those which will be remembered as her own. *La Bohème* was the last of these to be added, and she first sang in it at Philadelphia in 1898, having studied it with the composer in Italy earlier in the year. She was so much in love with the music that she would not rest until she had brought it to London, and it was largely by her personal influence that it was accepted at Covent Garden. Indeed, she persuaded the management to stage *La Bohème* with the promise to sing some favourite *scena* from her repertory in addition on each night that she appeared in it until the success of the opera was assured. She kept the promise, though the rapid success of the opera soon justified her faith. To most of the present generation of opera-goers "Melba nights" meant *La Bohème* nights, and, for several seasons before the War and when Covent Garden reopened after it, there could not be too many of them for the public. She bade farewell to Covent Garden on June 8, 1926, when, in the presence of the King and Queen, she sang in acts from *Roméo et Juliette*, *Otello*, and *La Bohème*. Actually her last appearance in London was at a charity concert in 1929.

It is difficult now to realize that 30 years or so ago *La Bohème* seemed to offer few opportunities for the special characteristics of Mme Melba's art, intimately associated as it then was with Donizetti, the earlier Verdi, and Gounod. But those characteristics in reality had full play in all music based on the expression of a pure vocal *cantilena*, and could appear in the simply held note at the end of the first act of *La Bohème* as completely as in the *fioritura* of "Caro nome" or "The Jewel Song." The essence of her power was due to such an ease in the production of pure tone in all parts of the voice and in all circumstances that there was no barrier between the music and the listener.

It is unnecessary to enlarge on the personal popularity of Melba here, or the almost passionate devotion which she inspired among her own countrymen on the various occasions when she revisited Australia. Her book of reminiscences, "Melodies and Memories" (1925), was disappointing, for it contained too little about her methods and experiences. She was generous in giving her services for good causes, and her work for War charities is remembered in the title conferred in 1918. She was then created DBE, and GBE in 1927.

Dame Nellie Melba, GBE, operatic soprano, was born on May 19, 1859. She died on February 23, 1931, aged 71

GERTRUDE JEKYLL

INNOVATIVE GARDEN DESIGNER
WHO PAINTED LIVING PICTURES
WITH GROWING PLANTS

DECEMBER 10, 1932

Miss Gertrude Jekyll died at her home at Godalming on Thursday evening, at the age of 89. She had been failing for some weeks and had felt the recent death of her brother, Sir Herbert Jekyll, very much. She was a great gardener, second only, if indeed she was second, to her friend William Robinson, of Gravetye. To these two, more than to any others, are due, not only the complete transformation of English horticultural method and design, but also that wide diffusion of knowledge and taste which has made us almost a nation of gardeners. Miss Jekyll was also a true artist with an exquisite sense of colour.

She was born on November 29, 1843, at 2, Grafton Street, the fourth child and second daughter of Edward Jekyll, captain in the Grenadier Guards, and Julia, *née* Hammersley. In 1848 the family moved to Bramley House, Surrey, and there she developed a strong interest in botany and gardening, in horses and all country pursuits, and especially in painting. About 1861 she began to study in the art schools of South Kensington, and in 1866 she worked in Paris. Later the British Museum, the National Gallery, the Louvre, the Brera, and the galleries of Venice and Rome offered her invaluable opportunity and experience.

A succession of German and French governesses of the early Victorian type left no more than a resentful impression on her independent mind and character. A brief incursion into boarding school life only deepened her sense of aloofness, and yet no one had a kinder heart, a more truly helpful and sympathetic spirit, a readier sense of humour and good comradeship. Not that her home circle was narrow, or wanting in intellectual or artistic opportunity. Her mother was a good musician, and Mendelssohn was a constant visitor at her London home. Leighton, Watts, and Poynter, among many others, gave help and encouragement to the young artist.

An early acquaintance with Charles Newton, then Keeper of the Greek and Roman collections in the British Museum, led to a fruitful friendship with him and his wife, Mary Severn, with whom, in 1863, she visited Rhodes, Constantinople, and Athens and acquired a knowledge of Greek art. While in Italy she obtained practical instruction in several handicrafts, such as the use of gesso, watergilding, inlaying, repoussé work, and woodcarving. Indeed, there was little her skilful fingers could not bring to perfection, from a piece of finely wrought decorative silver down to the making of her gardening boots. She could toss an omelette and brew Turkish coffee or elderberry wine, compose a liqueur, or manufacture her own incomparable pot-pourri. Embroideries designed by herself, repairs to ancient church work so skilful that they amounted to creation, patchworks of intricate pattern, quilting of medieval fineness, shell pictures such as only a real artist could conceive, banner-making for philanthropic friends, village-inn signs for Surrey neighbours — all were achieved with equal skill and enjoyment.

In 1871 Miss Jekyll formed an enduring friendship with Jacques Blumenthal and his wife, he a musician of distinction, she unusually gifted in all manner of minor arts. Their famous hospitalities in London and at their lovely chalet above Montreux brought her into happy relations with many artists, musicians, and social notabilities. Another inspiring friend of the seventies was Hercules Brabazon, who profoundly impressed a small circle in those days, but whose wide recognition only came after he had laid down his brush. He introduced Miss Jekyll to Mme Bodichon (Barbara Leigh Smith), a gifted painter, but better known in connexion with Girton College. Together they spent a happy winter in 1873-74 painting in Algiers and there making friends with the artist Frederick Walker.

Her father's death in 1876 at Wargrave Hill, Henley, led to the return of the family to West Surrey, and there Miss Jekyll settled with her mother in a house they built on Munstead Hill, above Godalming, in 1878. This soon became a meeting ground for a group of enthusiastic gardeners, amateur and professional, who helped her in the pursuit which henceforward was to be her main employment and delight. House decoration and furnishing, of which her most extensive work was done at Eaton Hall in 1882, had already for some years occupied and interested her, but these activities waned as her horticultural knowledge and taste developed.

In 1882 Canon Hole, afterwards Dean of Rochester, for ever preeminent among rose growers, brought with him on a visit to Munstead House Mr William Robinson, who in his championship of hardy flowers versus the prevailing bedding-out system, found in Miss Jekyll an enthusiastic fellow-worker. Their activities were soon shared by a remarkable group of ardent amateurs, all busy rediscovering neglected plants and popularizing better ways of gardening. The disability of restricted sight, which had prevented Miss Jekyll from painting pictures with brushes, was by the law of compensation turned into an unexpected development of painting living pictures with growing plants. The late Mr Lathbury first induced her to write for his paper, the *Guardian*, and she expanded her articles into a book, "Wood and Garden," published in 1899. This was followed in 1900 by "Home and Garden," and in the ensuing years by other books on "Lilies," "Wall and Water Gardens," "Children's Gardening," "Colour Schemes for the Garden," and "Flower Arrangements," besides one entitled "Old West Surrey," embodying recollections of bygone country ways, to be re-issued, with amplification, in 1925, under the title of "Old English Household Life." All these books were copiously illustrated by photographs, taken and developed by Miss Jekyll's own hand.

From the beginning of 1900, when the *Garden* newspaper became the property of *Country Life*, Miss Jekyll undertook its co-editorship with Mr Ernest Cook, and only relinquished it after two and a half years owing to the strain on her eyesight. But her interest in garden schemes, her own horticultural work including the distribution through the trade of improved strains of some of her favourite flowers, the recapture of many sweet and almost vanished climbing roses and garden plants, and the planning and beautifying of gardens of all sorts and sizes, went on to the end of her life. From 1895, when her mother died, onwards, this work was carried out from her own home at Munstead Wood, where she made herself, with the help of Sir Edwin Lutyens, who had begun his professional career in her workshop in the early eighties, the home of her delight, surrounded by some 15 acres of typical Surrey woodland. In that year she was gratified to receive from the Royal Horticultural Society the Victoria Medal of Honour, just then instituted, and again in February, 1929, the Veitchian gold cup and 50 guineas prize. In later years she kept in touch by correspondence with her numerous clients and private friends, and with a widening circle at home and overseas, attracted by her writings. To her correspondents, enthusiastic, but often horticulturally inexperienced, she owed many a humorous twinkle and quiet chuckle. "Could you spare me some of those lovely flowers I saw in your garden last time I came; I think you called them *Peacocks*?" Some moments of hard thinking ensued, and a parcel of *Narcissus Pallidus Praecox* was presently dispatched with an informative postscript. "What is the aspect of the flower border you ask me to plan?" inquired Miss Jekyll of an enthusiastic correspondent, who baffled her by replying, "Most of the day it faces south-east, but due north all the morning."

In the House of Nature there are many mansions, inhabited by widely divergent spirits. Darwin and Wallace took continents and oceans as their laboratories wherein to study strange and living creations; Wordsworth and Tennyson, lifting their eyes to the hills and the sky, discoursed of religion and philosophy. Gertrude Jekyll, to whom we now bid a grateful "Hail and Farewell," sought ever for practical knowledge allied to beauty, and in that quest, whereby she may truly be said to have transfigured the gardens of England, she never grew old at heart or wearied in mind, was never discouraged by difficulty or defeated by failure, neither did she cease to share widely the fruits of her long and loving apprenticeship to Nature.

Gertrude Jekyll, VMH, garden designer, artist and writer, was born on November 29, 1843. She died on December 8, 1932, aged 89

—♠—

MARIE CURIE

CHEMIST WHO WON THE NOBEL
PRIZE FOR HER DISCOVERY
OF RADIUM

JULY 5, 1934

Mme Curie had a worldwide reputation as the most distinguished woman investigator of our times. Her claim to fame rests primarily on her researches in connexion with the radioactive bodies and particularly for her discovery and separation of the new element radium which showed radiating properties to a marked degree. This was a discovery of the first importance, for it provided scientific men with a powerful source of radiation which has been instrumental in extending widely our knowledge not only of radioactivity but of the structure of atoms in general. Radium has also found an extensive application in hospitals for therapeutic purposes, and particularly for the treatment of cancerous growths by the action of the penetrating radiation emitted spontaneously from this element.

Marie Sklodowska, as she was before her marriage, was born on November 7, 1867, at Warsaw, and received her education there. She early showed a deep interest in science, and went to Paris to attend lectures in the Sorbonne. She had small financial resources, and had to teach in schools to earn sufficient money to pay her expenses. In 1895

she married Pierre Curie, a young scientist of great promise, who had already made several notable discoveries in magnetism and in the physics of crystals. Mme Curie continued her scientific work in collaboration with her husband, but the direction of their work was changed as the result of the famous discovery of Henri Becquerel in 1896, who found that the element uranium showed the surprising property of emitting penetrating types of radiation, which blackened a photographic plate and discharged an electrified body.

Mme Curie made further investigations of this remarkable property using the electric method as a method of analysis. She showed that the radioactivity of uranium was an atomic property, as it depended only on the amount of uranium present and was unaffected by the combination of uranium with other elements. She also observed the striking fact that the uranium minerals from which uranium was separated showed an activity four to five times the amount to be expected from the uranium present. She correctly concluded that there must be present in uranium minerals another substance or substances far more active than uranium. With great boldness she undertook the laborious work of the chemical examination of the radioactive mineral pitchblende, and discovered a new strongly active substance which she named polonium, after the country of her birth. Later she discovered another new element, allied in chemical properties to barium, which she happily named radium. This element is present in minerals only in about one part in 3,000,0000 compared with uranium, and shows radioactive properties more than a million times that of an equal weight of uranium. The Austrian Government presented Mme Curie with the radioactive residues necessary for the separation of radium in quantity, and she was in this way able to obtain sufficient material to determine the atomic weight and physical and chemical properties of the new element.

The importance of this discovery was at once recognized by the scientific world. In 1903 the Davy Medal of the Royal Society was awarded jointly to Professor and Mme Curie, while in 1904 they shared a Nobel Prize with Henri Becquerel. After the death of Pierre Curie in a street accident in Paris in 1906 Mme Curie was awarded in 1911 the Nobel Prize in Chemistry for the discovery and isolation of the element radium. In 1906 she was appointed to a special Chair in the Sorbonne and was the first woman to obtain this distinction. Later a special Radium Institute, called the Pierre Curie Institute, was founded for investigations in radioactivity, and Mme Curie became the first director. She held this post at the time of her death.

In the course of the last 20 years this institute has been an important centre of research, where students of many nationalities have carried out investigations under her supervision. Mme Curie was a clear and inspiring lecturer, and her classes at the Sorbonne were widely attended. Her scientific work was all of a high order. She was a careful and accurate experimenter, and showed marked power of critical judgment in interpreting scientific facts. She retained an enthusiastic interest in her science throughout her life, and was a regular attendant at international conferences, taking an active and valuable part in scientific discussions.

She had a deep interest in the application of radium for therapeutic work both in France and abroad, and during the War actively helped in this work. She was twice invited to visit the United States and was received with acclamation, while the women of that country presented her with a gram of radium, to allow her to extend her researches. In 1922 she was appointed a member of the International Committee for Intellectual Cooperation of the League of Nations and took an active part in their deliberations.

Mme Curie left two children. The elder, Irene, early showed marked scientific ability and married a co-worker in the Radium Institut, M. Joliot. It was a source of great satisfaction and pride to Mme Curie in her later years to follow the splendid researches made by her daughter and her husband, for they have made notable contributions to our knowledge of neutrons and transformations. During the present year, they observed that a number of elements became radioactive by bombardment with the a-particles from radium, and have thus opened up a new method for study of the transformation of the atoms of matter.

The many friends of Mme Curie of all nations, and the scientific world as a whole, will greatly lament the removal of one who was held in such great honour for her splendid discoveries in science, and one who by strength of character and personality left a deep impression on all those who met her.

Marie Curie, physicist and chemist, was born on November 7, 1867. She died on July 4, 1934, aged 66

———

AMELIA EARHART

THE FIRST WOMAN AVIATOR TO CROSS THE ATLANTIC

JULY 20, 1937

Hope has now been officially abandoned that Miss Earhart (Mrs G. P. Putnam) can have survived her last adventurous flight, after being missing for over a fortnight. Miss Earhart left Miami, Florida, on June 1 to fly round the world from west to east, with Captain Fred Noonan as navigator. Her machine was a Lockheed Electra, which was called the "Flying Laboratory" from its equipment of instruments and experimental apparatus. She arrived at Dumdum aerodrome, Calcutta, from Karachi on June 17, having covered about 15,000 miles, more than half her journey, at an average of 900 miles a day. From that point she had been working along the British air mail route. She arrived at Port Darwin on June 28, and started at 10am on July 2 from Lae, New Guinea, for Howland Island on the most hazardous part of her flight. Although signals for help are reported to have been received from her, she was never seen again, and prolonged searches by sea and air have failed to discover any traces of her machine.

Miss Earhart first became famous in June, 1928, when she crossed the Atlantic as a passenger, but afterwards, in 1932, she made a solo flight from Newfoundland to Ireland. In each case she was the first woman to accomplish the feat — if sitting in an aeroplane as a passenger can be called a feat. She was, however, a pilot of more than average ability, and at a time when sensational flights were constantly being made to advertise the name of the pilot, her modesty and her refusal to use her fame for commercial purposes made her very popular. In this she resembled Colonel Lindbergh, whom she was also supposed to resemble in features. In America she was popularly known as "Lady Lindy."

Amelia Earhart came from Atchison, Kansas, where she was born on July 24, 1898. During the War she served with the Canadian Red Cross, and afterwards entered Columbia University. She then learnt to fly, but her occupation in life was social welfare work among children in Boston. She was 30 years of age when she made her first crossing of the Atlantic by air. Mrs F. E. Guest, wife of the former Secretary of State for Air, and herself an American by birth, financed the flight to the extent of £8,000, and intended to fly in the machine herself. Finally she was persuaded to give her place to Miss Earhart. The machine was a Fokker with three 200-hp Wright Whirlwind engines, and was a twin-float seaplane. In the previous year, 1927, which had seen the greatest number of Atlantic flights, the successes of Lindbergh, Chamberlin, Byrd, and Brock, and also a regrettable number of fatal accidents, the three-engined Fokker had never failed its passengers on an ocean flight. The fitting of floats for wheels was an additional safeguard, and the machine also carried wireless. There were three on board — Commander Wilmer Stultz, the pilot, Mr Gordon, the mechanic, and Miss Earhart. The machine was named "Friendship." She left Newfoundland on June 17, 1928, and 21 hours later came down in Burry Port harbour in South Wales.

Not much was heard of Miss Earhart for a couple of years, but on April 8, 1931, she set up an autogiro altitude record, by reaching a height of about 19,000ft in a machine of that type with a 300-hp engine. She was also credited with two other aeroplane records for carrying certain weights at certain speeds.

It was not until after her marriage, on February 7, 1931, to Mr G. P. Putnam, of the famous publishing house, that she was able to gratify her ambition of

A welcoming committee for American aviation pioneer Amelia Earhart (centre) in June 1928

flying the Atlantic as a solo pilot, and being the first woman to do so. She was quite frank about her feelings. She did not profess that the flight would do any good to anyone or anything. "I did it really for fun," she said, "not to set up any records or anything like that." This time she chose a fast single-engined aeroplane, a Lockheed Vega with Pratt and Whitney 420-hp Wasp engine.

On May 20, 1932, she set off from Harbour Grace, Newfoundland, and after 13 and a quarter hours she made landfall off Donegal. This was the fastest Atlantic flight to date. She had trouble with various instruments and accessories on the machine during her flight, but she was then an experienced pilot, and doubtless her previous crossing stood her in good stead. When she was four hours out one section of the heavy exhaust manifold on the engine began to leak. At the same time she met bad weather and had to begin blind flying, and soon afterwards her altimeter failed her. She told our Aeronautical Correspondent that she then climbed up into the clouds until the tachometer (engine revolutions counter) froze, "and then I knew I couldn't be near the sea." She thought she went up to 12,000ft, but ice began to form on the wings and the clouds were still heavy above her. Meanwhile the intense heat at the leaking exhaust began to burn away the metal. She looked over at it and wished she hadn't as she saw the flames coming out, and it worried her all night. Other parts began to work loose and serious vibration was set up. The engine also "began

to run rough," petrol leaked into the cockpit from the petrol gauge, and there was the danger lest petrol fumes should reach the exhaust manifold and be exploded by the flames that poured from the gap. At last she made Ireland as she guessed, but could not be sure, and without an altimeter could not go high enough through the clouds to be sure of clearing the hills. So she turned north until she saw the hills above the river mouth west of Londonderry. Following the railway track, she made an almost perfect landing on a farm two miles from Londonderry, and was hospitably entertained by the farmer and his wife.

When she arrived in London she was given a great welcome. Afterwards she crossed to France, where her husband joined her, and was fêted and decorated there, as well as in Belgium and Italy, and the United States conferred a flying decoration on her.

In September, 1932, Miss Earhart set up another record for women by flying non-stop and solo across the United States from Los Angeles to Newark, New Jersey, in 19 hours 4 minutes, which was only 1 hour 25 minutes longer than the best time by a man pilot (Frank Hawks) over that route.

In January, 1935, Miss Earhart flew alone in her Lockheed Vega monoplane from Honolulu to Oakland, California, 2,408 miles, in 18 hours 15 minutes; and in the following May she made a non-stop flight from Mexico City to New York, 2,100 miles, in 14 hours 18 minutes. She had to cross mountains 10,000ft high.

On March 17 of the present year she left Oakland, California, on a flight round the world, but crashed at Honolulu on March 21. As the fuselage struck the ground a tongue of flame was seen to shoot from it, and it was believed that only Miss Earhart's prompt action in turning off the ignition saved the lives of herself and her two companions.

Amelia Earhart, aviation pioneer, was born on July 24, 1898. She, and the plane she was flying, disappeared on July 2, 1937; she was 38

—⁓—

LILIAN BAYLIS

MANAGER OF THE OLD VIC AND SADLER'S WELLS THEATRES WHO STAGED SHAKESPEARE, OPERA AND BALLET AT AFFORDABLE PRICES

NOVEMBER 26, 1937

Miss Lilian Mary Baylis's death takes from the English theatre a unique and important figure, whose name will always be associated with the Old Vic and Sadler's Wells Theatres. Miss Baylis was, moreover, in the best sense, a "character" with a rare directness of manner, a compelling faith — which she communicated to others — that what ought to be done could be done in spite of all obstacles, and a power of delegation that might have made the fortune of a Prime Minister — a power,

that is to say, of choosing unerringly the right men and women to do work for which she was not personally qualified, and of inducing them, as a team, to serve the cause to which she devoted a great part of her life.

Born in London on May 9, 1874, she came of musical stock, being the daughter of Newton Baylis, a baritone, and his wife, Liebe Konss, a contralto and a pianist. The girl was educated as a musician, practising five hours a day, looking after the younger members of her large family, and beginning to give concerts when she was 10 years old. When she was six her aunt, Emma Cons, opened the Old Vic, her niece being present with a ceremonial bouquet which, in the belief that princesses, like fairies, were always dressed in pink, she presented to the wrong lady. It was, perhaps, the only serious mistake she ever made in the theatre.

Her fortunes took her, as a young woman, to South Africa, where, between the ages of 17 and 22, she taught not the violin only, but the banjo, the mandolin, and the guitar. Overwork, illness, and an order to rest brought her to London, where she became her aunt's assistant as manager of the Old Vic, which she since described as "a coffee-music hall." She succeeded to management in 1912 and gradually built up a tradition of Shakespeare, opera, and ballet at low prices. She was justly proud not only of having produced all the works in the First Folio, together with *Pericles*, but of having given to her public a wide range of non-Shakespearian classics, from Ibsen's *Peer Gynt* to Tchehov's *The Cherry Orchard*.

In 1931 she increased her responsibilities by reopening Sadler's Wells, which was originally intended to exchange companies with the Old Vic, but this was found to be impracticable; the Old Vic held to the drama, and Sadler's Wells was devoted to opera and to the establishment of a permanent ballet company.

Miss Baylis's work for opera may perhaps be best described as the creation of a *Volksoper* for London in which popular operas like *Maritana* and *Faust*, outstanding masterpieces like *Tristan and Isolde* and *Don Giovanni*, native operas like Ethel Smyth's *The Boatswain's Mate*, and more recently Stanford's *The Travelling Companion* and Vaughan Williams's *Hugh The Drover* have been offered to the London public at philanthropic prices. The Old Vic originally had no dramatic licence, and in the early days only detached scenes from operas could be given. A chorus was first employed in 1895, but it was only in 1914 that operas could be presented in the normal manner. Miss Baylis solved her problem by a process of steady improvement, never outrunning, but always consolidating and extending the capacities of her company.

When Sadler's Wells was built it was possible to embark on a more generous policy which brought in many operas outside the normal repertory, of which Smetana's *The Bartered Bride*, Rimsky-Korsakov's *The Snow Maiden*, Mussorgsky's *Boris Goudonov*

in its original form, Tchaikovsky's *Eugene Onegin*, and only this week Beethoven's *Fidelio*, are conspicuous examples. The ballet was helped in its infancy by an inheritance from the Camargo Society, but under Miss Ninette de Valois Miss Baylis's youngest child has become in five years a permanent feature of London's artistic life, in which again native works like Vaughan Williams's *Job* have found a place beside the classics.

So skilful and so little selfish was Miss Baylis's work, and such was her power to join collaborators with her, that there is every reason to believe that, though her commanding personality is now withdrawn, the organization of which she was the head, and which has come to be thought of as an unofficial theatre of the nation, will continue to flourish and develop. There could be no more fitting memorial to her than the freeing of it from debt.

In England, organizations have often an unexpected growth. Lilian Baylis, though she believed that a divine voice commanded her to "put on Shakespeare as you do operas," was not in essence a Shakespearian, and, when she did put on Shakespeare, it was with the idea of giving performances of great plays to the very poor at very low prices. Since that time the standard of production has steadily risen, and so great has the reputation of her theatre become as a training-ground for young players and as a place of opportunity for leading actors and producers, that she seemed to have the whole profession at her command.

Men and women would work for her at salaries they would accept nowhere else, and when, at first nights, she appeared in academical dress with a bouquet she was greeted on both sides of the footlights with an affection that was good to watch and to share. She was a Companion of Honour, an honorary MA of Oxford, and an honorary LL.D of Birmingham.

Lilian Baylis, CH, theatre manager, was born on May 9, 1874. She died on November 25, 1937, aged 63

SUZANNE LENGLEN

FRENCH TENNIS PLAYER WHO DOMINATED THE WOMEN'S GAME IN THE YEARS IMMEDIATELY AFTER THE FIRST WORLD WAR

JULY 5, 1938

Mlle Suzanne Lenglen, the greatest woman lawn tennis player of her time, was taken ill on June 15, but as she complained of nothing more than undue fatigue there seemed no reason for alarm. She rapidly grew weaker, however, and a blood test revealed the true nature of her malady. Last Thursday the doctors decided on a blood transfusion, and a marked improvement followed, but on Friday she again began to weaken, though she insisted on discussing with her friends and family the lawn tennis championships at Wimbledon.

Late on Sunday night she herself realized that the end was near, telling her mother that she knew no more could be done for her. During the last few hours, ever-increasing feebleness and great suffering left her unable to say more than a few words at rare intervals, but she remained conscious and courageous until a few minutes before her death.

Our Lawn Tennis Correspondent writes:—

"It has become a journalistic custom to hail each successive champion as the best that ever was, but certainly no woman has played lawn tennis as Mlle Lenglen did. More than that, her influence on the feminine game throughout the world was extraordinary; she and Tilden may almost be said to have made Wimbledon as it exists to-day. So many people flocked to watch her that it soon became evident that the old ground in Worple Road was not nearly large enough to hold them. It seems all the sadder that she should have fallen ill during the Wimbledon meeting, which made her fame.

"Mlle Lenglen was more than a remarkably good player. Whether or not it was because she was French and burst upon an astonished world at the first Wimbledon after the War, hers was a positive, vital personality that made news. Even her *bandeau* achieved fame. Long after she left the amateur game she attracted much interest when she visited Wimbledon as a spectator;

at the Stade Roland Garros, in Auteuil, crowds would flock from a centre court match if 'Suzanne' were knocking up on a side court with Cochet. Curiously enough, however, it was on the English scene that her star shone brightest.

"I do not know whether Mlle Lenglen was ever beaten in a completed match. Certainly no one in Europe beat her after the War; from 1919 until 1926 her supremacy was unchallenged. At a time when J. D. Budge's feat in winning three Wimbledon championships is outstanding it may be recalled that Mlle Lenglen did so three times; in 1925 she won three events in the world championships at St Cloud as well, and Olympic honours fell to her at Antwerp in 1920. Her first Wimbledon in 1919 at the age of 20 was dramatic. In the last match she overcame Mrs Lambert Chambers, the established champion — whose record has just been beaten by Mrs Moody — after saving two match balls, one a little luckily, in the third set. Her score was 10-8, 4-6, 9-7, and Mlle Lenglen's reputation was made. No one after that really looked like beating her. She went on to win six singles championships at Wimbledon, six doubles, with Miss E. Ryan, and she won the mixed doubles with G. L. Patterson, P. O'Hara Wood, and J. Borotra. It was the same in France, where she won six times. Mlle Lenglen missed a year through illness in 1924, but her game was stronger than ever in 1925, when she won again at Wimbledon after beating the holder, Miss K. McKane (now Mrs Godfree) in two love sets. There is no counting her exploits in the South of France.

Suzanne Lenglen: "probably we shall not see her like again"

"Mlle Lenglen, like other champions, possessed what, for want of a better word, is called a 'temperament,' which more than once led to tears — French tears, remember — that may not have been understood by Anglo-Saxon audiences. In 1921 she undertook a tour of the United States in aid of the devastated areas of France, and had the misfortune to meet Mrs Mallory in her first match in the American championships. The draw was not seeded in those days, and Mlle Lenglen retired in tears amid general consternation after losing the first set. But earlier in the year at St Cloud she had beaten Mrs Mallory, and took ample revenge in the Wimbledon final of 1922, in which Mrs Mallory won only two games. In 1926 came disaster. Mlle Lenglen had become increasingly unamenable to the strict punctuality by which a great meeting like Wimbledon must be governed, and there came a day when she did not turn up for a match in the Centre Court which Queen Mary was waiting to watch. This unfortunate happening ruined everything. Mlle Lenglen retired after playing a mixed double in which Borotra displayed great tact, and shortly afterwards left the amateur game altogether. It had been in the spring of that year that Mlle Lenglen had played her historic match against Miss Wills (now Mrs Moody) in Cannes. Lord Charles Hope, one of the linesmen, intervened when the umpire awarded the match to Mlle Lenglen at 7-5 in the second set, and it was resumed in an uproar and won by Mlle Lenglen at 8-6. Miss Wills was taken ill early in the French Championships a few months later, and her challenge on Mlle Lenglen's dominion was not to be put satisfactorily to the test.

"Probably we shall not see the like of Mlle Lenglen again. Her fame belongs to the post-War period, but as a child, under the stern coaching of her father, who was always at the court side in her later matches, she had shown a remarkable aptitude for the game, and she won her first local championship at the age of 14. A year later she had won the French championship. Her genius lay in taking pains; her accuracy was such that she was supposed to be able to hit a coin in any part of the court. Her forehand drive was a magnificent stroke; no one else has had her dancing feet. M. Lacoste said of the first Lenglen match he watched: 'At first I was disappointed. I expected her to execute extraordinary strokes, but she played with marvellous ease the simplest strokes in the world. It was only after several games that I noticed what harmony was concealed by Mlle Lenglen's simplicity, what wonderful mental and physical balance was hidden by the facility of her play.' Apart from one or two tours Mlle Lenglen played very little as a professional, but in recent years her love of the game was devoted to running in Paris a State-aided lawn tennis school for children which was a great success. It had been truly said of her that she was incomparable; a host of English friends will miss 'Suzanne.'"

The funeral of Mlle Lenglen will take place to-morrow morning. At 11am a service will be held at the Church of the Assumption, and the burial will be in the cemetery of Saint Ouen.

Suzanne Lenglen, tennis player, was born on May 24, 1899. She died on July 4, 1938, aged 39

—◆◆◆—

AMY JOHNSON

FIRST WOMAN AVIATOR TO
FLY SOLO FROM ENGLAND
TO AUSTRALIA

JANUARY 8, 1941

Miss Amy Johnson, CBE, whose death is now confirmed, will always be remembered as the first woman to fly alone from England to Australia. That flight took place in 1930 and her name at once became world-famous.

In the early days of the war she was employed in "ferrying" material to France for the RAF. Her cool courage, flying unarmed through the danger zone, was much admired by the RAF pilots. Since that time she had flown a variety of aircraft many thousands of miles and she met her death while serving her country.

Amy Johnson was of Danish origin. Her grandfather, Anders Jörgensen, shipped to Hull when he was 16, settled there, changed his name to Johnson, and married a Yorkshire woman named Mary Holmes. One of their sons, the father of Amy, became a successful owner of Hull trawlers. Amy graduated BA at Sheffield University, and then went to London to learn to fly at the London Flying Club at Stag Lane,

Edgware. After taking her "A" licence she passed the Air Ministry examination to qualify as a ground engineer. Before starting on her flight to Australia her only considerable experience of cross-country flying was one flight from London to Hull.

Having acquired a secondhand Moth with Gipsy engine, she started from Croydon on May 5, 1930, on an attempt to beat the light aeroplane record of 15 and a half days from England to Australia. Considering her lack of experience at that time as a navigator, it was a marvel that she found her way so well. She arrived safely at Darwin on May 24. Thence she flew to Brisbane, where, probably through her exhausted condition, she overshot the aerodrome and crashed her Moth rather badly. Australian National Airways Limited arranged for her to fly as a passenger in one of their machines to Sydney, and in the pilot of that machine she met her future husband, Mr J. A. Mollison. She was accorded a great reception in Australia, and was received at Government House. King George V conferred on her the CBE and the *Daily Mail* made her a present of £10,000. On her return to England she was met at Croydon by the Secretary of State for Air, the late Lord Thomson, in person.

In 1931 she made a fine flight to Tokyo across Siberia, and then back to England, and in 1932 she started off in another Puss Moth, Desert Cloud, to beat her husband's record to the Cape, which she did by nearly 10 and a half hours. The skill with which she crossed

Amy Johnson sitting in her B A Eagle at the start of the King's Cup Race in February 1936

Africa proved that she had become a first-class pilot. In 1933 she and her husband acquired a D H Dragon aeroplane and set out to fly to New York. They successfully crossed the Atlantic, Newfoundland, Nova Scotia, Maine, and Massachusetts, but when they were approaching New York their petrol ran short and they therefore landed at Bridgeport, 60 miles short of New York, in the dark. The Dragon ran into a swamp and overturned. It was extensively damaged, and both of them were bruised and scratched. Her flight to the Cape and back in May, 1936, will rank as one of her greatest achievements. She beat the outward and the homeward records, the record for the double journey, and the capital to capital record. The Royal Aero Club conferred its gold medal upon her in October, 1936, in recognition of her Empire flights. Her book "Sky Roads of the World" was published in September, 1939.

Her marriage took place in 1932, but in 1936 she resumed her maiden name for the purposes of her career, and in 1938 the marriage was dissolved.

Miss Pauline Gower, Officer Commanding No. 5 Ferry Pilot School, writes:—

"Miss Amy Johnson was known throughout the world for her many famous flights, but in her private life and as a person she was less well known. I had the privilege of meeting her first in 1930, and during the years that followed got to know her as a friend. Although I always appreciated her brilliance as a pilot, the attributes which went to make her character were to me more impressive than her wonderful feats in the world of aeronautics. Her physical courage as an aviator was undoubted, her moral courage, her large-heartedness and her sense of humour were only fully appreciated by her friends. In her private life Amy Johnson was unassuming and entirely lacking in conceit. It is inevitable that the name of someone as famous as she was should be coupled with many extravagant stories. Those who knew Amy Johnson intimately saw her as an ordinary human being, keen on her job, brilliantly successful but always accessible. After her spectacular flight, when the world was at her feet, she could spare the time to give encouragement, help, and advice to any who asked her. Many have been assisted, encouraged, and cheered by her.

"When she joined the Air Transport Auxiliary she settled down to her new life with all the eagerness and enthusiasm of somebody who obviously had her heart in her work and was anxious to do a job for her country. The flying she was required to do was not spectacular, but it required steady application. Sometimes it was easy for one with her experience; at other times her skill stood her in good stead. Whatever the circumstances, however she was feeling, the job was done; and the conscientious manner in which she carried out her duties was an inspiration to all those who worked with her. Amy Johnson is not only a loss to aviation; those who knew her have lost the type of friend who cannot be replaced."

Amy Johnson, CBE, pioneer aviator, was born on July 1, 1903. She was killed in a flying accident on January 5, 1941, aged 37

———✸———

VIRGINIA WOOLF

INNOVATIVE BLOOMSBURY GROUP NOVELIST, ESSAYIST, AND CRITIC

APRIL 3, 1941

The death of Mrs Virginia Woolf, which must now be presumed, and is announced on another page, is a serious loss to English letters. As a novelist she showed a highly original form of sensitivity to mental impressions, the flux of which, in an intelligent mind, she managed to convey with remarkable force and beauty.

Adeline Virginia Stephen was born at Hyde Park Gate, London, in 1882, the daughter of Sir Leslie Stephen (then editor of the *Cornhill* and later of the *D.N.B.*) by his second wife, Julia Prinsep Duckworth (a widow, born Jackson). She was related to the Darwins, the Maitlands, the Symondses, and the Stracheys; her godfather was James Russell Lowell; and the whole force of heredity and environment was deeply literary. Virginia was a delicate child, never able to stand the rough-and-tumble of a normal schooling. She was reared partly in London and partly in Cornwall, where she imbibed that love of the sea which so often appears in her titles and her novels. Her chief companion was her sister Vanessa (later to become Mrs Clive Bell, and a distinguished painter). Her home studies included the unrestricted use of Sir Leslie's splendid library, and as she grew up she was able to enjoy the conversation of distinguished visitors like Hardy, Ruskin, Morley, and Gosse. She devoured Hakluyt's "Voyages" at a very juvenile age, and early acquired a love of the whole Elizabethan period that never left her. Her mother died when she was 13 and her father in 1904, when she was 22.

After Sir Leslie Stephen's death Virginia, Vanessa, and two brothers set up house together at Gordon Square, Bloomsbury, and as time went on the sisters, with Mr Clive Bell, the late Lytton Strachey, Mr T. S. Eliot, and some others, formed a group with which the name of that London district was associated, sometimes with ill-natured implications. But, so far as Virginia Woolf was concerned, she would have done honour to any district. She very soon displayed a keen and catholic critical sense which found expression in those brilliant and human articles written for *The Times Literary Supplement*, many of which are contained in her book, "The Common Reader." In 1912 she married Mr Leonard Woolf, the critic and political writer, and went to live at Richmond, Surrey.

The marriage led to much joint work, literary and in publishing; but Mrs Woolf's private interests remained primarily artistic rather than political. Despite friendships with Mrs Fawcett, the Pankhursts, and Lady Constance Lytton, she took no active part in the movement for woman suffrage, though as she showed in "A Room of One's Own," she passionately sympathized with the movement to secure for women a proper place in the community's life. It was not until she was 33 (in 1915) that she published her first novel, "The Voyage Out," which was a recension of a manuscript dating back some nine years. It was an immature work, but very interesting prophetically, as can be seen by comparing it with "To the Lighthouse." By this time Mr and Mrs Woolf had set up as publishers at Hogarth House, Richmond, calling their firm the Hogarth Press. The high level of the works published by this press is universally recognized. Among them are some of the best early works of Katherine Mansfield, Middleton Murry, T. S. Eliot, E. M. Forster, besides the works of Mrs Woolf herself. Later transferred to Bloomsbury, the Press acquired an additional reputation for the issue of books having a political trend to the Left.

In 1919 Mrs Woolf brought out a second novel, "Night and Day," which was still by way of being 'prentice work, but with "Jacob's Room" (1922) she became widely recognized as a novelist of subtle apprehensions and delicate reactions to life, with a method of her own and a finely wrought and musical style. Her subsequent novels, "Mrs Dalloway," "To the Lighthouse," "Orlando," and "The Waves," rightly earned her an international reputation. These books broke away from the orderly narrative style of the traditional English novel, and are sometimes baffling to minds less agile than hers; but their subtle poetry and their power of inspiring intense mental excitement in imaginative minds are qualities which far outweigh occasional obscurity. The flux of perceptions and the inexorable movement of time were two of her chief themes; and if there is some truth in the criticism that her characters are little more than states of mind, it is also true that they are very highly individualized by the author's remarkable power of observation. Above all, she had a perfect sense of form and of the unity — even if its expression were unattainable — underlying the whole strange process which we call human life. Mrs Woolf's last book, published in 1940, was a profoundly interesting biography of Roger Fry.

Virginia Woolf, writer, was born on January 25, 1882. She died on March 28, 1941, aged 59

————

ELLEN WILKINSON

LABOUR MP, KNOWN AS "RED ELLEN", WHO HEADED THE JARROW MARCH TO LONDON IN 1936

FEBRUARY 7, 1947

The Right Hon Miss Ellen Wilkinson, Minister of Education since 1945, and for many years a prominent personality among the middle generation of Labour Party politicians, died yesterday of a heart attack in St Mary's Hospital, Paddington, where she had been ill with bronchitis. She was 55.

Miss Wilkinson was indeed a politician, a woman of quick brain and shrewd administrative ability, adroit in debate, and tough and ambitious of temper, who knew how to exhibit to the best and liveliest advantage her Socialist convictions. It was not her red hair alone or her diminutive size that earned for her the familiar title of "Red Ellen" or "The Fiery Particle." The extremism of her left-wing views was not seriously abated for some time after she left the Communist Party, but Parliament and time together worked upon her, and experience of office completed what they began, and brought her more closely into line with the body of Parliamentary Labour opinion.

Ellen Cicely Wilkinson was born in Manchester on October 8, 1891, the third of the four children of a cotton operative. She went to an elementary school, by scholarship to a secondary school, by scholarship again to Manchester University, where she took a MA degree. For a time she was a pupil teacher, but her earliest thoughts of a career were in the direction of writing and journalism, and journalism indeed entered largely into her political career. She joined the Independent Labour Party in 1912. Small — she was no more than five feet in height — violently red-haired, and immensely at her ease, she proved a confident and effective speaker. In 1913 she became an organizer of the National Union of Women's Suffrage Societies, and then, after the outbreak of war (during which she maintained the characteristic ILP attitude), national organizer of the National Union of Distributive and Allied Workers.

Her association with all sorts of extreme left-wing bodies during and immediately after the war of 1914-18 inevitably carried her into the Communist Party on its formation in 1920. "Red Ellen" — who visited Moscow in the following year as a British Communist representative — became widely known as an advocate of "direct action." It was as the official Labour candidate, though she still retained her Communist Party membership, that she stood unsuccessfully for

Ashton-under-Lyne at the 1923 election. It was as a Communist that she was elected to the Manchester City Council in the same year. But by the next year, when she was elected to Parliament for Middlesbrough East, she had severed her connexion with the Communist Party. She held Middlesbrough until 1931. In the Commons she was fluent, well provided with facts, sometimes aggressive, sometimes impassioned, but inclined to weaken the force of her argument by resort to the scoring of debating points. Outside she engaged in her trade union affairs and in a good deal of public speaking and journalism.

Miss Wilkinson lost her seat in the election of 1931, was a bitter critic of Mr MacDonald and of the Baldwin administration, and came back to Parliament in 1935 as the member for Jarrow. She had in the meantime greatly widened her study of international affairs. The menace of Nazi Germany was not lost upon her, and visits to Germany in 1936 and to Spain in the following year sharpened her criticism of the policy of appeasement. In domestic politics she joined vigorously in the Opposition attack upon Government policy, or lack of policy, in regard to mass unemployment and the depressed areas, of which her own constituency was as tragic an instance as any. She headed the Jarrow marchers on their way to London in 1936, and three years afterwards produced a volume, "The Town that was Murdered," in which she set forth in detail the history of Palmer's shipyard and drew from Jarrow's bitter experience after it had

been closed an indictment of capitalism and a reasoned plea for a planned Socialist economy. In the previous year she had scored a notable personal success in Parliament in introducing a private member's Bill on hire purchase, designed to terminate various flagrant abuses of the system, and in securing its enactment with support from every quarter in the House.

At the outbreak of war in 1939 her attitude did not differ from that of the great majority of the Labour Party and of the country as a whole. When Mr Churchill became head of the Coalition Government she was appointed Parliamentary Secretary to the Ministry of Pensions, and, later in the year, one of the two Parliamentary Secretaries to Mr Herbert Morrison at the Ministry of Home Security. The inadequate and ill-provided shelter accommodation in London and other great cities at the start of the blitz roused her to a remarkable pitch of energy, which she maintained all through the prolonged phase of fire-watching and other civil defence precautions. It was apparently in deference to her own choice that she was appointed to the Ministry of Education, where the task devolved upon her of translating into practical effect the far-reaching changes embodied in the Education Act passed under the Coalition Government. The tragedy is that recurrent illness prevented her from achieving much of what she set out to do.

Active and resilient of temperament, Miss Wilkinson did not at any time spare her energies. The busy life of a member of Parliament between the wars matched her inclinations; the authority of a Minister during and after the second world war sustained her confidence. In the course of her career, during which she visited many parts of Europe, she suffered various physical mishaps and endured several bouts of illness, but always, in the homely phrase, she came up smiling. Her oddly picturesque person and shrewd debating style will be missed in the Commons, at Labour Party gatherings, and in the political life of the country as a whole.

Ellen Wilkinson, politician and campaigner, was born on October 8, 1891. She died of a heart attack on February 6, 1947, aged 55

—◦◦◦—

MARIA MONTESSORI

EDUCATOR WHOSE METHOD PREDICATES THAT THE BEST EDUCATION IS PROVIDED BY LEARNING FOR ONESELF

MAY 7, 1952

Dr Maria Montessori, who evolved the Montessori educational system, died at Noordwijk, Holland, last night, aged 81.

An Italian, she was for many years an important influence on the trend of educational practice. Her aims and technique have at times been travestied and misunderstood, yet she forced educationists everywhere to take stock of their ideas and was a powerful agency in the broadening of curricula and the humanization of instructional method. Moreover, her work has very wide social and philosophical implications.

Born at Chiaravalle, Ancona, on August 31, 1870, Maria was the only daughter of Cavaliere Alessandro Montessori. She entered the University of Rome as a medical student and was the first Italian woman to win the degree of M.D. She then became an instructor in the psychiatric clinic of her university, taking a special interest in pedagogical anthropology and the training of the mentally deficient child. The methods which she found the most congenial basis of experiment were those which Edouard Séguin had begun to apply some 50 years earlier in France. She rapidly came to the conclusion that for the cure of mental deficients the pedagogical approach was more important than the medical; and from her practical work at the clinic on these lines was to grow up the whole structure of her wider educational method. In 1898 she was appointed directress of the Scuola Ortofrenica in Rome. After due training she put several eight-year-old defectives in for the State examination in reading and writing. They not only passed, but gave better results than the normal children.

At last, early in 1907, came the great opportunity which enabled her to elaborate and test her method on a large scale. The Roman slum district of San Lorenzo had become a byword for filth, insanitary housing, overcrowding, and misery. The Istituto Romano di Beni Stabili now took it in hand and attached to each block a *Casa dei Bambini*, a kind of crèche. Dr Montessori was put in charge. She set out to discover whether principles that had worked so well with defectives would be equally efficacious with normal children. The infants went ahead by leaps and bounds under her system of free discipline. The Montessori method was established, and in 1909 its author issued her *Metodo della Pedagogia Scientifica*. A further two or three years of experimentation followed, and in 1912 she published her *Autoeducazione nelle Scuole Elementari*. In the previous year the method had been widely introduced into the Swiss state schools, and began to be employed in other schools, not only in Italy but in England, America, and elsewhere. At the Fielden Demonstration School, controlled by the University of Manchester, notable results were obtained with children aged from four to six.

In subsequent years many societies and institutions were founded for the study and exposition of the method, and Dr Montessori travelled widely, observing, lecturing, and demonstrating. A research institute was founded at Barcelona in 1917. In 1919 she gave the first of her London training courses, which were afterwards repeated biennially, under the aegis of the British Montessori Society. A teachers' training college was opened in Italy in 1928

and a year later a similar college began operations in London. From 1931 onwards annual congresses have been held. Besides controlling these various bodies and presiding over congresses, Dr Montessori acted from 1922 as Government inspector of schools in Italy. In 1923 she was awarded the honorary degree of D.Litt. by the University of Durham. Her books have been translated into many languages.

Her method is empirical, being built up on the observed results of actual teaching rather than conceived as a philosophical entity and imposed from above. Its two main principles are non-interference with the child's freedom and individuality and the use of sensory training in the earliest stages of education. Her claims to originality lie in the application of sensory training to normal children, in the working out of a systematic scheme, stage by stage, and in the provision of a set of didactic materials for handwork.

She believed that the best kind of education is provided by learning for oneself; and from this it follows that the teacher is a guide and observer, strongly adjured not to impose her personality on the pupils. In the *Case dei Bambini* work for its own sake was never imposed. Toys and common objects were provided, and it was left to the child to decide what his occupation should be. Ordinary household tasks like brushing, washing, and darning played a large part in the training. Discipline arose naturally out of the teacher's personality and the spontaneous interest of the children in what they were doing. Rewards and punishments were utterly abolished, and there was no insistence on remaining quiet and still.

Legitimate criticisms of Dr Montessori's method are that it tends to over-stress the manual side of education at the expense of the intellectual, that it gives insufficient scope to the natural imaginative faculty, and that its empiricism has not been confirmed by a philosophically coherent body of theory. There can, however, be no doubt as to the high status of this great woman in the line of educational reformers. The final judgment on the system may well be based not so much on the degree to which it has won integral acceptance in the schools as on the measure wherein its principles have been assimilated into the general consciousness of the race.

Maria Montessori, educator, was born on August 31, 1870. She died on May 6, 1952, aged 81

EVA PERÓN

CHARISMATIC FIRST LADY OF ARGENTINA WHOSE EFFORTS FOR THE POOR AND DISENFRANCHISED CULMINATED IN HER SOCIAL AID FUND

JULY 28, 1952

Señora Eva Perón, wife of the President of Argentina, whose death is reported on another page, was second only to her husband in power and influence in their country.

The republics of South America have in their brief histories abounded in men rising from obscurity like comets, to pass across the political horizon and to set again with equal speed. Señora Perón is the first woman to have had so spectacular a career in a part of the world where the tradition of feminine domesticity is still strong. True, she had a colourful personality, good looks, charm, and determination, but these gifts do not in themselves explain the hold she gained over her countrymen as well as her countrywomen, and though her marriage to the popular and forceful President of Argentina certainly contributed to her power, she was already a personality in her own right before her marriage. She thus remains something of an enigma, an enigma which her account of her political and social ideals published last year under the title *La*

Razón de mi Vida, does little to resolve. Perhaps the secret of the influence of this young and attractive girl of humble origin, who could, while wrapped in furs and sparkling with diamonds, address the workers of Buenos Aires as one of themselves, was that they saw in her all their cherished ambitions and aspirations fulfilled. To them she was Cinderella in real life and if she could make the grade so could they.

Eva Maria Duarte was, according to Argentine works of reference, born at Junin in the province of Buenos Aires on May 7, 1922, of relatively humble stock. The facts of her early life are obscure, but she seems to have gone to the capital before she was 20 and, aided by striking good looks and a vivacious manner, to have made something of a career for herself on the stage and in the cinema. Greater success attended her as a radio artist, in which in a number of historical serials she was cast for the heroine, generally encouraging and comforting South American liberators whose fortunes were temporarily in eclipse. Thus for millions of Argentines she became "Señorita Radio" and so was one of the people of nation-wide popularity on whom Colonel Perón, then Minister of Labour and Welfare, called when he wanted to make a great appeal for a national fund to help the victims of the San Juan earthquake. The attraction was mutual and together they set out to win support.

When her husband fell from power in October, 1945, and was arrested, she it was above all others who roused the workers to paralyse the country until he was released and placed on the way to supreme power. When that was attained, she organized the women workers, made female suffrage a live issue, and was behind every step taken to lend aid to the aged, succour the children, and alleviate distress — especially if these things could be done in such a way as to flout the former ruling classes — the "oligarchy," as Señora Perón called them. She had, indeed, little or no sympathy with those who sought salvation outside the ranks of "Peronismo." The tangible results of her vast work as an organizer exist in the great social aid fund — an institution whose enormous financial resources have never been estimated and whose income and expenditure could not be audited. The fund became under her guidance the most important single influence in Argentine life. Every form of out-relief, children's playgrounds, aid for earthquake victims, toys for destitute children, clothes for the needy — all were available under "Evita's" banner, and this fact explains much of her power and popularity in her own country.

Her popularity, however, received a check last year, when her candidature for the Vice-Presidency caused such opposition in the Army that she felt obliged to announce over the radio, in a voice shaken with emotion, that she had taken the irrevocable decision to renounce the high honour by her own free will. For this her husband awarded her the Grand Extraordinary Peronista Medal, "in recognition of her noble gesture." Her health was, in fact, already failing and last November she underwent a serious operation which led to a temporary recovery. She reappeared in public several times, but she was never able fully to resume her former activity. Masses for her recovery were said throughout Argentina, but it seemed unlikely that a fatal issue to her long illness could be far off. With her characteristic courage she accompanied her husband in the ceremonies of the inauguration of his second presidential term on June 4 and stood beside him in an open motor-car. This was her last public appearance.

Eva Perón, First Lady of Argentina, was born on May 7, 1919. She died on July 26, 1952, aged 33

—◆—

MARGARET BONDFIELD

LABOUR MP WHO WAS BRITAIN'S FIRST WOMAN CABINET MINISTER

JUNE 18, 1953

By the death of the Right Hon Margaret Bondfield, C.H., which occurred on Tuesday in a nursing home at Sanderstead, Surrey, the British Labour movement loses one of its most notable women, a trade union organizer of idealistic and practical temper during almost half a century.

The loss is not the Labour movement's only, for "Maggie" Bondfield was a woman of lovable temperament and unusually wide human sympathies. Though she was the first of her sex to attain Ministerial rank, her parliamentary career covered only six years in all. She was, first and foremost, a trade unionist rather than a politician, and the essential part of her work for what a generation ago was called social betterment was carried out elsewhere than at Westminster. The tribute to her energy and devotion was fully deserved when in 1923 she became the first woman chairman of the General Council of the TUC.

Margaret Grace Bondfield was born in humble circumstances at Chard, Somerset, on March 17, 1873, one of 11 children of a lace-maker. At the age of 13 she became a supply teacher to infants in a local board school. Two years later she left teaching and went to Brighton to serve in a colonial outfitter's shop, and for the next 11 years she worked in various London and provincial shops. Conditions under which the majority of shop assistants worked in those days were hard. Hours — a 70-hour week was not uncommon — and pay apart, the living-in system was the cause of many evils and abuses. "Maggie" Bondfield (the diminutive clung to her all through her career) soon reached the conclusion that the only hope of putting matters right lay in trade unionism. In 1894, four years before the formation of the National Union of Distributive and Allied Workers, she joined the Shop

Minister of Labour Margaret Bondfield with Stanley Baldwin, then Leader of the Opposition, in 1930

Assistants' Union; two years later, on its amalgamation with another union, she became its assistant secretary, remaining in that post until 1908, when she resigned to take up wider activities.

Sir Charles Dilke's Shop Bill had been introduced in 1896. Miss Bondfield made contact with him and Lady Dilke, and this association, together with her friendship with Mary Macarthur, led to vigorous propaganda on behalf of women in industry. In those days of trade union organization women who entered industry were regarded by many of the men with whom they worked as interlopers. Much of Miss Bondfield's prentice work as a union organizer was concerned with breaking down this prejudice. One instrument to her hand was the Women's Trade Union League. Another was the National Federation of Women Workers, founded in 1906.

On launching out into political activities Miss Bondfield threw in her lot with the Independent Labour Party, serving after a time on its executive. After the death of Mrs Ramsay MacDonald she became organizing secretary of the Women's Labour League, and in 1914 she occupied a similar post with the National Federation of Women Workers. During the war of 1914-18 she was a member of the Central Committee on Women's Employment, of the Trades Union Advisory Committee to the Ministry of Munitions, and of the War Emergency Workers National Committee. Like other prominent members of the ILP, she maintained an essentially pacifist attitude during the course of the war.

After the women's vote had been won Miss Bondfield pressed forward tirelessly with her work of labour organization. In 1920, as TUC delegate. she attended the convention of the American Federation of Labour and also visited Russia. The International Labour Office of the League of Nations had from the first awakened the liveliest hopes in her — with Mary Macarthur she went to its first conference, at Washington, in 1919 — and she attended further conferences at various times during 1921-27. In 1924 she was the official representative of Great Britain on the governing body. Mary Macarthur had died in 1921 and Miss Bondfield took over from her, among other responsibilities, the chairmanship of the Standing Joint Committee of Industrial Women's Organizations. She also became vice-president of the International Federation of Working Women. With the merging in 1920 of the National Federation of Women Workers in the General Workers' Union she also became the latter's chief woman officer and remained in the post until March, 1938.

She had received in 1923 the highest honour the British trade union movement could confer — the chairmanship of the General Council of the TUC. She was the first woman to occupy this office, just as 24 years earlier she had been the first woman to attend the annual union conference as delegate. In 1923 also she entered Parliament as the Labour member for Northampton. Her quality was recognized by her appointment, early in 1924, as Parliamentary Secretary to the Ministry of Labour in the first Socialist administration. That same year she headed a delegation sent to Canada by the Overseas Settlement Committee, and continued to serve on that body till 1929.

Miss Bondfield lost her seat at the General Election of 1924 and remained outside Parliament until 1926, when she was returned for Wallsend at a by-election with a majority of over 9,000. In the formation of the second Socialist administration she was an obvious choice as Minister of Labour. She held that office until 1931, having meanwhile been sworn of the Privy Council; she was one of the many conspicuous Labour casualties in the General Election of 1931. After a further defeat by the same candidate, Miss Irene Ward, she decided in 1936 not to stand again for Wallsend, but her interest in politics and industrial organization remained unabated. In 1938, at the age of 65, she undertook the journey to the United States and Mexico in order to study labour conditions there. More recently, however, she had withdrawn noticeably from public affairs, but some three years ago came again before the public as the authoress of her admirably written reminiscences, *A Life's Work*.

Her pioneering spirit and selfless devotion to the practical causes she made her own were widely recognized. Hers was not a sentimental humanitarianism. She appealed always to reason and presented a documented case innocent of rhetoric. As a speaker she was perhaps more successful on the public platform than in the House, though she had a good voice and a command of English which bore testimony to wide reading. Her generous nature and real sense of humour looked out from a pleasant, alert, bright-eyed countenance surmounted by a broad and thoughtful brow. She received the freedom of her native Chard in 1930 and was made an honorary LL.D. of Bristol in the same year. She was appointed a Companion of Honour in 1948.

Margaret Bondfield, CH, Britain's first female Cabinet minister, was born on March 17, 1873. She died on June 16, 1953, aged 80

—◆—

DAME CAROLINE HASLETT

ROLE MODEL AND
HIGH ACHIEVER IN THE
FIELDS OF ENGINEERING
AND PROFESSIONAL
ADMINISTRATION

JANUARY 5, 1957

Dame Caroline Haslett, DBE, who died yesterday at Bungay, Suffolk, at the age of 61, was a distinguished engineer and administrator, and a feminist who advanced her cause less by propaganda than by the attainment of high qualifications and responsible positions.

Dropping into an engineering career almost by accident, at a time when a woman engineer was a rarity, she excelled in her profession, and aspired to make posts in lighter engineering available to women generally. She founded the Electrical Association for Women, was secretary of the Women's Engineering Society, and founder and editor of its journal, *The Woman Engineer*, as well as of the *Electrical Age*. She carried out an educational programme for the Central Electricity Board, and after nationalization of the industry became a member of the British Electricity Authority. She was not a brusque or aggressive character and did not appear or behave like the typical woman executive of fiction. She was a person of methodical mind, who yet contrived to avoid being enslaved by system. Her work was her life. She shone as an organizer, and knew the virtues of judicious delegation, so that her time was not cluttered up with detail. Her valuable service and example were publicly recognized in 1931 by the conferment of the CBE and by her promotion to DBE in 1947.

Caroline Harriet Haslett was born at Worth, Sussex, on August 17, 1895, the eldest daughter of Robert Haslett, a railway signal fitter and a pioneer of the co-operative movement. After education at Haywards Heath High School she was offered a start in the engineering industry as a secretary with the Cochran Boiler Company. Before long she asked to be transferred to the works, and from 1914 to 1918 worked in London and Annan, qualifying first in general and then in electrical engineenng.

In 1919 there was founded the Women's Engineering Society, and Miss Haslett became its secretary, and for many years edited its journal, *The Woman Engineer*. Some of her most valuable work for this society was in breaking down the prejudices of employers against taking on female labour, and above all in persuading the various engineering institutions to allow women to qualify. She herself worked chiefly in the electrical sphere, perceiving that this form of energy was best adapted to household tasks. She edited the *Electrical Handbook for Women* and *Household Electricity*, and showed another kind of solicitude for the well-run house by becoming chairman of the home safety committee of the Safety-First Association and vice-president of the Royal Society for the Prevention of Accidents.

In November, 1924, she founded the Electrical Association for Women. Starting in a small way, in a one-room office, it was to grow in a quarter of a century into an organization having over 90 branches and 10,000 members, including housewives, educationists, and domestic science teachers. It founded the Caroline Haslett Trust, providing scholarships and travelling fellowships for these teachers. In 1925, meeting Sir Andrew Duncan, chairman of the newly formed Central Electricity Board, she persuaded him that a big educational programme was necessary if best advantage was to be had from the new facilities provided by the grid.

The board duly provided the necessary finance to enable the Electrical Association for Women to go ahead.

In 1930 Miss Haslett was the only woman delegate at a power conference in Berlin. During the next 20 years her public activities became legion. She became member of council of the British Institute of Management, of the Industrial Welfare Society, of the National Industrial Alliance, of the Administrative Staff College, and of King's College of Household and Social Science; a governor of the London School of Economics and Political Science, of Queen Elizabeth College, and of Bedford College for Women; a member of the Central Committee on Women's Training and Employment; a member of council and vice-president of the Royal Society of Arts; and president of the British Federation of Business and Professional Women. She was a member of the Women's Consultative Committee and the Advisory Council of the Appointments Department, Ministry of Labour; a member of the Correspondence Committee on Women's Work of the International Labour Office; a vice-president of the British Electrical Development Association, and the first woman to be made a Companion of the Institution of Electrical Engineers.

In September, 1947, came an appointment which crowned a many-sided career, the main part of which had been devoted to the electrical industry. Dame Caroline Haslett was named by the Minister of Fuel and Power a part-time member of the British Electricity Authority, formed to conduct the industry under national ownership. Another opportunity of public service in the post-war planning of Britain was her appointment to the Crawley New Town Development Corporation. In the last year or two ill health had obliged her to resign her more onerous posts.

Dame Caroline Haslett, DBE, engineer, was born on August 17, 1895. She died on January 4, 1957, aged 61

—⟋⟍⟍—

DOROTHY L. SAYERS

AUTHOR OF THE DETECTIVE NOVELS FEATURING LORD PETER WIMSEY, AS WELL AS WORKS OF CHRISTIAN APOLOGY

DECEMBER 19, 1957

Miss Dorothy L. Sayers died at her home at Witham, Essex, on Tuesday night at the age of 64.

Sudden death would have had no terrors for her. She combined an adventurous curiosity about life with a religious faith based on natural piety, common sense, and hard reading. She made a name in several diverse fields of creative work. But the diversity of her success was founded on an inner unity of character. When she came down from Somerville with a First in Modern Languages she tried her hand at advertising. The directness and the grasp of facts that are needed by a copywriter stood her in good stead as a newcomer to the crowded ranks of authors of detective fiction. During the 1920s and 1930s, she established herself as one of the few who could give a new look to that hard-ridden kind of novel.

Her recipe was deftly to mix a plot that kept readers guessing with inside information, told without tears, about some fascinating subject — campanology, the backrooms of an advertising agency, life behind the discreet windows of a West End club. Lord Peter Wimsey came alive as a good companion to the few detectives into whom an engaging individuality has been breathed.

This was not done by chance; she had made a close, critical study of the craft. Lecturing, once, on Aristotle's *Poetics* she remarked that he was obviously hankering after a good detective novel because he had laid it down that the writer's business was to lead the reader up the garden, to make the murderer's villainy implicit in his character from the start, and to remember that the *dénouement* is the most difficult part of the story.

But it is some 20 years since Miss Sayers wrote a detective story, and, shortly before her death, she said: "There will be no more Peter Wimseys." The detective writer had been ousted by the Christian apologist. Miss Sayers approached her task of making religion real for the widest public with a zeal that sometimes shocked the conventionally orthodox (with whose protests she was well able to deal) and always held the ears of listeners and the eyes of the reading public. *The Man Born to be King* became a BBC best-seller, attracting large audiences Christmas after Christmas.

She carried what she regarded as the central purpose of her life on to the stage and into books. Dogma had no terrors for her. She did not believe in putting water into the pure spirit of her Church. Dante, with his colloquial idiom and unselfconscious piety, naturally attracted her. The translations she published of his *Inferno* and *Purgatorio* caught the directness of the original but failed, as Binyon did not, to catch the poetry. But her prose comments have done more than those of any other recent English author to quicken interest in Dante.

Dorothy Leigh Sayers was born in 1893, the daughter of the Rev Henry Sayers and Helen Mary Leigh. She was in print before she was 21 with *Op I*, a book of verse, and followed it in 1919 by another, *Catholic Tales*. It was a medium in which she could be skilful, flexible, and effective, and readers of *The Times Literary Supplement* will, no doubt, remember her strong poem, *The English War*, which appeared in its issue of September 7, 1940. Lord Peter made his first appearance in 1923 in *Whose Body?* There followed *Clouds of Witness* (1926), *Unnatural Death* (1927), *The Unpleasantness at the Bellona Club* (1928) and *The Documents in the Case* (1930).

In 1930 Miss Sayers in addition to producing her *Strong Poison*, yet another detective book, made an interesting departure. Out of the fragments of its Anglo-Norman version she had constructed her *Tristan in Brittany*, in the form of a modem English story and produced it, partly in verse and partly in prose.

Have His Carcase (1932) introduced a companion for Lord Peter in the shape of Harriet Vane, a writer of detective stories. In *Hangman's Holiday* (1933), a book of short stories, she created another amateur detective, Mr Montague Egg, who was a simpler reasoner than Lord Peter, but almost as acute. In *The Nine Tailors*, though of the same genre, her theme was built round a noble church in Fenland, and possessed a majesty which disclosed powers the authoress had scarcely exerted until then. *Gaudy Night* (1935) took Lord Peter and Harriet Vane into the serene and serious life of a women's college at Oxford, and psychological problems deeper than those which belong to the detective convention arose.

In 1936 her *Busman's Holiday*, a play which presented Lord Peter married — Miss Sayers called it "a love story with detective interruptions" — was staged at the Comedy Theatre. She had a collaborator in M. St Clair Byrne, and between them they provided Lord Peter's public with an excellent entertainment. *The Zeal of Thy House* (1937), which was written for the Canterbury Festival and played there and in London, was set in the twelfth century and was a sincere and illuminating study of the purification of an artist, a kind of architectural

Gerontius purged by heavenly fire of his last earthly infirmity. *The Devil to Pay* (1939) was also written for the Canterbury Festival. It set the legend of Dr Faustus, one of the great stories of the world, at the kind of angle most likely to commend it to the modern stage. Later it was played at His Majesty's Theatre. By sheer alertness of invention and the power to fit her ideas into a dramatic narrative she accomplished an extremely difficult task with credit. *Love All* (1940) was an agreeable and amusing comedy.

In 1940 Miss Sayers published a calmly philosophic essay on the war, which she named *Begin Here*. Then, in 1941, she followed it with her *The Mind of the Maker*, in which she analysed the metaphor of God as Creator and tested it in the light of creative activity as she knew it.

Unpopular Opinions, a miscellaneous collection of essays, came out in 1946, *Creed or Chaos*, another series of essays, pungent and well reasoned, in 1947, and *The Lost Tools of Learning* in the following year.

She began her translations of Dante for the Penguin Series with the *Inferno* which came out in November, 1949; *Purgatorio* followed in May, 1955.

She found the third volume *Paradiso* the hardest and in August, 1956, her translation had reached Canto VII. Her commentary was one of the most valuable parts of her books. After she had finished her second volume, she slipped in, as a kind of relaxation, a translation of *Chanson de Roland*, published this year.

She was an honorary D.Litt. of Durham University. She married in 1926 Captain Atherton Fleming. He died in 1950.

Dorothy L. Sayers, novelist, was born on June 13, 1893. She died on December 17, 1957, aged 64

———

DAME CHRISTABEL PANKHURST

CAMPAIGNER FOR WOMEN'S SUFFRAGE AND CO-FOUNDER OF THE WOMEN'S SOCIAL AND POLITICAL UNION

FEBRUARY 15, 1958

Dame Christabel Pankhurst, DBE, who with her mother, Mrs Emmeline Pankhurst, founded the Women's Social and Political Union, which in the years before the First World War campaigned for women's suffrage, and who was the driving force behind the militant section of the movement and possibly its most brilliant orator, died on Thursday at Los Angeles. She was 77.

From the start of the campaign her power sprang from what was, in a very real sense, a magnetic personality. A most attractive young woman with fresh colouring, delicate features, and a mass of soft brown hair, a graceful figure on the platform, she spoke with a warmth, a passion, and a highly effective *raillerie*, which few who were prepared to give her a hearing could resist. Though the crowds in Hyde Park did not always spare her, the most familiar cry they set up in the neighbourhood of the WSPU platform there was "We want Chris." Courageous and resourceful in her extreme fashion in the years before 1914, she was a force to be reckoned with.

On the outbreak of war she and the other leaders declared a truce and lent their organization to the cause of national service. She made one or two attempts after the conclusion of hostilities to enter Parliament, but then abruptly abandoned public life and in her later years assumed the part of religious propagandist and proclaimed her belief in the imminence of the Second Advent.

Christabel Harriette Pankhurst was born on September 22, 1880. Her father, Richard Marsden Pankhurst, a man of some ability who had been the friend of John Stuart Mill, was a barrister and an ardent social worker. Her mother, Emmeline Pankhurst, was the daughter of Robert Goulden, a calico printer. Until she was 13 she was educated at home and then, after a spell at Manchester High School, at the age of 16 was sent to complete her education in Switzerland. Both parents were keenly alive to politics and both were what a generation ago would have been called feminists — her father had helped to form the original Woman's Suffrage Committee in 1865.

From an early age Christabel herself grew absorbed in political questions.

Her father died in 1898, leaving the family in straitened circumstances, and for some time she helped her mother, over whom she at all times exercised a strong influence, by acting as a deputy registrar of births and marriages. She shared — and deepened — her mother's sympathies with the Independent Labour Party, and in 1901, when she was appointed to the executive committee of the North of England Society for Women's Suffrage, she also became a member of the Women's Manchester Trade Union Council. In 1903 mother and daughter jointly set up the Women's Social and Political Union, which promptly began to carry resolutions on the suffrage question in trade councils all over the country.

In the following year, having studied law at what was then the Victoria University, Manchester, where later she took an LL.B. degree with honours, she sought admission as a student at Lincoln's Inn and was refused. This refusal, against which she entered an impassioned protest, marked what was perhaps the real starting-point in her career of militancy. Not, however, until her arrest, in 1905, together with Miss Annie Kenney, after their determined interruption of a meeting at Manchester addressed by Sir Edward Grey (Christabel had spat in a policeman's face, and, after refusing to pay the fine imposed, went to prison for a week) was the militant movement formally inaugurated. Mrs Pankhurst and other members of the WSPU gave it a start with their pilgrimages to the House of Commons, and the long series of conflicts with the law and the police followed.

All that was most dramatic in Christabel Pankhurst's career is bound up with the history of the militant phase of the "Votes for Women" campaign during the nine years before the outbreak of war in 1914. As organizing secretary of the WSPU, she was tireless and purposeful. In February, 1907, she was arrested and served a term of a fortnight's imprisonment. Not long afterwards she was charged with her mother and Mrs Drummond with inciting to riot and received a sentence of 10 weeks. During her trial she called the Home Secretary (Mr Herbert Gladstone) and the Chancellor of the Exchequer (Mr Lloyd George) as witnesses and with her legal training ably cross-examined them. In 1912, at the height of the window-breaking campaign, she escaped to Paris, where her mother, temporarily released from prison, joined her.

On the outbreak of war they both declared an immediate suffrage truce. With the announcement that as militant women she and her associates might be able to do something to arouse the spirit of militancy in men, she set herself the task of furthering national service and encouraging recruiting. From this point she planned somewhat vaguely to make of the body of future women electors a national, Imperial and international force. In November, 1918, she was adopted by the "Women's Party" (into which the WSPU had translated itself in the previous year) as a candidate for Parliament. At the "khaki election" she stood as a Coalition candidate for the Smethwick division and was only narrowly defeated. Later, she became prospective candidate for the Abbey division of Westminster. But her interest in politics waned rapidly, and the preoccupations of her later years are illustrated in various small volumes in which she turned to, among other sources, the Apocalypse of St John of Patmos for support for her belief in the imminence of the Second Advent. She had been created D.B.E. in 1936.

Dame Christabel Pankhurst, DBE, was born on September 22, 1880. She died on February 13, 1958, aged 78

—◦◦◦—

ROSALIND FRANKLIN

MOLECULAR BIOLOGIST WHOSE RESEARCHES CONTRIBUTED TO THE UNDERSTANDING OF THE STRUCTURE OF DNA

APRIL 19, 1958

Dr Rosalind Franklin died on Wednesday in a London hospital. She was 37.

Professor J. D. Bernal writes:—

"Rosalind Franklin's early and tragic death is a great loss to science. She has the distinction of having made her name successively in two very different branches of research, first in the study of coal and coke, and then in that of nucleo-proteins and virus structure.

"She discovered in a series of beautifully executed researches the fundamental distinction between carbons that turned on heating into graphite and those that did not. Further, she related this difference to the chemical constitution of the molecules from which the carbon was made. She was already a recognized authority in industrial physico-chemistry when she chose to abandon this work in favour of the far more difficult and more exciting fields of biophysics.

"Here, first in King's College London, she studied the structure of nucleic acid — the substance now recognized as the key to the regular functioning and inheritance of all living organisms. By the most ingenious experimental and mathematical techniques of X-ray analysis, she was able to verify and make more precise the illuminating hypothesis of Crick and Watson on the double spiral structure of this substance. She established definitely that the main sugar phosphate chain of nucleic acid lay on an outside spiral and not on an inner one, as had been authoritatively suggested.

"Moving to Birkbeck College, Miss Franklin took up the study of what is probably the most thoroughly studied of the plant viruses — that of Tobacco Mosaic disease — and almost at once, using the techniques she had already developed, made notable advances on it. She first verified and refined Watson's spiral hypothesis for the structure of the virus. She then made her greatest contribution in locating the infective element of the virus particle — its characteristic ribose nucleic acid. This she did by combining the study of the intact virus with that of a reconstituted virus without nucleic acid and using substituted mercury atoms as markers.

"Thus she was able for the first time to set out the structure on a molecular scale of a particle which if not in the full sense alive is capable of the vital functions of growth and reproduction in other cells. Her scale model of this structure is the central feature of the virus exhibit at the Brussels Exhibition.

"Her investigation of virus structure brought her widespread recognition in general biological as well as in biochemical and biophysical fields. One proof of that recognition was the generous grant from the Department of Health of the United States, which was just beginning to help her to extend her work on an adequate scale. Her work was, indeed, as much appreciated abroad as it was in Britain. She was particularly well known in France, where she worked for several years, and later in Germany and the United States, where she was recognized as one of the select band of pioneers who were unravelling the structure of nucleoproteins in relation to virus diseases and genetics.

"She was cut off in the middle of further plans which all who knew her work were confident she could have carried out with the same success. She had already started work on the virus of poliomyelitis and on the microsomal particles found in most healthy cells which are said to be responsible for protein synthesis and have marked similarity in size and structure to the small spherical viruses.

"Rosalind Franklin was not only a brilliant individual research worker with apparently effortless skill and precision in experiment, but also had the makings of a great organizer of research, as the small and devoted team she gathered round her bears witness. Her life is an example of single-minded devotion to scientific research."

Rosalind Franklin, molecular biologist, was born on July 25, 1920. She died on April 16, 1958, aged 37

—๛—

MARIE STOPES

AUTHOR OF THE SEX MANUAL "MARRIED LOVE" AND FOUNDER OF BRITAIN'S FIRST BIRTH-CONTROL CLINIC

OCTOBER 3, 1958

Marie Stopes, who died yesterday at her home at Dorking, Surrey, can fairly be said to have transformed the thoughts of her generation about the physical aspects of marriage and the role of contraception in married life.

Immediately after the First World War she began to issue the books which made her famous and notorious. In emotional, even rhapsodic, language far removed from the scientific precision in which she had been trained, she preached the gospel of marriage as a partnership of equals, sacramentally expressed both in its physical relations and in deliberate and joyous parenthood.

Attainment of this ideal of married love required the use of contraception to remove the fear of pregnancy at the wrong time and for deliberate family planning. Her books discussed the methods of contraception she favoured with uninhibited candour, though not always with medical accuracy; and she founded Britain's first birth-control clinic to give practical expression to a mission she pursued with religious fervour.

Addressed not to the learned or scientific public but to ordinary inarticulate men and women, and especially to wives and mothers, her writings at once achieved — and still retain — an enormous circulation. They helped innumerable humble folk to avoid unhappiness and ill-health. Before her advent the birth-control movement had been the preserve of a group of "Neo-Malthusian" intellectuals preoccupied chiefly by a rather academic concern about the balance between population trends and economic resources.

She transformed it into an openly discussed affair of the masses, directly and intimately concerned with the welfare of individual men and women and of their children. Her frontal attacks on old taboos, her quasi-prophetic tone, her flowery fervour aroused strong opposition from those who disagreed with her for religious reasons or felt she overstepped the bounds of good taste: and the launching of her pioneer clinics in London, Leeds, and Aberdeen was sometimes attended by stormy scenes.

Marie Carmichael Stopes was the eldest daughter of the late Henry Stopes, an anthropologist and archaeologist. Educated at St George's, Edinburgh, and the North London Collegiate School, she went on to University College London with a chemistry scholarship. Having there gained the gold medal in junior and senior botany and her BSc — she later took the DSc — she went to Munich and graduated as PhD. In 1904 she joined the science staff of Manchester University. In 1907 she travelled to Japan, where she spent nearly two years at Tokyo University and explored the country (including some remote areas) for fossils. She returned to Manchester as a lecturer in fossil botany. She was also a fellow and sometime lecturer in palaeo-botany at University College London. During this period she wrote a number of scientific papers, as well as books on plant life and on Japan. An early marriage was, at her suit, annulled.

In 1918, retaining her maiden name, she married Humphrey Verdon Roe, the aircraft pioneer and co-founder with his brother of the firm which made the Avro biplane. In the same year she produced her two best sellers, *Married Love* and its sequel, *Wise Parenthood*, forerunners of a series of similar books which sold in hundreds of thousands.

With the support of various well-known people she and her husband established "the Mothers' Clinic" in Holloway (now in Whitfield Street, St Pancras), and used the proceeds of *Married Love* and their own private resources to keep it going and to promote other clinics through her Society for Constructive Birth Control. In 1930 a play of hers, *Our Ostriches*, forceful propaganda but without dramatic merit, was staged at the Royalty Theatre. Her husband died in 1949.

In later life, after most of the separate birth-control societies had united and achieved acceptance and respectability in the Family Planning Association, the defects of her qualities became apparent. She remained aloof, for she could not co-operate on equal terms with others. Her dogmatism in scientific matters lost her the support of most doctors sympathetic to her aims. The shortcomings of her exuberant style and literary imagination (which could not readily transcend the plane of private bodily rapture) marred the verse she occasionally published.

Her home was near Dorking. She had two sons, one of whom survives her. *Marie Stopes, palaeobotanist and family-planning pioneer, was born on October 15, 1880. She died on October 2, 1958, aged 77*

—◦◦◦—

COUNTESS MOUNTBATTEN OF BURMA

CHARITY-WORKER AND WIFE
OF ADMIRAL OF THE FLEET
EARL MOUNTBATTEN OF
BURMA, WHO WAS ALSO LAST
VICEREINE OF INDIA

FEBRUARY 22, 1960

Tall, fair-haired and blue-eyed in the English tradition, Lady Mountbatten was the heiress of great wealth and made a brilliant marriage to one closely allied by blood and marriage to the Royal Family. Lady Louis gave early promise of the part she would play as the last Vicereine of India by her dedication to the interests of all those who care for the sick and helpless. No one did more to help that cause during and after the recent war than she, and her devotion was amply repaid by the love of the people of the sub-continent of India. Her influence there was immense and it was suitably acknowledged by Mr Nehru in 1948 when he recalled how she had moved from camp to camp in the stricken Punjab to bring help and cheer to the refugees.

She was the elder daughter of Lord Mount Temple, a grandson of the seventh Earl of Shaftesbury, and his first wife Amalia Maud, the only child of Sir Ernest Cassel. King Edward VII stood sponsor at her christening and she was named Edwina Cynthia Annette. Though the heiress to great wealth she was brought up strictly and up to the age of 21 she had a dress allowance of only £100 a year. Her grandfather's close personal friendship with King Edward VII and her father's prominent position in the House of Commons before he was raised to the peerage, ensured to her an *entrée* into the best circles, and it was at a Cowes Week soon after the end of the 1914-18 War that she was introduced by the Duke of Windsor, then Prince of Wales, to the first Marquess of Milford Haven's younger son, then Lord Louis Mountbatten, and serving in the Royal Navy. Their marriage was one of the great social events of the season of 1922 and was graced by the presence of King George V and Queen Mary. Both were young and full of life and they became by sheer force of character the leaders of the young fashion of the time. Sir Ernest Cassel had died in 1921 and had left between his two granddaughters the income from his immense fortune, subject to a number of provisions which were soon to become embarrassing. Only five years after his death Brook House, the great mansion in Park Lane which Sir Ernest Cassel had built and filled with an immensely valuable collection of objects of art, was sold and a block of flats was built on the site, with a penthouse on the roof to accommodate the Mountbattens. They also had a house at Bosham, a castle in the west of Ireland, and later Broadlands, near Romsey, once the home of Lord Palmerston.

Yet amid all this luxury neither of them forgot the more serious things of life. Lord Louis pursued his career in the Navy which his father had served with devotion throughout his life; Lady Louis took the greatest interest in dockland settlements and other charitable causes, but above all in hospitals and nursing. She became president of the London County branch of the St John Ambulance Brigade in 1939 and after the outbreak of war was indefatigable in the work of recruitment and organization. When her husband became head of Combined Operations in 1941 she added to her duties by organizing most efficiently the welfare branch of that immense inter-service body. Later on she proved a valuable stimulus in the same field in the even larger sphere of the South East Asia Command.

She had become Superintendent-in-Chief of the Red Cross and St John war organization and as such made an immense number of inspections of hospitals, welfare centres, schools, and clinics all over the world, but particularly in the Middle and Far East. In a three-month tour in 1945 she travelled some 34,000 miles, visiting many parts of India, Ceylon, Chungking, and the Burma front. Later in the year she visited Palestine and Jordan and after the collapse of Japan she did sterling work in Java in the early days of the organization for the recovery of allied prisoners of war and internees (RAPWI). She was gazetted DCVO in the New Year Honours of 1946, a recognition richly deserved. In the spring of that year she visited Australia and in Sydney was invited to march with the veterans of both wars to the Sydney cenotaph for the dawn service, a unique honour in recognition of her and her husband's work for service men.

She was therefore no stranger to India, Burma, and Malaya when she went to New Delhi as Vicereine in 1947. The staff at Viceregal House quickly found that she was determined to get to grips with the problems of Indian life. When her husband flew to the riot-torn Punjab she went with him, travelling thousands of miles by aircraft, car, and on foot in heat and dust to bring hope and solace to the despairing refugees. She was no great lady standing at a distance, but a mother and a nurse who took their soiled and trembling hands in hers and spoke quiet words of womanly comfort. In the short and difficult term of office of the last Viceroy of India she won the hearts of all, and nobody contributed more to the warm ties of friendship between the British and Indian peoples than she. In 1947 she was made CI [Imperial Order of the Crown of India]. She had been appointed CBE in 1943 and in 1948 she was advanced to GBE.

The year 1949 saw the introduction of a private Bill into the House of Lords with the object of varying the terms of her inheritance. Taxation had risen so steeply that her income had shrunk to less than a tenth of its original amount and some relief from the provision of Sir Ernest Cassel's will forbidding the anticipation of capital was urgently necessary, otherwise she and her husband would be compelled to curtail the public work they had so long and so devotedly performed. An Act giving relief from onerous provisions of settlement of married women's property had been passed in 1935, but it was not retrospective and as Sir Ernest Cassel had died in 1921 its provisions did not apply to Lady Mountbatten's case. The Bill passed through all its stages in the House of Lords, but there was considerable opposition from both sides of the House of Commons. After debate, the private Bill was withdrawn and a public Bill having similar force was eventually passed into law in November.

At the time of her death Lady Mountbatten was connected with a dozen and more bodies devoted to the welfare of youth, the sick and the underprivileged; among them the St John Ambulance Brigade (of which she was Superintendent-in-Chief), the Westminster Hospital, the Girl Guides Association, Save the Children Fund, the Royal College of Nursing, and the WVS. Yet her interest was never passive; she had an inquiring mind and it was never enough for her to be just a name on a letter heading. Once her sympathies had been roused she gave generously both of her time — she was often overseas — and her organizational experience. Of the two daughters she bore Lord Mountbatten, the elder, Lady Patricia, is married to Lord Brabourne and the younger, Lady Pamela, was married in January to Mr David Hicks.

Countess Mountbatten of Burma, GBE, DCVO, CI, was born on November 28, 1901. She died on February 21, 1960, aged 58

—⁓—

SYLVIA PANKHURST

A MILITANT SUFFRAGETTE WHO ALSO CAMPAIGNED ON BEHALF OF ABYSSINIAN INDEPENDENCE

SEPTEMBER 28, 1960

Miss Sylvia Pankhurst, who was one of the chief figures among the militant suffragettes in the years before 1914, died yesterday in Addis Ababa, our Correspondent there reports.

A woman of ardent temperament, devoted without emotional or any other reserve to the causes she made her own, Sylvia Pankhurst found in the women's suffrage movement an outlet for her somewhat tempestuous energies more satisfying than she was able to find afterwards. Her mother, Mrs Emmeline Pankhurst, and her elder sister, Christabel, were the chief forces in the Women's Social and Political Union; but she, as its honorary secretary and, later, in secession from the WSPU, was not the least dramatic personage in the movement as a whole.

An unqualified and vehement militant, she came frequently into collision with the law and suffered imprisonment on numerous occasions under the rigours of the "Cat and Mouse" Act. When in 1914 her mother and sister, together with most of the other militant leaders, called a truce in their campaign and lent their organization to the cause of national service, Sylvia Pankhurst took her stand upon violent opposition to the war. She attached herself to the extreme Left and continued upon occasion to find herself in serious trouble with the police. In later years, when the glory of the militant campaign had been dimmed, she devoted herself above all else to an all but private crusade against Fascist Italy and on behalf of Abyssinian independence.

At the time of her death she was editing the *Ethiopian Observer*.

Estelle Sylvia Pankhurst was born in Manchester in 1882. Her father, Richard Marsden Pankhurst, who had been a friend of John Stuart Mill, was a barrister and a sincere and high-minded social worker. Her mother, Emmeline Pankhurst, was the daughter of Robert Goulden, a calico printer. She was educated at the High School for Girls, Manchester; the Municipal School of Art; and the Royal College of Art, South Kensington. She won medals and scholarships and during her student days went to Venice, where she took a diploma at the Accademia. In 1903 her mother and her sister, Christabel, founded the Women's Social and Political Union, and in the course of time she became honorary secretary.

In 1912 and 1913 Sylvia Pankhurst formed branches of the WSPU in East London, which, developing upon other lines than the parent body, became a separate organization, under the name of the East London Federation. Thus she came to pursue her own feminist and other ideals, working in isolation from her mother and sister. In 1914 she established the *Workers' Dreadnought*, in which her pacifist attitude of mind was supported by a vaguely revolutionary social philosophy.

She was active all through the war years in organizing the work of a number of clinics and a day nursery in East London, though not in work of that character only; in October, 1918, she was fined £50 on a charge of attempting to cause mutiny, sedition, or dissatisfaction among His Majesty's Forces or the civilian population. Two years later, having in the meantime embraced with passion the cause of the Russian revolution, she paid a visit to Russia and on her return figured prominently among the communists in this country. Later in the year she was arrested again on a charge of publishing subversive matter, notably an article entitled "Discontent on the Lower Deck", and was sentenced to six months' imprisonment — a conviction that was upheld on appeal. She was expelled from the Communist Party in the following year after having refused to hand over to it the *Workers' Dreadnought*.

Abyssinia represented her chief devotion before, during, and after the war of 1939-1945, and there she settled finally in 1956. For her services she received from the Emperor the decoration of the Queen of Sheba, first class.

She wrote many books, most notably a history of the Suffragette movement (1931), an interesting enough volume, though characteristically it displayed little knowledge of the non-militant movement, a Life of her mother (1935), and in the last year of her life a number of works concerned with various aspects of Ethiopian life.

Sylvia Pankhurst, suffragette, was born on May 5, 1882. She died on September 27, 1960, aged 78

Editor's note: In response to the wave of hunger strikes by Suffragette prisoners, legislation that became known as the "Cat and Mouse" Act was passed in 1913, allowing hunger-striking prisoners to be released until they recouped their strength, at which point they could be re-arrested. In addition, this postscript appeared in *The Times* of October 27, 1960: "Dr Richard Pankhurst informs us that his mother, Sylvia Pankhurst, was never a member of the Communist Party and was therefore never expelled from it."

—⁓—

MARILYN MONROE

HOLLYWOOD LEGEND WITH A GIFT FOR COMEDY THAT SOME THOUGHT OUTSHONE OLIVIER'S

AUGUST 6, 1962

Miss Marilyn Monroe's career was not so much a Hollywood legend as *the* Hollywood legend: the poor orphan who became one of the most sought after (and highly paid) women in the world; the hopeful Hollywood unknown who became the most potent star-attraction in the American cinema; the uneducated beauty who married one of America's leading intellectuals.

The story thus dramatically outlined was in all essentials true. Marilyn Monroe began life as Norma Jean Baker in Los Angeles, where she was born on June 1, 1926. She was brought up in an orphanage and a series of foster homes, married first at the age of 15, obtained a divorce four years later and began a career as a photographer's model. From this, in a few months, she graduated to a screen test with Twentieth-Century Fox, a contract and the name which she was to make famous. Nothing came of this contract immediately, however, and her first appearance in a film was for another studio in 1948, when she played second lead in a not very successful B picture called *Ladies of the Chorus*. There followed a number of small roles in films such as *Love Happy* (with the Marx Brothers), *The Asphalt Jungle*, directed by John Huston, in which she was first seriously noticed, Joseph Mankiewicz's *All About Eve*, Fritz Lang's *Clash by Night* and others, until in 1952 she was given her first starring role in a minor thriller, *Don't Bother to Knock*, in which she played (improbably) a homicidal baby-sitter.

This was where she began in earnest to become a legend: during the shooting of the film it came to light that some years before she had posed nude for a calendar picture, and her career, hanging in the balance, was saved by the simple avowal that she had needed the money for the rent and was not

Marilyn Monroe and her new husband Arthur Miller in Surrey, in 1956. He wrote the screenplay of her final film, The Misfits, *for her*

ashamed. From then on her name was constantly before the public, even if the parts she played were not always large or important, and the advertising for her next major role, in *Niagara*, which showed her reclining splendidly the length of the Niagara Falls established the image once and for all.

At about this time she married the baseball star Joe di Maggio — the marriage was dissolved in 1954 — and began to show signs that she had talent as well as a dazzling physical presence. In *Gentlemen Prefer Blondes* and *How to Marry a Millionaire* startled critics noticed a real gift for comedy and by the arrival of *The Seven Year Itch* there was no doubt about it: she gave a performance in which personality and sheer acting ability (notably an infallible sense of comic timing) played as important a part as mere good looks. From then on she appeared in an unbroken string of personal successes: *Bus Stop*, of which as severe a judge as Jose Ferrer has said: "I challenge any actress that ever lived to give a better performance in that role", *The Prince and the Showgirl* in which many critics felt she outshone her director and co-star Sir Laurence Olivier, *Some Like It Hot* and *Let's Make Love*.

In 1956 Marilyn Monroe was married again — to the playwright Arthur Miller (they were divorced in 1960) and his next work, the original screenplay of *The Misfits*, was written for her. This was, in the event, her last film (the most recent, *Something's Got to Give*, being shelved after her failure to fulfil the terms of the contract) and in it under John Huston's direction she gave a performance which provoked its reviewer in *The Times* to a comment which might stand for her work as a whole: "Considerations of whether she can really act seem as irrelevant as they were with Garbo; it is her rare gift just to be in front of the camera, and, to paraphrase the comment of her apologetic employer in an earlier, more frivolous film, 'Well, anyone can *act*'."

Marilyn Monroe, actress, was born on June 1, 1926. She died on August 5, 1962, aged 36

—✺—

ELEANOR ROOSEVELT

VIGOROUS, LONG-SERVING US FIRST LADY, WHO CONTINUED IN ACTIVE PUBLIC LIFE AFTER HER HUSBAND'S DEATH IN OFFICE

NOVEMBER 8, 1962

Mrs Eleanor Roosevelt, the widow of President Franklin Roosevelt, whose death at the age of 78 is announced on another page, was perhaps the most distinguished of all the First Ladies who have graced the White House. It is true that Mrs Wilson, the second wife of President Woodrow Wilson, exerted more direct political power for a short period. But Mrs Roosevelt was more of an influential personality in her own right. To the men and women of America she became a figure of legendary earnestness, simplicity and devotion to the public good.

Her prominence derived in the first place, of course, from her husband. She had done more than most wives to help him in his political development, and her services to him were not curtailed when he achieved the Presidency. She was a charming and gifted hostess, interesting and interested in the many and varied guests whom it was her duty to entertain. But she was much more than that. She became the eyes and ears of a crippled man who could not move about as much as he would have wished. To him she presented the information and the views she acquired during her wide travels. As time went on she became herself a public commentator on the news in print and speech — and it must be confessed that on occasion her outspokenness proved a political embarrassment for her husband.

Her independent standing, however, was proved when she did not lapse into an honoured twilight of oblivion after Franklin Roosevelt's death. Indeed, her personal political influence became enhanced with the passage of years.

In a country where politics is so often regarded as a race for the spoils she stood out for her sense of *noblesse oblige*. Among a people where political manipulation is often considered one of the higher arts she was remarkable for her undeviating devotion to principle. She became the conscience of the Democratic Party.

Inevitably, she had the failings of her virtues. She may sometimes have been earnest to the point of the didactic. So uncompromising were her ideals that she lacked her husband's political skill. So unquestioned was her own righteousness that on occasion she did not notice her own prejudices. But overall she made a noble and healthy contribution to the public life of more than one American generation.

Anna Eleanor Roosevelt was born in 1884, the daughter of Elliot Roosevelt, a younger brother of President Theodore Roosevelt, by his marriage with Anna Hull. In 1892 her mother died and she went to live with her maternal grandmother. Two years later her father, to whom she was devoted, died also. Both her parents had belonged to affluent families of high social standing in New York and she had a sheltered and very careful upbringing. Her earlier youth was spent at her grandmother's homes in New York and the country. On occasion she stayed with her uncle Theodore at Oyster Bay. Lacking playmates of her own age she learned to amuse herself and became an omnivorous reader. Her mother had wished her to acquire part of her education in Europe, and in 1899 she went with an aunt to England, where she was placed at Mlle Souvestre's School at "Allinswood", near Wimbledon Common, frequently spending her holidays on the Continent.

Returning to New York, where she found herself somewhat out of touch with the younger generation, she was launched by her relations as a debutante. Soon, however, she met her distant cousin Franklin Delano Roosevelt, who was still at college. In 1903 he proposed to her and on St Patrick's Day, 1905, they were married. After a tour in Europe Mrs Roosevelt and her young husband returned to a New York house and, in due course, to the care of a growing family. (Their first child, a daughter, was born in 1906, and they also had five sons.) Then, however, with her husband's entry into politics, there came a new home in Albany and the dual existence of a politician's wife which was to continue through many active and crowded years. From girlhood she had had high ideals and one of them was that a wife should share her husband's interests.

In 1913 the future President became Assistant Secretary of the Navy, and the inevitable move to Washington ensued. It meant many social activities, into which she threw herself with characteristic energy. Then came the war and work for the Red Cross and in the Navy Hospital. After the armistice she was able to go with her husband to Europe. By that time his political future seemed assured, and in 1920 he was nominated for the Vice-Presidency.

The election was lost and the following year he suffered the attack of infantile paralysis that was to be a turning-point in his life. This was a period of stern trial for a devoted wife. She responded with superb courage and calm. One of the greatest services she ever rendered to him was in encouraging his determination some day to resume his political career in the active world. His mother would have had him lead the existence of an elegant invalid: his wife would have none of it. During his long convalescence she began to take an increasing interest in affairs, and after his election to the Governorship of New York a new field of public life opened for her.

In 1932 Franklin Roosevelt was elected President of the United States and Mrs Roosevelt became first lady in the land. She had immense energy and both enthusiasm and ability. The hesitancy of her earlier years had vanished and she threw herself into her new duties with vigour. She travelled immense distances, and was here, there and everywhere. Everything interested her. She talked with everybody she met, asked questions, examined everything. There was a cartoon of miners in the bowels of the earth looking with astonishment over their shoulders and exclaiming "Here comes Mrs Roosevelt". By this time she was a practised speaker and lecturer, and made speeches and broadcast. She also wrote books and in 1935 started her column, "My Day", which before long was reaching millions of readers. In it she was informal, chatty and friendly and the women in small homes absorbed her observations easily and felt they knew her. The profits she derived from her activities amounted to a large annual sum and she distributed it among her favourite charities.

Even if Mrs Roosevelt had played a less ambitious role her work would have been immense. Sacks of correspondence and endless gifts came as a matter of course to the President's wife. There was also the White House — she was soon to renovate its offices — and all its entertaining to look after. She seemed, however, to take her normal duties in her stride and to be always moving on to wider interests. In such spare moments as she had, however, she reverted to the kindly matriarch and knitted for grandchildren. Naturally she was a contentious figure and the political opponents of her husband did not spare her — "Nor Eleanor either" was a hostile slogan in one of his Presidential campaigns. But criticism she accepted as the natural lot of public life, and in spite of it she became and remained a great national figure.

In the war, kindly always in her recollections of her early days here, she proved herself a sympathetic friend towards Britain. She sent encouraging messages and adopted an East End boy for the duration of hostilities. In October, 1942, she flew across the Atlantic and stayed at Buckingham Palace. Her visit was full of incident. She saw the bombed areas and went to Dover, she visited American troops, the RAF and the women's services and paid special attention to the work of women in the war. She also crossed to Ulster to see the American troops there and travelled to Scotland. Everywhere she went she radiated encouragement and created an admirable impression. From England, moreover, she broadcast to her own country. In the summer of 1943 she went to New Zealand and Australia to be again a welcome and honoured guest. The next year she was in the West Indies.

At the President's death, in April, 1945, she was 60 but a whole new life and career and even more travel lay ahead of her. She continued her daily column of comment, "My Day", published several more books, was for years a delegate to the United Nations, visited half the countries of the world, and played an important role in American party politics.

Eight months after her husband's death President Truman asked her to be a delegate to the United Nations General Assembly meeting in 1945. The following year she was chairman of the Commission on Human Rights in Unesco. Thereafter she was constantly a delegate to the United Nations General Assembly meetings until the Democratic Administration gave way to the Republicans after the defeat of 1952. Even then she continued to be active in the American Association for the United Nations.

In 1948 she came to London at the invitation of the King and Queen to unveil the statue of her husband in Grosvenor Square. She had visited Germany immediately after the 1945 meeting of the General Assembly in London and thereafter she crossed the ocean so many times she described herself as a harassed commuter across the Atlantic. In addition to Britain, France and Germany her travels included Russia (as far as Samarkand and Tashkent), Yugoslavia, Greece, Turkey, Lebanon, Syria, Jordan, Israel, India, Pakistan, Burma, Siam, Indonesia, Hong-kong and Japan. On these travels she continued writing her daily column for various American newspapers and interviewed, as a newspaperwoman, important people around the world, including an interview with Mr Khrushchev at Yalta.

At home she remained pretty well aloof from domestic politics while she was representing her country at the United Nations although she did support Mr Adlai Stevenson for President in the 1952 campaign. He inspired her, as he did so many other people of deep liberal convictions, with the belief that he would have made a President of outstanding calibre. She remained his devoted supporter. In 1956 she campaigned for him in his fight for the Democratic nomination and in his contest for the Presidency itself. Nothing would have pleased her better than for him to be the Democratic standard-bearer once again in 1960.

It was not to be, but Mrs Roosevelt did not reconcile herself immediately to the choice of Mr Kennedy. Her doubts were occasioned not only by disappointment over the rejection of Mr Stevenson: she was disturbed by Mr Kennedy's ambiguous record on

Macarthyism and questioned whether he had the basic conviction and faithfulness to principle necessary for the highest responsibility. Eventually she did declare herself for him and campaign on his behalf, but there was always the suspicion that she was moved less by confidence in him than by concern at the thought of Mr Nixon in the White House.

Throughout these years, however, she was not preoccupied by national politics. Some of her most valuable work at this time was at the level of New York state affairs. In company with Mr Herbert Lehman and others she played a major part in freeing Democratic politics in the state from the control of Tammany Hall. It was on such an issue as this, where moral principles were closely involved, that she was at her best.

Her popularity with the American people transcended parties and politics. Many times during her widowhood she was voted, in annual polls by the Gallup organization, the most popular woman in America. In addition to her political labours, her travel and her daily journalism and her work for many charities, she found time to write a number of books of reminiscence. They included *This is My Story*, *My Days*, *If You Ask Me*, *This I Remember*, *India and the Awakening East*, and *On My Own*, this last the story of her life and activities following her departure from the White House in 1945. In the early thirties she had also published books for children and women, including *When You Grow Up to Vote*, and *It's Up to the Women*. She also edited various books including *The Moral Basis of Democracy*.

Eleanor Roosevelt, First Lady of the United States, was born on October 11, 1884. She died on November 7, 1962, aged 78

—◆—

NANCY, VISCOUNTESS ASTOR

FIRST WOMAN TO SIT IN THE HOUSE OF COMMONS

MAY 4, 1964

Nancy, Viscountess Astor, CH, the first woman to take her seat as a member of the House of Commons, died on Saturday at Grimsthorpe Castle, Lincolnshire. She was 84.

In any age or country, Nancy Astor would have been remarkable for outstanding vitality, personality, charm and will power. She was always a delight to the eye, small, compact, a finely drawn profile, a classic head, growing more and more exquisite with the years. She was made all of one piece, a perfect working model, always well-dressed. From the first day she entered the House of Commons in neat black with touches of white at collar, in appearance she struck the exact note and set the style for her feminine colleagues in years to come.

Nancy Witcher Langhorne was born of an old Virginian family on May 19, 1879, on the same day as her future husband William Waldorf Astor, was born in New York. In 1897 she married Robert Gerald Shaw, of Boston, from whom she obtained a divorce in 1903 and in 1906 she married Waldorf Astor. When he succeeded to the viscounty and resigned from the representation in Parliament of the Sutton Division of Plymouth Lady Astor was elected as Unionist member on November 28, 1919. She was the first woman to sit in the House of Commons, being introduced by Balfour and Lloyd George. Countess Markievicz, who did not take her seat, had been elected by an Irish constituency in the Sinn Fein interest at a slightly earlier date. From 1919 to 1945 Lady Astor continued to represent Plymouth and most of her life and work were closely identified with the city, of which during the Second World War she was Lady Mayoress.

In Parliament she naturally devoted herself mainly to the claims of women and children, speaking with gaiety or gravity according to her mood, but never dully and always briefly and sometimes brilliantly. Her worst fault was a habit of interruption which, however tempered with wit, was apt to cause annoyance. Temperance, education, nursery schools, women police were subjects which deeply interested her.

Like Zenobia, and also in St James's Square, Lady Astor was a famous political hostess and her house was the meeting place of distinguished visitors to the metropolis,

especially Americans. One day it might be Gandhi, the next Grandi and the following day a batch of social workers or Cabinet Ministers or Charlie Chaplin or Ruth Draper or G.B.S. And there were from time to time the huge party gatherings comparable with those of Londonderry House or of the Devonshire House of an earlier day. On the top of the staircase, sparkling with jewels, she welcomed each guest with a bantering quip or jest and was the central figure throughout the evening.

Her energy was extraordinary. After a long day in London and in the House she would return to Cliveden about seven, change into tennis clothes and play two or even three sets of singles with one of her nieces; then down to the river (before the war) in her cream-coloured car, driven at speed; she would swim across the Thames, talking all the time about God, or advising someone on the bank about the way to live his, or usually her, life, touch the bottom on the far bank, tell the swans to go away, and swim back still talking. In earlier years she was a dashing rider and a sure shot; later golf was her favourite game. She played it well and conversationally and distinguished herself in parliamentary matches.

She had a sharp sense of the ridiculous and could have made a fortune on the variety stage. No one who saw her Christmastide impersonations in the old days at Cliveden, egged on by her sisters Phyllis and Nora, will ever forget her clever performances. Dressed in a hunting coat of her husband's and her hair hidden under a large black velvet huntsman's cap she became the little foreign visitor, here for the hunting season; or with a row of celluloid teeth worn crookedly, an upper-class Englishwoman who thought Americans peculiar. Someone once said she was a cross between Joan of Arc and Gracie Fields. She wasn't courageous, if by courage is meant mastery of fear, for she did not know about fear. She was fearless of physical dangers, of criticism, of people.

No one could be kinder, more tender, generous, comforting and swift to help in time of trouble. She loved being needed and was at her best in a crisis. She would have denied it but she had an innate sense of drama and had a flair for dealing with people en masse.

American politicians and journalists of the old school were bewitched by her. The later, war-time journalists were scared by her outspokenness and refused to be charmed. It is recorded that Gladstone asked his wife whether she would prefer to know nothing and say anything she pleased, or to know everything and say next to nothing on matters of foreign and domestic policy. Lady Astor got the best of both worlds, knowing everything and saying anything she pleased.

Her matriarchal feelings were strong and she liked to feel in touch with the whole circle at all times. She held the family together, including nieces and nephews. Within this circle she loved to recall Virginia days, her father, Colonel Langhorne, her sisters and their beaux.

Nancy, Lady Astor, electioneering at Plymouth in 1922

During a visit to the States in 1922 she made 40 speeches, mainly in Virginia, "without a single faux pas," reported an American correspondent.

Her deep religious sense found its formal setting in the Christian Science Church and she was a diligent student of the Scriptures, with a strong horror of sin and a crusading spirit which spurred her to pursue reforms regardless of party divisions. There were four persons whose influence and friendship and characters she was never tired of acknowledging with gratitude and affection: Rachel Macmillan, Henry Jones, Arthur Balfour, and Philip Lothian.

After her withdrawal from Parliament in June, 1945, when she did not stand for re-election. Lady Astor continued her interest in the city she had represented so long and made regular visits while her health permitted.

On July 16, 1959, she was made an honorary Freeman of the City of Plymouth.

In the same year Lady Astor performed the launching ceremony for HMS Plymouth, first ship for 250 years to bear the name, presented a diamond and sapphire necklace to be worn by Lady Mayoresses of Plymouth, and gave her home at 3, Elliot Terrace, overlooking the Hoe, to the city for use as a Lord Mayor's residence. Its use was later modified to a place for the accommodation of official visitors.

She was made CH in 1937.

Her husband died in 1952 and she is survived by her four sons, Viscount Astor; David Astor, editor of the *Observer*; Michael Astor; Major J. J. Astor; and by her daughter, the Countess of Ancaster.

Nancy, Viscountess Astor, CH, first woman to sit as an MP, was born on May 19, 1879. She died on May 2, 1964, aged 84

—⁓—

DAME MYRA HESS

PIANIST WHO RAISED WARTIME MORALE IN LONDON WITH DAILY LUNCHTIME CONCERTS AT THE NATIONAL GALLERY

NOVEMBER 27, 1965

Dame Myra Hess, DBE, the concert pianist, died at her home at St John's Wood, London, on Thursday. She was 75.

That she was more than a distinguished pianist is attested by the honours which came to her.

Honorary doctorates of Durham, London, Cambridge, Manchester, Leeds, St Andrews, and Reading and her title, Dame of the British Empire, conferred in 1941, primarily in recognition of her establishment of daily concerts at the National Gallery as a war-emergency service, were public recognition that she gave to music more than virtuosity on her instrument, more even than many years of sane and poetical interpretation of pianoforte classics.

She was not in the least a solemn person, though she had a proper appreciation of music's significance and social value. There emanated from her presence on the platform as from her actual performances a combination of integrity and geniality. Her arrangement of Bach's figured chorale "Jesu, Joy of man's desiring" made her name a household word among amateurs and non-musicians.

Myra Hess was born in London on February 25, 1890, and began her education at the Guildhall School of Music under Julian Pascal and Orlando Morgan, but in 1902 she won a scholarship at the Royal Academy of Music and came under the late Tobias Matthay, becoming one of his earliest as well as one of his most distinguished pupils. In Matthay's textbook on muscular relaxation she and Mr Vivian Langrish are the models for the exercises which formed the basis of his method of teaching. In 1907 she came before the London public in a Queen's Hall concert conducted by Beecham, at which she played Beethoven's fourth piano concerto, an auspicious and prophetic choice. She must have played it hundreds of times — for many years it was a highlight of the Promenade concerts — yet more than 40 years afterwards it was still a revelation every time she came to it. Her success was immediate and engagements to play concertos, to give recitals and to take part in chamber music soon made her eminent. Her devotion to chamber music was never extinguished by the greater personal and material rewards of the other forms

of concert giving. When she stayed at home to establish the National Gallery concerts in 1939 instead of going off on a lucrative American tour she confessed that one of her rewards for so doing was the opportunity it gave her to take part once more in chamber music. This she did with the Menges and Rosé quartets, and with Miss Isolde Menges in duet sonatas.

She had a big repertory — the result of a remarkable facility in reading and an equally remarkable memory — and at an early stage in her career laid the foundations of it with the other concertos of Beethoven, all the concertos of Mozart, which she subsequently played at the National Gallery and during the Festival of Britain, 1951, the popular Schumann and Grieg concertos, which she treated as the small lyrical pieces they are, and the two big Brahms concertos, which perhaps suited her less but were well within her intellectual capacity. Her catholic taste embraced the virginalists, the sonatas of Scarlatti and late Beethoven, Bach and the romantics, and her own contemporaries and juniors. There was in her character and in her playing alike a mixture of strength and graciousness — she could be very pertinacious — which more than technical brilliance made her an artist of international reputation. She was one of the few English artists to establish herself as a musician of the front rank not only at home but in many European countries and in the United States.

The National Gallery concerts, which ran from the autumn of 1939 throughout the war to April, 1946, formed an episode of a unique character in her career and in English musical history. She had some help from Sir Kenneth Clark, then Director of the National Gallery, and from Mr Howard Ferguson, and encouragement from one or two other musicians, but the idea, the initiative, and the plan of giving daily lunch-hour concerts at a cheap flat rate price of admission was hers. She launched the scheme with a recital, planned the programmes, and presided over the committee which ran it. The concerts met an acutely felt need and immediately took their place as one of the stable features in London's disrupted life. They ran uninterruptedly all through the bombardments, nocturnal or matutinal, for six and a half years. Queen Elizabeth the Queen Mother went more than once and their value to the nation was recognized by the founder's promotion in the Order of the British Empire from Commander (conferred in 1936) to Dame. She was during that grim time the leader of our musical life. Only when, in 1946, the emergency was past and the concerts came to an end did she feel able to accept the many pressing invitations she had received to play abroad again. She continued to play for another 16 years when recurring arthritis brought about her retirement. She received affectionate tributes three years later when she celebrated her seventy-fifth birthday.

Dame Myra Hess, DBE, concert pianist, was born on February 25, 1890. She died on November 25, 1965, aged 75

ENID BLYTON

PROLIFIC AUTHOR OF BEST-SELLING BUT OFTEN CONTROVERSIAL CHILDREN'S BOOKS

NOVEMBER 29, 1968

Miss Enid Blyton, who died yesterday, was perhaps the most successful and most controversial children's author of the postwar period. Certainly she was the most productive: at her death something like 400 titles stood to her name.

Inevitably, her name is linked with her creation (or, as those who disliked her work called him) her creature, Noddy. Noddy became a household name. Though a figure of fiction, fiction could not hold him, he became a hot commercial property. At different times you could find him on the West End stage; on the back of breakfast food packets; on the handles of toothbrushes; and in the form of an eggcup. He was loathed by many adults — particularly librarians — and loved by many children. The antis found him odious, unwholesome, and wet — he was said to weep when confronted by some intractable Toyland problem. The case for the antis was crystallized some years ago in a witty article in *Encounter*. But it is probably true to say that those children who enjoyed Noddy were not much influenced by

*Enid Blyton reading one of her own
stories to her daughters in 1949*

the knockers. They looked on the
works of Miss Blyton and found them
good. They could not see what all the
fuss was about.

However, to judge the prolific
Miss Blyton solely on the merits of
the mini-adventures of Noddy, Big
Ears and Mr Plod would be unfair.
The enormous success of her Famous
Five and Secret Seven series and the
enduring popularity of such books as
The Island of Adventure, *The Sea of
Adventure* and *The Valley of Adventure*
was earned for she could write a readable tale, a tale with action in it, and
a tale that children, shrewd critics,
found credible.

The daughter of T. C. Blyton, her
early years are not easy to chart
exactly; she was not one to favour the
publisher's practice of printing on the
dust-jacket of a book a piece about
its author. She was born in the late
1890s and brought up and educated in
Beckenham; she was musical, taking
her LRAM at an early age. Her father
wished her to become a concert pianist
but she had already decided that she
would write for children and to prepare
for this left home and took Froebel
training. Subsequently she was governess to a family of boys in Surrey
and this experience encouraged her to
open a small school of her own. By now
she was writing stories, poems, and
plays for her pupils, the themes and
ideas for these often coming from the
children, and contributing regularly to
Teacher's World.

Her first published book, *Child
Whispers*, a collection of poems,
appeared in 1922. Her first stories
were published by George Newnes
and she was intimately connected
with the popular children's magazine
Sunny Stories. It was at Newnes that
she met and in 1924 married her
first husband, Lieutenant-Colonel H.
A. Pollock. After her marriage she
spread her wings yet further, editing
books on teaching and a children's
encyclopaedia.

Early in the 1940s it was suggested
to her by a London publisher that she
should emulate Angela Brazil and
write school stories for girls. She took
the advice and the tales she wrote went
like hot cakes. So successful were they

after the Second World War when there was a continuing shortage of paper and printing facilities that it was difficult to keep them in stock. At least three publishers were taking her work. Books of all kinds flowed from her pen: she produced an abridged edition of T. A. Coward's *Birds of the British Isles and their Eggs*, a children's life of Christ, some Old Testament tales, a version of *Pilgrim's Progress*, readers for class use, and books on botany and volumes of verse.

These, of course, in addition to her immensely popular Secret Seven and Famous Five series. Her success was not loved by the public librarians who in some cases imposed sanctions against her books. Children asked for her books and were told they were not in stock.

Cold war broke out. While the librarians were probably unwise to betray their prejudices so openly Miss Blyton was perhaps wrong in contending that children should have what they liked no matter what other books were squeezed out. Whoever was in the right the fact remains that though Miss Blyton's writings were not great literature they were harmless, as any adult who has worked through a bout of Secret Seven or Famous Five knows.

There are many children who can read but do not read much; they find *The Lion, the Witch and the Wardrobe* just a little too much for them; Miss Blyton they pick up and they are away; they are better catered for now but it was not always so. Undoubtedly she helped many a child on the frontiers of book reading to take his first step.

She did not frequently get what is called a good press and over the years became as cagey as Marie Corelli about herself and her affairs. Yet her relations with children were of the best. Many years ago she reluctantly agreed to speak at a children's book week and arrived not noticeably well turned out. She was a huge success. On the spot it was arranged that she should appear each day. For many years after that she was a first choice at one famous book fair and always drew packed houses.

Her second husband, Kenneth Waters, FRCS, whom she married in 1943, died in 1967. She leaves two daughters by her first marriage.

Enid Blyton, children's writer, was born on August 11, 1897. She died on November 28, 1968, aged 71

—◆—

PROFESSOR DOROTHY GARROD

PALAEOLITHIC ARCHAEOLOGIST WHO IN 1939 BECAME THE FIRST WOMAN TO HOLD A CAMBRIDGE PROFESSORSHIP

DECEMBER 19, 1968

Professor Dorothy Garrod, CBE, sometime Fellow of Newnham College, Cambridge, and former Disney Professor of Archaeology in the

University of Cambridge, died yesterday at the age of 76. For more than two generations she was the leading authority in this country on Palaeolithic archaeology, and the first woman to be appointed professor at the University of Cambridge.

Dorothy Annie Elizabeth Garrod was born in London in 1892, the daughter of Sir Archibald Edward Garrod, KCMG, FRS, Regius Professor of Medicine at Oxford. She was educated at Burklands School, St Albans, and at Newnham College, Cambridge. She went up to Cambridge in 1913 to read first history and then classics. In 1919 after three years of war work in France she returned to academic studies to read for the diploma in anthropology of Oxford, which she obtained with distinction.

In 1927 she undertook her first major piece of original fieldwork — the excavation of the Devil's Tower rock shelter at Gibraltar. The results were published in a long paper to the Royal Anthropological Institute in the following year and made a considerable impression both for the nature of the discoveries — the first important finds of Neanderthal man associated with cultural remains and geological evidences of age in the Iberian Peninsula — and on account of the admirable way in which the investigation had been planned and presented. In 1929 she was elected research Fellow of her old college, and in 1932 while holding a Leverhulme research fellowship she embarked on the greatest single task in her notable career as a field worker, the excavation of the immense stratified sequence of Palaeolithic cave habitations at Mount Carmel, Palestine.

Although followed soon after by comparable finds by a French expedition in the Judean desert, and a German expedition in Syria, the discoveries at Mount Carmel remain perhaps the most richly informative single contribution to the study of primitive man ever achieved by one investigator at any one locality. Thereby Garrod was able to reveal for the first time the essential features of the prehistoric succession of south-west Asia, from the final stages of the Lower Palaeolithic to the earliest signs of agriculture — a total period of human development now known to have lasted approximately 100,000 years. Moreover the conclusions set out in her well-known monograph "The Stone Age of Mount Carmel" in 1937 have been abundantly confirmed by later work, while the full significance of the material and observations is still after nearly 30 years by no means exhausted.

Garrod's remarkable capacity for field investigations was accompanied by a striking gift for the synthesis of the growing mass of data on the prehistoric past. At a time when most workers were content to elaborate knowledge of particular areas, Garrod played a leading part in stimulating conscious elucidation of the broader patterns of the Old Stone Age in much the same fashion as her contemporary Gordon Childe did for the European Neolithic. Her paper to the British Association as President of Section H in 1937, entitled, "The Upper Palaeolithic in the Light of Recent Research", is a landmark in the development of the geographical and historical approach to Palaeolithic problems. Its particular occasion, the historical relation between the eastern and western groups of the Upper Palaeolithic, remained with her an abiding interest that was undoubtedly stimulated in the first instance by the finds of this phase at Mount Carmel, and led to a long series of much discussed papers.

Professor Dorothy Garrod, CBE, archaeologist, was born on May 5, 1892. She died on December 18, 1968, aged 76

———

DAME ADELINE GENÉE

DANISH BALLERINA WHO RAISED STANDARDS IN THE PROFESSION AS FOUNDER PRESIDENT OF THE FUTURE ROYAL ACADEMY OF DANCING

APRIL 24, 1970

Dame Adeline Genée-Isitt, DBE, who died yesterday, at the age of 92, was not only one of the best and most loved dancers of her day, but through tireless effort as well as example one of the founders of British ballet as it exists today.

She was born at Hinnerup, near Aarhus, Denmark, on January 6, 1878. The survivor of twins, she was named Anina. From about the age of four she showed a love of dancing which was encouraged by her father's brother, a successful ballet master and dancer, who had taken the professional name of Alexander Genée. This uncle and his wife, a Hungarian ballerina named Antonia Zimmerman, offered to make themselves responsible for her upbringing as soon as she was old enough to undertake rigorous training.

She took the same adopted surname as her uncle, who also chose for her the first name Adeline (after Adelina Patti). What she was taught was the old pure classical style of dancing which had flourished in Paris nearly a century earlier, been brought from there to Copenhagen by August Bournonville, and passed on by him to Christian Johansson, with whom Alexander Genée studied in St. Petersburg.

She made her first public appearance at ten in a *Polka à la picarde*, but she was not encouraged to become a child prodigy. Instead, she took her place in due course in her uncle's corps de ballet, although her industry and good memory soon brought her the opportunity to dance solo roles when other members of the company were absent.

Alexander Genée's career took the family to Stettin, to Berlin, and then to Munich, where he decided to revive for his niece, then 18, what became one of her most famous ballets, *Coppélia*. Shortly afterwards came an invitation to appear in London at the Empire Theatre, and although the first offer (for Queen Victoria's diamond jubilee celebrations) had to be refused, Adeline Genée arrived there in November, 1897, with a six weeks' contract. She stayed, with only brief interruptions, for 10 years.

The ballets at the Empire were of a lighter nature than the kind Diaghilev's Russian Ballet was later to popularize. In almost all of them Genée as the star would be seen not only in her classical solo but also in at least one dance to display her gift of characterization. One of the most famous of her solos, first given in *High Jinks* in 1904, was *Return from the Hunt*, given in full long-skirted riding kit, portraying both horse and rider, the exhilaration of the one and the nimbleness of the other.

In October, 1902, Genée was invited as guest artist to the Royal Theatre, Copenhagen, where she danced *Coppélia* and *Flower Festival at Genzano* with Hans Beck, and a duet by her uncle with Gustav Uhlendorff. The Danish critics found her style exceptionally refined, although "a little hard and cool", and greatly admired her virtuosity which encompassed steps not then normally attempted by women, including *entrechat six* and double *pirouettes*.

In January, 1905, Genée took part in a Command performance at Chatsworth before Edward VII and Queen Alexandra, the first time a dancer had been so honoured. In 1907 she left for her first tour of the United States, where she enjoyed a success comparable to that she had long commanded in London. By now her reputation was such that works of a more serious nature could be produced at the Empire; in 1906 she danced *Coppélia* there and in 1909 Alexander Genée mounted for her a version of the ballet scene from *Robert le Diable* which, with Taglioni in the role Genée now played, had ushered in the Romantic ballet. Genée herself also produced a number of ballets, often based on historical models.

Marriage to a successful businessman, Frank S. N. Isitt, in 1910, brought her great happiness, and after further tours in the United States and Australia, and London seasons at the Coliseum, Genée in 1914 announced her farewell season. The subscription list for a farewell present was headed by five fellow ballerinas including Pavlova and Karsavina, but with characteristic generosity Genée asked that the money raised be given to relieve the poverty of another dancer who had fallen on hard times.

In fact Genée continued dancing for a time after this season, but withdrew from regular appearances in 1917. This was not, however, to be the end of her connexion with the dance. On December 31, 1920, the Association of Teachers of Operatic Dancing of Great Britain was formed to raise standards and Genée elected its first president. The post was no sinecure: she helped draw up a standard syllabus, organized performances for the benefit of the association, personally sought the patronage of Queen Mary which was granted in 1928, and eight years later had the pleasure of seeing the association granted its charter as the Royal Academy of Dancing.

Adeline Genée's last appearances were made in *The Love Song*, a duet with Anton Dolin which she produced for a charity performance in June, 1932, repeated on the programmes of a special group of English dancers which she took to Copenhagen later that year (appearing at the Royal Theatre during the British Industries Fair), and gave for the last time in a BBC television broadcast on March 15, 1933.

She was created DBE in 1950 for her services to ballet. She was made an honorary Mps.D. by London University in 1946. She was proud, too, of the links she maintained with her native land and of the several honours bestowed upon her by Denmark.

Dame Adeline retired from the presidency of the RAD in 1954, handing over the office to Dame Margot Fonteyn. She retained her interest in ballet, however, and in 1967 was present at the gala performance to open a new theatre named after her at East Grinstead. Her husband died in 1939.

It was Adeline Genée's blessing to bring happiness to many thousands who admired and enjoyed her art. It was her pride to conduct herself always so that her profession should be respected. It was her self-appointed task to give that art and profession a strong foundation in her second homeland. Purity and clearness of style were hers in her life as in her dancing, and for many she left the memory of "an art with the warmth and innocence of sunshine".

Dame Adeline Genée, DBE, ballet dancer, was born on January 6, 1878. She died on April 23, 1970, aged 92

JANIS JOPLIN

HARD-LIVING AMERICAN BLUES SINGER WHO SELDOM APPEARED WITHOUT A BOTTLE OF SOUTHERN COMFORT

OCTOBER 6, 1970

Janis Joplin, who died in Hollywood early yesterday at the age of 27, was the foremost female blues singer of her generation. Born in Port Arthur, Texas, she heard the blues at an early age, and began singing when a student at Austin University. For several years she drifted in and out of music and various other jobs all over America, until in 1966 she moved to San Francisco, where she joined the resident band at the Avalon Ballroom, an easy "psychedelic" dance hall which spawned many top groups.

Her band, Big Brother and the Holding Company, rapidly rose to fame and really broke through with a stunning performance at the Monterey pop festival in 1967. Inevitably she was given the star treatment and broke away from the group the following year to form her own outfit.

After a disastrous debut in Memphis she triumphed in New York early in 1969, and visited Britain in April of that year to play at the Royal Albert Hall to an enraptured audience. A few months later she was voted World's Top Female Singer by the readers of the *Melody Maker*, but since then her career had been quiet until, a month before her death, she began recording with a new band.

Her harsh delivery and sensual stage act put her in direct line of descent from Bessie Smith, the greatest of all female blues singers. and she cultivated the outrageous image by seldom being seen without a bottle of Southern Comfort whisky near to hand. This quickly became her trade mark, as did the tough, hard-boiled exterior which hides the tensions and fears inside all women who choose to sing the blues for a living.

Janis Joplin, blues singer and songwriter, was born on January 19, 1943. She was found dead on October 4, 1970, aged 27

—◆◆◆—

"COCO" CHANEL

FRENCH DESIGNER WHO MADE FASHION HISTORY WITH THE COLLARLESS CARDIGAN JACKET

JANUARY 12, 1971

Mlle Gabrielle Chanel, "Coco" Chanel, *la grande couturière*, reached a peak of fame and popularity in the 1920s when she succeeded in replacing the extravagant pre-war fashions with simple, comfortable clothes. The same cardigan jackets and easy skirts that she popularized then were revived in her successful come-back in the late fifties, and her famous Chanel No. 5 scent kept her name in the public eye throughout her long career.

She became something of a legend in the world of fashion, and a Broadway musical, based on her career and starring Katharine Hepburn, was put on in 1968.

Most sources suggest that "Coco" Chanel was born in 1883, although this fact, like so many others about her life, was a jealously guarded secret. Traditionally, her nickname "Coco" was earned by her habit of riding in the Bois when the cocks were still crowing "cocorico", but she later claimed that it was merely a respectable version of "cocotte".

Orphaned at an early age, she worked with her sister in a milliner's in Deauville, where she finally opened a shop in 1912. After a brief spell of nursing in the war, she founded a couture house in the Rue Cambon in Paris. There she worked, lived and entertained for much of the rest of her life, although she actually slept in the Ritz hotel on the other side of the road.

Chanel sensed the profound need for change, renewal and emancipation that was sweeping the world in 1914 and set out to revolutionize women's clothing. It was her talent, drive and inspiration that brought about a complete metamorphosis of fashion in post-war years. She began by liberating women from the bondage of the corset. In 1920 she made the first chemise dress and the "poor girl look", in contrast to the rich woman of pre-war years, was born. She succeeded in making women look casual but at the same time elegant by using the then revolutionary combinations of jersey, tweed and pearls. Dior was to say of her later: "with a black sweater and 10 rows of pearls Chanel revolutionized fashion".

In 1925 she made fashion history again with the collarless cardigan jacket. Her bias-cut dress was labelled by one critic "a Ford because everybody has one". It was Chanel who introduced the shoe-string shoulder strap, the strapped sandal, the flower on the shoulder, the floating evening scarf, the wearing together of "junk" and real jewels. Chanel launched the vogue for costume jewellery, particularly rows of fake pearls, bead and gold chains and gee-gaw-hung bracelets.

At the height of her career, Chanel was said to be the wealthiest *couturière* in Paris. She was at that time controlling four businesses: the couture house, textile and costume jewellery factories and perfume laboratories for her famous scent. At this time also her private life, particularly her friendship with the second Duke of Westminster, became a subject of constant public interest and speculation. But although Mademoiselle Chanel's engagement to Paul Iribe, a well-known artist and fashion sketcher, was reported in 1933, she never married.

In 1938, after a losing battle with the rising influence of Schiaparelli, Chanel retired from the couture scene. Sixteen years later she staged a spectacular comeback, roused into action it is said by irritation of seeing Paris fashion taken over by men designers. Her first post-war collection in 1954 was ill received by fashion critics, for instead of launching a new fashion revolution, she went on from where she had left off — cardigan suits, short pleated skirts, crisp little blouses, short chiffon and lace dresses, masses of "junk" jewellery. But her timing proved to have been perfect. Rich and famous women once again adopted the Chanel look and when the French magazine *Elle* ran a Chanel pattern they received a quarter of a million requests for it.

In 1957 Chanel won the American Nieman Marcus award for fashion, but even without this official recognition, her continuing influence was indisputable. Many different factors contributed to her success as a dress designer, but chiefly it was the result of immense flair coupled with ruthless good taste. In her own language she described all that she most disliked as *vulgaire*. Her clothes were the antithesis of that.

"Coco" Chanel, fashion designer, was born on August 19, 1883. She died on January 10, 1971, aged 87

—◦◦◦—

DAME KATHLEEN LONSDALE

CRYSTALLOGRAPHER WHO WAS
THE FIRST WOMAN PRESIDENT
OF THE BRITISH ASSOCIATION

APRIL 2, 1971

Dame Kathleen Lonsdale, DBE, FRS, Professor of Chemistry and Head of Department of Crystallography, University College London from 1949 to 1968, died yesterday at the age of 68.

Crystallographer, Quaker and pacifist, she was the first woman president of the British Association for the Advancement of Science. Her presidential address delivered in 1968 was a characteristic utterance aiming darts at a variety of targets: the uses of science and technology; the sale of arms; the narrowness of many scientists and responsibility of scientists as a whole for the use made of their discoveries.

Born January 28, 1903, Kathleen Yardley was the youngest of a large family which had a distant connexion with the makers of perfume. Certainly in later life her appearance was more suggestive of lavender than of the Professor, Dame of the British Empire, vice-president of the Royal Society. The camera could catch her, when she was serious, to give a typical slightly grim look, partly attributable to a depth of eyes exaggerated by lenses, but normally she looked quietly happy. Simply dressed, she was in no way unfeminine. Her hair was usually allowed to blow in the wind and could take on a slightly golliwog form. When she was summoned to Buckingham Palace, on the same day as the leading ballerina, she made herself a neat hat for a few shillings.

After taking her first London degree from Bedford College for Women she became research assistant to Sir William Bragg at the Royal Institution in 1922. At that time X-ray diffraction methods, pioneered by the Braggs, had been applied to determine the arrangement of atoms in the crystalline forms of a few fairly simple chemical substances. The possibility of determining almost any crystal structure, however complex, could be seen but the practical difficulties seemed very great. The relative position of a few atoms could be found; no one yet thought of tackling the detailed structure of a protein containing thousands of atoms though the possible revolutionary effects on the biological sciences could be foreseen.

In fact the general forms but not the dimensions and structural details of the simplest molecules of organic compounds were still known almost entirely from chemists' inferences. In particular the form of the benzene ring, a group of six carbon atoms, the basis of "aromatic" chemistry and perhaps the most disputed of all molecular structures, had not been determined. Kathleen Lonsdale investigated some other organic substances, and years later recalled with glee that her doctorate was awarded for a structure that later was found to have errors, but her first outstanding achievement was to find the structure of the hexamethylbenzene molecule. This showed that the benzene ring consisted of a flat regular hexagon of the six carbon atoms with the other six carbon atoms of attached methyl groups coplanar with the ring. Previously there was no certainty that it was not a puckered non-planar ring and though it was expected by many that all the sides would be equal there were as many who would not have been surprised had it been otherwise. Even today the aromatic ring is for convenience often represented by a drawing suggestive of alternate longer and shorter sides though this first aromatic crystal structure, and a host of others that came after it from the Royal Institution and elsewhere, established the essential equivalence of many carbon-to-carbon bonds which, in a single graphic formula of the molecule, are misrepresented. Much theoretical work on the nature of aromatic compounds followed this demonstration.

She held research appointments as Amy Lady Tate Scholar at Leeds University 1927-29, Leverhulme Research Fellow 1935-37, Dewar Fellow at the Royal Institution 1944-46, Special Fellow of the United States Federal Health Service 1947, and in 1949 became Professor of Chemistry and Head of the Department of Crystallography at University College London. In all these posts she was active in research. Her interest was not in the determination of great numbers of crystal structures or in the unravelling of those of the greatest novelty or complexity. She dealt rather with some aspects of the physics of crystals, the fundamentals of structure determination and some key structures.

Her work included extensive investigations of diamonds, both natural and synthetic — by no means the simple matter that a first examination of this form of elementary carbon might suggest. This work was partly linked with the study of diffuse scattering of X-rays by crystals, which is often related to the movements of atoms in crystal lattices and so may be exploited as an aid to structure determination. She also made detailed studies of thermal movements of atoms in selected lattices at room temperature and at much lower temperatures. One series of investigations contained fundamental work on the magnetic susceptibilities of crystals. From magnetic measurements alone it was possible to calculate the orientations of aromatic molecules in crystals and independent proof of the nature of the complex atomic ring system in the phthalocyanine molecule was obtained.

She also played a great part in the development of her subject, stimulating and in a remarkable way assisting others engaged in it. She wrote a book on crystals and X-rays but is better known for a number of invaluable aids to crystal structure determination. With Astbury, early in her career she put out fault-free descriptions of the 230 Fedorov space groups, a tiresome and difficult feat. In 1936, when the need was felt, she published the first simplified and practical forms of tabulated mathematical formulae for X-ray crystal structure analysis, first working them out and then, in her own neat script, writing nearly two hundred pages of them so that they could be reproduced without the possibility of printer's errors. Later she was general editor for the International Union of Crystallography of the several massive volumes of its International Tables. She served on national and international committees which foster the subject. Her work can be seen in great numbers of scientific communications which do not bear her name.

Many honours came to her from universities and scientific societies at home and throughout the world and she visited many countries to lecture on her work. In 1945 she was elected Fellow of the Royal Society, one of the first women to join it. She was awarded the society's Davy medal in 1957.

It is quite clear where the pursuit of scientific knowledge stood in relation to her adherence to Quaker principles. "We utterly deny all outward wars and strife, and fightings with outward weapons, for any end, or under any pretence whatever: this is our testimony to the whole world." These are the words of the Declaration to Charles II, 1660, which she repeats as preface to *Quakers Visit Russia*.

Once, as a result of her writing to *The Times* complaining about the difficulty of getting funds for certain scientific purposes, a military organization offered support in the form of research contracts. Her reply must have been polite, powerful, and final. When asked, for purposes of obtaining an entry visa, whether she belonged to any peace societies she replied "as many as I can afford". When similarly asked to state her race she said "human". The visit of seven Quakers to Russia in 1951 was made to explain the methods which they believed essential if peace was to be achieved. They did not succeed in seeing Stalin, Gromyko, or Vyshinsky but were received by Malik at the Foreign Office and talked for some hours. The talk seems to have been straight and followed lines that might have been predicted. They met representatives of the Soviet press, the Soviet Peace Committee, and leaders of the Baptist and of the Eastern Orthodox Churches. Kathleen Lonsdale said that the party and those they represented may have been idealists but not simpletons. They were not being "used" by others. What the effect was or may be is not for those of limited knowledge to conjecture. Her other public contributions to peace causes include the Swarthmore Lecture 1953 on "Removing the Causes of War" and the Penguin Special *Is Peace Possible* in 1957.

To the Quaker, conscription for military training is an offence against the human spirit. What service the individual may voluntarily undertake is a matter of conscience. When compulsory fire-watching for civilians was introduced after some of the great air raids in Britain no one bothered about a conscience clause similar to that applicable to ordinary military service. Men and women were called upon to register. Kathleen Lonsdale responded in a way that was inevitable. She did not object to fire-watching — in fact was already doing it — but the Act, without the clause, was contrary to principle. She knew that her three small children would exempt her but she failed to register. Authority could not budge so eventually she refused to pay the fine and went to Holloway. Someone else paid the fine so her stay was short, but she learnt a lot, including the reason for the temporarily assumed religious adherence of the more knowing ladies in detention. It has something to do with lipstick-substitutes and she must have learnt it when they heard, probably for the first time, of the Quaker way of things. She would not wish this incident to be suppressed though she certainly never used it in any boastful way.

Aggressiveness had to show somewhere. She was forthright in committee and inclined, with the best intentions, to stick to rules sometimes to the extent of blocking action. Sessions of the Assembly of the International Union of Crystallography, over which she presided, in Moscow, 1966, were prolonged until she was satisfied that the right things were done and were done in the right way. Walking down the staircase at the British Embassy from a pleasant party, broken off too soon for him, her successor, Professor Belov, as she dragged him on to another committee meeting, was heard to say "Kathleen, you are a martinet".

In 1927 she married Dr T. J. Lonsdale, physicist (and Quaker) like herself. She had a son and two daughters.

Dame Kathleen Lonsdale, DBE, FRS, crystallographer, was born on January 28, 1903. She died on April 1, 1971, aged 68

—◦—

DAME BARBARA HEPWORTH

SCULPTOR WHOSE ABSTRACT AND MONUMENTAL FORMS ECHO THEIR NATURAL SURROUNDINGS

MAY 22, 1975

Dame Barbara Hepworth, who died on May 20, aged 72, was a sculptor of abstract and monumental works in stone, wood and bronze of a quality which gained her an amount of international recognition which few English artists have received. In some ways her work might be compared with that of Mr Henry Moore and it is by no means irrelevant to recall that they came from the same district of Yorkshire, she from Wakefield and Moore from Castleford, a few miles away; that they were students at the same time at the Leeds College of Art and the Royal College of Art. Later in London they had artist friends and ideas in common.

She seems to have developed, somewhat earlier than Moore, the relation of solids and hollows, of exterior and interior forms which they both used to striking effect, though with less of the energy with which he drew forms out of the material. In the comparatively passive shapes she treated with great refinement she might be said to show a feminine quality in contrast with his essentially masculine expression though there is also the difference between her "classic" and his more romantic sense of form.

The formative influences on her art included those of nature. She was responsive in youth to the landscape of the industrial West Riding and the Pennines. Cornwall, where she worked in later life, also evoked an uplift of mood akin to that she derived from Greece. She wrote of the carving in yew ("Nanjizal"), now in the Tate Gallery, as "really my sensations *within* myself" when resting in a Cornish cove with archways through the cliffs. In sculpture the revival of carving found in her a devoted adherent, the texture of surface obtained by this means being one of her main preoccupations. Carving, she defined, in a statement in *Unit One*, 1934, as "a perfect relationship between the mind and the colour, light and weight which is the stone, made by the hand which feels".

From early stylized figures (which found an appreciative buyer in the collector George Eumorfopoulos) she turned towards the abstract in the 1930s. Her ideas in this respect were parallel with those of her second husband, Mr Ben Nicholson. There was much in her work at this period that shows the influence of Brancusi in the simplicity of ovoid shape. Visits to his studio and those of Arp, Picasso, Braque and Mondrian made for a great sympathy with the trend of art on the Continent. In the highly productive post-war years, when she also pursued the study of anatomy and structure in drawings and added proficiency in bronze casting to her accomplishment in carving, she showed most conclusively her ability to conceive a formal and geometrical completeness in harmony with natural surroundings.

Jocelyn Barbara Hepworth was born at Wakefield, on January 10, 1903, the daughter of H. R. Hepworth, CBE, county surveyor, and Gertrude A. Hepworth. After study at the Leeds College of Art, 1920-21, she went to the Royal College of Art, 1921-24, competing for the Prix de Rome in sculpture, which she missed winning by a narrow margin. A West Riding travelling scholarship enabled her to go to Italy, where she met Mr John Skeaping, the sculptor, who had won the Rome competition. They were married in Florence in 1925 and exhibited together. For some years thereafter they were members of the mildly avant-garde "Seven and Five" Society and contributed to its exhibitions but their first comprehensive joint exhibition was held at the Beaux Arts Gallery in 1928.

Both by this time were enthusiasts for direct carving, giving much

Barbara Hepworth working in her garden studio at St Ives, Cornwall, in May 1952

attention to the different qualities of the marble, stone and wood they employed. At a second joint exhibition at Tooth's gallery in 1930 Miss Hepworth was especially praised for her "Mother and Child" in Honiton stone, her work at this stage being more of note for its sensitive treatment of material and craftsmanship than for new departure in style.

From 1931 she worked in association with Mr Ben Nicholson, whom she married after divorce from Mr Skeaping in 1933. They exhibited together at the Lefevre Gallery, where a number of Barbara Hepworth's later exhibitions were held (1933-54) and became jointly active in the groups promoting abstract art, "Unit One", 1933-34,

and in Paris "Abstraction-Création", 1933-35. London remained her headquarters until 1939 when she moved to St Ives, Cornwall. This remained her home and place of work. In 1960 she bought the building that had formerly been the "Palais de Danse" and made it into a studio. In the church nearby is the "Madonna and Child" which she carved in memory of her son Paul, who was killed in action while serving with the RAF in Malaya in 1953.

An increasing interest in modern sculpture brought her work prominently into notice at home and abroad in the 1950s. Monumental commissions included the "Single Form" (bronze) for United Nations, New York, 1963, the Dag Hammarskjöld memorial and the 15ft bronze for the office building in Holborn, State House, a dynamic system of curves.

Perhaps her culminating achievement was the completion in 1972 of the monumental nine-piece group "Family of Man" which she designed to occupy a special hillside setting in Cornwall.

She was the recipient of many awards and honours and was created CBE in 1958 and Dame Commander of the Order of the British Empire in 1965. Her works are widely distributed about the world in museums and private collections. There are monographs by William Gibson, 1946, Sir Herbert Read, 1952, Professor A. M. Hammacher, 1959, Dr J. P. Hodin, 1961, and Michael Shepherd, 1963. A film about her work, *Figures in a Landscape*, was made in 1952-53.

In person she was broad of brow, firm and precise in speech, neat in habits of dress and with a fondness for the outdoors which extended to carving in the open.

The abstract nature of her art implied no coldness of feeling. She was as sensitive to beauty in any form as she was bitter against ugliness, the ugliness she found, for example, in much modern architecture. Undertaking drawings in a hospital in 1947 she feared she might not be able to bear the sight of an operation but in fact found herself absorbed, as she put it in her own words, by "the extraordinary beauty of purpose and coordination between human beings dedicated to the saving of life". She dated her sculpture, it was noted, from intimate and emotional circumstances, a change of style for instance from the birth of her children. Domestic life and children were as important to her as to any woman. She spoke of "this wonderful business of having children" and the care they needed as something that "flowed back" into her work.

Sensitiveness was combined with a strong will and fighting spirit that supported her during the lean years of unpopularity. She was never intimidated by the idea of competing with men in sculpture. The woman's approach, she said, had a different emphasis and a special range of perception. She thought of "the sensation of being a woman" as "another facet of the sculptural idea".

She had four children, the first by her marriage to Mr Skeaping and triplet children, a son and two daughters, born in 1934 by her marriage to Mr Ben Nicholson. Their marriage was dissolved in 1951. She herself designed the tombstone for her grave though it was reported in 1967 to be a problem for local officials as it was 3ft over the permitted height.

Dame Barbara Hepworth, DBE, was born on January 10, 1903. She died in a fire at home, on May 20, 1975, aged 72

DAME AGATHA CHRISTIE

WRITER OF DETECTIVE
FICTION, WHOSE PRINCIPAL
SLEUTHS, HERCULE POIROT
AND MISS MARPLE, HAVE
PROVED ENDLESSLY POPULAR

JANUARY 13, 1976

Dame Agatha Christie, DBE, died yesterday at the age of 85. She belonged to the great period of English detective fiction. Her work typified the *genre*, and, after Dorothy Sayers died, she was recognized as the undoubted queen of her profession.

The popularity of her books not only survived into an era when other crime writers had abandoned detection and were trading in sex and violence, but continued to grow. According to a Unesco report, she was the most widely read British author in the world, with translations into 103 languages — 14 more than Shakespeare. Her principal detectives, Poirot and Miss Marple, hold a secure place on the roll of classic sleuths which is headed by Sherlock Holmes.

She was born in September, 1890, at Torquay, the youngest daughter of Frederick Alvah Miller, an American from New York. "My father", she recalled, "was a gentleman of substance, and never did a handsturn in his life, and he was a most agreeable man". She received little or no formal education, but was brought up in a house full of books and by a mother who encouraged her to read and tell stories. Further encouragement came from Eden Phillpotts, who was a neighbour. When she was 16, she went to Paris to be trained as a singer, but found her voice not strong enough for opera or the concert platform. She wrote some poems and "rather gloomy stories of unrequited love".

In 1914 she married Archibald Christie (later Colonel Archibald Christie, CMG, DSO). While he was in France, she did VAD work at a local hospital and qualified as a dispenser. Her first detective story, *The Mysterious Affair at Styles* (1920), not only utilized her knowledge of poisons but introduced Hercule Poirot, with his egg-shaped head, comically broken English and his reliance on "the little grey cells", who was based on Belgian refugees she had met. The book enjoyed a modest success, but it was her seventh novel, *The Murder of Roger Ackroyd* (1926), which brought fame. In that same year a curious episode occurred: she vanished from her Surrey home, and was found 10 days later, after a nationwide search, staying under a false name in an hotel at Harrogate, apparently suffering from amnesia.

She divorced Colonel Christie in 1928. Left with a daughter to educate, she began to write seriously, and to travel. Two years later, while visiting Sir Leonard Woolley in Iraq,

Agatha Christie at home in 1966

because her readers insisted, she came to think him too artificial a character and she totally discarded the Watson-figure of Captain Hastings. She preferred, and increasingly used, Miss Marple, the inquisitive spinster from *Murder at the Vicarage* (1930), who found the solution to all mysteries in her experience of human behaviour in an English village.

Mrs Christie (as she continued to call herself for professional purposes) also wrote, more or less for her own pleasure, a series of "straight" novels under the strictly guarded pseudonym of "Mary Westmacott", but year after year, throughout the Second World War and the decades which followed, her detective stories continued to be, and usually deserved to be, best sellers. Her style scarcely changed and her inventiveness showed little decline: *Mrs McGinty's Dead* (1952), *4.50 from Paddington* (1957) and *At Bertram's Hotel* (1965) are every bit as good as *Cards on the Table* (1936) or *The Moving Finger* (1943). Her occasional experiments with different formulae, as in *Endless Night* (1967) and *Passenger to Frankfurt* (1970), were perhaps not altogether happy, but her public bought them as enthusiastically as ever and they did serve to demonstrate her continued alertness to social trends and quirks.

she met another archaeologist, Max Mallowan, now Sir Max Mallowan, CBE, Emeritus Professor of Western Asiatic Archaeology in the University of London. They were married almost at once, and she subsequently accompanied him on many of his expeditions to the Middle East, learning to help with photography and the piecing together of shards. Several of her detective stories had a Middle Eastern background, and one, *Death Comes As The End* (1945), was set in Ancient Egypt.

Although she continued to write about Hercule Poirot — *Murder on the Orient Express* (1934) and *The ABC Murders* (1936) were *tours de force* to equal *Roger Ackroyd* — largely

Meanwhile she continued, almost to the end, to publish prolifically with *Nemesis* (1971); *Elephants Can Remember* (1972); *Akhnaton* (1973), a play written in 1937 which had remained unpublished and which she did not intend to be staged; *Poems* (1973); *Postern of Fate* (1973); *Poirot's Early Cases* (1974), and a final salute to her detective hero Poirot entitled *Curtain*, which she had written during the Second World War intending it for posthumous publication, but in fact releasing it in 1975.

She had achieved spectacular success in another field. The stage adaptations of several of her early books (including one of *Roger Ackroyd* with Charles Laughton playing Poirot) had dissatisfied her; so, in 1943, she made her own dramatization of *Ten Little Niggers*, and followed it with a series of other plays, culminating in *The Mousetrap* (1952) with its fantastic London run (at her death it is at the St Martin's Theatre in the 24th year of its world record breaking course) and *Witness for the Prosecution* (1935), the film rights of which were bought by Hollywood for what was then the record price of £116,000.

She never cared much for the cinema, or for wireless and television (though *The Mousetrap* was originally a short radio play, written at the special request of Queen Mary). The famous stage play, *Love from a Stranger* (1936), taken from one of her short stories, was filmed twice, however, and there was a series of adaptations for the screen with Margaret Rutherford as Miss Marple,

notably *4.50 from Paddington. Witness for the Prosecution* was also a notable box office success and, more recently, *Murder on the Orient Express* was launched with a host of stars including Ingrid Bergman, Lauren Bacall and Albert Finney.

Dame Agatha's private pleasures were gardening — she won local prizes for horticulture — and buying furniture for her various houses. She was a shy person — she disliked public appearances — but she was friendly and sharp-witted to meet. By inclination as well as breeding she belonged to the English upper middle-class. She wrote about, and for, people like herself. That was an essential part of her charm.

She was not, in fact, a particularly good writer, certainly not the equal of Dorothy Sayers. But she had a real and subtle narrative gift. Her stories could be gulped down as smoothly and pleasantly as cream. Her handling of the plot-structures, too, was very skilful. She brought a peculiarly English form to its perfect, and perfectly English, flowering. She was, beyond question, one of the half-dozen best detective story writers in the world.

She was created CBE in 1956, and advanced to DBE in 1971.

Dame Agatha Christie, DBE, writer of detective fiction, was born on September 15, 1890. She died on January 12, 1976, aged 85

—◇◇◇—

DAME SYBIL THORNDIKE

HARD-WORKING,
NO-NONSENSE ACTRESS WHO
STARRED IN ROLES RANGING
FROM HECUBA TO ST JOAN

JUNE 10, 1976

Dame Sybil Thorndike had a long and very distinguished career as actress, actress in management, actress on tours overseas, senior actress, and actress in dramatic recitals. To those who worked with her she appeared to be all actress, while to those who knew her in other contexts she appeared to be all daughter, wife, mother, grandmother or great-grandmother; all churchwoman; all musician; all Christian-Socialist and worker for the causes of the left. She deserves to be remembered not only as Lilian Baylis's first regular leading lady in Shakespeare at the Old Vic, as Hecuba and Medea in Gilbert Murray's translations of Euripides, and as Shaw's Saint Joan, but also in her own right, as Canon Thorndike's daughter, Lewis Casson's wife, Dame Sybil.

Born at Gainsborough on October 24, 1882, Agnes Sybil Thorndike grew up at Rochester, where her father, the Rev Arthur J. W. Thorndike, was appointed a minor canon of the cathedral in 1884. As a child she acted in home-made plays, "supported" by her brother Russell and in time by her younger brother Frank and sister Eileen, all of whom went on the stage. But the first art she seriously studied was her mother's art, music, which she took so seriously that she strained her wrist and had to give up professional playing.

Scarcely had she started, at the prompting of her brother Russell, on a new career as an actress than an accident, in the course of her third season with Ben Greet's Shakespearian Company in the United States, threatened to deprive her of her speaking voice. Complete silence effected a cure, and in 1908 she joined Miss Horniman's Repertory Company at Manchester, there renewing acquaintance with Lewis Casson, a young actor of Welsh extraction and, unlike Canon Thorndike, a Socialist. She married him at her father's parish church at Aylesford in December of that year.

Summoned by Ben Greet in 1914 to the Old Vic, where he was directing plays during Lilian Baylis's first Shakespearian season, she remained there, while Casson served in the Army, almost four years, becoming the first great favourite of Lilian Baylis's new audience for Shakespeare in the Waterloo Road. Miss Baylis then encouraged her to return to the West End, but in 1919 allowed the Cassons to present matinees at the Old Vic of Gilbert Murray's translation of the after-the-war play, *The Trojan Women*. Sybil Thorndike's Hecuba and Medea, presented at matinees at the Holborn Empire during the Cassons' first venture into management, were felt to be, with all their faults, performances of tragic stature no other actress of her age in England could have given.

The reward of almost two years' continuous work in Jose G. Levy's experiment in Grand Guignol at the Little was an invitation to the Cassons to associate themselves with Lady Wyndham and Bronson Albery in management at the New. Here, during their first season, she was seen by Bernard Shaw as Shelley's Beatrice Cenci. GBS mentally cast her as Saint Joan in the play that he was considering writing. When written it had to go first to the Theatre Guild in New York, but for England he entrusted it in 1924 to the Albery-Casson management and to Sybil Thorndike. She might still incur criticism on the score of restlessness, hardness, lack of charm, but in this play, which was not a poet's play nor a tragedy, but a Shaw play about a warrior saint, an eccentric worthy, a queer fish, her faults were negligible. Shaw himself admitted it by giving her permission to continue playing the part as long as she wished.

She played it for some eight years in London, Paris, South Africa and Australia. In the intervals she appeared in new plays by Susan Glaspell and Clemence Dane, in Shakespeare under the Albery-Casson management (*Henry VIII* and *Macbeth*) and with Lilian Baylis's Old Vic Company. She also appeared in silent films, notably as Nurse Edith Cavell in *Dawn*. In 1931, when she was approaching 50, she was created DBE.

Dame Sybil's managerial activity now decreased, and her opportunities as an actress were less rewarding, though they included characters in plays by Van Druten and J. B. Priestley — in both of which she was seen on Broadway — and Volumnia to Olivier's Coriolanus. Then Emlyn Williams's *The Corn is Green* showed her at the top of her form as an English spinster with a vocation for teaching, and obtained for her and the author, who himself played the Welsh mining lad who was her star pupil, a heartening success on the eve of war and of new developments in theatrical life.

One of the first professional companies to go out under the auspices of the Council for the Encouragement of Music and the Arts, after it had received financial support from the government, was an old Vic Company led by the Cassons, which in 1940 took *Medea* on a tour of the Welsh coalfields. During the next two years they toured extensively and also appeared at their former West End address, the New, with Old Vic Companies. In 1943 when yet another Old Vic Company began operations at the New, this time in repertoire, with Ralph Richardson and Olivier for leading men and with Tyrone Guthrie directing, Sybil Thorndike was the "heavy" woman, opening as Peer Gynt's mother to Richardson's Peer. She toured with the company in Western Europe and remained with them for the first postwar season, which was regarded as the peak of the English theatre's attainment in state-aided classical work up to that date. She played Mistress Quickly to Richardson's Falstaff in *Henry IV* and Jocasta to Olivier's Oedipus Rex.

She did not go with the company to New York for their guest-season in 1946, but stayed in England, and appeared once again in a play with Casson, who had been knighted in the previous year. There were roles for them both in Priestley's *The Linden Tree* and in a revival of Home's tragedy *Douglas* at the Edinburgh Festival in 1950, but not in *Waters of the Moon*, N. C. Hunter's long-running play at the Haymarket, in which Dame Sybil co-starred with her old friend Dame Edith Evans.

The Cassons rejoined forces in Hunter's next play at the Haymarket, in time for the celebration of her stage jubilee in 1954. During the years that followed they appeared together in many different parts of the world: in India, the Far East and Africa in dramatic recitals; in Australia and New Zealand in plays by Terence Rattigan and Enid Bagnold; in New York in Graham Greene's *The Potting Shed*; and in England in Clemence Dane's *Eighty in the Shade*, a production that commemorated the fiftieth anniversary of their marriage.

In 1962 Dame Sybil undertook with her husband another series of poetry recitals in Australia, appeared with him in Chekhov on the "horse-shoe" stage of the new Festival Theatre at Chichester, this being the type of stage that she said she preferred to all others. A few weeks after attaining the age of 80, she acted, this time without Casson, and sang one number, in a musical version of *Vanity Fair*.

All-star cast: Dame Sybil Thorndike (centre) with Irene Worth, Sir Ralph Richardson, Sir John Gielgud and Sir Lewis Casson at the Haymarket Theatre, London, in 1953

She was also without Casson in the production of William Douglas-Home's political comedy *The Reluctant Peer*. In 1966 she was invited to launch the *Morning Star*, the enlarged successor to the *Daily Worker*. In that year also, the public was invited to subscribe to the building of a theatre at Leatherhead to be called the Thorndike, and the Cassons worked together again, in *Arsenic and Old Lace*, one matinee of which was cancelled to allow them to visit Oxford in order to receive a dual honorary degree — she already had honorary degrees from Manchester, Edinburgh and Southampton — from Mr Harold Macmillan. In 1970 Durham made her an honorary DLitt. In 1967 she was heard once more as Saint Joan during the BBC's Sybil Thorndike Festival, and in 1968 she played, at Oxford, a very long part in a new play by Enid Bagnold, and, on tour, a part that was new to her in a revival of Emlyn Williams's *Night Must Fall*, in which her co-star was the former pop singer Adam Faith.

Sybil Thorndike saw it as her task as an actress to identify herself with as many other characters as possible, especially those whom she would not have wished to associate with had she met their counterparts in actual life. The wish to be at one with them through her work, and to enable audiences to have the same experience, was for her a part of religion, and the attempt to realize it was for her, again, an exercise that could be called religious. This did not come easily to her, except perhaps in *Saint Joan*,

for, if she herself is to be believed, her spirit was always larger than her capacities. In developing the latter she owed much to the inspiration of music; something to her film work and to film directors such as Hitchcock (in *Stagefright*) and Olivier (in *The Prince and the Showgirl*), who encouraged her to play "down" and to aim at being 10 times smaller than life and yet true to it; and as much to her sense of humour, which had once, in the wartime blackout, cautioned her against wailing too loud off-stage as Medea, lest audiences might be deceived into supposing that her voice was an air-raid warning.

Her husband died in May, 1969, at the age of 93, but she remained undefeated and was present with ticket No 1 at the gala opening night of the Thorndike Theatre in September. Soon afterwards she appeared at the theatre in *There Was an Old Woman*. In June, 1970, she was created a Companion of Honour and two months later exuberantly opened the new adjunct to the National Theatre known as the Young Vic.

By her marriage to Casson she had two sons, John and Christopher, and two daughters, Mary and Ann, all of whom have at some time acted. In 1929 the freedom of the city of Rochester was conferred on her. In 1938 a memoir of Lilian Baylis by Sybil and Russell Thorndike was published. Never can biographers have been more in sympathy with their subject, or the subject of a biography have owed more, while she lived and worked, to those who described her work afterwards. Dame Sybil also edited a personal anthology of prose and verse, *Favourites*, which appeared in 1973. Of this daughter of the vicarage and parish worker it may be said that she lived to become the best-loved English actress since Ellen Terry.

Dame Sybil Thorndike, CH, DBE, actress, was born on October 24, 1882. She died on June 9, 1976, aged 93

———

DAME EDITH EVANS

VERSATILE AND ADVENTUROUS ACTRESS BEST REMEMBERED FOR ONE CRESCENDO OF SCANDALIZED HORROR

OCTOBER 15, 1976

Dame Edith Evans was an actress of genius with an assured place in the history of English acting. Her genius, though primarily comic, expressed itself in an extraordinarily wide range of parts. In Restoration comedy she was unrivalled. Her playing in romantic comedy, Elizabethan and modern, made precious additions to playgoing memories. She could etch in melodrama a figure of macabre terror such as Agatha Payne in *The Old Ladies* (1935). She emerged from her rare ventures into tragedy never without honour and sometimes, for instance as the Rebecca West of *Rosmersholm*

(1926), with the highest distinction. Her unforgettable stage personality was shaped by an exuberant vitality which technical accomplishment held delicately in check and by an imagination that flashed across the character impersonated penetrating glances of mischief, irony, gaiety and pathos.

To each of her parts she appeared to bring the special acting technique of the period to which it belonged. As Millamant (1924 and 1927); as Lady Wishfort (1948); as Mrs Sullen (1927 and 1930); as Lady Fidget (1936); she induced the audience to believe that now they knew exactly what fine Restoration acting was like. Yet her nurse in *Romeo and Juliet* (England 1926, 1932, 1935, 1961; New York 1934), a piece of boisterously chuckling low life with overtones of rough pathos, seemed the epitome of earthy Elizabethan humour. A vicar's troubled wife; a staunch Welsh servant maid; a half-insane old sadist of a provincial lodging house; the brandy-drinking lady of *Daphne Laureola* (London 1949; New York 1950), startling a crowded modern restaurant with a burst of contralto song and a stream of embarrassing reminiscence — the treatment of all these diverse creatures exhibited the same nice adjustment of appropriate technical means to dramatic ends.

But nobody was ever so foolish as to measure the pleasures Edith Evans offered with a technical yardstick. What makes acting an art is not the imitation of external things but the spirit that informs the imitation. The comic spirit of the actress was ever ready to sally forth with gay knight-errantry to make "a new conquest over dullness." Some familiar passage in classic comedy would solicit her attention, and then every word, every syllable even, would appear to spring in her some fresh delighted sense of the humour inherent in the whole; and when she had been happily delivered the audience knew that an old jest had been born anew. She could turn a piece of Restoration bawdry with such delicacy that it took on a delusive air of fine wit, and when she was Millamant mocking Mirabell the mockery was drawn out so deliciously that we wished it never to end.

Edith Evans played Cleopatra in two different plays, Dryden's *All For Love* (1922) and Shakespeare's (1925 and 1946). If she was not meant by nature to play tragic heroines she was certainly meant to speak Shakespeare's verse. She had a strong internal word-sense which enabled her to challenge, if she wished, the conventionally accepted colours and resonances of a famous speech. No other actress has made so much of the soliloquy in which Viola considers the possibility that her disguise has fatally charmed Olivia: in a score of lines she explored depths of comic irony that have not been hinted at since. Was there ever a Rosalind more alive than hers to the pure humour of being happily in love? Her internal word-sense served her not only in the speaking of verse. From William Poel

she had learned that the voice, to be audible in a theatre, must be kept running up and down the scale. She put this serviceable general rule to highly individual comic use. She could turn a single word, the "hand-bag!" of Lady Bracknell when she hears that her prospective son-in-law has been born in one, to a wondrous crescendo of scandalized horror.

Only at the very end did Edith Evans sometimes give way to the temptation to parody her own mannerisms. At the height of her powers she was an actress of unending subtlety and perpetual surprises, compelling laughter or tears as she wished. When she burst on the town at Hammersmith in 1924 in *The Way of the World* she made Millamant appear the supreme heroine of the English comic stage. Millamant has never appeared so since, though Edith Evans many years later brought that comedy to life with Lady Wishfort, appallingly funny in her stark reality, as its central character.

Born on February 8, 1888, in London, the only child of Edward Evans who was a civil servant in the Post Office and not of Welsh descent — nor was his wife Welsh — Edith Evans was apprenticed at the age of 14 to a milliner. She remarked in later years that she loved rich and beautiful materials but had nevertheless found it hard to make two hats alike. At 16 she began attending a dramatic class in Victoria Street, which developed into a club known as the Streatham Shakespeare Players. William Poel saw her play Beatrice at Streatham in 1912, and chose her for the part of Cressida in a production of his own at King's Hall, Covent Garden, later in the same year. Immediately afterwards she gave up her milliner's job in Wood Street, Cheapside. Her professional stage career seems in retrospect to fall into three periods, the third coinciding with a film career which began in 1948 when she was 60.

The first began with a Stage Society production of a comedy by George Moore in 1913 — Moore had intended her to play the lead in this, but was overruled —and culminated in *The Way of the World* at the Lyric, Hammersmith (1924). The triumph of her Millamant was founded on the experience of such early campaigns as a Shakespearian tour in Ellen Terry's company (1918), Lady Utterword in the original *Heartbreak House* (1921), the first cycle of *Back to Methuselah* at the Birmingham Repertory Theatre (1923) and special appearances for the Phoenix Society in *Venice Preserv'd* and *All for Love* and for the Stage Society in *The Witch of Edmonton.*

The second period covered the next 20 years, from *The Way of the World* at Hammersmith to the end of the Second World War, and was that of the definition of her full range as an actress: of the things she could do as well as, or better than, anyone else, and of those she could do only moderately or not at all. The positive and the negative were both adumbrated in the course of her first season at the Old Vic (1925-1926) under Andrew Leigh as director, with Mr Baliol Holloway as leading man: a season beginning with her Portia of Belmont, continuing with her Cleopatra, and ending, during the General Strike, with Beatrice — and in which, on her only free day from rehearsals, she married George Booth, a petroleum engineer. He died in 1935. Performances of absolute assurance given by Edith Evans during the second period included those in *Tiger Cats* (1924 and 1931), *The Beaux' Stratagem* (1927 and 1930), *The Lady with a Lamp* (London 1929, New York 1931), *The Apple Cart* (1929), *Evensong* (London 1932, New York 1933), *The Late Christopher Bean* (1933), *The Seagull* (1936, under Komisarjevsky), *Robert's Wife* (1937) and *The Importance of Being Earnest* (1939).

She was again seen in Wilde's comedy during the war years, and also both at home and overseas in *Heartbreak House*, on this occasion as Mrs Hushabye. Other wartime appearances of hers were in two editions of the revue *Diversion* at Wyndham's; in a revue at Gibraltar for the forces; in new plays by Miss Clemence Dane and Van Druten; at the Garrison Theatre, Salisbury; and in India in *The Late Christopher Bean* for ENSA. This period also included two ventures in management: one jointly with Leon M. Lion at Wyndham's in 1927, opening with a short-lived comedy adapted from the French, and the other at the Prince of Wales' in 1930. Her part in the play presented there was Delilah. She had invested all her savings in it. It ran for just three days.

Her return to London as Mrs Malaprop in September, 1945, shortly before she was created a DBE in 1946 inaugurated the third period. Though it was to include other classical parts — Shakespeare's Cleopatra (this time opposite Godfrey Tearle) in 1946; Lady Wishfort, Mme Ranevsky and Henry VIII's Queen for the Old Vic Company — as well as appearances in films, perhaps the most distinctive feature of these years was the quality of her work in a series of new plays: *Daphne Laureola* (London, 1949, New York, 1950), *Waters of the Moon* (1951), *The Dark Is Light Enough* (1954) and *The Chalk Garden* (1956). In 1959, she went to Stratford for the first time since 1913, to play the Countess in *All's Well That Ends Well* for Tyrone Guthrie; and Volumnia to Olivier's Coriolanus, followed in 1961 by Queen Margaret in *Richard III*, in which year she also played the Nurse in *Romeo and Juliet*. Roles in *Hay Fever* (1964) and *Dear Antoine* were only two in a seemingly never-ending stage career.

If she did not necessarily show new aspects of her art in these plays, she added a dimension to what was there already. Her performances were now like comments not only on human nature, but also on acting generally, on her own acting, and on herself. She told us less, and what she told us was sometimes repetitive; but in a sense it implied more than it used to do. Bridie's Lady Pitts, Mr Fry's Countess Rosmarin and Miss Bagnold's Mrs St Maugham would not have been such "high women" as they seemed, unless they had felt inside them, and caused us to feel, too, the Millamant, the Rosalind, the favourite of Shaw's King Magnus, that Edith Evans had been in her own prime.

Her film career had begun in 1948 with a version of Pushkin's *The Queen of Spades*, followed in the same year by *The Last Days of Dolwyn*, written and directed by Emlyn Williams. In the cinema she was able, as in the theatre, to place her experience of life, clarified as she had said earlier, by Time, fully at the service of acting. *The Importance of Being Earnest* (1951) gave us another peerless performance, as Lady Bracknell, and her fourth and fifth films, Tony Richardson's *Look Back in Anger* and Fred Zinnemann's *The Nun's Story*, were both shown in 1959. Tony Richardson's *Tom Jones* followed in 1963, succeeded by *The Chalk Garden* (1963); *Young Cassidy* (1965); *Fitzwilly Strikes Back* (1966); and *Prudence and the Pill* (1967).

Bryan Forbes's film *The Whisperers*, in the same year, won her the best actress award at the 1967 Berlin Film Festival and later films included *David Copperfield*, *Scrooge* (both 1970); and *A Doll's House* (1973). Many of her old stage roles were heard again on radio during this period and she appeared on television where a version of Dostoevsky's *The Gambler* was screened by the BBC to celebrate her eightieth birthday. In the 1950s she had had honorary doctorates conferred on her by the Universities of London (1950), Cambridge (1951) and Oxford (1954).

Had Edith Evans died in her fifties, she would probably be remembered chiefly as a comedienne: for her Millamant; her Mrs Sullen; her Rosalind; for — as James Agate called it — her smile of happy deliverance on uttering an author's wittiest conceits. Having lived long enough to show us also the pensioner subject to illusions in *The Whisperers* and the grandmother who lost a fortune at the tables in *The Gambler* — but not Lady Macbeth, a part she always refused because she found the character incredible — she deserves to be remembered not only as a comedienne, but also as an actress of the highest dedication.

Dame Edith Evans, DBE, actress, was born on February 8, 1888. She died on October 14, 1976, aged 88

—∾∾—

CECIL WOODHAM-SMITH

INSIGHTFUL BIOGRAPHER AND HISTORIAN OF THE VICTORIAN ERA

MARCH 17, 1977

Cecil Woodham-Smith was one of the most gifted biographers and narrative historians of her generation. She did not begin writing seriously until her children were at boarding school, and it is in the context of only four books

— *Florence Nightingale* (1950), *The Reason Why* (1953), *The Great Hunger* (1962) and *Queen Victoria* (1972) — that she displayed an attention to detail, a flair for storytelling, and an historical and human intelligence that set her work apart. She was doubly fortunate in possessing both the means to take time over her work and the talent to use her good fortune wisely and well. She organized her material brilliantly.

Cecil Blanche Woodham-Smith was born in April 1896, the daughter of Colonel James Fitzgerald, of the family of Lord Edward Fitzgerald, hero of the Irish Rising in 1798. Although her home was never in Ireland, she set great store by her Irish ancestry and during her time at St Hilda's College, Oxford, her pro-Irish sympathies were much in evidence; more than thirty years later these sympathies were directed into her most sombre and relentless work, *The Great Hunger*. In 1928 she married George Ivon Woodham-Smith, a lawyer of distinction who became the enthusiastic manager of her literary affairs; by him she had a son and a daughter and the marriage was exceptionally close and deep. When he died in 1968, some of the impetus behind her work died with him.

Before marriage she had written articles and short stories, and in the late 1930s wrote three pot-boiling novels under the name of Janet Gordon, but she did not begin research on *Florence Nightingale* until 1941. She was always a meticulous worker and the book was not ready for publication until nine years later, when it was acclaimed on both sides of the Atlantic, its rare combination of scholarship and readability commending it to professional historians and general public alike. An authoritative life of Florence Nightingale had been long overdue, and here was one at last to do justice to the complexity — part commonsense, part saintliness — of the subject. It stands as a milestone in the reviving study of the Victorians that distinguished the middle years of our century.

The Reason Why must be seen in the same light, a brilliant analysis of that central Victorian episode, the Charge of the Light Brigade. It is constructed on the two fatally converging biographies of Lords Lucan and Cardigan, and is as memorable for its characterization of these men and their colleagues as for its grand landscape painting of Victorian society, the festering Balkans and the cruel, glittering plains of the Crimea itself; few women have written so well of armies on the march.

These two are masterpieces of refined information. If there is a slight falling-off in the two later works, it is from this very high standard and has nothing to do with accuracy or scholarship, both of which remained impeccable. It is rather because the process of documentary investigation seemed to become an absorbing pleasure in itself, sometimes at the expense of the narrative line. In *The Great Hunger* she was writing of the subject perhaps nearest to her heart, the distress of Ireland, and did not always know when to let well — or rather, ill — alone, and get

on with the terrible tale. It remains a formidable and moving account, with a mass of invaluable matter, much of it almost parenthetical ("In Erris today there are many people who have never seen a train; in 1847 there were many who had never seen a living tree larger than a shrub").

With *Queen Victoria*, the first volume of which appeared in 1972, she entered for the first time a field already claimed by a talent the equal of hers — Elizabeth Longford's *Victoria RI* had been greeted as definitive for its time in 1964, and some commentators questioned the need for another Life so soon. In fact, both books hold their place: Mrs Woodham-Smith was careful not to read her predecessor and, whilst covering much of the same ground in great detail, produced a very different work. No other life of Queen Victoria has defined quite so sharply the exact nature of the young Princess's horrible childhood (Mrs Woodham-Smith perused the Conroy Papers at Balliol with particular thoroughness) or shown quite so clearly the emotional violence recurrent in the Queen's marriage to Albert.

In this, of course, she prepared the way for Victoria's hysterical mourning to open the second volume of the biography, on which she had been working since 1972. Characteristically she unearthed such a wealth of attractive new information on such figures as Sir John Conroy, Princess Feodora, the Queen's half-sister, Henry Cole, planner of the Great Exhibition, and George Anson, Albert's private secretary, that she was actively looking forward to assembling a further volume of "brief lives" to complement the main work.

In life as in scholarship and literature Cecil Woodham-Smith was a perfectionist, content only with the highest standards even in such everyday matters as dress, furniture and food. A good lecturer and most entertaining in conversation, she was sharply witty in speech, but sympathetic and generous in action, especially to her fellow-writers and to young people. In 1960 she was made a CBE, made an honorary Doctor of Literature at the National University of Ireland in 1964 and at St Andrews in 1965. She was an honorary Fellow of St Hilda's.

Cecil Woodham-Smith, CBE, historian and biographer, was born on April 29, 1896. She died on March 16, 1977, aged 80

—◇◇◇—

JOAN CRAWFORD

A HOLLYWOOD STAR PERSONALITY IN THE GRAND MANNER

MAY 12, 1977

Her most devoted admirers would never have claimed that Miss Joan Crawford was an actress of great range or adaptability: her secret lay rather in doing one thing at a time and doing it superlatively well. She never puzzled her public by appearing in quick succession in a wide variety of parts; at any given period of her career the filmgoer who went to a Joan Crawford film knew just what sort of thing to expect, and knew too that he could expect it to be the best of its kind. Nevertheless, during her long reign as uncrowned queen of Hollywood she showed a remarkable ability to remodel her public personality in accordance with the demands of the public, a quality which betokens, if not necessarily a great actress, at least a great star.

She was born at San Antonio, Texas, at a date variously placed between 1901 and 1908 and her real name was Lucille Le Sueur. She did not take the name of Joan Crawford until after her success in *Sally, Irene and Mary* in 1925. She once wrote of herself that she was convinced from childhood that she possessed talent, but was uncertain what that talent might be. At first it appeared to be for dancing, and she began her professional career as a song-and-dance performer in a small café in Chicago. From there she graduated to the chorus of a J. J. Shubert revue in New York called *Innocent Eyes*, and then into that of one called *The Passing Show of 1925*. Here she was seen by an MGM talent scout and invited to Hollywood.

She appeared in her first film the same year. This was *Pretty Ladies*, which starred Norma Shearer and ZaSu Pitts. During the next three years she appeared in a number of films, among them comedies with Harry Langdon and Charles Ray, but did not make any great mark until *Our Dancing Daughters* (1928), which first established her as one of the most potent and enduring legends of the American screen: indeed, since the death of Gary Cooper, Joan Crawford could claim to be the only major star of silent films still at the top of the acting profession in Hollywood.

After this film her progress was rapid: a number of similar films followed — *Our Modern Maidens* in 1929, *Our Blushing Brides* in 1930 — which all served to strengthen her position as the foremost representative of "flaming youth" on the screen. In the early 1930s, however, she began to broaden her scope with dramatic roles in such films as *Grand Hotel* (with Garbo, Wallace Beery and John and Lionel Barrymore) and the first talking version of *Rain*. But in 1936 the mood of the times was changing, and in accordance with the new demands of the public a new, "mature" Joan Crawford was seen in a series of sophisticated comedies, most notably *The Gorgeous Hussy* (1936), *The Last of Mrs Cheyney* (1937) and *The Women* (1939). It was at this period that an American exhibitor made the much publicized statement that a number of top stars, among them Katharine Hepburn and Joan Crawford, were "box-office poison" — which, though frequently quoted, did not prevent any of the people concerned from continuing their highly successful careers for, in several cases, another 20 years or so.

During the 1940s, after appearing with notable improbability as a mink-clad heroine of the French resistance in *Reunion in France* (1942), Joan Crawford was absent from the screen for three years through illness. Her return in 1945 with *Mildred Pierce* gave her one of her most spectacular successes and an Academy Award, as well as setting the pattern for her next few films, all of which, with slight variations, recounted the rise of a girl "from the wrong side of the tracks" to fame and fortune, though seldom to happiness. Particularly memorable were *Humoresque* (1947), from a screenplay by Clifford Odets about a rich music-lover who becomes too closely involved with her protégé, and *Flamingo Road* (1949) with its intriguing glimpses of Miss Crawford as a dancer in a fifth-rate roadshow. *Sudden Fear* (1952) marked a further development; from now on a new toughness and sometimes even savagery marked the characters she portrayed in such films as *Torch Song*, *Johnny Guitar* and *Female on the Beach*. In 1957 she came to this country to make her first British film, *The Story of Esther Costello*.

After a year or two away from the screen after the death of her fourth husband Alfred Steele, she returned in a series of strong roles in more or less horrific films, starting with *Whatever Happened to Baby Jane?*, in which she starred for the first time with her one-time greatest rival Bette Davis; after this came *The Caretaker*, *Straitjacket*, another film with Bette Davis, *Hush... Hush, Sweet Charlotte*, and *Trog* (1971).

Of her performances perhaps the most memorable were those in *Grand Hotel*, *The Women* (as Crystal Allen, the shopgirl vamp), *Sudden Fear*, *Torch Song* (as a savagely successful stage-star who is wooed at last to reason and domesticity) and *Autumn Leaves*, the story of a middle-aged woman who marries a man half her age. Joan Crawford was a personality in the grand manner; Hollywood will never be the same without her.

She was four times married, to: (1) Douglas Fairbanks, junior, (2) Franchot Tone, (3) Phil Terry, (4) Alfred Steele. Steele, who died in 1959, was chairman of the Pepsi-Cola Company and after his death Joan Crawford joined the board.

Joan Crawford, actress, was born on March 23, somewhere in the period 1901-1908. She died on May 10, 1977, aged between 69 and 76

———

MARIA CALLAS

POWERFULLY DRAMATIC OPERATIC SOPRANO

SEPTEMBER 17, 1977

Miss Maria Callas, the most colourful, exciting and traditionally powerful *prima donna* of the mid-twentieth century, whose career showed the hallmarks of genius, died yesterday at the age of 53.

Ever since 1948 she has added something intensely flamboyant and vividly personal to the world of international opera, for in the age of the common man, when even sopranos, whatever their quality, are expected to be rather like everybody else, she insisted upon being entirely herself.

Maria Meneghini Callas was born in New York, of Greek parents, on December 3, 1923; her second name she took from her Italian husband, Giovanni Meneghini, whom she married in 1947, but she took Greek citizenship in 1966 to facilitate a lengthy divorce suit which ended the marriage. She had returned to Greece with her family in 1936, and studied at the Athens Conservatoire. She was seen several times at the Athens Opera during and immediately after the Second World War — her first role was that of Martha, in d'Albert's *Tiefland* — before marriage took her to Italy and the beginning of the most spectacular career in modern operatic history. After an initial appearance in the Verona amphitheatre in Ponchielli's *La Gioconda*, she was at once accepted as a brilliant exponent of the "heavy" soprano roles: Aida, Turandot, Isolde, Brünnhilde, and Kundry fell to her advance without a struggle, but the note of the incredible was sounded when within a single week in 1949 she not only sang Brünnhilde in *Die Walküre* but also deputized for an indisposed coloratura as Elvira in Bellini's *I Puritani*, dealing accurately and spectacularly with the elaborate vocal gymnastics of the role.

From then onwards she began to drop the great heroic roles from her repertoire and to specialize in the bel canto heroines of Rossini, Bellini and Donizetti, to which she added those of the early and middle period Verdi operas. The unhappy Lucia of Lammermoor, Verdi's Violetta and Gilda, Bellini's Norma and Cherubini's Medea were roles in which she spectacularly succeeded, and she found herself in demand, with audiences at her feet, wherever such works were sung. Rossini's *Il Turco in Italia* provided her with a great success as Fiorilla; she sang Euridice in the first modern performance of Haydn's *Orfeo ed Euridice* in Florence in 1951. The change in her repertoire was no more startling than the change in her appearance; her Brünnhilde had been an imposingly Wagnerian figure, but the new Callas of the great Italian operas was slim, elegant, "glamorous" in the sense that Hollywood has applied to that adjective, and as fiery in her dealings with conductors and impresarios as was her Tosca — a role she never relinquished — in dealing with Baron Scarpia. Like any of the great sopranos of the past she knew her worth and expected to dominate conductors and colleagues as well as her audiences. Unlike most singers of the twentieth century, she never moved outside opera, although her versatility within that wide field suggests that she might have sung other things no less memorably. When asked why she never gave a song recital, the story goes, she replied that she had never found time from operatic engagements to learn the songs that she might sing.

The effectiveness of her style and the magnetism of her personality made her one of the most powerfully effective instruments in the revival of interest in *bel canto* opera after 1945. There have been, and are, voices more sensuously beautiful in themselves than was that of Maria Callas, capable of a more moving pathos and equally attractive throughout as wide a register: in vertiginous regions towards the high E flat that was her upper limit, Callas's voice was usually thin and, when she was in less than her best form, it could be shrill. It was, however, remarkably athletic and accurate, so that Norma's *Casta Diva*, an aria published, and usually sung, in F was, in her performances, put up to the G that is supposed to have been Bellini's original key for the aria. Her florid singing, especially in her lower register, was always brilliant and exciting.

It was, however, the dramatic truth of her performances which conquered the operatic world. Her greatest days coincided with those of Joan Sutherland, and whilst the Australian *prima donna* seemed incapable of singing a note which sounded less than perfectly and fully moulded, Maria Callas held her own against the tremendous opposition of Miss Sutherland's well-nigh perfect voice because she was, in reality, an actress of genius whose field of action was opera and not spoken drama. She developed to an unusual degree the power of timing action and gesture along the line of their music in a way which seemed always dramatically true and could, by the force of her personality and the exactitude of her characterization, convince any audience that the speed or slowness of such actions and gestures was that natural to the character at the moment in question. Not only, as she played them, were Isolde and Aida real personalities whose tragedies referred to the depths of human experience; the harassed heroines of Bellini and Donizetti too became equally real personages of heightened intensity. The music of the closing scene of *La Traviata* may itself suggest that Violetta is weak and mortally ill, but Callas's interpretation went beyond that; it had the somewhat frenetic gaiety which can be associated with tuberculosis and it added to the halting pathos of the last act a voice made husky and veiled by the progress of the disease.

For many years Maria Callas's relationship with the late Aristotle Onassis, the shipowner, was the most widely

The glamorous and fiesty Maria Callas at her London hotel before her appearance in La Traviata *in 1958*

publicized *affaire* in the world. She denied, however, that after Onassis married Mrs Jacqueline Kennedy, widow of the American President, she attempted suicide.

Almost as well publicized was the action which, in the late 1960s, Onassis and Callas brought alleging non-fulfilment of an agreement made with their former friend, Mr Panaghis Vergottis, another Greek shipowner. The case went finally to the House of Lords, with Vergottis seeking a retrial, but the Lords upheld Mr Justice Roskill's earlier decision that Callas was entitled to receive shipping shares in return for an advance of £60,000, the venture having been made to provide for her on her eventual retirement.

By 1965, when she last appeared at Covent Garden, she had no more operatic worlds to conquer, and her dramatic genius seemed to express itself powerfully in these domestic fields. Her withdrawal from the opera stage was not, however, a complete retirement. In autumn 1973, with the tenor Giuseppe di Stefano and the pianist Ivor Newton, she undertook a series of recitals — her first with piano accompaniment — in Europe, ending with two performances in the Royal Festival Hall. Her programmes consisted mainly of arias and duets from Italian opera, sung with her accustomed dramatic intensity. Though, in other respects, her personality seemed to have mellowed into a new cooperativeness and warmth, she generated in the calm surroundings of the Festival Hall the intensity of feeling that had belonged to her stage performances. Her audiences, refusing to leave the hall, or to end their tumultuous homage, will remember her as a splendidly elegant, slim, and gracious personality at whose command they sorrowed, rejoiced, feared and adored.

The greatness of Maria Callas was that of an actress able to impress on the improbably romantic heroines with whom she was associated, or upon the melodramatics of Tosca, a passionate reality which she had found, earlier in her career, in the more profound and exalted works of late Verdi and Wagner. Singing was not, for her, an end in itself through which she could express all there was to say about a character; it was another instrument in the hands of a powerful, vivid and exciting romantic actress.

Maria Callas, operatic soprano, was born on December 3, 1923. She died on September 16, 1977, aged 53

—⁓—

NADIA BOULANGER

TEACHER, CONDUCTOR
AND COMPOSER WHO MADE
AN UNRIVALLED IMPACT ON
THE MUSICAL LIFE OF THE
20TH CENTURY

NOVEMBER 13, 1979
Mademoiselle Nadia Boulanger, the remarkable all-round French musician,

died on October 22 at the age of 92 after a long life of intense activity in more than one branch of music. Famed chiefly as a teacher, who attracted to Paris students from all over the world, she was also a conductor specialising in vocal music of all periods and in her time had been assistant to her former teacher, Alexander Guilmant, at the organ of the Madeleine in Paris. As a composer she won the second Prix de Rome in 1908 with a cantata, *La Sirène*, and had songs, orchestral pieces and incidental music (to d'Annunzio's *Città morte*) to her credit, but it is chiefly through others that her great influence was exercised, either through her interpretations of other composers, or through her pupils.

Her family had a tradition of music going back to her grandfather, who had won a prize for cello playing in 1797. His son, her father, taught singing at the Paris Conservatoire for 27 years. Her mother was a Russian, née Princess Mychetsky, who was an accomplished singer. Her younger sister Lilli, who died in 1918, made a mark as a composer.

Nadia Boulanger was born in Paris on September 16, 1887. She was trained at the Paris Conservatoire under Fauré for composition and obtained first prizes in harmony, counterpoint, fugue, organ and accompaniment, so that whatever her imaginative endowment as a composer she could not be other than a first-class musician, as the rest of her career showed. On her first visit to England in 1936 she introduced Fauré's *Requiem* and in the following year she conducted a whole programme for the Royal Philharmonic Society, which included works by Monteverdi, of whom she became (and remained) an expert interpreter. Years later she came to England to take part in Bath Festivals, when she directed programmes that exactly represented her taste, consisting of Monteverdi, Stravinsky and Fauré. It was observed on one of these occasions that this unlikely conjunction of styles indicated that Mlle Boulanger's musical personality favoured clarity, objectivity and serious devotion, which are the qualities that her pupils find most strongly marked in her.

There is no doubt that she was a great teacher — and teachers of composition are rare, since if they are too strong minded they will suffocate their pupils' individualities. Mlle Boulanger did not altogether escape this danger and was sometimes charged with teaching an arid form of pseudo-Stravinsky to all comers. Indeed her disciples were sometimes jocularly called products of *la Boulangerie*. But there is other testimony to her ability to preserve and stimulate the individual personality. Among her American pupils were Copland, Harris, Bernstein and Piston; among her English ones, Lennox Berkeley and Professor Lewis. She taught at three institutions, the Paris Conservatoire, the École Normale de Musique and the American Conservatory at Fontainebleau, and was indefatigable into her seventies in exerting her magnetic personality upon her pupils and upon the groups of singers and players she gathered round her for carrying her ideas of interpretation into effect. As far back as 1925 she first made a lecture-tour of the United States; she came to Britain pretty frequently during the past 30 years usually to broadcast for the BBC, sometimes to take master-classes at the Royal College of Music; she made records of Monteverdi; indeed she impressed herself upon the musical life of the twentieth century as few but great composers and international virtuosi have done, and certainly as no other woman did. As long ago as 1937 she conducted a concert given by the Royal Philharmonic Orchestra, the first woman to conduct a whole programme for that society.

In the 1960s she conducted both the New York Philharmonic and the Hallé orchestras. She was a Grand Officier of the Legion of Honour and an honorary CBE and was the recipient of several honorary doctorates.

Nadia Boulanger, CBE, teacher, conductor and award-winning composer, was born on September 16, 1887. She died on October 22, 1979, aged 92

GOLDA MEIR

PRIME MINISTER OF ISRAEL WHO NEGOTIATED WITH HENRY KISSINGER THE DISENGAGEMENT OF TROOPS IN SINAI AND THE GOLAN HEIGHTS

NOVEMBER 16, 1979 (*The Times Obituaries Supplement*)
Mrs Golda Meir, who died on December 8, 1978, at the age of 80, was Israel's fourth Prime Minister, having taken over the office in March 1969 on the sudden death of Mr Levi Eshkol.

Golda Meir had previously served as Minister for Foreign Affairs, Minister of Labour, Ambassador to the Soviet Union and Secretary General of Mapai — the largest political party in the country, approximately the same political colour as the British Labour Party. She had retired from public life, or so she had said, but had been at leisure for only a very short time before she was called upon to take up the highest political position. She retired in June 1974.

Mrs Meir (née Mabovitch) was born in Kiev, in southwest Russia, on May 3, 1898. Her family and background were much the same as those of the many thousands of Jews who went to Britain and the United States at the turn of the century. Members of an underprivileged and discriminated against minority, they sought their fortune in

the west where they had been told freedom and equality were there for the
taking, and wealth could be earned or
seized. They found the freedom, but too
often it was accompanied by poverty
and misery.

Golda was the middle one of three
sisters — survivors of eight children born to their parents. Her father
left Kiev in advance to prepare a
place for his family in Milwaukee.
Mrs Mabovitch and the three girls
went to wait in the mother's home town,
Pinsk. There Golda's older sister, a
teenager, joined a revolutionary youth
movement and the Mabovitch home
was one of their secret meeting places.
Golda heard the whispered arguments
of the ideal society that would one day
come, and the socialism she learnt at
the time remained with her all her life.
Only later as Prime Minister did she
mellow into a more muted political
colour, when she realized that national
economic needs did not always fit into
left-wing slots.

When eventually the family were
reunited in Milwaukee, the father was
not even making an adequate living,
and the parents saw no possibility
— nor even any need — for a higher
education for their daughter, although
she had done well at school. She ran
away to her older sister, by then married
and living in Denver. They quarrelled
and Golda went to live on her own,
working first in a laundry and then in
a department store. Eventually, her
parents hearing of her plight became
reconciled and she returned home,
went back to school and finished her
training to become a teacher. A slight
"schoolmarmy" tinge in her attitude to
those who opposed her views remained
with her.

While still in Denver she met and fell
in love with Morris Myerson, but at that
period also she became imbued with
the Zionist aim and joined the Poale
Zion — the labour wing of the World
Zionist Organization, which in the State
of Israel became the party of Mapai.
She married Myerson although he was
not a Zionist and even persuaded him
that they must go and live in Palestine.
They set sail in May, 1921, when Golda
was 23, already mature and determined
to follow the path she had set herself no
matter what. The twenties were a time
of almost economic bankruptcy for the
small Jewish community in Palestine.
The Myersons went to live on a kibbutz
— as most newcomers did then, having
very little choice in the matter, but also
an idealistic urge to do so.

However, this was altogether too
much for Morris. He wanted to return to
the United States. They compromised
by going to live in Tel Aviv, where
they barely made two ends meet. Yet
for Golda it represented the opportunity for taking on public work. Though
they had two children, she more and
more became involved in politics —
her family life was the price she paid.
She and her husband separated. At
first she spent long periods abroad on
behalf of the Labour Women's Council,
but later she became a member of the
executive of the General Federation
of Labour (the Histadrut), and of the
World Zionist Organization, the then

de facto government of the Jewish community in Palestine. When in 1946 the conflict between the Zionist leaders and the British Mandatory Government reached its peak with the arrest of a number of Zionist leaders — among them Moshe Sharett (then Shertok), the political secretary — Golda Meir, as much because she was English-speaking as for her abilities, became acting political secretary. Her fearless and outspoken response to British pressure set the pattern of her future political image, and was the fruitful seed which was to ripen into a most successful career. When the British left Palestine and the State of Israel was proclaimed on May 14, 1948, the members of the Zionist Executive painlessly and smoothly transformed themselves into the Provisional Government.

A short time before this, David Ben-Gurion had foreseen the probable attack by Arab states once a Jewish State was established, and he sent Golda Meir on a mission to the United States to raise money and/or arms. Her achievement at the time was another step forward in the esteem in which Ben-Gurion and other colleagues held her. The recognition of Israel only minutes, almost seconds, after it was proclaimed, by both the United States and the Soviet Union, made Israeli representation in both those countries of great importance. A delegation was already in New York and Washington because of the negotiations held there, but Ben-Gurion sent his strongest card — Golda Meir — as the first Israeli Ambassador to Moscow.

For her, as indeed for all the Jews in Israel, it was as much a mission to Soviet Jewry as to the Soviet Government. Six million brethren, among them relatives, perhaps even parents, certainly brothers and sisters, had been done to death in Europe. How precious was it then to break through the barrier that separated them from this Jewish community in Russia, though somewhat decimated yet still great.

The sight of the many thousands of Jews who followed Golda Meir through the streets of Moscow to Synagogue on the New Year festival appears to have been the foundation on which later Soviet hostility to Israel was built. Yet Mrs Meir herself never gave up belief that one day the doors of Russia would open to let Jews go out to return to their ancient homeland. And this despite the ever increasing unfriendliness of the Soviet Government, and their stubborn resistance to every overture made by Israel throughout the years to try to win back the initial support. It must have been a source of great satisfaction to Mrs Meir that, just during her term as Prime Minister, Jews reached Israel from the USSR in their thousands. It was the realization of a dream which had for long been dreamt both by the immigrants and by those who received them.

In February, 1949, the first general elections were held in Israel resulting, expectedly, in Mapai emerging as by far the largest party but without an overall majority, a situation which was still unchanged when Mrs Meir became Prime Minister. Ben-Gurion, forming his first Government, wanted Golda

Meir at his side and called her back to Israel to become Minister of Labour.

As Labour Minister her tasks included finding work for immigrants who in the early fifties reached Israel in their hundreds of thousands. Despite an impossible budget her Ministry managed to shoulder the burden.

In 1956, Mr Ben-Gurion returned to the Premiership after retiring for about a year and a half to a kibbutz in the arid south. He decided to drop Moshe Sharett who had been Prime Minister in his absence and Minister for Foreign Affairs from the beginning of the State till then. Instead he gave that portfolio to Mrs Meir, his loyal adherent. Mrs Meir's outstanding achievement as Foreign Minister was undoubtedly the relationship she built with the newly emergent states in Africa, with whom Israel felt a close affinity. It was largely held at the time that the United States' sharp reaction to the Sinai campaign was motivated, among other things, by the effect on peoples who had just thrown off the shackles of colonialism. Mrs Meir therefore toured these countries and created friendships with them, which owed a good deal to her personal contacts.

When the excitement of the Sinai campaign and its aftermath had died down, conflicts which had been brewing within Mapai boiled over and scalded, in the process, the harmony which had always existed between Mrs Meir and Mr Ben-Gurion. The clash was between the veterans of the party on one side, and the "younger" element led by Moshe Dayan and Shimon Peres

on the other. Mrs Meir and those of her generation never forgave Mr Ben-Gurion for completely siding with the younger group. Though Mrs Meir did not carry out the threat she made that she would not serve in Mr Ben-Gurion's Government after the elections at the end of 1959, she had to swallow her dislikes and accept among her Cabinet colleagues both Moshe Dayan and Abba Eban, with Shimon Peres as Deputy Minister of Defence.

She had her revenge, however, when the famous "Lavon affair" split the party completely. Mrs Meir led the veterans against Ben-Gurion. Thereafter her strength lay in that leadership, for the party machinery was too tightly held in their hands for them to be dislodged. So much so, that there are many political observers who contend that she was largely responsible for Mr Ben-Gurion's resignation in 1963. Certainly, she gave her full support to Mr Levi Eshkol as Prime Minister and fought strongly against the group who, with Mr Ben-Gurion at the head, broke away from Mapai and formed their own party, Rafi.

Shortly afterwards Mrs Meir resigned from the Government and became secretary-general of Mapai. It was the time of perhaps her greatest influence on internal politics. Her power did not diminish even when the split in the party was healed, and it was joined by two other left-wing groups, although she suffered one or two reverses. The most important was that in the emergency of May, 1967, Moshe Dayan was appointed Minister of Defence against her strong opposition. She had wanted Mr Yigal Allon. Nevertheless, before relinquishing her position as secretary of Mapai, which she did shortly before Mr Eshkol's death, she saw to it that her nominee, Pincus Sapir, took her place, although it meant his giving up the post of Minister of Finance to do so. And she insisted that Mr Yigal Allon be made Deputy Prime Minister. Her retirement, so far as the power she wielded in Mapai affairs was concerned, was only nominal. When Mr Eshkol suddenly died it was therefore almost inevitable that she should take his place. She was at first seen as a compromise choice to avert the otherwise inevitable struggle for the leadership which was expected.

She was very much a mother-figure as the first Premier, David Ben-Gurion, had been a father-figure; and indeed towards the end of her term of office she was often referred to as "grandmother". She was thus firmly in control, the matriarch holding her "family" together at a time of great difficulty from without and growing discord within the county and particularly within her own party.

This reached a climax with the sudden onslaught of war in October, 1973, on Yom Kippur, the holiest day in the Jewish calendar. The fact emerged that the Israeli armed forces were apparently caught unawares and sustained heavy losses in the first three days, not compensated for by the Israeli gains by the time a halt was called to the fighting.

The nation was in a turmoil: appeasement was possible only by finding someone to blame.

It was somewhat ironic that as Prime Minister she was compelled to rely to a great extent on matters of security on her Defence Minister, who was Mr Moshe Dayan: even more so that in the criticism over the war — levelled at both of them and the military leaders — she had publicly to express her support of him.

In the general elections which followed in December, 1973, her party therefore lost many votes and left her in a weak position to form a new coalition government. She nevertheless persisted and had succeeded, but the inner-party strife reached a new dimension and she resigned, to make way for Mr Yitzhak Rabin, a much younger man, a former Chief of Staff of the armed forces and a former Ambassador to the United States.

Under Israeli procedure, in the period between the elections till Mr Rabin had formed his government and obtained a parliamentary vote of confidence in it, the outgoing government remained as a "caretaker". Mrs Meir was thus still Prime Minister and led the negotiations with Dr Kissinger which resulted in the disengagement of Egyptian-Israeli troops in Sinai, and Syrian-Israeli troops in the Golan Heights: the crowning achievement of her political career, immediately after which, in June 1974, she retired.

She was without doubt the voice of the majority of her people in those negotiations: tough enough to wrest the best terms possible, flexible enough to give way when the limit was reached.

Her strength lay in her total single-mindedness. For her the cause of the Jewish people, their right to territory won in wars they saw as forced upon them, their claim to sovereignty, independence and security, were so self-evident that she was able to present them with perfect conviction and unequivocalness, possible only to someone uninhibited by even a glance at the other side. She was, at the same time, intolerant of any slight, explicit or implicit, against her people.

When she made history by being the first Israeli Prime Minister, or leader, to be received by the Pope, she entered with due reverence, and remarked beforehand: "That I, the daughter of Moshe Mabovitch, a carpenter, should call on the Pope!" But in the interview itself, she reacted very sharply when the Pope told her he was surprised that the Jews who had suffered so much should act so fiercely to the Arabs: "When we were homeless and merciful", she declared to His Holiness, "we were led to the gas chambers!" It was this kind of "talking straight from the shoulder" which endeared her to fellow Jews and won her disciples.

Her obvious honesty and straightforwardness, devoid of guile or dissembling, earned her the respect of foreign politicians with whom she came into contact. Though outwardly severe looking, her face reflecting the strains and stresses through which she had lived her whole life, she was inwardly warm-hearted, compassionate and even sentimental.

Her passing ends an era for Israel, for she is the last of the group which,

as the executive of the World Zionist Movement, led the transition of the Jewish settlement in Palestine into a sovereign State, and then led that State as its Government. Their outlook, and even policies, were influenced by their own experiences in their countries of origin, of anti-Semitism and persecution. They fled from these to find hostility and hardship in their ancient homeland. But they had the exaltation of reaching in their lifetime the goal of Statehood which they had set for themselves: they were tough, granite-hard and uncompromising. They were in the forefront in the battle for the rebirth of a nation, in overcoming economic crises and winning four wars; and during that time immigration continued on a massive scale and the development of Israel raced on at a spectacular rate. They set a pace it will be difficult to match, impossible to increase, by the new generation, either Israeli-born or almost entirely Israeli-bred, who have already taken over completely.

Among those older leaders Golda Meir has an honoured place: her role was vital and she gave the whole of herself to it. She was at the same time one of the masses and yet their leader. Mrs Meir, whose autobiography, *My Life*, was published in Britain in 1975, celebrated her 80th birthday in May, 1978, but was in hospital three times during the following autumn.

Golda Meir, Israel's first woman Prime Minister, was born on May 3, 1898. She died on December 8, 1978, aged 80

Editor's note: Mrs Meir died while publication of *The Times* was suspended; this obituary appeared in *The Times Obituaries Supplement* almost a year later.

———◦◦◦———

DAME GRACIE FIELDS

FORMER MILL GIRL WHOSE
FINE VOICE AND SENSE OF FUN
LED HER TO BE A PRE-EMINENT
ENTERTAINER ON STAGE,
RECORD AND FILM

NOVEMBER 23, 1979 (*The Times Obituaries Supplement*)

Dame Gracie Fields, DBE, who died on September 27, at the age of 81, was perhaps the most popular entertainer of the day. She was, moreover, one of those few who are able to step beyond the strict limits of their profession and become a national figure. To many thousands of people who never saw her "Our Gracie" was a beloved character, the very embodiment of that fairy-tale quality in our age which allowed a poor mill girl to rise, by talent, personality and character, above the circumstances of her birth to astonishing heights of success.

Born at Rochdale, Lancashire, on January 9, 1898, her real name was Grace Stansfield, and she was only eight when she first sang in a local cinema. She used also to sing outside the lodgings of music hall performers in the hope of attracting their attention, but the only engagement she got in this way was one to assist an artiste by singing choruses from the gallery. The child's efforts to do so were, however, promptly suppressed by a woman sitting near her, who did not realize that she was part of the show. Later she danced and sang with Haley's Juveniles — long a famous troupe of children on the music halls — and in 1912 with Cherburn's Young Stars. In 1913 she made her first appearance as a single turn, and the following year, at Oldham, played in her only pantomime. If she could not obtain theatrical engagements she worked, at this period, in a cotton mill, a shop, or a paper-bag factory, and when in 1915 she joined a touring revue her mother told her that if she did not then "make good" she would have to go back to the mill as a permanency — a fate which happily for the world she avoided. Her first revue was *Yes, I Think So*, which was produced at Hulme, Manchester, early in 1915, and in July of that year paid a visit to the Middlesex Music Hall, in Drury Lane, where Gracie Fields made her first London appearance.

The principal comedian in that revue was Archie Pitt, with whose productions she was for many years associated and whom later she married. For two years from February, 1916, they played together in *It's a Bargain*, and in 1918 began a tour of seven years in *Mr Tower of London*, probably the most successful touring revue ever produced. It several times filled the bill at London music halls, including notably the Alhambra, and in it the charm, humour, and freshness of Gracie Fields began to attract general notice. After a period in another revue, *By Request*, she appeared again as a single act, and in February, 1928, was engaged by the late Sir Gerald du Maurier to act as Lady Weir with him in *SOS*. The fact of one of the most popular "legitimate" actors of his day thus choosing a young music hall singer for a leading part in one of his productions caused a considerable stir at the time. This was, however, her only "straight" part, and before long she was back again in variety and revue, one of her chief successes being in *The Show's The Thing*, at the Victoria Palace, and subsequently at other London theatres. In 1930 she paid her first visit to America, to perform at the Palace Theatre, New York.

The following year saw the beginning of her screen career, her first film being *Sally in Our Alley*, in which she introduced "Sally", the most popular of all her songs. Her later films included *Looking on the Bright Side, Love, Life and Laughter, Sing As We Go*, and *Look Up and Laugh*. She signed in 1935 what was then stated to be the biggest contract ever made by a film or stage artist in this country, computed to bring her in about £150,000 in two years. The sale of her gramophone records, too, was vast, four million of them being sold in less than five years. In 1937 she received the freedom of her native town of Rochdale, and in 1938, she was created CBE. A woman of great generosity, she established an orphanage at Peacehaven in Sussex.

Gracie Fields's first marriage was dissolved in 1940, and she then married the Italian-born entertainer Monty Banks. It was typical of her lively generosity of spirit that during the Second World War she appeared wherever she could to strengthen morale and enliven servicemen and workers. One almost legendary tour took her, in six weeks, from Scapa Flow to Plymouth, giving three performances a day in army and air force camps and in factories. The performances were themselves unstintedly generous, and the last was no less fresh and vigorous than the first.

After the war, and the death of her second husband in 1950, the pace of her career slackened still further. Her third marriage, to Boris Alperovici, in 1952, saw her partial retirement to a home in Capri.

The comparative rarity of her public appearances seemed not to lessen her popularity or her place in the normally fickle memory of the public. She was, in her later days, less a legend than a personal friend of every member of her audiences, a happy, honest, and good-hearted visitor to whose appearances everybody looked forward. Her autobiography, *Sing as We Go*, was published in 1960. It conveyed a good deal of the directness, simplicity, and reticence of an artist who never lived or could have tolerated the idea of living her personal life in public. Between the lively, adored entertainer and her private concerns, with their great generosity and secretive kindness, a tactful curtain was always drawn.

She toured Britain, Canada and Australia in 1964 and the United States a year later. She returned to Rochdale in 1978 to open a theatre named after her and was warmly greeted (which warmth she returned in good measure and in characteristic uninhibited style) and subsequently made a surprise appearance at what was to be her last Command Performance. In the New Year Honours List (of 1979) she was advanced to DBE and in February received the insignia at an investiture held by Queen Elizabeth the Queen Mother.

Undoubtedly Gracie Fields was the outstanding figure of the music hall in the years between the wars. To compare her hold upon the public with that of the great personalities of an earlier generation — say Marie Lloyd or Miss Vesta Tilley — would be pointless, since she worked in such changed circumstances and was able to supplement her music-hall work with the new media of the talking film and the wireless. But though the screen and the radio helped to build up her tremendous reputation, though she made some extremely successful and enjoyable films of an unsophisticated kind and was a tremendous draw also upon the air, she was, first and foremost, a music hall performer, and those who never saw her in the flesh, singing to an audience actually present, never knew the essential Gracie Fields.

Slender, rather tall, with a slight stoop, thin lips and strongly marked, somewhat pointed features, she caught the attention immediately she appeared. Her face, crowned with a mass of hair rippling back from a broad, high forehead, was intelligent rather than beautiful. As a performer she had two great gifts, a delicious sense of burlesque and genuine, homely fun, and an exceptionally beautiful and flexible voice, with a wide range. Her vocal technique improved steadily throughout her career, and even late in life the beauty of her high notes and the precision and neatness of her phrasing were remarkable. The excellence of her singing, indeed, at one time seemed a menace to her performance, for the sentimental ditties, on which she lavished so much artistry, were quite unworthy of her talent. Early in her career she had an entrancing trick of indicating her real opinion of these tearful ballads by introducing into the middle of her song some ludicrous trick of voice, or by absentmindedly scratching her back between high notes. Then for a time she became, to the disappointment of her more discerning admirers, more and more a serious sentimental singer, and her charming little buffooneries and her comic songs in her native Lancashire dialect became less and less prominent in her act. Later, however, though she did not return to the burlesque of her sentimental numbers, she restored a proper proportion of comic singing, and would give eight or 10 songs on end, alternately sentimental and humorous.

As a comic singer she was delicious. Her fun, which was always good-humoured, inoffensive and full of character, seemed to bubble out of herself, and needed none of the extravagant make-up or costume upon which many comediennes have relied. Gracie Fields could change in a second from the heart-broken night-club frequenter begging for "Music, Maestro, Please" to the Lancashire mill girl who owned "The Biggest Aspidestra [sic] in the World" or had been to the christening of "Mrs Binns's Twins" without changing her dress or even altering the set of her hair. Just as quickly and easily she could become the young Welsh girl whose family had "Got to Keep up with the Joneses". Gracie Fields had a very great spontaneous comic talent, a lovely voice and a personality (perhaps the most important asset of all, since the basis of the art of the music hall is personality) which made her, whether she was being funny or senti-mental, always unaffectedly good and likable company.

Dame Gracie Fields, DBE, popular entertainer, was born on January 9, 1898. She died on September 27, 1979, aged 81

Editor's note: Dame Gracie Fields died while publication of *The Times* was suspended; this obituary appeared in *The Times Obituaries Supplement* two months later.

DAME REBECCA WEST

WRITER WHO BROUGHT
A NOVELIST'S FLAIR TO
HER POWERFUL WORKS OF
JOURNALISM

MARCH 16, 1983

Dame Rebecca West, DBE, the author, journalist and critic, died yesterday in London. She was 90.

Into no one of these departments of literary activity did Rebecca West fit with entire ease, though she shone in them all. As a novelist, she had an analytical mind, somewhat too ruthless, perhaps, at stripping away pretence and pathetic disguise in the character she was exploring or the human motives she was exposing, entirely to win the reader's allegiance. It is as though one watched a brilliant surgeon operating rather than admired a physician at the gentler work of healing.

Somewhat at odds with this sharp method of dissection was an impres-sive, but occasionally orotund literary style, the perfect instrument for catch-ing a scene of tension, but, in involved passages of deduction and comparison, demanding from the reader a close attention to the argument which not everyone was capable of offering. Yet when she was reporting direct, and analysing only in brilliant asides and sharp descriptive cuts, no writer of her time could excel her. The *New Yorker* early recognized her as a valuable contributor, and her association with that magazine, the iconoclastic nature of which so perfectly reflected her own temperament, was a long and happy one. It is, perhaps, as a Great Reporter of our time, rather than as a novelist, that she is likely to be remembered. Nevertheless, at least one of her novels *The Fountain Overflows* (1957) was of a stature to encourage a higher estimation of her as a novelist, though planned sequels on the life of the Aubrey family never appeared.

She was born in London on December 21, 1892, the third and youngest daughter of Charles Fairfield, who has been variously described as a journalist, a war correspondent and pamphleteer. He was of Irish extraction. Her mother was a Mackenzie, a native of Edinburgh, and an excellent fictional portrait of both parents appears in *The Fountain Overflows*.

Born a few months after her family's return from Australia, whither her father had followed one of his passionate quests to right some injustice, she was christened Cicily Isabel Fairfield. It was not until she was 19 that she assumed the name of Rebecca West by which she was later to become so well known. The first 10 years of her life had been spent in the huge house in South London in which she was born. After her father's death, her mother moved the family to Edinburgh and the girls received their education at George Watson's Ladies' College.

At the age of 18 she descended upon London to make a career. The moment was propitious for the encounter, but strong characters who are to make a mark on the world are often kept waiting in the wings for a little, and it was not until after she had been trained for the stage at a London dramatic academy and had appeared briefly in Ibsen's *Rosmersholm* that she abandoned the prospect of an acting career. Her pen name "Rebecca West" was a reminder of an Ibsen role she had once played in an empty theatre.

The rights of women were being hotly debated. H. G. Wells's *Ann Veronica* had shocked one section of society. To another, the intelligent, ambitious, younger people of Rebecca's generation, it was accepted as a great pronouncement. The establishment of women's rights was not hastened by Wells's most intelligent novel, but it had a very wide public. It led to some dramatic gestures, and it had its part in the loosening of the rigid bonds of Victorian society in the post-war freedom of the 1920s.

Into this exciting debate Rebecca flung herself with the enthusiasm for a cause she had inherited from her father but with the cool detachment she had got from her mother. In 1911 she joined the staff of *The Freewoman* and in the following year, when she was only 20, became a political writer on *The Clarion*. She continued to play an active part in the fight for women's suffrage, while contributing a whole stream of political essays and literary criticisms to *The Star*, the *Daily News* and the *New Statesman*.

Attractive in appearance, with a quick mind, a biting wit, and an iconoclastic outlook, it is not surprising that H. G. Wells, then in his "phase of imaginative dispersal", when he was beginning "to scandalize the whisperers", should have found this young disciple a good deal more to his taste than some of those who, inspired by *Ann Veronica*, were prepared to throw off family ties and fling themselves at his feet. Rebecca's first encounter with him was when, as a young reporter, she was sent to write him up. The attraction between them was immediate, in spite of the considerable difference in age.

What Wells may not have recognized at first was the vein of seriousness beneath the girl's daring talk. Between the shy, sensitive Scots-Irish girl of upper class origin, her romantic heart constantly being directed by her intelligent brain, and the successful, hard-headed son of the lower classes vibrant with life and intelligence and the charm these qualities exercise over others, there was a strong attraction but a profound difference of outlook, and a union between them, especially one of an irregular kind, was bound to end in disaster. But the association lasted for some years. A son was born to them who was given the name Anthony West. It was this relationship which was probably responsible for the iconoclastic views on marriage which Rebecca was to enunciate with such firmness for many years to follow.

It was in this period that she published her first book, a critical study of Henry James. Her first work of fiction,

The Return of the Soldier, appeared in 1918. This was followed by *The Judge* (1922), *The Strange Necessity* (1928), *Harriet Hume* (1929), and *The Thinking Reed* (1936). These books demonstrated both the remarkable range of her powers of observation, and at the same time her limitations as a novelist. The theme and background of every book was different from its predecessor, ranging from the shell-shocked soldier in the first, to the fashionable heroine of the last one. She seemed to penetrate beneath the surface of human conduct, and to find new and convincing motives for behaviour: the reader is compelled to admire her craftsmanship and to accept the explanations of her narrative. Her style imitated no one; she brought to her story-telling a fresh use of language, and these novels stand high above most of those that appeared in the 1920s and 1930s.

Yet they are not great novels. Something that Hardy, Wells, Conrad, or Henry lames could communicate in their different ways to the reader is missing here. It is intuition, that last and greatest gift that is given to true genius. Hardy and Tess, Dickens and David Copperfield, Tolstoy and Natasha, Wells and Kipps, that deep intuitive understanding between the creator and his creation is missing from these admirable works of fiction, and they are lost in the mists of time with other works of far less quality. Rebecca West's brain had come to command her heart; which is sensible in life but is a loss to the great novelist. But this loss was to be recovered in her last work of fiction, *The Fountain Overflows*, published 20 years after *The Thinking Reed*. For the background to this work, designed to be written in three parts, she turned back to her own childhood and the image of a beloved mother. It had a large public.

This work might have appeared earlier but for the interruption of the Second World War. In 1930 she had married Henry Maxwell Andrews, a private banker with literary tastes, who did much to encourage and help her in her literary work. In the mid-1930s they made several journeys to Serbia, Macmillan having commissioned from her a travel book of 80,000 words. Her interest in the subject deepened as her knowledge of the country widened. She went back again and again, collecting and sifting her material. The war had been going on for more than a year, and the bombs were beginning to fall in London when she delivered to her publishers the book which they had contracted for several years before. It had grown to a quarter of a million words, but it had grown from a travel book to a masterpiece of biography, not of a man but of a whole people. It was published in 1941 in two volumes under the title of *Black Lamb and Grey Falcon*, and was immediately recognized as a magnum opus, as astonishing in its range, in the subtlety and power of its judgment, as it is brilliant in expression. As a result of this work she was invited during the war to superintend the BBC broadcasts to Yugoslavia.

The trials that followed the war offered her talents a fresh opportunity for pyrotechnic display. She was present at the Nuremberg Trials. Her graphic accounts appeared in the *New Yorker* and were subsequently published, together with accounts she gave of other trials following the war arising out of the relation of the individual to the state, in two memorable books, *The Meaning of Treason* (1949) and *A Train of Powder* (1955). These she followed with a critical work of originality and brilliance, *The Court and the Castle* (1958), which is an enlargement of a theme first stated in some lectures she was invited to give at Yale University.

Later books were *The Vassall Affair* (1963), *The New Meaning of Treason* (1964), and a final novel *The Birds Fall Down* (1966), a parable of disloyalty and espionage worked out within the framework of a historical romance. This was translated into a BBC television serial in 1978.

In an age when broadcasting and the style of reporting developed by such magazines as *Time* have accustomed us to the declamatory and breathless, her descriptions of great events caught the reader's imagination by emphasizing the ordinariness of the men given outsize parts in them. Her description of the scene of the attempted assassination of Dr Verwoerd, the patient beasts at an agricultural show, the Boer farmers, and one farmer like a beast that has broken away from the stall stumbling towards the Prime Minister with a gun in his hand, caught the imagination of the reader and fixed the scene in his mind far more vividly than did the breathless messages of other journalists less gifted. She was a novelist who used her great gifts for journalism. At the same time, a journalist who brought to that fleeting work the powers of observation, the absorption with the motives of human conduct, the complexity of human character which his more leisurely production allows a novelist, but not a journalist, time to explore.

She was created CBE in 1949 and advanced to DBE 10 years later. In 1957 she was made a Chevalier of the Legion of Honour, and in 1968 a Companion of Literature. Her husband died in 1968.

Dame Rebecca West, DBE, writer, was born on December 21, 1892. She died on March 15, 1983, aged 90

—⁓—

LILLIAN HELLMAN

UNCOMPROMISING AMERICAN PLAYWRIGHT, BLACKLISTED DURING THE MCCARTHY ERA

JULY 2, 1984

Lillian Hellman, who died in Boston on June 30 at the age of 77, was one of the most distinguished playwrights of the twentieth century.

Born in New Orleans on June 20, 1907, she came of an old-established if somewhat stormy deep Southern background; when she wrote of her own life in two indirectly autobiographical collections of character studies (*An Unfinished Woman* published in 1969 and *Pentimento* published in 1974) it was clear that her recollections of childhood were marked by an uncertain affection for many of her relatives and a feeling of alienation from the more conservative traditions of the American South in the early years of the century.

In 1925 she married the writer Arthur Kober and went with him to Paris where she began to write short stories for a magazine with which he was involved; the marriage did not last long however — it was her only one — and by 1926 she was back in New York working as a reader for the celebrated publishing house of Horace Liveright.

Early in the 1930s Lillian Hellman met Dashiell Hammett, the writer who was to share her life until his death 30 years later and with whom she was to be blacklisted during the McCarthy era. Her first produced play, *The Children's Hour*, reached Broadway in 1934 and dealt prophetically with the tragic effects of manipulated public opinion and subsequent victimisation: it was first filmed as *These Three* and later remade as *The Loudest Whisper*.

Throughout the rest of the 1930s and early 1940s Miss Hellman continued to work as a playwright. *The Little Foxes* (1939) and *Another Part of the Forest* (1946) told the tangled and tortured history of a decadent Southern family, while *Watch on the*

Rhine (1941) was about dogged anti-Nazis. Miss Hellman had also by this time been involved with the Spanish civil war, and with the early anti-Nazi underground; her life had moved some way from its sheltered and cloistered beginnings. A section of *Pentimento* made into the film *Julia* was about an American woman involved in getting Jews and dissidents out of Nazi Germany.

Her playwriting and her later autobiographical work was marked by a lean, spare, uncompromising and peculiarly American style — seeing her plays in Britain, she once said, was "like seeing them in translation".

It is tempting to see in her one of the first of the modern feminists — the kind of lady played most often by Katharine Hepburn in Hollywood films of the 1930s. More seriously, her refusal to compromise with the changing times got her into trouble in California where she had gone to write screenplays in the late 1940s.

Taken before the House Un-American Activities Committee in 1952, and refusing to answer questions about the politics of her friends, she stated: "I cannot and will not cut my conscience to fit this year's fashions". This experience formed the basis of another autobiographical work,

Scoundrel Time (1976); *Maybe* (1980) was also autobiographical.

In later years Miss Hellman turned to theatrical adaptations — Anouilh's *The Lark* in 1955, Voltaire's *Candide* as the book for a musical in 1956, and Blechman's *How Much?* as *My Mother, My Father and Me* in 1963. She also edited some of Hammett's short stories as well as a collection of Chekov letters, but much of her later life was spent travelling and working on the character sketches which made up her first two part-autobiographical collections. The cast for these included such friends and enemies as Hemingway, Scott Fitzgerald and Dorothy Parker as well as Hammett and her many relatives from the deep South, but she retained the observer's distance — she once described herself as a loner, not by choice but certainly by temperament.

Dedicated as Lillian Hellman was to the principles of freedom and tolerance, she took a lighter view of her own calling. "Despite many disillusions," she once wrote, "I still cling obstinately to the belief that writing can be done with your left hand while your right is busy with something else".

Lillian Hellman, playwright and screenwriter, was born on June 20, 1907. She died on June 30, 1984, aged 77

—◡◡◡—

INDIRA GANDHI

RULER OF INDIA WITH A
TALENT FOR POLITICAL
MANOEUVRE BUT WHO,
FATALLY, COULD NOT CURB
THE DISAFFECTION OF THE
SIKHS OF PUNJAB

NOVEMBER 1, 1984

Mrs Indira Gandhi, who was Prime Minister of India for most of the last 18 years, and who came to dominate the country's affairs through her combination of personal aura and sheer political toughness, was assassinated yesterday in Delhi at the age of 66.

Much of her appeal derived from the fact that she was the only daughter of Jawaharlal Nehru, the first Prime Minister of independent India and widely revered as a father figure. This gave the impression of a Nehru dynasty ruling India, and she herself lent strength to this by the way in which she closely associated first her younger son, Sanjay, and after his death his elder brother, Rajiv, with her political activities. It was clear that she was preparing the way for a possible succession.

But she herself could not have achieved the pre-eminence she did without considerable gifts of her own: she showed a talent for political manoeuvre

and, frequently, ruthlessness. It was this latter quality which led her to declare a state of emergency in June, 1975, which in turn led to severe restrictions on democratic liberties, and fears of the installation of a dictatorship.

To her credit, however, she decided to call a general election in March, 1977; this revealed a decisive repudiation of her and her associates' policies, and the attachment of the Indian electorate to democratic principles. She accepted the verdict, and in a remarkable recovery, admittedly helped by the incompetence of her successors, fought her way back to the Prime Minister's office.

India, a vast country of disparate peoples, widespread poverty and turbulent climate, is a hard country to rule, let alone lead to greater achievement. The difficulties with outlying regions are demonstrated by the fact that Mrs Gandhi met her death at the hands of Sikhs, only months after she had ordered the Indian Army to storm the Golden Temple at Amritsar, where Sikh extremists had holed up. Another problem area, among many, was Assam, where some 3,000 people are estimated to have died in ethnic clashes in the past two years.

Mrs Gandhi's response to such situations was to try to impose control, if not rule, from Delhi — often by less than scrupulous means. It can be argued that just as the Indian economy has shown a modest improvement over the years, so she, by her own personal presence and determined style, did much to hold the country together.

In international relations she aimed, by her own account, to steer a middle course between the two superpowers — though to Western eyes this appeared to involve a particularly close relationship with the Soviet Union, and an attitude of suspicion towards the United States. Certainly there was no doubt of her pursuance of Indian national objectives, seen in her intervention in the war between East and West Pakistan in 1971, and the explosion of a nuclear device in 1974, putting India among the nuclear powers.

Mrs Gandhi was not a political thinker, or a skilled administrator. But she inherited from her father an intolerance of linguistic or religious fanaticism, which stood her in good stead, as well as a belief in state intervention in the economy. Perhaps most important of all, she understood power and, under a deceptively mild exterior, was determined to do what appeared necessary to attain and retain it.

Indira was born in Allahabad on November 19, 1917, into a wealthy Kashmiri Brahmin family. Her father, educated at Harrow, Cambridge and the Inner Temple, had married Kamala Kaul the daughter of a Delhi Kashmiri businessman. She was beautiful but, compared with the Nehru family, unsophisticated and she was not made welcome by some of the women of the family. This brushed off on Indira, only child of the marriage, and the residual effect later marred relations between her and her father's distinguished sister, Mrs Vijaya Lakshmi Pandit, and other members of the family.

The rich Allahabad household provided a fascinating, but sometimes uncomfortable background for Indira's childhood. Although highly westernized and Anglophile in style, it became a centre for India's growing nationalist movement and she grew up in an intensely political atmosphere among the Congressmen of the day.

It was a very lonely life for the child as her father and mother were often in jail and her grandfather, Motilal Nehru, joined the movement led by Mohandas Gandhi for independence, abandoned his lavish life style and spent an obligatory spell in prison.

It was during these years that she decided that she would model her life on that of Joan of Arc and could be observed practising poses suitable to that famous and feminine opponent of the British.

Her education was spasmodic and varied; she spent some time at the International School in Geneva, at various schools in India, happy days at Shantiniketan, the university established in Bengal by Rabindranath Tagore, and finally at Oxford. She went up to Somerville in 1937, a year after her mother had died of tuberculosis in Switzerland. She enjoyed her stay at Oxford, but was longing to return to India and to her father, and she finally arrived in Bombay in 1941, without a degree but escorted by the man she was later to marry. He was Feroze Gandhi, a Parsi student who had courted her assiduously but with great discretion since she was 16.

Indira visited her father in prison and told him that she had made up her mind to marry Feroze. He was not at all pleased and there was also something of a public outcry because marriage between members of different communities was not as common then in India as it is now. Mahatma Gandhi, however, spoke up for the young couple whose love was breaking through traditional barriers, and in early 1942 they were married.

They had two children — both boys, Rajiv and Sanjay — but it was an unusual marriage, particularly for the conservative society in which they lived. With the coming of independence, Nehru became India's first Prime Minister, and Indira felt it her duty to act as his hostess and to look after him. Relations between father-in-law and son-in-law were uneasy and as his own political career as an MP developed, Feroze lived apart from his family although they frequently met.

He died in 1960, and although Indira was aware of the vicious gossip among Delhi socialites about her married life, she would never accept that it had been less than successful. She and her husband had both been jailed by the British on their return from their honeymoon in Kashmir, and each of them in their own fashion was absorbed in politics for the rest of their lives.

As hostess to her father from 1947 until his death in 1964, Indira not only travelled with him on his many journeys abroad and helped to entertain the world's leaders who visited Delhi, but gained a unique insight into the Indian political scene. She lived right in the eye of the many storms that shook the country, and had a privileged position from which to observe the motivation and methods of many of her father's colleagues. She was observing them while they largely ignored her and when the time came for her to deal with them as Prime Minister, she demonstrated a penetrating understanding of their weaknesses.

She also had seen her father often seeking agreement through conciliation and losing ground by vacillation, and seems to have made up her mind that her style would be different, without undue concern for constitutional niceties, the claims of personal loyalty or the opinions of critics.

The first indications she gave of her own style came in 1959 when she accepted the post of Congress President. She showed dynamism and a certain lack of principle in fostering the agitation which led to the unseating of the Communist Government of Kerala State and the return to power of a Congress Ministry in somewhat dubious alliance with Socialists and the Muslim League.

Mrs Gandhi was elected leader of the Congress party, and thus Prime Minister, in February 1966, after the sudden death of Lal Bahadur Shastri in Tashkent. She was then Minister of Information, having been brought into the cabinet by Shastri when he succeeded her father less than two years before.

Her term in the Congress presidency had been brief, but those who had called on her ailing father for discussions on party or even policy matters had become accustomed to being told to "talk it over with Indira", and the idea of her becoming prime minister had even been in the air on Nehru's death in 1964, though Shastri was then more acceptable.

Even in 1966 it was primarily for negative reasons that Mrs Gandhi was advanced to the prime minister-ship. From the point of view of the Congress party's organization men, the man to stop was Morarji Desai (the former Finance Minister, who had been dropped from the Cabinet by Nehru and passed over in favour of Shastri after Nehru's death). Mrs Gandhi, hail-ing from Uttar Pradesh, the heartland of Congress politics, and even more significantly from the Nehru family, had wide acceptability in the party.

There were, however, setbacks to Congress in the polls in the early days of her prime ministership, and dis-satisfaction with her leadership — or, as her critics had it, the absence of leadership — was openly expressed. The "queen-makers" who backed her original election as leader of the party and therefore prime minister began to consider alternatives.

The opportunity to assert their dominance came with the death in the summer of 1969 of Dr Zakir Husain, the president of India. The party lead-ership moved to fill the office with one of their own men, Sanjiva Reddy, who was known to be personally ill-disposed to Mrs Gandhi. The party leadership appeared united behind Reddy's candi-dacy, and at first Mrs Gandhi seemed to bow to the inevitable — going so far as to nominate Reddy herself.

But in fact — and naturally — she was strongly resistant to the nomina-tion; she had her own candidate, and she meant to fight for him. She came into the open, opposing Reddy, putting her weight behind the then vice-presi-dent, V. V. Giri.

In this struggle Mrs Gandhi showed her true mettle. She used every weapon at her command, challenging normal party conventions and in con-sequence splitting Congress. By using the powers of her office to legislate by ordinance she outmanoeuvred her opponents (and that her manoeuvres were later ruled unconstitutional by the supreme court did not make them any less effective); she succeeded in presenting a pure struggle for office as if it were an ideological contest, a battle for the socialist soul of Congress — and she won hands down.

The extent of her victory was not at first apparent. Two parties, each claim-ing to be the true Congress, emerged from the struggle. But Mrs Gandhi was Prime Minister, her candidate had won the presidency, and the rival (or "organization") Congress was left in very poor shape.

At this time, however, the decisive-ness and effectiveness she had shown in the party's internal struggles were not complemented by equivalent achievements in the field of govern-ment. Measures such as the cutting off of the princes' privy purses and the nationalization of the major banks were not in themselves of great significance, when judged against the problems Mrs Gandhi's government faced. The late

1960s were years of great difficulty; bad food years combined with the consequences of the short 1965 war with Pakistan had left the economy in worse straits than usual.

Elections for the central parliament were due again in 1972, but Mrs Gandhi seized the initiative, obtained a dissolution a year in advance, and won an astounding victory. Far from seeing her majority reduced, she saw it increased beyond anything conceived as possible. Her Congress party was returned to a more than two-thirds majority in the Indian parliament — a strength nearly as great as the most it had achieved in the first, heady years after independence.

If 1971 began with Mrs Gandhi's triumph at the polls, it was to end with an even greater triumph, and one that, like the election, was taken to be very largely a personal one. At the end of March, 1971, as a result of demands for autonomy in what was then East Pakistan, the Pakistani army acted to put down the autonomy movement, and return the province to the centre's authority. The army acted with great ferocity, and killing and counter-killing spread and intensified.

Refugees by the scores of thousands and then by the million poured into India, presenting the government there with a huge and explosive problem. Even before the refugee problem reached such magnitude, the Delhi government was seized of course with the question of what India's role should be: to stand back, and watch the Pakistani army crush the Bengalis?

Or to intercede and bring the dissolution of Pakistan, the emergence of the new state of Bangladesh? The multitude of refugees made an answer to the question imperative, and the record of events suggests that towards the end of April the Indian government decided on support for the Bengalis, including military intervention if need be.

The eventual Indian intervention on behalf of Bangladesh (as East Pakistan now became) was brilliantly successful on both the military and the diplomatic level. Except for Washington and Peking — where the Indian action was strongly criticized — most world capitals were at least silent, while some praised India.

Understandably, this triumph too redounded solidly to the credit of Mrs Gandhi in her own country.

Every Indian felt, it seems, more confident of his identity and future, more alive to his role as an Indian, than he had been able to do in the preceding years of doubt and failure in India; and

Indian Prime Minister Indira Gandhi attracting crowds in London on a visit in 1978

for this they all thanked Mrs Gandhi. In response she arranged for state elections, which she had originally wanted to postpone, to be held in early 1972, and her Congress Party was returned to power in every state where an election was held.

It was, perhaps, inevitable that the high hopes of 1971 and 1972 could not be sustained. Externally, the groundswell of international support for India's intervention on the side of the Bengalis against Pakistan ebbed steadily away. It must in fairness be said that Mrs Gandhi showed both the authority and the magnanimity to resist the jingoistic demands from some political quarters in India which would have seen the country taking a wholly unyielding approach to the defeated rump of Pakistan. The 1971 military victory encouraged nevertheless in Indian foreign policy a disregard for the opinions of the outside world which sprang from the renewal of national confidence. This was shown in the explosion of India's nuclear device in the Rajasthan desert in May, 1974, and the incorporation of Sikkim later that year.

If the events of 1971 seemed to have left India and Mrs Gandhi in a position of unchallenged hegemony in South Asia, the social and economic problems facing the country internally were not thereby eased. At the beginning of the decade there had been hopeful signs that India might at last be on the threshold of self-sufficiency in food production. This optimism and in particular premature claims made on behalf of the "green revolution" were rudely shattered by droughts in 1972 and 1974.

With industrial production stagnant, and, labour unrest widespread, the economic future was not bright. Admittedly, many of the causes for this state of affairs were beyond Mrs Gandhi's control; among them, worldwide inflation, a precipitate deterioration of India's terms of trade, and, most savage of all, the fourfold increase in the price of oil at the end of 1973.

Politically, Mrs Gandhi soon found that the huge majorities she enjoyed in the central parliament and in most state legislatures could not insulate her from the popular unrest born of economic dissatisfaction.

In the states of Bihar and Gujarat, in particular, this opposition assumed formidable proportions, and parties of the right, left and centre began to coalesce under the leadership of the veteran Gandhian socialist, Mr J. P. Narayan. It was in this movement that Mrs Gandhi saw the threat to national security which provoked her to proclaim the Emergency in June, 1975; her critics, on the other hand, believed it was a threat to her position from within her own party which led her to impose such draconian discipline upon the entire country.

There was certainly some basis for the critics' doubts. The Allahabad High Court had found her guilty of certain technical offences in connexion with her own election to Parliament which while trivial in themselves were an embarrassment involving automatic disbarment from office unless the

Supreme Court ruled the conviction out of order. Mrs Gandhi had staked her personal reputation on victory in an election in Gujarat state forced on an unwilling Congress Party by a threatened fast to death by her old rival Morarji Desai; she had lost.

Opposition newspapers were making much scandal about corruption alleged to involve some of her closest associates, even her family, and in Parliament there were almost daily accusations of dishonesty against her Government. The tension in Delhi in June built up with the oppressive heat to breaking point and a vast opposition rally called for Mrs Gandhi's resignation and threatened the kind of civil disobedience in the capital which even neutral observers feared could lead to grave disorders.

Mrs Gandhi struck on the night of June 25-26. Opposition leaders and cadres all over the country were arrested. So were some Congressmen. The press was subjected to total censorship and decree after decree followed restricting civil liberties and stifling protest. It was known that the Cabinet only learnt what had happened some hours afterwards, but if there was any disapproval voiced nobody knew about that, and when Parliament met it was without most of the Opposition leaders. It endorsed all the constitutional changes Mrs Gandhi wanted, some plainly designed to secure her own position.

There were many Indians who believed that Mrs Gandhi had acted for the safety and security of the state, and that the discipline which followed the emergency was beneficial and necessary to end a period when liberty had degenerated into licence. Businessmen welcomed the sudden end to strikes and constant agitation in factories and offices, and the public were happy to find India's vast army of civil servants politer and more punctual about their duties.

Alongside the benefits of the emergency, however, some very disturbing factors were developing which, because of the effectiveness of internal censorship and the control over the foreign press, were not widely known outside the areas affected. Measures taken to control the growth of the population, however well-intended, led to great resentment. Sterilization was the favoured method and stories of compulsory operations spread like wildfire over northern India. Many dwellings were bulldozed in Delhi's old city as part of a slum clearance campaign without consideration for the residents. Police and officials behaved in a very high-handed fashion, and more and more public attention was focused on Sanjay Gandhi.

He took over the leadership of the youth wing of the Congress party and his influence on the development of the emergency was watched with growing apprehension by Congress politicians and public alike. Arrests were widespread and the suspension of the normal processes of the law whereby prisoners could appeal against continuing detention was seen as a further step towards the establishment of a dictatorship.

If there were still plenty of syco-phants ready to reassure Mrs Gandhi that the people were enthusiastically supporting her measures she must have also heard other voices indicating that all was not in fact well. In any case, within weeks of announcing the post-ponement of the general election, she decided after all to go to the country and chose March, 1977, for polling. Political prisoners were released and emergency restrictions began to be eased. Nevertheless, in a remarkably peaceful election, right across northern India, where the emergency measures had pressed the hardest, the Congress party was defeated.

Mrs Gandhi lost her seat to an old enemy, Mr Raj Narain; Sanjay was humiliatingly beaten in a neighbouring constituency and many of the ministers who had been Mrs Gandhi's closest allies were also rejected by the elector-ate. The Janata Party, composed of four somewhat disparate political parties with their latest ally, the Congress for Democracy, formed a Government. For Mrs Gandhi, her cup of bitterness was filled when her old rival, Mr Morarji Desai, whom she had imprisoned throughout the emergency, was chosen as Prime Minister and Mr Jagjivan Ram, the man she regarded as an arch-traitor, became Defence Minister.

It was nevertheless a public sensation when Mrs Gandhi was arrested early in October 1977 on charges of alleged misuse of her official position. The mag-istrate before whom she was produced ordered her unconditional release and there was widespread disquiet over what was seen as Government bungling of a vital matter. Mrs Gandhi, however, lost no time in making much political capital out of the affair.

In May 1978, interim reports from Mr Justice J. C. Shah's commission appointed to investigate allegations of misuse of power and other excesses during the emergency were laid before Parliament. Mrs Gandhi and Sanjay came under heavy criticism; she, it was said, had imposed the emergency in a desperate effort to continue in power despite a judicial verdict against her and she was also held responsible for the illegal arrest and detention of a number of persons.

The Government accepted the findings in full and they were widely publicized; many voices were raised demanding that Mrs Gandhi and her associates should be brought to trial. There was, however, some conflict within the Janata leadership about the procedure for punishing the Gandhi caucus, with Mr Desai firm in his belief that whatever was done should be strictly in accordance with the coun-try's legal system. As the result of this and the Indian courts' susceptibility to procrastination progress was slow and by the time Mrs Gandhi became Prime Minister again in January 1980, any action against her was at an early stage.

Mrs Gandhi, 20 months after her party's crushing defeat in the post-emergency general election, served notice that she was determined to stay in public life by winning a remarkable victory in a by-election in Chikmagalur in the southern state of Karnataka where her faction of the Congress party was in power. Her decision to seek re-election to Parliament from the south was an interesting one. A defeat in her home state would have been disastrous, so with characteristic political acumen she chose to return to the political limelight by an easier, if unorthodox, route. She won by over 77,000 votes after a bitter campaign.

Mrs Gandhi took her seat in Parliament on November 20, 1978. A month later, she was found guilty of contempt of the House and breach of privilege. The charges related to the period when she was Prime Minister just before the Emergency; they alleged that she had harassed four minor officials who had been instructed to collect facts for a parliamentary inquiry into her son's people's car project. She would almost certainly have been given a nominal sentence had she not chosen to deny the charges in a defiant and unrepentant speech which angered even MPs anxious to exercise clemency and avoid obliging her the accolade of temporary martyrdom. In the event, she was expelled from Parliament and sent to jail for the rest of the session, which turned out to be one week.

Before she left for Delhi's Tihar jail where so many of her political opponents had found themselves, this astonishing woman sang a verse of a popular English wartime song: "Wish me luck as you wave me goodbye".

The suicidal activities of the Janata leadership continued, however, and as its political standing collapsed a new election was called for the first week of 1980. Mrs Gandhi had ample ammunition for criticism of the lack of firmness and direction in its rule and, after a further split in her own Congress (I) Party, she entered the fray with no rivals in her own party and a divided opposition.

The voters turned back to the woman they knew. Her party won 351 seats out of 542 in the Lok Sabha, the lower house of the Indian Parliament. It was a party with only one star; Mrs Gandhi signified her supremacy by standing in two constituencies, one in the south and also in Rae Bareli where she had been humiliatingly defeated in 1977. She won both seats handsomely and, more surprisingly, Sanjay Gandhi won in Amethi, the Uttar Pradesh constituency which had rejected him in 1977, by more than 120,000 votes over his Janata opponent. Mrs Gandhi's new cabinet was notable chiefly for names omitted rather than those included. None of the men regarded as responsible for the worst excesses of the Emergency were included but observers were quick to detect friends of Sanjay in the list.

India's difficulties were no less than before when Mrs Gandhi moved back into the Prime Minister's office. In Assam an agitation began against the growing presence of what were described as foreigners — people from West Bengal, Bangladesh and Nepal. There were also economic difficulties, and one of Mrs Gandhi's first acts was to nationalize six large Indian banks in addition to the 14 taken over by the State in 1969 — an action regarded as populist rather than economically necessary.

Abroad, Afghanistan presented a particularly tricky problem. The world wanted to know where the Indian government stood in relation to the Soviet invasion of a non-aligned Muslim country, with which India had traditionally close ties. It soon became clear that Mrs Gandhi's suspicions of the United States had not abated. She coupled regret at the Soviet intervention with the charge that the Western nations were also guilty of meddling in the area.

What seemed to worry her most was the possibility that the United States might re-arm Pakistan, and that those arms might eventually be used against India.

Then, in June, 1980, she suffered a totally unexpected blow when Sanjay Gandhi, on whom she had come to rely as a close adviser, was killed when the aircraft in which he was stunt-flying over Delhi crashed. Her response was to call on his elder brother, Rajiv, who until then had led an entirely non-political life as an airline pilot; he became a general secretary of the Congress (I) Party and an adviser in Sanjay's place.

Her most serious crisis, however, came with the growth of agitation by the Sikhs of Punjab. There was widespread resentment in the Sikh community arising from a feeling that they did not have proper control of their own resources, and a demand by some for new boundaries and a new, Sikh, capital. The extremists wanted virtual autonomy, and terrorism flared up. At the centre of the extremists was Sant Jarnail Bhindranwale, who based himself with his close supporters in the Golden Temple in Amritsar.

Mrs Gandhi's attempts to resolve the crisis through political means — including some ill-advised moves by local representatives of her party — came to nothing, and on June 6 of this year she ordered the Army into the temple. The operation was successful, but at least 300 people were killed, and she provoked a wave of revulsion among Sikhs across India.

Indira Gandhi, India's third prime minister, was born on November 19, 1917. She was assassinated on October 31, 1984, aged 66

—⁓—

LAURA ASHLEY

FABRIC AND FASHION DESIGNER WHO DREW ON TRADITIONAL ENGLISH STYLES TO CREATE A ROMANTIC VOGUE

SEPTEMBER 18, 1985

Laura Ashley, the fabric and fashion designer, died yesterday at the age of 60 as a result of injuries sustained during a fall last week.

The name Laura Ashley became synonymous with a style of dressing which flew in the face of the successes of the designers who had made London the fashion capital of the world in the 1960s.

Eschewing the short skirts, revealing lines and bright colours of that era, the Laura Ashley success — which was to prove far more enduring than that of its competitors — was based upon the solidly English virtues of a previous century.

Flowing lines, traditional Victorian prints and traditional, natural fabrics, not only restored the romance to dress for young women, but also provided an idiom in which the middle-aged woman could see herself as looking attractive in clothes which manifestly suited her and emphasized the dignity of maturity. Thus the Laura Ashley appeal was made right across the rigidly drawn battle lines of generation, and from modest beginnings in the sale of a few printed scarves to a London department store, was to expand remarkably quickly to cross international frontiers as well.

Owing its business success to Mrs Ashley's husband Bernard with whom she enjoyed a mutually inspiring partnership, Laura Ashley expanded from clothes and fabrics into wallpapers and soft furnishings and had this year been about to go public with an annual turnover of over £100,000,000 and more than 180 shops all round the world.

Laura Ashley was born Laura Mountney in Dowlais, Glamorgan, in 1925. The daughter of a civil servant, she was brought up a strict Baptist. She was educated in London but evacuated back to Wales at the outbreak of the war in 1939 and finished her schooling there before training as a secretary. A short spell at the War Office was followed by service in the WRNS — she was afterwards to say she preferred that uniform to any clothes she had subsequently worn. After that she held a post with the National Federation of Women's Institutes.

She married Bernard Ashley in 1949. He was trying to make a career in the City and his wife had apparently settled down to domestic orthodoxy when she began printing fabrics, with a silk screen of her husband's devising, on the kitchen table of her flat during her first pregnancy in 1953.

She sold her first designs, a mere twenty scarves, to John Lewis in Oxford Street who immediately sold out and requested more. When it became apparent that her design flair was much in demand, her husband left his City job and they went into business, printing fabrics together.

Their first ventures into garments were smocks and aprons and in 1961 they graduated to dresses, blouses and other clothes.

But it was not until 1967 with the opening of the first Laura Ashley shop in Kensington that the Ashley appeal made its first great impact on fashion consciousness at large. From then on the 18th and 19th century designs collected by Laura from museums all over the world, the sturdy fabrics, the high necked blouses and, of course, the highly accessible prices, created a vogue which swept the country.

Locating their headquarters in a disused railway station at Carno in Wales, the Ashleys prepared an assault on the values purveyed by the fevered world of contemporary fashion. And the Laura Ashley qualities of natural fabrics and natural, unforced designs, came to seem to be logical corollary to the move towards healthy, whole-food eating which was also gaining ground under the surface glitter of the 1960s.

By the early 1970s the Ashleys had opened in Shrewsbury, Bath, Edinburgh and Oxford and had licensed operations in Canada and Australia. Very soon clothes, wallpaper and scent were being sold throughout Europe and across America under the familiar blackberry sprig motif.

The wholesome virtues propounded by Laura Ashley dresses were echoed in the conditions in Laura Ashley factories. Fried food was not served in Ashley staff canteens and smoking was discouraged. There were no night shifts and the working week ended at Friday midday.

Inevitably under the pressure of success a homely style of living for the Ashleys themselves was bound to be a thing hard to maintain. Fear of death duties necessitated a move abroad and the acquisition of a château in Picardy and a town house in Brussels. Communicating between the various parts of the Ashley empire meant private aircraft and the other logistical necessities behind the ability to be in many places in quick succession.

However Mrs Ashley continued to the end to give forth an invincibly homely air to the beholder, and to seem always rather to belong to the Welsh dressers and fireplaces of her valleys upbringing than to the world of international fashion which she did in fact inhabit. At the time of her death the Laura Ashley look, though it had undergone some modifications of the more "sensible" sort, showed not the slightest sign of waning in its appeal.

Laura Ashley, fashion designer, was born on September 7, 1925. She died on September 17, 1985, aged 60

—⁓—

SIMONE DE BEAUVOIR

WRITER, PHILOSOPHER
AND EXPONENT OF
REVOLUTIONARY FEMINISM

APRIL 15, 1986

Simone de Beauvoir, who died yesterday, was, in partnership with Jean-Paul Sartre, a leading philosopher-novelist of the existentialist school and later, on her own, a theorist of radical feminism.

She was born in Paris on January 9, 1908, into a prosperous and cultivated though not exceptionally distinguished family. Her father dabbled in the theatre both as actor and director, but was too conscious of his status as a gentleman to do so for profit. He upheld the traditional French upper-class ethos with something of the same humourless rigidity with which his daughter afterwards attacked it.

Simone de Beauvoir's earnestness and intensity revealed itself at an early age. Even as a child she was tormented by doubts about the existence of God and the moral order of the universe, and these doubts prompted her first essays into metaphysics. As an adolescent she resolved to study philosophy, not merely as part of an ordinary student's syllabus, but as a specialist. Her parents and teachers were discouraging. Philosophy, she was told, was a man's subject.

She studied philosophy in Paris together with Simone Weil with whom she might be thought to have much in common, but friendship did not ripen between the two women, and the reason may perhaps be seen in a remark of Simone de Beauvoir's that while Simone Weil was wholly concerned with problems of social justice, she herself was absorbed with the problem of the meaning of existence.

Simone de Beauvoir herself was to come in time to be absorbed with problems of social justice, but in her younger days metaphysics was her chief concern.

Preparing for the *agrégation*, she specialized in Leibniz and was nominally the pupil of Brunschvig, but in practice she was coached by two fellow students with whom she had liaisons, first René Maheu and then Sartre.

She passed the competition successfully when she was 21, the youngest *agrégée* in philosophy in France. Maheu, a future director-general of Unesco, soon proved too much a discreet establishment personality for her liking (she had to refer to him in her memoirs in his lifetime under a pseudonym, André Herbaut); by contrast, the uncompromising, unconventional Sartre thrilled her; meeting him she felt she "could share everything with him always".

Sartre, three years older than she, became in effect her guru. They formed a union which, though painstakingly distinguished from "bourgeois marriage", remained a settled partnership until his death in 1980. In both her philosophical and her political thinking, she follows his lead, and like him she tried to express her ideas in a variety of literary forms — novels, stories and plays as well as straight theoretical essays.

Her best philosophical work, of an academic kind, was her earliest, *Pour une morale de l'ambiguité* (1947) and *L'Existentialisme et la sagesse des nations* (1948) in which she attempted to revise the conventional existentialist notion that life is "absurd" by defining it instead as "ambiguous".

The meaning of life, she suggested, is what each one of us can discover or create for himself. Similarly, she argued that there can be moral values insofar as men construct them for themselves.

Simone de Beauvoir's most successful novel was *Les Mandarins* (1954) a *roman à clef* about Sartre, Camus, herself and other luminaries of the French left-wing after the *Libération*. The book won the Prix Goncourt, and was a best-seller, but precisely because it was so "realist", it was also her least characteristic and distinctive work.

In an essay on *Littérature et métaphysique* (1946) she explained that her aim was to write a "metaphysical novel", and the two books that came closest to realising this ambition were written at about the same time: *Le Sang des Autres* (1945) about a young girl who thirsts for the Absolute and then solves the problem of life by dying a noble death, and *Tous les Hommes sont Mortels* (1946) about a woman who dreads death and then discovers that life is an even heavier burden.

Death was a constant theme in Simone de Beauvoir's writing and became more prominent with the passage of time. *Une Mort Très Douce* (1964) is about the painful death of her mother; *La Vieillesse* (1970) is as much concerned with dying as with ageing; *La Céremonie des Adieux* (1981) is about Sartre's death — it ends with these words: "Sa mort nous sépare. Ma mort ne nous reunira pas. C'est ainsi: il est déjà beau que nos vies aient pu si longtemps s'accorder".

Simone de Beauvoir reached a wide audience with her journalism. She also wrote a number of travel books, one about the United States, which was bitterly hostile, and others about China and Cuba, which were correspondingly eulogistic.

In some respects her most substantial literary achievement was her autobiography. In the first volume, *Mémoires d'une Jeune Fille Rangée* (1958), she describes the family and the world in which she grew up. In *La Force des Choses* (1963) she wrote about her reaction against that background, and about her life with Sartre.

She recalled that, after their *agrégation*, they were separated by their teaching duties, which kept Sartre in Le Havre while she was in Marseilles, and Sartre suggested that they should marry so as to be appointed to the same town.

De Beauvoir firmly resisted such a compromise with her principles; if they intended to have children, she would have agreed, but as they did not, she stuck to her "radical freedom". Sartre himself seems to have been relieved, continuing to live with his mother until her death many years later, and pursuing on the side his various sexual adventures.

In her efforts to keep pace with him, and enact the role of the fully liberated woman, she threw herself, according to her memoirs, into affairs with such unlikely people as Nelson Algren, a Chicago novelist, and Claude Lanzmann, a Marxist journalist 16 years her junior. In the end, she always returned to Sartre.

It was Sartre's financial success which enabled her, after 12 years of teaching, to quit the *lycée* as he had done; and soon she was earning her own living. Her tastes were frugal; Sartre and she always met, in her words, "as equals". The chief difference that de Beauvoir noted between Sartre and herself was that he "was shaped by books" whereas she was affected by "immediate experience". Sartre himself, in his memoirs, *Les Mots*, confirmed that diagnosis. Simone de Beauvoir was also more robust than Sartre. As a young teacher in Marseilles she would hike for 20 miles a day in espadrilles; on visits to Greece, she would try to drag Sartre on long walks in the midday sun.

In the third volume of her autobiography, *La Force de l'âge* (1960), she wrote about the years in which she had become rich and famous. Fame she wore gracefully enough, but riches posed problems for her. She could rarely bring herself to spend money on clothes; with an effort of will she bought herself a small car and a modest flat near the cemetery of Montparnasse.

After *L'Age de Discrétion*, which came out in 1968, she forsook the novel as a literary medium. A book entitled *Quand Prime le Spirituel* appeared in 1979, but it turned out to be an experiment in fiction from the pre-war years, the title an ironical reference to the "spiritual" philosophy of Jacques Maritain which the book was designed to refute from a perspective of atheist existentialism.

Simone de Beauvoir did not participate in Sartre's later enterprise of "integrating existentialism with Marxism", although she had to some extent to nurse him through the ordeal of composing his later mammoth works, and in the last years of his life, when he grew progressively more blind, she spent more and more time in his company, reading aloud to him, and helping to manage his money, which he was apt to lose or give away with reckless generosity. Sartre once compared his life with her to that of George Henry Lewes with George Eliot and indeed, however unlike Lewes Sartre may have been, Simone de Beauvoir did have a lot in common with George Eliot.

She certainly took more seriously than Sartre some of the ideas they shared. A streak of Voltairean impishness in Sartre prompted him to proclaim himself a Marxist, for example, without the least willingness to submit to any authority, even that of Marx himself.

Simone de Beauvoir made more earnest efforts to be a good Marxist. Her most conspicuous endeavour was to work out a Marxist theory of women's liberation, and she undoubtedly succeeded in giving feminism a new look. This was a field in which she reached her widest public.

Her long study of the predicament of women, *Le Deuxième Sexe*, came out as early as 1949, and although its impact was not immediate, it did much to make the demand for women's rights a key factor of the radicalism which emerged in Europe and America in the 1960s and 1970s. Feminism was one thing she did not learn from Sartre. Indeed in an interview she once reproached Sartre for being a "phallocrat", and he denied the charge with only a mock indignation. In 1972, she helped found a society called Choisir, to promote the cause of abortion and contraception on demand. Two years later she was elected President of the Ligue du Droit des Femmes. She refused, however, to have anything to do with the UN Women's Year in 1976, claiming that the Mexico Women's Conference was designed "only to integrate women in a masculine society". She supported the alternative "revolutionary feminist" congress in Brussels.

As an active editorial director of the review *Les Temps Modernes*, Simone de Beauvoir made "revolutionary feminism" one of its favoured causes, and she devoted most of her articles, interviews and television appearances to this subject in the later years. Although she remained on the far left all her life, she became with time more critical of the

Soviet Union because of its persecution of dissenters and of the French Communist Party because it stood for "population not contraception". Simone de Beauvoir was always a very readable writer, and a very likeable person. Her honesty, her sincerity, her almost Victorian high seriousness, commanded widespread respect, even from those who disagreed with her somewhat extreme opinions.

Simone de Beauvoir, French writer and philosopher, was born on January 9, 1908. She died on April 14, 1986, aged 78

———ᴧᴧᴧ———

BERYL MARKHAM

THE FIRST WOMAN AVIATOR TO FLY THE ATLANTIC SOLO FROM EAST TO WEST

AUGUST 5, 1986

Beryl Markham, who in 1936 was the first person* to fly the Atlantic solo from east to west and whose book describing the flight recently became a best-seller when it was republished after 40 years, died in Nairobi on August 3. She was 83.

She was born on October 26, 1902, at Melton Mowbray, in Leicestershire, but most of her life was spent in Africa. In 1906 she was taken to Kenya by her father, Captain Charles Clutterbuck.

Her parents were already divorced and her mother, who remained in England, played no part in her upbringing.

As a child she had little schooling, but acquired from her father the love of horses which was to dominate much of her life. She was eager for adventure and early cultivated the sporting pursuits of male settlers in the White Highlands, spending her time, as she put it, "hunting barefooted in the Rongai Valley or in the cedar forests of the Mau Escarpment." On one occasion she survived mauling by a lion.

When she was 17 her father was ruined and went off to repair his fortune in Peru, leaving Beryl with a horse significantly (in view of her future) called Pegasus. She began her career as a trainer, and the following year one of her horses won the Kenya St Leger. In the 1920s she learnt to fly, and before long was a professional pilot flying around Kenya and into neighbouring territories, sometimes carrying mail or medical supplies. She pioneered the scouting of elephant and other wild game from the air.

Tall, blonde and attractive in a tomboyish way, she made a number of male conquests at this time, including probably — to the extent that he could ever be conquered — Denys Finch Hatton, whom she had the chance (luckily turned down) to accompany on his fatal flight in 1931. Her first marriage, to a Scottish international rugby player, Jock Purves, ended in divorce after two years. In 1927 she married Mansfield Markham, rich younger son of a Liberal MP and coal magnate.

While she was married to him, Henry Duke of Gloucester, as yet unmarried, visited Kenya with his brother the Prince of Wales, and became besotted by her. Her husband, much aggrieved by this romance, threatened to sue, and the matter was only settled when a substantial sum was privately paid over. But she and Markham were soon separated, though not formally divorced until 1942.

In September, 1936, she made her famous transatlantic flight, without radio, and in appalling weather. In her De Havilland Gipsy she took off from Abingdon and landed 24 hours and 25 minutes later with the nose of her aircraft in a Nova Scotia bog. She was slightly injured, but her reputation was made. Immediately she was treated as a heroine, receiving, like Lindbergh, a tickertape welcome in New York. Her looks also contributed to her success in America, since they were compared with Garbo's.

After the flight she went to live in California, where she met the man who was to become her third husband, Raoul Schumacher. With his assistance (for she would have been quite incapable of writing a book on her own) she produced the selective account of her early life, culminating in the great flight, which appeared in 1942 entitled *West With the Night*. Schumacher was a professional editor and ghost-writer, to whom she was able to give the best story he ever handled. Later, he wrote several other stories under her name.

West With the Night was not a success at the time, and was soon forgotten amid all the excitement of a World War in which the United States had just become involved. But it caught the eye of Ernest Hemingway, who described it as "bloody wonderful" in a private letter to Maxwell Perkins. Discovery of this letter inspired the triumphant republication of the book in 1983. Later this year a television documentary on her life will be shown nationwide in the United States, to mark the 50th anniversary of her flight.

In 1947 she and Schumacher were divorced and in the early 1950s she was back in Kenya where she resumed her career as a trainer of race horses, winning the top trainer's award five times and the Kenya Derby six times. Later she trained for a time in South Africa and in Southern Rhodesia (as it then was), but in the early 1970s she returned to Kenya for good. During the last phase of her life her home was a bungalow on the edge of Nairobi racecourse, and she continued to live dangerously, being robbed, beaten up, and on one occasion shot at while driving in her car during an attempted coup.

She had one son by Mansfield Markham. He was killed in the 1970s, but she is survived by two grandchildren. *Beryl Markham, aviator, was born on October 26, 1902. She died on August 3, 1986, aged 83*

* *Editor's note*: Beryl Markham's obituarist was overlooking Scots aviator Jim Mollison's prior achievement, in 1932, when he flew from Portmarnock Strand in Ireland to New Brunswick in Canada.

JACQUELINE DU PRÉ

IMPASSIONED CELLIST
WHO EARNED HER TOWERING
REPUTATION THROUGH
INTERPRETATIONS
OF ELGAR

OCTOBER 21, 1987

Miss Jacqueline du Pré, OBE, who died on October 19, at the age of 42, was regarded as one of the cello's most brilliant exponents when her playing career was tragically cut short by multiple sclerosis at the age of 26.

Though she had her critics among the sterner sort of purist, her wealth of natural talent, which expressed itself in a warm-blooded, romantic approach to her material, made her a favourite on the concert platform, and made the sound of the cello popular with lay audiences. Over the last few years she had established an enviable reputation as an interpreter of the solo cello repertory. Her name was particularly linked with the Elgar cello concerto, which she had played on many occasions all over the country and abroad.

Jacqueline du Pré was born on January 26, 1945. After being inspired by her mother, who, she once said, "guided my first steps, wrote tunes for me to play, and drew pictorial descriptions of the melodies", she went to the London Cello School at the age of six. When she was 10, she went to William Pleeth, whom she always described as "my cello Daddy". She felt that she owed almost everything to him.

Her first public success came when she gave a Wigmore Hall recital at the aged of 16. Then she went to study with Tortelier in Paris and Rostropovich in Moscow. At the same time she began a concert career which took her all over the world.

At the end of 1966 she met the pianist and conductor Daniel Barenboim, and they were married in the following year. He exerted a strong influence on her (as Barbirolli previously had done), particularly in the realm of chamber music. She became one of several players, soloists in their own right, who came together at fairly frequent intervals to tackle the chamber-music repertory. The most common combination was Zukerman, Barenboim and du Pré.

Du Pré's style could, perhaps, be most aptly described as impassioned and grainy. She threw herself into the classical and more modern repertory with her whole body and soul. Some even found her wholehearted approach too subjective, too emotional. If that was a fault, it was one on the right side.

In any case, it is inconceivable that one of her natural gifts would not, as she grew older, have developed a riper, more rounded approach to the cello's repertory. But it was not to be. During a performance of the Brahms Double Concerto at the Lincoln Centre, New York, in 1971, she began to experience extreme difficulty fingering and bowing her cello. She was found to have contracted multiple sclerosis, and her concert career was over. The rest of her life was a brave battle against the ravages of the disease, and she was an example and inspiration to other sufferers.

With her husband she set up the Jacqueline du Pré MS Society Research Fund, which has been administered by the Multiple Sclerosis Society of Great Britain since 1977.

She was appointed OBE in 1976, and had honorary doctorates from numerous universities.

Besides the memory of her concert performances Miss du Pré also leaves a considerable legacy of recordings to console her admirers for her cruelly early death. Among these, her playing of the Elgar will inevitably take first place, but her interpretations of the Delius and Dvorák concertos and of various sonatas are equally rewarding memorials. Alexander Goehr wrote his evocative *Romanze* for her.

As a person, she was as outgoing and lively as she was as an artist, and her friends in the musical world were legion. *Jacqueline du Pré, OBE, cellist, was born on January 26, 1945. She died on October 19, 1987, aged 42*

BETTE DAVIS

STAR WHOSE SCREEN
PORTRAYALS OF SCHEMING
WOMEN AMPLY LIVED UP
TO THE STUDIO SLOGAN,
"NOBODY'S AS GOOD AS BETTE
WHEN SHE'S BAD"

OCTOBER 9, 1989

Bette Davis, who died in a Paris hospital on October 6, at the age of 81, was one of the most durable of all Hollywood film stars, and what does not necessarily follow: one of those most unmistakably gifted with an acting talent. She was an actress of striking presence, rather than conventional beauty, whose main physical asset was her large eyes. She first made her reputation as the suffering heroine of melodrama, in a genre popularly known as the "woman's picture". Later, as she matured towards middle age, she played a gallery of steely, wilful and scheming women, who knew exactly what they wanted and were usually able to get it. In a third, though less distinguished phase of her career, she became a mistress of the grotesque in a series of horror films.

The resolution and capriciousness Bette Davis displayed on screen was very much part of her private character and during her career she had inevitable battles with studios who tried to curb her independence of spirit. It was a spirit that enabled her to survive an unhappy childhood and three broken marriages, and long before feminism became a rallying cry she was the epitome of the liberated woman.

She was born on April 5, 1908, in Lowell, Massachusetts, and christened Ruth Elizabeth — the name Bette (so spelt in tribute to Balzac's *La Cousine Bette*) was adopted in her teens, when her mother became a professional photographer and began to consider some kind of show business career for her.

She early began studying, acting and dancing, and made her professional debut while still at school in a production of *A Midsummer Night's Dream*. In 1928 she entered John Murray Anderson's school in New York, where she studied acting under Anderson and dancing under Martha Graham. A year in repertory led to her first Broadway appearance in a play called *The Earth Between* (1929). Two more Broadway plays later, after her second screen test, she was put under contract to Universal and went out to Hollywood for the first time. From then until the mid 1970s she was rarely away from the studios, and with few intervals she made in regular succession some 90 films, frequently at the rate of three or four a year.

She began, in the traditional fashion, with small roles — in her first film, *Bad Sister*, she played, improbably, the good sister and was apparently regarded as something of a problem: not glamorous enough to be a siren, not conventional enough to play classy, ladylike roles, with a strange nervous intensity which made her difficult to cast.

There her career might have stayed had she not been cast by George Arliss as the female lead in his talkie version of *The Man Who Played God* (1932) at Warner Brothers — her Universal contract having meanwhile expired. In this she was widely noticed, the association with Arliss gave her a new standing in Hollywood, and, perhaps most important, as a result of the film she was put under contract to Warner Bros, the company which controlled her career, and one of whose chief box-office attractions she was, for some 17 years.

Her first great role came in 1934 with her extraordinary creation as Somerset Maugham's unscrupulous Cockney waitress in *Of Human Bondage*, a performance which, despite some obtrusive mannerisms and uncertainties, still holds up remarkably well. It was widely felt that Bette Davis should have won her first Academy Award for this film, and that the award she got the following year for *Dangerous*, in which she gave a virtuoso performance as an alcoholic ex-actress (at the ripe old age of 27), was something in the nature of a consolation prize.

Immediately after *Dangerous* she made another of her most famous films, *The Petrified Forest*, a rather stagy adaptation of Robert E. Sherwood's play in which she starred opposite Leslie Howard, a teaming repeated bizarrely in *It's Love I'm After* (1937), where they were uncharacteristically called upon to play broad comedy.

The teaming was famously not repeated in *Gone With The Wind*, Scarlett O'Hara being a role Bette Davis passionately wanted to play. But, again, she received compensation with a very similar role in the Goldwyn production *Jezebel*, directed by William Wyler, and, again, she was given an Oscar for it. This inaugurated the 1940s, perhaps the greatest period in her career, with classic following classic. Not that all of them were classics on the same level: some of them were classics, in particular retrospectively, of camp rather than true quality. But among them were films in which Bette Davis was a remarkable part of a remarkable whole, such as William Wyler's *The Letter* and *The Little Foxes*, William Dieterle's historical drama *Juarez*, and John Huston's *In This Our Life*. And the shameless vehicles for a display of big-star fireworks, like *Dark Victory*, *The Old Maid*, *Now, Voyager*, *Old Acquaintance*, *Mr Skeffington* and *Deception* are somehow given a conviction which transcends the nonsense elements in them by the sheer intensity of Bette Davis's involvement in her roles.

The Private Lives of Elizabeth and Essex (1939) was her first film in colour and saw her famous portrayal of Queen Elizabeth I, her favourite role and one she repeated 16 years later in *The Virgin Queen*.

In 1949 her long-lasting contract with Warner Bros, the subject of some famous litigation in the 1930s when Bette Davis spearheaded a revolt of Hollywood stars against the restrictions of the contract system, ended with one of her most peculiar films, King Vidor's *Beyond The Forest*, in which she was called upon to disport herself in a Charles Addams wig as a femme fatale of the Mid-West: "Men turned and stared when Rosa Moline passed by" — as well they might. For this film the publicity department coined the immortal slogan "Nobody's as good as Bette when she's bad", a line which nicely if simplistically summed up much of her work during these years.

Strangely enough, this seeming low in her career led, quite by chance (she was the third choice for the role), to what remains perhaps the definitive Bette Davis portrayal, Margo Channing in Joseph L. Mankiewicz's *All About Eve* (1950) — the temperamental actress, betrayed by her young protégée but finding true love in the process. This used — as nearly as any character she played — the full range of her talents and an extra something of total instinctive identification between actress and role.

The years that followed brought ups and downs, the most important up being the title role in *Whatever Happened to Baby Jane?*, in which Robert Aldrich brought together two arch rivals of Hollywood, Bette Davis and Joan Crawford, as rival sisters, both Hollywood has-beens, with vicious designs on each other's health and sanity. This inaugurated a period of horror and semi-horror films, such as *Dead Ringer*, *Hush... Hush, Sweet Charlotte*, and *The Nanny*, with Bette Davis, as usual, gallantly trying her hand at anything that offered, absorbed in her craft and the necessity of continuing to exercise it, even in decidedly less than propitious conditions. During this time she also made occasional returns to the stage, notably in a revue, *Two's Company* (1952) with her then husband, Gary Merrill, and in Tennessee Williams's *Night of the Iguana* (1961). She also wrote her autobiography, *The Lonely Life* (1962), one of the franker and more personal of as-told-to Hollywood books.

Though she had lost her looks, and some of her stamina, and had a serious operation for cancer, Bette Davis continued to be busy well into her seventies. Much of her work was now for television, where she enhanced many a routine drama. But there were cinema films as well and when playing an imperious American matron in Agatha Christie's *Death On The Nile* (1978) she showed she could still hold her own in an all-star cast. Four years before a stage comeback in *Miss Moffat*, a musical version of one of her cinema successes, *The Corn Is Green*, proved abortive when she withdrew through illness. Her last important film role was opposite another veteran actress, Lillian Gish, in Lindsay Anderson's *The Whales of August* which appeared in 1987.

Bette Davis was on her way home to California via Paris when she died, after having attended this year's San Sebastian Film Festival in Spain where she had been specially honoured.

Star quality — the ability to project personality, to just exist interestingly on screen — is one thing, and acting talent — the ability to create a variety of different characters, to bury the actor in the role — quite another. Bette Davis was the supreme example of their coexistence in one and the same performer — the most starry of film actors, the most actorly of film stars. Her unmistakable vocal mannerisms, even her distinctive ways of smoking a cigarette, made her the delight of imitators — yet, though herself a symbol of Hollywood and the star system, she managed to transcend them both often enough to make the whole thing worthwhile. There never was, and never will be, anyone like her.

Her acting ability appealed to the widest audiences and in the most diverse circumstances. One such testimony of her success was from wartime Britain. "Jock" Colville, Churchill's secretary, in a diary entry of January 1945, wrote: "After dinner there was a film in an Air Ministry room on the ground floor in King Charles St. The PM bid us all cast care aside... and so all the typists, drivers, servants, etc, saw. .. Bette Davis in *Dark Victory*, a brilliantly acted film and one of the few I have seen end as a tragedy".

Of her four marriages, the second ended with the death of her husband and the other three in divorce. Her fourth husband was the actor, Gary Merrill, with whom she appeared in films and on stage. "I have not been very fortunate; I think it is very difficult for a famous woman," was her own comment on married life when talking to reporters in San Sebastian last month.

She is survived by one daughter, as well as two adopted children.

Bette Davis, film star, was born on April 5, 1908. She died on October 6, 1989, aged 81.

—◆—

PROFESSOR DAPHNE JACKSON

PHYSICS PROFESSOR WHO
TIRELESSLY PROMOTED
CAREERS IN SCIENCE AND
ENGINEERING FOR WOMEN AND
SCHOOLGIRLS

FEBRUARY 14, 1991

When, in 1971, Daphne Jackson was appointed professor of physics at Surrey University she was the only woman professor of physics in the United Kingdom and was to remain so for many years. As well as doing distinguished work in nuclear, medical and radiation physics, she exerted herself to make the sciences an attractive career for women and was active, for example, in seeking ways and means to enable women who had had to bring up children to return to professions in the scientific world.

Daphne Jackson was educated at Peterborough County Grammar School for Girls and at Imperial College, London, where she read physics. In 1958 she moved to Battersea College of Technology as a research assistant in physics. There she began to research in theoretical nuclear physics with

Professor Lewis Elton. She became a lecturer at Battersea in 1960 and was awarded her PhD in 1962. In 1967 she was promoted to reader in physics at the University of Surrey (as Battersea had by then become). She was dean of the faculty of science from 1977 to 1980 and from 1984 to 1988. Her publications included *Nuclear Reactions* (with R. C. Barrett, 1970), *Nuclear Sizes and Structure* (1977) and *Imaging with Ionising Radiations* (with K. Kouris and N. M. Spyrou, 1982) besides many contributions to learned journals. The latter consisted not only of papers on nuclear science but also contributions to the debate on education and science policy.

Besides her scientific work Daphne Jackson was greatly in demand to provide advice and guidance to numerous bodies. These covered a wide range of interests and activities, in both the professional and public domain; to mention but a few: the Science and Engineering Research Council, the National Radiological Protection Board, the Civil Service Commission final selection board, local health authorities, the Department of Energy and the Meteorological Office. But she will perhaps be best remembered for her work with the Women's Engineering Society of which she was president from 1983 to 1985.

She was tireless in her efforts to promote the idea that a career in science and engineering could be exciting to women, and carried her gospel energetically into the schools. She personally raised substantial sums from industry to support her Women Returners Scheme, which provided flexible, part-time fellowships for women qualified in science and engineering who wanted to return to their profession after a career break. In recognition of her work in this area she was appointed OBE in 1987 and she also received honorary doctorates from the Open University and from Exeter and Loughborough universities.

Although very much in demand outside the university, Daphne Jackson also worked long and hard within. She firmly believed that a head of department should teach undergraduates, particularly in the first year, so that they got to know her and could approach her if they had any difficulties. She was a fine research leader and the fact that Surrey's physics department was rated very highly in both of the UGC's research selectivity exercises owed much to her high standards and leadership. She promoted close links with schools not only to encourage greater numbers to consider a career in science but also to inculcate the idea of the University of Surrey as an exciting place to study. She was also active in providing advice on public relations about which she had a great deal of personal knowledge since she had a gift to express complex scientific information in a way which the general public could understand and hence was much in demand by the media. Among the recreations she listed in her *Who's Who* entry was "encouraging women in science education".

Although she had suffered from cancer for some years, it was only in December of last year that she became seriously ill and even then she worked from home until last week. She was unmarried.

Professor Daphne Jackson, OBE, physicist and campaigner for scientific education, was born on September 23, 1936. She died of cancer on February 8, 1991, aged 54

━━◦◦◦◦━━

DAME MARGOT FONTEYN

BALLERINA OF OUTSTANDING LYRICAL GIFTS AND CONSUMMATE ARTISTRY

FEBRUARY 22, 1991
Dame Margot Fonteyn, the ballerina, died yesterday in Panama City aged 71. She was born at Reigate, Surrey, on May 18, 1919.

Margot Fonteyn was one of the great dancers not just of her own time but of all time; her name will live as surely in the history of ballet as those of Taglioni and Pavlova. She was also one of the rare artists whose names mean as much to the ordinary man and woman as to the devotees of their own particular art. Many dancers have excelled her in virtuosity or in the theatrical intensity they brought to dramatic roles. Fonteyn's special gift was for grasping completely the intention and balance of the dance and the music and bringing them to life for the audience. She never lost the enthusiasm which marked her dancing from childhood, and the ability to communicate her own enjoyment was perhaps the supreme secret of her art.

During the course of an extraordinarily long career she brought that gift to ever wider audiences in many parts of the world where she performed on stage; millions more saw her on television or in films. Consequently, even more than Anna Pavlova in the early years of this century, Fonteyn awakened a love of dance in untold thousands of spectators.

She was born Margaret Hookham, the child of an English father and a mother half Irish, half Brazilian. She claimed to have inherited her enthusiasm and response to rhythm and music from her mother; and from her father the tenacity and perfectionism to put those qualities to use. From the age of four she attended dancing classes with a local teacher, and continued them in various places abroad where her father's work as an engineer took the family. The liveliness of character dancing attracted her more than the pure classicism which was later to bring her fame.

It was not until she saw Alicia Markova dance *Les Sylphides* during a visit home in 1931 that Peggy Hookham became really ambitious to be a dancer herself. Her father was then working in China and the child was lucky in finding an exceptionally gifted teacher, George Goncharov, in Shanghai. After two years with him she returned to England and studied with Seraphine Astafieva (Markova's teacher) before joining the Vic-Wells Ballet School in 1934. Within a few weeks she was performing with the Vic-Wells Ballet, and before the year was out she had her first solo role as the child in Ninette de Valois's *The Haunted Ballroom*, under an interim version of her stage name, Margot Fontes.

Before her sixteenth birthday Frederick Ashton gave Fonteyn the leading part in a new production of *Rio Grande*, and when Markova left the company soon afterwards, Fonteyn was one of the dancers who shared the ballerina's roles among them. It did not take long for her to emerge as the front runner, and by the time she was 20 Fonteyn had danced the lead in three of the great classics, *Giselle*, *Swan Lake* and *The Sleeping Beauty*, besides creating roles in a series of ballets by Ashton: *Le Baiser de la fée*, *Apparitions*, *Nocturne*, *Les Patineurs*, *A Wedding Bouquet* and *Horoscope*.

Fonteyn was fortunate in the colleagues under whose professional influence she found herself at this time. De Valois, directing the young company, had a far-sighted grasp of strategy in repertoire and casting. Ashton, choosing Fonteyn as his new muse in the flush of his youthful creative energy, developed her interpretative gifts and also advised her on how to dress and behave off-stage. She had Robert Helpmann as her most frequent partner, a man with a keen theatrical flair, and the company's music director, Constant Lambert, a man of wide culture, took her particularly under his wing.

The outbreak of war in 1939 brought a more urgent tempo to the company's work. Instead of only two or three performances a week, they began dancing nightly, with matinées besides, to provide entertainment for war workers and troops on leave; long gruelling tours were undertaken between short London seasons. The company was in Holland at the time of the German invasion and escaped with nothing more than what the dancers stood up in. Fonteyn by now was the company's undisputed ballerina, with a consequent demand for her to appear as often as possible. And there were still new roles to add, most notably two by Ashton which extended her range with the passion of *Dante Sonata* and the glitter of *The Wanderer*.

This experience must have helped develop the stamina that made her later career possible, but at the time it did more to consolidate her talent than to advance her artistry. The performances she gave in *The Sleeping Beauty* when the ballet moved to Covent Garden in 1946 seemed impressive at the time but would be only promising by today's standards. Luckily Ashton created in *Symphonic Variations* a work that showed Fonteyn's lyrical gifts to supreme advantage.

A turning point in her career came in 1948 when she went as guest artist to Paris to create the role of Agathe, the cat-woman, in Roland Petit's *Les Demoiselles de la Nuit*. The frank admiration of this glamorous young choreographer, and being treated as a star, seemed to add a new assurance and crispness to everything she did on returning to London. The acclaim she received in New York the next year, opening the Sadler's Wells Ballet's first season there with *The Sleeping Beauty*, completed the transformation into a ballerina of international quality.

Before the American tour, an injury during the first night of Ashton's *Don Juan* had kept her from the stage for several months and prevented her from dancing the premiere of his first three-act ballet, *Cinderella*. When she took over the role later, however, she made it peculiarly her own, showing new qualities of humour and romance.

Fonteyn's career was subsequently interrupted more than once by serious injury or illness, setbacks that might have precipitated early retirement in other dancers. Each time, however, she returned apparently stronger than before, and she went on dancing long past the age when a dancer's powers usually decline. In Fonteyn's case the physical loss was compensated by continually developing expressiveness and artistic maturity. The initial impetus to extending her career came, however, when, in her early forties, she first danced with Rudolf Nureyev in 1962. He was, as she remarked, young enough to be her son, but there was such immediate rapport between them, such a chemistry between them on stage and such unanimity of purpose in their preparation that they became a partnership of uniquely satisfying quality. Both learned much from the

Dame Margot Fonteyn in 1975

other, enriching their performances with other partners as well as their joint appearances.

Fonteyn's long career on stage was made easier because her performances had never depended primarily on virtuosity, although in fact her technique was stronger than was often said. It was she who introduced the long-sustained balances now expected of Aurora in the Rose Adagio; and when younger dancers took over some of her created roles they revealed unexpected difficulties, probably for lack of her gift of phrasing steps to the music. It can be said that Fonteyn never lacked the technique needed for any role she was cast in.

These covered a wide range. Among the many leading parts created for her with the Royal Ballet were *Scènes de ballet*, *Daphnis and Chloë*, *Tiresias*, *Sylvia*, *Homage to the Queen*, *La Péri*, *Birthday Offering* and *Marguerite and Armand*, all by Ashton; de Valois's

Don Quixote, Helpmann's *Hamlet*, Petit's *Paradise Lost* and *Pelléas et Mélisande*. As guest elsewhere, John Cranko created *Poème de l'extase* for her in Stuttgart, Martha Graham mounted *Lucifer* for Nureyev and her, and Peter Darrell presented her as a Beardsley seductress in *Scarlet Pastorale* with the Scottish Ballet. She was (against the choreographer's wish but at the insistence of the Royal Ballet's American impresario Sol Hurok) the first Juliet in Kenneth MacMillan's production, and danced also in revivals of Massine's *Three Cornered Hat* with the choreographer, Balanchine's *Ballet Imperial* and *Night Shadow*, Fokine's *Firebird* and *Petrushka*, and Limón's *The Moor's Pavane* among others, also Nureyev's productions of the *Corsair* pas de deux, *La Bayadère*, *Raymonda* and the Grand Pas from *Paquita*.

With the Royal Ballet, Fonteyn occupied a position of complete supremacy. It has sometimes been said that her presence held back the advancement of other dancers, but there was never any among her contemporaries or juniors to equal her. By 1959 the demand for seats when she appeared was such that special prices were charged, and in that same year she began to be billed as a guest artist so that she should be free to accept more of the engagements she was offered all over the world. Nevertheless the Royal Ballet remained her base until after Ashton's retirement in 1970, although she also danced with more than 30 other companies and specially assembled groups.

She continued dancing until after her sixtieth birthday, which was marked by Covent Garden with a special gala including a *Salut d'amour* by Ashton which they danced together. Even after that she took on a new role as the leading nymph in Nijinsky's *L'Après-midi d'un faune* during Nureyev's 1979 summer season, and was persuaded by him to dance also two final performances of *Le Spectre de la Rose*. Occasionally thereafter she appeared on special occasions but only in roles that required no dancing.

In 1955 Fonteyn married Dr Roberto de Arias, a sweetheart of her girlhood who had meanwhile married and had a family before re-entering her life. Immediately after their wedding he was appointed Panamanian ambassador to the Court of St James's. Fonteyn managed to combine the duties of an ambassador's wife with her already demanding career, and when her husband fell from political favour she supported his attempts to regain power in his own country. This led at one point to her arrest. She also found herself in police custody once after attending a party in the hippie district of Los Angeles. The dignity with which she endured such incidents showed one aspect of her character. Another was revealed by the devotion with which she personally nursed her husband for 25 years until his death after he had been shot and crippled by an associate with a personal grudge.

Two careers, as ballerina and as politician's wife, would have been enough for most women, but Fonteyn also became in 1954 president of the Royal Academy of Dancing and committed herself wholeheartedly to its well being.

In later years, Fonteyn developed a great interest in her husband's farm in Panama, and she continued to live there even after his death with few creature comforts because she had spent most of her money on caring for her husband and then incurred considerable costs having treatment in Texas when she developed cancer.

In spite of her illness she undertook some teaching and coaching, and also visited England each year for the Assembly of the RAD and for the degree ceremony at Durham University, which had elected her chancellor. She wrote and introduced a six-part television series *The Magic of Dance*. This was also the subject of one of several books she wrote; they included an autobiography, a study of Pavlova, and an account of *A Dancer's World*.

Fonteyn was created CBE in 1951 and DBE in 1956. She had honorary degrees from many universities and the Order of the Finnish Lion. A greater tribute however was the affection she inspired all over the world. The purity and musicality of her work won admiration; its liveliness and dedication inspired much warmer and deeper feelings, manifested in a special tribute performance at Covent Garden last May for which Nureyev danced and Plácido Domingo sang.

Dame Margot Fonteyn, DBE, ballerina, was born on May 18, 1919. She died on February 21, 1991, aged 71

EILEEN JOYCE

AUSTRALIAN-BORN CONCERT
PIANIST WHO PROGRESSED
FROM PLAYING A BEER-STAINED
PUB PIANO TO A SENSATIONAL
PROMS DEBUT

MARCH 29, 1991

Because in mid-career she opted for an emphasis on personal popularity, Eileen Joyce's undoubted musicality and virtuosity were for a while overlooked. She was a player of extraordinary skill, at home in Mozart as in Shostakovich and encompassing Chopin, Liszt, Grieg and Rachmaninov along the way, as her many excellent records, recently reissued, reveal. These capabilities had been on display before the war, during which her good looks and charm, allied to her pianistic flair, brought her playing to the attention of a much broader section of the public than generally listened to classical music at that time. At this period she revelled in playing three concertos in a programme, often appearing in a different dress for each. Their glamour attracted some comment at a time when it was unexpected, but she said: "Changing fills in the intervals when I might be biting my nails with nervousness. Would the critics prefer that I should wear black?" She played the piano for Ann Todd in the film *The Seventh Veil* and made a film of an autobiographical nature called *Wherever She Goes.*

Joyce was born of immigrant parents of Spanish and Irish descent. Her mother told her she was born in a tent; her father was a labourer and she was called "Ragged Eilie". They were terribly poor and she first played falteringly on a beer-stained piano from a local pub that was trundled round to her father's house. She was educated at a convent school sitting in the back row reserved for the non-paying pupils. She became well known in Boulder City for her playing and money was collected so that she could go to a larger convent school at Perth.

Her talents were spotted first by the composer Percy Grainger and then by the pianist Backhaus who was touring Australia. They urged that she be sent abroad to study. Grainger was helpful in raising funds so that she could go to the conservatoire in Leipzig. Her teachers there were Max Pauer and the fearfully strict Robert Teichmüller who was responsible for giving her a magnificent technique. After three years at Leipzig she moved to London and continued her studies with Tobias Matthay and Adelina de Lara. Finally she went to work with Schnabel in Berlin.

With such a comprehensive training she astonished the conductor Albert Coates at an audition in 1930. He recommended her to Sir Henry Wood with whom she made a sensational debut that year, playing a Prokofiev concerto. She quickly established an appreciable reputation in recitals and concertos and began a long series of recordings for Parlophone. Her repertoire eventually consisted of more than

70 works, some of which, such as the John Ireland Concerto, were written especially for her.

After her war-time fame she resumed a fairly normal concert career touring all over the world. She could be out-spoken publicly, once complaining, in 1957, that there was not one grand piano available for public recitals in three county towns — Winchester, Exeter and Gloucester, home of the Three Choirs Festival. At a musical competition in Geneva she walked out on her fellow judges, complaining of outside influences being brought to bear on the jury. At the Proms in 1958 she gave the first performance in England of Shostakovich's piano concerto, Opus 101.

Her career was hard work. Some of her strong stubby fingers were in 1958 taped to prevent cuts and others had corns. Her hands became weary, her back strained and Harley Street became a second home. Towards the end she was spending more on doctors' bills than she was earning on the concert platform.

In the early 1960s she retired precipitately although in 1967 she was persuaded to reappear to play Rachmaninov's Second Concerto, one of her greatest successes, once more. She was made an honorary Doctor of Music at Cambridge in 1970 and appointed CMG in 1981. Her retirement was spent in Kent, near Chartwell, where she would often entertain friends with her playing.

She was married twice and had a son by her first husband.

Eileen Joyce, CMG, concert pianist, was born on November 21, 1912. She died on March 25, 1991, aged 78

Editor's note: Other authorities claim January 1, 1908, or November 21, 1910, as Eileen Joyce's birthdate.

DAME PEGGY ASHCROFT

BOLD AND VERSATILE
FIRST LADY OF THE ENGLISH
STAGE, FOR WHOM THERE WAS
NO SUCH THING AS
A TYPICAL ROLE

JUNE 15, 1991

Since the death of Edith Evans, Peggy Ashcroft had held the undisputed place of first lady of the English stage. Her performances were among the Shakespearian peaks of the past 60 years, but she is no less vividly remembered for her work in the modern repertory and for the television and film roles that won her a huge audience during her final decade. She also had a larger vision of the theatre than can be conveyed by summarising her acting career.

From her girlhood reading of Stanislavsky she was, from the start, an actress in search of a company. She briefly glimpsed her goal during the 1930s and finally achieved it after the war with the foundation of the English Stage Company, the Royal Shakespeare Company and the National Theatre. To each she gave wholehearted support at a crucial time in its fortunes. What they gained from her was not only the services of a great classical star but a moral force which was as visible in her performances as it was in her personal life. She was seen as an embodiment of British integrity, a factor that was turned against her by such critics as James Agate and Kenneth Tynan who persisted in regarding her as a class-bound home counties lady who had no business to be essaying Cleopatra or the Duchess of Malfi. In fact these parts were fully within her range and if one point emerges from the roll-call of her most successful performances it is that there was no such thing as a typical Ashcroft role.

What did set her apart from actors who simply disappear into whatever they are playing was the presence of a central moral intelligence authorising whatever imaginative leap the character demanded. When she became the first establishment actress to play Brecht, or when she first hurled a four-letter word at a West End audience, she left a landmark behind. To recount her life is to tell the story of the English theatrical renaissance.

Edith Margaret Emily Ashcroft was born in Croydon, the second child of a land-agent father and a Danish-German mother herself an amateur actress who had taken lessons from the poetic speech pioneer Elsie Fogerty, at whose Central School of Speech and Drama the 16-year-old Peggy Ashcroft enrolled on leaving Woodford School. "I learned very little about acting there," she later declared, being as resistant as her fellow student Laurence Olivier to the school's stress on the Voice Beautiful. Her theatrical education began with her reading of Stanislavsky's *My Life in Art* and her discovery of his émigré compatriot Theodore Komisarjevsky who was then revolutionising the English stage from his tiny theatre in Barnes. She made her professional debut in 1926, playing opposite Ralph Richardson in a Birmingham Repertory revival of Barrie's *Dear Brutus* after which except for illness or personal choice she was seldom out of work.

In the early years, like any newcomer, she took what was going, though even then she was more at home in London's adventurous little theatres than in the commercial machine. Critics of the time were struck by her freedom from any kind of stage trickery and by the transparent honesty which remained one of her sovereign qualities. One conspicuous early event was her 1930 performance of Desdemona to Paul Robeson's Othello, which also marked her political awakening (a star in the Savoy Theatre, Robeson was unwelcome upstairs in the hotel). The turning point came not on the professional stage but in the 1932 OUDS production of *Romeo and Juliet* which brought her into contact with undergraduate George Devine and his guest director, John Gielgud, her two closest allies over the next 25 years.

The alliance was delayed by her marriage to Komisarjevsky and a season with the Old Vic where she piled up a succession of Shakespearian leads at breakneck speed under the direction of Harcourt Williams. By then a member of the unofficial "family" that grew up in the Motleys' Studio (Gielgud's designers), hatching theatrical revolution over endless cups of tea, she came into her own as Gielgud's leading actress when he embarked on the untried adventure of setting up a classical company in the West End. Beginning as Juliet in the legendary 1935 New Theatre production, she returned for Gielgud's subsequent seasons at the Queen's and the Haymarket, playing Nina in Komisarjevsky's The Seagull, Irina in Michel Saint-Denis's Three Sisters, and the Duchess of Malfi (then a controversial novelty) for George Rylands: productions that left an indelible mark on theatrical memory. True to her company loyalties, she also joined in Saint-Denis's ill-fated 1938 Phoenix season before the "family" was dispersed by the war.

Had Gielgud's companies not kept breaking up, she would gladly have stayed inside them. As it was, she rebuilt her career at the Stratford Memorial Theatre (under Anthony Quayle) and in the West End. She often undertook parts with severe misgivings but then turned them to triumph: as with the alcoholic wife in Robert Morley's Edward, My Son, the victim-turned-avenger in The Heiress, and (originally her prime bête noire) the suicidal Hester Collyer in Rattigan's The Deep Blue Sea.

The pattern of her career underwent its second great change in the 1950s with the dawning of the age of subsidy. First she resumed her alliance with Devine in the 1954 Hedda Gabler and when Devine launched the English Stage Company two years later, Ashcroft at the height of her commercial success in Enid Bagnold's The Chalk Garden forsook the Haymarket for the wilderness of Sloane Square to double as Shen TeShui Ta in his production of Brecht's The Good Woman of Setzuan. The ESC, however, did not maintain a permanent troupe so, although she subsequently joined Devine in revivals of Chekhov and Ibsen, her main allegiance went to Peter Hall's newly-formed Royal Shakespeare Company. She began in 1960 by reclaiming two shrews, Kate and Paulina, in The Taming of the Shrew and The Winter's Tale, before going on, in 1963-64, to play Margaret of Anjou in The Wars of the Roses, in which (then in her late fifties) she began as a young girl and aged into a demonic septuagenarian. This was a woman, Philip Hope-Wallace wrote, "kept alive by sheer passion of inner hate". With Hall, she also became an incomparable advocate of Pinter, Albee, and (when Hall moved on to the National Theatre) Beckett. Just as she had championed the young Peter Hall at the start of the RSC, so she supported his younger successor, Trevor Nunn, with whom she achieved her crowning stage performance as the Countess of Roussillon in the 1981 All's Well That Ends Well, in which she lent something Chekhovian to Shakespearian comedy.

Nunn once made the point that actors achieve greatness only in old age when "life has tested them and they've come through." This was clearly true of Ashcroft, both on stage and in her final creative breakthrough on film. Three times married, CND supporter, and veteran campaigner against social injustice (so much so that when she was created DBE in 1956 Hugh Beaumont nicknamed her "the Red Dame"), she was not short of living experience. In her youth an epitome of the intelligent *ingénue*, in middle age a radical actress exploring the desperation of women of violently contrasted classes and cultures, she finally took on a quality in which acting became wisdom. Nunn again: "You simply lose yourself in the largeness of her spirit."

In her film and television work she was able to take the spectator straight to the heart of character. One of her most remarkable small screen roles was Barbie Batchelor in Paul Scott's *The Jewel in the Crown* (1984), where she showed the development of character from robust decency to ferocious despair with minimal reliance on external effects. This performance won her a BAFTA award. She had acted in films from *The Wandering Jew* of 1933 and had a role in Hitchcock's *The Thirty-Nine Steps* of 1935. But she picked her film parts. She had a success as the Mother Superior in *The Nun's Story* (1958) and won an Oscar as the best supporting actress for her portrayal of Mrs Moore in David Lean's film version of E. M. Forster's *A Passage to India* (1984). At 81, in 1989, she shared the best actress award, the Coppa Volpi Prize, with Geraldine James at the Venice Film Festival for her performance in Sir Peter Hall's film *She's Been Away*. It was a remarkable achievement for an actress who had made her debut 60 years before. Her most recent public appearance was at the Olivier Awards in London in April when she was given a special award to mark her life's service to the theatre.

Her work was always hard to describe. She herself called it a process of arriving at psychological truth by means of tonal accuracy. Externally it was made up of innumerable small details of gesture and facial expression; but what she was clearly mattered more than what she did, with the result that any attempt to express it in words was liable to turn into gush. Colleagues habitually summed her up by contrasts: "English containment and wild passion", "fearlessness and vulnerability", "ferocity and tenderness." Anthony Quayle put it more simply: "She's a crusader, she's *Pilgrim's Progress* to the end."

Besides Komisarjevsky, she was married to Sir Rupert Hart-Davis and to Jeremy Hutchinson (now Lord Hutchinson of Lullington), by whom she leaves a son and a daughter.

Dame Peggy Ashcroft, DBE, actress, was born on December 22, 1907. She died on June 14, 1991, aged 83

MARLENE DIETRICH

MESMERISINGLY
EROTIC, HUSKY-VOICED
HOLLYWOOD FILM STAR AND
CABARET SINGER

MAY 7, 1992

"Though we all might enjoy/ Seeing Helen of Troy/As a gay cabaret entertainer/ I doubt that she could/ Be one quarter as good/ As our legendary, lovely/ Marlene."

Thus Noël Coward, introducing Dietrich to a London nightclub audience at the Café de Paris in 1954 by which time the star was well into her fifties and a second career. In her first career she had conquered the screens, first as Lola in *The Blue Angel*. Others have taken the role of Heinrich Mann's temptress, on screen — and on stage a version is about to open on Shaftesbury Avenue. But none could match Dietrich. Hollywood seized her and Paramount turned her into a star. She became synonymous with the erotic: no one could light a cigarette more sensuously than she or tell, in the huskiest of voices, the boys in the backroom what they should have. Unlike most actresses who are compelled to evolve with age the image of Dietrich, once established, was amplified rather than altered as time went on. The insolent,

ironic style of her youth did at one point mellow into approachability, but it re-emerged in maturer form to haunt her later performances on the screen and in cabaret. But the soul of the Dietrich secret, a quality which kept crowds queuing for her one-woman shows at an age when such a thing came to seem almost preposterous, was something, perhaps, more fundamental.

Reduced to its simplest terms, Dietrich's appeal was, indeed, sex appeal. But it was a sex appeal which involved not merely the face, the million dollar legs and the air of Do Not Touch, which were all part of the armoury. Essentially, it embodied the idea of the eternal woman and like Garbo it began with beauty of an order calculated to overwhelm the senses, suspending criticism of the roles (frequently in Dietrich's case tawdry ones) represented by the actress. The crowds who later flocked to see and hear the septuagenarian Dietrich came not to judge the performance but simply to be part of the ambience it created.

The biggest mystery about Dietrich was, for a long time, her date of birth. This was carefully concealed and suggestions for the date ranged from 1894 through to 1912. Then the secret came out when an East German clerk located in his registry and somewhat tactlessly published the entry relating to the birth of one Maria Magdalene (hence the contraction Marlene) Dietrich on December 27, 1901, in the suburb of Schöneberg.

Marlene Dietrich was born Maria Magdalene, the second daughter of an officer in the Prussian police and a mother who came from a well-known family of Berlin jewellers. She grew up against a background of clenched social and financial respectability. A year or two after her birth Dietrich's father died and her mother married another military man, Edouard von Losch, who was killed on the Russian front in the closing weeks of the first world war, leaving his widow and her daughters in severely straitened circumstances. But her mother strenuously supported her daughter's intense desire to be a performer and she in turn remained proud of her Prussian ancestry.

By 1919 Dietrich was enrolled in the Berlin Hochschule für Musik, since it was thought she had a future as a violinist. Damage to her wrist put an end to that idea, and she soon afterwards auditioned for Max Reinhardt. But he gravely doubted her acting ability and her first attempt was not successful. For some time after that she worked as a chorus girl in a touring company before he eventually gave her small roles at the Deutsches Theater.

While there Dietrich, like many of her contemporaries, also began to play small roles at the UFA studios.

It was in 1922, though she often denied it, that she made her debut at the age of 21 as a maid in *The Little Napoleon*. For the next seven years she divided her time more or less equally between the theatres of Berlin and its film studios: on stage, guided by Reinhardt, she worked in Shaw's *Misalliance* and *Back to Methuselah*, establishing a local reputation second

"Calculatingly lit and evocatively dressed": Marlene Dietrich at the Queen's Theatre in London in 1964

only to that of Elisabeth Bergner who once remarked: "If I were as beautiful as Marlene, I wouldn't know what to do with my talent."

But on screen Dietrich's talents were confined to rather less demanding or rewarding scripts until in 1929 the Austrian director who was to become her guide, mentor and guardian, Josef von Sternberg, while searching for a Lola to play opposite Emil Jannings in *The Blue Angel*, saw her on stage one night. He was later to write: "There was a woman whose face promised everything. I took a beautiful woman, instructed her, presented her carefully, edited her charms, disguised her imperfections and led her to crystallise a pictorial aphrodisiac."

The success of *The Blue Angel* in Berlin confirmed rather than created Dietrich as a star in Germany: a year earlier she had already been sharing German movie-magazine covers with Garbo. But internationally it was the film in which she was born, and which was to characterise her forever. "What happened to you before *Blue Angel?*" she was once asked at a Hollywood press conference. Dietrich, who was never renowned for courtesy when dealing with the press, replied curtly and none too accurately, "Nothing".

Paramount immediately signed her to a two-picture deal and she moved to California with von Sternberg, sending only some months later for the husband and daughter with whom she had started her family in Berlin during the late 1920s.

Her first American picture was *Morocco* (1930) for which Paramount made her lose 33 pounds in weight. Thereafter she appeared in films ranging from such von Sternberg classics as *Blonde Venus* (1932) and *The Scarlet Empress* (1934) through the considerably less impressive *Garden of Allah* (1936) to George Marshall's great western *Destry Rides Again* (1939). But it became increasingly clear that with von Sternberg's determination to end their partnership in the middle 1930s the focus of Marlene's interest in cinema became blurred. Her last film with von Sternberg was *Devil is a Woman* (1935).

So when the war came, it was with a kind of relief that she went off around the world on extended army concert tours, beginning to work as a singer with live audiences that were to occupy more and more of her time in the second half of her career. She had rejected an offer by Hitler — the only person she ever "hated" she said in her 1979 memoirs — to return to Germany and become a star of the Nazi-controlled film company UFA, and in 1937 she took United States citizenship.

During the second world war she participated in the US war effort by keeping the troops' morale high as a singer in benefit performances for the US army's welfare services in North Africa, Italy and other European war theatres. This first work as a singer with the live audiences was to occupy more and more of her time in the second half of her career. Quite extraordinarily it was her version of a German first world war soldiers' song, "Lili Marlene", that propelled it to fame, in spite of the initial attempts of both British and American army authorities to have it suppressed as subversive. Her version of the song eventually made it popular on both sides of the fighting lines. "Falling in Love Again" was another huge wartime success, as popular with German PoWs as it had been with American GIs.

After the war, an affair with Jean Gabin led her back to the cinema for *Martin Roumagnac*, but from now on her films were to get fewer and further apart. Her next venture was Billy Wilder's *A Foreign Affair* (1948), a hard-edged comedy of post-war Berlin. In 1950 she starred in Alfred Hitchcock's *Stage Fright* and Henry Koster's *No Highway* (1951).

But between the films she had begun to develop a cabaret talent second to none. Cocteau once said that her beauty was its own praise, and Hemingway, a lover of blondes in general and Dietrich in particular, noted: "her voice alone could break your heart". Beyond the heartbreak was the expression of an immensely theatrical talent for going out alone on stage and holding an audience with all the power of a great dramatic actress that many of her songs, from "Lili Marlene" of the second world war to "Where Have all the Flowers Gone?" of the Vietnam conflict, required.

Although she worked once with Hitchcock, once with Kramer and most memorably with Orson Welles in *A Touch of Evil* (1958), few directors were able to follow in the footsteps of "Svengali Jo" von Sternberg. So she took to travelling more and more alone on solo cabaret. Her last cameo role was in *Just a Gigolo* in 1976. The "Marlene" of the 1930s, a German-American creation of von Sternberg and some excellent lighting cameramen, was gradually translated into "Dietrich", a somewhat tougher and lonelier figure who, around the world, learnt the greatest of all theatrical lessons: waste nothing. Money, time and herself were all exquisitely preserved against need, and, although sometimes cold to frosty and distant before the footlights, she passed again and

again that final test of stardom — the ability not just to do something, but to stand there.

Her war activities tarnished her reputation in Germany, where she was regarded as a traitor long after hostilities ceased. When she returned to West Germany in 1960 for a series of performances, she found that the image of her wearing an American uniform was still vivid in the minds of many Germans. Her homecoming was marred by bomb threats, pickets carrying signs in English that read "Marlene Go Home" and editorials calling her a "traitor". Despite a unanimously acclaimed performance with two encores and 11 curtain calls, she said she would never return.

Towards the end of her career, in concert seasons for the West End and New York and Australia through the middle 1970s, she would take centre stage, an elderly German lady with a slight limp swathed in acres of white fur. She was Dietrich, a constant reminder of the survival of the human spirit and of endurance. She was a theatrical Mother Courage without Brecht, belonging with Lotte Lenya and Edith Piaf and precious few others to a band of dramatic singers who had spanned much of the century. Having her sing to you was not unlike being entertained by the Statue of Liberty. Her greatest achievement was perhaps to evoke memories and the past and then to transcend them.

As the years went on her one-woman show with its battery of the old, irresistible songs, "Lili Marlene", "Falling in Love Again" and "Honeysuckle Rose", established her beyond the reach of any criticism that might have accrued to her films. Audiences that included large numbers of women to whom she had an appeal as electrifying as she did to men packed in to see her wherever she appeared. In a way, her image regained its pristine Sternbergian remoteness (although, owing to her creator's lack of charity to her in his autobiography, she did for a while stop alluding to his contribution to her early success).

As she passed 60 and then 70, an older generation went to see her out of nostalgia for an age of elegant and beautiful women that seemed to have departed, while their children were fascinated anew by the timeless distillation of the experience of being a woman she communicated. In the end, perhaps, the act was more and more in the nature of a carefully planned assault on the emotions, meticulously orchestrated, calculatingly lit and evocatively dressed. But nobody minded. The idea of the woman who had been a close friend of Cocteau and Remarque, of whom Hemingway had characteristically remarked: "The Kraut's the best thing that ever came into the ring", had long outlived its physical embodiment.

By the time the famous legs did fail and Marlene Dietrich fell on stage and broke a thigh bone in Sydney on September 29, 1975, she had passed unassailably into the legends which it is Hollywood's peculiar power to create. She retired to her home on the Avenue Montaigne in Paris. Like Callas and Garbo before her, she shunned publicity and declined interviews, especially from those trying to chronicle her life in one or other of the media. "No one will ever trespass on my private world," she said and she kept to her word.

The Dietrich image was well preserved elsewhere. In 1947 she was awarded the Medal of Freedom, the highest US decoration for civilians, for her contributions to the American war effort, and made French Chevalier of the Légion d'honneur in 1951 and Officier of the Légion d'honneur in 1972.

Dietrich leaves her only child, a daughter Maria born in 1925 to the husband, Rudolph Sieber, whom she had married a year earlier and to whom she remained distantly married until his death a decade ago in California.

Marlene Dietrich, actress and cabaret entertainer, was born on December 27, 1901. She died on May 6, 1992, aged 90

—◈—

ELIZABETH DAVID

INFLUENTIAL COOKERY WRITER WITH A POWER TO AMUSE AS WELL AS INSTRUCT

MAY 23, 1992

Elizabeth David was the doyenne of English cookery writers. She influenced the generations who came after her, whether they, too, were intending to be culinary experts or merely taking a well-thumbed Elizabeth David Penguin from the kitchen shelf for the next day's dinner party. "Elizabeth David says…" was the regular way of resolving how much spice and which spices should be added to a stew and how much garlic should be put in a dressing.

At its best, her prose was as precise as her instructions, unlike that of some of her predecessors who sometimes wrapped up advice on what to do in the kitchen with impenetrable sentences. She was a pleasure to read, a stylist of true distinction. Perhaps only in Britain would she have been classified as a "food writer", too often rather a damning phrase. Elizabeth David combined a scholar's feeling for history with the traveller-aesthete's gift of conveying a sense of place.

Elizabeth David's father was the Conservative Member of Parliament for Eastbourne; her mother the daughter of the 1st Viscount Ridley. At the impressionable age of 16 she was sent from her English boarding school to study French literature and history at the Sorbonne, living for 18 months with a family in Passy. It was then that she first became aware of food, the daily fare of the French *bourgeoisie* coming as a startling contrast to the bland food to which she had been accustomed.

On her return to London she worked briefly as an actress, then as a *vendeuse* for Worth, where her striking looks stood her in good stead. She was living in Greece at the outbreak of war and was evacuated to Egypt, where she lived first in Alexandria and later in Cairo. There she worked as a librarian for the ministry of information. In 1944 she married an English officer, Anthony David, and went to live in India, where he was stationed. The marriage was not a success, and she rarely referred to it. There were no children.

In the winter of 1946 she returned to England alone and went to live in a small hotel in Ross-on-Wye. Here, amid the gloom and deprivation of post-war England, she began to write about the food of the Eastern Mediterranean. In 1950 *A Book of Mediterranean Food* was published by John Lehmann, with drawings by John Minton, another expert on the eastern reaches of that sea. Its impact was colossal, both on those who were too young to remember the pre-war years, and on an older generation. Other books followed in rapid succession: *French Country Cooking* (1951), *Italian Food* (1954) and *Summer Cooking* (1955). The following year she started writing regularly for *The Sunday Times*, *Vogue* and *House & Garden*. In 1960 *French Provincial Cooking* was published, based on a series commissioned by *Vogue*. The next year she gave up working for Condé Nast and *The Sunday Times*, and began writing for *The Spectator*, which freed her from the chore of writing recipes.

In 1965 she opened her kitchenware shop in Elizabeth Street in Belgravia. This involved her in annual trips to France searching for merchandise, a distinct pleasure and rarely a chore. Over the next years she published a series of pamphlets for sale in the shop, one of which was the basis for her next book: *Spices, Salt and Aromatics in the English Kitchen*, which came out in 1970. Three years later she fell out with her partners and severed all connection with the shop, although it continued to trade under her name. In 1976 she was appointed OBE, in 1986 CBE, and in 1977 *English Bread and Yeast Cookery* had been published, destined to be her last original work.

The same year she was made Chevalier du Mérite Agricole, and two years later she received an honorary degree from Essex University. In 1982 she was made a fellow of the Royal Society of Literature, but despite repeated efforts on the part of her friends and colleagues she was never given the accolade she merited. Her last published work, *An Omelette and a Glass of Wine*, came out in 1984.

As the years passed she became more and more obsessed with research, and the *joie de vivre*, which had filled so much of her earlier writing, became muted. Her very first books shared an infectious enthusiasm for the joys of eating and living well, while the recipes were often sketchy, probably written from memory. With *Italian Food*, however, the first book written in situ, her tone became more scholarly, the recipes more precise. After a return to her former style in a short book, *Summer Cooking*, she resumed her research with *French Provincial Cooking*, probably her greatest book and the one no amateur or professional chef is likely to be without. Ten years passed before her next book, originally intended as the first in a series on English food. The title alone of *Spices, Salt and Aromatics in the English Kitchen* shows the change in attitude, as it defines with typical accuracy its range of contents. This interesting book proved a watershed in her career, for after it her passion for research seemed to get out of control.

Seven years later her long-awaited *English Bread and Yeast Cookery* finally appeared, a disappointment to many of her admirers. A heavy tome, over-filled with intricate variations on the same theme, this was a work of reference rather than a pleasure to read. The following years were spent researching a book on sorbets and ices which was never completed. But the academic period towards the end of her life was balanced by the publication of *An Omelette and a Glass of Wine*, a collection of pieces written mostly between 1955 and 1965. These provided a timely reminder of her powers to amuse and entertain, as well as to instruct. Her wit was devastating, often caustic, usually at someone's expense.

She was highly critical, but fair, giving praise rarely, for her standards were very high. She did not suffer incompetents and the dim-witted gladly, if at all, as customers in her Elizabeth Street shop often found, to their discomfiture. This may have been a family trait, for her sister Félicité could be equally crushing with foolish enquiries in Sandoe Books, just off the King's Road, where she worked. Many people found Elizabeth David intimidating, yet she could be friendly and encouraging to younger writers. She had beautiful manners and was an accomplished letter writer. She was shy, unwilling to talk in public, or even to give interviews. In latter years she refused to be photographed, preferring to re-use earlier pictures by Cecil Beaton or the painter Derek Hill on her dust jackets. She became more and more reclusive and rarely went out except to see close friends. These had always been important to her, and included such figures as Norman Douglas, almost 50 years her senior, Derek Hill, and her publisher and editor, Jill Norman.

But even friends were kept at a distance. One, returning from abroad, tried to get her telephone number from directory enquiries, only to be told they were under strict orders not to divulge it under any circumstances, even in case of death.

For more than 34 years she shared a house in Chelsea with her younger unmarried sister Félicité, who died in 1986. Despite mutual regard and affection they lived quite separately. Elizabeth David was a solitary figure in old age, living alone with her books, and memories of a warmer, more enchanting past, as in 1939, when she "fell under the spell of the Levant, the warm flat bread, the freshly pressed tomato juice, the charcoal-grilled lamb, the oniony salads, the mint and yoghurt sauces, the sesame seed paste, the pistachios and the pomegranates and the apricots, the rosewater and the scented sweetmeats, and everywhere the warm spicy smell of cumin".

Elizabeth David, CBE, cookery writer and expert on the cuisine of the Mediterranean, was born on December 26, 1913. She died on May 22, 1992, aged 78

———

BARBARA McCLINTOCK

AMERICAN SCIENTIFIC VISIONARY AND NOBEL PRIZE-WINNER WHO DISCOVERED "JUMPING GENES"

SEPTEMBER 5, 1992

There was never a scientist quite like Barbara McClintock. She lived and worked alone, never gave lectures, delayed publication of her most revolutionary observations for many years, and did not even possess a telephone until 1986. Anyone who wanted to talk to her, said McClintock, could write a letter.

For more than half a century, almost until her death, she followed her own course at Long Island's Cold Spring Harbor Laboratory, where the director is Dr James Watson, co-discoverer of the structure of DNA. In a tribute to McClintock, Watson described her as one of the three most important figures in the whole history of genetics, linking her name with those of Gregor Mendel and Thomas Hunt Morgan.

McClintock's ruling passion was the genetic construction of maize; so much so that she spent her entire professional lifetime studying that one plant. She used the tell-tale patterns of the coloured kernels to disclose the breaking, joining and re-arranging of genes and chromosomes inside the cells. Because the pigments of the kernels are inherited, McClintock was able to use them to trace the genes. In this way, using her uncanny ability to understand the nature of genes and how they interact, McClintock made important discoveries about the role of chromosomes in heredity.

In the 1930s she discovered the fact that chromosomes break and recombine to create genetic changes in a process known as "crossing over", which explained puzzling patterns of inheritance. She also discovered a structure called the nucleolar organiser of the chromosome, which seemed to control the genetic material during cell division. It was to be three decades before molecular biologists could explain and confirm the finding.

Much of McClintock's early work was done at Cornell University's College of Agriculture, where she began to study as an undergraduate in 1919. Her bent towards science, which had begun in high school, had been strongly resisted by her mother who feared that her daughter was failing to develop "appropriate feminine behaviour". But McClintock's persistence won in the end, and by her junior year she was already taking graduate courses in biology.

In her first year of graduate school, McClintock found that she could identify individual maize chromosomes under the microscope — a discovery that opened the door to the integration of plant-breeding experiments with chromosomal analysis. She gained her PhD from Cornell in 1927, published a series of radical research papers and soon became recognised as one of the leading scientists in her field.

But despite a two-year fellowship from the National Research Council and the subsequent award of a Guggenheim fellowship in 1933, McClintock was soon to discover that the avenues of professional advancement available to women were severely limited. Cornell refused to give her a faculty position, and she became increasingly irritated by the favourable treatment given to male colleagues with inferior qualifications. Finally, in 1936, she left Cornell to take a teaching position at the University of Missouri, but there, too, her independence and maverick behaviour, coupled with the continuing prejudice against female academics, precluded any chance of promotion.

She left the university in 1941 and went to work at the Cold Spring Harbor Laboratory, where at last she achieved recognition. It was here, during the 1940s, that McClintock performed the experiments that led to her discovery of transposable genetic elements, or "jumping genes".

Observing successive generations of maize, she noticed colour changes in the leaves and kernels of some plants that failed to follow a predictable hereditary pattern. When she compared the variant specimens with their parent plants under the microscope, she found that parts of the chromosomes had changed position. She eventually concluded, after six years of painstaking research, that the genes were being manipulated by genetic "controlling elements," whose locations on the chromosome were not fixed.

The discovery of transposable elements had far-reaching implications for the understanding of cell differentiation in the growth and development of an organism, and was at total odds with scientific theory at the time. Most scientists then believed that genes were immovable beads on a string, and when McClintock presented her findings at a Cold Harbor symposium in the summer of 1951 virtually no one understood the significance and implications of her work.

Although she had been elected president of the Genetics Society of America and was listed among the top 1,000 scientists in the United States, McClintock found herself laughed out of court. "They called me crazy, absolutely mad at times," she recalled later. Disappointed by the reception of her peers, she stopped publishing the results of her experiments, though she continued her research.

Vindication finally came in the 1970s, when a series of experiments by molecular biologists proved that pieces of bacterial DNA do indeed "jump around" on the chromosomes. Suddenly, McClintock found herself recognised as a scientific visionary and was showered with awards from every quarter. In 1981 she became the first recipient of the MacArthur Laureate Award, giving her a lifetime income of $60,000 a year, and in 1983 her Nobel Prize in Physiology or Medicine made her the first woman to receive an unshared Nobel Prize in that category.

When asked by a reporter if she was bitter about the long years of neglect, Barbara McClintock replied: "If you know you're right, you don't care. You know that sooner or later it will come out in the wash."

Reviewing *The Dynamic Genome: Barbara McClintock's Ideas in the Century of Genetics*, a book published to celebrate her 90th birthday, J. R. S. Fincham said in the August 20 edition of the science magazine *Nature*: "Her solitary style of work, total independence of thought, and extraordinary record of getting things right, have elevated her to the status of a prophet in the eyes of some."

She never married, and is survived by one sister and one brother.

Barbara McClintock, geneticist who discovered the "jumping gene," was born on June 16, 1902. She died on September 2, 1992, aged 90

MARIAN ANDERSON

AMERICAN CONTRALTO
WHO SURVIVED RACIAL
PREJUDICE TO BECOME
THE FIRST BLACK SINGER
TO APPEAR AT THE
METROPOLITAN OPERA,
NEW YORK

APRIL 9, 1993

The life of Marian Anderson is not merely the story of a successful concert and opera singer, eminent though she was in those fields, in her day. It is also the story of a struggle against poverty and racial prejudice to earn for her vocal gifts their due. For years in her own country this prejudice denied her the rewards of her artistry, long after she had been hailed in Europe as a great voice. When she was finally admitted to the Metropolitan Opera in 1955 it was, in reality, almost too late. She was by then in her late fifties and getting past her peak. Nevertheless by that time, through her conduct and her singing she had established a place for herself in the struggle for civil rights in America. Her concert at the Lincoln Memorial in Washington on Easter Sunday 1939 is a landmark in the history of the movement.

Marian Anderson was the daughter of a Pennsylvania coal and ice dealer. While still of tender years she displayed astonishing precocity and versatility as a singer. She was singing before the age of three and at six was in the choir of the local Baptist chapel, where she went on to sing in the soprano, contralto and tenor ranges. At a religious concert when she was in her early teens, she was heard by the famous black tenor Roland Hayes, who was impressed by her singing and gave her name to concert promoters. As a result she was asked to appear in oratorio performances and began to specialise in Bach.

She was refused entrance to a Philadelphia music academy on racial grounds: "We don't take coloured," she was told brusquely. But she received much encouragement and financial support from well-wishers and family friends, who dipped into their none too well stocked purses to raise money to help with her musical education. She went to New York where she studied with Giuseppe Boghetti. While still Boghetti's pupil she began giving successful recitals in the New York area. She then participated in a competition to sing with the New York Philharmonic and won the prize against 300 other entrants. As a result she appeared with the orchestra at the Lewisohn Stadium in 1925.

In any normal circumstances such an occurrence would have marked the lift-off point in a singer's career. It was not to be so for Anderson. Though well received by the critics she found herself obstructed by racial prejudice at every level. In travelling about the country on a recital career she found doors shut against her and hotel accommodation difficult to obtain.

In 1927, at thirty, she decided to try her luck in Europe and found a completely different reception awaiting her. She was lionised in Britain, the Soviet Union, Scandinavia, Austria and Germany. In London she sang with Henry Wood at the Wigmore Hall. She gave royal command performances for the kings of Denmark and Sweden. In Helsinki she sang for Sibelius who was so moved that he dedicated his work "Solitude" to her. When she gave a recital in the ballroom of a Salzburg hotel Toscanini, who was among the audience, went backstage in the interval and told the nervous singer: "What I have heard today one is privileged to listen to once in a hundred years."

She had offers to appear in opera in Europe (one from Stanislavsky to sing the role of Carmen in the Soviet Union) but she refused them because she lacked confidence in her own acting ability. Although she often sang operatic arias at her concerts — "Softly awakes my Heart" from Saint-Saëns's *Samson et Dalila* became one of her most popular records —Lieder and spirituals remained her favourites.

Sol Hurok, the famous impresario, heard her in Paris in the early 1930s, put her under contract and went on to promote her in the US, where at last she seemed to be on the verge of becoming a big name. In 1935 she sang at New York Town Hall and her reputation thereafter began to burgeon. On the occasion of a visit to Washington by

King George VI and Queen Elizabeth in 1939 she was invited to sing at the White House, an event which helped project her public image. However, the Daughters of the American Revolution were not to be moved even by these marks of official approval.

When she was engaged to sing a concert at Washington's Constitution Hall, the organisation, which owned the building, refused to let her sing there because of her colour. It was a piece of racial discrimination which in fact rebounded on them and provided Marian Anderson with an opportunity to strike a blow for civil rights in America. Outraged at the behaviour of the Daughters, Eleanor Roosevelt arranged for Anderson to sing at the Lincoln Memorial on Easter Day 1939, a date which has gone down in the annals of the struggle for equal rights for blacks in America. Before an audience of 75,000, the largest public tribute since the return home of Charles Lindbergh after his solo transatlantic flight in 1927, she sang a programme which included "America", Schubert's "Ave Maria" and the spirituals "Gospel Train", "Trampin'" and "My Soul is Anchored in the Lord". When the final notes of her programme died away this vast crowd gave her an ovation.

After the war she continued her successful concert career. In 1953 she became the first black to perform at the Japanese imperial court in the 2,000 years of its history. Then, finally, on January 7, 1955, the Metropolitan, through Sir Rudolf Bing's efforts, opened its doors to her, and she sang Ulrica in *Un Ballo in Maschera*.

In truth, her rendering was not of her best. Not only was her voice not quite what it had been but, as she later admitted, she was so overcome emotionally by the reception she received when she stepped on stage that she could hardly focus some of the notes as she would have wished. Nevertheless this landmark in American opera history was received with rapturous acclaim by the Met audience.

Marian Anderson gave her farewell concert at the Carnegie Hall, on April 18, 1965, symbolically another Easter Sunday. It was understandably a moving occasion, for here was the artist who more than any other broke down the barriers of racial prejudice in operatic and concert singing in the US, and thus enabled later generations of black singers: Leontyne Price, Grace Bumbry, Jessye Norman and more recently Kathleen Battle and Cynthia Haymon to emerge and establish themselves of right in the opera field. Marian Anderson's voice was a rich, true, vibrant contralto of great intrinsic beauty. She used it expressively in the wide variety of music she sang. At her recitals her warm personality won all hearts. In her autobiography *My Lord, What a Morning* (1956) she described her life thus: "My mission is to leave behind me a kind of impression that will make it easier for those who follow". Indeed it was more by her example than through anything she said that she was able to make this aim effective.

She married, in 1943, the architect Orpheus H. Fisher. He died in 1985. There were no children.

Marian Anderson, American contralto, was born on February 17, 1897. She died on April 8, 1993, aged 96

—*∿*—

DAME FREYA STARK

WRITER AND ARABIST WHO "TRAVELLED THE HARD WAY IN MALE LANDS"

MAY 11, 1993

It is not unusual for travellers to write well about their travels. Doughty, Burton, Kinglake, to mention only a few from Freya Stark's own territory, belong as much to literature as to geography. What was so rare about Freya Stark was that she was a woman who travelled the hard way in male lands, and that she would have been a writer if she had never got further than her front door. The movement and colour of words in many languages fascinated her; so did the nobility and absurdity of human beings; so did the world of ideas. Of course, travel provided her with the material for most of her books, but when she grew older and travelled less she wrote more, finding memory an even more productive vein than novelty.

For obvious reasons Freya Stark was often compared with that other intrepid female orientalist, Gertrude

Bell; but the comparison is misleading. Gertrude Bell was a rich, masculine person, who "floored the pashas flat". Freya Stark was extremely feminine, without money or any worldly advantages and with a constitution which, though fundamentally tough, was continually letting her down at critical moments, so that on more than one of her journeys she very nearly died. But a will of iron, infinite patience and powers of persuasion, an exact knowledge of her own aims and a sublime egoism, overcame all obstacles. Woe betide anyone — tribal sheikh, general officer, Italian greengrocer, Levantine merchant, guest sitting down at the Scrabble board — if they thought they were going to be let off with anything less than total surrender.

With all this strength of character went a matching generosity. Freya Stark drew out the talents of others. She believed most men and some women capable of distinction, and they responded accordingly. Only the deliberately second-rate angered her. She regarded the world as a place thrown open for individual achievement, and she herself achieved much.

Freya Stark was born in Paris where her parents were briefly resident. Her mother and father were first cousins, both belonging to an old family with its roots in Devon. Here her father's branch had remained, but her maternal grandmother had settled in Italy. It was Italy that was to be Freya Stark's home (when eventually she had one) but her roots remained in Devon and, more particularly, in Dartmoor. No more fervent lover of everything connected with England has ever been a permanent and voluntary exile.

Both parents were artists of more than ordinary ability (some of her father's sculptures are to be seen at the Tate). Freya Stark's childhood was highly mobile. Houses were rented, bought, and built in London, Italy, France and on Dartmoor, but none occupied for long. "My parents were moderately well off people of good taste, with a liking for the arrangement of houses, and yet it is astonishing how much of our childhood was spent in dingy lodgings."

One place only came to rival Dartmoor in her childhood affections, and that was Asolo, the small fortress town which looks out under

Dame Freya Stark, intrepid explorer and sensitive author

the lee of the Dolomites across the Venetian plain towards Padua. Before Robert Stark married he had taken the advice of Robert Browning's son, Pen Browning, and with an artist friend, Herbert Young, had escaped to Asolo from the summer heat of Venice. Within a week Herbert Young had bought a house in the city walls with a wild garden enclosing the remains of a Roman theatre. Here he settled for the rest of his life, and when he died in 1941 house and garden passed by his will to Freya Stark.

For Robert and Flora Stark Asolo also became an early home, though a less permanent one. In the first volume of her autobiography, *Traveller's Prelude*, Freya Stark described the growing incompatibility and eventual separation of two beings whom she loved with parallel but distinct devotion. With her sister Vera, a year younger than herself, the small Freya was a sorrowful spectator of a process which ended with her father's departure to Canada and her mother's settling in another hill town, Dronero in Piedmont.

Freya Stark had no regular schooling, but learnt to speak French and German almost as naturally as Italian. She read universally in the literature of all countries, including Greece and Italy. It was not until she was 19, and entered Bedford College, London, that her formal education began, and two years later the outbreak of war brought it to an end.

One great benefit of this brief academic interlude was that it gave her the friendship of W. P. Ker, who was quick to recognise the unusual qualities of this small, shy creature who spoke English (on the rare occasions when she opened her mouth) with an Italian accent. He directed her imagination and guided her literary taste, and in the vacations transformed her from a lover of mountains into an intrepid mountaineer.

When the first world war came, Freya Stark trained as a nurse and served with the Trevelyan hospital unit on the Italian front, finding herself caught up in the chaos of the Caporetto disaster of 1917, in which the Italians were utterly routed by the Austrians. Peace brought family complications and years of poverty and increasing ill-health, including three years as a bedridden and despaired of invalid. It was partly for distraction, but always ultimately with the idea of travel, that she began taking lessons in Arabic from a white-bearded Capuchin in San Remo. By 1927, a course at the London School of Oriental Studies behind her, improved health, plus a minuscule but assured income and the traveller's prelude was completed.

Poor health and lack of funds remained troublesome, though successful authorship eventually counteracted the latter. In other respects Freya Stark was now, at the age of 34, well equipped for the hazards of the next 12 years. She had great curiosity and no narrow prejudices; she liked people, treating them as equals without condescension or diffidence; she was used to hardship; she knew languages, had acquired the elements of surveying, and was a competent nurse. Two other things she quickly learnt — that journeys must be minutely planned if they are to be successful, and how to take photographs. Armed with the cheapest instruments she became an artist in photography.

Freya Stark first set foot in Asia in November 1927. She settled for the winter at Brummana in Lebanon, spent some time in Damascus, and with a friend completed her first proper expedition, through the then disturbed Jebel Druze country, subsequently moving on to Jerusalem and Cairo. The literary product of this period was *Letters from Syria*, not published until 1942.

Two years later she was in Lebanon again, on her way to Baghdad. Here she established herself in the house of a shoemaker overlooking the Tigris, much to the disgust of the British community which considered such behaviour "a flouting of national prestige". Freya Stark never ceased to marvel at the blinkered views of expatriates. Upbringing and predilections made her in a sense "unconventional" though she cherished the traditional British virtues — courtesy, restraint, self-reliance — to an infinitely greater degree than most of her critics. She was, in fact, like her father, a High Tory anarchist as well as an artist.

There were, however, some British in Baghdad without blinkers who were quick to appreciate the newcomer. These included Sir Kinahan Cornwallis, then adviser to the Ministry of Interior and later ambassador, and Lionel Smith, adviser to the Ministry of Education. These two became lifelong friends, joining the ranks of the older men whose society always meant so much to Freya Stark. Such had been her father and W. P. Ker; such, too, were Sydney Cockerell and Lord Wavell.

Having absorbed oriental ways and languages in Baghdad, she used it as a base for invasions of Iran. Three tough but extremely rewarding solo journeys were carried out in 1929-31, two in Luristan and one in the mountains of Mazanderan, south of the Caspian sea. It was on this occasion that she "first stood consciously on the edge of death" as the result of severe malaria and dysentery combined. Out of these journeys came *The Valley of the Assassins* (1934), the book which made her reputation as a writer, and which remains probably the most popular of all those she wrote. In it can be seen in all their freshness the qualities which combined to make Freya Stark so attractive a personality in print — strong sensitivity to places and people, humour, and a clear narrative style, free from the somewhat conscious adornment which sometimes accumulated later. (She herself said of her style: "There is nothing to it except a natural ear for cadence and the wish to get the meaning right." True enough.)

The first truly Arabian journey came in the winter of 1934-35. Her route was from Mukalla on the coast, northward into the Wadi Hadhramaut and to Shibam and Tarim. The episode ended with her rescue by the RAF, from Aden, after she contracted measles and carried on, not properly recovered, so that her heart was strained and very nearly stopped altogether. Prolonged convalescence, and a return to Iraq, were followed by a second Arabian journey, again with Mukalla as a starting-point, in the winter of 1937-38, this time ending in dengue fever but no RAF rescue. These journeys were recorded in *The Southern Gates of Arabia* (1936), *Seen in the Hadhramaut* (1938), and *A Winter in Arabia* (1940).

The war engaged Freya Stark in political and publicity work, for the most part in Arab lands. She served in Aden, Yemen (showing propaganda films under the noses of Mussolini's ubiquitous agents), Cairo and Baghdad (where she was one of those besieged in the British embassy by Rashid Ali's revolt). She had, needless to say, her own ideas of how things should be run, and these ideas, more than directives from a remote ministry, governed her actions. Much of her time was devoted to an association she founded in Egypt and later developed in Iraq called the Brotherhood of Freedom. This consisted of groups of autonomous cells devoted to the cult of self-help, encouraged and to a limited extent financed from a centre which mainly consisted of Freya Stark herself. By a characteristic twist of fate, a lecture tour of the United States, arranged for her by the Ministry of Information in the autumn of 1943, involved her in what she was later to describe as much the worst of all her journeys — during which she suffered a burst appendix on the Halifax-bound liner *Aquitania*, then a troopship. Again, she cheated death by inches.

After the armistice of 1943 she went back to Italy where she worked for the British embassy. When, towards the end of the war, she was able to return to her house at Asolo she found it intact, in spite of its having been used as headquarters by both the retreating Germans and the Salò fascists. Its possessions had been hidden and preserved by loyal friends.

In 1947 Freya Stark married Stewart Perowne, diplomatist and orientalist, and accompanied him to his posts in Barbados and Cyrenaica, but five years later the marriage, which appears to have been based on a misunderstanding of his sexual orientation, ended in an amicable separation. She was now writing her autobiography, three volumes of which appeared in swift succession: *Traveller's Prelude* (1950) the best of them, a graphic and at times most moving portrait, *Beyond the Euphrates* (1951) and *The Coast of Incense* (1953). A fourth volume, dealing with the war years, *Dust in the Lion's Paw*, came out in 1961.

Now, at 60, she looked for new worlds to conquer, and found them in Anatolia and its history. She learnt Turkish (with the aid of a Turkish bible and Turkish detective stories). She made several arduous journeys, often on horseback, in the remoter parts of Turkey, acting as guide, interpreter and goad to younger friends whom she thus initiated into the joys of oriental travel. She brushed up her classics. Out of this came *Ionia: a Quest* (1954), *The Lycian Shore* (1956), *Alexander's Path* (1958), *Riding to the Tigris* (1959), and finally the product of three years' concentrated labour, *Rome on the Euphrates* (1966), a scholarly study of Rome's eastern limes, illuminated by her own unique knowledge of the topography of the region about which she was writing.

Freya Stark had now all the resources for a graceful and comfortable old age — a beautiful house filled with beautiful things, troops of friends, a solid reputation, a contented mind. But she had, besides, an unconquerable restlessness. In 1962, on the eve of her 70th birthday, she suddenly bought a hill near Asolo on which she proceeded to build an enormous house to her own design. The Balzacian complications of the sale of her old house and the financing of the new one at times strained even her composure. She sought relief in revisiting old haunts — Iran, Turkey, Greece — as well as discovering new ones, notably Afghanistan and Nepal.

After a few years the big house was abandoned for the final refuge of a flat in Asolo. There was more travelling, well on into her late eighties on horseback in Nepal and the Pamirs, down the Euphrates on a raft for the BBC — continuing to outpace many of those half or even a quarter of her age. She enjoyed watching the publication in many volumes of her letters, the form in which her career as a writer had begun and in which she excelled. Fortunately, since for the last five years the world had passed her by, she knew nothing of the publication of a shallow and hostile biography of her, produced to coincide with her 100th birthday earlier this year.

Freya Stark was appointed CBE in 1953 and created DBE in 1972. She received many geographical awards, including the Burton Medal from

the Royal Asiatic Society in 1933, the Founder's Medal from the Royal Geographical Society in 1942, and the Percy Sykes Memorial Medal from the Royal Central Asian Society in 1951. She received an LLD from Glasgow University that same year and a DLitt from Durham in 1971. Her godson was her publisher, John (Jock) Murray.

Dame Freya Stark, DBE, writer and traveller, was born on January 31, 1893. She died on May 9, 1993, aged 100

—⁓—

TATIANA NIKOLAYEVA

RUSSIAN PIANIST AND BACH INTERPRETER, TO WHOM SHOSTAKOVICH DEDICATED HIS 24 PRELUDES AND FUGUES

NOVEMBER 25, 1993

For decades Tatiana Nikolayeva was, like so many Russian pianists of her generation, an unseen, mysterious name, known only to Western connoisseurs who would scour record shops for her 1960s LPs of Bach and Shostakovich. Yet in the 1980s Nikolayeva's roles as mother, grandmother, composer and teacher gradually were overtaken by that of performing artist. Her fame in the West reached its climax in a remarkable debut at the last of the BBC Henry Wood Proms at the

Albert Hall in 1992 — her small, comfortable, endearing figure enrapturing both the millions watching on television and the concert audience who chorused messages to her in Russian. The concert finally confirmed her "arrival" as a musician with a serious following in this country. She had also made a warm impression the previous year when she was given one of the *Gramophone* magazine's awards. Her unassuming speech delivered in German again captivated her audience.

Born into a Russia of great uncertainty, fear and arbitrary disappearances, Nikolayeva — like her mother — studied with Goldenweiser at the Moscow Conservatoire. While she was still young, the aged Goldenweiser who himself had been a friend of Tolstoy noticed her polyphonic gifts and enormous memory and encouraged her to memorise as much as she could. (At his instigation, she learnt all 48 of Bach's Preludes and Fugues, which were to become so central to her repertory.)

As the Germans advanced into Russia, she and her family escaped to Saratov on the Volga, her father and grandmother dying en route. After the war she graduated in both piano and composition and in 1950 was selected to participate in the first international Bach competition held in the ruined city of Leipzig.

Her prize-winning performance at Leipzig led, in her own words, to a far greater prize — the lifelong friendship of Dmitri Shostakovich, a juror at the competition. Shostakovich was delighted with her playing of Bach because, he felt, it was not belonging to a museum, but "modern", and played unapologetically with all the dynamics a piano is capable of — this at a time when many Bach performers were demanding a return to the authentic instruments (the clavichord and harpsichord) for which Bach originally wrote. "I have no time for this asceticism," said Nikolayeva, "Bach was a human being, after all."

Upon their return to Moscow, and inspired by her rendition of Bach's Preludes and Fugues, Shostakovich immediately started work on his own piano cycle — 24 Preludes and Fugues — trying each piece out on his young *protégée*. He himself then demonstrated the finished work to the Union of Composers (with Nikolayeva turning the pages), but his interpretation was not a success, partly because he was racked by nerves, and it took Nikolayeva's subsequent performance of it for other pianists to show interest. She was the dedicatee of this huge collection which many consider to be the finest piano music of the 20th century.

Nikolayeva's career until the mid-1980s was largely confined to the Soviet Union and remains substantially undocumented. Although she made the occasional trip abroad, she was not one of the favoured artistes regularly allowed out to the West. She spent, it seems, most of her time based at the Moscow Conservatoire where her name has been engraved on the marble rolls of honour as both pianist and composer.

It was the Leeds International Piano Competition that first invited Nikolayeva to the United Kingdom in 1984 as a juror. At an unscheduled concert there she gave a performance of Bach's *Art of Fugue* which enchanted her audience of piano-lovers. She attracted a cult-like following and her greatest fan, a Cambridge don, frequently travelled the world to hear her. It was fitting that it should have been Hyperion Records, with its legion of devotees, that was responsible for the first Western release of her playing the Shostakovich cycle. The recording, which introduced her to a fresh host of admirers, coincided with her performance of the same work at the Wigmore Hall in 1989. This led, in turn, to the *Gramophone* award, an invitation to the Edinburgh Festival and an opportunity for the BBC to film her playing the cycle.

As it had been in Britain, so it later was in America. Her fame was growing across the New World at the time of her death. It was while in the middle of a concert in San Francisco last week that she suffered a stroke that proved fatal.

Looking, and indeed at times behaving, like one of the legendary babushkas of Moscow, Tatiana Nikolayeva was always an improbable star of the concert platform. She would greet her audience with a cheerful smile and, without further ado, sit down at the keyboard to play with a natural musicality, full of expression and devoid of self-advertising tricks. But her prowess was based firmly on technique and she brought an authority to the keyboard, in particular in her interpretation of Bach, that was matched by few of her contemporaries

and none of her successors. Especially in her later years she set herself a punishing schedule but, as she once remarked, "The important thing is to love music, then you'll have enough time and energy to cultivate it".

Twice widowed, Nikolayeva leaves a son and two grandchildren.

Tatiana Nikolayeva, Russian pianist, was born on May 24, 1924. She died on November 22, 1993, aged 69

—◈—

JACQUELINE KENNEDY ONASSIS

ELEGANT WIFE OF US
PRESIDENT JOHN F. KENNEDY
AND INSTIGATOR OF A
COMPLETE RESTORATION OF
THE WHITE HOUSE

MAY 21, 1994

For the two years, ten months and two days that her husband was President of the United States, Jacqueline Bouvier Kennedy brought an unprecedented degree of youthful glamour to the role of First Lady. Unlike those staid matrons in whose paths she trod, the young and always exquisitely turned-out Jacqueline Kennedy proved to be her husband's best political asset during the primary campaign of 1960 (she sat out most of the actual election through being pregnant) and very rapidly became a celebrity in her own right. This despite the fact that John F. Kennedy had feared that she would be something of an embarrassment to his career possessing, as he put it, "too much status and not enough quo" to appeal to the average voter.

Her family was the American equivalent of aristocracy — rich, Republican, and Catholic. Their ancestry could be traced back much further than the more boisterous Kennedy clan, on whom she tended to look down at first in consequence: 24 of them had come over from France to fight in the American War of Independence, returning with Lafayette to France, but a younger cousin, inspired by tales of frontier life, came back to Philadelphia in 1814, and subsequently made a fortune through importing and real-estate transactions in West Virginia.

If the initial response to Jacqueline Kennedy as First Lady was rather cool, what really swung not just Seventh Avenue but the grassroots American public behind her was the extraordinary reception she received from the people of France on the Kennedys' state visit there in May 1961. She completely stole the show from her husband, charming not only President de Gaulle but the entire French nation with her fluent French and her famous pill-box hats. On the final day of the visit, her husband began his farewell speech, not entirely without justification: "I do not think it altogether inappropriate to introduce myself. I am the man who accompanied Jacqueline Kennedy to Paris."

For the next two years she was taken unconditionally to the nation's heart and idolised by press and public alike. She became Washington's premier hostess, not just in name, as previous Presidents' wives had been, but in fact, holding fashionably informal parties at a White House which she had restored to its former elegance. But the idyll ended abruptly on November 22, 1963, when Lee Harvey Oswald assassinated Kennedy in Dallas.

Her extraordinary show of courage and dignity in the days immediately following his death — especially as displayed at the President's funeral — endeared her to the world. For the next few years, she was still prominent in high society, still consistently voted one of the most admired women in America. But in October 1968 the announcement of her engagement to Aristotle Onassis profoundly shocked the American people, not because her remarriage was unexpected, but for her choice of a man more than 20 years her senior, a rough-mannered, jet-setting Greek shipping tycoon.

Jacqueline Bouvier was the daughter of John Vernou "Black Jack" Bouvier III, a wealthy Wall Street stockbroker. He was a hard-drinking man and a philanderer, but she adored him and it was perhaps for this reason that she tolerated her husband's later infidelities. Her father and her mother, Janet Lee Bouvier, an attractive society woman, separated when she was eight, divorcing in 1938. Her mother went on to marry Hugh D. Auchincloss, a wealthy lawyer and stockbroker from Washington. From then on Jacqueline played the two men off against each other, enjoying holidays both with her father and her horses in East Hampton, Long Island, and at her stepfather's estates.

It was her stepfather's third marriage. His second had been to Nina Gore Vidal, the mother of the writer, and for this reason, Jacqueline saw a good deal of the young Gore Vidal as a child. Her other early companion was her younger sister Lee, who was to marry an ex-Polish nobleman, and later London businessman, Prince Stanislas "Stas" Radziwill.

Jacqueline was educated at the fashionable Chapin School in New York, where her mischievousness earned her the label of "the very worst girl in school," and at Holton-Arms, a blue-chip girls' school in Washington. She was soon displaying an unusual degree of social poise. When she came out in New York at the age of 17, the society columnist, Igor Cassini, described her as the "Queen Deb of the Year... a regal brunette who has classic features and the daintiness of Dresden porcelain." But she had no intention of being married off too soon to any of the young men she had grown up with. After two years at Vassar, she spent a year in Paris at the Sorbonne, an experience which gave her a lasting love for the country and put the final polish on her fluent French. Her education was completed at George Washington University.

Afterwards she won the first prize in a *Vogue* talent contest, with essays on Diaghilev, Baudelaire and Oscar Wilde. Her prize consisted of spending six months working in the New York office of the magazine and six months in Paris, and, because of the latter period away from home, she decided to turn the offer down. But she was sufficiently interested in journalism to approach Arthur Krock, a friend on *The New York Times*, who found her a job on the *Washington Times-Herald* in 1952. This lasted for 18 months and led to interviews as a photojournalist. Jacqueline had her difficulties with the job — "I always forgot to pull out the slide," she admitted — but pulled off some minor coups, interviewing Pat and Richard Nixon, and the junior senator from Massachusetts, John F. Kennedy.

It was not the first time they had met. Indeed, by the time of her interview, they had known each other for a year or so, having been brought together by a matchmaking friend at a dinner party in Washington. Their relationship began to intensify after Kennedy had launched his bid for the Senate in 1952 — he was beginning to realise that marriage to the right woman would enhance his political prospects though even then he never played the devoted lover. He once sent her a rather perfunctory postcard from Bermuda saying "Wish you were here. Cheers, Jack," which Jacqueline held up to friends as her sole piece of courtship correspondence.

That was not entirely true, for the following year, when she was sent to England to cover the Coronation in 1953, he sent her a telegram:

"ARTICLES EXCELLENT. BUT YOU ARE MISSED." The day after she returned they were engaged and they married in September that year in an extravagant wedding attended by 1,700 friends and family, and officiated over by Archbishop Richard Cushing of Boston, who brought with him the blessing of Pope Pius XII. Not everything went smoothly: Jacqueline's father, who had planned to walk his daughter down the aisle, had started celebrating a little too early in his hotel room before the ceremony, and, being deemed unfit for the task by Jacqueline's mother, was replaced by Hugh Auchincloss.

Jacqueline devoted her early years of marriage to her husband — grooming his appearance, teaching him about art and encouraging him to mend his occasionally abrupt social manners. Already there were early signs of strain: Jacqueline was not particularly interested in politics and saw her role as being primarily one of supporter. She was happy enough to switch from Republican — her family's party — to Democrat for her husband, though there was no evidence that she ever really understood the politics involved: "She breathes all the political gases that flow around us, but she never seems to inhale them," Jack once complained. She was also, even at this point, notoriously extravagant with her personal expenditure, particularly on clothes.

For her part, though she had had no illusions about his cavalier attitude to women before the wedding, she was hurt by her husband's frequent infidelities. But what rocked the marriage most was Jack's reaction in 1956 following the ending of her second pregnancy (the first had resulted in a miscarriage in 1955) in a premature and stillborn birth. Jack was then enjoying a Mediterranean cruise and, on being told the news, was reluctant to return home and comfort his wife. It was only when a friend bluntly put it to him, "You better haul your ass back to your wife if you ever want to run for President," that he caught the next plane out. His behaviour was bad enough to prompt a rumour — never denied — that she had been offered $1 million by her father-in-law, Joe Kennedy, to stay with his son.

Eventually they did have three children — Caroline in 1957, John in 1960, and later Patrick in 1963, though the latter died almost immediately after his birth. Jacqueline became pregnant with John early in 1960 just after her husband had declared his candidacy for the Democratic nomination. Kennedy at first rebuffed his wife's offer to help him with his campaign — "The American people just aren't ready for someone like you," he told her, "I guess we'll just have to run you through subliminally in one of those quick flash TV spots so no one will notice".

This rather unflattering appraisal of her usefulness was not borne out by events. Jacqueline grew, over the next few months, into a very effective campaign wife, holding fund-raising teas and the occasional press conference, even delivering a couple of pretty speeches in her famously whisper-soft voice, and providing her husband with an endless source of campaign jokes

Jackie Kennedy on a family holiday in Ireland in 1967, the year before her marriage to Aristotle Onassis

on the subject of her heavily pregnant condition. Above all, she was visually pleasing to the electorate and the prospect of a young family in the White House at the dawn of a hopeful new decade was an invigorating one.

Her husband was sworn in as 35th president of the United States on January 20, 1961. At first Jacqueline found it more difficult than she had foreseen to accustom herself to the loss of privacy that went with being First Lady — she complained of feeling like a fish in a fishbowl, or a moth on a windowpane. But she adapted by trying to define her own areas of responsibility. Typically for the period, these centred around the First Lady's traditional domain, the home, although in her case they went far beyond a little light redecoration.

She decided to take on the complete restoration of the White House which, she complained, looked as though it had been furnished from "discount stores" — launching a campaign to restore it to its former glory and to make it a "national historical object" which would reveal something of the history of the Presidency, back to Lincoln's day, through its furnishings, paintings and sculpture. To this end, she persuaded Congress to designate the building a national museum, and enlisted the help of museum directors and historians, forming committees to supervise and fund the project. Finally she published an *Historic Guide to the White House*, and appeared on television in 1962, watched by 48 million viewers, giving a guided tour through the newly-restored rooms. The success of the project produced an enormous increase in the numbers of visitors to the White House, and proved to be another breakthrough in the public's growing estimation of her.

She became a successful political hostess, bringing together in informal dinner parties a stimulating mixture of artists, musicians, businessmen and politicians. But it was perhaps abroad that she was most appreciated. The sort of adulation she received in France set a pattern for future foreign visits, where her poise, charm and effortless linguistic skills endeared her also to the Canadians, to Nikita Khrushchev, who was then holding talks with her husband in Vienna, to the Queen in London, and to the peoples of India and Pakistan which she toured in 1962. She became, for the American public, the nearest thing they had ever had to a queen.

For all the adulation she was receiving, she could still insist at times on withdrawing from the public gaze, much to her husband's annoyance. Once she even refused to appear at a Distinguished Ladies' Reception held in her honour (Jack eventually went in her place). And as rumours about her husband's infidelities continued to circulate around Washington, Jacqueline and her children, perhaps in retaliation, began to spend more time away from the White House, visiting friends and relatives, hunting from her country estate in Middleburg, Virginia, and spending holidays in Greece and Italy. But the death of her third child, Patrick, in August 1963, less than two days after his birth, drew the family close again, though Jacqueline became depressed.

To try to raise her spirits, her sister Lee Radziwill invited her in October to join a group for a short break in the Mediterranean on the yacht belonging to the Greek shipping tycoon, Aristotle Onassis. She accepted, travelling without her husband again, but chaperoned this time by Franklin Roosevelt Jr, then under-secretary for commerce, and his wife Suzanne. It was not the first time she had been on board *Christina*. That had been in 1957 in Monte Carlo, when the Kennedys had been invited to meet Winston Churchill, Onassis's guest. The meeting had not been a success — Churchill, then very old, was not on his best form, and Jacqueline later teased her husband, "Maybe he thought you were a waiter". Nor did Kennedy approve of his sister-in-law's infatuation with Onassis (who was invited to stay at the White House during Kennedy's funeral).

Jacqueline returned from the trip restored and eager to give the world a most ostentatious show of marital happiness for the President's final public appearance, in Dallas in November that year. The full horror of the scene in Dallas after the shooting — Jacqueline's suit being drenched with the blood of her dying husband — was captured by television cameras and relayed around the world. Afterwards the fact that she was still wearing the suit during President Lyndon B. Johnson's swearing-in on Air Force One was seen by a grieving nation as an extraordinarily poignant and fitting tribute to her husband, as too was her quiet dignity at his funeral, when she stood frailly by his graveside supported only by their two small children. In those days immediately following the president's death and after her very statesman-like television performance when she thanked the American nation for their words of support, she became fixed in the mind of a traumatised nation as the necessary symbol of chief mourner.

Even after it was all over, it remained difficult for her to escape the attentions of the press, who were now more than ever intent on examining her private conduct, eager for proof of some indiscretion. She decided to move to a New York apartment with her children, and set to work on building up the memorial to her husband. She persuaded President Johnson to change the name of Cape Canaveral to Cape Kennedy (it was changed back in 1973), and launched the project of a John F. Kennedy Memorial Library in Boston.

She found it hard to completely escape the possessive attentions of the Kennedy clan. She became particularly close to Jack's brother, Bobby Kennedy, supporting him in his 1968 campaign for the Democratic presidential nomination. His murder in June that year, which shook her badly, may well have precipitated her rush into marriage with Aristotle Onassis, a man of whom Bobby strongly disapproved. The fact that she managed to keep their romance a secret for so long was partly because

of the physical and social incongruities between them — it seemed impossible to outsiders — and partly because she had been seen very publicly with other men — the widowed Lord Harlech, a former ambassador to the United States, and Roswell Gilpatric, undersecretary of defense in the Kennedy administration.

They were married, after some hard bargaining on Jacqueline's part over the fine print of a marriage contract, on October 20, 1968, less than a week after word of their engagement had been broken on the front page of the *Boston Herald-Traveler*. The uproar with which the news was greeted was not the only complication. Onassis was a divorced man, whose first wife was still living, and a member of the Greek Orthodox Church. The Vatican was extremely critical of the match, announcing that Jacqueline Kennedy would be living in a state of mortal sin, despite a refusal to condemn the marriage by Cardinal Cushing who had officiated at her first wedding. Maria Callas, the opera singer, with whom Onassis had been conducting a very open affair for years, was also enraged.

Ignoring the outcry, the couple were married on Onassis's private Greek island of Skorpios, ejecting some 90 passengers from a scheduled flight of the bridegroom's Olympic Airways in order to make the trip.

It was a measure of the public disapproval of the marriage that stories now began to circulate, indicating that Jacqueline Kennedy Onassis had been something less than perfect, even as First Lady. Her former personal secretary, Mary Barelli Gallagher, published a book, *My Life with Jacqueline Kennedy* (1969), in which Jacqueline was portrayed as both extravagant and tight-fisted; a woman who spent more than her husband's entire salary on herself, yet insisted that her staff shop at stores that gave trading stamps. The book was serialised world-wide.

The marriage to Onassis, meanwhile, was not going well and before he died, in March 1975, he was reported by *The New York Times* to be intending to sue for divorce. His bequest to Jacqueline — an income of $250,000 a year — was considerably less than the lump sum of $250 million she had expected, and the will contained a clause that would stop the allowance if she tried to lay claim to the estate. Instead, Onassis left the bulk of his fortune to his daughter Christina, who had never been on friendly terms with her stepmother.

It was not until September 1977 that the legal wrangle between Jacqueline Kennedy Onassis and her stepdaughter over the provisions of Aristotle Onassis's will was finally resolved when Christina, who had reportedly inherited about $250 million, agreed to pay Jacqueline $20 million to settle the matter. This virtually doubled her inheritance, and was considerably more than the $3 million which Onassis had reportedly told friends he was offering for a divorce settlement.

In her own way, she continued to support the Kennedy clan, turning out for Ted Kennedy in his 1980 bid to win the Democratic nomination from Jimmy Carter, and putting in an appearance with the family in Florida in 1991 when William Kennedy Smith was charged with rape — although she always refused to allow her children to be exploited politically. She had never been like any of the other Kennedy women — she was too dignified to join in with the rough family games of touch football — but beneath the elegant, slightly vulnerable façade she shared their survivor instincts.

She returned, after her second husband's death, to New York and found her niche there in the last two decades of her life as a publisher, first as an editor at Viking — a connection she severed after a disagreement — and later as an associate editor at Doubleday, where she worked up to her death.

Her companion in later years was Maurice Tempelsman, whom she had first met in the late 1950s when he had arranged a meeting between Jack Kennedy and Harry Oppenheimer. She tried to protect their privacy and that of her family to the end, although even the smallest appearance or public comment was considered worthy of intense press speculation. Gradually she retired from public view as, in the last few months, she succumbed to the cancer that killed her. One of her last public appearances was hosting a party on board a yacht in Martha's Vineyard for one of Jack Kennedy's greatest admirers, Bill Clinton.

Jacqueline Kennedy Onassis is survived by her daughter Caroline and her son John.

Jacqueline Kennedy Onassis, widow of President John F. Kennedy, was born on July 28, 1929. She died from lymphatic cancer on May 19, 1994, aged 64

———⁓⁓⁓———

DOROTHY HODGKIN

SCIENTIST WHO WON
THE NOBEL PRIZE FOR
CHEMISTRY IN 1964

JULY 30, 1994

The world recognised Dorothy Hodgkin as one of the outstanding scientists of the 20th century. She will always be remembered for her discovery of the structure of penicillin, of the anti-pernicious anaemia factor, Vitamin B12, and of the diabetic hormone, insulin.

However, she will also be remembered as a unique human being — a woman with no enemies, a woman of infinite understanding, compassion, simplicity and an enduring serenity. She was never too busy to help both the deserving and the undeserving in distress, caring about individuals as well as the needs of universities and society whether at home or abroad. Besides being a scientist she was a wife, a mother and a grandmother, and her home welcomed scientists, politicians and the down-and-out with unfailing warmth. This was based on the depth

of love and understanding that existed between her and her husband Thomas, a distinguished Africanist and Arabist.

She had a modest but engaging approach to formal occasions. When summoned to the Palace to receive the Order of Merit it is said that she arrived on foot, approached one of the guards and simply said, "I want to see the Queen."

Dorothy Mary Crowfoot, as she was before she married, was educated at the Sir John Leman School, Beccles, and at Somerville College, Oxford, where she later became a tutor and fellow, building up in the college a tradition of scientific scholarship in the days when few women read science. At Somerville one of her undergraduate students was Margaret Thatcher.

In 1946 she became a university lecturer and demonstrator; in 1956 University Reader in X-ray Crystallography; and in 1960 Royal Society Wolfson Research Professor.

Her own scientific work began with H. M. Powell in Oxford and concerned certain compounds of thallium. In 1932 she moved from Oxford to Cambridge and, working with J. D. Bernal, began to explore the structures of an enormous range of molecules, many of them of biological importance. Amid a great deal of distinguished work, some of the crystals she studied at this time were to be particularly significant and of life-long interest.

The most exciting of the discoveries at Cambridge was to be longest in coming to fruition. In 1934 the first X-ray photograph of a crystalline protein, pepsin, was taken in Bernal's laboratory. A year later Hodgkin photographed, for the first time, insulin crystals of the form used when the structure was finally solved in 1969. Following an examination of suitably prepared (wet) crystals, a year or two later, she used the mathematical technique introduced by Patterson in 1935 to obtain some objective information about the arrangement of atoms within the molecules. Such an awareness of the possibilities of new methods always characterised her work.

At the time, in the absence of computers, a detailed determination of the arrangement of the atoms of a molecule as large as insulin, with more than 1,000 atoms, was impossible. After obtaining the important result which indicated the regularity of this molecule, Dorothy Hodgkin returned to the structures of smaller biologically interesting molecules, which were also entirely unknown. The first structures to which she applied the new objective methods were derivatives of the sterols, which had been the subject of her PhD thesis with Bernal, and her investigations confirmed their previous conclusions.

Work on penicillin began in 1942, an investigation fraught with difficulties caused both by the nature of the crystals and by the fact that the chemical structure of the molecule was not known. Throughout this investigation, the chemical and crystallographic evidence were compared, and much ingenuity was required to obtain the correct structure in a problem so close to the limits of possibility. The important results led the way to the structures of a large number of antibiotics over the years, particularly of the cephalosporins. In 1970 the structure of the large and interesting compound, thiostrepton, with antibiotic properties, was determined. This molecule required, in its time, as much genius for its solution as did penicillin in the 1940s. Such an ability to choose and solve important problems at the limit of the technique was a continuing feature of Dorothy Hodgkin's work.

This was particularly evident in the determination of the structure of vitamin B12, the anti-pernicious anaemia factor. The first X-ray photographs were taken before even the size of the molecule was known, and from these the size was determined. The investigation, from 1948 to 1956, demanded not only a great deal of painstaking hard work from many people, but also enormous insight. The structure of the important central part of the molecule was obtained by combining information from four slightly different compounds, one of which was a degradation product of vitamin B12. Again, the investigation showed the complementary nature of crystallographic and chemical investigations.

It is, perhaps, the insulin structure which Dorothy Hodgkin had most wanted to see in full detail. Her early pictures in 1935 were taken when even the first principles of protein structure were in dispute. Advances in technique and in computer technology made determination of structures of this complexity possible. The early 1960s saw structures of important protein molecules such as haemoglobin, larger than insulin. For several years after that, the very close packing of insulin molecules in the crystal, commented on in her first papers, made the structure still difficult to solve.

However, in 1969, the structure of "two zinc" insulin was solved in such detail that the positions of the individual chemical groups could be seen. The tightness of the packing of the molecules of insulin now became useful, allowing even greater detail to be discovered. This detail was required by Hodgkin who expected to be able to define the position of each atom in order to understand the structure. Recent work has been directed toward increasing such detail and toward understanding the action of this molecule in the body.

Her many and far-flung former students and colleagues will remember with gratitude and amazement her uncanny ability to choose the right from the wrong features, despite apparent evidence to the contrary, and even more her generosity and her ability to let them follow their own paths under an ever-watchful eye.

After her retirement from her Wolfson chair in 1977 she became a fellow of Wolfson College. But she had already, in 1970, become Chancellor of Bristol University and continued as such until 1988. There she is remembered for the intense interest she took in student affairs, particularly in the lives of overseas students. A facility in Bristol which offers accommodation to overseas students, opened in 1986, is named Hodgkin House in honour of her and her husband.

Another concern of hers during her time at Bristol was the Hodgkin scholarship for which she encouraged Bristol students to raise the money themselves. It was officially a scholarship "for students from southern Africa", but no one was in any doubt that what was really intended by it was to raise money for students from South Africa, who were battling apartheid and would certainly have not been able to get government backing for studies overseas. It was an initiative typical of her radical nature.

Another offshoot of this was her becoming, with another Nobel laureate, the physicist Sir Cecil Powell, a founder-member of "Pugwash". This was an international organisation of scientists whose aim was to keep lines of communication open between those working on this and the Warsaw Pact side of the Iron Curtain in the days of the Cold War.

A woman of indomitable spirit, she refused to let even severe arthritis call a halt to her scientific activity. Only last year, although wheelchair-bound, she flew to an international crystallography conference in Peking, to the astonishment of the other delegates who attended it.

Dorothy Hodgkin was awarded the Gold Medal of the Royal Society in 1956, the Nobel Prize for Chemistry for 1964 and was made a member of the Order of Merit in 1965. At the time of her death she was the senior member of the order. She was also a member of many of the great national scientific academies and the recipient of many honorary degrees from universities here and abroad.

Her husband Thomas died in 1982, and she is survived by two sons and one daughter.

Dorothy Hodgkin, OM, FRS, scientist, was born on May 12, 1910. She died on July 29, 1994, aged 84

—∿—

ODETTE HALLOWES

RESISTANCE HEROINE WHO SURVIVED WARTIME TORTURE TO BECOME A BEACON OF POSTWAR HEALING

MARCH 17, 1995

Of all the women who took part in wartime special operations in France, Odette — as she was universally known in spite of having borne three married surnames in her lifetime — perhaps best symbolised the indomitable spirit of resistance to the horrors of Nazism. Captured by the Gestapo in France in 1943 and consigned, after being cruelly tortured in Paris's notorious Fresnes prison, to Ravensbrück concentration camp, she emerged emaciated, weak and gravely ill at the end of the war.

But, in the years that followed, her undiminished mental and moral energy, combined with a complete absence of bitterness towards her tormentors and the nation that had spawned them, became a beacon to others who had suffered disfigurement, pain or bereavement. Indeed, the theme of her postwar working life, with its service to various charities and help for the underprivileged, was the healing of those wounds, both physical and mental, which had been inflicted upon individuals by the war.

Her George Cross, she always maintained, was not to be regarded as an award to her personally, but as an acknowledgement of all those, known and unknown, alive or dead, who had served the cause of the liberation of France. Her wartime experiences had taught her two great truths: that suffering is an ineluctable part of the human lot, and that the battle against evil is never over.

Fame came to her notably through the film *Odette*, which celebrated her life, but she never sought it. In her entry in *Who's Who* she styled herself simply: housewife.

She was born Odette Marie Céline Brailly in Picardy, the daughter of Gaston Brailly, who was killed towards the end of the First World War. She was educated privately and at the Convent of Ste Thérèse in Amiens.

She always said that she had been determined at the outset to marry an Englishman, after a series of young British officers were billeted on the family house during the First World War. At any rate, when the son of one such man, whom her mother had nursed back to health, visited the family after the war to improve his English, romance soon blossomed. She married Roy Sansom, who worked in the hotel industry, in 1931 and settled in London, where she had three daughters.

British domiciled she might be, but her heart remained French. After the catastrophe to French arms in the early summer of 1940, she longed to do something more active than looking after her young ones. By a stroke of luck she got in touch with the independent French section of the Special Operations Executive.

Yet when she was first interviewed there were some doubts about her suitability as a clandestine SOE courier. Would she be able, as a mother of three young daughters who might be constantly on her mind, to undertake missions requiring steely nerves and an ability to concentrate on the task in question to the exclusion of all else? On the other hand, from certain points of view she seemed an ideal candidate. She was young, attractive, vivacious. She knew France; she had a winning manner. Furthermore, she had a burning desire to redeem by direct action the disgrace her country had suffered in its capitulation of June 1940.

Accepted, she joined the First Aid Nursing Yeomanry (since membership of a service organisation was a prerequisite of working for SOE, and the FANY provided basic training in such matters as driving, wireless operation, etc) and did well in all her courses. She returned to France secretly, by small boat from Gibraltar to Antibes, on the last night of October 1942, with orders to join a new circuit in Burgundy. There she got on so well with Peter Churchill, SOE's organiser on the spot, that he secured London's leave to keep her on the Riviera.

Within a fortnight, the Germans and Italians overran all southern France. Churchill and Mme Sansom continued to try to provide contact between London and a large and, as it turned out, a purely imaginary secret army that was supposed to be organised by a friend of Churchill's codenamed "Carte", the father of Danielle Darrieux the film star. Unfortunately quarrels among "Carte's" friends became so acute that next February Churchill took Mme Sansom and his wireless operator, Adolphe Rabinovitch, away to St Jorioz near Annecy in the French Alps. Churchill then returned to London for instructions.

While he was away, Odette was approached by a "Colonel Henri", who represented himself to be a German officer who wanted to defect to the Allies. She was highly suspicious of "Colonel Henri" with some justification since he was in fact Sergeant Bleicher of the Abwehr. But one of the more impetuous of the "Carte" members was taken in by him and imparted some names and numbers of the members of the circuit in and around Annecy. Churchill returned to France by parachute on April 14-15, 1943, and was met by Odette, with whom he returned to St Jorioz.

He had already been warned against "Colonel Henri" in London. But their operation had been fatally undermined by the indiscreet disclosures of their "Carte" comrade. After dark next evening Bleicher and a detachment of Italian troops arrived at the hotel in St Jorioz where Odette and Churchill were staying. He arrested her in the hall and, going upstairs, where he found Churchill sound asleep in bed, arrested him too.

Churchill and Odette passed themselves off as married, and as relations of Winston Churchill (he claimed to be Churchill's nephew). They were, therefore, for a time treated with a mixture of savagery and deference. Odette was sent to Paris where, at the notorious Fresnes prison, she endured excruciating torments including having her toenails pulled out (for a year after her homecoming she could not wear shoes and had to walk on her heels until several operations restored her to normal mobility).

Both she and Churchill were eventually sent to the vast concentration camp at Ravensbrück, north of Berlin, where, in June 1943, Odette was condemned to death. That sentence was not carried out, but for the remainder of her stay there her lot was one of alternate mollycoddling and beating which is the traditional procedure of the interrogator. Neither of them, however, made any admissions of importance. Meanwhile, Rabinovitch, who had evaded arrest, escaped to England only to be dropped back by an unhappy staff error straight into the arms of the Gestapo next year.

At the end of the war, when the Red Army's advance approached Ravensbrück, Fritz Suhren, the camp commandant, drove in a sports car with Odette beside him into the American lines, in the hope that he could use her charm to save himself. She at once denounced him and he was hanged after trial.

Odette became a national heroine, subject of innumerable newspaper articles, a book by Jerrard Tickell and the film *Odette* (1950) which starred Anna Neagle in the title role. She was appointed MBE in 1945 and in the following year awarded the George Cross. In 1950 she was made an officer of the Légion d'Honneur.

She believed that the George Cross had been given to her, not because she had been especially gallant, but because she had had the good fortune to survive, unlike 11 other women in her section who had died in German hands, some of them shot within earshot of her cell.

Her first husband died and she married Peter Churchill in 1947. In 1956 that marriage was dissolved and she married Geoffrey Hallowes, a wine importer, who had also served in another section with the SOE in France. He was a constant support to her throughout the years when her life was lived in the glare of often unexpected bursts of publicity, not all of them welcome; there were, for example, criticisms of the effectiveness of SOE's operations in southern France.

But there was also publicity of a more light-hearted kind. On one occasion her mother's house in Kensington was burgled, the thief making off with some silver spoons and Odette's George Cross and Légion d'Honneur. Distraught at the loss of her daughter's treasures, Mme Brailly appealed through the press for their return. The thief, evidently a humane soul, obliged. His letter accompanying the decorations read: "You Madame, appear to be a dear old lady. God bless you and your children. I thank you for having faith in me. I am not all that bad it's just circumstances. Your little dog really loves me. I gave him a nice pat and left him a piece of meat out of fridge. Sincerely yours, A Bad Egg."

Odette was active in many organisations: she was on the committee of the VC and GC Association; she was a vice-president of the FANY; an honorary member of the St Dunstan's Ex-Prisoners of War Association; and President of 282 (East Ham) Air Cadet Squadron.

Last year, though already frail, she revisited Ravensbrück. For her it was the first time since 1945. The occasion, the unveiling of a plaque remembering the courage of the SOE women who had died there, was for her a profoundly moving experience.

Her husband and the three daughters of her first marriage survive her.

Odette Hallowes, GC, MBE, wartime heroine of the Special Operations Executive, was born on April 28, 1912. She died on March 13, 1995, aged 82

GINGER ROGERS

DANCING FILM STAR WHO "DID EVERYTHING FRED ASTAIRE DID, BUT BACKWARDS AND IN HIGH HEELS"

APRIL 26, 1995

Ginger Rogers was a vivacious film star from the golden age of Hollywood whose screen career was made by her celebrated screen partnership with the late Fred Astaire. This ran from 1933 to 1939 and embraced some of the cinema's most celebrated musicals. She was outstanding neither as a singer nor as a dancer but she responded triumphantly to Astaire's immaculate professionalism and sense of style. Theirs was art that concealed art and what appeared on the screen was a total effacement of a painstaking quest for spontaneity and grace.

In the context of her career the musicals she made with Astaire formed a relatively small part. In other films stretching over a period of nearly 30 years, she revealed herself as an expert comedienne and a serviceable dramatic actress with a particular talent for impersonating children.

Above all, Ginger Rogers was a star who never lost the common touch. She remained at heart the ordinary, jolly working girl, not very different from scores of others who dreamt of making it into the movies and getting to dance with Fred Astaire.

She was born Virginia Katherine McMath in Independence, Missouri, an only child, and owed her early success in show business to the shrewd guidance of her formidable mother, Lela Rogers, who later became a Hollywood scriptwriter. It was mother who decided that she was not ready to sign the film contract of a child actress. The name Ginger was given to her by a cousin, Helen, who could not say her "v"s. Because of this, Virginia became Dinda and then Ginger.

Her professional debut still came at the age of 14, as a dancer with Eddie Foy's troupe at Fort Worth, Texas. She went on to win a charleston contest, and thus launched her professional career. She worked extraordinarily hard as a young girl, criss-crossing the country in trains with her mother, performing in theatres, clubs and on the New York stage, living out of suitcases in hotel rooms. It was this discipline which gave her the strength to shoulder such an extraordinary workload later in Hollywood. She appeared in some nine films in 1933 alone.

Having formed a Vaudeville act, Ginger and Pepper, with her first husband, Jack Pepper, and appeared in several short films, she arrived on Broadway in 1929 when she played the second female lead in the musical *Top Speed* and went into another Broadway show, George Gershwin's *Girl Crazy*. The Gershwins had written "But Not For Me" especially for her and she opened the show with the lovely "Embraceable You". During rehearsals, the producers were dissatisfied with this last number and called in the expert help of Astaire, then starring on Broadway with his sister Adele. Astaire watched the routine in the theatre lobby and said: "Here, Ginger, try it with me."

In 1930 she made her first feature film *Young Man of Manhattan*, singing and wise-cracking as the girlfriend of Charles Ruggles and uttering a famous line: "Cigarette me, big boy." After serving an apprenticeship in broad comedy she switched with immediate success to musicals. She was the social climbing Anytime Annie in *42nd Street* (1933) and had a strong supporting part as a wisecracking bottle blonde in *Gold Diggers of 1933* (1933), a Busby Berkeley extravaganza and her first real break.

One day on set she was handed the opening song, "We're in the Money", and told to learn it by the evening, ready for the next day's shooting. She went into a corner and after three hours had become so confident that she started improvising on the lyrics with nonsense words: "Er'way in-hay the oney-may." Darryl Zanuck stopped to listen and was so impressed that he insisted she do it exactly the same way to open the film. This is how the film starts, the camera zooming in on Rogers wearing nothing but a coin-specked gold bikini.

She first appeared with Astaire in *Flying Down to Rio* (1933). The nominal female lead was Dolores del Rio and Astaire was making only his second film but Fred and Ginger stole the picture. They were paired again in *The Gay Divorcee* (1934) and while Rogers continued to make a string of excellent non-musicals, her international popularity rested on her work with Astaire.

In films like *Top Hat* (1935), *Follow the Fleet* (1936), *Swing Time* (1936) and *Shall We Dance* (1936) the couple gave cinemagoers some of their happiest moments. With banal plots, usually Astaire in romantic pursuit of Rogers, they were the sheerest escapism and at the same time consummate art, even if Rogers's feet were often raw and bleeding by the time the demanding Astaire decided that a take was good enough to print.

Despite the inevitable speculation, their partnership in fact never strayed from a professional footing. They rarely saw each other on a social basis, and Astaire's wife, who insisted on coming on to the set, would sit on the sidelines and knit. She would also vet scripts with Astaire to make sure there was no kissing between Astaire and Rogers. Ginger was mildly amused by this, and by the fact that critics never quite judged her on the same level as Astaire as a dancer. Her favourite cartoon had a couple commenting on a poster for Astaire: "Sure he was great, but don't forget Ginger Rogers did everything he did, backwards and in high heels."

After playing real-life dancers in their ninth film, *The Story of Vernon and Irene Castle* (1939), Astaire and Rogers went their separate ways. Wanting to prove herself as a dramatic actress, Rogers found no difficulty striking out on her own and during the 1940s she was one of America's highest-paid women. Notable among her films during the period were the comedy *Bachelor Mother* (1939), with David Niven, as a shopgirl who finds an abandoned baby, and the drama *Kitty Foyle* (1948), for which she won her only Oscar as a proud young Irish salesgirl who marries above her class and comes to regret it.

In 1943 she played the title role in *Roxie Hart*, sporting a bubble cut for a boisterous piece about a showgirl taking a murder rap. After *Kitty Foyle*, her best juvenile role was in *The Major and the Minor* (1942), a comedy about a girl posing as a child to travel halffare. It marked the American directing debut of Billy Wilder.

Rogers remained a star until the mid-1950s, though her films became gradually less distinguished. Replacing Judy Garland, who withdrew through illness, she partnered Astaire again, in the MGM musical *The Barkleys of Broadway* (1949). The reunion proved popular with the public but the film was not up to the standard of their 1930s work.

In 1952 she played opposite Cary Grant and a chimpanzee in the Howard Hawks comedy *Monkey Business*, and the pick of her later roles was as the gangster's moll in *Tight Spot* (1955), with Edward G. Robinson. Her last film appearance was as Jean Harlow's mother in *Harlow* in 1965.

Long before this she had been trying to widen her options through television and the stage. A bizarre and forget-table television project was a live BBC musical, *Carissima*, transmitted in 1959, in which she neither sang nor danced. She was luckier in the theatre, taking over from Carol Channing in the Broadway production of *Hello Dolly!* (1965) and starring in a London pro-duction of *Mame* (1969) for which her fee of £250,000 was the highest then paid to an artist in the West End. In the late 1970s she had her last incarnation as a revue artist touring America and appearing at the London Palladium. She published her autobiography, *Ginger: My Story*, in 1991.

Like her mother, Ginger was a devout Christian Scientist. This gave her an almost puritanical streak in some respects, a determination never to let her standards slip, or to be influ-enced by Hollywood habits of which she disapproved. For example, in keep-ing with her Christian Science faith she never drank, and though she threw many Hollywood parties, they were tee-total affairs.

Her five marriages all ended in divorce and there were no children. Her second husband was the actor Lew Ayres; her third, Jack Briggs; her fourth another actor, Jacques Bergerac; and her fifth, William Marshall, an actor and producer.

Ginger Rogers, actress and dancer, was born on July 16, 1911. She died on April 25, 1995, aged 83

ALISON HARGREAVES

THE FIRST WOMAN
TO CONQUER MOUNT
EVEREST SOLO WITHOUT
SUPPLEMENTARY OXYGEN

AUGUST 21, 1995

Alison Hargreaves was always deter-mined to meet the toughest challenges head on. It was this that drove her for-ward to earn both a place in the record books and an international reputation as a superlative mountaineer. In May this year she became the first woman and only the second person ever to conquer Everest solo, without supple-mentary oxygen. Undeterred by the long-frozen corpses of two previous climbers which she passed on the way, she braved night-time temperatures dropping as low as minus 30 degrees centigrade and an agonisingly rarefied atmosphere to make her ascent to the roof of the world.

"There is no gain without risk," Hargreaves said. She climbed not because of some deep-rooted death wish, but because she loved mountains with a passion. "Most climbers," she said, "enjoy living more than normal people because they have so much to live for."

Hargreaves joked that she had an ego as big as Mount Everest, but she firmly counteracted the opprobrium of those who accused her of selfishly putting her career as a climber before her duties as a mother. She felt that by going out to tackle challenges she had more to offer than if she had settled to be a housewife. "By climbing I can give my children 100 per cent rather than be a frustrated mother at home," she said. It was with her children in mind that she balanced her ambition with an eminently practical caution, showing herself wise enough to turn back even when much effort and money had been invested in a trip.

In 1994 her first attempt on Everest was abandoned just 1,500ft from the summit because of threatening weather conditions. It felt, Hargreaves said, "as though someone had scraped away everything inside and left me empty". When on a second attempt she finally achieved her goal on May 13 this year she once more proved her devotion to her children in a radio message transmitted amid tears of joy and exhaustion from the summit: "I am on top of the world and I love you dearly."

First introduced to rock climbing at Belper High School in Derbyshire, by the age of 14 Hargreaves was travelling all over Britain in search of testing rock faces. At 18, instead of following family tradition and going to Oxford to read mathematics, she outfaced parental disapproval and announced that she was going to move in with her boyfriend Jim Ballard, an amateur rock climber who was later to become her husband. Together they set up an outdoor equipment business in Matlock.

By 21 Hargreaves was building up a formidable stamina by running for two hours every day up the steep hillsides of the Derbyshire Peak District, and by 1986, when she travelled to the Himalayas for the first time, she knew that she had made the right decision and that she wanted to become a professional mountaineer.

Hargreaves was five-and-a-half months pregnant when she tackled the 4,600ft north face of the Eiger. But her first child, Tom, was in the end nearly born out in the wilds of Derbyshire when Hargreaves's waters broke while she was out bouldering with her husband. After that her life calmed a little as she settled into a four-year career break. She had a second child, Kate, in 1991. During these years she enjoyed taking up a very different sort of challenge as chairman of the local playgroup, yet she still kept herself in peak physical condition, running early in the mornings before the household had arisen.

In 1993 the family sold their home and business to finance a trip to the Alps where they travelled and lived in an old Land Rover so that Hargreaves could climb. There she broke previous records by becoming the first person to climb solo, and in one season, the classic six north faces of the Alps: those of the Eiger, Matterhorn, Dru, Badile, Grandes Jorasses and Cima Grande mountains.

With this first major achievement under her belt, she returned to Britain, and bought a house at Spean Bridge in Inverness-shire, in the shadow of

Ben Nevis. But it was not long before Hargreaves was off again to make her famed ascent of the 29,028ft Everest, from which she returned back to base camp on May 16 this year.

Most mountaineers would have hung up their crampons for a while, but not Hargreaves. By June 12 she had set off for the Karakoram range, ready to conquer the Himalayan K2, which at 28,244ft is the second highest and technically the most difficult mountain to climb in the world. It has a reputation for unreliable weather and terrible storms.

There have been hundreds of ascents of Everest, and comparatively few fatalities. But, since the first conquest of K2 in 1954, out of just 113 confirmed ascents there have been 37 deaths. The body of Julie Tullis, the first and only British woman to climb the peak, is buried in the snow up there, after she died in a blizzard in 1986.

It is little wonder that K2 has been called the Savage Mountain. But Hargreaves was hopeful. If she had succeeded on K2 she already had plans under way to go straight on to Kangchenjunga, the world's third highest peak on the Sikkim-Nepal border. Hargreaves set out to climb K2 via its southeast ridge without bottled oxygen, fixing ropes, high-altitude porters or fixed camps. She reached the summit with two other climbers on August 13 but, on her descent, was overcome by a fierce storm. Exactly how she died remains unclear.

She is survived by her husband, and by their son and daughter.

Alison Hargreaves, mountaineer, was born on February 17, 1962. She died on August 13, 1995, aged 33

———— ∿ ————

PAT SMYTHE

INTERNATIONAL SHOWJUMPER
WHO WAS THE FIRST WOMAN TO
WIN AN OLYMPIC MEDAL
IN THE SPORT

FEBRUARY 28, 1996

In international showjumping, one of the few sports in which men and women come together on level terms, Pat Smythe was the world's most successful woman ever. Lieutenant-Colonel Sir Harry Llewellyn, an Olympic gold medal winner, described her as "an all-time great, the best lady rider I have ever seen".

With Prince Hal and Tosca in particular, two difficult and temperamental horses, bought for a song, she had an amazing run of successes. This led to other people sending her their horses to jump, including Lord King of Wartnaby; the Hon Dorothy Paget, the eccentric racehorse owner, and Robert Hanson, master of the Grove and Rufford Hunt and father of Lord Hanson.

But Pat Smythe was not one of today's sponsored sports stars. In order to get into showjumping, pay her horse's keep and show entry fees, she worked weekends and in school holidays, milking cows, repairing farm walls and selling vegetables.

She became a household name because, during her 17 years at the top, television seemed besotted by showjumping. At the start of her international career the sport was still largely dominated by the officers of such smart pre-war cavalry schools as Saumur, Tor di Quinto and Fort Riley. They rode big horses and they rode in uniform. The TV audiences warmed to the fresh young woman in black coat and cap, riding a pony-size horse, yet still able to beat the men on big occasions — even to beat them with ease.

Smythe won grand prix events on her own horses in more countries than any man or woman has done since. She won in the United States, France, Belgium, Spain, Portugal, Italy, Switzerland, The Netherlands, and Denmark. In Australia, South Africa and South America she won grand prix events on borrowed horses that she had first seen less than a week before. In 1956 she was the first woman to ride in the showjumping at the Olympic Games and the first to win a medal, a bronze. Women had previously been banned by the Olympic authorities on the ground that it was not fair to them to compete against the men. Indeed in her early days Smythe sometimes inadvertently caused embarrassment. "Sorry about this, we were not expecting a woman rider to be as good as you," said Mr Justice Wylie, chairman of the Royal Dublin Horse Show, presenting her with the prize for the show's most successful international rider — the prize was a silver cigar box.

Yet Smythe had neither the strong leg nor strong back thought to be essential for a leading rider at international level. Her gift was rather the rapport she developed with each and every horse. Horses were treated as friends with whom to co-operate for the best results, and never as machines to be booted into the winning slot. Horse and rider blended with a harmony seldom seen in top sport. Together they would saunter into a big arena, always at the walk, and not looking at all like winners. But Smythe seemed to imbue her mounts with her indomitable will to win.

Her favourite was Prince Hal. She saw him finishing last in the Kim Muir Chase at the Cheltenham Gold Cup meeting. It was love at first sight. Closer inspection revealed a bowed tendon. Amazingly in the circumstances, she and her mother reckoned they could get the horse sound and turn him into a showjumper. They paid £300 for him. He won them thousands in return. On the North American jumping circuit, Smythe was to win all five international events at Harrisburg on Prince Hal. The headlines in the local paper ran: "One Girl Beats All the Americans." Smythe repeated the performance on the same horse at the even more competitive Brussels International.

She was brilliant on the big occasions. She won the Gold Buttons of Algiers on Prince Hal, Africa's most coveted showjumping prize. But perhaps the most memorable aspect of this win was the outstandingly high quality of the competition. Smythe beat three men who between them had taken four Olympic gold medals and one world championship.

Prince Hal was at the height of his powers at the time of the 1960 Rome Olympics. Smythe was near to tears when she was picked for the team without him but the team trainer, Colonel Jack Talbot-Ponsonby, declared that he would not have "a thin-skinned broken-down racehorse on his team". A Weedon cavalryman of the old school, his idea of an Olympic horse was one that looked like a pre-war officer's charger. Smythe had the last laugh. Riding Prince Hal at the very next show after the Rome Olympics she beat both the gold and silver medallists in a major event.

There is always danger and sometimes damage when competing at the highest level on a fiery, difficult horse. On Tosca's first international abroad, at Nice, Smythe took a crashing fall. She lay on the ground motionless and spectators wondered if she was still alive. She did not jump again at that show. But four months later horse and rider took the most important national title of them all, the Leading Showjumper of the Year championship at Wembley. And for two years they were to be the biggest money-winners in British showjumping.

Smythe took four individual European titles. She was the first woman to win the famous international, the Hickstead Derby, riding Robert Hanson's Flanagan. Lord King's Mr Pollard finally won her the Queen Elizabeth Cup, after a string of seconds on other horses. On two of the four occasions that she won the Royal International Show supreme championship it was on the Hon Dorothy Paget's Scorchin, a horse she was later to drive to a Ralli cart round the Gloucestershire roads near her home.

However, though showjumping was Smythe's career it was not one that dominated her life. In her spare time at international shows she would be polishing up her languages, visiting an incredible number of local sights, and in the evening in the hotel she would strum local songs on her guitar, while everybody joined in the singing. She also became a bestselling author of children's books, as well as spending the latter years of her life working for the preservation of rare animals and the environment.

Pat Smythe was born in Barnes. Her childhood was in many ways difficult, especially during the Second World War. Her father, a civil engineer Major Eric Smythe, was already an invalid by 1939 and her mother had to give up her job schooling horses for the polo proprietor, Billy Walsh, to nurse him herself. He died in 1944.

Smythe had attended six different schools by the age of 15. From Oakhill in Wimbledon, she then went to Downe House, Seaford, Fern House and also Fonthill Abbey in Wiltshire, Pate's Grammar School and later St Michael's in Cheltenham, and Thornton Heath, Bournemouth. Relatives who had lost their own children in the war helped out with school fees. They hoped that she would go on to higher education, offering to finance it.

She matriculated at 15 and won the school's top biology prize. Later she was to say that her biology studies at school were a great help to her when she travelled the world decades later on conservation work. But higher education was not for her. She announced to the formidable Miss Freda Sykes, who was headmistress of Thornton Heath at the time, that she was quitting after five terms. She wanted to be a showjumper, and she had a sick horse, Finality, that needed nursing. It was necessary for her to earn money to pay for the horse's keep.

At this time Smythe, her mother and her elder brother Ronald were living in a rented house in the Gloucestershire countryside. They grew vegetables in the garden and at weekends Pat would harness up the pony Pixie to a cart, drive into Cheltenham and sell the produce to hotels and boarding houses. During the school holidays she worked on a nearby farm. She also learnt to repair the Cotswold stone walls of the area.

Later the family moved to two rooms in Bath. Mrs Smythe gave children riding lessons and got to work, together with her daughter, repairing the stables at Bath racecourse which had been damaged by wartime bombing. Their next move was to the country, to Miserden, where they turned their home into a guest-house for 12 students from Cirencester Agricultural College during the term and took in foreign children wishing to learn English in the holidays. This provided them with sufficient income to live and to finance Pat's showjumping. She was then 20. But though the guest-house flourished, Pat's mother died three years later when her car skidded on an icy road.

Despite all her struggles, friends could only remember Smythe being bitter once — the afternoon that her mother died. The bank manager rang to say that he had to call in a debt of £1,500 that had been loaned for the conversion of the house. Always practical, Smythe sold Leona, her most promising international horse at the time, to Swiss friends for £1,500. The guest-house continued, staff being hired to take the place of her mother.

Smythe began to write books and had 11 published by the age of 30. Her children's series, *The Three Jays*, an ongoing story of children, their ponies and their farm animals, was translated into several languages. She published her autobiography *Jump For Joy*, to be followed by *Jumping Life's Fences*. This dramatically changed her financial position, at least for a time.

She purchased Sudgrove, a fine country house in the Cotswolds with stables and paddocks for her horses, and invited showjumping friends, Sir Harry and Lady Llewellyn, to come and see it. They were appalled at its dilapidated state and the erratic electricity and water supplies, neither of which came from the mains. Smythe nonetheless decided to go ahead. She craved a home of her own after all the years of lettings and leases. When she went to live in Switzerland, Sudgrove continued to be a guest-house for students.

In 1963, aged 35, she married Sam Koechlin, a Swiss lawyer and businessman. Sir Malcolm Sargent, the conductor, chose the singers for the ceremony and Lord Beaverbrook lent his London flat for the honeymoon. The couple had met 12 years before when he had come to study at the London School of Economics and his horse had come with him for him to ride in the Badminton Horse Trials and been accommodated in his future wife's stables.

For some twenty years Smythe accompanied her husband on business trips all over the world, finding an outlet for her second love, the preservation of rare animals and conservation of the environment. In summer there were visits to the family villa on an island on Lake Lucerne. In winter they would ski from the family chalet at Wengen where Pat kept up with British friends at the Downhill Only Club. Their home was a house of Cotswold-coloured stone which they had built on the sunny side of the Jura mountains. Building work was slow until Smythe hung on the biggest tree in the village an open invitation to supper and a dance. A great evening for the builders and all their friends resulted in the house being finished with astonishing rapidity.

After her husband's death Smythe returned to Sudgrove. She had had a succession of illnesses, many of them developing from bad falls from her very early days of showjumping. She had several leg operations. Both her hips were replaced and at the age of 56 she was found to have a genetic heart fault. She also developed crippling osteoporosis.

But Smythe never really retired. She redoubled her efforts on behalf of the World Wildlife Fund, travelling the world on inspections as a member of its international committee. She was involved with a number of conservation groups, and always actively so. Local events such as church fetes always meant much to her.

Long after she had been forced to give up showjumping she remained involved in the sport as an international selector, and, sometimes, *chef d'équipe* of British teams abroad. From 1986 to 1989 she was president of the British Showjumping Association. She was appointed OBE in 1956.

She is survived by her two daughters. *Pat Smythe, OBE, international showjumper, was born on November 22, 1928. She died from heart disease on February 27, 1996, aged 67*

—⁓—

DIANA, PRINCESS OF WALES

THE WIFE AND MOTHER OF FUTURE KINGS

SEPTEMBER 1, 1997

Not since the heyday of Jacqueline Kennedy Onassis had there been an international icon to match Diana, Princess of Wales. Her picture on the cover of magazines was enough to guarantee sales worldwide, and no personality in history was ever the subject of more unremitting attention on the part of the paparazzi. In that sense, the fact that she should have met her death — with her new boy-friend Dodi Fayed — while apparently seeking to escape a motorcycle pursuit by photographers carries its own cruel irony along with it.

In an age when stars have become drabber and more ordinary, she achieved unrivalled glamour and respect. She developed from being a relatively unprepossessing kindergar-ten teacher into a stylish and beautiful young woman, always well dressed, and beloved for her gentle and loving nature.

The most successful princesses in history have been those who loved children and cared for the sick. The Princess enjoyed a natural affinity with both children and the sick. She devoted much energy to their care, in a way entirely in tune with the age. Her warmth and kindness found many outlets, particularly in regard to those struck down with HIV. She was spon-taneous in manner, happily ignoring royal protocol to bestow a kiss on a child in the crowd, and writing letters to members of the public signed "love Diana".

Almost from the day she emerged into public life, the British people took her to their hearts. She brought to the Royal Family not only her very English beauty, but the enthusiasm of youth, combined with an innate dignity and a good-natured sense of humour.

She was not an intellectual: neither a good passer of exams nor a noted reader. But she possessed a canny and straightforward form of common sense. She listened and she learnt, and whereas she may have found her schooldays boring, she relished her role as Princess of Wales. She loved fashion and dancing, and pop stars and groups such as Phil Collins and Spandau Ballet. In the early years of her marriage she was as excited at meeting stars like Elizabeth Taylor as they were to meet her.

Though she was born into the far from stimulating world of the conventional upper-class girl, reared in the counties of Norfolk and Northamptonshire and veering in youth towards the world of the "Sloane Ranger", her character had great possibilities for development, and develop she did, into a figure of inter-national importance, confident of her place on the world stage.

She was given little support, it would seem, by her own family or that into which she married. Perhaps one of the reasons that the British public loved her as they did was that they always feared for her, and were concerned that she might be unhappy, while admiring her for being a fighter who refused to give up in the face of adversity.

The world's press loved her, too. Newspapers built her up into the epitome of a fairy-tale princess. Occasionally they were fickle and turned on their creation, but it was generally more comfortable to let the world love her, and their onslaughts were accordingly short-lived. The press interest was relentless, however, and it began long before the engagement was in any sense firm. After her marriage, her every movement, her every outfit, her every mood, was the excuse for many column inches of press comment. She was a natural joy for photographers, being both photogenic and having an innate understanding of the needs of journalists. Her face could sell a million copies of any publication, and both they and she knew it. She adorned many a magazine cover by editor's choice, and once, memorably, that of *Vogue* by her own wish.

In this great love for a public figure there was bound to lurk danger. When she flourished the press supported her, but when life was dark it deserted her. In the summer of 1992, the forthcoming publication of a biography by Andrew Morton, a journalist from the lower echelons of the trade, caught the attention of Andrew Neil, the Editor of *The Sunday Times*. Several weeks of serialisation damaging to the monarchy followed. Despite complaints from the Press Council and pleas from the Archbishop of Canterbury, the campaign raged on. It could be seen as a major destructive force in the Princess's life.

Diana, Princess of Wales, was born at Park House, Sandringham, as the Hon Diana Frances Spencer. She was the third and youngest daughter of Viscount Althorp (later the 8th Earl Spencer, who died in 1992), and his first wife, the Hon Frances Roche (later married for some years to the wallpaper

heir, Peter Shand Kydd). She became Lady Diana Spencer on the death of her grandfather in 1975.

Her Spencer forebears had been sheep farmers in Warwickshire, who settled at Althorp, Northamptonshire, in 1506. Cousins of the Spencer-Churchills, they included many connoisseurs and patrons of the arts. Having inherited a considerable fortune from Sarah, Duchess of Marlborough, they were able to spend large sums on antiquities, paintings and sculpture.

For many generations they served their Sovereigns, and the tradition continued. The Princess's father was equerry to King George VI and to the present Queen. Both her grandmothers, the Countess Spencer and Ruth Lady Fermoy, were close members of the court of Queen Elizabeth the Queen Mother, as were no fewer than four Spencer great-aunts. To her two sons, the Princess of Wales passed strong physical Spencer traits, considerably diluting the Hanoverian strain in the Royal Family.

While the Princess's paternal ancestors were representative of the Whig oligarchy of the 18th century, she also descended through several lines from the Stuart Kings Charles II and James II, who were not ancestors of the Prince of Wales. Other paternal forebears included the great Duke of Marlborough, Sir Robert Walpole, the Marquess of Anglesey (who lost a leg at Waterloo), and the Earl of Lucan, of Balaclava fame. On her mother's side there was Irish and Scottish blood,

Princess Diana: "In this great love for a public figure there was bound to lurk danger"

with a sprinkling of pioneer New England stock. Her closest relationship to the Prince of Wales was that of seventh cousin once removed, through their common descent from the 3rd Duke of Devonshire.

The Princess was educated at Riddlesworth Hall in Norfolk, and then at West Heath, a boarding school in Kent. She achieved no O-level passes. Later she attended a finishing school, the Institut Alpin Videmanette at Rougemont in Switzerland, for six weeks. Her childhood was somewhat unsettled and unhappy because of the separation of her parents when she was six, and their divorce in 1969. She had more natural affinity with her father than with her mother.

During the period after leaving school, the Princess worked as a nanny, a babysitter and a skivvy. She attended a cookery course in September 1978, and soon after this her father collapsed with a grave cerebral haemorrhage, from which it took him months to recover. In 1979 she worked briefly as a student teacher at Miss Vacani's dance studios. Later she was invited by friends to help at the Young England Kindergarten in Pimlico, where she was popular with the children. She worked at the kindergarten three days a week and at other times she looked after a small American boy.

In London the Princess shared a flat at Coleherne Court, Earls Court, with three girlfriends. They found her a kind and thoughtful flatmate, keen on housework and evenings in front of the television, a lover of ballet, opera and cinema. She loved to dance and sometimes they returned to find her dancing happily around the flat. At the time of the pre-wedding press siege, these girls were to prove staunchly loyal allies. Fortunately, they were content to spend hours in each other's company. Years later, one of them, Mrs William Bartholomew, the former Carolyn Pride, was a source for the Morton biography of the Princess.

The Prince and Princess of Wales claimed to have met in a ploughed field at Althorp where Prince Charles was staying as a guest of Lady Sarah Spencer, the Princess's elder sister, in November 1977. The accepted version of the story is that Prince Charles and Lady Sarah were romantically involved, though not deeply so. The younger sister fell in love with everything about the Prince, was keen to be Princess of Wales, and saw in him a challenge.

She knew from an early age that she would have to tread carefully, and she never put a foot wrong. It was not until the late summer of 1980 that Lady Diana Spencer's name came to the attention of the world. The Prince of Wales was nearly 32 and the subject of his eventual marriage had been of consuming interest to the media for nearly a decade. Nor had he helped his difficulty by pronouncing that he thought 30 a good age at which to marry. As November 1978 loomed, the pressure increased. But he remained a bachelor, and there were times when he looked a less than happy man.

Lady Diana's appearance on the scene refocused press attention on the

Prince's bachelor state. While a discreet and low-key courtship was executed in private, Lady Diana was pursued to and from work by determined cameramen and reporters and had to resort to complicated manoeuvres to rescue the last vestiges of her privacy. Her subtle handling of the press earned her not only universal respect but the real affection of these normally hard-hearted men. At one point after she had broken down in tears, a note of apology was placed under her windscreen wiper. But the press pursuit persisted to such an extent that Lady Diana's mother wrote a letter of appeal to *The Times*. Later the Queen was obliged to complain to newspaper editors through her press secretary. The Prince proposed early in February 1981.

The engagement was announced on February 24, after which Lady Diana was better protected. From that day on she was surrounded by what she described as "a mass of smiling faces". Indeed the engagement was greeted with universal approval — though the Princess herself found her immediate pre-marriage days in Buckingham Palace both tense and lonely.

The Royal Wedding took place in St Paul's Cathedral on July 29, 1981, by the shared wish of both bride and groom. Prince Charles ensured that it was a "marvellous, musical, emotional experience", with three orchestras playing and Kiri te Kanawa (soon afterwards appointed a Dame) and the Bach Choir singing. Lady Diana chose her favourite school hymn, *I vow to thee my Country*.

Many heads of state attended, including nearly all the crowned heads of Europe, President Mitterrand of France, and Mrs Nancy Reagan, wife of the then President of the United States. The King of Tonga required a special chair to be built to support his mighty frame. A last-minute absentee was King Juan Carlos of Spain, because of the decision of the Prince and Princess to embark on the Royal Yacht *Britannia* at Gibraltar. The wedding day was such that for a brief while it seemed that all strife was set aside, the sun blazed richly and, at the end of it, the police thanked the public for their vigilance, and the public praised the police, and, as one commentator put it, "the world was a friendlier and easier place for everyone".

The honeymoon was spent first at Broadlands, the home of Lord and Lady Romsey, and a favoured retreat of the Prince when he had stayed there with the late Lord Mountbatten in his youth. Then they cruised on *Britannia* in the Mediterranean. A long holiday at Balmoral followed.

Returning to London in October, the Prince and Princess took up residence at Kensington Palace and at Highgrove House in Gloucestershire. These were their homes for the next 11 years. Their first royal engagement was a 400-mile tour of Wales, the first such visit of a Princess of Wales for 113 years. The tour included a visit to Caernarfon Castle where the Prince had been invested in 1969. The Princess of Wales was given the Freedom of Cardiff, made her first public speech and spoke a few words of Welsh. Despite the ever-present threat of incendiary devices, the tour was a resounding success.

The Princess made an immediate impact on the world of fashion. The British fashion industry, long in a precarious state, was given a welcome boost by her arrival. Her style was fresh, attractive and original. She became the personification of current trends in British fashion, with felicitous results for the trade.

The Princess soon revealed a penchant for outfits of considerable glamour. On her first outing with her fiancé, she had arrived at Goldsmiths' Hall in a *décolleté* black taffeta dress, a considerable contrast to her formerly discreet image, which caused the octogenarian Lady Diana Cooper to joke: "Wasn't that a mighty feast to set before a King?" Her wedding dress with its lavish detail and lengthy train matched the magnificence of St Paul's Cathedral and her going away outfit was chic and stylish. The fair fringe she favoured early in the marriage was widely copied for a time.

Very soon the Princess was pregnant, giving birth to a boy, Prince William of Wales, on June 21, 1982. A second son, Prince Harry, followed in September 1984.

In the early years of the marriage the Waleses normally undertook joint engagements. This was the period of the Princess's apprenticeship. But it soon became clear that of the two it was her that the public most wished to see, and Prince Charles was to some extent reduced to a male dancer supporting his glorious ballerina in her pirouettes.

While the popularity of his bride should have delighted him, it added a sense of pointlessness to his slightly frustrated life. Equally, he was irritated when he tried to make an important speech, and the next day the papers merely reported his wife's outfit. He failed to grasp that one of the things the world wanted was a recurring series of images of a young couple enjoying a happy family life. He always appeared reluctant in such photo-calls, fearing that this diminished the import of his more serious endeavours. The Princess, on the other hand, fulfilled all such demands to perfection.

The respective backgrounds of the Prince and Princess of Wales were an additional challenge in the creation of a happy family atmosphere. She had come from a broken home, while his upbringing had been formal to say the least. His early companion had been his nanny, and he lacked any close involvement with his parents.

The love of solitude to which the Prince adhered even after marriage, combined with his love of polo and hunting, inevitably left the Princess on many occasions without him. But both parents shared an adoration for their children.

Even as the world rejoiced on their wedding day, the Princess was aware that she had not entirely captured Prince Charles's heart. Yet she always felt that she would win him. He most probably felt that the marriage was akin to an arranged one, and some have said that he did not enter into it in the same spirit as his bride. When the Princess realised that Prince Charles was never entirely to reciprocate the love she felt for him, she, like many mothers, transferred much of her devotion to her sons.

The Princess celebrated her 21st birthday in July 1982, and that September she represented the Queen at the funeral of Princess Grace of Monaco in the cathedral at Monte Carlo.

The Princess was soon busily involved in the world of public duty. As the years went by, she evolved into a deeply committed member of the Royal Family. She swiftly became better informed — in the early days of her marriage a Fleet Street editor was surprised to hear Prince Charles explaining to her at lunch that Chancellor Kohl was the leader of West Germany. She also learnt the tricks of the royal trade, speaking easily to individual members of the public of all ages and possessing a good instinct as to what to talk about.

Yet in the early days she seldom made speeches in public, and when she did they were of the most formal sort. As she gained confidence, she began to write her own speeches, delivering them from the podium with calm assurance. She spoke of the importance of the family in everyday life, the rehabilitation of drug-users, and urged more compassion for those dying of Aids. When she and the Prince of Wales appeared together in television interviews it was not long before she was the more articulate of the two, leaving him almost monosyllabic, despite an earlier reputation for fluency.

The modern manner is for members of the Royal Family to be actively involved with any organisation of which they are patron or president. Until she gave up most of her charitable commitments at the end of 1993, the Princess was never merely a figurehead, but served directly as fundraiser, promoter, chairman of meetings — and, of course, as public spokesman.

She gave her support to an enormous number of charities, in a wide range of fields. Among her key presidencies or patronages were Barnardo's; the Great Ormond Street Hospital for Children; Centrepoint; English National Ballet; RADA; the Royal Academy of Music; the Leprosy Mission; the National Aids Trust; the Royal Marsden Hospital; Help the Aged; and the National Meningitis Trust.

An exhausting round of overseas travel was also a feature of her marriage. Her first big overseas tour occurred in March and April 1983, when she accompanied Prince Charles on a visit to Australia. The infant Prince William went with them. They travelled extensively from the Northern Territory to Canberra, through New South Wales, Tasmania, Southern Australia, Western Australia, Queensland and Victoria. At that time the Australian Prime Minister, Bob Hawke, was a committed republican, but he was forced to concede that the Princess was "a lovely lady".

The Australian trip (followed on that occasion by 12 days in New Zealand) was the first of three such visits. In June they went to Canada where there was an outbreak of "Di-mania", a 1980s equivalent of Beatlemania.

In February 1984, the Princess made her first major solo visit abroad, to Norway to attend a gala performance of *Carmen* by the London City Ballet. Arriving in the snow, she was at once dubbed "The Snow Princess". In the spring of 1985 she and the Prince of Wales went to Italy, a 17-day tour which included a visit to Sir Harold Acton at La Pietra, and to the Pope in Rome. Venice was perhaps the highlight of the tour, and here they were joined by Prince William and Prince Harry.

In October the Princess spent two days with the 1st Battalion The Royal Hampshire Regiment (of which she was Colonel-in-Chief until she relinquished her military commitments on her divorce in 1996) in West Germany. Following their second Australian visit, they paused briefly in Fiji, and rested in Hawaii before visiting the Reagans in the United States. The White House dinner and dance was typical of the mid-Eighties bonanza-style entertainment favoured during the Reagan era, and the highlight of the evening was when the Princess accompanied John Travolta in a sensational dance to *You're the One that I Want* (from the film *Grease*), an experience which both enjoyed and which served to resurrect Travolta's flagging career.

Other destinations during these years included Austria, Japan (where there was more "Di-mania"), the Gulf states, Portugal and France.

In 1989 the Princess returned to the United States, this time for a less glitzy trip to New York, where she visited centres for the homeless and dying children in the Aids ward of Harlem Hospital. She was dubbed, in American parlance, "Bigger than Gorby, Better than Bush". There was a visit to Kuwait (where security was intense following the Salman Rushdie affair), and the United Arab Emirates. In June she and the Prince revisited Australia, and in November they went on a Far East tour, taking in Indonesia and Hong Kong.

Visiting Nigeria in 1990, the Princess saw much suffering at first hand, and pointedly shook hands with the chief of a leper colony. In May the same year she and the Prince paid the first royal visit to a Warsaw Pact country, when they travelled to Hungary. In October the Princess went alone to Washington for a ballet gala and to further understanding of Aids. In November she and the Prince went to Japan for the enthronement of Emperor Akihito (a visit surrounded by controversy in Britain). There were also visits to Brussels, to British troops in Germany, to Prague, and to Expo 92 in Seville.

Besides the birth of her two children, there were other events of significance in her years of marriage. She much encouraged the union between Prince Andrew and her friend Sarah Ferguson, and she was delighted when they married in 1986. For some years they remained close friends and confidantes, and it was a cause of distress to her when that marriage came apart in the spring of 1992.

The Duchess of York had appeared to be a good ally at court, never as glamorous as the Princess, never likely to threaten her place in the esteem of the general public, but certainly her friend. But the arrival of the Duchess of York was, in retrospect, a damaging thing for the Princess of Wales, for she began to be tarnished by the new Duchess's fun-loving and sometimes irresponsible attitude.

The two may have seemed alike in character, but they were essentially different, the Princess being a great deal more dutiful and less interested in the perks. But the Duchess of York influenced her somewhat and it was during the time when they were close that the two then Royal Highnesses prodded their friends with the tip of their ferrule at the Royal Ascot meeting, one of a number of incidents that caused Establishment eyebrows to be raised.

Each girl represented an alternative fantasy for the young: to be like the Princess of Wales was to diet rigorously and undertake regular aerobics. The Duchess of York, on the other hand, made few concessions and her attitude was more one of "Take me as I am". In 1988 they were both in Klosters when their friend Major Hugh Lindsay was killed in an accident skiing off-piste with the Prince of Wales. This tragedy long dampened the spirits of all three.

For many years a small circle was aware of the not altogether happy state of the Princess of Wales's marriage. Much was written about this over the years, but the situation continued until *The Sunday Times* adopted the story in 1992 and blew it up to sensational proportions. The public was left with another dream shattered, and the monarchy's image was tarnished.

The 1992 revelations suggested that the Prince and Princess of Wales had failed to establish a mutually happy rapport during their marriage. There were many obstacles to natural happiness. With nearly 13 years between them, they were almost of different generations, he being born in the late 1940s, she in the early 1960s. The Prince was always of a serious disposition, inflexible in his way of life, not noted for his willingness to accept change. The Princess was initially more light-headed, though she developed considerably in the first decade of the marriage. She certainly entered the union with a more generous heart than her husband, who did not disguise his anxiety that the taking of a wife was an additional burden in an already busy life.

Despite her enormous popularity with the public, the differences in their interests seemed to divide them increasingly as the years progressed. Though they were both energetically and successfully involved in public life, the framework of their home life gradually eroded. He began to entertain separately. She spent more time in London, frequently away from Highgrove. Their problems were the focus of more attention than any couple could bear. Not only did they have to face their respective difficulties, but they had to do so in the full blast of media attention.

The strain began to show. The Prince of Wales had resumed his earlier association with a former girlfriend, Mrs Camilla Parker Bowles. The Princess's name was linked with those of two men nearer to her age, the Old Etonian James Gilbey and the Life Guards officer James Hewitt. There were clear signs of marital discord during a visit to India in February 1992, when the Princess spent time alone looking miserable at the Taj Mahal, and during a four-day trip to Korea in November that year, when the Prince and Princess, clearly unhappy in each other's company, were dubbed "The Glums" by reporters.

By the end of 1992, speculation about the state of the royal marriage had come to a head, fuelled by the release of a tape of an intimate conversation between the Princess and James Gilbey. There was talk of separate living arrangements, and a suggestion that reconciliation was now impossible. In December, John Major confirmed to the House of Commons that the couple were to separate.

Separation did little to reduce public interest, particularly after the discovery in 1993 of another intimate tape recording, this time of a conversation between the Prince and Mrs Parker Bowles. In December 1993 the Princess tearfully bowed out of public life, severing her links with most of the charities she had supported and begging to be left alone by the press. In 1994 Prince Charles admitted his long-standing and continuing relationship with Mrs Parker Bowles in a television interview with Jonathan Dimbleby.

Despite her pleas for privacy, the Princess remained very much in the public eye. As she set about putting her life in order during the period of personal confusion that followed the separation — visiting gymnasiums one day and psychotherapists the next — her every step was dogged by photographers and reporters. Yet her relationship with the media was always more complicated than she was prepared to admit. She may have been unhappy about some of the press ambushes, and about speculation on her association with married men such as the art dealer Oliver Hoare and the England rugby captain Will Carling, but there were undoubtedly occasions when she courted the attention, in an attempt to influence perceptions of her marriage and its breakdown.

Nowhere was this more evident than in her extraordinary decision — taken without consulting the Royal Household or even her own advisers — to appear on a special edition of the BBC *Panorama* programme in November 1995. She spoke frankly about her unhappy relationship with the Royal Family, her eating disorders, and her own and her husband's adultery. She announced her desire to be seen as "a queen of people's hearts". On August 28, 1996, the Prince and Princess of Wales divorced.

Throughout her marital difficulties, the Princess had remained devoted to her sons. After the divorce, when she and the Prince were given joint custody, she continued to invest considerable energy in their upbringing. She was an adoring mother, and there were many images of mother and children together, the most celebrated when the children ran to their mother's arms on *Britannia* after a period apart. The devotion was reciprocated, and her boys were a great source of comfort to her.

After her divorce the Princess made a return to public life, associating herself particularly with the work of the Red Cross, and taking a leading — and sometimes controversial — role in the international campaign to ban landmines. Earlier this year she auctioned many of her dresses to raise money for charity. She also seemed to find new happiness in her private life, spending much of the past few weeks in the company of Dodi Fayed, who died with her.

When she married the Prince of Wales, Diana said on television that she saw her life as a great challenge. Realistic though she was at 20 years of age, she underestimated how great that challenge would prove and at what cost to personal happiness it would be met.

The Princess made a lasting impression on the public. On the whole, they loved her; and even when she tried their patience, she remained a source of fascination. Outwardly shy, she had no lack of inner strength and common sense. Before her marriage she cast her head down, hiding behind her fringe. After the marriage she gained confidence, the head came up, and she began to acquire that star quality that drew all eyes in crowds and preoccupied fellow lunchers in restaurants. That quality, and that strength of character, saw her through her marital difficulties, and remained with her once the marriage was over.

Soon after her marriage to the Prince of Wales she was given the Royal Family Order by the Queen, but she was never given any other honours, such as the Grand Cross of the Royal Victorian Order, which she perhaps merited. On her divorce she assumed the title Diana, Princess of Wales, and remained a member of the Royal Family. She received various foreign orders on state visits.

Her two sons survive her.

Diana, Princess of Wales, was born on July 1, 1961. She died on August 31, 1997, after a car crash in Paris, aged 36

———

MOTHER TERESA

ROMAN CATHOLIC NUN WHO FOUNDED THE ORDER OF THE MISSIONARIES OF CHARITY DEDICATED TO THE WELFARE OF THE POOR

SEPTEMBER 6, 1997

More than anyone else of her time, Mother Teresa came to be regarded by millions as the embodiment of human goodness. By her compassion, humility and, it also has to be said, shrewd eye for publicity she raised public concern for the destitute; by devoting herself with single-minded vigour to the relief of human suffering, she galvanised individuals, both believers and non-believers, and even governments into action. Not since Albert Schweitzer has any one person had such an inspirational effect.

Mother Teresa's simplicity of purpose and approach hid a formidable personality and a determined strength of character. Despite a seemingly frail stature, she was physically strong and exercised a sometimes stern, unbending authority over her followers. Her personal philosophy was of a distinctly conservative kind, and she caused some disquiet in more liberal quarters by her highly public stance in opposition to abortion.

Her magnetism built the order she founded in Calcutta, the Missionaries of Charity, into a global movement. Without the benefit of image-makers, she captivated the attention of the international media, but was never herself captivated by it — or by the attentions of politicians. During a visit to London in 1988, she visited both Downing Street and the homeless of the capital; she praised Margaret Thatcher for supporting her sentiments, but when no progress was made against the homelessness problem, she spoke out against the Government's inaction.

Mother Teresa first became aware of the absolute deprivation of India's poor in the *bustees*, the slums of Calcutta, in the 1930s when she was involved in taking girls who were members of the Sodality of the Virgin Mary, together with some Hindu girls, to visit the sick in hospital. At the time she was a teacher at St Mary's, a Roman Catholic school in Entally, a rich residential area of Calcutta. They visited a few of the thousands of *bustees* hidden from the view of the rich residential houses and offices in Calcutta.

The contrast between the *bustees* and the oasis of beauty and security of the well-established community of the Congregation of the Loreto nuns where she lived gave a new direction to her vocation. "I knew that I belonged to the people of the *bustees*," she said. "The problem was how to get there and live with them."

It was on a train journey back to Darjeeling, on September 10, 1946 (a day now celebrated annually by her missionaries and co-workers), that Sister Teresa, as she then was, received what she described as "the call within a call" — a directive from God, that she was to have the courage to fulfil her ambitions and work with the poorest of the poor. "It was a command — I had to obey," she said.

By this time she had become the Principal of St Mary's. She then began applying for permission to leave her congregation, which she dearly loved. It took two years before this was granted by the Roman Congregation. On August 16, 1948, just before her 38th birthday, she exchanged her habit for a cheap white sari with a blue border, pinned a cross on her left shoulder and with five rupees in her pocket left the safety of the convent walls.

She applied to stay with the Medical Missionary Sisters in Patna, who condensed her medical training into four hectic months. They knew she wanted to start a new congregation whose members would devote their lives to the service of the destitute. Her nuns would be expected to live exactly as the *bustee* people, and she originally planned a diet of rice and salt — the poorest food of all. The Medical Missionaries persuaded her that this would be morally wrong, for if her future congregation were to give "their all", it was her responsibility to see that they would have a diet suited to their obligations. It was indeed sound advice which she accepted, and the food at her Home for the Destitute and Dying in Calcutta and her other missions around the world, although simple, is nutritious and adequate.

Mother Teresa — known simply as "Mother" — was a woman of courage and spirit. She was born of Albanian parents in Skopje, christened Agnes Gonxha Bojaxhiu, and educated at the local government school. She was first inspired by the writings of Pope Pius XI and also by the letters written to the school by Jesuit missionaries who were working among the poor in India, in the archdiocese of Calcutta.

She felt called to join a religious order, and entered the congregation of Loreto nuns who worked in Bengal. Before going to India she was sent to learn the English language in Dublin. From Ireland, she went to Darjeeling, situated in the most beautiful and wealthy part of the country, and found herself completing her novitiate in the famous Loreto School, where the daughters of the rich Indians and colonials obtained the best public school education for

their children. On March 24, 1931, Agnes Bojaxhiu made her first vows and took the name of Teresa.

The young Sister Teresa was transferred to St Mary's School, Entally, where she taught geography and history for 17 years. It was here that she took her final vows on May 24, 1937, and eventually became the Principal of the school.

In December 1948, after her medical training in Patna, Sister Teresa returned to Calcutta and initially stayed with the Little Sisters of the Poor. Bengal had been torn by riots resulting from the religious conflicts between Hindu and Muslim. In the city there were tens of thousands dying of starvation, tuberculosis, leprosy and other diseases resulting from malnutrition. Teresa was not afraid, although she knew the immensity of her task, and she began work by starting a pavement school for the *bustee* children, teaching them to write using the mud and dust as a blackboard.

On March 19, 1949, a small, shy former Bengali pupil, Subhasini Das, became Mother Teresa's first postulant, and took her old name of Agnes. She was followed by nine other former students who formed the nucleus of her community, the Missionaries of Charity, which today numbers over 3,000 novices and professed nuns supported by nearly 40,000 lay co-workers operating more than 400 homes in nine countries.

The community was recognised as a new, separate order and in addition to the customary religious vows, a fourth promise was added: "to give wholehearted, free service to the very poorest". The majority of the sisters were from the Third World. Unlike many other religious organisations who insist that novices should be at least second generation Christians, Mother Teresa was happy to accept girls from Indian families who wished to work with her. There were many parents who, faced with the crippling dowry prospects, were only too relieved that their daughters could be accepted into the security of such a community.

In 1952, through the Missionaries of Charity, Mother Teresa opened the Nirmal Hriday (Pure Heart) Home for Dying Destitutes. In 1965, the order was recognised as a papal congregation under the protection of the Vatican and in 1967 a Congregation of Brothers was formed. Mother Teresa was well aware that, although her community was increasing at an alarming rate, it was still important that lay people should be involved with the work among the destitute, and in 1969 a constitution was drawn up in Rome to unite these co-workers into one association. There were eventually tens of thousands of lay people — including a special group called the sick and suffering co-workers — from more than 40 countries.

Mother Teresa was a tireless worker, and it was surprising that her small frame managed to keep up with the speed of her activities. "God gives me the strength," she said. "There is no need to worry." When other nuns were ordered to rest, Mother Teresa was writing letters or attending to the queues of people who would be waiting outside the parlour to tell her their problems, and ask for her advice, or answering questions to the press, who were constantly around her.

The most important part of the day was the early morning when the daily Mass was celebrated, and Mother Teresa would lead her nuns in prayer, as she did for all the services throughout the day. Sometimes she would be found alone in the chapel, sitting barefoot, her hands folded, her head bent in silent private devotion. Wherever the Missionaries of Charity worked, they tried to set up a Shishu Bhavan, a children's home, for all unwanted babies and children in need — and a Nirmal Hriday (The Place of the Pure Heart) named after the first home for the dying which was in two rooms given for her use in the Hindu temple of Kalighat. The temple to this goddess of destruction, Kali, was felt to be a fitting home for the "place of the pure hearts".

Mother Teresa was proud of the fact that 50 per cent of the dying were brought "back to life" by the care of her community who, for six hours each day, washed, fed and gave medical attention to more than one hundred dying men and women brought in from the streets of Calcutta. Whenever Mother Teresa built new homes, she would have nothing that looked too Western and, therefore, might make the building appear over-bright and expensive to the very poor, for they would then be afraid to enter and to bring those who were ill and in need.

With her fame spreading, journalists and broadcasters began trekking to her home for the destitute and dying in Calcutta. One of them was Malcolm Muggeridge, who in 1969 made a documentary called *Something Beautiful for God*. He described it as the most important programme he had worked on and later said the experience had caused him, 12 years later, to become a Roman Catholic. In 1971 the Vatican awarded Mother Teresa the Pope John XXIII Peace Prize and she travelled to London to open a novitiate for the training of novices of her order in Southall — the first to be established outside India.

The next year she visited Northern Ireland to set up a small community of her nuns in Belfast. But she refused to abide by the unwritten sectarian rules of the divided Northern Ireland society and withdrew them two years later. On another visit, in 1981, she condemned an IRA hunger strike as an act of violence.

A year earlier the Prince of Wales was one of the VIP visitors to her children's orphanage in Calcutta and in 1983 the Queen also came to make Mother Teresa an honorary member of the Order of Merit, the only non-British subject to be so recognised, for her work among the sick and destitute.

In spite of her international renown, Mother Teresa continued to live and work without ostentation. When she travelled she did so either alone or accompanied by just a few of her white-veiled sisters. She never deviated from her rejection of personal reward. Her philosophy was based on a simple belief in divine intervention; she forbade her co-workers from raising

money in her name and relied on uninvited donations, which — as her fame spread — were not slow in coming.

With the growth of the community, there were many other activities which Mother Teresa encouraged among the poor. She arranged for food to be collected and given to thousands of destitutes — feeding 7,000 each morning at Shishu Bhavan in Calcutta. Some said the distribution of free meals made people too dependent, and that for them to make payment in kind would encourage dignity and independence.

There were medical clinics which gave free medicines donated from many countries. Here, too, some questioned whether medical treatment should not extend to more advanced rehabilitation programmes, and that patients with long-term illnesses should learn how to become self-sufficient and take pride in earning their living. The few who were able to weave provided sheets, clothing and bandages for the Missionaries of Charity homes. But Mother Teresa was particularly insistent that money should never change hands.

The community ran family planning clinics, where only the thermometer method was used (for Mother Teresa gave credence solely to the official teaching of the Roman Catholic Church); mobile clinics for leprosy and tubercular patients; schools; malnutrition centres and night shelters. Prison work was carried out and troubled and lonely families were visited. Mother Teresa once said: "I have come more and more to realise that it is being unwanted that is the worst disease that any human being can ever experience." Those who were unwanted, uncared for and deserted were to be respected by her nuns, cared for and cherished and recognised as people with their own human dignity in their own right.

She always maintained that those in her community were really contemplatives rather than social workers, hence, although they cared for the dying, handicapped and even minute premature aborted babies, the nuns were never to be considered a nursing order. Because she saw Christ in all people, then their work was contemplation. When she first heard that she was to receive the Nobel award she said: "I accept the prize in the name of the poor. The prize is the recognition of the poor world. Jesus said: 'I am hungry, I am naked, I am homeless.' By serving the poor, I am serving Him."

She made use of the opportunity to expound her total opposition to abortion. "The world has given me the Nobel Prize," she said as she was about to leave for Oslo in December 1979, "but I ask the world for a gift — I want the abortion laws abolished. This would be a real gift." At her request, the traditional dinner at the prize-awarding ceremony was cancelled and the money it would have cost was added to her prize money.

Mother Teresa was a hard-working and selfless woman, helped by the fact that she came of strong peasant stock and by her simple faith. She knew the meaning of loneliness by the very nature of her position. On her visit to London in 1988, she was as moved by the fate of London's homeless as she had been by the destitute of the Calcutta streets, and personally appealed to the Prime Minister for help in setting up a hostel to relieve their wants.

Speaking at the Global Forum on Human Survival in Oxford, she described abortion as the greatest threat to the future of the human race and said she would never allow a family which had practised contraception to adopt one of the orphans her missionary order cared for. She also complained that Aids victims were much more cruelly treated in Western countries than in Africa. That year she also visited the Soviet Union, China and South Africa to set up missions among the poor.

In September 1989, she was taken to hospital in Calcutta suffering from an irregular heartbeat and a high fever and doctors fitted her with a heart-pacemaker. Seven months later the Vatican announced that she would be resigning as head of her Missionaries of Charity order on grounds of ill-health, but in September that year she abandoned her retirement plans when the mission's electoral college unexpectedly failed to agree on a successor. In December 1990 she returned to her Albanian roots, visiting Tirana where she was awarded the Order of Maim Frasheri, the country's highest honour.

Showing little regard for her increasing frailty, she continued to work and travel. In March 1991 she was again in Albania, opening a mission there, and two months later she visited Bangladesh to survey the cyclone damage which

*Surrounded by children, Mother Teresa
photographed in India in 1980*

had devastated the country. When not travelling, she remained much in evidence at her Home for the Destitute and Dying in Calcutta where, unless her fellow nuns hid her alarm clock, she would be the first to rise. "I want to be the first to wake and see Jesus," she would say before attending the 6am Mass, sitting indistinguishably from the other nuns on reed-mats.

In November she began a tour of her missions worldwide with a visit to Tanzania. But becoming ill on December 26 in Tijuana, Mexico, during the last leg of her journey, she was taken for treatment to the Scripps Clinic and Research Foundation in La Jolla, across the border in California. In 1993 she was admitted to hospital four times suffering from heart trouble and malaria. She underwent heart surgery but returned to Calcutta.

In 1995 she published her book *A Simple Path*, urging materialistic Westerners to ponder the value of "prayer, meditation and silence". But, increasingly frail, in 1996 she fell and broke her collarbone and was admitted to hospital once again. From then on she was in and out of hospital, finally facing the inevitable when in March 1997 she resigned from running the Missionaries of Charity.

Mother Teresa had her human failings: she was the spokesman for her community so that, until her retirement, one rarely heard the views expressed of any of her nuns; she was adamant in what she believed and dictatorial within her houses, which she visited regularly all over the world.

In 1994 a television profile of her was broadcast on Channel 4 in which the journalist Christopher Hitchens presented her as a publicity-hungry egotist, and he followed it up with a book claiming that she promulgated "a cult based on death, suffering and subjection". But to most of the world she remained the "living saint of Calcutta" and she was loved by people from all countries and all faiths. She had a magnetic aura. Crowds flocked after her and yet held her in awe.

Mother Teresa, Roman Catholic missionary, was born on August 27, 1910. She died on September 5, 1997, aged 87

JOYCE WETHERED

GOLF CHAMPION WITH PERFECT BALANCE, AND A SEEMINGLY EFFORTLESS SWING

NOVEMBER 21, 1997

Joyce Wethered was the most stylish and successful woman golfer of her day, and is still widely regarded as the best the world has seen. Becoming English Ladies' Champion in 1920 when she was not quite 19, she held the title for five consecutive years, playing 33 matches without defeat. She went on to be four times winner of the British Ladies' Open, in 1922, 1924, 1925 and 1929. She also played several important international matches, captaining the British team in three competitions; and she won the mixed foursomes at Worplesdon eight times in fifteen years, with seven different partners. Bobby Jones, the great American golfer, after playing her at St Andrews in 1931, said he doubted whether there had ever been a better player, man or woman.

Joyce Wethered was born at Brook near Godalming in Surrey and educated privately there, being considered too frail for school. It was on childhood holidays that she first experienced golf. At Bude in Cornwall there were games on a windswept headland, and at Dornoch in the Highlands, where the family took a house overlooking the links, there were highly competitive contests with her brother Roger, captain of the Oxford team as an undergraduate and himself prominent in the British game as a gifted amateur for a decade after the First World War.

Apart from a single golf lesson from Tom Lyle, the professional at Bude, Wethered learnt her golf mainly by imitation, talking to her brother and his friends about technique, and watching and studying such great players as Harry Vardon, John H. Taylor and Jones. She had perfect balance, and a seemingly effortless swing, economical yet full of power. She was a perfectionist, and an outstanding stylist, with sound judgment and a full range of accurate, elegant shots.

Her temperament was perhaps her greatest strength. Calm and purposeful in competition, she liked to say that she aimed always to play the course, not her opponent. Her concentration was famous. A railway line runs alongside the course at Sheringham in Norfolk, and the story was often told of how, having brought off a crucial putt as a train rattled past the 17th, she was asked whether she had not been distracted by the noise. "What train?" was her response.

It was at Sheringham that she began her long run of championship form in 1920. Hers was an improbable and unexpected national debut. Still five months short of her 19th birthday, and playing no higher than number 6 in the Surrey county team, she travelled to Norfolk for that year's English Ladies'

Golf Championship only because a Surrey team-mate, Molly Griffith, persuaded her to come along. Despite being on the point of coming down with whooping cough, she played through to reach the final, where she won a remarkable victory over the redoubtable Cecil Leitch, then the dominant figure in women's golf. "It was throughout a match full of dramatic incident," *The Times* observed.

The most dramatic thing about it was that Leitch should have been defeated at all, let alone by a young unknown. She had not been beaten in a ladies' match on level terms since 1913. Wethered's surprise victory marked the start of an exciting and absorbing rivalry, keenly followed by the public. The two women's styles were very different, with the powerful Leitch appearing almost flamboyant by comparison with the graceful younger woman.

Wethered, who was to retain the English Ladies' Golf Championship for the next four years, met Leitch twice in 1921. On both occasions — at Turnberry in the final of the British Ladies' Open Amateur Championship, which Leitch had held since 1914, and in the final of the French Open at Fontainebleau — the older woman had the upper hand. In the British Ladies' of 1922, however, Wethered triumphed once more, impressing spectators at Sandwich (and rattling Leitch) with her inspired strokes and extraordinary coolness under pressure. "A new golfing queen has arisen," one newspaper headline proclaimed.

Wethered won the Ladies' Open again in 1922, 1924 (when she knocked out Leitch in the fifth round), and 1925 (when she beat her in a gripping and hard-fought final). After the last of these wins she retired from competition, but was persuaded back to contest the Ladies' Open once more, on the Old Course at St Andrews in 1929. There she met another formidable opponent, the American champion Glenna Collett, and came back from five down after 11 holes to prevail in a memorable final.

She retired from competition once more, but captained the British women's team in the first Curtis Cup in 1929, against France in 1931, and against America in 1932. In 1933 she took a job as a golf adviser in the sports department of Fortnum and Mason. In 1935 she was paid £4,000 for a tour of America, in which she played more than 50 exhibition matches and advertised equipment. She was not entirely happy with her new-found professional status, however, and was eventually reinstated as an amateur in 1946.

By then she was married to Sir John Heathcoat-Amory, 3rd Bt, a noted Devon sportsman, and proprietor of a long-established family business making lace. An earlier engagement to the Scottish golfer Major Cecil Hutchinson had been broken off. Golf was no longer such an important part of her life after her marriage in 1937, though in 1948 she and her husband reached the final of the Worplesdon mixed foursomes, a competition which

she had done much to promote since
1921 and which she had won eight
times before her marriage, despite
being hampered by the occasional
hopeless partner.

She and her husband lived at
Knightshayes House, near Tiverton,
an elaborate and eccentric Victorian
Gothic edifice, where they built up a
fine collection of pictures and a celebrated garden; Lady Heathcoat-Amory
was awarded the Royal Horticultural
Society's Victoria Medal of Honour.

She continued to live at Knightshayes
after her husband's death in 1972,
when the house passed into the custody
of the National Trust and the best of the
pictures, including works by Lancret,
Poussin and Memling, were donated to
museums. She retained her interest in
golf, having become the first president
of the English Ladies' Golf Association
in 1951. She had no children.

*Joyce Wethered (Lady Heathcoat-
Amory), golfer, was born on
November 17, 1901. She died on
November 18, 1997, aged 96*

MARTHA GELLHORN

FEARLESS AMERICAN WAR
CORRESPONDENT, ADEPT AT
GETTING CLOSE TO
THE ACTION

FEBRUARY 18, 1998

Martha Gellhorn was famous on two
counts. She was a war correspondent
of high calibre, one of the first women
— someone would argue the first — to
enter that area of journalism. And she
was the third wife of Ernest Hemingway,
dedicatee of *For Whom The Bell Tolls*.

She was fiercely proud of her reputation as a reporter. For many years she
always managed to get to where the
action was, often using subterfuge or
downright trickery to reach her destination: Madrid in the Spanish Civil War,
the D-Day landings, Dachau, Vietnam,
El Salvador.

But on the subject of Hemingway she
refused to say a word as she entered old
age. She began by remarking caustically that she had no intention of being
a footnote to someone else's life. But
her silence on the subject gradually
became obsessive.

Gellhorn who, as a journalist, had
conducted interviews by the score
herself began to make the stipulation
that the name of Hemingway was not
to be mentioned in any interview she

permitted. A profile on BBC TV as she approached her 83rd birthday contained no mention of the Hemingway marriage, or any other liaison for that matter. (She was married in all three times, finally in 1954 to T. S. Matthews, whose secretary she had once been on the *New Republic* in Washington.)

Gellhorn saw herself as a champion of the oppressed. Wherever they were in the world she sought them out and reported on what she found in cool, crisp prose, which could be emotive through its almost laconic cadences. She remained true to her left-wing credentials.

She was brought up in St Louis, where her father was a successful gynaecologist and her mother an early suffragette. She went to Bryn Mawr, retaining something of its accent and style, but she left both further education and the family home abruptly, with $50 borrowed from the cook, to seek her fame and fortune. She arrived in Paris, favourite location for American expatriates, in 1929 and did some journalism for American magazines, including *Vogue*. Her first novel, *What Mad Pursuit*, came out in 1933.

The following year was crucial. She left her first husband — the French writer, Bertrand de Jouvenel — deciding that America in the midst of the Depression was more worthy of her attention than Europe. She became an investigator for the Emergency Relief Administration and her reports from poverty-stricken areas, especially in Massachusetts, brought her national attention and an invitation to Franklin Roosevelt's White House.

Those reports provided the source for her first major book, *The Trouble I've Seen*. This was in the style, which Gellhorn was to perfect, of fact only lightly clad in fiction. One particular portrait of a child prostitute called "Ruby" remained in the minds of all who read it. *Trouble* had an introduction by H. G. Wells, who was much taken by the author's blond beauty at a White House encounter, although Martha Gellhorn was to complain that this contribution was forced on her.

Hemingway was similarly struck shortly afterwards when Martha Gellhorn picked him out in a bar called Sloppy Joe's in Key West, where the Gellhorn family was on holiday following the death of Martha's father. There were other meetings in America between the dishevelled literary lion and the svelte young tigress just making a name for herself, before both made their separate ways to the Spanish Civil War. There it was perfectly clear to fellow reporters and supporters of the Republican cause that they were lovers. Martha duly emerged as Maria in *For Whom the Bell Tolls*.

She was already determined not to be that "footnote" to the history of a more famous writer. Her work for *Collier's* magazine had established her as a first-rate war correspondent, adept at getting to the front line and apparently impervious to the dangers once she was there. She went to Czechoslovakia when it was occupied by the Germans in March 1939 and covered the Russo-Finnish War of 1939-40. The Prague visit inspired one of her best books, *A Stricken Field* (1939), in which — under the disguise of "Mary Douglas" — she shows a cool outrage at a people living in fear and fury towards the passivity of those countries which let it happen.

When Hemingway's divorce from his second wife, Pauline, came through in 1940 he married Martha Gellhorn in Wyoming. The marriage was to last five years and was to be stormy. The divorce, when it came, was predictably acrimonious.

When they were together, as they were at Finca Vigia, the house Hemingway bought in Cuba outside Havana, the loud clash of egos could be heard. Gellhorn, as usual, continued to do her own thing, including smuggling herself aboard a hospital ship to cover the D-Day landings in Europe. She was with the Allied forces when Dachau was liberated and her report was one of the first to reveal the dark secret of the Holocaust — and one of the most harrowing.

With the end of the Second World War it looked as though Martha Gellhorn might be short of causes to espouse and battlefronts to describe. Vietnam altered all that and, she remarked bitterly, for the first time she found herself on the wrong side, the American one. She also found difficulty at times in getting where she wanted to be. By now she was too well known to open doors with disingenuous excuses along the lines that she was "just there for the woman's angle". Even the dimmest bureaucrats were not going to fall for that. She railed against paying her American taxes to support a war she believed to be evil.

Other conflicts attracted Gellhorn's attention, notably those in Lebanon and El Salvador. But as she moved through her sixties she became more content to roam quieter and remoter parts of the world and write about what she saw. Fiction, she said, was so much harder than reportage and she wrote less of it. But there was a revival of interest in her early work and especially in *Ruby*, almost certainly her best piece of fiction, when the short novels were reprinted in 1991.

Even in her eighties, before her eyesight started giving her trouble, she betrayed little sign of old age. The considered phrases would still roll out through a curtain of cigarette smoke — initially at her home in Wales and latterly at her flat in Eaton Square. The old poise was still there and so were the old dislikes: "I am profoundly unliterary. Literary stuff? I hate it."

Not that this stopped her being inordinately proud of the fact that some of her last writing appeared in *Granta* — though she also rallied to the defence of Bill and Hillary Clinton in the columns of the *New Republic* during their first term in the White House. The only thing that no one seems to have dared to ask her is why she had settled for living the last part of her life in Britain, which she had once described as "that accursed island".

Martha Gellhorn's three husbands predeceased her. She and her third husband, T. S. Matthews, adopted a son.

Martha Gellhorn, war correspondent and novelist, was born on November 8, 1908. She died on February 15, 1998, aged 89

DAME IRIS MURDOCH

WRITER AND PHILOSOPHER
WHO USED FICTION TO
CHART THE PROGRESS OF
A METAPHYSICAL BATTLE
BETWEEN EVIL AND GOOD

FEBRUARY 9, 1999

"It had been his fate not to be interested in anything except everything," Iris Murdoch once wrote of one of her characters. In many ways this was her own fate, too. As a lecturer in philosophy and Fellow of St Anne's College, Oxford, she shied away from the narrower analytical studies which interested such contemporaries as A. J. Ayer, and turned her attention instead to the expansive, though unfashionable, discipline of metaphysics.

Lecturing and publishing in the field of moral philosophy, she engaged with the Post-Modernist Jacques Derrida and his flanking armies of deconstructionists, arguing that fact could not be separated from value. She sought to place moral inquiry back at the heart of philosophy, embarking with Casaubon-like fervour on her extensive study *Metaphysics as a Guide to Morals* (1992) which was greeted by some critics as a ramshackle collection of essays and by others as a grand philosophical synthesis.

As a novelist, Iris Murdoch was similarly broad in her outlook, taking the "dramas of the human heart" as her subject. Fiction, she said, was a "hall of reflection" which can encompass every form of tragedy and comedy. She used it to chart the progress of a metaphysical battle between evil and good, usually played out within the confines of a leisured upper-middle-class society.

Distrusting the constricted focus of much modern fiction, she created large casts of characters so that her novels, at their worst, spun like an emotional merry-go-round, while at their best they were persuasive and amusing commentaries on the contemporary world and the intricacies of human relationships.

She was energetically prolific, and her output seemed as much a show of stamina as of inspiration. Novels such as her 1978 Booker prizewinner *The Sea, the Sea*, or *Nuns and Soldiers* (1981), or *The Philosopher's Pupil* (1983), expanded to more than 500 pages, as she painstakingly knitted their protracted and typically mysterious plots, slowly chewing over unfashionably long descriptions and quasi-philosophical themes. Yet, although some critics suggested that adroit editorial excision would have increased the impact of her work, there were others who acclaimed her as the most accomplished novelist in postwar Britain.

Murdoch's personal beliefs were as expansive and accommodating as her fiction. She did not believe in a personal God, she said, which is why she found Buddhism especially appealing.

Iris Murdoch: "a persuasive commentator on the contemporary world"

But the religious dimension was essential to her and she bewailed the lack of faith in the modern world.

A woman of immense practical kindness, she was soft-voiced and courteous, with a warm, open manner and a large capacity for sympathetic listening, which in many ways she preferred to talking. She seemed rarely to be bored by anything, taking advantage of every encounter to find out as much as possible. "There is never a moment," one of her friends once said, "when she would think it inappropriate to ask: 'Do you believe in God?'"

Murdoch was a familiar figure on the literary scene, youthfully pink-cheeked and with a softly enigmatic smile, dressed in her donnish clothes: woolly jerseys and tweedy A-line skirts. Although there was a natural authority and decisiveness to her conversation,

her language was oddly peppered with old-fashioned schoolgirl jargon: "Hello, old thing" and "cheerio".

Jean Iris Murdoch was very much a product of her benign and cultivated background. She was born in Dublin after the end of the First World War, during which her father had served as a cavalry officer. But he was a bookish, intellectual man who, on demobilisation, joined the Civil Service. Her mother was also a cultured woman, who had trained as an opera singer before her early marriage. Iris was the only child, brought up as part of what she famously described as a "perfect trinity of love".

From the age of nine she was brought up in suburban London, but she always felt herself to be at least partly Irish, and throughout her childhood the family would spend their summer holidays there. She was educated at the Froebel Educational Institute in London, and, from the age of 13, at a vaguely progressive school, Badminton, where she was a contemporary of Indira Gandhi.

Iris Murdoch began writing at an early age, partly, she believed, as compensation for having no siblings to play with. "I'm the only child in search of the imaginary brother or sister. That is probably why I like to invent characters," she once said. Her first published work appeared in a school magazine in 1933. A comic poem about a girl with "bluebottle eyes and a sense of vocation" whose chief interest is fishing for stars in the Milky Way, it shows the vein of humour mixed with the philosophical solemnity which was to characterise her work.

In 1938 Murdoch won the Harriet Needham Exhibition to Somerville College, Oxford, where she read Mods and Greats. There she found herself mixing with such stimulating figures as Raymond Williams, Philip Larkin, Edward Heath, Denis Healey and Roy Jenkins. Politically she was, at that time, on the far Left, and when Roy Jenkins wrote her a modest letter on some matter of party business, she penned him an impassioned reply, addressing him as "Comrade Jenkins". Her political preferences thereafter followed a well-trodden path. She moved to Gaitskellism in the 1950s, through the muddled attitudes of the Sixties, to moderate Conservatism in the 1970s and then to Thatcherism in the 1980s.

Graduating with a first in Greats, she left Oxford to work during the war years in the Treasury under the formidable Evelyn Sharp. From there she was seconded to the United Nations Relief and Rehabilitation Administration and was sent first to Belgium and then to Austria, where, in her job in a camp for displaced people, she proved most adaptable, whether operating the switchboard or negotiating narrow roads behind the wheel of a heavy lorry.

In all this time she scarcely read a book, exhausted by the strenuous work. But passing through Brussels on the way out she had got what she described as a heady whiff of philosophy. She had met Sartre and, although previously she had considered archaeology or art history as her calling, she became fascinated by Existentialism. In Brussels she came across a bookshop owner who had pressed L'Être et le néant into her hands. "It was wonderful," Murdoch said. "People were liberated by that book after the war, it made people happy, it was like the Gospel. Having been chained up for years, you were suddenly free and could be yourself."

On her return to England she decided that she wanted to return to academic life and applied for and won a scholarship to pursue her studies in the United States. But as a former member of the Communist Party — which she had briefly joined under the influence of a boyfriend, Frank Thompson, who was later killed in Bulgaria — she was refused a visa. The next year, 1947, she was awarded the Sarah Smithson Studentship in philosophy at Newnham

College, Cambridge, and she studied there for a year before returning to Oxford as a tutor in philosophy and fellow of St Anne's. She was to hold this post for the next 15 years.

Her first book, *Sartre: Romantic Rationalist* (1953), reflected her youthful passion for Existentialism, though intellectually she was always to remain at a distance from Sartre, and he was later to become the subject of some of her most acute criticism. She found his view of lonely, self-determining man quite inaccurate, and her collection of essays *The Sovereignty of Good* (1970) showed a widening of her work into a general attack on analytic philosophy. Plato, however — about whom she wrote in *The Fire and the Sun* (1977) — was to remain her abiding interest, as she probed for a wider metaphysical system from which to answer the questions of philosophy.

However, as she was the first to admit — and her detractors were quick to point out — she was not a philosopher of true originality. "Unless one is a genius, philosophy is a mug's game," one of her fictional characters says. Only a genius, Murdoch maintained, could ever make a real contribution to the subject. At the age of 35 she turned her hand to writing novels.

In her first novel, *Under the Net* (1954) — which was actually her fourth, since she discarded two and another did not find a publisher — she harked back to Existential themes as she traced the journey of a posse of rootless individuals traipsing round London in search of their identities.

But unlike Sartre's, her novels were not simply the lumbering vehicles for philosophical ideas. "I might put in things about philosophy because I happen to know about philosophy," she said. "If I knew about sailing ships I would put in sailing ships."

Once she had begun to write, Murdoch scarcely seemed to pause, producing a new novel every year or so, with perhaps a break of half-an-hour between ending one and beginning the next. She began each with a period of "hard reflection" at the end of which every chapter would have been delineated and the characters moulded and given their names — usually improbable ones. At the end of the process, hefty shopping bags of manuscript would be presented to her publishers, Chatto & Windus, where the boast was that never a word was changed. She professed herself impervious to reviews. "A bad review," she used to say, "is even less important than whether it is raining in Patagonia."

Those who reproached her with publishing too much were perhaps missing the point: her project was one of imperfection, or imperfectibility even, as if the perfect — like the good, about which she meditated so deeply — was fundamentally beyond human achievement. If for her every novel was a fresh attempt to attain her ideal, she found each time that her ideal had moved on. She was always alert to the dangers of complacency. "I'm in the second league," she said, "not among the gods like Jane Austen and Henry James and Tolstoy."

Critics mostly felt that she was at the height of her powers in the 1960s and early 1970s, with works such as *A Severed Head* (1961), *The Italian Girl* (1964), *A Fairly Honourable Defeat* (1970), *The Black Prince* (1973) and *The Sacred and Profane Love Machine* (1974). Several of these were made into plays and films. *The Severed Head*, for instance, ran for nearly three years at the Criterion Theatre, and was made into a film starring Richard Attenborough. In 1978 she also published a collection of poems, *A Year of Birds*.

She received many honours in her life. She was appointed CBE in 1976 and advanced to DBE in 1987. She was six times shortlisted for the Booker Prize, and won it in 1978 with *The Sea, the Sea*.

In 1956 Iris Murdoch married John Bayley, later Warton Professor of English Literature and a fellow of St Catherine's College, Oxford. He looked out of his college window one day, he said, and seeing her cycling by knew at once that he would marry her. Together they lived a life of cosy intellectual companionship, haphazard domestic arrangements and bizarre culinary creations. It was reported by friends who had them to stay early in their married life that when taking up a pot of tea in the morning, they found Iris sitting bolt up in bed with her nose in Wittgenstein, while her husband lounged at her side perusing *Woman's Own*. They were to remain constant companions throughout their long marriage, and together were familiar figures in the literary world, both dressed from their favourite "good as new" shop. John Bayley cared for her with devotion and tenderness throughout her final years when Alzheimer's disease took an increasingly tenacious grip upon her once fine mind. He charted the cruel progress of the illness in his poignant and unflinchingly honest memoir *Iris*, published last year.

He survives her. There were no children.

Dame Iris Murdoch, DBE, novelist and philosopher, was born on July 15, 1919. She died on February 8, 1999, aged 79

—◈—

DUSTY SPRINGFIELD

POP SINGER BLESSED WITH
A HUSKY EROTIC VOICE
WHO BECAME A GAY
AND LESBIAN ICON

MARCH 4, 1999

Dusty Springfield was acknowledged on both sides of the Atlantic as the finest female soul singer Britain has produced. Her croakily erotic voice — which belied the shy, vulnerable convent girl who produced it — created a string of hit records during the Sixties' beat boom. After three successful years teamed with her songwriter brother Tom as two-thirds of the folk-music based group, the Springfields, she made her 1963 solo debut with "I Only Want to Be With You", sung with jaunty fervour. It was an immediate hit, remaining in the charts for 18 weeks, and it has endured as a pop classic.

More hits followed throughout the Sixties, including "Stay Awhile", "I Just Don't Know What to Do with Myself", "Losing You", "In the Middle of Nowhere", and the poignant "You Don't Have to Say You Love Me", which in March 1966 took her to No 1. The following year she was back in the Top Ten, at No 4 with "I Close My Eyes and Count to Ten".

Dusty Springfield took her enjoyment of her fame right down to the wire in those heady years. As part of the swinging London club scene, she found she had become a model for teenage girls, who slavishly copied her startling beehive blonde hairstyle and dark "panda" eye makeup.

On concert tours she played to packed houses, and adoring fans writhed and screamed when the myopic star appeared hesitantly from backstage to belt out her first number. The Sixties were her apogee. She consistently won the top female singer award, outshining such contemporaries as Lulu, Cilla Black and Sandie Shaw.

But the golden years did not last. Her career, spanning more than four decades, was a turbulent one even by the standards of the pop world. Persistent tabloid interest in her sexual proclivities — largely engendered by her confessing that she was as much attracted to women as to men — drove her to live in Los Angeles for much of the Seventies. There, although she became something of an icon for gays and lesbians, her talent was largely neglected. "I became bored with being a pop singer," she confessed. A rare success was "Son of a Preacher Man", taken as a single from an otherwise stonily received LP, *Dusty in Memphis*.

Despondent, and fighting what was to be a lifelong weight problem, she followed a downward spiral of drug and alcohol abuse. Known for her impulsive candour during interviews, she once said: "I lost nearly all the Seventies in a haze of booze and pills. I couldn't have one or two drinks. I had to get loaded. Vodka and the pills helped ease my shyness. Then I got into cocaine and in seven months I was a brain-scrambled wreck."

But she went on to overcome her addictions and then revived her career, courtesy of the Pet Shop Boys, and enjoyed an inspired period in the late Eighties and Nineties. The group began by inviting her to sing on what was to become their worldwide triumph, "What Have I Done to Deserve This?", and went on to write much of her album *Reputation*.

In 1994, however, she discovered that she had breast cancer. She was forced to cancel her singing dates and undergo surgery and months of chemo and radiotherapy at the Royal Marsden Hospital, London. After the initial shock, her attitude was typically wry: "Why me? Why not?" she said, and added: "I never expected to live this long anyway, so it's uncharted territory."

Dusty Springfield was born Mary Isabel Catherine Bernadette O'Brien in Hampstead, of Irish parents. Her father was a tax consultant and her mother, as the singer once described her, was "a free spirit who married to escape spinsterhood; they both bitterly regretted it." Staunch Catholics, they stayed together for the children but quarrelled endlessly. Dusty recalled a troubled childhood. "I was so unhappy as a kid." She would challenge her hot-tempered father when he hit her, and she became "very jealous of my brother Dion. He was older and the blue-eyed boy."

She grew up at first in Buckinghamshire and then in Ealing, where she went to a convent school. On leaving she took a part-time job in Bentalls department store, meanwhile joining a syrupy all-female vocal trio, the Lana Sisters, which sang mostly at air bases. In 1960 she and Dion, who was already writing songs, adopted the stage names Dusty and Tom Springfield, and launched themselves as the Springfields, a folk-singing duo. Dusty supplied the guitar accompaniment.

Success was elusive to begin with, but when they were joined by Tim Feild they quickly became one of the country's top vocal groups. They had two Top Five singles with "Island of Dreams" (1962) and "Say I Won't be There" (1963), by which time Feild had been replaced by Mike Hurst. The Springfields had a million-seller in America with the country standard "Silver Threads and Golden Needles" (although it did nothing in Britain) before splitting up in 1963.

Inspired by the ear-thumping "wall of sound" style pioneered by the American producer Phil Spector, Dusty Springfield recorded her first solo hit, "I Only Want to Be With You", which got to No 4. It was the first record ever played on a new television programme called *Top of the Pops*.

By 1967 she was in full flow, with a string of hits including "Middle of Nowhere", "Some of Your Lovin'", and "Look of Love", which featured in the James Bond film *Casino Royale*. She was also a regular on the TV pop music show *Ready, Steady, Go*. At the time she used her celebrity to campaign on behalf of the then little-known American soul and Motown artists. Her eclectic taste in music tended to set her apart from most of her peers in this country. She became popular in America, where she made numerous appearances.

In all she had 16 hits almost successively during the 1960s before her career began to falter. She exiled herself to California for 15 years, living in a two-bedroom house with up to a dozen cats for company. She made sporadic visits to Britain, each time attempting a come-back. But renewed success eluded her until 1987, at the start of her collaboration with the Pet Shop Boys (the singer Neil Tennant and keyboard player Chris Lowe). Not only did she have a share in the duo's No 2 hit "What Have I Done to Deserve This?", but she featured on the soundtrack of the film *Scandal*, about the Profumo affair, singing their theme tune "Nothing Has Been Proved".

She was still bedevilled by her past, however. In 1991 she sued and won undisclosed damages in the High Court as the result of a sketch on a television show in which the comedian portrayed her performing while drunk.

After extensive chemotherapy she was in 1995 pronounced to be clear of cancer. But the disease returned in the following year.

She was appointed OBE in the last New Year's Honours.

Dusty Springfield, OBE, pop and soul singer, was born on April 16, 1939. She died of cancer on March 2, 1999, aged 59

——✺——

BARONESS RYDER OF WARSAW

FORMER SOE WORKER WHOSE EXPERIENCES IN POSTWAR EUROPE LED HER TO FOUND AN INTERNATIONAL CHARITY FOR THE SICK AND DISABLED

NOVEMBER 3, 2000

It was the Second World War that confirmed Sue Ryder's desire to help relieve suffering, the task which shaped her life and gave rise to the international charity named after her. The Sue Ryder Foundation for the sick and disabled of all age groups grew from the misery she witnessed in postwar Europe, particularly in Poland, where its work came to be focused. It grew to run more than 80 homes worldwide and 500 charity shops.

From 1959 she worked in harness with her famous husband, the former bomber pilot Leonard Cheshire, who had founded the Cheshire Homes for the Disabled. Together they made a formidable team, tireless in works of mercy.

During her Yorkshire childhood she had cared for people who lived in slums, but the war, which brought her childhood to an end, showed her more extreme cases of human suffering, and shaped her resolve to relieve suffering wherever she found it. Sue Ryder grew up in a pleasant home near Leeds, but she was within walking distance of terrible slums. Her mother and her friends worked hard to raise funds to buy more taps, lavatories and even communal baths for the slums. From a young age, Sue Ryder helped her mother. The family gave up their second house in Yorkshire because of the Depression, and lived permanently at Great Thurlow in Suffolk.

When the war broke out she was a 16-year-old schoolgirl at Benenden. She joined the First Aid Nursing Yeomanry (FANY), and was posted to the Special Operations Executive, the unit responsible for coordinating resistance to the Third Reich in countries occupied by Nazi Germany. She joined the Polish section of the SOE, and later said that the optimism and sense of sacrifice which the Polish agents, or "Bods", as they were known, made an indelible impression on her. She began to think of ways in which their faith, courage and humour might be perpetuated. In 1942 she volunteered to do relief work in Poland and elsewhere, when she could be released from SOE duties.

After the end of the war she went to France, where she worked in a relief unit. She was told to collect a lorry in London and load it with stoves and drugs for the relief of tuberculosis and typhus. The lorry broke down in the Vauxhall Bridge Road, but she got it into the gutter with the help of passers-by. She then cleaned the carburettor and the petrol pump, replaced the sparking plugs and was off. She later drove a mobile clinic with the women of the Croix Rouge; nine of them slept and ate in a stable.

In Germany she drew attention to the fate of former prisoners-of-war who had been held in German prisons, sometimes for stealing food in places where there were severe food shortages. She found work for many former prisoners, tried to make contact with their families, and continued to work for them for the next thirty years. In 1980 there were just a handful remaining, out of the original thousands. She also brought many survivors of the concentration camps to a holiday home in England. It was for her work with prisoners in Germany that she was appointed OBE in 1957 at the age of 34.

She wanted to found a living memorial to those who had died in the two world wars in defence of humane values. The work in hospitals and prisons grew so quickly that by the time she returned to England in the winter of 1951-52 she had decided to form a small committee and register the living memorial with the Church Commissioners.

In 1953 the Sue Ryder Foundation was established with the help of a small legacy, credit from the bank and plenty of optimism. She bought her mother's house in Suffolk to serve as the foundation's headquarters and the first Sue Ryder Home. It was to look after physically disabled individuals, and cared for many people who would otherwise have occupied hospital beds. A friend provided quantities of secondhand furniture, and nurses, carpenters and secretaries flocked to help.

Sue Ryder might have missed meeting the war hero and commander of the famous 617 Squadron, Group Captain Leonard Cheshire, out of diffidence. He had been awarded the VC during the war for his service in Bomber Command, and had later found a different kind of fame by establishing the Cheshire Homes for the physically handicapped. When she arrived one day at his home for the disabled at Ampthill, she came to the wrong gate. It was locked, and in a moment of uncharacteristic shyness she was tempted to go home. But she persevered, they met, and they were married four years later, in 1959.

It was to be a marriage of true minds and common purposes. They made it clear to their fellow workers that their intention as a team was to strengthen their work for those who depended on them. The birth of a son and a daughter were hardly allowed to interrupt their work. The two foundations remained largely separate, although they did found a joint centre at Dehra Dun, in India. They named it after Raphael, the archangel of healing, and among others it cared for lepers, many of whom were taught to use their hands and learnt a trade.

In her autobiography Ryder wrote, "I feel I belong to Poland", and the country eventually had 28 Sue Ryder Homes. Most of the material came from Britain, but the Polish authorities ran the homes, and provided the staff. For many years she drove thousands of miles to Poland in lorries named after such prophets as Daniel and Ezekiel. Poland lacked the most basic medical provisions, and they were filled with everything from condensed milk to pillows. On one occasion a few orthopaedic pillows aroused the suspicions of an East German border guard; on another, the guards wasted so much time that an impatient colleague of Ryder's blessed them with water from the shrine at Lourdes. The guardsmen were amazed, but the team was allowed to proceed without further ado.

She also established 22 homes in Yugoslavia, where one helper said that the conditions reminded her of descriptions of the Crimean War. Some of the homes were destroyed in the Bosnian War.

By the 1980s the six Sue Ryder Homes for continuing care were nursing almost 900 people in Britain. Fundraising was always a priority: methods included a wellington-boot throwing competition and the "fastest bedmaker in town" competition. One Sue Ryder Home was at Leckhampton Court, near Cheltenham. The medieval house had been abandoned for nearly ten years when she found it; she converted its ruins into a working home within 18 months. There was a desperate need for after-care facilities to work in conjunction with the radiotherapy centre at Cheltenham General Hospital, and the home relieved the pressure on beds at the hospital, reducing the waiting list.

Sue Ryder expected her colleagues to show as much dedication as she could display herself. Since she had a formidable appetite for work, and typically got up shortly before 4.30am, she was a difficult woman to work with; but it may be that a congenial woman would not have achieved so much. She also found it difficult to delegate, wanting to stay in control, but her personal concern for everyone in her care was genuine and a strength. She was a devout Roman Catholic.

Sue Ryder was appointed CMG in 1976, and created a life peer as Baroness Ryder of Warsaw in 1979. Poland was so important to her that she insisted, unconventionally, on associating the peerage with Warsaw (usually only service chiefs were allowed to associate a peerage with a foreign place). She also received a host of Polish and Yugoslavian honours. Her autobiography was published in two volumes, *And the Morrow is Theirs* (1975) and *Child of My Love* (1986).

In recent months Ryder had become estranged from the organisation, which changed its name to Sue Ryder Care. Before entering hospital in September she had founded a new organisation, the Bouverie Foundation, to continue charitable work, particularly that overseas.

Leonard Cheshire, who had by then been made a life peer, died in 1992; she is survived by her son and daughter.

Baroness Ryder of Warsaw, CMG, OBE, founder of Sue Ryder Homes, was born on July 3, 1923. She died on November 2, 2000, aged 77

Editor's note: The Sue Ryder organisation, and other authorities, give Baroness Ryder's year of birth as 1924.

—⁓—

ELIZABETH ANSCOMBE

BOLD AND ORIGINAL
THINKER WHOSE IMPACT
ON THE INTERNATIONAL
PHILOSOPHICAL COMMUNITY
WAS DEEP AND ENDURING

JANUARY 8, 2001

Elizabeth Anscombe was a giant in the world of 20th-century Anglo-American philosophy. An internationally known author and speaker, she worked on the history of philosophy, logic, philosophy of mind and human action, philosophy of causation, philosophy of religion, political philosophy, and moral philosophy. She retired as an active teacher some years ago, but her impact on the philosophical community endures to this day. As a contributor to a Festschrift in her honour once put it: "Philosophy as she does it is fresh; her arguments take unexpected turns and make unexpected connections, and show always how much there is that had not been seen before."

Gertrude Elizabeth Margaret Anscombe was born in 1919, the youngest child of Alan Wells Anscombe, a schoolmaster at Dulwich College, and his wife, Gertrude Elizabeth. She had two older twin brothers. Educated at Sydenham School and St Hugh's College, Oxford (of which she later became an honorary Fellow), she was a research student at Newnham College, Cambridge, and a Research Fellow, and then Fellow, at Somerville College, Oxford (in which her portrait now hangs). She became a Fellow of the British Academy in 1967 and was a foreign honorary member of the American Academy of Arts and Sciences.

In 1970 Anscombe was appointed to the chair of philosophy at Cambridge University. Ludwig Wittgenstein (arguably the greatest philosopher of the 20th century) had held the same position before her, and her name will always be associated with his. Her teacher and friend, he nominated Anscombe as one of his literary executors (together with Rush Rhees and G. H. von Wright).

Following his death in 1951, she spent years working to get his prodigious literary remains into print. Many of them were written in German and Anscombe translated some of them herself. English-speaking readers are particularly indebted to her for her thoughtful translation of the *Philosophical Investigations*, probably Wittgenstein's best-known and most influential work. She always reflected with thanks on the fact that Wittgenstein had been one of her teachers. His readers should reflect with thanks that she was one of his students.

Anscombe travelled widely and lectured in many countries including the US, Canada, Poland, Finland, Austria, Germany, Sweden, Spain and Australia. In 1941 she married Peter Geach, who also achieved considerable philosophical renown. They had seven children together, but she did not like to be called "Mrs Geach" and, in academic circles, she continued to be known as "Miss Anscombe". It has been said that someone looking for Mrs Geach at the door of their Cambridge residence was told that there was no such person there. Whatever the truth of that story, there is no doubt that Elizabeth Anscombe and Peter Geach were a devoted couple. And their intellectual interests were more than purely philosophical; they both shared a deep commitment to the teachings of the Roman Catholic Church.

Anscombe became a convert to the Church in 1940 and her Catholic loyalty is evident in much that she wrote. But she had problems making the leap into Catholicism. For instruction on Catholic doctrine she went to Father Richard Kehoe of Blackfriars, Oxford.

She was worried about the teaching of the 16th-century Jesuit Luis de Molina, according to whom, in Anscombe's words, "God knew what anybody would have done if, eg, he hadn't died when he did". She found that she could not believe this doctrine. As she subsequently wrote: "It appeared to me that there was not, quite generally, any such thing as what would have happened if what did happen had not happened, and that in particular there was no such thing, generally speaking, as what someone would have done if... and certainly there was no such thing as how someone would have spent his life if he had not died as a child." Father Kehoe was amused by her reaction and rightly thought it compatible with Catholicism. So Anscombe made the leap.

Apart from her work as Wittgenstein's literary executor, Anscombe will probably be best remembered among philosophers for her 1957 book *Intention* (widely regarded as a classic in its field); for her 1959 work *An Introduction to Wittgenstein's Tractatus* (a magisterial exposition and discussion) and for the contents of her three-volume *Collected Philosophical Papers* (1981), much of which has had a considerable impact in academic circles.

Particularly worth mentioning is her paper *Modern Moral Philosophy* (1958), which played a significant role in the contemporary revival of interest in the Aristotelian notion of human virtues. In it Anscombe argued that "it is not profitable at present to do moral philosophy", that "the concepts of obligation and duty — moral obligation and moral duty, that is to say — and of what is morally right and wrong, and of the moral sense of 'ought', ought to be jettisoned... because they are survivals, or derivatives of survivals, from an earlier conception of ethics which no longer generally survives". The words might seem to represent an attack on ethical thinking. Their effect was to make "virtue ethics", as it is now often called, one of the central areas of current philosophical inquiry.

Anscombe also published a number of more popular texts which were straightforwardly written from the position of a firm doctrinal commitment. An example is her Catholic Truth Society pamphlet *Contraception and Chastity* (1975), in which she strongly condemns contraception and argues that we shall be committing ourselves to more than we might want to if we think of it as a viable moral option. As she put it later: "You might as well accept any sexual goings-on, if you accept contraceptive intercourse."

Such a verdict is not common among philosophers, but Anscombe was a courageous woman who had no qualms about defying popular opinion when it came to a cause in which she believed. She was an outspoken Catholic, working among people who largely had little time for religion.

She was no pacifist, but in 1939 she publicly argued that it was morally wrong for Britain to go to war since the war was not just. In 1956 she strenuously opposed the conferment of an honorary degree by Oxford University on America's former President Harry S. Truman because of the bombing of Hiroshima and Nagasaki. "Choosing to kill the innocent as a means to your ends is always murder," as she later wrote when reflecting on the episode.

She gave a talk for the BBC (published in *The Listener* in 1957) in which she ingeniously and ironically argued that the moral philosophy then prevalent in Britain was a corrupting influence on the young. And she was unafraid to adopt unconventional positions even with respect to technical debates within philosophy. In a much discussed paper, *The First Person*, she argued that "I" is not a word that refers to anything. In a number of other papers she challenged a huge amount of what many philosophers think they know about causality and freedom of the will. In 1985 she presented an ingenious defence of St Anselm's so-called "Ontological Argument" for God's existence (commonly regarded as a philosophical dead duck).

She was a bold, inventive, and original thinker. She was also a loyal and helpful friend who, though an unusually busy person, took time to correspond with students. It is hard for any generation to know which of its members will be read and admired in years to come. But Anscombe's work made an important and permanent contribution to philosophy.

Her writings demand patience and effort from their readers since they are often intricate and subtle. But they are always hugely stimulating. For Anscombe had what all great philosophers share: the ability to be struck by simple yet teasing questions, and the capacity to pursue them.

She is survived by her husband Peter and by their three sons and four daughters.

Elizabeth Anscombe, Professor of Philosophy, Cambridge University, 1970-86, was born on March 18, 1919. She died on January 5, 2001, aged 81

——∿∿——

DAME NINETTE DE VALOIS

BENEVOLENT AUTOCRAT
WHO GAVE UP HER
CAREER AS A DANCER AND
CHOREOGRAPHER TO CREATE
A NATIONAL INSTITUTION AS
FOUNDER-DIRECTOR OF THE
ROYAL BALLET

MARCH 9, 2001

Ninette de Valois was the founder and chief architect of the Royal Ballet, which under her iron control grew quickly from its tiny origins in 1931 to become world-famous as one of the handful of really great international dance companies. Its move to the Royal Opera House, Covent Garden, in 1946, was the beginning of that theatre's career as the home of important national companies, and was accompanied by the formation of a second troupe which

in turn has grown into the Birmingham Royal Ballet, England's first large-scale regionally based dance company.

De Valois also created, as a necessary forerunner and now a vital adjunct of the companies, one of the world's leading ballet schools, which has long attracted pupils from every continent.

She laid down the lines of development for this great organisation and herself ran it for more than three decades. Then, with uncommon generosity, she stood down from responsibility early enough for others to learn how to run it after her. With hindsight one might wish she had continued longer in office. She did remain as director of the Royal Ballet School until 1971 and thereafter maintained her links as a life governor.

Even in official retirement she remained intimately involved with the activities of the companies and the school as their most valued adviser, particularly interested in the development of young choreographers. In spite of increasing frailty as the years went by, she kept her wits about her. A benevolent autocrat, she was loved as well as respected, as was shown by the warm response to her 100th birthday in June 1998.

More than once de Valois reproved audiences who wanted to applaud her achievements by remarking that "It takes more than one person to make a ballet company". Of course, a great deal of the success of the Royal Ballet depended on her ability to find and encourage able collaborators. Frederick Ashton as principal choreographer and Constant Lambert as the company's first music director were the most invaluable, but the work of hundreds of choreographers, dancers, musicians, designers, administrators and others was needed. Without the vision, determination and clear-headedness of Ninette de Valois, however, the work of all these would not have flowered in the way it did.

A few disgruntled dancers and others complained that their personal hopes had been sacrificed to her vision of the company's long-term development. But de Valois sacrificed her own potential career as dancer and choreographer far more than anyone else's. Happily, the outcome was an achievement more glorious than she could otherwise have hoped for.

She was never afraid to take advantage of an unexpected opportunity, such as the availability of Rudolf Nureyev to join the Royal Ballet in 1962, and she welcomed him in spite of the opposition of some long-standing colleagues who feared his different background and approach would prove incompatible. Time proved her right, not only through the incomparable partnership he formed with Margot Fonteyn (the greatest star attraction the company ever possessed) but also through his enrichment of the Royal Ballet's classical repertoire and his dramatic effect on the ambitions and qualities of the male dancers. She maintained her admiration and affection for Nureyev to the end, and was much saddened by his early death, as also that of another of her discoveries and special protégés, Kenneth MacMillan.

Yet the tactic of seizing the lucky moment, exemplified by her taking up of Nureyev, and earlier of linking Leonide Massine with her company, was combined with ability to fit such benefits into a carefully planned long-term strategy. As early as 1937 her first book, *Invitation to the Ballet*, revealed immense, deep and detailed thought about the nature of ballet and of theatre, and what was needed to put her ambitions for her company into practice.

Born in the last years of the 19th century at Baltiboys, the family home in Co Wicklow, the second of four children, she was christened Edris, the family name being Stannus. Her father died in the First World War as Lieutenant-Colonel Stannus, DSO; it is possible to think that any inheritance of a military aptitude for discipline and for planning campaigns was as important to her career as the artistic side contributed by her mother, who both collected and made glassware (and also chose her daughter's stage name on the basis of a distant family link with the French royal house).

Her first dancing lessons (after the family had moved when she was seven to Walmer, on the English coast, and then, when she was 11, to London) were in what she described later as "fancy dancing", but as a child she was taken to see Genée, Pavlova and the Diaghilev Ballet, and from about 12 or 13 she began to study for a theatrical career.

At 14 she danced The Dying Swan in a touring pupil show called *The Wonder Children* organised by her then teacher. They appeared, she later said, "on every pier in England". At 16 she was principal dancer in the Lyceum pantomime. Subsequent engagements included being principal dancer in the Covent Garden Opera session of 1919, appearing in musical comedies and revue, and taking her own small group of dancers on the touring circuit.

She was, according to contemporary accounts and photographs, a most accomplished dancer, at her best in roles calling for lively characterisation, and able to bring the house down by her speed and brilliance in classical solos. As important as her performances during this early period was the fact that she methodically developed her knowledge of dance by studying with the leading teachers in three different traditions: Espinosa for the French school, Cecchetti for the Italian and Legat for the Russian. Her analytical mind tried to draw the best from each of these for herself and her eventual pupils.

Her first connection with the Russian Ballet came in 1921 as a dancer in the Massine-Lopokova company. Two years later she was invited to join Diaghilev's company without even an audition, apparently on the recommendation of another British dancer, Lydia Sokolova (Hilda Munnings), and of her teacher Cecchetti. During two years with Diaghilev, de Valois proved a useful soloist: valuable enough for Diaghilev to invite her more than once to return as guest to dance the hostess in *Les Biches* or a solo in *Aurora's Wedding*. She said, however, that it was the experience of working as a member of the ensemble in many ballets which she enjoyed most and from which she gained invaluable knowledge. When she left, it was with the determination to try to start in England a tradition of ballet as firmly grounded as the Russian.

Others had the same idea, but de Valois' methods were more shrewd and more tenaciously pursued than most. The first steps towards her aim must have seemed tiny ones. She still danced occasionally to support herself, and she opened a ballet school in South Kensington called, rather grandly, the Academy of Choreographic Art. With her pupils she presented occasional ballets (including one, *Rout*, to music by Arthur Bliss, which achieved quite a reputation). She also took every opportunity of working with the increasingly important repertory theatre movement, being convinced that the future of ballet lay in becoming a part of this. She arranged dances and ballets for the Festival Theatre, Cambridge; the Abbey Theatre, Dublin, where Yeats regarded her as the ideal exponent of his "plays for dancers"; and at the Old Vic.

It was the support of Lilian Baylis at the Vic which led eventually to the beginnings of a permanent company, although before being accepted there de Valois had also applied in vain to Barry Jackson's Birmingham Rep. However, the meeting of Baylis with the smart, well-mannered, highly intelligent and extremely well-organised ballet teacher was an immediate success. Their collaboration started with little ballets given as curtain-raisers before the operas: *Les Petits Riens*, arranged by de Valois to Mozart's music, was the first, given at Christmas 1928. Just over two years later, with the opening of Sadler's Wells Theatre, de Valois closed her own school, moved with her pupils to the Wells, and officially formed the Vic-Wells Ballet, which gave its first full evening of ballet at the Old Vic on May 5, 1931.

The existence of other organisations also aiming to establish a British ballet helped rather than impeded the enterprise. *Job*, the young company's most ambitious production, was the fruit of collaboration with the Camargo Society, and the rival companies of de Valois and Marie Rambert shared many dancers.

The presence of Alicia Markova as ballerina and the guest appearances of Anton Dolin, Stanislas Idzikovsky, Lydia Lopokova and others made it possible for de Valois to mount the 19th-century classic ballets (*Coppélia*, *Giselle*, *Swan Lake*) which she regarded as the cornerstones of the repertoire. At the same time she set out to develop new stars within the company, and by the time she produced *The Sleeping Beauty* in 1939 she was able to present Margot Fonteyn, Robert Helpmann and other home-bred dancers in the leading roles.

It was also during the 1930s that de Valois produced the most important of her own choreographies: *La Création du Monde* to Milhaud's score and *Job* to Vaughan Williams's music

were major works, both in 1931. *The Haunted Ballroom*, to a romantic score by Geoffrey Toye, proved a highly popular melodrama in 1934, and *The Rake's Progress* (music by Gavin Gordon) was even more successful as vivid dance theatre.

That, with *Job* and *Checkmate*, her 1937 collaboration with Arthur Bliss, are the works she is likely to be remembered by, although Robert Helpmann's comic solo in *The Prospect Before Us* (1940) must remain unforgettable by those who saw it. Thereafter, however, she left the creation of new works mostly to others (Roberto Gerhard's *Don Quixote* in 1950 was her last big work, taken on only when the intended choreographer withdrew), although she played a vital part in new productions of the classics.

The rapid development of the company (renamed Sadler's Wells Ballet) during the war years, meeting a greatly increased demand for serious entertainment, is well known. So is the story of the post-war move to Covent Garden, the international tours and wide acclaim that followed, and the grant in 1956 of the royal charter. With this, de Valois' work was in a sense complete. She had ensured that the company would live after her. What had begun as one woman's effort had become a national institution.

She remained artistic director until 1963, after which she devoted herself primarily for almost another decade to directing the Royal Ballet School. She also maintained a close interest in the ballet school and company which she had founded in Turkey at the request of the Turkish Government, for which she continued to find suitable teachers and directors.

With a little more time in hand, de Valois wrote further books, not only about ballet but a book of poems which she published to raise funds for the Royal Ballet School. For the same good cause she also undertook a gruelling lecture tour of the United States. Her capacity for driving herself on must have been phenomenal; at first (until the war years) she had to be company manager and administrator as well as artistic director, choreographer and, at first, leading dancer. All this was in addition to being the wife of a general practitioner, Dr Arthur Connell, whom she married in 1935.

Little of de Valois' individual contribution will survive her. Of the many ballets she created, few have been seen lately. Birmingham Royal Ballet mounted *Job* (after an absence of more than 20 years) in honour of her 95th birthday in June 1993, giving it not only in Birmingham and London but also in Coventry Cathedral for the 950th anniversary of the original foundation. To mark her centenary, the Birmingham company reconstructed *The Prospect Before Us* with unexpected success. But only *Checkmate* and *The Rake's Progress* have maintained a continuing — if tenuous — place in the repertoire, exemplifying the drama, the robust humour and theatrical flair which were her main virtues as a choreographer.

The memory will remain, however, of a gracious, efficient and kindly person, devoted to the work she had set herself, and concerned deeply for the well-being of all professional dancers. Her work, for instance, to expand the scope of the Royal Ballet Benevolent Fund to relieve distress among professional dancers is too little known, but was a significant supplement to her main achievement. She also more than once spoke up forcefully on behalf of the small, struggling London City Ballet when its existence was threatened by lack of public funding.

The Covent Garden management has tended latterly to let the London-based Royal run down through too small a share of resources, while its artistic policy has been left to freewheel on the lines she laid down, without her commitment and capacity for renewal. Nevertheless, de Valois leaves, for future British dancers, the prospect of a career that did not exist when she was young; for audiences, two great companies that would not have existed without her; and for her country, a national asset beyond price.

Dame Ninette de Valois, OM, CH, DBE, founder and director of the Royal Ballet, was born on June 5, 1898. She died on March 8, 2001, aged 102

KATHARINE GRAHAM

PUBLISHER OF *THE
WASHINGTON POST* WHO
BROUGHT DOWN NIXON OVER
WATERGATE, AND BECAME
ONE OF THE MOST POWERFUL
WOMEN IN AMERICA

JULY 18, 2001

As controlling shareholder and publisher of *The Washington Post*, Mrs
Katharine Graham was for decades
one of the half-dozen most influential people in the American capital.
Presidents, cabinet secretaries, sena-
tors and White House staffers came
and went; Kay Graham remained a
force to be reckoned with: wealthy,
determined and with a reputation for
absolute integrity.

Her decisions were an important
factor in the *Post*'s campaigns to publish
the so-called Pentagon Papers about
the Vietnam War, and in the decision to
pursue the Watergate scandal, which led
to the resignation of President Nixon in
1974. Her moral courage in these two
crises helped to win the *Post* a position
alongside or only slightly behind *The
New York Times* as the most influential
newspaper in the country.

It had not always been so. The *Post*
had been bankrupt when it was bought
at auction by her father, the successful

Wall Street investor Eugene Meyer, who
had put together the Allied Chemical
company out of confiscated German
chemicals and dyestuffs businesses.

Katharine's mother, Agnes Meyer,
was a journalist, the first woman
reporter on *The New York Sun*. She was
a domineering personality with strong
liberal views, and she and her daughter
never got along easily.

Katharine was born in New York and
educated at Vassar and the University
of Chicago, where she shed her
Republicanism and became a left-wing
Democrat. In 1938 she too became a
reporter, on *The San Francisco News*,
where she specialised in labour news.

In 1940 she married Philip L.
Graham, a brilliant lawyer from Florida
by way of the Harvard Law School, to
whom she had been introduced by
John Oakes, of the family which owns
The New York Times. Graham, who
was a close friend of the future presidents John F. Kennedy and Lyndon
B. Johnson (and a protégé of the arch-
networker Justice Felix Frankfurter of
the Supreme Court), was expected to
have a great career of his own either
in the law or in politics. When Graham
came back from the war, however,
Eugene Meyer persuaded his son-in-
law to help him run the paper.

Philip Graham decided to buy
Newsweek magazine, persuaded Meyer
to buy up the *Post*'s only remaining rival of substance in Washington,
the *Times-Herald*, and became one
of the most influential figures in the
Washington of the late 1950s. It was
he who brokered the deal by which

Lyndon Johnson stood down to allow Kennedy a clear run for the Democratic presidential nomination in return for the vice-presidency.

He was, however, psychologically very ill, and by 1963 the mental strain and imbalance had become impossible to hide. He began to drink heavily and became publicly involved with a young woman who was a correspondent for *Newsweek*. With her, after several attempts to break off the relationship, he began careering around the country, his escapades culminating in his beginning to strip in front of an audience of his peers at the Associated Press convention. Finally he shot himself at the Grahams' farm in Virginia. His wife was in the next room.

Graham, a mother of four young children, now found herself sole owner of *The Washington Post*. Most of the executives and journalists expected her to hand the reins to them. Instead, with an extraordinary effort of will, she overcame the shock and took control herself.

Although at first nervous about her own inexperience, she soon showed that she was determined to play an active part in running the paper and the group as a whole. (By this time the Washington Post Company owned several television stations in Washington and in Florida as well as *Newsweek* and minor properties.) She loved the buzz of the news, of the editorial conference and the newsroom, and for the next quarter of a century she was at the centre of a series of political storms and business dramas.

One moment of decision came in June 1971, when Graham learnt through a social contact that *The New York Times* — chief obstacle in the way of her ambition of making the *Post* the best paper in the country — had obtained copies of a secret report on American policy towards Vietnam. It came to be known as the Pentagon Papers.

The *Times* had had access to the papers long enough to mount a careful checking operation. The *Post* faced a dilemma: let the *Times* have its great scoop to itself, or risk publishing the material imperfectly checked and lose all credibility by getting something seriously wrong. The choice was the more agonising for coming on the eve of the first public flotation of Washington Post Company shares on the stock exchange.

The lawyers warned her against publishing. The journalists, led by the dashing Editor Ben Bradlee, were all for taking the risk. Graham overruled the legal advisers and agreed to publication — and she held to this course despite heavy threats of criminal prosecution from the Nixon Administration. The *Post* itself had, she felt, supported the war in Vietnam for too long.

The experience of the Pentagon Papers added sulphur to the atmosphere when, 18 months later, Bradlee and two of his young reporters, Carl Bernstein and Bob Woodward, began to follow the trail of the various misdeeds and criminal activities in the Nixon White House that came to be known as Watergate.

Especially in the earlier months, when the *Post* stood almost alone against an electorally triumphant and furiously vindictive Administration — which was determined to ruin her paper's reputation — the personal pressure on Graham was formidable. But she never wavered.

The Washington Post emerged from the Watergate struggle covered with glory — too much, it turned out, for its own good. Graham, meanwhile, was changing. Even before the Watergate showdown, she had distanced herself from some of the *Post*'s journalists, who were bitter opponents of the Nixon Administration. She was, in particular, on excellent terms with Dr Henry Kissinger.

Although the paper continued to take a broadly liberal approach, in those same years she took a hard line with its unions. When the journalists went on strike, she reverted to her youthful experience as a reporter and even worked, taking down classified advertisements over the phone.

During the far more bitter strike by the pressmen which followed, the underlying steel of her character became even more clearly apparent. She made no secret of her anger at strikers who physically attacked journalists and did millions of dollars-worth of damage to her presses. This shy woman first brought in helicopters to fly out plates to be printed elsewhere, and ended up seeking the help of the Newspaper Production and Research Center, a conservative organisation in Oklahoma, to break the union, which she effectively did.

In 1979 Mrs Graham handed over her job as publisher to her son, Donald Graham, although she continued to play an important part in the affairs of the company as a whole. As a result of the victory over the pressmen, the company became more valuable than ever — and *The Washington Post* was only the flagship of a considerable business empire, which included television stations (which the Nixon Administration threatened to remove), as well as other communications companies and paper-making interests.

As early as 1971 Graham was made nervous by a letter from Warren Buffett, then a comparatively unknown investor out in Omaha, which said that his investment vehicle, Berkshire-Hathaway, had bought 5 per cent of the Post Company's stock. Over the following years, Buffett and Graham developed a close business and personal friendship. She claimed that he was her instructor in business. Together they weathered a number of business storms, and the Washington Post Company's shares soared steadily higher.

Graham had taken to the business world with enthusiasm, and she took great pleasure in passing various milestones, such as seeing the company's stock passing $300 a share, and an award that listed it as one of the five best-managed corporations in the United States. Its revenues multiplied nearly 20-fold under her management.

The paper's reputation, however, was badly dented by the disastrous Janet Cooke affair of 1981. Cooke, an African-American reporter, won a Pulitzer prize for what turned out to be an almost wholly untrue story about a child heroin addict; and on inspection it turned out that she had conned the editors about her own background and credentials as well as her story.

Meanwhile, Graham's politics were changing. She greatly enjoyed her participation in the Brandt Commission, which in 1978 produced the report *North and South*, about imbalances in the world economy, but by the 1980s it was really no longer accurate to identify her as a liberal. As she grew older she travelled a good deal and enjoyed meeting the world's movers and shakers. Among her friends were the Reagans, Vaclav Havel, Diana, Princess of Wales, and Bill Gates. She also had a number of relationships of a more or less romantic nature with men, most of them distinctly rich and powerful.

She remained, however, a strong feminist, and over the years her commitment to equality for women only intensified. She once interrupted a statement at an Allied Chemicals shareholders' meeting to insist that female employees must be called "women" and not "girls", a modest enough demand by today's standards, but daring at the time. On another occasion she sent for her car and swept out of a dinner party at the British Embassy because she was expected to join the ladies in withdrawing from the men after dinner.

In 1997 she finally confounded those — if there were any left — who still patronised her abilities by publishing an autobiography, *Personal History*, which instantly became a bestseller and won a Pulitzer prize. Like its author it was frank, courageous and full of ideas; it confronted the most painful aspects of her husband's traumatic end and she even found the generosity to say something good about the young woman whose affair with her husband led to his final catastrophe.

Graham is survived by her daughter and three sons.

Katharine Graham, publisher of **The Washington Post,** *was born on* **June 16, 1917.** *She died on July 17, 2001, aged 84*

———

QUEEN ELIZABETH THE QUEEN MOTHER

A UNIQUE PUBLIC PERSONALITY, WHOSE SERVICE TO THE MONARCHY WAS SECOND TO NONE IN THE 20TH CENTURY

APRIL 1, 2002

The wife of King George VI was the first non-royal queen consort since Catherine Parr in the 16th century, and the first non-royal mother of a sovereign since Anne Hyde in the 17th. But these achievements — interesting as they may be for the record book — say nothing of the individual, whose achievements were of a quite different order.

By virtue of qualities peculiarly her own, not the least of which was an extraordinary, even awe-inspiring, longevity, Queen Elizabeth came to occupy a special position in the country and throughout the world. As queen consort from 1936 to 1952, she was immensely popular and an incalculable asset to the monarchy. As queen mother she was, if possible, more popular still, and continued to make an outstanding contribution to the work of the Royal Family.

It was not in her nature to behave as though her privileged position was a crushing burden. By temperament an enjoyer of life, she entered into everything she did with gusto, and never forgot what she owed to people whose lives were less comfortable, pleasant and interesting than her own. With this attitude, she could turn even an intrinsically tedious occasion into a party. As a *Times* leader once said of her: "She lays a foundation stone as though she has discovered a new and delightful way of spending an afternoon."

When she married Albert, Duke of York in 1923 she had no reason to imagine that he would ever be king. But 13 years later, she was more than equal to the double challenge of supporting him in a role for which, in many ways, he seemed to be unfitted, and of making a success of her own role as first lady. Though it is absurd to suggest that the monarchy itself was seriously endangered by Edward VIII's abdication, it is true that, but for her, the institution might, at that time, have suffered some loss of glamour and prestige, if only temporarily.

Without doubt it was her devotion and strength of character that enabled the new king to rise above the natural disadvantages of a stammer, and almost crippling shyness, to become a competent and, in time, a well-loved monarch. At the same time she took to her new position with apparently effortless ease, showing from the first the star quality that was never to desert her.

During the Second World War, Queen Elizabeth was unchallenged as the woman to whom people looked for inspiration. If she had not been there, the monarchy might have been comprehensively upstaged by Winston Churchill (however unwillingly, on his part). Her conduct during the war showed her at her brilliant best, and deepened the affection and respect in which she was already held.

By contrast with his father, King George VI was able, with the help of Queen Elizabeth, to give his children a home life that was as warm and intimate as any in the land; and it is immensely to the credit of both parents that they never thought of sending their daughters to invidious and probably unhappy safety overseas during the war.

On the education of her children Queen Elizabeth's instincts were conservative. As a result, the princesses Elizabeth and Margaret were not sent to school but taught by governesses. It may be argued that after 1945 her essential conservatism may have somewhat delayed the process of evolution and adaptation of the royal household that the times required. But her relatively old-fashioned views never cost her any popularity, partly because they were widely shared in the community, but also because her personal charm prevailed over any criticism.

However, behind the famous smile was a character that was tough as well as sweet and gracious. Without this toughness she could not have achieved what she did. In general, her strength was exerted to good ends, and helped to make her a unique public personality, whose service to the monarchy was second to none in the 20th century.

Elizabeth Angela Marguerite Bowes-Lyon's exact place of birth remains a mystery, although it was probably in London. It was always assumed to have been at St Paul's, Walden Bury, the Hertfordshire home of her parents, the 14th Earl and Countess of Strathmore and Kinghorne, whose ninth child she was, but she herself denied it without ever elaborating on where precisely she entered the world. Lord Strathmore was a dignified but unremarkable backwoods peer. Lady Strathmore, daughter of a parson with ducal (Portland) connections, was the more forceful parent.

Elizabeth and her younger brother, David, were respectively 17 and 19 years younger than their eldest sister, and their mother used to say that they might have been her grandchildren. Their upbringing and education had a distinctly Victorian flavour. The future queen's early life was passed in an almost royal routine, alternating between the estate in Hertfordshire, with its Queen Anne house, a big London house in Grosvenor Gardens, and the historic seat of the family, Glamis Castle, which was used largely for holidays and shooting parties.

A pretty child with striking eyes, she early showed the companionable disposition which was later to win her so many friends, as well as the not entirely friendly description of "a simple, chattering, sweet-hearted, little round-faced woman in pink". (Her other distinctive dress colour was to be powder-blue.) As with most young women of her class, there were no plans for her to have a career beyond that of marriage. Her education was at home, apart from brief attendance at "select classes for girls" at a school in Sloane Street. For the rest, her childhood before 1914 was more or less happy and carefree.

War changed all this and brought her into contact with harsher realities. Personal sorrows struck her family. One of her brothers, Fergus, was killed, and another, Michael, taken prisoner. The circle of friends which had gathered annually for the three-month holiday at Glamis was similarly reduced. But the war had positive value for Lady Elizabeth. The drawing-room at Glamis was converted into a convalescent home for wounded Australian soldiers discharged from Dundee Infirmary; their presence gave her an opportunity for service, which she relished.

With the inventiveness of youth she and David improvised trivial comforts for the soldiers, ran errands for them and entertained them with stories and games. With her beguiling ways she became immensely popular with them — as later with a worldwide public. It was also good for her to find, at an impressionable age, that she could get on with men from backgrounds of which she had absolutely no knowledge. She liked to listen to what they had to say, and in return talked to them about herself without embarrassment or condescension.

But when the war ended she returned to the conventional round. She belatedly "came out" (though she was never actually presented at court) and then threw herself into the social activities appropriate to a girl of her standing. She loved parties and was known as one of the best dancers in London, though she never became a familiar name to the readers of social gossip columns. Her reputation as a charming, eligible girl was confined to a fairly limited circle. She seemed to have no desire for early marriage and turned down a number of proposals before coming of age.

The first postwar meeting with her future husband, Albert, Duke of York, took place in 1920 at a party given by his father's friend, Lord Farquhar (later — posthumously — exposed as a crook). Soon the duke was visiting Glamis and beginning his long courtship, which was not to end until his third proposal was accepted by Elizabeth at St Paul's, Walden Bury, on January 14, 1923. Joyfully, he sent a telegram to his mother —"ALL RIGHT BERTIE". It was, indeed, a providential moment for him, and not for him only.

They were married in Westminster Abbey on April 26, 1923. It was the first marriage of a sovereign's son for nearly half-a-century, and popular enthusiasm vindicated the decision to hold it in Westminster Abbey rather than in the privacy of a Chapel Royal. Queen Alexandra attended — one of her last public appearances — as did her sister, the Dowager Empress of Russia. The Archbishop of York preached a somewhat wordy sermon. In the afternoon the couple drove away to Polesden Lacey, which had been lent to them by Mrs (Maggie) Greville, who later favoured the Royal Family with substantial legacies.

Before there was any question of her becoming a royal personage, Elizabeth had been described by an observer, at a British Embassy ball in Paris, in these words: "The most charming sight there was Lady Elizabeth Bowes Lyon, a bewitching little figure in rose colour, which set off her lovely eyes and dark eyebrows to perfection. She seemed to me the incarnation of fresh, happy, English girlhood." (She would have corrected the word "English".) It was not expected, in 1923, that a royal duchess should necessarily become an active public figure. All the same, Elizabeth began to undertake engagements in her own right. The first were modest enough, connected with local organisations or charities that friends persuaded her to support. But national presidencies and patronages followed.

Her most important work at this time was done out of the public eye in helping her husband to fight his natural handicaps. Her easy, relaxed temperament was balm to him, and the change in his bearing was soon noticed. With her encouragement he set about tackling the worst obstacle to his performance in public, his stammer. Visiting the Australian speech therapist Lionel Logue in 1926, he began a course of treatment which certainly improved, though it could never completely eliminate, what had seemed to be an insuperable problem.

She fitted well into the tightly knit family circle of King George V, who astonished other members of his family by treating her unpunctuality — particularly at meals, where it would normally have driven him to fury — as a venial fault. She was fond of him and, unlike his own children, never afraid of him.

During the winter of 1924-25, she accompanied her husband on a visit to East Africa and the Sudan, which was largely recreational, but broadened their horizons. On safari in Kenya she was no mere spectator of the Duke's marksmanship, but did a lot of shooting herself with a 0.275 Rigby rifle.

The birth of her first daughter on April 21, 1926, was a highly popular event. The child was given her mother's first Christian name, which could also be seen as a gesture to England's, though not Scotland's, past. The second daughter, Margaret — or Margaret Rose, as she was always known at the time — was born four years later, on August 21, 1930.

At first the Yorks could hardly compete with the dashing Prince of Wales

as a royal attraction. He was the star, while they were essentially only members of the supporting cast. In 1927, however, they had an opportunity to shine on their own, when they went on a world tour which included state visits to New Zealand and Australia. For a time during their visit to New Zealand the Duchess was out of action with a throat infection, but this was almost a blessing, however disguised. It pleased her that the Duke was able to cope on his own, and that the undiminished enthusiasm with which he was greeted relieved him of the suspicion that the crowds had previously turned out to see only his wife.

In Australia, the Duchess's good humour and informality made a strong appeal. She bore the turbulent welcome of crowds as cheerfully as she bore the extremes of temperature. At a ball at Government House, Melbourne, she insisted on dancing with a man whom she had met as a wounded officer at Glamis during the war.

After this tour the couple returned to a more settled existence. Their first married home had been the White Lodge in Richmond Park, but in 1927 they took up residence at No 145 Piccadilly, which remained their London address until they moved to Buckingham Palace. In 1931 the King gave them the Royal Lodge in Windsor Park, which was expanded and done up for their benefit; it became their favourite home.

As the years passed and the Prince of Wales remained unmarried, the prospect that their elder daughter might one day succeed to the throne came to seem less remote. But any idea that the Duke of York might be called to it himself was still beyond the wildest speculation. With George V's death in January 1936, however, the crisis which produced this result became imminent. Already aware of the new King's attachment to Wallis Simpson, the Yorks soon realised that it was much more than a passing affair: that he was, in fact, determined to marry her, and that if he could not marry her as king, he would abdicate forthwith.

The Yorks were genuinely distraught, he doubting his capacity to do the job of monarch, she anxious on his behalf and not at all wanting him to be exposed to such a test. But when it became apparent that the British and Dominion governments would not accept Mrs Simpson as queen, or even as the king's morganatic wife, Edward bowed to constitutional necessity and promptly abdicated. In his farewell broadcast he made a graceful reference to his brother and to the happy family life that he enjoyed.

So far as the State was concerned, the transition was perfectly smooth. The constitutional crisis ended the moment Edward signed the instrument of abdication, and the fairy-story appeal of the monarchy was doubly enhanced: by the Yorks' brave assumption of office for duty's sake and by Edward's renunciation of it for love.

But the new King and Queen did not see it that way. In their view, Edward had let the monarchy down, and the woman who had inveigled him into doing so was beyond the pale. As a result, a family feud developed and the Duke and Duchess of Windsor (as the former king and his wife became) entered upon a life of exile, with the duchess denied the title "Royal Highness" to the end of her days. Queen Elizabeth's relentless disapproval of the Duchess of Windsor arose from the belief that the duchess's behaviour had imposed an intolerable strain on King George VI and had eventually contributed to his early death.

The new king, though much improved since his marriage, was still painfully conscious of his limitations and inadequacies, more especially by comparison with his elder brother. When he told Queen Mary that Edward was abdicating, he broke down and (in his own words) "sobbed like a child". The new Queen accepted her destiny with a serene self-confidence. In her first letter to the Archbishop of Canterbury she wrote: "I can hardly believe that we have been called to the tremendous task and (I am writing to you quite intimately) the curious thing is that we are not afraid". It was certainly true of her, and her courage was vital in sustaining the King.

She made few public appearances between her husband's accession and the Coronation on May 12, 1937. In this she acquitted herself with dignity and reverence, and people were touched also by her air of youthfulness. She was the youngest queen consort since George III's wife, Queen Charlotte, had been crowned in 1761. As the crown was placed on Queen Elizabeth's head,

Winston Churchill (who had been a staunch and romantic supporter of Edward VIII) turned to his wife, his eyes full of tears, and said: "You were right; I see now the 'other one' wouldn't have done."

With the dark clouds of war gathering on the horizon, Neville Chamberlain's policy of appeasement was tried and failed. Queen Elizabeth and her husband were enthusiastic supporters of the policy, to the extent of appearing with Chamberlain on the balcony of Buckingham Palace after his return from signing the Munich agreement, even though the agreement was to be the subject of a party vote in the House of Commons. This extraordinary constitutional lapse escaped censure because the royal couple were reflecting overwhelming popular sentiment at the time.

Earlier in 1938 they had paid a successful state visit to France, which had to be postponed from June to July because of the sudden death of Queen Elizabeth's mother. In Paris the Queen chose to wear white as a mark of mourning, and her all-white trousseau was much admired, as was her appearance for the first time in crinoline dresses inspired by Winterhalter portraits of the young Queen Victoria. She also benefited, then as later, by being able to converse with a fair degree of ease in French.

In the spring and early summer of 1939 they undertook a more ambitious journey, first to Canada and then to the United States. After landing at Quebec in mid-May they travelled across Canada to the Pacific coast, everywhere evoking loyal demonstrations. Returning eastwards they made history by entering the United States, at Niagara, on June 9. In Washington a senator congratulated the King on being "a great Queen-picker". While staying with the Roosevelts at Hyde Park the Queen was able to talk to her daughters in England by transatlantic telephone, a novel experience for both her and them.

At about this time Sir Harold Nicolson wrote of her in his diary: "She really does manage to convey to each individual in the crowd that he or she has had a personal greeting. It is due, I think, to the brilliance of her eyes. But she is in truth one of the most amazing Queens since Cleopatra."

During the Second World War she came into her own, more especially, of course, after the fall of France, when invasion seemed imminent. At this time a number of people sent their children out of the country, and the possibility of sending the princesses to Canada was, in fact, discussed. But the King and Queen decided firmly against it, realising that in a supreme national emergency it was quite wrong for children of the rich and privileged to be made invidiously safe; also that it was desirable, in any case, for their family to stay together.

The Queen's attitude was summed up in words that are, justly, the most famous of her life: "The Princesses would never leave without me, and I couldn't leave without the King, and the King will never leave."

The Queen Mother visiting The Times *offices at Wapping, with Richard Williams (left) and Charles Wilson, then editor (far left), showing her around*

The children lived at Windsor during the war, which meant that their lives were considerably more at risk than those of many children from poor families, who were removed to remote parts of the country. The King and Queen normally slept at Windsor, but drove into London for the day. Buckingham Palace was hit several times by bombs, which enabled the Queen, as she put it, to "look the East End in the face". The East End of London and other blitzed areas were able to look her in the face when she and the King visited them after raids. Her combination of glamour, serenity, friendliness and genuine sympathy made her uniquely effective in lifting people's spirits.

She did not, however, go around wearing any of the uniforms that were available to women in the war effort, though she could have worn any or all of them if she had wished. Her essentially feminine nature recoiled from the somewhat Amazonian connotations of a uniform, and she continued to dress in her usual style.

But in 1943 "Chips" Channon detected a change in her walk, which may have been associated with the slight amplification of figure that came to her in middle age. As she entered St Paul's for a service to celebrate the victory in Tunisia, she was, he wrote, as ever "gracious and smiling", but also "leaning back, a new walk she has acquired."

She and the King were sympathetic towards sovereigns and governments in exile. In particular, they treated General de Gaulle with an understanding and consideration that he did not, as a rule, receive from the British

Government. Their kindness was handsomely acknowledged in his memoirs, and in later years he never failed to show special regard for the Queen Mother in her widowhood.

They were unable to return President Roosevelt's hospitality, because he did not visit Britain during the war. But Mrs Roosevelt stayed at Buckingham Palace in 1942 and suffered acutely from the cold there, since there was limited electric heating even in rooms with windows patched-up after bombing. She was also served simple wartime food on gold and silver plates, perhaps a studied attempt to emphasise the truth that the royal family had submitted themselves to all the rigours of wartime austerity.

The Queen also had the bulldog courage of that slightly unrealistic type which the British people are not ashamed to display in moments of dire peril and have no aversion to seeing reflected in their leaders. Thus she practised with both .303 rifle and .38 service revolver in the grounds of Buckingham Palace, telling Sir Harold Nicolson, who had expressed surprise at this martial activity from one so diminutive, "Yes, I shall not go down like the others," referring, perhaps not entirely fairly, to the capitulation of the monarchs of the continent in the face of the German onslaught.

The victory of Labour in the 1945 general election restored the monarchy to its normal position of unchallenged prestige. Churchill, who in spite of himself had in some ways eclipsed the sovereign, was replaced by the uncharismatic Clement Attlee. Yet Attlee was no less of a traditionalist than Churchill, and he and his colleagues showed, like Ramsay MacDonald and the first Labour Government, that they yielded to none in reverence for the throne.

Queen Elizabeth was not the one to contemplate making any unnecessary concessions to the spirit of the age, and shrewdly judged that virtually none were, in fact, necessary, since politicians and press were equally reluctant to demand any. The prewar royal routines, including some that were beginning to seem out of date even then — such as the presentation of debutantes at Buckingham Palace — were brought back without significant modification.

Between February and May 1947 the King and Queen toured the Union of South Africa. The visit was stage-managed by the country's illustrious prime minister, Field-Marshal J. C. Smuts, who must have hoped that it would serve to counteract the appeal of the Nationalist party. Although it was embarrassing for the royal family to have to leave Britain en route for a land of sunshine when the British people were experiencing one of the worst winters on record, with the added misery of fuel shortage, the tour went ahead on firm ministerial advice and was, on the face of it, a triumphant success. The Queen's part in it was from first to last outstanding, and when speaking to Afrikaners resentful of England she would sometimes imply, a little speciously, that as a Scotswoman she could understand their feelings.

Soon after her arrival in Cape Town she returned to the family of President Kruger a family Bible of his that had fallen into British hands during the Boer War. And at Bloemfontein she called on the octogenarian widow of President Steyn of the Orange Free State. But along with such conciliatory gestures to former enemies, she also showed to the full her appreciation of those South Africans who had fought beside Britain in two world wars, more especially wounded veterans.

Travelling in a white and gold train, the royal party visited Southern Rhodesia and the three British protectorates of Bechuanaland, Basutoland, and Swaziland, as well as most parts of the South African Union. They saw all the sights of the region, including the Victoria Falls and any amount of wildlife, and it meant much to the King and Queen that they had their daughters with them on such a spectacular trip.

Before they re-embarked for home (they travelled both ways by sea, in the Royal Navy's most modern battleship, HMS *Vanguard*), the Queen received an honorary doctorate from Smuts himself as Chancellor of the University of Cape Town. In acknowledging it, she made her only speech of the tour, in which she listed the qualities to which academics should aspire as honesty, justice and resolve, all needing to be sustained by religious faith. The speech was highly praised. However, conversation was her natural medium, and her supreme gift was for putting people at their ease in informal talk.

In July 1947 the King and Queen announced the engagement of their elder daughter, Princess Elizabeth, to Lieutenant Philip Mountbatten, and the wedding took place in Westminster Abbey on November 20 with a show of pageantry that brightened the rather dreary postwar scene. Within a year the Queen was able to celebrate the birth of her first, and perhaps favourite, grandchild, Prince Charles.

Meanwhile, she and the King had celebrated their Silver Wedding, on April 26, 1948. Publicly, the day was marked by a service at St Paul's, followed by a 20-mile drive through the streets of London in the afternoon. In the evening she and the King appeared on the balcony of Buckingham Palace, and were repeatedly called back by an enthusiastic crowd.

But in November the King was diagnosed as suffering from incipient arteriosclerosis and a projected tour of Australia and New Zealand had to be postponed. In the event, it never occurred, because the King's health, never robust, was entering an irreversible decline. In September 1951 he was found to have lung cancer and his left lung was removed. He seemed to recover from the operation, while looking much aged. But during the night of February 5-6, 1952, after a day's shooting at Sandringham, he died in his sleep.

His death left Queen Elizabeth a widow in her early fifties, faced with the challenge of adapting herself to a new life. Beyond question, she was profoundly sad to lose her husband.

Despite her initial reluctance to marry him, she had become a most loving as well as a most devoted wife, and they were a very close couple. All the same, the task of supporting him had been quite a strain and inevitably involved some cramping of her own style. Now that she was alone, it was some compensation for her loss of private happiness that her public role became less difficult and demanding.

Without wishing in any way to stand in her daughter's light, she showed no desire to withdraw into the traditional reclusion of a dowager. The title that she chose for herself, Queen Elizabeth The Queen Mother — with its curious and somewhat unyielding repetition of the royal title — had an unmistakably assertive ring. She remained a star, as she had been as queen consort — the more so, perhaps, for being able at last to perform on her own.

And she continued to live in style. In London her residence was Clarence House. Out of London she had the use of her old home, Royal Lodge, at Windsor, while on the Balmoral estate Birkhall was placed at her disposal. In addition, she soon acquired a dilapidated castle overlooking the Pentland Firth, did it up and renamed it the Castle of Mey — visited, at most, for a few weeks every year. Later, another castle, Walmer, was added to her residences, when, in 1978, she became Lord Warden of the Cinque Ports in succession to Sir Robert Menzies.

Her widowhood was clouded by a family crisis. When the King died she asked Group Captain Peter Townsend, a much decorated Battle of Britain fighter ace who had been an equerry since March 1944, to stay on as comptroller of her household. Townsend was already estranged from his wife; he was therefore romantically footloose and a likely focus of romantic thoughts. It was hardly surprising that he and Princess Margaret fell in love with each other.

The affair trailed on until October 1955 with Townsend meanwhile getting divorced and being rusticated for a time in Brussels. By then the princess was free to marry without her sister's consent, though it was made clear that if she married Townsend she would have to forfeit her royal title and perquisites. In the end she renounced him, "mindful of the Church's teaching" and of her "duty to the Commonwealth". Five years later she married Antony Armstrong-Jones, who became Lord Snowdon, and from whom, in 1978, she was divorced.

These events must have caused the Queen Mother, an Anglican traditionalist, a lot of distress. Yet she was also adaptable and worldly-wise. It was noteworthy that some of her best friends were divorcees and when the Snowdons' divorce occurred she appeared to accept it with equanimity, remaining on good terms with her daughter's ex-husband.

As Queen Mother she travelled far more than she had ever done as Queen. In 1954 she revisited the United States to receive money which had been raised there in commemoration of her husband. She also received an honorary doctorate at Columbia University in New York, where the citation described her as "a noble Queen, whose quiet and constant courage in time of great stress sustained a nation and inspired a world"; and in Washington she was a guest of the Eisenhowers at the White House. Thereafter her peregrinations were unremitting. Canada she visited nine times, Southern Rhodesia (now Zimbabwe) four times, Australia and New Zealand twice, Northern Rhodesia (Zambia) and Nyasaland (Malawi) twice, Uganda twice, as well as Kenya, Tunisia, Jamaica and other places in the Caribbean, Cyprus and Iran. In Europe, she was a frequent visitor to France, and she went several times to Italy. Germany, though never her favourite country, was visited too.

Nearer home, she was seen in the Channel Islands and the Isle of Man. And, of course, she visited every part of the United Kingdom itself, including Northern Ireland, to which she was particularly devoted. When the Queen was out of the country she would often act as a Counsellor of State, or carry out investitures.

One of the posts that gave her most satisfaction was the chancellorship of London University, which she held from 1955 to 1980. In this she showed her capacity to disarm even radical lecturers and students, and it must have been a tribute to her, as well as to her grand-daughter, that when she eventually stood down Princess Anne was elected to succeed her by a convincing majority, in a secret ballot, against strong competition.

Among recreations, none meant more to the Queen Mother than racing. Her passion for National Hunt racing made her the most popular owner in the land by a long way. Both through her understanding and love of horses and her immense enjoyment of steeplechasing and its world, she became, over half a century, the embodiment of the sport, as well as its greatest ambassador. As such, she helped to transform the image of National Hunt racing and enhance its prestige.

Yet it all came about by accident. Whoever made the seating plan for the Royal Ascot dinner at Windsor Castle on June 15, 1949, must take the responsibility. Lord Mildmay, that idol of National Hunt racing, later tragically lost in a bathing accident, happened to be seated between Queen Elizabeth and her daughter, then Princess Elizabeth. It was he who suggested that they should try their luck at owning a steeplechaser. There was a ready response. Mildmay would find a suitable horse to be trained by Peter Cazalet. It was Monaveen. Owned in partnership, he was the first of the Queen Mother's more than 450 winners.

Monaveen had to be put down in 1950. But he had fired the Queen Mother's ambition to go into racing and register her subsequently famous blue colours with buff stripes. The first horse to carry these successfully was Manicou, who appropriately triumphed in the King George VI Chase on Boxing Day, 1950. There followed many more important winners, including Laffy (1962 Ulster Harp National); Makaldar

(1965 Mackeson Hurdle); Inch Arran (1973 Topham Trophy); Tammuz (1975 Schweppes Gold Trophy); Insular (1986 Imperial Cup); Special Cargo — one of her special favourites (1984 Whitbread Gold Cup and three times in a row successful 1984-86 in the Grand Military Gold Cup which his owner also captured with The Argonaut in 1990 and Norman Conqueror in 1996).

The Queen Mother's most prolific jockey was David Mould who, between 1966 and 1973, rode 106 of her winners. Her big disappointments came in the Grand National, particularly when Devon Loch looked a certain success in 1956 but slipped on the run-in. Against that, she had a remarkable steeplechaser in Game Spirit who ran up an astonishing 21 victories between 1971 and 1976. His name, above that of any of her horses, perhaps most fittingly represented her own character.

Another outdoor sport that she much enjoyed was fishing, particularly salmon-fishing. She was very fond of gardens, as was her brother Sir David Bowes-Lyon — whose death in 1961, while staying with her at Birkhall, was a great blow to her — but she did not do much active gardening herself. She was, however, an energetic walker.

During a time when royal patronage of the arts was not very conspicuous, she was the principal exception. Advised by Kenneth Clark, she became a modest collector of relatively modern paintings, including works by Augustus John, Sickert, Wilson Steer, Matthew Smith and Paul Nash. She also bought a Monet that had belonged to Clemenceau, and it was at her invitation that John Piper produced his series of drawings and watercolours of Windsor.

In 1964 she had an emergency operation for appendicitis, and two years later underwent a colostomy. But her basically strong constitution enabled her to weather these vicissitudes and throughout the 1960s and 1970s she maintained an extensive diary of royal engagements. Among other things she was occupied by her patronage of no fewer than three hundred charities and was colonel-in chief of 13 regular regiments, eight of them in the British Army and five in the forces of Commonwealth countries.

Among these her colonelcies of both the Black Watch and the Black Watch of Canada emphasised her ties with Scotland. She was also honorary colonel of three Territorial Army units, the Royal Yeomanry, the London Scottish Regiment and the Inns of Court Regiment, and was commandant-in-chief of women in the Royal Navy and RAF and was patron of the Women's Royal Army Corps Association.

In the summer of 1980, on the occasion of her 80th birthday, she drove to St Paul's in a landau with Prince Charles through cheering crowds. Her 90th birthday was the cause for even more extended congratulations. Though she had specifically asked that no fuss be made, there were celebrations in Scotland, Wales and England lasting well over a month. These included a recorded concert featuring works especially commissioned by young composers, organised by the Prince of

Wales to raise funds for his charitable trust. In his foreword to the recording, the Queen Mother's favourite grandson described it as: "a wonderful reason for commissioning some new music: to celebrate a very special occasion and an even more special grandmother." On the day itself a crowd of 4,000 stood for hours outside Clarence House with the temperature in the nineties, waiting for her to appear.

But clouds were gathering again over the personal lives of members of the royal family. The marriage of her granddaughter Princess Anne had already failed in the 1980s. Now, in quick succession in the early 1990s the marriage of her second grandson, the Duke of York, foundered and was closely followed by the separation of the Prince and Princess of Wales. Both events were accompanied by unsparing reporting of details of private conflicts and sexual infidelities that would have been undreamt of a generation earlier.

The disintegration of the Prince of Wales's marriage affected the Queen Mother deeply and, given her predilection for her eldest grandson, involved her in undoubted partisanship. Relations between the Queen Mother and the Princess of Wales had never been good. Under the pressure of the publicity which accompanied the painful steps towards the dissolution of the heir to the throne's marriage, they cooled even further. But, though a staunch churchwoman to whom divorce was anathema, the Queen Mother studiously avoided giving any public hint of her feelings.

At this time the popularity of the royal family was sinking to its lowest level during the present reign. The indulged lives of the younger generation, with their seemingly incessant round of parties and beach or skiing holidays, grated on a British people which was having to tighten its belt in the worst economic recession since the war. Even the Queen, with her untaxed millions, found that the nation's sympathy had its limits when a part of Windsor Castle was destroyed by fire, and the initial assumption appeared to be that the public would pay. A spate of unprecedented royal-bashing was unleashed in the popular press.

The Queen Mother alone escaped censure. Her popularity continued undimmed. A public appeal, launched in 1990, for a monument to celebrate her life with an ornamental gate (named the Queen Elizabeth Gate) at Hyde Park raised the necessary £2 million within two years. This quite confounded her own sensitivities about the wisdom of such an appeal in a time of recession.

Almost to the end the Queen Mother demonstrated remarkable robustness, both physical and mental, in her round of duties. In May 1992, when verging on her 92nd birthday, she insisted on unveiling a statue of Bomber Command's wartime leader, Air Chief Marshal Sir Arthur Harris, at St Clement Dane's Church in the Strand. This was in spite of the fact that she had been advised that there might be demonstrations of a more than merely vociferous character. In the event there were, but in spite of all the shouting and paint-throwing she delivered a speech of tribute to Bomber Command's dead, in a clear and resolute voice.

Physical frailty was hinted at in her absence from Royal Ascot in the following year. Yet, in July of the same year, on a day of brilliant sunshine, she appeared much recovered when she strolled through the Queen Elizabeth Gate on its official opening by her daughter, the Queen. During her later years there were the occasional health scares which are generally associated with those many years her junior. At 95 and then 97, she underwent hip replacement operations.

The Queen Mother was to live to play the central role in a celebration which, perhaps more than any other, summed up her life of unstinting service to the British people — the 50th anniversary of VE day on May 8, 1995. In a moving echo of the original ceremony in 1945, though this time without Winston Churchill and King George VI at her side, she stepped out onto the balcony of Buckingham Palace, followed by both her daughters, to wave to the 400,000-strong crowd which thronged the Mall. Joining in with them in the singing of some of the old wartime favourites, this astonishingly sprightly 94-year-old seemed more than ever a symbol of the nation's fortitude in dark years of adversity.

By the time of her centenary in August 2000, the royal family was recovering some, though certainly not all, of its popularity. There were several reasons for this. The Princess of Wales was dead, killed in a high-speed car crash in a Paris underpass. It was an event which led to a powerful, if ultimately short-lived, outpouring of public grief, particularly among the young — especially young women — to whom, it seemed, she had been such an icon. More broadly, the awkward position of the Prince of Wales at that time reminded people that he was, after all, another human being and was no more to be protected from the grief of such a tragedy than anyone else. The censure attaching to his relationship with his paramour, Camilla Parker Bowles, gradually abated.

A return visit to St Paul's Cathedral on July 11 marked the start of the Queen Mother's 100th birthday celebrations. Almost all of her descendants, as well as distant relations and in-laws from several European royal families, were present to hear the Archbishop of Canterbury lead the nation in tribute to her. Meanwhile, members of parliament heard the Prime Minister's congratulation in the form of a Humble Address in the House of Commons.

Certainly, there were words and actions of dissent. A Channel 4 television programme made insinuations about her steely nature and extravagant lifestyle, but they made no great impact on the population at large. Dissident Irish Republicans tried to disrupt a colourful parade that was part military and part fun held at Horse Guards on July 19 through a series of security alerts which paralysed most of London's rail, underground and bus routes.

With no precedent for celebrating such longevity in the Royal Family, her advisers had dreamt up the colourful occasion which was an effervescent and eccentric 90-minute spectacular involving more than 7,000 participants, from schoolchildren to holders of the Victoria Cross. On her birthday itself, August 4, 2000, the Queen Mother, like all centenarians, received a personally signed card from the monarch. Standing outside Clarence House beside the Prince of Wales, she struggled for a moment with the envelope until her equerry stepped forward to slit it open with a ceremonial sword. Touchingly, it was signed "Lilibet", Queen Elizabeth II's childhood pet name.

Meanwhile, the crowds had gathered in their thousands and, escorted by the Prince of Wales, the Queen Mother travelled in an open landau, garlanded with flowers in her racing colours of blue and buff, to Buckingham Palace for a celebratory lunch with the extended family. But before sitting down there was, much to the delight of the crowds, time for a wave from the balcony.

Certainly it was a tribute to her person that while the popularity of lesser royals ebbed and flowed, hers seemed to remain constant. Her role always as consort but never monarch had given her a detachment from any constitutional entanglements. There was also a genuine public admiration of the behaviour of a queen who, having been widowed at a relatively young age, had not, as she might well have done, retired into pampered seclusion, but had continued to make a positive and colourful contribution to public life. Above all, she gave the impression always of making herself available to people and of placing herself and her time at their disposal.

Astonishingly, to those who might have imagined that her 100th birthday would be her last, she courageously negotiated another 12 months, at the end of which she was able to celebrate her 101st. She did so shortly after having had a blood transfusion which, though it had seemed to be a prognostication of irreversible decline, left her evidently much invigorated.

On August 4, 2001, she entertained a dozen of her closest family to lunch at Clarence House, and when she rounded off the birthday celebrations with a visit to the Royal Ballet at Covent Garden, it was not so much her health which gave cause for concern as that of Princess Margaret, who attended her in a wheelchair, visibly a shadow of her formerly vivacious self.

As the year drew on Princess Margaret could be seen to be in palpable decline. In 2002, while the Queen Mother made a very slow recovery from a cold caught over the Christmas period, it began to seem to be a distinct possibility that her daughter might precede her to the grave. And, indeed, the Queen Mother was herself still struggling against the effects of a chest infection which, worryingly to those around her, continued to confine her to bed, when the death of Princess Margaret was made known on February 9.

What her private feelings were in a moment of such painful bereavement cannot be known. In a spirit which was characteristic of her, she declared that she would travel from Sandringham to her daughter's funeral service at St George's Chapel, Windsor, and she did. Even a fall in her sitting room at Sandringham two days before, as a result of which she sustained a cut arm, could not shake this resolve, despite the Queen's efforts to dissuade her.

The Queen, her elder daughter, survives her.

Queen Elizabeth the Queen Mother was born on August 4, 1900. She died on March 30, 2002, aged 101

—◈—

BARONESS CASTLE OF BLACKBURN

LABOUR FIREBRAND WHO LAUNCHED CHILD BENEFIT AND THE BREATHALYSER — AND A DOOMED ATTEMPT AT TRADE UNION REFORM

MAY 4, 2002

For more than 20 years Barbara Castle was Britain's best-known woman politician. As a minister she was astute, accomplished, combative and controversial, her successes eclipsing memories of Margaret Bondfield, Ellen Wilkinson and Florence Horsburgh, the only three previous women Cabinet ministers. She was the favourite of party activists, frequently topping the poll in the constituency section of the national executive. Ladbroke's regularly took bets on her becoming the first woman Prime Minister. This alerted some of her political opponents to the possibility of having a woman at No 10 and, to that extent, Castle, to her dismay, was sometimes said to have played a part in the election of Margaret Thatcher as Conservative leader and the longest-serving 20th-century inhabitant of No 10.

Barbara Castle was an easily identifiable figure from the moment she arrived at the Commons in the Labour landslide of 1945. Her temperament matched the fiery colour of her hair. Inevitably, the popular papers called her the Red Queen as she exhibited from her backbench seat below the gangway a pent-up fury about the slow pace of socialist reform. She had joined the Independent Labour Party when she was 16 and her fundamental beliefs never changed.

She once summed up her nature as being constitutionally incapable of turning down a challenge, however risky, and claimed that once she was embroiled in anything she had to try to make it work. This attitude was responsible for some of her greatest achievements: equal pay, the introduction of seat belts, the state earnings-related pension scheme (Serps), equal pension rights for women, child benefit, the statutory right to belong to a trade union — and, of course, the Breathalyser. "I suppose the Breathalyser's what I shall be remembered for," she used to say.

Unfortunately her self-confessed inability to resist a challenge means that she will be remembered also for her brave but forlorn bid to reform the trade unions, a move which almost ended her career and at one time endangered the position of her ally and patron, Harold Wilson. Her plan in 1969 to modernise the unions and stop unofficial strikes caused alarm even among her traditional friends on the Left. Opposition in the Parliamentary Labour Party, mobilised by James Callaghan and the late Douglas Houghton, proved too strong: the vital elements of her scheme were abandoned when the Chief Whip, Robert Mellish, told the Cabinet her Bill would never get through the Commons. That failure cost Castle any chance she might have had of becoming the first woman Prime Minister.

This was one of her few misjudgments about her party: her ministerial career was almost entirely successful. Although she was a woman operating in what was largely a male environment she hated being credited with a masculine mind. She managed to dominate most of her civil servants and colleagues without losing her essential femininity. She demanded to be taken for what she was and not for what she was born, though she was not above tears when all else had failed.

She was a socialist from childhood. Her father, Frank Betts, a tax inspector, was an enthusiastic propagandist for the ILP and it was not surprising that her first election address, written when she was six, consisted of a ten-word promise: "Dear citizens, vote for me, I will give you houses."

Betts was an unusual tax inspector. He was a voracious reader and Castle maintained that she was brought up in an aura of Greek plays, Irish ballads, medieval romances and Icelandic sagas — with Betts teaching himself various foreign languages at the breakfast table. His wife, Annie, was in the same mould. She was a milliner who became a William Morris socialist and Castle's early memories included dancing round the maypole every spring in her family's series of neglected gardens.

The gardens were numerous because of her father's profession. The Inland Revenue believed in keeping tax inspectors on the move and, though Castle was born in Chesterfield, her father was soon posted to Hull and on to Pontefract before moving to Bradford, where Castle went to Bradford Girls' Grammar School and won a scholarship to St Hugh's College, Oxford.

She fell in love with Oxford, but then began to hate it. She thought her college dull and stifling. She went up to read French but soon switched to philosophy, politics and economics, as she had decided her future lay in journalism or politics. She found Oxford in the early 1930s a mixture of sexual discrimination and sexual frustration. She found a welcome lack of discrimination in the Labour Club, where she became a leading figure, to the neglect of her studies. Her general unhappiness was reflected in her degree. She went down with a third.

By then her family had moved on to Hyde in Cheshire. She had no money and no prospects. The only job she could find was selling crystallised fruits in a Manchester department store, dressed improbably as Little Nell. She was considered bright enough to be transferred to the store's London headquarters; but there her ideas were thought too bright altogether, and she was sacked. She was saved from despair by the great love of her life, William Mellor, a former Editor of the *Daily Herald*.

She had met Mellor through the Socialist League. The attraction was immediate. Mellor, married, with a child, was in no position to marry her immediately and made this clear. Frank Betts told Barbara appreciatively: "I never expected a man to come and tell me his intentions towards my daughter were strictly dishonourable."

Mellor, 22 years older than she was, dominated their relationship. He launched a local government magazine and she became its secretary. Then, in 1937, he became Editor of a new magazine. It was called *Tribune*. The magazine was the brainchild of George Strauss, Aneurin Bevan and Sir Stafford Cripps — who provided most of its finance. Castle wrote a column for it in conjunction with a new friend, Michael Foot. But Mellor soon ceased to be Editor and in 1942 he died from a duodenal ulcer. Castle was desolate but next year she went as a delegate to her first Labour Party conference. The conference changed her life. It brought her fame, a job and a husband.

She spoke on the Beveridge Report and her speech was a sensation. The next day her picture was on the front page of the *Daily Mirror* and she was hailed as "The Voice of Youth" (she was actually 32). The paper immediately appointed her its housing correspondent. The night editor who made the all-important decision to make her the *Mirror*'s main story was Ted Castle. His first marriage had broken up and they began meeting regularly. He was also a left-winger and they shared speaking engagements. In July 1944, with the V1s falling on London, they were married. Nye Bevan and Jennie Lee were two of the four guests at their wedding breakfast at the Savoy.

The marriage lasted until Ted Castle's death 34 years later. In one way, their partnership was difficult. Ted Castle was a talented journalist who longed to be a politician but his only successful bid to get a constituency to fight ended in 1953 in a by-election defeat. He had to be content with a local government aldermanship, an appointment as Member of the European Parliament and a belated life peerage. This was probably just as well. In the Commons he would never have been more than a run-of-the-mill backbencher, while his wife — with many of the characteristics of a leading actress — always seemed destined to be a star. It nevertheless proved to be a successful marriage, despite their failure to have children, which Barbara Castle always described as the greatest sorrow of her life. Ted Castle's death in 1979 was an event from which she never fully recovered.

He was at her side during her triumphs and occasional disasters and never more so than during the 1945 general election. Her *Mirror* column and more platform successes brought her the chance to fight one of the two Blackburn seats, where she was selected after the constituency's women revolted against an all-male list. Her husband chauffeured and encouraged her throughout an exhilarating but exhausting campaign which she duly won.

In the Commons she lined up automatically with the Left. She was one of the Labour MPs who supported Dick Crossman's 1947 amendment calling on the Attlee Government to recast its foreign policy. She backed the new Keep Left Group. None of this prevented her political advancement. Cripps appointed her his PPS at the Board of Trade and his successor, Harold Wilson, retained her in the post and began an association which lasted 40 years.

In 1950 she was elected to the women's section of her party's national executive. Showing considerable courage, she decided to stand the next year for one of the seven seats in the constituency section. To her astonishment, she came second, only Bevan being ahead of her. The following year the left-wingers won six of the seven seats and the Bevanite movement became a reality.

The Bevanites were a curious organisation: despite right-wing allegations, they never truly developed into a party within a party. They were not tightly knit. Most of them mistrusted each other. Bevan himself, with a tendency to indolence, had no talent for conspiracy, unlike his front man, Ian Mikardo. Castle once summed up her leader: "Bevan wanted Bevanism without the Bevanites. He hated teamwork." But while Bevanism may have helped Castle's popularity with party members, it did not appear to have helped her in her constituency, where she scraped in at the 1955 election by just over 500 votes.

The next Parliament was not her happiest. She spoke largely on colonial affairs, concentrating on apartheid in South Africa, the Hola camp massacre in Kenya and the struggle for Enosis in Cyprus. It was a visit to Cyprus, where she was interpreted as having been critical of British troops, that got her into trouble with the right-wing press. She even launched a libel action against Christopher Chataway (which she lost), but she rode the storm, increasing her majority at Blackburn in 1959.

Then, in 1960, Wilson stood against Gaitskell for the party leadership and Castle nominated him. Predictably, Wilson lost and, just as predictably, Gaitskell dropped Castle from her post as front-bench spokesman on Ministry of Works affairs. But, when Gaitskell died in 1963, Wilson replaced him and Castle's star rose again. Once Labour won the 1964 election, Wilson made her Minister of Overseas Development. After nearly 20 years spent almost entirely on the back benches, Castle was in the Cabinet.

Office gave her the fulfilment her restless spirit demanded. Her civil servants appreciated the battles she won to obtain aid for developing countries. Even her enemies, who were plentiful by this time, were forced to admire the burning social conscience which caused the Cabinet and the Treasury to give more to her department than they ever intended.

Promotion came soon. Wilson appointed her Minister of Transport in 1965, using an advertising slogan of the time to flatter her by saying that he needed "a tiger in the tank". But at first her appointment was ridiculed as she had never held a driving licence, though this was not for want of effort. Michael Foot had once given her lessons, but after a series of near disasters, including being expelled from the Regent's Park circuit as a danger to other road users, both decided that regard for each other's safety demanded an end to the experiment.

She took advantage of preparatory work done by Tom Fraser, her predecessor, and produced no fewer than four White Papers before introducing her Transport Bill. This set up three new state bodies — the National Freight Corporation, the National Bus Company and the Scottish Transport Group. The Bill was an impressive achievement, though it failed in her original hope of solving the problem of the railways, where it soon became clear that there was no core of profitable lines and that continuing and increasing subsidies would be needed.

Her most spectacular act was the introduction of the Breathalyser. She was denounced by sections of the liquor trade, but fewer road deaths, reliably attributed to the consequent change in driving habits, made it one of the most beneficial acts of her career. At the time, she was against random breath-testing, but later, as a backbencher, she reversed her position.

Her time at Transport was a golden period. No section of new motorway was opened without a photograph of her. In 1967 she was voted the best-known member of the Cabinet after Wilson, and people began to talk of her, with some reason, as Wilson's successor. When she was promoted in 1968 to become Secretary of State for Employment and Productivity, with the rank and additional title of First Secretary, she seemed the Prime Minister's closest colleague.

But her new post, which carried such promise, always contained the possibility of disaster. Ray Gunter had famously described the old Ministry of Labour — before Castle renamed and reshaped it — as "the bed of nails". On the night of her appointment she wrote in her diary: "I am under no illusion that I may be committing political suicide." In her case she was nearly right.

Castle's first inheritance was a Prices and Incomes Bill about which she had reservations. She believed in the policy as a whole but her trouble was that large sections of the Labour movement did not. At the 1968 party conference a resolution to abandon the policy was carried by five million votes to just over a million. Castle ignored the warning. She came top of the voting for the executive's constituency section and, encouraged by this, she returned to London determined to do something about the unions.

Wilson, harried by unofficial strikes, had set up a royal commission under Lord Donovan in an effort to find a solution. The report was on Castle's desk. She accepted the general tenor of the report, which was fairly acceptable to the unions, but she went well beyond it. With her advisers she produced her own plan to delay and possibly defuse unofficial strikes. It called for pre-strike ballots, a 28-day conciliation period and settlements to be imposed where unofficial action came from inter-union disputes. It also proposed penalties — the hated penal clauses — if the new rules were breached.

At her husband's suggestion, she called the White Paper outlining her proposals *In Place of Strife*, an obvious echo of the title of Aneurin Bevan's book *In Place of Fear*. If she hoped by this to gain left-wing support, she failed. Her proposals produced more strife in her party than anything since the dispute over nuclear disarmament.

But Wilson was captivated by her plan. He saw it as a vote-winner and believed it could get through the Commons. He was soon disabused. In the spring of 1969, when it was debated in the House, 55 Labour MPs voted against it and some 40 abstained. Worse was to come.

Three weeks later, at a meeting of the national executive, James Callaghan, then Home Secretary, opposed the scheme. With the active help of Douglas Houghton, his old colleague from the tax officers' union who was now chairman of the Parliamentary Labour Party, he worked diligently to organise opposition. By this he risked being sacked from the Cabinet, but Wilson, fearful of union reaction, held back. Castle realised the danger, calling Callaghan "the snake lurking in the grass". They had been old opponents when on different wings of the party. Now they became outright enemies and remained so for the rest of their careers.

Wilson, who had hoped for a short, quick Bill, found himself bogged down. His Cabinet was divided. He began to display irritation, petulance and, it was said, some evidence of fear at Cabinet meetings. His position seemed in genuine danger, and supporters of Callaghan and Jenkins began seriously to weigh up their chances for the succession. But they could never combine and Wilson scraped through.

But the plan to tackle the unions did not. Robert Mellish, the new Chief Whip, announced it would never get through the Commons. Castle's original backers, including Peter Shore, Wilson's particular *protégé*, and Roy Jenkins, the Chancellor, withdrew their support. Wilson and Castle were isolated. The Prime Minister railed against the deserters, calling them "the weak sisters". The decisive meeting with the TUC ended with the unions offering "a solemn and binding undertaking" — later a much derided phrase — to intervene in unofficial strikes.

In fact, the unions kept to the agreement pretty well and unofficial strikes were reduced. But that was not the way

Parliament, the press and the public saw it. The next day many papers carried the headline "Surrender". And that was the impression which remained at the 1970 general election.

Castle was shattered by the experience. There was some consolation soon afterwards when her Equal Pay Bill got through Parliament, but her defeat by the unions haunted her. Eventually there was grudging admission by some of her opponents that perhaps they would have done better to accept the reforms proposed by Castle rather than wait for the swingeing limitations imposed by Margaret Thatcher. But this acknowledgement came too late to revive any chance she might have had of becoming the first woman Prime Minister or even the first woman Foreign Secretary. She was even voted out of the Shadow Cabinet.

Wilson, somewhat to his surprise, won a narrow victory in the first election of 1974 and Castle, equally to her surprise, was recalled to Government as Secretary of State for Health and Social Security. It was Wilson's tribute to her loyalty as well as testimony to her undiminished energy.

She repaid his confidence by showing all her old spirit in her new post. She launched an ambitious pensions plan and fought a series of battles with the hospital consultants in a bid to phase out pay-beds. She considered that her main achievement was the introduction of the Child Benefit Act, switching the male tax allowance for children directly to the mothers. This was in its final stages in 1976 when Wilson resigned. Callaghan sent for her almost immediately and said he wanted her post in order to make way

Barbara Castle: an "astute, accomplished combative and controversial" minister

for younger people. She said she was tempted to say: "Why not start with yourself?" She was 66; he was 64.

She had realised her Commons career was coming to end but wanted to see her Child Benefit Act through its final stages. She was devastated by her sudden dismissal. She felt she had been "discarded like a piece of old junk".

She sat out the rest of the Parliament and then, to general surprise, she left Westminster in 1979 and was elected to the European Parliament. She had been a consistent opponent of entry into what was then still called the Common Market and had campaigned in the 1975 referendum for Britain to leave. Now she came to work in Strasbourg herself. Though she could never be described as *communautaire*, she gradually relaxed her outright opposition.

While she continued to maintain that Britain had entered on the wrong terms, she now believed that her country should try to change the European Union from within. She became quite a figure at Strasbourg, leading the British Labour MPs and becoming vice-chairman of the Socialist Group. When she retired from the Parliament in 1989 she moved almost immediately to another — to the House of Lords as Baroness Castle of Blackburn.

Although she spoke occasionally in the Upper House her activities tended to diminish. Her eyesight was failing and so was a little of her spirit — which made the cruel caricature of her in David Hare's play *The Absence*

of War (1993) all the more hurtful. Despite voting for John Prescott in the 1994 leadership election, she initially became reconciled to the prospect of a Blair Government.

But before long she grew restive under the regime of new Labour. Although Tony Blair had put in an appreciated appearance at her 85th birthday party at Brighton in 1995, her attitude towards the leadership had by the following year become distinctly more critical. Just as in 1943 she had seized the headlines with a fiery speech calling on her leaders to show boldness in introducing the welfare state, so more than half a century later at Blackpool in 1996 she repeated the performance with another firework display that the party leadership could well have done without.

Within a few days of her 86th birthday, she had to be helped to the rostrum. But she soon proved that she knew how to use her frailty to her own advantage. She achieved what must have been a record for a speaker from the floor. She not only gained a standing ovation at the end of her speech but she also received one before she even reached the microphone.

In the early days of the Blair leadership she had been careful to support it — "anything for a Labour Government, dear" was the view she expressed in private — but she became increasingly anxious about the way new Labour was developing. Her apprehensions surfaced at the 1995 conference when she pleaded eloquently for more money to be spent on pensions. She savaged

Gordon Brown and Harriet Harman as effectively as she had assailed other leaders in the past. It was a Bevanite speech from one of the last survivors of the Bevanites.

By her last days, she was almost completely blind. This did not prevent her from enjoying being entertained at luncheons in London. "Read me the menu, dear, but don't tell me the prices," she would say. *Tribune* remained one of her great interests. It brought back memories of her first lover, Will Mellor, and her first triumphs. Recently she attended a lunch — at the Gay Hussar, inevitably — to produce ideas for invigorating the paper. Her idea was for a greater role for herself. She never underrated her worth. But blindness meant that she could never play the active role she wanted again.

In her last days she would refer often to her husband Ted. She had had other lovers, and so had he. But this apparently open marriage did not seem to diminish their relationship. When they entertained she insisted on giving Ted his role as the head of the household. "Of course Ted will carve" was her introduction to many a meal.

For a woman so conscious of her appearance, her blindness must have had an added terror. But to the end she was never less than beautifully dressed.

She is survived by her nephews and nieces, to whom she was devoted.

Baroness Castle of Blackburn, former Labour Government Minister, was born on October 6, 1910. She died on May 3, 2002, aged 91

JOAN LITTLEWOOD

LIFELONG REBEL WHO TRANSFORMED BRITISH THEATRE WITH HER COMMITMENT TO POLITICAL DRAMA AND WORKING-CLASS WRITERS AND PERFORMERS

SEPTEMBER 23, 2002

The British theatre revolution of the 1950s took place at opposite ends of London. George Devine ruled at the Royal Court in Sloane Square with the help of Tony Richardson, John Osborne and others. At the Theatre Royal, Stratford, E15, Joan Littlewood was running a totally different operation, with the almost single-handed support of her partner, Gerry Raffles.

Littlewood professed to have little time for the Court, declaring it to be soft-centred and middle-class. Her favourite writer of the period, Brendan Behan, added more fuel to the flames by describing Osborne as being "about as angry as Mrs Dale". But then Littlewood attacked most of those connected with the theatrical establishment. Olivier, Hall, even Peter Brook received her vituperation, often in unprintable terms, although several at the top of the profession were generous about her. Her special invective, though, was reserved, to the end of her life, for the gentlemen of the Arts Council, who at one time had refused even to pay the gas bill at the Theatre Royal.

Joan Littlewood believed in the class struggle and she preferred to engage working-class actors, many of whom had little education. Her familiar peaked cap, worn jauntily on the back of her head to keep her unruly hair in place, was a throwback to Bertolt Brecht.

She had put on the first British performance of his *Mother Courage*, playing the title role herself when needs be. But Brecht was no hero — Joan did not have heroes — and she complained when he sent in his "Gauleiters" to ensure that his work was being properly interpreted. Littlewood believed that art should emerge from life and to this end she sent her actors out to discover it in the local cafés and pubs.

There were plenty of both in Stratford, and some of her greatest successes grew out of straightforward East End language and attitudes. Among them were *Fings Ain't Wot They Used T'Be*, fairly early on, and *Oh What a Lovely War*, the biggest hit of all, which was translated into numerous languages and closed the Littlewood régime at E15.

Scripts were of little importance and often considered to be simply the basis for company improvisation. Brendan Behan's play *The Quare Fellow* comprised a few scraps of paper before Littlewood got to work. Shelagh Delaney's *A Taste of Honey* was little more than the experience of one teenage girl until more characters were fed into it. A Littlewood production generally contained a great deal of Littlewood script, although she rarely took any credit in the programme.

The Theatre Royal stands as Joan Littlewood's monument in a street now renamed Gerry Raffles Square. But she claimed never to have liked it. It was, she said, the only theatre they could get in 1953 at a rent of £20 a week, payable six and a half weeks in advance. It was decrepit and smelly, but Raffles and Littlewood restored it to a kind of Edwardian plush dowdiness, making sure that the huge stalls bar provided a music-hall atmosphere. There was no sentimentality on Littlewood's part. When she left Stratford in 1963, not yet 50 and at the height of her fame, it was without regrets.

Joan Maud Littlewood was born to be a rebel. She was the illegitimate daughter of a Cockney maidservant. Her grandfather, who laid cables for the GPO and remained illiterate to the end of his life, according to Joan, tracked down the man responsible and made him pay six shillings a week upkeep for his child until she reached 16. Joan grew up in Stockwell with three legitimate stepbrothers and sisters, but soon showed her independence. She started going to the Old Vic, not far away; was befriended by a female art teacher and shown Paris for the first time; and she won a scholarship as a teenager to RADA. She stayed there just long enough to have George Bernard Shaw tell her how to play Ellie in *Heartbreak House*, before deciding to seek her fame and fortune in America by way of hitch-hiking to Liverpool.

She did not even get as far as the Mersey. She was taken beneath the wing of a producer for BBC Manchester and found herself, still well under 20, as part of Mancunian literary life with a strong left-wing flavour. She met a young writer and poet called Jimmie Miller, who had just returned from Germany, completely under the influence of Brecht and the agit-prop theatre. Miller was applying to the North West the lessons he had learnt in Europe, performing plays and sketches with a political message for the workers of the area's factories and mills.

Joan was quickly roped in to Miller's company, which by the end of 1933 was calling itself Theatre of Action. Its manifesto was uncompromising: "The Theatre of Action realises that the very class which plays the chief part in contemporary history — the class upon which the prevention of war and the defeat of reaction solely depends — is debarred from expression in the present day theatre. This theatre will perform, mainly in working-class districts, plays which express the life and struggles of the workers. Politics, in its fullest sense, means the affairs of the people. In this sense the plays done will be political."

That, more or less, was Littlewood's credo for the rest of her career. Another constant would be the mix of directness and sophistication already evident in Theatre of Action's work. Littlewood liked amateur performers, free of the mannerisms that may come with a drama-school training. She would always encourage her actors to retain their regional accents, and she would show, time and again, that working-class people and working-class speech had a place on the serious stage.

But if the political message was simple, the dramatic methods showed a familiarity with theatrical traditions from Commedia dell'arte to Jacobean drama and Chinese theatre, not to mention the well-assimilated influences of Meyerhold, Brecht, Piscator, Laban and the rest of the international avant garde. Miller and Littlewood were in 1934 even offered scholarships by the Soviet Academy of Theatre and Cinema to study in Moscow, but they ran out of funds while waiting for their visas to come through.

Theatre of Action and its equally short-lived successor Theatre Union drew some of their material, in the "living newspaper" tradition, directly from the lives of those to whom performances were addressed. (During the run of one of these topical shows, *Last Edition*, staged in Manchester just after the start of the Second World War, Miller and Littlewood were arrested, fined £20 each for disturbing the peace, and bound over for two years.) But the repertoire also embraced Hans Schlumberg's ambitious anti-war play *Miracle at Verdun* (with a cast of eighty), Lope de Vega's *Fuente Ovejuna*, staged as a fundraiser for the Republican cause in the Spanish Civil War, and the first European production of *Waiting for Lefty* by Clifford Odets.

Formally innovative, the company aimed always, so Miller would recall, "to find a theatrical language and style that people understood, which would move them, but not talk down to them".

Littlewood and Miller were married, but the partnership did not last. There was another member of the group, three years younger than Littlewood, who had taken her eye: Gerry Raffles. His dark wavy hair and delight in singing ballads suggested that he was an Irish rover, an image he did nothing to dispel. In fact he was a Manchester Grammar School boy, who had run away from his Jewish home to join the theatre. Jimmie Miller was to become better known as the folk-singer Ewan MacColl. Littlewood, in later life, remembered him less than fondly: "He became boring. He went down the drain. He was a snob, Jimmie, a great talent but always plugging the same thing. That beard, it was very bad."

Littlewood joined the payroll of the BBC. Her programmes there included *The Classic Soil*, a 1939 radio documentary on social conditions in Manchester which took its cue from Friedrich Engels's famous survey of nearly 100 years before. But she was dismissed during the war because of her left-wing connections. A similar stance was taken by ENSA and both facts are gleefully recorded in Littlewood's *Who's Who* entry. At the end of the war members of Theatre of Action regrouped under the title of Theatre Workshop, with Manchester still as its base. It was funded mainly by the demobilisation grants of its members. Productions on a shoestring were taken up the mill valleys and Miller, writing as James T. Miller, had a success with a version of *Lysistrata* and his own original *Uranium 235*. Both were directed by Littlewood and both were seen in London, with *Uranium 235* transferring to the Comedy Theatre.

Theatre Workshop became known as an impeccably left-wing company, winning the support of politicians such as Nye Bevan and, most particularly, Tom Driberg. The Arts Council, however, was suspicious and unenthusiastic. A long war between Littlewood and the men from the Council began. Raffles had been made company manager and it was his energy, coupled with a readiness to travel with little cash in hand and even fewer foreign words at his command, that got Workshop its first overseas engagements.

There was a triumphant visit to Czechoslovakia and more success in Stockholm. But at home the company worked from a dilapidated truck, not unlike Mother Courage's canteen.

Both Raffles and Littlewood saw that this itinerant existence could not go on for ever and they looked for a permanent home, with its attendant permanent audience. The only place on offer at the right rent was the Theatre Royal, Stratford. Littlewood was not enthusiastic and declared roundly — and accurately — that "it stank". It was not even on the main road, but was conveniently close to the Tube station. Raffles and Littlewood set about cleaning it up themselves. The tradition continued: years later, when Barbara

Windsor came to audition, she was greeted by a woman with a duster whom she took to be the char, but who was, of course, Littlewood.

Theatre Workshop began with their normal repertory, which mixed Jonson and Marlowe with politically committed contemporaries such as Sartre and Hasek. The locals were friendly enough, but slow to buy tickets. Littlewood was keen to find new plays — Miller had long since gone off to devote himself to folk-songs. In 1956 a bundle of 17 beer-stained pages arrived, which turned out to be the beginnings of Brendan Behan's *The Quare Fellow*. Raffles sent the price of an air fare to the author in Dublin, asking him to come over and work on the play. Behan promptly drank the cash, so Raffles then posted the air ticket itself, non-convertible into Guinness. *The Quare Fellow* became Theatre Workshop's first big success, not without trouble from Littlewood's new enemy the Lord Chamberlain, and transferred to the West End. Behan became a familiar figure in the Stratford pubs and followed up with *The Hostage*.

Shelagh Delaney's *A Taste of Honey* was turned into something actable, also transferring "up West" (in the Stratford argot) as well as being filmed. Littlewood was none too pleased when Delaney took her next play to the Royal Court, but cheered up a little when it turned out a failure. Joan had gathered around her a proper company of regular collaborators which included Victor Spinetti, Howard Goorney, Murray Melvin and James (David) Booth. She disliked calling them actors. "It's an insult to them. I called them nuts, crackpots, tossers... I love them, the bastards. I never told them so." A Stratford style was emerging based on improvisation, ensemble and sheer exuberance. There was no hanging about in a Littlewood production: if things started to become boring, then a song and dance livened them up.

Nothing exemplified Joan Littlewood's ability to transmute the skimpiest of material into gold than *Fings Ain't Wot They Used T'Be*. Frank Norman's original script was wafer-thin and rested heavily on its use of then unfamiliar East End slang. Some of Lionel Bart's songs were all too familiar. But *Fings* took off, another Stratford money-spinner.

Any cash from transfers to the West End was carefully ploughed back into the Theatre Royal. But Littlewood almost resented her success and did not care for her dealings with theatre impresarios. She became restless and at one point walked out on the company to set up a film in Nigeria based on a story by Wole Soyinka. The project turned into a disaster. Back in London she did succeed in filming *Sparrers Can't Sing*, which was not one of Stratford's better plays. The camera crew was mildly surprised about the ripeness of language that flowed from the lips of the film's director (who knew nothing about cinema technique). But at least it survives, and with it one of the few mementoes of the Stratford style.

The idea of Stratford's last and greatest success, *Oh What a Lovely War*, came to Gerry Raffles through a long-running radio programme by Charles Chilton based on the songs of the First World War. Littlewood pieced them together, showing false optimism changing into the enforced contemplation of mass death.

Richard Attenborough later filmed it, but this was a starry and inflated version of what struck home harder at the Theatre Royal.

Littlewood knew that the Stratford days were almost over. She was bored with the theatre and had not succeeded with film. Efforts to combine with Lionel Bart on a Robin Hood musical, *Twang!*, turned into one of the West End's biggest flops of the decade. So she devoted her energies to trying to create a Fun Palace, a Utopian 20th-century equivalent of the Vauxhall Pleasure Gardens, where children and adults alike could have a good time. Foreign governments offered her the sites and the money, but the project came to nothing.

Then in 1975 Gerry Raffles died suddenly, mainly as a result of consistent overwork. Littlewood, who throughout her life had despised all sentimentality, became a changed woman. She left Britain and set up her home in the small French town of Vienne, where Raffles had his final illness. She formed an unlikely friendship with Baron Philippe de Rothschild, which began as a literary correspondence. She called him "Guv". Together they collaborated on a book, *Milady Vine*. She wrote her own autobiography, *Joan's Book*, an honest, rambling and lengthy account of her life. But its 800 pages stop short of Gerry's death.

In her eightieth year she came back to London to promote the book, allowing some of the interviews she had given so reluctantly in the past. ("I hate the bloody book. It's not much good," she said.) She also, for the first time in 20 years, revisited the scene of her earlier success. She had vowed not to return to Stratford after Raffles died, but the death of one of her protégés, the writer and director Ken Hill, made her change her mind, and when the musical Hill had been rehearsing went on at the Theatre Royal, she was in the audience for the first night. To the end, the Bert Brecht cap still sat askew on auburn frizzy hair, the features were those of a perky pug, she was combative, ungrateful, rude — and still tossing obscenities at the Arts Council. The old rebel had not changed.

She had no children.

Joan Littlewood, theatre director and writer, was born on October 6, 1914. She died on September 20, 2002, aged 87

ELIZABETH, COUNTESS OF LONGFORD

BIOGRAPHER, HISTORIAN AND
THE INDOMITABLE MATRIARCH
OF A LEFT-LEANING DYNASTY
OF WRITERS

OCTOBER 24, 2002

Elizabeth Longford was matriarch of the most powerful and well-connected literary dynasty in the land — that of the Pakenhams, Frasers, Pinters and Billingtons — and her life was spent among intellectuals for whom the production of books of all kinds was at least as natural as the production of children. Her own historical writings combined erudition and thorough research with wide appeal. As Countess of Longford, wife of the 7th Earl (Frank Pakenham), she was a notable crusader in society and in Labour politics for many a losing cause.

It was a grand and indomitable life, which has already been the subject of a biography. In her early years she occasionally overlapped with the Bloomsbury Group, and her own clan has some of the same fascination. Like them, the Longford family are pillars of the left wing of the Establishment, and sure enough, Elizabeth Longford kept a diary and encouraged all her children to do the same. Longford thinking was progressive, though always sensibly, never militantly so, yet their life perfectly represented the conservatism of comfort, divided as it was between Chelsea in the week and an 18th-century house at Hurst Green, East Sussex, at weekends.

Elizabeth was the daughter of N. B. Harman, a Unitarian Harley Street ophthalmic surgeon, and Katherine Chamberlain, a niece of Joseph Chamberlain; she was thus a second cousin of Austen and Neville. She was educated at Headington School, Oxford, where her main talent was thought to be drawing, though she wrote a Gothic novel at 13 and dreamt of becoming an actress. But her mother was a determined proponent of proper education for girls, so she applied to Oxford. Rejection stiffened her resolve: she took coaching for a year and applied again, winning a place at Lady Margaret Hall.

There she was regarded as one of the cleverest and most attractive women undergraduates of the day. She became a friend of W. H. Auden, Stephen Spender, John Betjeman and David Cecil — and Quintin Hogg later said: "There was not an undergraduate in Oxford who wouldn't have considered it a privilege to hold an umbrella over her head."

She received five proposals of marriage. Two were from her tutors, Maurice Bowra, who persuaded her to switch from English to Greats, and Hugh Gaitskell, who had a considerable effect on her left-liberal convictions. After going down — without the expected first, perhaps because a friend of hers had just been killed in an accident — she spent six years lecturing in English, politics and economics for the Workers' Educational Association.

Gaitskell was instrumental in her social as well as her socialist development. In 1927 he took her to Magdalen College ball, at which she first glimpsed Frank Pakenham. The following evening, at the New College ball, she saw him again, and kissed him. Yet it was four years before they married, and she remembered that, in a year's courtship while they were at Oxford, she never invited him to anything on his own.

When they married he was a committed Conservative, working for the party. Nevertheless she stood unsuccessfully as Labour candidate for Cheltenham in 1935. She was subsequently Labour's candidate for King's Norton, Birmingham, until 1943, and stood for Oxford City in 1950. She was never elected, but she did make one convert, her husband joining the party in 1936.

Conversely, she became a Roman Catholic in 1946, six years after her husband had converted without telling her. She was won over by reading Evelyn Waugh's biography of Edmund Campion, not knowing that Waugh had opposed her marriage — as became apparent when his letters were published.

Frank Pakenham's political career began in earnest after he resigned his commission because of ill-health in 1940. He soon became personal assistant to William Beveridge, and from 1948 to 1951 he was Minister for Aviation. For six months he was First Lord of the Admiralty, and by 1964 he was Leader of the House of Lords. He went on to campaign against pornography and for penal reform and clemency in several high-profile cases; "hate the sin, love the sinner" was his maxim. For 60 years he was also a prolific, didactic author.

Meanwhile, the Longfords had four sons and four daughters in quick succession, claiming to be able to determine their sex by attention to the body chemistry. It was a most extraordinarily energetic and driven family. "When there were eight of them at home with all their activities and high spirits and me being so ambitious," she said, "we were all very competitive and quarrelsome. I transferred the intellectual snobbery on to the children and pushed the eldest ones too much." On the other hand, she felt that too many parents nowadays abandon their responsibility towards their children when they reach their teens, out of misplaced regard for their independence when they are still too young to know how to exercise it.

The Labour Party took exception to a potential MP having so many children, and when the choice came, she put family first without much regret. As it turned out, her *métier* was not politics but writing, which she began to do at the behest of newspapers wanting her to dispense advice on family life.

She produced some excellent historical books and a fine volume of memoirs, although she turned out potboilers too.

Yet it was not until she was in her fifties that she published her first book, *Jameson's Raid* (1960). This was at the time the best account of that controversial episode of 1895-96, although later investigations and C. M. Woodhouse's publication of the famous "missing telegrams" in his life of Cecil Rhodes suggested that Joseph Chamberlain was more deeply involved than she had believed.

In 1964 Longford published the book that made her name, *Victoria RI*, a superbly sympathetic yet realistic portrait. There had not been a substantial life of the Queen for many years, and it is not too much to say that she was the first biographer to make Victoria into a living and understandable human being. It was deservedly a bestseller and she was awarded the James Tait Black Memorial Prize for non-fiction.

Next, at the request of the late Duke of Wellington, she tackled the monumental task of writing a two-volume biography of the Iron Duke, whose unhappy wife, Kitty Pakenham, was a great-great aunt of her husband. The first volume, *Wellington: Years of the Sword*, appeared in 1969 and won the *Yorkshire Post* Prize. It was widely acclaimed and certainly disproved the suggestion then current that women could not write about war. The description of Waterloo is a wonderful set piece, and the whole book is one of the finest historical biographies in the English language. That year Longford was one of six authors in the family who were collective guests of honour at a unique Foyles lunch.

Wellington: Pillar of State came out in 1972. Although both scholarly and highly readable, it was not quite on the level of the first volume — but then the duke's career after 1815 was something of an anticlimax, so it may be that the problem was intractable.

None of her later books was of the calibre of *Victoria RI* and *Wellington*, but all were sensible, stylishly written and gave pleasure to many. Having met Winston Churchill at Chartwell in 1938, she produced a pictorial biography of him in 1974, which was followed by one of Byron in 1976. She then spent three years in the archives of the Fitzwilliam Museum, Cambridge, reading the papers of the poet Wilfrid Scawen Blunt, who married Byron's granddaughter. Her biography did full justice to his lurid sexual life, though she was disgusted to find that he had once sent the same love poem to three women on the same day. Her anthology of verse by poets interred in Westminster Abbey, *Poets' Corner* (1992), was an excellent idea but displayed evidence, in the editing at least, of too much haste.

Meanwhile, she made something of a corner in books about royalty, beginning in 1974 with a splendidly illustrated and very enjoyable short survey of *The Royal House of Windsor*. This was followed by *The Queen Mother* (in a series published by Marks & Spencer, 1981), *Elizabeth R* (1983), *The Oxford Book of Royal Anecdotes* (1989) and *Letters to Princess Louise* (1991).

Needless to say, an aristocrat writing about royalty was an irresistible recipe for publishers, readers and Americans, and she was a staunch monarchist, whatever others in the Labour Party might say.

She abhorred the Andrew Morton school of graphically revealing biography, but could not entirely avoid becoming caught up in the controversies over the Prince of Wales's marriage. While writing *Royal Throne: The Future of the Monarchy*, which appeared in 1993, she was granted an interview by Prince Charles, but as his separation from his wife became public, she found herself rewriting chapter after chapter. "I don't like the philosophy of 'doing your own thing' which was injected into social life about 20 years ago," she commented. "One can see why it's caught on, but your own thing may not be other people's thing. You've to try to do your best for those around you as well as yourself."

Having been granted permission by the Queen to investigate Queen Victoria's correspondence with her eldest daughter, Longford published a final short life of Victoria in 1999.

Her autobiography, *The Pebbled Shore* (1986), was a stylish account of the social and political scene before and after the Second World War. She was not, she confessed, an introspective person, and she was surprised at the effect that writing the book had on

her: "It brought home that all these happy times really were past, the children being born, and Frank and I being young. I'd never quite acknowledged that these things were over and were never going to happen again. It was a melancholy discovery."

To the end she retained immense charm and great beauty and remained active, attending the funeral earlier this year of the Queen Mother, and appearing on *Desert Island Discs*. She read widely (*War and Peace* counted as holiday reading), and dabbled happily in watercolour. She was a trustee of the National Portrait Gallery, 1968-78, and a member of the advisory committee of the Victoria and Albert Museum, 1969-75. She received an honorary doctorate from Sussex University in 1970 and was appointed CBE in 1974.

Her husband died last year. She is survived by four sons and three daughters. Among the children are the historians Antonia Fraser and Thomas Pakenham, the novelist Rachel Billington and the poet Judith Kazantzis. The journalist Catherine Pakenham was killed at 23 in a car accident in 1969, and a prize for women journalists was established in her name. *Elizabeth, Countess of Longford, CBE, author, was born on August 30, 1906. She died on October 23, 2002, aged 96*

KATHARINE HEPBURN

THOROUGHLY ORIGINAL
ACTRESS WHO THRIVED ON
BEING AS HAUGHTY AND
INDEPENDENT OFF SCREEN
AS SHE WAS ON IT

JULY 1, 2003

Katharine Hepburn was not one of Hollywood's more lovable stars, nor did she ever aim to be. She once observed of the young Maggie Smith: "She has the real star thing, the quality to irritate," and that same quality was very important throughout Hepburn's six decades of screen stardom. There were always those filmgoers who could not stand her at any price, to such an extent that when, in 1938, a leading distributor labelled about a dozen top box office stars "box office poison", Hepburn was the only one on the list that anyone afterwards remembered.

This was partly because her reaction was so characteristic: while all the rest shrugged and went on with their careers, she stormed out of Hollywood, vowing vengeance, and promptly achieved it by scoring her biggest success on Broadway in Philip Barry's play *The Philadelphia Story*, to return to Hollywood in triumph in the film version of the play. By the end of her career she had won a record four

Oscars for best leading actress — the first for *Morning Glory* and the last for *On Golden Pond*, almost 50 years later. In between she forged a famous alliance with Spencer Tracy, and their partnership in *Guess Who's Coming to Dinner?* led her to an Oscar in 1968.

Where so many other stars were pathetically dependent on feeling that the audience loved them, she was always an awkward customer, determined to do things her own way or not at all. When one of her later films, *Olly, Olly, Oxen Free*, was widely accounted by preview audiences a disaster that could be turned into a hit with some judicious re-editing, she firmly turned down the assistance, freely proffered, of such expert friends as George Cukor and Anthony Harvey, choosing rather to let the film go its own way to oblivion.

On screen she never hesitated to play difficult, aggressive, unlovable characters, though the cynic might observe that she always (or nearly always) made audiences love her before the final fade-out. Certainly it is true, and probably significant, that the two roles of her maturity that she remained unhappy with and did not care to discuss were in *Suddenly, Last Summer* and *Long Day's Journey into Night*, neither of which, in different ways, allowed this final access of audience sympathy.

Many leading traits of her character, personal and professional, must have come from her early background, which was exceptional by Hollywood standards. Katharine Houghton Hepburn's family was socially distinguished and guaranteed her financial independence from the outset. Her father, Thomas Norval Hepburn, was a famous urologist and supported her mother, Katharine Houghton, in her militant campaigns for women's suffrage and birth control; she became the chairwoman in Washington of the National Committee on Federal Legislation for Birth Control. The young Katharine took part in suffrage marches and met prominent feminists such as Margaret Sanger and Emmeline Pankhurst. She was always encouraged to think for herself.

After education at Bryn Mawr, the exclusive women's college near Philadelphia that her mother had attended, she determined that she wanted to become a professional actress, and no one stood in her way. She had previously wanted to be a surgeon, but said that acting seemed to provide unlimited opportunities for both sexes and she was assisted by letters of introduction to leading figures in the theatrical world. Though she paid her dues with a succession of small parts and time in the sticks, she managed to get herself fired from, or walked out of, a number of promising situations before making it to Broadway, playing the Amazon heroine in *The Warrior's Husband* in 1932. Her entrance was a spectacular 15ft leap on to the stage, which she performed each night without breaking a bone.

From there it proved an unexpectedly quick passage to Hollywood stardom in her first film role, the daughter of a veteran who returns unexpectedly to haunt his family after years in a mental institution, in the film of Clemence Dane's controversial play, *A Bill of Divorcement* (1932). Visibly unsure, and already very mannered, the 25-year-old Hepburn at once commanded the screen (which she had always affected to despise), particularly in an early scene in which she crossed the room and lay in front of the fireplace. The director, George Cukor, was to become a lifelong friend and counsellor, and had a house built specially for her lover, Spencer Tracy, on his estate. He went on to direct Hepburn in many of her most successful films, including *Keeper of the Flame* (1942), *Adam's Rib* (1949) and *Pat and Mike* (1952), in all of which Tracy co-starred.

Hepburn was emerging as one of the most effective and individual new stars of the early sound cinema. Less successful was her return to the stage; when she appeared in *The Lake* in 1933, the play closed after only 55 performances and inspired Dorothy Parker's famous line that Hepburn ran "the gamut of emotions from A to B". But her position on the silver screen was confirmed that same year in *Morning Glory*, for which she won the first of her Oscars in the tailor-made role of a difficult but aspiring young actress.

Until the "box office" slur in 1938 Hepburn's career was an almost uninterrupted succession of triumphs in Hollywood. Her way of dealing with Hollywood was a perfect demonstration of "if you want them to run after you, just walk the other way", though whether this was by design or because she was incapable of behaving differently has remained unclear. She certainly did not do any of the usual things a Hollywood aspirant would do, insisting on striding around in slacks, keeping her private life entirely private and retaining a distant hauteur in her relationships with tycoons unless, like Howard Hughes, they were as eccentric and unpredictable as herself. Her motto could have been "let them hate, provided they fear", and undoubtedly many Hollywood high-ups did both.

But there was no arguing with the success of films such as *Little Women* (1933), *Alice Adams* (1935), *Quality Street* (1937), *Stage Door* (1937) and *Bringing Up Baby* (1938), the archetypal screwball comedy of the 1930s; it could even excuse the occasional misfire like *Sylvia Scarlett* (1935), which teamed her with Cary Grant and the director George Cukor in an uneasy version of Compton Mackenzie's transvestite comedy, insisted on despite all advice to the contrary.

In all of these films she played variations, pushed towards farce, comedy or occasionally pathos, of her own perceived character: headstrong, independent and at times arrogant, the sort of person people wanted to shake even while they loved her to distraction. This was fair enough as a Hollywood style — what else, after all, did any important star do at the time? — though, remarkably, Hepburn continued to be taken seriously as an actress rather than dismissed as a mere movie star.

She departed from Hollywood after the *succès d'estime* of *Holiday* (1938), also co-starring Cary Grant and directed by Cukor, only to return on her own terms in triumph with the film version of *The Philadelphia Story* (1940), written by the same playwright as *Holiday*, Philip Barry. Howard Hughes offered to finance it even before he had read it and, with a loan from Hughes, she put up a quarter of the costs and bought the screen rights from Barry for $25,000. It was a hit and within a few days of opening, MGM offered her $175,000 for the rights.

This meant that she could dictate that her salary was $75,000, the director was Cukor and that her co-stars would be James Stewart and Cary Grant. Tracy Lord was the definitive Hepburn role and the film version was a hit. It could hardly have done more to confirm everything that everyone had ever thought about her.

For her next film, *Woman of the Year* (1942), her chosen director was George Stevens — with whom she had had a fling when he directed her in *Alice Adams* and *Quality Street*. This film would also change the course of her life since it brought her together for the first time with Spencer Tracy. They starred together in nine films and remained deeply involved for the remaining 27 years of his life.

When they first met she was 33 and he was 42. The story went that she had just come from a meeting with MGM executives, for which she had worn heels which added four inches to her 5ft 7in; Tracy was two inches taller. "I'm afraid I'm a little tall for you, Mr Tracy," she said. "Don't worry, Miss Hepburn," he replied. "I'll cut you down to my size." And he did. Years later, she said: "I struggled to change all the qualities I felt he didn't like. I was his."

Tracy and Hepburn were together for years, but neither lived together nor went out together; it was said that Tracy and his wife, Louise, could not get divorced on account of being Catholics, but in fact Louise was Episcopalian. Hepburn's relationship with him was an open secret, handled with great dignity by all parties — even, surprisingly, the Hollywood press. She was his secretary, companion and chauffeur — and frequently his nurse.

On screen they were chalk and cheese: he was the roughneck made good, she the society lady able to keep her end up in any amatory and professional tussles through class and gender. But as she grew older — and she did nothing to disguise or hinder the ageing process — her standard characterisation of the difficult but magnetic young woman, relations with whom tended to be a minefield worth traversing, gradually shifted into that of the prickly, cranky old maid whose life might yet be transfigured by affection and romance. A key film in this transition was John Huston's *The African Queen* (1951), in which she was a missionary navigating dangerous waters with Humphrey Bogart as a hard-drinking captain of a disreputable motor launch. The film was shot in the Belgian Congo, from where she wrote long letters to Tracy every day.

The transition was complete when she made *Summertime* (1955), in which she enjoyed a romantic interlude with the deceptively seductive Rossano Brazzi in Venice. In one scene she had to fall backwards into a canal, from which she caught a form of conjunctivitis that led to the teary look that remained with her for the rest of her career. In 1959 and 1962 came the two effective but aberrant, unsympathetic characterisations: as Tennessee Williams's implacable Southern matron in *Suddenly, Last Summer* and Eugene O'Neill's drug-addicted mother in *Long Day's Journey Into Night*, both of which, despite her dislike of the roles, won her Oscar nominations.

In the early 1960s Tracy's health deteriorated. Hepburn retired from the cinema to care for him, and by 1966 he was recovering. It was then that the producer Stanley Kramer offered them roles in *Guess Who's Coming to Dinner?* (1967), as an upper-middle-class couple whose only child — eventually played by Hepburn's niece, Katharine Houghton — surprises them with her fiancé, a black doctor, played by Sidney Poitier. It was completed 17 days before Tracy's death, and Hepburn said that she was never able to watch the film.

It won Hepburn her second Oscar, which was widely felt to be an award for her work with Tracy over the years, and to mark the end of their careers. But with typical perversity she bounced back the very next year with one of the finest of all her performances, as Eleanor of Aquitaine in Anthony Harvey's distinguished version of James Goldman's play *The Lion in Winter* (1968). This time the Oscar was won in earnest, even if it was shared with Barbra Streisand as a result of the only tie in the history of the Academy Awards.

Her subsequent films were mostly more distinguished than popular, including two grand movies for television directed by her old mentor George Cukor, *Love Among the Ruins*, which teamed her for the first time with Laurence Olivier, and a new version of Emlyn Williams's classic *The Corn Is Green*.

But she could still command popularity if she wished it. In 1969 she returned to the Broadway stage, after a long absence, in, of all things, a musical based on the life of Chanel called *Coco*, in which she scored a great personal triumph, making no claims to a singing voice but working out her own form of speech song as effectively as Rex Harrison's in *My Fair Lady*. Six years later she was back on Broadway, with less success, in *A Matter of Gravity*. Even on film she could still reach a considerable audience, and did so in 1975 with John Wayne in a comedy Western called *Rooster Cogburn*, which was really a crafty reworking of *The African Queen*, in a different setting.

It must have seemed to everybody that her career, somewhat impeded in its later stages by Parkinson's disease, was coasting to a dignified conclusion, when along came *On Golden Pond* (1981) to confound all expectations.

She played the brusque but understanding wife of crabby old Henry Fonda — who throughout the film wore the favourite hat of Tracy's that Hepburn had given him — in a rosy but not too sentimentalised view of old age. It was the first time that they had worked together, and it proved to be one of the great hits of the decade. Both won Oscars, hers an unprecedented fourth.

Subsequently Hepburn made occasional appearances on stage and on television, most notably in *One Christmas*, a television movie based on a short story by Truman Capote. She devoted much of her energy to writing a short book about the making of *The African Queen* and a more ambitious autobiography, *Me*, for which she earned a $4 million advance. It was cranky and teasing in what it revealed and what it glossed over — as both her admirers and her detractors must by then have expected.

Hepburn began by being, and remained throughout her life, totally original and quite unlike anyone else who starred in Hollywood. For six decades she was an inescapable fact of Hollywood life, more durable than any of the companies she battled with, and more honoured than any other star. Unlike many of those whom she met along the way, she did not bow to celebrity; she considered the greatest luxury imaginable to be "nobody telling you to get out of the bathroom".

Nor she did bow to the studios. During the hearings of the House Un-American Activities Committee in

1947, she spoke out publicly against censorship, against the wishes of her studio boss, Louis B. Mayer. As a result, J. Edgar Hoover wanted to expose her relationship with Tracy to the public. Hoover was advised by Richard Nixon that this would backfire.

Though her private life was kept scrupulously to herself, it is known that Hepburn, who said that marriage was not a natural state, married in 1928 the socialite stockbroker Ludlow Ogden Smith, and that the marriage was quietly dissolved in 1934. "I married him, spent all his money, broke his heart and discarded him," she said. Though her biographers have hinted at other relationships, notably with Howard Hughes, the central emotional involvement of her life was clearly the 27 years that she spent with Spencer Tracy.

Katharine Hepburn, actress, was born on May 12, 1907. She died on June 29, 2003, aged 96

———

GERTRUDE EDERLE

FIRST WOMAN TO SWIM THE CHANNEL, WHOSE CROSSING KNOCKED TWO HOURS OFF THE FASTEST TIME BY A MAN

DECEMBER 2, 2003

Gertrude Ederle was the first woman to swim the English Channel, a feat accomplished despite widespread belief at the time that this was impossible for any female, let alone one aged only 19.

However, when the American landed at Kingsdown in Kent, on August 6, 1926, her time of 14 hours 39 minutes was almost two hours faster than any of her five male predecessors, a dynasty which had begun with Captain Matthew Webb in 1875.

After a crossing completed despite severe weather conditions, she was taken by escort boat to Dover. There, she had to wait for two hours for the immigration authorities to allow her to disembark, because they did not believe that she had swum the Channel. Her comment to the world was: "I knew it could be done. It had to be done. And I did it."

She was subsequently accorded a ticker-tape parade in New York, met President Coolidge, toured in vaudeville and played herself in a film entitled *Swim, Girl, Swim.*

Gertrude Ederle was born into a New York family, which was devoted to swimming. She said in 1926: "I have three sisters and two brothers and they all swim like fishes, even my youngest brother, who is only six years old." She was renowned for her excellence at shorter distances, taking part in the 1924 Olympics in Paris. Although travelling to Europe took the edge off her form, she still took bronze medals in the 100 and 400 metres freestyle and then swam the lead-off leg for the US team that set a world record in winning the 4 x 100 metres relay.

Ederle then started a long-distance swimming career. In 1925, she completed the 21 miles from the tip of Manhattan to Sandy Hook, New Jersey, in seven hours 11 minutes, breaking the men's record. She then tried the English Channel but was forced to give up seven miles off the English coast after swimming for about nine hours. A worried trainer grabbed her when she started coughing, and under the rules of Channel swimming she was immediately disqualified.

She began preparing for another attempt the following year. Ederle was slightly built, and so did not possess much subcutaneous fat, which is valuable for warding off some of the worst effects of the cold water. However, she presaged the later development of marathon swimming because she was sufficiently fast to complete the course before becoming overcome by hypothermia. She used the crawl stroke, which was then still unusual for long-distance swimming. Many people preferred the trudgen because, they believed, wrongly, that the crawl was too tiring to sustain for many hours. One of her American contemporaries, Aileen Soule, also pointed to a key attribute for her success, remarking: "She had the stubbornness."

On August 6, 1926, she set off at 7.05am on the ebb tide from Cap Gris Nez, with Thomas Burgess, who had been the second man to complete the crossing, as her trainer on the accompanying boat. Little was then known about the importance of a regular intake of carbohydrates and she did not take her first meal until midday, when she consumed some chicken broth and cold chicken. With weather forecasting also less precise than it is nowadays, she then had to combat conditions that would have postponed the attempt had she known about them in advance.

The tide, choppy sea and driving southwest wind forced her off-course and Burgess tried to persuade her to give up. But she replied: "What for?" The morale of those in the escort boat, rather than of the swimmer herself, was maintained by a phonograph playing records such as *Let Me Call You Sweetheart* and *After the Ball is Over*. Soon, however, the phonograph began to jump grooves because of the movement of the boat.

The weather continued to worsen, with white-capped waves being commonplace, but Ederle survived the ordeal to land at Kingsdown. *The Times* was so impressed that it devoted a leader to her performance, stating that "her intention not to try again is sensible". Her record time stood for 24 years until another American, Florence Chadwick, achieved 13 hours 23 minutes in 1950.

Ederle returned to the US to be fêted as a national celebrity, a role which she performed, with attractive modesty, until 1933, when she fell down a flight of stairs, damaging her spine. Although she took part in the 1939 World's Fair, she was now suffering from deafness, something with which she had been afflicted since a childhood bout of measles. By the 1940s she was completely deaf, and she then devoted her life to teaching deaf children to swim, saying: "Since I can't hear either, they feel that I am one of them."

In her last days, she lived at the Christian Health Care Centre in Wyckoff, New Jersey. She did not complain about her incapacity, telling one interviewer: "I am not a person who reaches for the moon as long as I have the stars."

Gertrude Ederle, swimmer, was born on October 23, 1906. She died on November 30, 2003, aged 97

———

DAME ALICIA MARKOVA

DANCER OF GREAT TECHNIQUE AND STYLE WHO BECAME AN INTERNATIONAL STAR WHILE HELPING TO ESTABLISH A BRITISH BALLET TRADITION

DECEMBER 3, 2004

Alicia Markova was still two months short of her 20th birthday when British ballet effectively began in October 1930 with the foundation of the Ballet Club (which later became Ballet Rambert) and the first performances of the Camargo Society. This was a producing organisation which put on special programmes bringing together all available local talent, including Rambert's dancers and those of Ninette de Valois, who were soon to become the

Vic-Wells Ballet although at that time still only supplementing the operas at the Old Vic. But the teenager Markova already had experience in leading roles with Diaghilev's Russian Ballet; she was blessed with a phenomenal technique and beautiful style.

Inevitably, she became the first ballerina of all these emerging ventures. Just as inevitably, they were unable, with their limited resources, to contain her talent for long and she left for international fame. Most of her career was spent touring the world at the head of various companies and later as a guest star.

However, her presence at a critical time proved invaluable in founding a British ballet tradition, not only by attracting audiences to the early efforts of the young companies but by the inspiration she provided both to creative artists and to other dancers.

To a later generation, Markova's fame has been hidden by the universal admiration for Margot Fonteyn; but Fonteyn, a decade younger, was one of the dancers who learnt much from Markova's example, and while they were both working there was no need for rivalry because their gifts were different and complementary.

Lilian Alicia Marks was born in Stoke Newington, North London, and showed an early interest in theatre, music and dancing, encouraged by her Irish mother. But her first formal lessons in "fancy dancing" were taken on medical advice to correct weak feet and legs. She revealed an astonishing facility and at ten earned the considerable sum of £10 a week as principal dancer in the pantomime *Dick Whittington* at Kennington Theatre, billed as "Little Alicia, the Child Pavlova".

This unwise sobriquet caused Alicia and her mother to be angrily turned away when they first applied for her admission at the age of 11 as a pupil of Seraphine Astafieva, the leading teacher in London; but the child's tears led to an audition and acceptance. In Astafieva's studio in King's Road, Chelsea, her serious education began; here too she first met Anton Dolin, with whom her career was to be closely linked, and she was shown off to Serge Diaghilev.

When the Marks family were in straitened circumstances following the sudden death of her father (a mining engineer of Polish ancestry), it was Astafieva who persuaded Diaghilev to consider the child, still only 14, for his Russian Ballet, and after a long audition with his new choreographer George Balanchine she was accepted. Diaghilev renamed her Markova and placed her at first in the care of Ninette de Valois, whose initial reluctance to be saddled with her quickly turned to the beginning of a lifelong friendship and mutual admiration.

Markova was so tiny that it was difficult to cast her except in carefully chosen solos. In her first season, Balanchine created for her the role of the Nightingale in his *Chant du Rossignol*; he also made solos for her in the world premiere of Ravel's *L'Enfant et les Sortilèges*. There were child roles she could play in *La Boutique Fantasque*, *Petrushka* and *Aurora's Wedding* (as Red Riding Hood) and she was given Papillon's solo in *Le Carnaval*. Later she grew sufficiently to be put into the corps de ballet, which Diaghilev thought an essential step in her development, but she also danced leading parts for him in Balanchine's *La Chatte*, Massine's *Cimarosiana* and (laying the foundations of her future fame in classic roles) the "Bluebird" pas de deux and a single performance of *Swan Lake* Act II.

On Diaghilev's death in 1929 the company broke up. Markova returned to London and had no employment, except for a three-month opera season in Monte Carlo, until Frederick Ashton invited her to appear in dances he was doing for Nigel Playfair's production of *Marriage à la Mode* at the Lyric, Hammersmith.

With the beginnings of regular ballet seasons by British dancers later that year, Markova was immediately in heavy demand, and she became Ashton's first muse. At the Ballet Club and for the Camargo Society he made a great many highly contrasted roles for her: among them the title part in his languorously poetic *La Pen*, the witty polka in *Façade* (ending with a double *tour en l'air* in pointe shoes which nobody attempts nowadays), a sexy Creole girl in *Rio Grande*, the insolently proud ballerina in *Foyer de Danse*, the immensely chic and naughty lady friend in *Les Masques*, and the tragic Marguerite in *Mephisto Valse*. Many roles she took brought out a gift for shrewd comic characterisation far removed from the pure classic perfection for which she was widely celebrated.

But the tiny fee which was all Rambert could afford was only enough to keep Markova in ballet shoes; to support herself she also had to dance three times a day between films in a cinema at Marble Arch, the choreography again by Ashton.

During 1932 Markova began dancing sometimes for de Valois's company at Sadler's Wells, too, and staged *Les Sylphides* for them (the first evidence of her exceptional memory for choreography, largely based on her great musicality). In 1933 Markova and Ashton both joined the Vic-Wells Ballet. The first role he made for her there was in *Les Rendez-vous*, a triumphant display of her wit, charm, romantic lyricism and brilliant technique.

Markova's arrival as her regular ballerina enabled de Valois to begin mounting the old classics: *The Nutcracker*, *Giselle* and *Swan Lake*. These were to provide a staple of Markova's repertoire from then on. For many years her Giselle was acknowledged as the best in the western world, unrivalled for the tragic depth of her acting, her phrasing of the solo in Act I or the illusion of ethereality she brought to the act. But the apparently less profound ballerina role in *The Nutcracker* almost equally revealed her supreme artistry, with its crystalline delicacy and beautiful detail.

During this early period of her career Markova performed for other choreographers too, most notably in ballets by de Valois, who created for her the wickedly vulgar, riotously funny role of La Goulue in *Bar aux Folies-Bergère* as well as the gullible pure young girl in *The Rake's Progress*.

In the summer of 1935 Mrs Laura Henderson, owner of the Windmill Theatre with its famously undressed revues, underwrote a West End season and a provincial tour for the Vic-Wells Ballet, with Markova and Dolin as its stars. This led to the idea of their starting the Markova-Dolin Ballet which toured successfully for two years with a repertoire including Nijinska's *Les Biches*, with Markova as the ambiguous person in blue, and what may have been the first murder-mystery ballet, Keith Lester's *Death in Adagio*, where, wearing a blonde wig, she was improbably but enjoyably cast as a homicidal typist. But the strain of eight performances a week prompted Markova in 1938 to accept Léonide Massine's invitation to join the new Ballet Russe de Monte Carlo. Her new roles there included creations in two of Massine's symphonic ballets, *Seventh Symphony* (Beethoven) and *Rouge et Noir* (Shostakovich No 1).

Her commitments with the Ballet Russe resulted in Markova's finding herself in America during the war and (with no obvious work for her at home) she joined Ballet Theatre in 1941, creating further roles including Princess Hermilia in Michel Fokine's last ballet, *Bluebeard*, the gypsy Zemphire in Massine's *Aleko*, and Juliet in Antony Tudor's hauntingly beautiful *Romeo and Juliet* to music by Delius. She also played Taglioni in Dolin's *Pas de*

Quatre with a subtle mixture of charm and aloofness that eluded all successors, as did too her apparent ability to soar across the stage with no regard for the power of gravity. During her Ballet Theatre days, Markova took time off to dance with Dolin in the world premiere of Stravinsky's *Scènes de Ballet* for a revue, *The Seven Lively Arts*, and to tour central America with a new Markova-Dolin group.

Further tours with this group followed, and guest appearances with Ballet Russe de Monte Carlo, where John Taras created Camille for her (in beautiful costumes by Cecil Beaton), and de Basil's Original Ballet Russe, where she appeared in one of Jerome Robbins's early works, *Pas de Trois*.

These occupied her time until she and Dolin reintroduced themselves to British audiences through a guest season with the Sadler's Wells Ballet at Covent Garden, summer 1948, during which they both danced the full *Sleeping Beauty* for the first time.

Next they pioneered the use of vast arenas for ballet with seasons at the Empress Hall and at Harringay; these were followed by long tours with a supporting group as a forerunner of Festival Ballet which they founded in 1950. Injuries forced Markova to leave the company in 1952 and subsequently she worked entirely as a guest artist and in concert performances, continuing however to take on new roles including Bournonville's *La Sylphide* which she danced with the de Cuevas company. Among her wide-ranging appearances at this time were programmes with the Indian dancer Ram Gopal, others with Pilar Lopez and her Spanish company, an Italian opera season at Drury Lane, and Ruth Page's ballets *The Merry Widow* and *Revanche* (based on *Il Trovatore*) in Chicago.

Her last stage appearance was in 1962, but even she did not realise that until, interviewed at Heathrow on January 1, 1963, en route for New York while recovering from a tonsillectomy, she said without premeditation that her new year resolution would be to stop dancing. After this decision, Markova became from 1963 to 1970 director of ballet at the Metropolitan Opera House, New York, and subsequently lectured at the University of Cincinnati. Even in later retirement she still staged ballets (especially *Les Sylphides*, which she had studied with its choreographer, Fokine) and coached dancers in some of the roles specially associated with her. Her enthusiasm remained undimmed, especially for the many activities she undertook to help the progress of young pupils.

She was appointed CBE in 1958 and DBE in 1963. Her book *Giselle and I*, published in 1960, records her thoughts and experiences of her most famous parts, and her reminiscences *Markova Remembers* (published 1986) provide a remarkably frank, informal account of her career, written with a lively humour surprising to those who knew her only in more formal circumstances. Her oft-time partner Dolin also interrupted his own stream of autobiographies for a book on her: *Markova, Her Life and Work*.

A dancer's work is ephemeral and no worthy record of Markova's dancing remains on film, although some of her masterclasses were shown on television. But her performances all over the world brought pleasure to innumerable spectators, and her example fired many young dancers to follow the career she herself irradiated with such lustre.

Dame Alicia Markova, DBE, ballerina, was born on December 1, 1910. She died on December 2, 2004, aged 94

———〜〜〜———

DAME MIRIAM ROTHSCHILD

REVERED NATURALIST
WITH A LIFELONG LOVE OF
CONSERVATION AND THE
COUNTRYSIDE

JANUARY 22, 2005

A scientist of scholarship and distinction, Dame Miriam Rothschild was known primarily for her writings on butterflies and fleas, though she also published more than 300 highly technical papers on subjects such as bird behaviour and parasitic castration. Several of the papers concern a group of odoriferous chemicals called pyrazines which — as she noticed in 1961 — are widespread in nature and play a part in triggering brain functions such as memory and alertness.

Her major academic work was the *Catalogue of the Rothschild Collection of Fleas*, the six volumes of which appeared over thirty years. It was an area of research, as she wrily recognised, that was not always appreciated socially, as for instance when her children were at school. Nonetheless, her results were remarkable. She found, for instance, that the widely underestimated flea develops an acceleration of 149g when taking off — twenty times more than a Moon rocket re-entering Earth's atmosphere. The Rothschild collection of hundreds of thousands of specimens was transferred to the Natural History Museum in 1971.

Yet Rothschild carried her erudition lightly and whimsically, as befitted a member of her remarkable family (she was sister of the 3rd Lord Rothschild). Her lyrical writing, in particular in *Butterfly Cooing like a Dove*, published in her eighties, is in the best tradition of authors who combine science, literature and a sense of wonder, from Sir Thomas Browne to Vladimir Nabokov. "Nobody has really thought about what is so satisfying in nature," she once said, "but people really do benefit from contact with plants, animals, birds and butterflies. Without them we are a deprived species."

Between 1899 and 1913, the Rothschild family won 374 awards from the Royal Horticultural Society. Each Rothschild strove to outdo the others — Alfred, for instance, planted one of every British species of tree in his garden — and altogether they created

100 gardens all over Europe, which Miriam Rothschild documented in her book *The Rothschild Gardens* (1997).

Miriam Rothschild's own gardening, however, took a different turn. As a child she had her own vegetable patch, as well as a cactus collection in a miniature greenhouse, and she went on to win prizes at Chelsea for orchids. But later she returned to her childhood love of wild flowers, allowing them to reclaim much that had been artfully denatured by Edwardian garden planning. Greenhouses that were once devoted to exotic fruit were turned over to the cultivation of wayside flowers.

"One day the penny dropped," she said, "and I realised with dismay that wild flowers had been drained, bulldozed, weedkillered and fertilised out of the fields, and that we now had a countryside reminiscent of a snooker table." Gardeners, she proclaimed, should not battle against nature — the endless struggle to keep the weeds down — but should allow it to flourish.

She began her first meadow garden in 1970 — "John Clare's countryside resurrected," she called it — and eventually 150 acres were filled with wild flowers. One field was later said to contain 115 different species. The Prince of Wales listened to her ideas, and asked her to sow her "farmer's nightmare" mixture of seeds at Highgrove, and she was delighted to find that she had started a fashion.

In her zeal she even planted a bypass with primroses and cowslips, ladies' smocks and buttercups, to brighten the verges and encourage butterflies. In her seventies she sponsored the distribution of seeds to schools, and experimented with caterpillars which might destroy cannabis before the crop ripened.

She was a tremendous friend to the cause of conservation, which came entirely naturally to her. She pioneered humane livestock methods and campaigned against the widespread use of insecticides. The tone was set in *The Butterfly Gardener*, which opened with the words: "I garden purely for pleasure. I love plants and flowers and green leaves and I am incurably romantic — hankering after small stars spangling the grass."

Entranced by the worlds she saw out of the window and through the microscope Miriam Rothschild continued her "scientific play" into her nineties. She continued to publish, too, contributing notes and papers to journals and providing passionate introductions to books on gardening and wildflowers.

Born in 1908, Miriam Louisa Rothschild reached the scientific heights despite — or, as she delighted to say, because of — having had no formal academic instruction (her eight doctorates of science were all honorary). She claimed to have been "self-non-educated", but this understated the remarkable experience of her childhood, much of it spent at Tring Park, the Wren house at the foot of the Chilterns which was the country seat of her grandfather (the first Jewish member of the House of Lords). Such a home could not help but be an education.

Long before most people were aware of environmental issues, her father, Charles Rothschild, campaigned for a national network of nature reserves. One of the first people to realise the importance of preserving habitats as well as species, he nominated 280 potential sites, before dying in his forties in 1923. In 1997 Miriam wrote *Rothschild's Reserves* with Peter Marren (she liked to have a collaborator, to focus her projects), and found that 80 years had devastated the nature reserves, with species counts falling even where the reserves themselves had not disappeared under concrete. The book concluded that nature cannot live in reserves alone, but depends on the practices that farmers adopt, guided by the incentives and restrictions of governments.

The senior Rothschild at Tring was Charles's elder brother Walter, the 2nd Lord Rothschild, who built up a vast private museum of stuffed animals, birds, insects and reptiles (now a large part of the Natural History Museum). By any standards he was one of England's greatest eccentrics. He kept kangaroos, emus, cassowaries and salamanders, and once drove himself along Piccadilly and into Buckingham Palace in a buggy pulled by zebras.

A child at Tring learnt much about animals and perhaps more about humans. Large sums were spent on financing expeditions to remote places to fill gaps in the collections, and 5,000 new species were discovered. Live creatures arrived too, and giant turtles, kangaroos and wild horses roamed the grounds.

As a child Miriam Rothschild had an owl as a pet, and a quail; at the age of 4 she was *Country Life*'s "youngest milker". In 1983 she honoured her uncle's memory by publishing a highly praised biography, *Dear Lord Rothschild*.

Her father was given a 1,200-acre rural estate near Oundle, where he built Ashton Wold, and renewed the village of Ashton, bringing running water to the residents and organising village events. Later, Miriam Rothschild, who lived there until her death, rehabilitated the watermill to supply electricity to the house, and established the National Dragonfly Museum there.

After her home education she attended evening classes in zoology at Chelsea Polytechnic and took classes in literature during the day at Bedford College. Meanwhile, she was asked to play both cricket and squash for England. Her earliest scientific research was on marine parasitology, some of it carried out at the marine laboratory in Naples, where she won a scholarship — because, she said, "no one else applied".

During the war she worked at the Foreign Office, and then for several years she was a visiting professor in biology at the Royal Free Hospital.

Voluble, argumentative and brimming with vivid observations, she felt that study of the variety of nature broadened the mind. "Human beings are apt to regard their own personal structure as 'normal' and everything that differs from it as distinctly humorous."

Discovering an insect that urinates out of its head — and why not? — widens the realm of possibility. It was in that spirit of tolerance, during the 1950s, that Rothschild campaigned with the geneticist E. B. Ford for the legalisation of homosexual acts. She also kept a collection of art by schizophrenics, inspired by her sister Liberty (Elizabeth), who lived for some years with Miriam at Ashton Wold until her death in 1988.

She was a trustee of the Natural History Museum, and her honours included an honorary fellowship of St Hugh's College, Oxford, and the Royal Horticultural Society's highest award, the Victoria Medal. She was also president of the Royal Entomological Society. She was appointed CBE in 1982, elected a Fellow of the Royal Society in 1985 and advanced to DBE in 2000.

Disapproving of the methods of slaughter used in Britain, she did not eat meat, or use cosmetics. She also refused to wear leather shoes, and instead liked to wear white wellingtons in summer and moonboots in winter. Her wellingtons caused a considerable stir at Prince Charles's 40th birthday ball at Buckingham Palace.

In 1943 she married Captain George Lane, and they had two sons and four daughters. The marriage was dissolved in 1957 — "I don't really like marriage", she concluded. She is survived by a son and three daughters.

Dame Miriam Rothschild, DBE, FRS, naturalist, entomologist, gardener and conservationist, was born on August 5, 1908. She died on January 20, 2005, aged 96

———*w*———

DAME MOURA LYMPANY

CONCERT PIANIST WHOSE
BRITISH CAREER SURVIVED
YEARS DOMICILED OVERSEAS
AND BLOSSOMED AGAIN IN
THE 1980S

MARCH 31, 2005
According to Sir Neville Cardus, there have been just two great English women pianists this century: Dame Myra Hess and Dame Moura Lympany. Hess died in 1965 and from then on Lympany, who had long been a favourite in the concert hall and on record, occupied a special place in the hearts and minds of British and Anglophile music lovers across the world.

Her career, which spanned seven decades, epitomised that of the international virtuoso concert pianist. Her repertoire, though broad, centred on the standard Classical and Romantic concertos, enriched with the French Impressionists, Spanish nationalists, Russian warhorses from Rachmaninov to Shostakovich, and British post-Romantics such as Delius and Ireland.

Born Mary Johnstone, she was known within her family as Moura, the Russian diminutive of Mary reflecting her mother's love of pre-revolution St Petersburg, where she had once taught the daughters of wealthy aristocrats.

The surname Lympany, an early version of her mother's maiden name Limpenny, came at the suggestion of the conductor Basil Cameron who offered the 12-year-old prodigy her first concerto engagement at a time when it was fashionable for British artists to adopt foreign-sounding names.

That debut, with Cameron, took place in Harrogate on August 8, 1928, and her interpretation of the youthful Mendelssohn's glittering G minor Concerto earned glowing reviews, including the headline from the *Daily Express*: "Two plaits and a symphony orchestra".

At the age of 6 Lympany was sent to a convent in Tongres, Belgium, where she studied with Jules Debèfve of the Liège Conservatoire. Four years later, and enriched with Belgian culture and the French language, she moved to a convent school in Bayswater. She won an early scholarship to the Royal Academy of Music, where she won several awards and was equipped for further studies at the Vienna Hochschule with Paul Weingarten.

Back in London a period with Mathilde Verne, a pupil of Clara Schumann, the teacher of Solomon, and a firm believer in making a beautiful, effortless sound, preceded ten years' work with the octogenarian Tobias Matthay, teacher of Eileen Joyce, Harriet Cohen, Clifford Curzon and Myra Hess. "Uncle Tobs", as Lympany invariably referred to him, had a profound influence on her career. She once said: "Uncle Tobs taught me not to resist the inclination to be a virtuoso player." He was also instrumental in teaching the beautiful phrasing that invariably characterised a Lympany recital, particularly in the music of Chopin.

In 1938 she returned to Belgium and, thanks to a dazzling rendition of Liszt's First Concerto, came second in the Ysaÿe Competition behind Emil Gilels. The virtuoso Arturo Benedetti Michelangeli, incapacitated through overpractising, was placed seventh. After the competition she lunched with Queen Elisabeth of the Belgians and recalled how, years before, she had been scheduled to play for the Queen when Her Majesty had visited Moura's convent school. The day before the great occasion the Reverend Mother had cancelled her performance, claiming: "It might turn the head of one so young; you must be humble."

Three weeks before war broke out in 1939, Lympany made a thrilling debut at La Scala, Milan, but the hostilities meant that her international opportunities dried up. Like her compatriot Hess, Lympany recognised the need for morale to be boosted back home, and how better than through music. She gave numerous recitals for factory workers, dockers and others involved in the war effort.

Lympany's ability to learn music quickly proved beneficial in 1940, when Clifford Curzon, pleading too heavy a workload, declined the opportunity to give the first performance outside Russia of Aram Khachaturian's Piano Concerto. The music was delivered to Lympany while she sat under the drier at the hairdressers. Conducted by Alan Bush in the Queen's Hall, the premiere received great acclaim, and Lympany's international standing grew enormously.

A concert in Bristol in 1944 coincided with the home leave of one of her two brothers, Joseph. He hitch-hiked to the West Country to hear her play the John Ireland concerto, with its beautiful melody at the beginning of the second movement. She recalled: "When my darling brother came to see me after the concert there were tears in his eyes. 'You played as if you were crying,' he said, 'and I cried too'." Weeks later he was posted to Italy and killed in fighting on the Adriatic coast near Rimini.

After the war Moura Lympany played at the Proms in the summer of 1945, having first played the Grieg concerto there a decade earlier with Henry Wood. In Paris she collaborated with Sir Adrian Boult and L'Orchestre de la Société des Concerts du Conservatoire in the Khachaturian and Alan Rawsthorne's first concerto. The following year she and Boult visited the Prague Spring Festival with the John Ireland concerto, and two years later her New York debut was a triumph. Concerts under the batons of such great conductors as Sir Adrian Boult, Rafael Kubelik, Erich Kleiber and Herbert von Karajan came thick and fast.

A marriage in 1944, to Lieutenant-Colonel Colin Defries, was dissolved in 1950. Married for a second time, to the American television producer Bennet

Korn, Lympany took up residence in New York in 1951 and during the following decade was mainly active in the New World, making just occasional forays to Britain.

When this marriage, too, was dissolved and she returned to her homeland in the early 1960s Lympany discovered that she had been all but forgotten and struggled over the next 15 years or so to attract the degree of attention she had previously enjoyed.

On the advice of a doctor treating her for a constantly croaking voice, she sought solitude one summer in Rasiguères, near Perpignan in the south of France. She fell in love with the place, bought a vineyard and, in 1981, established a music and wine festival there. The villagers entitled one vintage Cuvée Moura Lympany. Every year artistic friends from all over the world flocked to Rasiguères to participate. Among the first was Victoria de los Angeles, and later visitors included Larry Adler, Cécile Ousset and Elizabeth Harwood. The Manchester Camerata made the pilgrimage each year. Sadly the festival faded out in 1993 when the local organisers fell into dispute with the mayor.

Financial problems and the difficulties of housing a piano in an affordable London flat persuaded Lympany to move to Monte Carlo in 1984. Prince Louis de Polignac, a cousin of Prince Rainier, persuaded her to help him to establish Le Festival des Sept Chapelles in seven chapels he had rescued from being sold and converted into discotheques. She was happy in

Monte Carlo, enjoying her correspondence and travelling to performances.

Towards the end of the 1980s her career was blossoming once again. Her Royal Festival Hall recital in 1989, marking her 60th anniversary on the concert platform, and her BBC Prom two years later, in which she played the Mendelssohn G minor Piano Concerto, the same work as in Harrogate with Basil Cameron all those years before, were splendid occasions demonstrating the finest and most lyrical of music making. Her ability to learn new works did not diminish either, and when the opportunity came in 1992 to learn Richard Addinsell's Warsaw Concerto for a concert at the Barbican with the London Symphony Orchestra, she seized it with as much zest as she had the Khachaturian more than half a century earlier.

Her recordings earned her a host of admirers. The 1951 Decca LP of Rachmaninov's Preludes is one of the most memorable, but even in her late seventies she was making successful forays into the studios. Many of her greatest records have recently appeared on CD, including the Khachaturian, Rachmaninov's First, Second and Third and Saint-Saëns's Second concertos as well as the Chopin nocturnes, waltzes and études.

Her appointment as DBE in 1992 brought her — and her many admirers — much pleasure.

Dame Moura Lympany, DBE, concert pianist, was born on August 18, 1916. She died on March 28, 2005, aged 88

DAME CICELY SAUNDERS

VISIONARY FOUNDER OF THE MODERN HOSPICE MOVEMENT WHO SET THE HIGHEST STANDARDS IN CARE FOR THE DYING

JULY 15, 2005

Dame Cicely Saunders earned gratitude, admiration and international renown for helping to alleviate the suffering of terminally ill people. Hundreds of hospices in Britain and more than 95 other countries are modelled on St Christopher's, Sydenham, the hospice which she established in 1967.

St Christopher's, on her initiative, attempted for the first time to provide patient-centred palliative care for the terminally ill, combining emotional, spiritual and social support with expert medical and nursing care. Its practices have since been widely copied and developed. Today St Christopher's cares for about 2,000 patients and their families each year and, in training more than 60,000 health professionals, has influenced standards of care for the dying throughout the world.

Despite coming late in life to her vocation — she trained in turn as a nurse, almoner, medical secretary and doctor, before opening St Christopher's — by the time she died Saunders had gained a place in public esteem almost comparable to that occupied by Florence Nightingale.

She had, in fact, begun her training in 1940 as a Nightingale nurse. A shy, tall, gawky young woman, she had felt the need for some stronger wartime commitment than the completion of an Oxford degree — a task to which she returned when a lifelong back defect made a nursing career impossible, before going on to qualify as a hospital social worker. But for all her dedication, much strengthened by her conversion to evangelical Christianity, Saunders was for long uncertain how best to deploy her passionate concern for the sick and suffering.

She was in many ways an old-fashioned woman, a charismatic *grande dame* with strong values and a great talent for leadership. She was such a remarkable innovator in the treatment of physical and psychological pain that she eventually held fellowships in the Royal College of Physicians (1974), the Royal College of Nursing (1981) and the Royal College of Surgeons (1986). She was awarded the esteemed Templeton, Onassis and Wallenberg prizes, a score of honorary degrees and medals, was advanced from OBE (1967) to DBE in 1980 and appointed to the Order of Merit in 1989. In 2001 she was awarded the million-dollar Conrad N. Hilton Humanitarian Prize.

None of this was easily achieved. Born Cicely Mary Strode Saunders in Barnet, North London, in 1918, she was the eldest daughter of a prosperous, domineering estate agent, whose unhappy marriage to a dependent wife broke up in 1945, the critical year in which Saunders graduated from Oxford and abruptly exchanged the agnosticism in which she had grown up for an earnest religious search for a mission.

She was unhappy at home, even more unhappy at Roedean, eager for a partnership in life which she could not find among her widening circle of colleagues and friends. Seeking a better-matched relationship than her parents, she found it only in middle age, with the émigré Polish painter Marian Bohusz-Szyszko, a Catholic, whom she married in 1980, after the death of his separated wife in Poland.

Other Poles had earlier played a decisive role in her life. Saunders herself wondered why she felt such a lifelong attraction towards things and persons Polish. She attributed much of it to an intimate but unconsummated love for a dying patient, David Tasma, a refugee from the Warsaw ghetto, whom she met on her first rounds as an almoner at St Thomas's. He was a friendless waiter with no family, and there was no consolation for him except in the love which she discovered to be within her reach. It was then that she saw how the pain of cancer could be tamed by modern drugs and that unavoidable distress could be made tolerable by a form of care that ranked the physical and spiritual needs of the patient together.

Tasma bequeathed her all his worldly goods, £500, which she treasured for years until she found a way to give full effect to his cryptic wish that it should be "a window in your home". His gift is now commemorated in the entrance to St Christopher's.

Her experience as a volunteer in St Luke's, the Bayswater Home for the Dying Poor, persuaded Saunders to challenge the received medical wisdom about dying, death and bereavement. She put herself back to school, studied physics and chemistry and qualified as a doctor when she was 38. She then combined membership of a research group on pain, set up at St Mary's, Paddington, with her continuing ward work — this time at St Joseph's Hackney, where the Sisters of Charity showed her how much might be done for the dying by sustained loving care; and where she, in turn, began to bring into play her more unorthodox ideas about pain relief.

What she then demonstrated, and what is now widely adopted, was that intermittent reactive sedation of surging pain was far less effective than achieving a steady state in which the dying patient could still maintain consciousness and even life with some quality.

At St Joseph's Saunders met the second of the Poles who changed her life. The transfiguration of Antoni Michniewicz showed her what dying might be like when love could be given and received. His death inspired her in her plan to found St Christopher's — named, appropriately, after the patron saint of travellers — as a place to find shelter on the most difficult part of life's journey. St Christopher's was to cater primarily for cancer patients because Saunders had seen a gap in

NHS provision, highlighted by a 1952 Marie Curie Foundation survey of their needs and a later Gulbenkian report on the care of the chronic sick — a perspective which today carries the principles and practice of palliative care beyond the initial concern with cancer.

It took years of planning and financing to open a purpose-built hospice on the Sydenham site. There Saunders explored all the possibilities for matching quality medical care with support for patients and their families at home, changing existing medical and social attitudes about the care of the dying. Through the struggles for financial and professional backing, in which Saunders proved herself as a medical director, a fundraiser of quiet genius, a relentless administrator and a proponent of the hospice idea on the world stage, it was clear that she was achieving exactly what she set out to do.

The change she accomplished in medical attitudes was most notably recognised when the Royal College of Physicians established palliative medicine as a distinct medical specialism.

When the Cicely Saunders Foundation was launched in 2002, her reputation attracted leading specialists from North America and Australia to its international scientific advisory panel. The foundation aims to promote research into all aspects of palliative medicine and care for the dying, with particular emphasis on collaborations between different professions in healthcare, clinical and non-clinical services, to improve the integration between research and practice.

Many years ago, in response to a question at a symposium about the prospect of death, Saunders declared that she would hope for a sudden demise but would prefer to die — as she has — with a cancer that gave due notice and allowed the time to reflect on life and to put one's practical and spiritual affairs in order.

Her husband, Marian Bohusz-Szysko, died in 1995, aged 92.

Dame Cicely Saunders, OM, DBE, the founder of the modern hospice movement, was born on June 22, 1918. She died on July 14, 2005, aged 87

—⁓—

ROSA PARKS

THE "MOTHER OF THE CIVIL RIGHTS MOVEMENT" WHOSE REFUSAL TO YIELD HER SEAT ON A BUS LAUNCHED A SOCIAL REVOLUTION IN THE US

OCTOBER 26, 2005

On the evening of December 1, 1955, Rosa Parks boarded a bus in downtown Montgomery, Alabama. It was to be the most famous bus ride in American history, a bus ride that would spark civil rights protest across the American South and propel Parks to iconic status as the "mother of the civil rights movement".

At the time, Parks was a 42-year-old black seamstress returning home, weary from her day's work and in some pain from an inflamed shoulder. As was customary for black passengers, she got on the bus at the front door and paid the driver, then got off the bus and boarded again through the back door. She then took her seat just behind the sign marking the "coloured" rear section of the bus. This was a movable sign, allowing the bus company maximum flexibility while upholding Alabama's strict racial segregation laws.

As more white passengers boarded the bus, the white section at the front of the bus filled up, and one white man was unable to sit down. The bus driver decided to move the sign marking the coloured section back a row, and told Parks to give up her seat. As there were no black seats left either, Parks would have had to stand. She refused to move. The driver called the police, who arrested Parks and took her to the city jail.

Racial incidents on buses were common across the South. From the end of the 19th century, the 11 states of the old Confederacy had imposed a system of white supremacy that included the disenfranchisement of black voters, discrimination in employment and education, and strict segregation in all areas of public life. It was a system sanctioned by the law and often upheld by violence.

But it was never a settled system. Black southerners challenged segregation repeatedly, never more so than on buses. Indeed, blacks in Montgomery had boycotted the buses for more than a year when segregation was first introduced in 1900. After the Second

World War there were frequent skirmishes and arrests on the buses, but at the end of 1955 segregation seemed firmly entrenched across the South. However, the arrest of Parks precipitated a mass bus boycott by blacks in Montgomery that lasted for more than a year and culminated in the end of segregated transport and the first big breakthrough in the struggle against white supremacy.

When the bus driver challenged Rosa Parks, he picked the wrong person. She was one of the most educated and politically engaged black women in Montgomery. She was born Rosa Louise McCauley in 1913, to James McCauley, a carpenter, and Leona Edwards, a teacher. Her mother sent her to Montgomery Industrial School for Negro Girls, where she trained as a stenographer and a typist. When her mother fell ill, Rosa had to cut short her education. But after marrying a local barber, Raymond Parks, Rosa resumed her schooling and at 20 she became one of the very few black high-school graduates in the city.

At the time of her arrest Parks was also one of the most active and knowledgeable opponents of white supremacy in the state. Unable to get a job as a stenographer on account of her colour, Parks worked as a seamstress. But she put her typing skills to work in the service of the local branch of the National Association for the Advancement of Colored People, the main civil rights organisation of its day. By the time of her arrest Parks was secretary of the branch, adviser to the branch's youth council and had been involved in efforts to register black voting. She had also recently attended a two-week training course at the Highlander Folk School in Tennessee, a militantly liberal training school for civil rights campaigners, where she met the inspirational civil rights leader Ella Baker.

Black leaders in Montgomery had been pushing for a test case to challenge the treatment of black passengers on the buses. Even so, Parks's refusal to stand up on the bus was not premeditated. "I did not get on the bus to get arrested," she said later. "I got on the bus to get home." But it was conditioned by her increasing resentment at white supremacy and segregation. As she recalled later, "I was thinking that the only way to let them know I felt I was being mistreated was to do just what I did... I simply decided that I would not get up so a white person could sit. That I would refuse to do."

Nevertheless, Parks's arrest was opportune in every respect. She was mild-mannered, a committed Christian and well-known to many, and her arrest prompted an outcry and galvanised her community. E. D. Nixon, president of the NAACP branch, called a meeting of black leaders. Jo Ann Robinson, the feisty leader of the town's Black Women's Political Council, distributed leaflets calling for a boycott. When the black leaders met, and to the consternation of some, community support for a boycott was unstoppable.

The Montgomery Improvement Association was founded to organise the boycott. A 26-year-old pastor, Martin Luther King Jr, was appointed president. (King was appointed less for his talents than for being new to town and thus acceptable to the factions in the local black leadership.) On December 5 Parks appeared in court. She was fined $10 plus costs. She refused to pay the fine. The boycott started the same day. It lasted for another 380 days.

Ironically, boycott leaders did not initially demand the end of segregation, but called for more courtesy from white drivers and the appointment of black drivers on black routes. Such was the intransigence of the white city authorities, however, that boycott leaders raised the stakes and filed suit against segregation.

Meanwhile, a spate of violence united the black community further.

Parks lost her job and received death threats. King was arrested and fined $500. A stick of dynamite was thrown onto King's porch. The Ku Klux Klan forced one black truck driver to jump to his death in the Alabama River. Despite the attacks, the boycott continued, and on December 20, 1956, the federal court declared segregation illegal.

The court ruling ended the boycott — and began a new chapter in the long history of civil rights protest. In the wake of the triumph in Montgomery, Martin Luther King rose to national and international prominence as the spokesman for the civil rights movement. In Montgomery itself the racial situation hardened. After the buses integrated, white snipers shot at black

passengers, forcing a temporary suspension of buses. But across the South protests gripped the nation. In 1960 students in many cities sat in the "wrong" areas of segregated cafes and refused to leave until they were served. In 1961 an integrated group boarded the front portion of a greyhound bus in Washington on a "freedom ride" and tried to travel to New Orleans. King led massive city-wide demonstrations in Birmingham, Alabama, in 1963 and Selma, Alabama, in 1965 to put pressure on the federal government to legislate.

Faced by this mounting protest and by growing white supremacist violence, Congress passed the Civil Rights Act of 1964 and Voting Rights Act of 1965 that decisively ended racial segregation and disenfranchisement.

For Parks the boycott marked the end of her time in the front line of protest. The perpetual harassment during the boycott took its toll, and her husband suffered a nervous breakdown. To gain some respite, she, Raymond and her mother moved to Detroit in 1957.

Parks, though, continued to support the civil rights movement, and joined King on several marches in Alabama. In 1965 she joined the staff of a black Congressman, John Conyers Jr, for whom she worked until her retirement in 1988. Much of her time was spent working to house the homeless in Michigan.

In memory of her husband who died in 1977, Parks founded the Rosa and Raymond Parks Institute for Self-Development, the primary aim of which was to motivate young people to achieve their potential. She was beaten in her own home in August 1994 by an unemployed young black man, but was much praised for her dignified response: "I pray for this young man and the condition of our country that has made him this way".

She remained an outspoken advocate of civil rights throughout her later life, lending support to a wide range of black leaders including the controversial Louis Farrakhan. She also remained one of the most celebrated figures not just in black history but also in US history. *Time* magazine named her as one of the 100 most important people in the history of the US. In 1999 she received the Congressional Gold Medal of Honor from President Clinton, the highest award which the US government can bestow.

Rosa Parks, civil rights campaigner, was born on February 13, 1913. She died on October 24, 2005, aged 92

Editor's note: A number of authorities, including the American organisers of Rosa Parks Day, give Mrs Parks' birthdate as February 4, 1913.

DAME MURIEL SPARK

WRITER WHOSE CONVERSION TO CATHOLICISM INSPIRED HER TO WORKS OF WIT AND VARIETY, INCLUDING *THE PRIME OF MISS JEAN BRODIE*

APRIL 17, 2006

The Sparklet was her nickname, and anyone who met her could tell why. Perhaps Scotland's most important modern novelist, Muriel Spark was a small, striking woman, with a coruscating mind. She brought a vivacious imagination to her writing, backed by pitiless powers of observation. "You may not call Spark's novels lifelike," her fellow Scottish author Allan Massie once wrote, "but it is probable, even certain, that you will some day, sometimes, find life to be Sparklike."

She wrote more than 20 novels, as well as stories, plays and children's books, and was a master of taut, quirky plots, often focusing on a small group of people whose lives are altered by a strange twist of fate. She admired what she called a literature of ridicule — "the only honourable weapon we have left" — and even in her own social life, she said, she picked up the craft of being polite while people were present and leaving the laughter until later.

She made her name with the character of Miss Jean Brodie, the unconventional and incorrigibly romantic Edinburgh schoolmistress with an admiration for Mussolini and dedication to the *crème de la crème* of her pupils. A restrained comedy of manners, mocking the old Edinburgh politesse, *The Prime of Miss Jean Brodie* (1961) sold hundreds of thousands of copies. It was adapted for the Broadway stage and made into a film in which Maggie Smith took the schoolmistress's starring role.

Spark wrote rapidly, rarely revising what she scribbled in the spiral-bound notebooks, which she had sent to her in consignments from the Edinburgh stationers James Thin. She claimed to have dreamt up *The Public Image* (1968) — about a film star's struggle with the scandal industry — while asleep: "When I woke up every detail was in my head. I just wrote it all down." In *A Far Cry from Kensington* (1988), she dispenses authorial advice. Write as if you are writing to a friend, she suggests. "Write privately, not publicly; without fear or timidity, right to the end of the letter... as if it was never going to be published, so that your true friend will read it over and over and then want more enchanting letters from you... Remember not to think of the reading public. It will put you off."

In 1992 Spark published her autobiography, *Curriculum Vitae*, a series of vignettes and flashbacks of a life full of intriguing characters and peculiar subplots. But she detested intrusion into her private life, and the book tells very little about Spark herself. She could be prickly and had a reputation for falling out with friends and associates. A former editor, for example, with whom she once shared the ownership of a racehorse, fell from grace when he described her in an interview as "really quite batty".

Muriel Spark was born Muriel Sarah Camberg in the genteel Edinburgh suburb of Morningside. Her father, Bernard Camberg, an engineer in a rubber factory, was a Jew whose family had settled in Scotland. Her mother, Sarah Uezzell, was an English Presbyterian from Watford, who was later to take to drink.

The religious divide in her parents' marriage was to influence Spark's imagination considerably. In her only long novel, *The Mandelbaum Gate*, set in Jerusalem during the trial of Eichmann, a Roman Catholic woman finds herself in peril because of her part-Jewish ancestry. In later life Spark was to become involved in a bitter feud with her son Robin (a painter) about her Jewishness, and the quarrel snowballed in a blizzard of birth and marriage certificates, claims and counterclaims. Spark's relationship with her son was not improved by her comments about his paintings: "He always wanted me to say they were good but I didn't think they were", she said. "Art is important to me and I'm not going to commit perjury."

Spark's native city remained very important to her. Wherever she went in her long life, its puritanical ethos remained with her, and her religious faith came to be symbolised by Edinburgh's Castle Rock. "To have a great, primitive black crag rising up in the middle of populated streets of commerce, stately squares and winding closes," she said, "is like a statement preceded by 'nevertheless'. In the middle of worldly enterprises there is, nevertheless, the inescapable fact of God."

At James Gillespie's School for Girls, a merchant foundation where pupils started classical languages at seven, Spark encountered Miss Christina Kay, the inspirational teacher who was the model for Miss Jean Brodie. "She entered my imagination immediately. I started to write about her even then. Her accounts of her travels were gripping, fantastic," Spark later wrote in her autobiography. "Her dazzling non-sequiturs filled my heart with joy."

And Miss Kay encouraged Spark to write. She had written her first poem at nine — a version of *The Pied Piper of Hamelin* called *The Piper Pied* — and, being reared on the *Border Ballads*, she had a taste for a good yarn. By adolescence she was composing torrid love letters that she signed with fictitious men's names and hid under the sofa cushions in the hope of shocking her mother.

On leaving school, she went briefly to a technical college, but in 1936 ran away on a romantic impulse to Salisbury in Southern Rhodesia to marry Sidney Oswald Spark, a schoolteacher more than 12 years her senior. "I don't quite know why I married SOS," she later said. "I suppose I was attracted to a man who brought me bunches of flowers when I had 'flu. But my husband was very much a nut." He became increasingly quarrelsome and violent, often shooting his revolver at the walls.

Spark separated from him shortly after her son was born in 1938, and the marriage was later dissolved, although Spark kept the name because "it possessed some ingredient of life and fun". She was never to marry again, and although there were several subsequent love affairs she was always "a very bad picker of men", she said. "Maybe I was subconsciously protecting myself as I didn't really want anything that rivalled my work in attraction," she said.

In 1944 she returned to Britain and, depositing her seven-year-old son with her parents, took a room at a London club for "ladies of good families" — later to serve as a model for the boarding house in *The Girls of Slender Means* — and found work in the Political Intelligence Department at Woburn Abbey, where her creative talents were put to use inventing bogus news items for "black" propaganda broadcasts.

Once the war was over she found employment with a jewellery trade paper and then as a press agent for businessmen before, in 1947, joining the Poetry Society. A fiercely determined autodidact resolved to make a literary career, she soon became general secretary and editor of *Poetry Review*, opening it up to young writers, who were paid ten shillings for successful submissions.

The magazine had previously been little more than a forum for fossilised Georgian poets who paid to be published, and with this revolution the Poetry Society soon found its finances drained, so Spark was ousted. Undeterred, she founded her own magazine, *Forum*, but it folded after two issues.

In 1951 Spark won a short story competition in *The Observer* with *The Seraph and the Zambesi*, in which a tawdry troupe of travelling actors, staging a Christmas pageant on the banks of an African river, are interrupted by an argumentative angel.

Encouraged by this small success, she continued to write, scribbling through the nights, while working part-time during the day as an editor in the offices of Peter Owen Publishers. She also reviewed occasionally under the nom de plume Evelyn Cavallo.

In 1952 she published a collection of poems, *The Fanfarlo and Other Verse*. She also worked in collaboration with Derek Stanford, who had co-edited the second edition of *Forum* and was to remain her literary partner until 1957 on a number of publications, including *Selected Poems of Emily Brontë* (1952), *My Best Mary: The Letters of Mary Shelley* (1953) and *The Brontë Letters* (1954). But it was when she came to edit the *Letters of John Henry Newman* (1957) that she found her life changed. Newman's writings inspired her, and she decided in 1954 to be received into the Roman Catholic Church, in a process which she later described as "both too easy and too difficult to explain".

With conversion came her freedom to write. "Everyone said that I would be so restricted, but in fact the very opposite happened," Spark said. "I didn't get my style until I was a Catholic," she explained, "because you haven't got to care and you need security for that. That's the whole secret of style in a way. Its simply not caring too much, it's caring only a little." Her fiction was to reflect her religious beliefs in its fierce sense of good and evil. And faith provided a framework for her surreal, even grotesque, inventions as well as her discomfitingly acute awareness of the folly of human life.

Her first novel, written at the suggestion of her publishers, Macmillan, was intended simply as a way of working out the technique of what she considered at the time an inferior literary form. Aided by a stipend from Graham Greene — given on condition that she didn't say thank you or pray for him — and by a loan of a cottage in the country, she completed and published *The Comforters* in 1957. Inspired by dreams resulting from the appetite-suppressing drug she was taking at the time, it describes the spiritual and psychological crisis of a Catholic convert called Caroline, who hears a phantom typewriter tapping out her thoughts, writing a third-person novel about her life, even as it happens. It was a daring piece of metafiction, before the term had been coined.

Hailed by Evelyn Waugh as a masterpiece, *The Comforters* made her literary reputation. She followed it in 1958 with *Robinson*, in which another convert, a young widow, finds herself marooned with three men on a desert island.

Spark had honed her humour to a sharp, unsparing edge by 1959 when she published *Memento Mori*, in which a group of octogenarians are plagued by an anonymous caller who tells them "remember you must die" and produces ever more absurd reactions. The novel was adapted for the London stage in 1964 and later televised by the BBC in 1978.

The biting verbal humour of *The Ballad of Peckham Rye* (1960) — in which the Devil is sent to one of the tattier boroughs of South London — lent itself to a prizewinning radio adaptation, and *The Bachelors* followed in the same year, about a phoney spiritualist medium. But it was for her 1961 *The Prime of Miss Jean Brodie* that Spark was to be most remembered.

It was shortly after that success that Spark, now slavishly courted by the London literati, left Britain. "If people know you are famous," she said, "they quiver in a different way. You don't get the same natural response." This was important for a novelist whose ear for dialogue was acute, and who was alert to the jargon and pomposities of speech. She was also fed up with her alcoholic mother, who kept falling down and breaking her bones.

So Spark left for New York City, procuring an office overlooking Times Square. "I had lots of fun," she later said, "I bought pretty clothes, went to the hairdresser and travelled a great deal — I think I felt free for the first time." Friends recall how a tight-permed English frump was transformed within weeks into an elegant New York socialite, breezing through circles that included Norman Mailer, John Updike and W. H. Auden. She also developed an internal sophistication. Being an expatriate helped her writing, she thought. It put her at a slant to society, offering her a different perspective on life — "a new angle of absurdity".

In 1967 she was appointed OBE. But by then she was ready for another move. She changed her wardrobe, recoiffed her hair, and set off for Rome where, taken up by a succession of English-speaking monsignors and expats such as Anthony Burgess, Gore Vidal and William Weaver, she indulged in a dramatic *dolce vita*, hosting glamorous parties in a palazzo drawing room that had once been the library of Cardinal Orsini. When she wanted to write she would withdraw, persuading a doctor friend to sign her into a private hospital room where nobody could contact her.

Novels from this period included *The Driver's Seat* (1970) — her own favourite, and technically perhaps the neatest of her novels — in which a young woman seeks out the perfect sex maniac to hack her to death, *Not to Disturb* (1971), a black farce centering on three enraged aristocrats who, on the brink of committing murder and suicide, lock themselves into a Geneva mansion while their servants lay plans to cash in by writing their memoirs, and *The Abbess of Crewe* (1974), most commonly described as Watergate in a nunnery.

By the 1980s, however, Spark had begun to retreat more frequently to the Tuscan countryside, where she eventually moved to a converted 14th-century monastery house set in a garden of olive trees and vines on precipitous slopes above a village. Here, protected from the press by her longstanding companion, Penelope Jardine, a painter and sculptress, she would relax watching the interminable South American soap operas whose tortuous and protracted plots she so enjoyed.

In later years she was a familiar figure to locals, speeding through the Tuscan lanes in an Alfa Romeo brought from part of the proceeds of the David Cohen Literature Prize, awarded for a lifetime achievement in literature. Part of this prize money she also presented to her old school, the place where Miss Jean Brodie was born.

Spark's later novels include *Symposium* (1990), in which a stylish London dinner party turns dark as the reader learns that one absent guest "is dying, now, as they speak"; *Reality and Dreams* (1996), in which a film director's fall from a crane prompts him to reconsider the relationship between art and life; and *Aiding and Abetting* (2000), which was based on a real London murder case.

She had continued to write even when slowed down by a long series of hip operations; her last book, *The Finishing School*, a tense and comic portrayal of a creative writing teacher's consuming jealousy of his teenage pupil's talent, was published in 2004.

Spark was appointed DBE in 1993. She is survived by her son.

Dame Muriel Spark, DBE, novelist, was born on February 1, 1918. She died on April 13, 2006, aged 88

―᷍᷍―

DAME ELISABETH SCHWARZKOPF

GERMAN SOPRANO WHOSE PARTNERSHIP WITH HER RECORD-PRODUCER HUSBAND LEFT AN INDELIBLE MARK ON OPERA

AUGUST 4, 2006

Radiant was an adjective applied frequently to Elisabeth Schwarzkopf by critics and others. It was used with justification. The word well described the famed and inimitable Schwarzkopf interpretations of certain heroines in Strauss operas, such as the Marschallin in *Der Rosenkavalier* and the Countess in *Capriccio*. It was altogether appropriate to her performance in lieder, with Wolf and Strauss (again) to the fore, to which she turned when she gave up the stage.

And it was quite right for Elisabeth Schwarzkopf herself, with her mane of hair acting almost like a halo, which remained golden well into old age. She was totally professional in all that she did, right through to her personal appearance. She used to tell the story of her arrival, with her mother, in gloomy, bomb-torn Vienna. They had little or no money, but her mother insisted that their meagre luggage contained one impressive and expensive-looking dress for auditions.

It was in Vienna that Schwarzkopf came to the ears of Walter Legge, the recording manager of EMI. They met in the Café Mozart in a Harry Lime world, went directly to the Musikverein, where Legge gave her an audition of an inordinate length, which even Herbert von Karajan, who was present, described as cruel. But that started a partnership — with quite substantial involvement from Karajan — on stage and on record which was to last almost 30 years.

In 1953 Legge married Schwarzkopf and he guided every stage and step of her career. With him she made all her records, apart from song recitals recorded in Germany during the war, many of which remain unsurpassed in their field. When, just before her 75th birthday, Schwarzkopf was asked whether anyone else had acted in the recording studios as her producer she was faintly surprised by the question and replied that she had never considered anyone else, adding: "In any case Walter would never have allowed it."

Legge was equally punctilious about her stage appearances. He recognised that the voice was supremely musical, intelligently coloured, capable of conveying extremes of meaning. But it was neither exceptionally large, nor did it have the high notes of the coloratura range. On the one hand Schwarzkopf steered away from heavy parts, such as Beethoven's Leonore, which she sang only in concert performance, and on the other from parts such as Strauss's Arabella for which she was physically ideal but which lay a little too high.

The Legge-Schwarzkopf combination was a redoubtable one, combining a huge breadth of musical knowledge with a total understanding of the practicalities of music-making in theatres, studios and concert halls. Together they gave some notable masterclasses until Legge's premature death in 1979. Thereafter Elisabeth Schwarzkopf went on telling singers, young and some of them not so young, how to develop their potential. "Think about what you are going to sing before you sing it," she used to warn, "not when you are halfway through. That's not just my advice. It was Stanislavsky's."

Elisabeth Schwarzkopf was born in 1915 in Jarotschin near Posen (now Poznan). Her father was a teacher and classical scholar and the family moved around Silesia before coming to Berlin when she was 17. She studied voice and piano at the Hochschule für Musik, and immediately set her sights on joining the Deutsche Oper. Her first appearance on record was as a member of the chorus of a *Zauberflöte* made in Berlin by Sir Thomas Beecham. His technical assistant was a young man called Walter Legge. Neither Schwarzkopf nor Legge could have guessed at the future influence they were to have on one another.

By the next year her first ambition was achieved. She was engaged by the

Deutsche Oper and made her debut in 1938 as a Flowermaiden in *Parsifal*. During that first season she sang quantities of supporting roles in both opera and operetta, mixing Wagner with Lortzing, before she was cast as the soubrette Zerbinetta in a new production of Richard Strauss's *Ariadne auf Naxos*. In the early years of the war she joined the National Socialist Party, according to Alan Jefferson's punctilious but at times contentious biography of her. It caused a considerable stir when it was published in 1996 and certainly did not please its subject. Schwarzkopf appeared in a handful of propaganda films under Goebbels' banner and sang too in a single performance of *Die Fledermaus* in Paris in 1941, put on for the benefit of the German occupying forces.

These moves were purely pragmatic. Schwarzkopf was determined to get to the top and was not inclined to go looking for obstacles. At the Deutsche Oper one or two of the older sopranos were none too pleased with the presence of a young rival who was exceptionally good-looking as well as talented. But she was not content with being a star in wartime Berlin. Encouraged by Karl Böhm, who was considering her as Blonde in a production of *Entführung* he was planning, she went to Vienna, with that audition dress in her suitcase. There she made her debut in her regular role of Zerbinetta. The Deutsche Oper was abandoned and she threw in her lot with Vienna for such performances as were going in the last months of the war.

During 1946 Schwarzkopf, in common with other prominent musicians including Furtwängler and Karajan, came under the scrutiny of the Allied Denazification Bureau. But while the process was continuing they were allowed to appear from time to time. On Karajan's suggestion Legge, who was working for ENSA but looking for future artists for EMI, heard Schwarzkopf in *The Barber of Seville*. He recognised the talent at once but believed that she should be a lyric soprano — but not before he recorded her singing Johann Strauss's *Frühlingsstimmen*, one of the first of their many discs together.

Supported by Legge, Schwarzkopf rejoined the Vienna State Opera in their temporary home of the Theater an der Wien. She was part of an extraordinary company, which included Erich Kunz, Irmgard Seefried, Paul Schöffler and Anton Dermota. Superb Mozart was performed in a city short of food and that was still in ruins. In 1947 the Vienna State came to Covent Garden for a short but memorable season in which Schwarzkopf made her London debut as Donna Elvira in *Don Giovanni*.

Covent Garden at the time, like Vienna, was trying to rebuild its company. But it recognised in Schwarzkopf a natural talent. The problem was that Covent Garden was committed to opera in English, in which Schwarzkopf was then far from fluent. But she accepted the challenge and in the late 1940s and early 1950s London heard her as Pamina (*Zauberflöte*), Eva (*Die*

Meistersinger), Violetta (*La Traviata*) and Susanna (*The Marriage of Figaro*) among other roles. There was an outstanding Mimi, with Welitsch as Musetta, in *La Bohème*.

But the honeymoon with London soured. William Walton composed the role of Cressida in his opera *Troilus and Cressida* for Schwarzkopf, but there were arguments and the first night found another soprano in the role. She was never to sing the part. And as far as non-British opera was concerned Schwarzkopf saw no reason to continue in a language where the words did not always fit the music. A growing band of critics started to complain that, even when she was singing in German, her performances were too artificial. Matters came to a head in the *Rosenkavalier* of 1959 where her Marschallin came in for some harsh words. She was the leading exponent of the role, as Paul Czinner's film of the Salzburg production of the same period demonstrates, and she had every right to be cross. She was not to appear in opera at Covent Garden again and she selected any friendships with London critics very carefully.

Indeed, she had little need of London, which henceforth was to hear her in lieder recitals, especially of works by Wolf, Schubert and Brahms, which always attracted full houses. During the 1950s, with Legge's hand on the tiller, she had become EMI's leading soprano. There was a series of Viennese "champagne" operettas devised by Legge and conducted, with the exception of *Fledermaus*, by

Otto Ackermann using a team of singers highly skilled in this genre. With Karajan she recorded Mozart, Eva in *Meistersinger*, a witty Alice Ford in *Falstaff* and, perhaps best of all, Humperdinck's *Hänsel und Gretel*. For the young Wolfgang Sawallisch there was a *Capriccio* which has not been surpassed.

On stage she was always a figure of poise and extreme elegance, penetrating the meaning of each phrase she had to sing. In opera she was probably at her peak in the early 1950s, when she was an outstanding Eva in the Bayreuth *Meistersinger* and created the role of Anne Trulove when Stravinsky's *The Rake's Progress* was heard for the first time in Venice. She was a regular visitor to La Scala, where she first appeared in *Figaro* in 1949, and was to be heard in most of the following 14 seasons.

During her career Schwarzkopf sang 74 different operatic roles. But as she approached her fifties she concentrated on just five. Mozart provided Elvira, Fiordiligi (*Così*) and the Countess (*Figaro*). Strauss gave another Countess (*Capriccio*), and the Marschallin. Schwarzkopf's last full performance in an opera house was in *Der Rosenkavalier* at the Monnaie in Brussels just after Christmas 1967. She chose the same theatre for her official farewell to opera on New Year's Eve 1971, *Rosenkavalier* again, but just the first act.

Quantities of lieder recitals continued, usually with Geoffrey Parsons as accompanist and always carefully masterminded by Legge who was ever attentive to the hall and the potential audience. These eventually came to an end in 1978 with a farewell at the Wigmore Hall, followed by a final appearance in March 1979 in Zurich. Switzerland had become the Legges' home, but he died from a heart attack three days after that last recital.

Schwarzkopf tried her hand at directing in 1981. Inevitably the opera was *Der Rosenkavalier* and she went back to her beloved Monnaie. But the venture was not the success she had hoped for, partly because of a chill that developed between her and the chosen Marschallin, Elisabeth Söderström. The two women were too similar in musical style and temperament for the combination to work. Thereafter Schwarzkopf devoted most of her energies to teaching, which she had already developed by the side of Legge. A number of singers who went on to international careers passed through her hands, usually getting individual coaching at her Zurich home. She rarely accepted payment, although those receiving advice were sworn to secrecy lest too many came knocking at her door.

A six-CD set, containing some previously unissued tracks, came out to celebrate her 75th birthday. When she had passed 80 she personally supervised a re-press of the *Rosenkavalier* recorded with Karajan. Her numerous awards included an honorary doctorate in music from Cambridge University (1977) and life membership of the Vienna State Opera (1993). She was appointed DBE in 1992.

Dame Elisabeth Schwarzkopf, DBE, soprano, was born on December 9, 1915. She died on August 3, 2006, aged 90

———༄༅———

JEANE KIRKPATRICK

US AMBASSADOR TO THE UN WHO FOUGHT TO GET PRESIDENT REAGAN TO SIDE WITH ARGENTINA IN THE FALKLANDS CONFLICT

DECEMBER 9, 2006
By far Britain's least favourite American during the Falklands War was the US Ambassador to the UN, Jeane Kirkpatrick. Only hours after the 1982 invasion of the Falklands she notoriously attended as guest of honour a reception at the Argentine Embassy in Washington. She then went on television to assert that if the islands rightly belonged to Argentina its action could not be considered as "armed aggression".

Her efforts to tilt the Reagan Administration in favour of Argentina and against Britain provoked a most undiplomatic row with the US Secretary of State, Alexander Haig. Haig charged that Kirkpatrick was "mentally and emotionally incapable of thinking clearly on this issue because of her close links with the

Latins". Kirkpatrick dismissed Haig's policy as "a boy's club vision of gang loyalty". She accused him of being blindly pro-British and said that he and his advisers were "Britons in American clothes".

Kirkpatrick, who was close to the Argentine junta headed by General Galtieri, argued that America should not jeopardise its relations with Latin America by supporting Britain in a colonial war. Haig and the US Defence Secretary Caspar Weinberger (obituary, March 29, 2006) took Britain's side, and Weinberger was later awarded an honorary knighthood for his role in the victory.

Had Kirkpatrick prevailed, Britain would have been deprived of American fuel, Sidewinder missiles and other arms, and the vital US satellite intelligence that enabled it to win the war. And Galtieri and his junta would not have been replaced by a freely elected government.

President Reagan found himself in the midst of the tug-of-war between the West's two most formidable conservative women — Jeane Kirkpatrick and Margaret Thatcher. Thatcher prevailed, but though the two shared a similar ideology, the British Prime Minister never forgave Kirkpatrick for her role in the Falklands.

Kirkpatrick first came to Reagan's attention on the eve of his first Administration over an article she had written for *Commentary*, a publication backed by the American Jewish Committee. Entitled *Dictatorships and Double Standards*, it argued that right-wing "authoritarian" governments, such as those in Argentina, Chile and South Africa, suited American interests better and were "less repressive" than pro-Soviet "totalitarian" regimes. She castigated the emphasis placed on human rights by the previous, Carter Administration and blamed it for undermining right-wing governments in Nicaragua and Iran.

Overnight Kirkpatrick, a not particularly well-known academic and political scientist, and a paid-up Democrat, became one of the most powerful women in America as Ambassador to the UN with a seat in the Reagan Cabinet and a member of the National Security Council. As the US Representative to the UN for four years after the 1980 election, she came to be regarded as the ideological conscience of the Reagan Administration. Combative and confrontational, she symbolised the assertiveness that characterised American foreign policy after Reagan took office. She declared at the time: "I am not a professional diplomat. I've not signed over my conscience and intellect."

Adored by the neo-conservatives and despised by the liberal foreign-policy establishment, she provided the intellectual foundations for a policy which aimed to confront Soviet expansionism and restore US pre-eminence in world affairs. She endeared herself to Reagan by lecturing Third World nations that the US would no longer put up with the sort of abuse it had suffered during the Carter Administration.

Many of her fellow ambassadors found her abrasive and uncompromising, but for others she was a refreshingly cold blast through the cynical corridors of the UN, attacking hypocrisy and the double standards of the Third World. She was a formidable figure with cropped hair, a jutting lower lip and a growl in her voice. She berated delegates for failing to condemn the Soviet invasion of Afghanistan and said it was hard to understand "why we support some UN agencies, which are undermining the work of the US and some of its allies". She frequently vetoed sanctions against Israel and South Africa. On one occasion, after an attack by the Non-Aligned Movement in the UN, she wrote personally to each delegate demanding an explanation for their support of "base lies and malicious attacks upon the good name of the United States".

The only Democrat in the Reagan cabinet, and for a while the only woman, Kirkpatrick was a professor of political science at Georgetown University and resident scholar at the American Enterprise Institute before joining the Administration.

Jeane Duane Jordan was born in Oklahoma in 1926, the daughter of an oil-well engineer. She was educated in New York, receiving her PhD from Columbia University in 1968. She married Evron Kirkpatrick, another political scientist and 15 years her senior, and had three sons.

Although a registered Democrat, until becoming a Republican in 1985, the party to which she looked back was that of Presidents Truman and Kennedy. She subsequently became disillusioned with liberal Democrats during the counter-culture of the 1960s and the violence of the anti-Vietnam War movement. In the late 1970s she became highly critical of the policies of Jimmy Carter and observed that the Soviet Union had become "a major power in the Western hemisphere" during his Administration. When she first took office she felt completely at home with President Reagan's hard-line approach to Moscow and his depiction of the Soviet Union as an "evil empire". But she lost ground in Washington as Reagan began to move towards a deal with Moscow.

After battling for four years at the UN with the Soviet bloc and a hostile Third World, Kirkpatrick announced that she would resign her post at the end of the first Reagan Administration and made it clear that she would return to office only as Secretary of State or National Security Adviser.

At the Republican National Convention in 1984 she made the inaugural address to great acclaim and was the toast of the party's right wing. But the new Reagan team were uneasy about bringing such a loose cannon to Washington (and the President may have sought a quieter life for his second term), and Kirkpatrick was offered neither of the posts of her choice. Kirkpatrick then returned to academic life in Washington, based at Georgetown University and the American Enterprise Institute.

In 1986, in an open break with her past, she expressed doubts about Reagan's capacity for superpower diplomacy, indicating that she felt the Soviet leader Mikhail Gorbachev was too clever for the President and his advisers. Later she claimed that she had been eased out of the Reagan Administration because her hard-line views had caused problems for Reagan's "be nice to Gorby" aides.

Kirkpatrick was the author of numerous scholarly articles and a number of books. These ranged from *Political Woman* (1974), a study of the role of women in modern politics, to *The Withering Away of the Totalitarian State — and Other Surprises*, which appeared in 1992. In 2003 she became chairman of the US delegation to the UN Human rights Commission.

Her husband died in 1995.

Jeane Kirkpatrick, US diplomat, was born on November 19, 1926. She died on December 7, 2006, aged 80

———

DAME ANNE McLAREN

DISTINGUISHED GENETICIST
WHO MADE NOTABLE
CONTRIBUTIONS TO THE
SCIENCE, TECHNIQUES
AND ETHICS OF FERTILITY
TREATMENT

JULY 12, 2007

Anne McLaren was an exceptional scientist. She made fundamental advances in genetics which paved the way for the development of human *in vitro* fertilisation. She played an important role in discussions of ethical issues relating to embryos and stem cells, serving on the Warnock committee and later on the Human Fertilisation and Embryology Authority. As foreign secretary and vice president of the Royal Society — elected FRS in 1975, she was the first woman in the 331 years of its existence to become one of its officers — she travelled widely. In addition to promoting scientific exchanges and raising awareness of the medical and educational needs of developing countries, she was also a role model for women in science.

Anne Laura McLaren was born in 1927, the daughter of Henry McLaren, the 2nd Baron Aberconway, and Christabel MacNaghten. The family were industrialists with an interest in Liberal politics, women's suffrage and the beautiful gardens created at Bodnant in North Wales. She was educated at Longstowe Hall and Lady Margaret Hall in Oxford where she took a first in zoology and, in 1952, a DPhil. She studied mite infestation in fruit flies with J. B. S. Haldane, the genetics of rabbits with Peter Medawar and mouse viruses under Kingsley Sanders.

She moved to London as a research fellow, first at University College and then at the Royal Veterinary College. She worked with Donald Michie, later her husband, on mice, which became her preferred animal. She studied the effects of the mother on the development of the spinal column in her offspring, and on the influence of "super-ovulation" on fertility. In 1958, working with John Biggers, she produced the first litter of mice grown from eggs that had developed in tissue culture and then been transferred to a surrogate mother. This advance led to the development of successful treatments for infertile women using *in vitro* fertilisation and embryo transfer.

She spent the next 15 years, 1959-74, at the Institute of Animal Genetics in Edinburgh, eventually becoming a principal scientific officer. Here she successfully nurtured a large group of graduate students. Her particular mixture of unstinting support, tolerance, sense of fun and a highly developed critical faculty made her an ideal supervisor. Her refusal, even when she had done a considerable amount of the work, to include her name on the scientific papers generated (an honourable practice rarely seen today) was deeply appreciated.

McLaren was actively involved in many research projects on infertility and embryonic development. This work involved developing the techniques needed for the successful transfer of embryos. She also studied reproductive immunology, contraception and the characteristics of chimeras produced by the fusion of different embryonic cells.

In 1974 she left Edinburgh to be the director of the Medical Research Council's new Mammalian Development Unit at University College London. Here she carried on her research, and was made a Fellow of the Royal College of Obstetricians and Gynaecologists in 1986. In 1991 she became foreign secretary and vice president of the Royal Society.

In 1992 McLaren moved to the Gurdon Institute in Cambridge. She continued the research, developed in London, on primordial germ cells that mature into sperms or eggs. She described these as "the most fascinating cells of all — still deeply mysterious". Interested in how they converted into stem cells, she studied their properties by putting them back into early embryos and monitoring their contributions to the developing adult. She compared them with the stem cells that can be obtained from early embryos. The reprogramming of germ cells into stem cells is crucial to understanding how a cell in an adult can be turned into one capable of generating many other kinds of cells. She maintained her interest in the formation of sperms and eggs, in the influence of sex chromosomes on the development of germ cells and in the activity of these chromosomes in modifying other chromosomes in the germ cells.

She was appointed a Fellow of King's College, Cambridge, in 1992 and became a Fellow Commoner at Christ's College. In 1994 she was made an honorary Fellow at Lucy Cavendish College. She was appointed DBE in 1993, and was president of the British Association for the Advancement of Science in 1993-94.

Throughout her working life she endeavoured to promote the careers of women in the sciences, and in 1995 became president of the Association for Women in Science and Engineering. She was a trustee of the Natural History Museum London, 1994-2003, where she was much appreciated for her wisdom and vision.

Membership of the Government's Warnock committee on human fertilisation and embryology was followed by ten years working on the Human Fertilisation and Embryology Authority that served to regulate IVF and the research and use of human embryos.

McLaren — she always preferred to be addressed as Dr McLaren rather than Dame or Professor — received numerous honorary degrees and awards, including the Japan Prize for her work in developmental biology, the Scientific Medal of the Zoological Society of London, the Royal Medal of the Royal Society and the Marshall Medal of the Society for the Study of Fertility. She was a foreign member of many academic institutions overseas, including the Polish Academy of Science, the American Academy of Arts & Sciences and the Russian Academy of Sciences. In 1986 she was made a Fellow of the Royal College of Obstetricians and Gynaecologists for her outstanding contribution to the field of fertility. In 1991 she became a Founder Fellow in the Academy of Medical Sciences and the Fullerian Professor of Physiology at the Royal Institution.

In addition to writing two academic books and more than 330 research papers, she served on many committees, councils and editorial boards, often as chairman or scientific adviser. They included the World Health Organisation's Special Programme on Human Reproduction and the Panel on Sustainable Development. A lesser-known early achievement, at 9 years of age, was when, with charming confidence, she appeared with Raymond Massey and Ralph Richardson in the film Things to Come (1936) based on a story by H. G. Wells.

During her last few years McLaren served as trustee of the Frozen Ark project which she had co-founded. This aims to preserve the DNA and viable cells of the world's endangered animal species before they become extinct. She was convinced that the stored material would provide an invaluable source of genetic information for future generations, and a "back-up" for conservation breeding programmes.

Her research interests in stem cells led her to make a notable contribution to the ethical debate about their generation and use, in particular those made from early human embryos. She became a member of the Nuffield Foundation's Bioethics Council and the European Group on Ethics that advises the European Commission on the social and ethical implications of new technologies. She was a long-term member and council member of the Pugwash Conferences. This group, which was awarded the Nobel Prize for Peace in 1995, is devoted to reducing the danger from all forms of armed conflict and seeks to raise awareness of the ethical issues that arise from scientific advance.

McLaren died in a car crash. Donald Michie, her former husband, scientific colleague, father of her children and lifelong friend, was travelling with her and also died in the accident. Her death is a tremendous loss to the world of science and to her colleagues, students, many friends and all those who were lucky enough to enter her orbit. Her particular blend of idealism, effectiveness and all the splendid personal qualities for which she was held in such high regard will make her greatly missed.

McLaren is survived by two daughters and her son.

Dame Anne McLaren, DBE, FRS, geneticist, was born on April 26, 1927. She died in a car accident on July 7, 2007, aged 80

———

BENAZIR BHUTTO

COURAGEOUS PRIME MINISTER OF PAKISTAN WHOSE REFORMING ZEAL WAS NO MATCH FOR THE CONSERVATIVE FORCES RANGED AGAINST HER

DECEMBER 28, 2007

Benazir Bhutto was one of several women who were collectively South Asia's greatest political paradox, each rising to heights of power on the backs of dead husbands and fathers for the sole reason that they possessed famous names. Bhutto's ambition and guts were beyond question, but without her name and family political pedigree — and vast wealth — she could not have become the first female leader of a contemporary Muslim country.

It also happened in Muslim-majority Bangladesh, where two women who hated each other, Begum Khalida Zia and Sheikh Hasina Wajid, carved up the political landscape because one was the widow of the liberation war hero against Pakistan and the other the daughter of the founder of the nation. Sirimavo Bandaranaike of Sri Lanka became the world's first female head of government in 1960 because her husband had held the job before her — paving the way for their daughter, Chandrika Kumaratunga, subsequently to become Prime Minister and President. Indira Gandhi led India because her father was Jawaharlal Nehru, and Sonia Gandhi became political kingmaker because she was Rajiv Gandhi's widow.

Benazir Bhutto rose to power because she was the daughter of Zulfikar Ali Bhutto, a former populist Prime Minister who was hanged by the military dictatorship of General Zia-ul Haq in 1979. The dignity with which she handled herself after his judicial assassination — she called it murder — drew admiring comparisons with the Kennedy family, and touched the hearts of a nation sick of austere military rule. Her beauty and powerful oratory caught the imagination, and army rule weakened as her popularity soared.

It was a measure of Bhutto's political ambition that in 1987 she submitted herself to an arranged marriage to somebody she did not love — the son of a Karachi cinema owner — aware that the highly conservative electorate would not tolerate being led by an unmarried woman. She constantly endured the sometimes salacious taunts of clerics who accused her of dating men while she was studying at Harvard and Oxford.

She was elected leader of the Pakistan People's Party, founded by her father, and in national elections in November 1988 swept to power. She had returned from exile in London to be cheered by hundreds of thousands of people who were as confident as she was that a new and prosperous era was beginning and that the Army would at last allow democracy to take root.

Never had Pakistan been more optimistic or certain of itself. In less than two years, however, the military engineered Bhutto's dismissal on the grounds of incompetence and corruption, and a new era of failed democracies and squandered hopes began.

Almost her entire time in her first term of office was spent fighting political battles with clerics and others determined to get her out. There was little opportunity for policymaking or economic planning, and the country reeled in financial crisis as the rich grew richer through corruption. Reports of rampant fraud by her husband, Asif Zardari, sullied the Bhutto name. Downtrodden women and the poor, groups which she had pledged to help, felt betrayed.

Three years after her dismissal, however, following even worse misrule and corruption under the government of Nawaz Sharif — also dismissed at the Army's behest — she was re-elected Prime Minister. But circumstances did not improve, and nationwide loathing of the antics of Asif Zardari, openly branded "Mr Ten Per Cent" by the press, helped to wreck Bhutto's credibility at home and abroad. There was widespread speculation about the obvious power Zardari exercised over his wife, and about her apparently inexplicable refusal to curtail his activities even though they were helping to destroy her credibility and undermine her leadership.

In 1996 the Army once again arranged her dismissal, clearing the way for another chaotic period of misgovernment by Nawaz Sharif. This endured until the military seized direct power once more in 1999, with Pervez Musharraf, the chief of staff of the Army, effecting a bloodless military coup.

Benazir faced imprisonment on a range of charges, including corruption, but she was allowed to go into exile, which she spent mostly in London, while an exiled Nawaz Sharif occupied a borrowed palace in Saudi Arabia. The two old enemies passed many years plotting to see who could be first to return to power when military rule ended. Even in exile Bhutto maintained a wary contact with Musharraf, in which power-sharing came under discussion.

With the stock of Musharraf falling lower within Pakistan in the opening years of the new millennium, with his uneasy alliance with the US as its principal partner in the "war on terror" coming under constant attack, both verbal and physical, from Muslim clerical leaders and their followers, and with a groundswell of demand in the Western countries that supported him that he submit his presidency to ratification by a popular vote, the return of Bhutto to Pakistan, to play some sort of role in the political process, suddenly began to be spoken of again as a possibility.

On October 5 this year Musharraf signed a national reconciliation ordinance which gave amnesty to Bhutto and other opposition political leaders — though significantly not, at first, to Sharif. All corruption charges against her were dropped. The following day Musharraf won a parliamentary election which legitimised his tenure of the presidency. On October 18, Bhutto returned in triumph to Pakistan, assuming on-the-spot leadership of the opposition Pakistan People's Party (PPP).

Two suicide bombs exploded shortly after she arrived at Jinnah International Airport, Karachi. She was unharmed, but among the 136 killed in the blasts were 50 security guards of the PPP who had formed a human chain around the truck that was carrying her away from the airport. It was a portent of things to come, and an indication that the old enmities that had twice forced her from power were never far from the surface in Pakistan.

Benazir Bhutto was born in Karachi in 1953, the eldest daughter of Zulfikar Ali Bhutto, a Pakistani of Sindhi extraction, and his wife Begum Nusrat Bhutto, who was of Iranian-Kurdish extraction. The Bhutto family was not a happy one. Benazir's mother openly supported one of her sons as the rightful heir of the political dynasty before he was killed in a shoot-out in Karachi, saying that as a man it was his right to take over the party.

Zulfikar Ali Bhutto adored his daughter but never hid his contempt for both his sons. His ancestors had grown rich by helping the British to rule Sind province (now Sindh), for which they were handsomely rewarded. Although presenting himself as a man of the people he never gave up the family's huge feudal landholdings. Neither did his daughter. It was often said of her that her political life was driven by a need to vindicate her father, a foul-tempered man who made enemies easily. She was to fail, just as she failed to fulfil the dreams of the millions who had believed passionately in her and in her father.

She was educated in Karachi at Lady Jennings Nursery School and the Convent of Jesus and Mary. She then had two years at Rawalpindi Presentation Convent before going to the Jesus and Mary Convent in Murree, where she took her O-levels at the age of 15. She then went to Karachi Grammar School where she took her A-levels. She continued her studies in the US, from 1969 to 1973 at Radcliffe College. From there she went to Harvard, where she took a good BA in comparative government and was elected to Phi Beta Kappa. From the US she came to Britain to read philosophy, politics and economics at Lady Margaret Hall, Oxford, while also doing a course in international law and diplomacy. In 1976 she became the first Asian woman to be elected President of the Oxford Union.

After completing her education she returned to Pakistan. Her father, who had been deposed, was in jail, and she was placed under house arrest. She was to be intermittently with him during his last days. It was some years before Bhutto talked in detail of the day that her father was executed inside Rawalpindi Central Jail while she and her mother were held at a deserted police training camp at Sihala. She recalled waking suddenly at 2am and screaming "No!" Her father's body was taken away immediately for burial, with no family members present, and his clothes were handed over to Benazir and her mother by a junior jailer who told them that the end had been peaceful.

"The scent of his cologne was still on his clothes, the scent of Shalimar," Bhutto wrote in her 1988 autobiography, *Daughter of the East*. For two years she had done nothing but fight in the courts and on the international stage to save her father, and now she felt shattered and empty. On her last visit to his cell she asked: "What will I do without you to help me?" He shrugged helplessly, unaware that he was to be hanged the next day. After 30 minutes Bhutto and her mother were ordered to leave.

Bhutto used her speaking skills — she was more comfortable in her first language of English than Urdu — to campaign relentlessly against the Zia regime after her father's death, and was frequently placed under house arrest. That only heightened her popularity. She spent the summer of 1981 in an insect-infested jail cell in Sindh, fighting heat and insect bites, and in 1984 was allowed to travel to England to be treated for a serious ear infection. She remained in exile until Zia lifted martial law in December 1985. She returned to a massive welcome on the streets and instantly began to organise mass protests and civil disobedience campaigns to force Zia out. His death in a still-unexplained air crash in 1988 — there was apparently an on-board explosion — cleared the way for elections.

No one ever doubted Bhutto's resilience and determination, but few could praise her for effective governance. She fought formidable objects — she was young, attractive, inexperienced and, above all, female in a political system controlled jealously by men. In her early days of power she tried to calm tensions with India, but a strong and entrenched rightist parliamentary opposition scuttled any attempts at progress at home or abroad. She was perhaps doomed from the outset. As a head of government she relied heavily on Washington — a vital paymaster — to keep her in power, and she presented Pakistan as a frontline state in the fight against Islamic extremism, making her the darling of the US before corruption and incompetence soured her name.

Her husband went to jail for corruption but was later allowed to leave the country. When Bhutto, threatened with jail on corruption charges, also went into exile in 1999 a sickly Zardari did not join her. The marriage appeared to be dead.

In spite of her failures in the past, her return to Pakistan in October 2007 at the head of the PPP as opposition leader was greeted with wild enthusiasm by large numbers of the party's followers who still saw in her a liberal middle way in Pakistani politics. Her launch of the PPP's electoral manifesto stressed that if elected the party would concentrate on the "Five Es" — employment, education, energy, environment, equality.

Her optimism was high for a convincing performance for the PPP in elections scheduled for January 8. But continuing physical attacks on the party's personnel and premises were a constant reminder of the dangers lying in her path. Already this month three PPP workers had been killed in an attack by gunmen on the party's headquarters in Quetta, Baluchistan province. Bhutto herself was fatally injured in a suspected suicide attack as she left a rally in Rawalpindi after addressing an audience of thousands. *Benazir Bhutto, Prime Minister of Pakistan, 1988-90 and 1993-96, was born on June 21, 1953. She died of injuries sustained in an attack by a suicide bomber on December 27, 2007, aged 54*

HELEN SUZMAN

IRREPRESSIBLE ANTI-APARTHEID CAMPAIGNER AND POLITICIAN WHO WAS A CONSTANT THORN IN THE SIDE OF SOUTH AFRICAN GOVERNMENTS

JANUARY 2, 2009

The most celebrated white champion of the anti-apartheid movement, Helen Suzman was the South African MP who, over a period of 36 years, consistently denounced the iniquities of racial segregation. Often, she was the sole politician in South Africa's parliament to campaign vociferously against apartheid legislation and highlight the frequent instances she discovered of institutional racial abuse. For six years, she was also the only woman among 165 MPs, enduring the contempt of male parliamentarians who viewed white supremacy as a birthright, and to whom "liberal" was a dirty word.

Undeterred, Suzman used her privileges as an MP to gain access to areas forbidden to the general public: prisons, black townships and "resettlement areas" in the tribal homelands. At every step she highlighted the evils of the system. She disseminated her findings and presented alternative policies to the outside world through the parliamentary press gallery.

Suzman began her parliamentary career as a United Party MP in 1953, but left in 1959 to co-found the Progressive Party after the UP split on the question of allocation of land to blacks. Thereafter hers was often the lone voice of dissent on the parliamentary benches. For 13 years she was the only representative in Parliament of the Progressive Party. But she persevered, using the paradoxical circumstance of the authoritarian Government's respect for the parliamentary system to challenge it and its policies at every turn. Her most relentless campaign was against the notorious pass laws, which restricted the movement of blacks and prevented them from selling their labour in the open market. The repeal of these odious laws towards the end of the life of apartheid government in South Africa owed much to her obduracy.

Slight of build though she was, Suzman had great reserves of courage and stamina. She readily held the attention of the House, particularly in her clashes with successive prime ministers and ministers of justice. She used question time to good effect, drawing attention to abuses in the police force and other departments of state and ensuring that these gained the widest publicity.

Helen Suzman was born in Germiston, a small mining town outside Johannesburg, in 1917. She was the daughter of Samuel Gavronsky, a Jewish immigrant who had come to the Transvaal from Lithuania with, as she used to say, "a bundle on his back".

She was educated at Parktown Convent in Johannesburg and at the University of the Witwatersrand where she read commerce and economics. She married in 1937 before graduating, and dropped out of university to give birth to her first child. She returned to her studies and completed her degree with first-class honours.

After the Second World War Suzman taught economic history at Witwatersrand for eight years before going into politics. She entered Parliament with the United Party representing the Houghton constituency of Johannesburg in 1953. At that time Dr D. F. Malan's Nationalists had completed five years in office and were enforcing the first apartheid legislation. Elected as a member of the old United Party of General Smuts, Suzman was one of a group of liberal-minded MPs who broke away from the UP to form the Progressive Party in 1959. In the general election of 1961 this new party was all but wiped out at the polls: Suzman was the only survivor. It was a situation to be repeated at the elections of 1966 and 1970.

In the 1960s, with the Vorster Government introducing the first legislation providing for detention without trial, hers was frequently the only dissenting voice on the opposition benches. It was this legislation, later supplemented by the Terrorism Act and consolidated in the Internal Security Act, which gave the State powers to hold detainees incommunicado and in solitary confinement. It also gave rise to abuses such as torture during interrogation — and a spate of deaths in detention.

Suzman was witty and irrepressible in debate, a master of the pungent aside and cutting rejoinder. She often faced roars of disapproval from the government benches as she argued the case against the Nationalist Government's ideological legislation. In the 1960s, she frequently had to stand her ground in debate amid intense anger and abuse. The three successive prime ministers whom she confronted over a period of 25 years, Hendrik Verwoerd, John Vorster and P. W. Botha, she was subsequently to describe as "as nasty a trio as you could encounter in your worst nightmares".

She later admitted that Verwoerd was "the only man who has ever scared me stiff". Yet she stood up to him across the floor of the House, notably on one occasion in 1961 when he was at his most aggressive and sarcastic, telling her that "the country has written you off". Suzman replied: "The world has written you off."

Her spell as the only Progressive MP came to an end in 1974 when the party won five more seats. Indeed, as the United Party continued to lose ground at the polls, the Progressive Party gradually became the official Opposition, and Suzman's onslaughts on apartheid policies gained welcome reinforcement from a new breed of vigorous parliamentarians.

From the outset Suzman had taken a special interest in conditions in South African prisons. She visited Nelson Mandela on Robben Island in the early 1960s, continuing to do so in later years. She was one of the first MPs to visit the squatter camps such as Crossroads and bring them to the attention of Parliament. In latter years she paid particular attention to what she believed were deteriorating standards in the South African judicial system and, in particular, the recurring cases in which whites who beat blacks to death in the most brutal fashion were given scandalously light sentences.

In 1989 she introduced the first censure motion ever before Parliament on a judge, J. J. Strydom, who had given a five-year suspended jail sentence, and a fine equivalent to a few hundred pounds, to a farmer, Jacobus Vorster, who had beaten a black labourer to death. Vorster was also to pay a small stipend to the widow and five children of the deceased for the next five years.

Describing the entire judgment as "a travesty of justice", Suzman found herself subjected to a barrage of sarcastic remarks from the Minister of Justice, who also saw fit to make the extraordinary observation that in addition to his punishment the convicted man would face humiliation because he would be known by fellow whites to be working for the next five years to support a black woman. It goes without saying that in an atmosphere of such moral inversions, Suzman's censure motion was thrown out.

Yet, South Africa was on the verge of change. P. W. Botha had given up the leadership of his party in February 1989 after suffering a stroke, though still retaining the State Presidency

Helen Suzman at a Christmas party for South African pensioners in 1979

(the office of Prime Minister had been abolished in 1983). His successor, the Education Minster, F. W. de Klerk, though not previously noted as an advocate of reform, was soon to be calling for a non-racist South Africa and for full-scale, open, negotiations about the country's future.

But 1989 was also the year in which Suzman decided to retire from politics. She had reached the age of 70 and felt that much of what she had striven for was about to be achieved. In October that year she came to London and was appointed an honorary DBE. She also received prizes and honorary degrees from institutions and universities all over the world.

Back in South Africa she then watched from the political sidelines the heady events leading to the release of Mandela and the transition to majority rule, with a mixture of apprehension and hope.

Her autobiography, *In No Uncertain Terms*, was published in 1993. She was appointed to the Order of Merit of South Africa in 1997.

The Helen Suzman Foundation, an independent think-tank dedicated to the promotion of liberal values in post-apartheid South Africa, was founded in her honour, and Suzman acted as patron.

Helen Suzman's husband, Dr M. M. Suzman, died in 1994. She is survived by their two daughters.

Helen Suzman, South African parliamentarian and civil rights campaigner, was born on November 7, 1917. She died on January 1, 2009, aged 91

—✺—

DAME JOAN SUTHERLAND

AUSTRALIAN SOPRANO WHOSE
DRAMATIC COLORATURA
VOICE BECAME THE TOAST
OF THE WORLD

OCTOBER 12, 2010

On a raw mid-February night in 1959 one of the most remarkable performances in the postwar history of opera took place in London — a night that transformed the career of Joan Sutherland, a 32-year-old soprano from Sydney. The occasion was the premiere of Franco Zeffirelli's production of Donizetti's *Lucia di Lammermoor* at Covent Garden. The opera had not been heard there since 1925, although in recent years Maria Callas had been restoring the reputation of Donizetti and bel canto in general.

The production was mounted especially for Sutherland, who had previously performed a wide repertoire as a company member for six and a half years. The soprano's skill in the florid style had been carefully brought out by the coaching of her husband, Richard Bonynge. Zeffirelli had also worked meticulously to help her to build a convincing physical characterisation (in the unforgettable Mad Scene, he had her darting frantically from one guest to another, which

she accomplished while continuing to maintain perfect vocal control).

The performance launched Sutherland's reign as the world's leading Lucia over the next quarter-century, and helped to establish her as one of the greatest of all bel canto interpreters. The *Lucia* was immensely gratifying not only for Sutherland herself, but also for those who had believed in her — above all her husband; her mother, whose voice had been Sutherland's initial inspiration; her teacher, Clive Carey; her dramatic coach, Norman Ayrton; Covent Garden's backstage personnel, who had constantly encouraged her; and Sir David Webster, the house's general administrator at the time. Webster had watched Sutherland gain confidence on stage over the years, and had known full well that he would need to find a suitable vehicle for her. *Lucia* was the fulfilment of his astute judgment of Sutherland's talent and his faith in it.

Over a quarter of a century later, in 1985, the Covent Garden audience heard Sutherland's Lucia again. The Zeffirelli production by that time was looking its age, but Dame Joan, as she had now become, was in tremendous form, as was the tenor Carlo Bergonzi, who sang Edgardo. These two veterans gave the public an unforgettable performance, which at the same time provided a priceless lesson for artists of the next generation.

The 1985 *Lucia* should have come as no surprise to anyone who had followed Sutherland's career over the years. She had been unfailingly vigilant in preserving her voice; as a result, her command of trills and florid passages proved as dazzling as ever. Beyond that, she exhibited the sheer authority that comes only from long experience in applying superb technique to formidable stylistic demands. "Without technique we cannot take a single artistic step forward," she once said, and her career demonstrated the supreme wisdom of that assertion.

Joan Sutherland was born in Sydney, New South Wales, in 1926. Even as a child she absorbed a great deal from the singing of her mother, who possessed a remarkable mezzo-soprano voice. The budding singer studied at the conservatory in Sydney and in her early twenties was performing everything from *Acis and Galatea* and *Dido and Aeneas* to excerpts from the operas of Wagner. One of her early successes was the title role of Sir Eugene Goossens's *Judith* (1951). The composer believed that here was the true successor to Sutherland's compatriot of the 1920s, the great Wagner soprano Florence Austral. Shortly thereafter Sutherland won the Sun Aria competition, and Australian sponsorship money made possible her trip to Britain for the continuation of her studies.

Sutherland arrived in London in August 1951. She attended the Royal College of Music where another Australian, Richard Bonynge, who had studied piano at the Sydney Conservatory, was already installed.

After four auditions, Sutherland made her debut at Covent Garden as the First Lady in *The Magic Flute*. During her first two seasons she sang supporting and leading parts — Clotilde in *Norma* (for Callas's debut, 1952), the Priestess in *Aida*, Frasquita in *Carmen*, but also Lady Rich in *Gloriana*, Agathe in *Der Freischütz* and, on tour, the Countess in *Le nozze di Figaro* and Amelia in *Un ballo in maschera*.

Bonynge introduced his fellow Australian not only to musical London but also to the bel canto repertoire, which was to remain their joint passion throughout their professional lives. Hearing Callas helped Bonynge to prove to Sutherland that a large-scale soprano voice, with sufficient technique, could easily manage the demands of bel canto singing.

Bonynge, whose original intention had been to become a concert pianist, increasingly chose to spend his time coaching and guiding Sutherland — not necessarily in a direction that pleased Covent Garden, where bel canto repertoire was not one of the management's major interests. Sutherland and Bonynge were married in 1954.

Shortly after the wedding Bonynge gave a Wigmore Hall recital, but during the next several years he was generally heard only with Sutherland, either as accompanist or conductor. By the mid-1960s he was leading nearly all of Sutherland's performances, both on stage and in the studio (major exceptions were recordings of *Turandot* under Mehta and the Verdi *Requiem* under Solti).

Eventually, however, Bonynge branched out to make his own superb contribution internationally as both a conductor and scholar, restoring innumerable neglected scores to public attention.

The five years prior to *Lucia* found Sutherland acquiring a vast amount of stage and concert experience. At Covent Garden she sang brilliantly as Jenifer in Tippett's *The Midsummer Marriage* (world premiere, 1955) and also shone in such leading roles as Gilda, Eva in *Die Meistersinger*, and Mme Lidoine in *Dialogues of the Carmelites* (British premiere, 1958).

In other venues she took on operas not associated with her later on (*La clemenza di Tito*, *Euryanthe* and *Aida*). She also revealed her flair for Handel: as Alcina with the Handel Opera Society, then later at the Garden where, as the Israelite Woman in *Samson*, she stopped the show with *Let the Bright Seraphim*. Once *Lucia* brought Sutherland to the front rank she was able to choose what she wished to sing, both in London and in major theatres abroad.

The offers came swiftly, including *I Puritani* at Glyndebourne, *Beatrice di Tenda* at La Scala, and, in 1960, *Alcina* for her American debut in Dallas (following the premiere of Zeffirelli's production in Venice). Sutherland toured America the following year, ending at the Metropolitan Opera, where she made her debut as Lucia. She returned to La Scala to star opposite Giulietta Simionato in Rossini's *Semiramide*, one of many neglected works she helped to return to the repertoire (others over the years would include Meyerbeer's *Les Huguenots*, Verdi's *I Masnadieri*, and two operas of Massenet, *Esclarmonde* and *Le roi de Lahore*).

The soprano's recording career was launched in 1959 with a magnificent Bellini/Donizetti/Verdi recital for Decca. Her voice was revealed as that rarity, a dramatic coloratura soprano; the combination of gleaming tone, huge range, and infallible command of florid passages, in an instrument of Wagnerian amplitude, seemed unparalleled in modern times. Sutherland also recorded Donna Anna in Columbia's *Don Giovanni* under Giulini and then, in 1960, a two-disc recital entitled *The Art of the Prima Donna*. That set rightly positioned Sutherland as the successor to the greatest sopranos, from Mrs Billington and Giuditta Pasta to Melba and Tetrazzini.

Sutherland's New York debut with the American Opera Society in a concert performance of Bellini's *Beatrice di Tenda* (1961) brought her together for the first time with the American mezzo-soprano Marilyn Horne. Vocally, musically, and personally, their rapport was complete, as witnessed in *Semiramide* (Los Angeles, Boston, Chicago, concert performance in London) and *Norma* (their role debuts in Vancouver were followed by new productions at Covent Garden, the Met, and San Francisco).

In 1965 Sutherland first encountered another frequent partner, Luciano Pavarotti: first for the tenor's American debut in Miami, then for Sutherland's return to Australia with an ensemble created for the occasion, the Sutherland-Williamson International Opera Company. In 1966 she and Pavarotti recorded *Beatrice di Tenda* for Decca (many more complete operas would follow), and they later sang together in new Met productions of *Il Trovatore*, *I Puritani*, and *La Fille du Régiment*. This last work reprised a staging in which the two had triumphed at Covent Garden, with Sutherland — to general amazement — revealing the instincts of a born comedienne. The first half of her career included few comic roles, but she would make up for it later, enjoying herself tremendously as leading lady of *Die Fledermaus* and *The Merry Widow*.

The Bonynges had a villa in Switzerland as their home base, but for three decades they travelled the world, with appearances in every major concert hall and opera house. Their recitals were enchantingly old-fashioned events, with Sutherland often singing French and English material that would have graced programmes of the Victorian era. (She generally sang from a music stand, blaming this on what she described as "my rotten memory".) Her concerts with orchestra were invariably memorable occasions, in which she would frequently delight audiences with arias from operas she had little or no chance to sing on stage.

Audiences who heard Sutherland during her three decades as an international star will long remember portrayals as varied as Cleopatra (Hamburg); Rodelinda (Amsterdam);

Marguerite de Valois (La Scala, also in concert at the Royal Albert Hall); Anna Bolena (Toronto, San Francisco, Houston, Chicago, and in a telecast from New York's Lincoln Centre); Ophélie (Toronto); Esclarmonde (San Francisco, the Met, Covent Garden); Adriana Lecouvreur (San Diego); and an extraordinary variety of roles — among them Alcina, *Idomeneo*'s Elettra, Desdemona, Lakmé, Suor Angelica and Mme Lidoine — in Sydney.

Over the years Sutherland was able to exploit her statuesque presence to increasingly effective dramatic purposes. She always responded to stage direction as long as it was honest and remained faithful to the work.

Other than *Lucia*, her finest achievement as an actress was perhaps the four *Hoffmann* heroines, the greatest possible challenge to her versatility. She sang Olympia, Giulietta and Antonia individually in her early years at Covent Garden (Olympia helped to awaken management to her possibilities in coloratura roles). Not until 1970 did she add Stella to the other three, singing them all for the director Bliss Hebert's Seattle production. She reprised *Hoffmann* at the Met (in New York and on tour), in Sydney, and for a justly praised Decca recording under Bonynge, with Plácido Domingo as her partner.

Sutherland husbanded her resources in the final decade of her career, choosing less strenuous roles and eliminating others from her active repertoire. In October 1990 the Australian Opera presented the soprano's final complete role on stage, Marguerite de Valois in *Les Huguenots.*

On New Year's Eve that year, Sutherland made her last stage appearance as the special event of a gala *Fledermaus* at Covent Garden. As guest of honour in the second-act party scene, with her husband conducting, she sang from *La Traviata* with Pavarotti and from *Semiramide* with Horne (for *The Times* her appearance served as "a fitting reminder of the reason she has dominated the bel canto repertoire for three decades: nobody ever produced coloratura singing of more purity or accuracy"). Her single, utterly appropriate solo contribution was Sir Henry Bishop's ballad *Home Sweet Home*, sung with immense affection.

On disc one can hear all of Sutherland's greatest stage roles, as well as several she sang only in the recording studio, among them Adina in *L'Elisir d'Amore*, Elvira in *Ernani*, Turandot (an enthralling portrayal, this), and Ah-Joe in Franco Leoni's *L'Oracolo*. One can also hear a wide variety of songs and arias — not just the expected Rossini and Donizetti, but also off-the-beaten-track French repertoire, operetta, and songs by the Bonynges' devoted friend Noël Coward. On video several concerts are exceptionally rewarding, as are *Lucia* (Met), *Norma* (Toronto), *Lucrezia Borgia* (Covent Garden), and numerous portrayals taped in Sydney. Sutherland was also captivating as host and leading performer in a television series for youngsters, *Who's*

Afraid of Opera?, originally shown on American television.

Sutherland was appointed CBE in 1961, AC (Companion of the Order of Australia) in 1975, DBE in 1978, and to the Order of Merit in 1991. She was patron of the BBC Cardiff Singer of the World competition.

The soprano was beloved by fans and friends not simply for her artistry but for her charm, humour and feet-on-the-ground attitude to life. Her autobiography, *A Prima Donna's Progress*, appeared in 1997.

She is survived by her husband and their son.

Dame Joan Sutherland, OM, AC, DBE, operatic soprano, was born on November 7, 1926. She died on October 11, 2010, aged 83

—⁓—

DAME ELIZABETH TAYLOR

INTUITIVE AND ALLURING SCREEN ACTRESS WHO PROVED FASCINATING TO THE CAMERA AND THE PUBLIC LONG AFTER HER FILM CAREER HAD GONE INTO DECLINE

MARCH 24, 2011

From the age of ten, Elizabeth Taylor was a superstar, perhaps one of the biggest Hollywood ever made. Her career, its rise and decline, was inextricably linked to the story of that town, to the glory days of the studio system and to the advent of the modern age of film-making. But her talents as an actress went only a small way to explaining her rumbustious, headline-making appeal.

Married eight times to seven different husbands, she conducted her affairs like a Beverly Hills Wife of Bath. Plagued by accidents as she was, she was also blessed with apparent indestructibility. She bounced back after divorce, bereavement, alcohol and drug addiction, career droughts and the venom of the world's press.

In her youth she was often described as the brunette counterpart to Marilyn Monroe. But there was nothing remotely vulnerable about Taylor. She proved to be tougher than any of her husbands, and she claimed, after a lifetime's hard work, the right to enjoy her money and celebrity.

Her greatest gift as an actress was her face. She was incomparably photogenic, with jet-black hair, so dark it seemed almost blue on screen, and eyes the deep purple colour of an aubergine skin. Her figure presented more problems for cameramen. Small, curvaceous and top-heavy, she had the bust of a much taller woman. Beauty aside, she could strike those who met her, particularly when she was sober, as rather ordinary, happiest talking about her children and dogs. It was that streak of normality which saved her.

Her acting talents were peculiarly limited to the big screen. Both Paul Newman and Richard Burton, when they first rehearsed with her, complained to their directors that Taylor was wooden and gave them nothing to act against. Both had to agree, when they saw what the camera had picked up — her instinctive, understated gestures, the flicker of her eyes — that she knew what she was doing. Even so, there were some critics who made a living out of lambasting Taylor, those who could never look past the awfulness of some of her early work, or who could not admit that such a pretty girl could act.

While they conceded that she had been excellent in *National Velvet* and *Who's Afraid of Virginia Woolf?*, they complained that these roles were merely aspects of Taylor's own character, and therefore required no effort. They were right, to the extent that Taylor could be lazy as an actress. She never attempted to improve her worst faults, which were her high-pitched voice and weight problem, and she was at her best when the plot revolved around sex. But it was her misfortune to be hitting her stride as an actress just as she reached middle age, and the plum roles began to dry up.

Elizabeth Rosemond Taylor was born in London, near Hampstead Heath. Though Hollywood fan magazines later liked to stress her upper-class English background, she was, in fact, the daughter of two Americans. Her mother, Sara, was a promising actress who had given up her career to bring up the children, and her father was Francis Taylor, a handsome art dealer, whose job in London was to ship Constables home for the American market.

The family's entrée on to the bottom rungs of British high society was guaranteed by their friendship with the Cazalet family. Victor Cazalet, the gregarious Conservative MP, acted as unofficial godfather to the young Elizabeth. In truth, he was also her father's lover for several years — one reason, perhaps, why Elizabeth, as she grew up, seemed happiest in the company of homosexual men.

On the outbreak of the Second World War, Francis Taylor left England with crates of drawings by his friend Augustus John and set up an art boutique in the Beverly Hills Hotel. The Cazalets' family friend Hedda Hopper gave the boutique a good notice, and also announced in her column "a new find — eight-year-old Elizabeth Taylor".

In the beauty-obsessed culture of Beverly Hills, Elizabeth enjoyed being at the centre of attention. She was a compliant child who danced for guests and allowed herself to be fussily dressed and ringletted. Having watched Shirley Temple, she also harboured ambitions to act, ambitions which her mother eagerly encouraged.

A year's contract at Universal gave her her first screen outing, *There's One Born Every Minute* (1942). It was a flop. But her father, who had got to know a producer at MGM, persuaded him to take a look at his little girl. Sam Marx was then casting for *Lassie Come Home*. He already had six children lined up in his office when in walked his friend's daughter, Elizabeth. "It was like an

eclipse of the sun," said Marx. "The child, dressed in blue velvet with white trim and matching hat, was breathtaking. She looked so splendid that we opted to forgo a screen test. I walked her to the casting office and we drew up a contract."

For the next two decades, Louis B. Mayer's MGM was Taylor's teacher, surrogate parent and eventually, in her eyes, her jailer. After *Lassie Come Home* (1943), in which she was cast opposite Roddy McDowall, her career stalled momentarily. The next year she played the consumptive Helen Burns in *Jane Eyre*, such a tiny part that she did not even receive a screen credit. However, backed by her resourceful mother, she accosted Clarence Brown, who was to direct *National Velvet*, and, legend has it, talked him into giving her the lead. The film was about a little girl who rides her horse to victory at the Grand National, disguised as a boy.

Taylor was very short, with a high-pitched voice that tended to screech. But the real problem was that Velvet Brown was an adolescent with breasts. "Don't worry," Taylor is supposed to have said. "You'll have your breasts." Three months later, as if by willpower, she had grown three inches and graduated to a B-cup bra.

Her performance put her in the top rank of child stars. But considering that she was still a child, Elizabeth was blossoming into a surprisingly adult-looking creature, with the face — slightly oversized for her short body — of a much older woman. Even at this age, she had a disconcertingly sexual effect on men around the MGM block, an effect of which she seemed fully aware.

Studying during her afternoons at MGM's Little Red Schoolhouse, she made a film a year steadily through her adolescence: with another dog in *Courage of Lassie* (1946); in Victorian costume in *Life With Father* (1947); and in a blonde wig for *Little Women* (1949).

When she moved on to adult roles, Vincente Minnelli drew a charming performance from her in *Father of the Bride* (1950), opposite Spencer Tracy, as the eager young virgin, ready for marriage but tearful at the prospect of leaving her still beloved father. *A Place in the Sun* (1951) showed what she was capable of with another good director, when George Stevens cast her as the spoilt rich girl who proves to be Montgomery Clift's nemesis.

In real life, with two broken engagements behind her and an enamoured Howard Hughes in pursuit, Taylor's love life was worryingly out of control. Her parents persuaded her to marry, and in 1950, disastrously, she chose Nicky Hilton Jr, heir to the Hilton hotel chain. After a spectacular MGM stage-managed wedding, the marriage barely outlasted the honeymoon in Europe. Taylor returned to Hollywood covered in bruises and determined on divorce.

Elizabeth Taylor bringing glamour to the premiere of The Lady with the Lamp *in 1951. She married one of the film's leading actors, Michael Wilding, in 1952*

While she enjoyed a little plate-smashing with her men, she would not stand for being beaten.

In 1952, seemingly as a reaction to Hilton's temper, she married the much older, kindly British actor Michael Wilding, by whom she had two sons. But Wilding proved too mild-mannered for Taylor. Not content with having destroyed his career by transplanting him to Hollywood, she proceeded to humiliate him with her affairs with Victor Mature and Frank Sinatra, much as she was later publicly to emasculate the gentle Eddie Fisher.

Eventually she left Wilding for the producer Mike Todd. They were married in 1957, when he was in the middle of a publicity drive for *Around the World in 80 Days*, and she bore him a daughter. Having declared twice before that all she wanted was to settle down to a happy marriage, Taylor now seemed genuinely to have met her match in Todd.

Professionally, too, she was riding high after several years of drubbings from the critics. One, who had watched her performance as Rebecca the Jewess in *Ivanhoe* (1952), wrote that he would never forget her being led to the stake with the expression of a girl who has just been stood up on a date. *Giant* (1956), in which she played the wife of a Texan cattle rancher, gave her a chance to change their minds. *The Times* talked of "a long-sustained achievement by Elizabeth Taylor which is an astonishing revelation of unsuspected gifts". The film was aided at the box office by the untimely death of its co-star, James Dean.

By the mid-1950s Taylor was a role model. A new hairstyle or strapless dress worn by her could change fashions. As a sex symbol, she was in the same league as her slightly older blonde equivalent, Monroe.

Oscar nominations followed for *Raintree County* (1957), in which she played a Southern belle, and *Cat on a Hot Tin Roof* (1958), in which she was the frustrated wife of a homosexual (played by Paul Newman). During filming of the latter, Todd was killed in a plane crash, and production ground to a halt as Taylor grieved. *Suddenly, Last Summer* (1959) brought a third nomination, despite the ludicrous nature of her role — an unstable woman who has witnessed her homosexual cousin being eaten by cannibals, and who is being threatened with a lobotomy.

In the interim Taylor had flouted public opinion after her bereavement by almost immediately being seen out on the town with her dead husband's best friend, the crooner Eddie Fisher, who was then married to Debbie Reynolds. Hedda Hopper, when she heard the rumours, rang Taylor to find out what was happening. "Mike's dead and I'm alive," Taylor snapped down the telephone. "What do you expect me to do — sleep alone?" Taylor never expected an old family friend to publish her ill-judged words, but Hopper did and the column fanned Taylor's growing notoriety as a man-eater.

It seemed ironic, therefore, that the last film which MGM wrung out of her contract was *Butterfield 8* (1960), in which she played a prostitute. She had wanted to go straight on to film *Cleopatra*, for a reported $1 million. (In due course it was to pay her several times that much.) Incensed to be forced to make the film before her old studio would release her, she behaved badly on set. It was the last film she made as a contract player. From then on, like other stars of her generation, she became independent, and started making real money.

However, *Butterfield 8* did bring her her first Oscar, though she called it a sympathy vote. Filming on *Cleopatra* was held up when she was stricken with pneumonia. Her health had never been robust. She had suffered from chronic back pain since a fall in 1956 on Lord Beaverbrook's yacht, and despite surgery she took handfuls of painkillers daily for the rest of her life. This time the pneumonia had the benefit of restoring public affection.

That affection was tested again when the cast of *Cleopatra* continued filming in Rome, where Taylor, her new husband Fisher and their entourage took a villa. The former Shakespearean actor Richard Burton, playing Mark Antony, lived in a villa nearby. He first met Taylor on the set when he was suffering from a hangover. She was solicitous and their friendship rapidly became a passionate and not very discreet love affair.

The director Joseph Mankiewicz did not have time to contain "le scandale" as Burton jokingly called it, as he was battling with budgetary problems of his own. *Cleopatra* eventually cost about $40 million to make, and to pay for it

Twentieth Century Fox had to sell many acres of its backlots. No studio could bear that kind of expense, and the fallout from *Cleopatra* changed irrevocably the way Hollywood did business.

Once the critics had seen the laboured product, they agreed unanimously that its cost and the Taylor/Burton affair were the only aspects of *Cleopatra* worth remembering — "The mountain of notoriety has produced a mouse," wrote Judith Crist in *The Herald Tribune*.

After filming ended, Burton wavered for a while between Taylor and his wife Sybil, before eventually getting a divorce and marrying Taylor in 1964. Her fifth marriage introduced Taylor to a more normal life than she had ever known. Burton took her to rugby matches, to his Welsh home town and taught her to drink beer and eat fish and chips. The daughter she had intended to adopt with Fisher became instead her adopted daughter with Burton.

Just as after Todd's death she had converted to Judaism in his memory, so now she took up British citizenship in honour of Burton.

Even as respectably married tax exiles living in Switzerland, the Burtons were still big news, and they cashed in by making a run of films together. Films such as *The VIPs* (1963) and *The Sandpiper* (1965) were good as well as lucrative. *The Taming of the Shrew* (1967), for which Burton threw out two fifths of Shakespeare's lines and concentrated on gorgeous pictures, was rewarded with excellent box-office takings. *Who's Afraid of*

Virginia Woolf? (1966), in which Taylor played the frowsy, academic wife, Martha, was the high point of their collaboration, and won Taylor her second Oscar. It was one of her most brilliant performances, vulgar yet truly passionate. Taylor yelled her "Screw-yous" and "God-damn-yous" at top volume, daring to abandon glamour to show life's underbelly.

The pendulum began to swing the other way at the end of 1967 with *Reflections in a Golden Eye* and *The Comedians*, followed the next year by *Boom!* — all of them flops. Audiences were staying at home, perhaps out of boredom with the Burton-Taylor double act, perhaps because Taylor, despite giving good performances, was looking out of date. Modern bare-faced actresses such as Vanessa Redgrave were casually stripping for the camera, where Taylor was still clinging to low-cut gowns.

Having bordered on chubby since the late 1950s, she was now becoming uncontrollably fat. In the film of *Under Milk Wood* (1971) her personal photographer, according to one observer, "kept flinging himself to the ground to photograph her from below so that her double chins wouldn't show".

But if Taylor was not such good box office, her personal life was still as big news as ever. As the Burtons had become richer, so their lifestyle had become more ostentatious and imperial. Her habit of arriving late on set, which had been a minor annoyance to directors in MGM days, seriously threatened to undermine some of the independent productions in which she now appeared. Directors would be alerted to her arrival by a stately procession of secretaries and hairdressers.

It was during the 1960s that Taylor became the owner of some of the world's costliest diamonds. Princess Margaret asked to try on one of them, the 33.19-carat Krupp, when she met Taylor at a wedding. "How very vulgar," she said when it was on her finger. "Yeah, ain't it great?" was Taylor's response. Besides the Krupp, she also owned the 69.42-carat pear-shaped Taylor-Burton diamond, a gift from the actor. A book, *My Love Affair with Jewellery*, appeared in 2002.

It was Burton's yearning for a more normal life, as much as his wife's professional slump, which led to their divorce in 1974. To a noisy fanfare they were remarried in Botswana in 1975, but the second marriage was upset almost immediately by Burton's womanising and drinking. He went on to marry Suzy Hunt, the former wife of the racing driver James Hunt, and Taylor, in 1976, wed the Republican Senator John Warner.

In 1981 she leapt at the chance to act in a stage play, *The Little Foxes*, and, meeting Burton in London, she agreed to do another with him, Noël Coward's *Private Lives*. The plot about two middle-aged divorcees who still love each other would guarantee good box office.

Taylor divorced Warner in 1982. But any hopes that the old Burton-Taylor magic would be renewed on the American tour of *Private Lives* in 1983 were soon dashed. In rehearsal they were quarrelsome; in performance they were unexciting (and, in Taylor's case, not always audible). Taylor had other problems too. Although not at her heaviest, she was 12 stone, and no amount of whalebone could conceal it. The show limped on to Los Angeles where it closed in November.

The next month Taylor was persuaded to book herself into the Betty Ford Centre in California to tackle her addiction to painkilling drugs and alcohol. Though the cure appeared to work, she readmitted herself in 1988, and it was then that she met her eighth husband, a recovering alcoholic builder named Larry Fortensky. Not many gave the Fortensky marriage more than six months. But Taylor, who had always enjoyed thumbing her nose at Hollywood, seemed genuinely happy with her young husband — until their divorce in 1996.

Her feature-film career never recovered after the 1970s. There was an ill-fated attempt at a comeback as an ageing diva in *Young Toscanini* (1988). And there were also unworthy television movies, mini-series and cameo roles. She hardly needed the money. Apart from her fortune invested in jewels and Impressionist paintings, she was making a tidy sum from the launch in 1987 of a new scent, *Passion*. But a shortage of good roles hardly affected her popularity. As she weathered the 1980s, in particular the deaths of Burton and her friend Rock Hudson, she was as newsworthy as ever. Her friendship with the singer Michael Jackson made her visible to a younger generation; and her charity work for an Aids foundation used up much of her formidable energy.

When she became 60 Taylor appeared on Oprah Winfrey's talk show, and, for a moment, became introspective: "I worked all during my childhood, except for riding horses. My peers were all grown-ups. The child in me was really suppressed. I worked, and was paid. And it was on the screen, but it wasn't me." Typically, the introspection did not last long. A moment later she raised her fist, triumphantly and said: "I feel great. I am happy. My life is wonderful. I never think about growing old. I barely think about growing up."

That vulgar *joie de vivre* was the key to Taylor's longevity in the business. At home she looked at ease with herself, a plump, suburban grandmother in a tracksuit. And, at Hollywood parties, garishly dressed and pasted in diamonds, she showed that she could still play the *grande dame*.

As her film career wound down she concentrated on charitable work, notably in the field of combating Aids, through her own foundation and through the American Foundation for Aids Research, which she established in 1985. In 1982 she had initiated the Elizabeth Taylor-Ben Gurion University Fund for the Children of the Negev.

In 1987 France bestowed on her the Legion of Honour (she was also a Commander of Arts and Letters); in 2001 President Clinton awarded her the Presidential Citizens Medal in recognition of her philanthropic works. In 2000 she had been appointed DBE, and in 2005 she received the Britannia Award for Artistic Excellence in International Entertainment.

She had two sons from her marriage to Michael Wilding, and a daughter with Mike Todd. She and Burton adopted a daughter.

Dame Elizabeth Taylor, DBE, actress, was born on February 27, 1932. She died on March 23, 2011, aged 79

———ᴧᴧ———

BRIGADIER ANNE FIELD

Head of the WRAC who played a significant role in the full integration of women in the British Army

JUNE 29, 2011

From the moment she joined the Auxiliary Territorial Service (ATS) as a private aged 21, after leaving the LSE without taking a degree, it was clear that Anne Field's strong suit was leadership. If she ever let up until she became the Head of her Corps, it can only have been during quiet moments in her beloved Lake District. After official retirement she continued to work for the better recognition of the place women had won in the Army. Yet she was always at ease with soldiers — one of the boys.

Born in Keswick, the daughter of Captain Harold and Annie Hodgson,

she attended Keswick School and St George's, Harpenden, before going to LSE. Commissioned in 1948 she applied for overseas service. Subsequently, she commanded 4th Independent Company WRAC in Singapore and Malaya from 1951 to 1953, the most dangerous years of the communist insurrection.

She attended the six-month course at the WRAC Staff College, Frimley Park, in 1953, and on graduation was posted to Staff Duties branch in the War Office. She married Captain Anthony Field in 1956. The marriage was dissolved in 1961.

Regimental and staff appointments in London, Catterick and Scotland, where she was Adjutant of 317 (Scottish) Battalion WRAC of the Territorial Army, followed, before she went as a major to the WRAC training depot at Guildford as Chief Instructor in 1961. In September 1963 she joined HQ Middle East Command in Aden as the staff officer responsible for the conditions, discipline and welfare of soldiers and their families in South Arabia. The spring of 1964 saw the outbreak of rebellion by the Radfan tribes of the Western Aden Protectorate and a brigade and supporting units were sent there to deal with it.

As staff officer responsible for the notification of casualties to the next of kin at home, she got herself up-country to see conditions for herself. Her straightforward way of questioning and no-nonsense attitude to roughing it were well remembered 40 years later when she became patron of the Aden Veterans' Association.

Two appointments in the MoD preceded her advance to lieutenant-colonel to become Assistant Director WRAC in the Army of the Rhine. In 1971 she was appointment Commandant of the WRAC College at Camberley, in the rank of colonel. The next three years projected her — and her increasingly confident personality — as an advocate for additional roles that WRAC officers could take on, relieving male officers for more dangerous work. The Northern Ireland emergency intensified during her tenure as college commandant, and she was quick to suggest new posts for women officers in the Province, some as hazardous as those undertaken by their male counterparts.

The strain of the Northern Ireland emergency on the Army's manpower ceiling finally broke the taboo on the wider employment of women in "teeth arm" units on active service. It had long been standard practice for a proportion of members of the WRAC to specialise in communications, supply and transport, and wear the insignia of the appropriate corps. As this system became extended, it was decided to carry it to the conclusion of women joining the corps in which they wished to specialise from the outset. Anne Field promoted this concept and put in the groundwork during her tenure first as Assistant Director at HQ UK Land Forces and then as Director WRAC from 1977 to 1982.

Although another decade would pass before the WRAC was formally disbanded in 1992, much of the credit for initiating the changes to direct commissioning and "badging" was due to Field. In her honorary position as Deputy Controller Commandant to the Duchess of Kent — as Controller Commandant — from 1984 to 1992, she continued to contribute to the debate for this reform and served for a further two years as Deputy Colonel Commandant of the new Adjutant-General's Corps, into which many WRAC women were absorbed, from 1992 to 1994.

She was appointed an Honorary ADC to the Queen in 1977 and CB in 1979. (A decade earlier she would have been appointed DBE as head of her service.) After leaving the Army in 1982 she devoted herself to the interests of the WRAC Association and the ATS and WRAC Benevolent Fund, serving as chairman of Council from 1991 to 1997. She was appointed CBE (Civil) in recognition of her continued service to past and present members of the ATS and WRAC in 1995.

She was a director of the London Regional Board of Lloyds Bank, 1982-91, a special commissioner of The Duke of York's Royal Military School, Dover, 1989-2004, a member of the main grants committee of the Army Benevolent Fund, a Freeman of the City of London and a Liveryman of the Spectacle Makers' Company.

A woman of immense warmth and friendliness, despite a steely determination to bring about results she deemed necessary, she kept her friendships bright. Generals she had known since they were subalterns received, whether or not they welcomed it, the benefit of her advice and experience, but always delivered with a reassuring twinkle. She kept her finger on the Army's pulse through living in London in retirement, but her holidays in the Lake District were sacrosanct.

Her younger brother predeceased her. *Brigadier Anne Field, CB, CBE, Director, Women's Royal Army Corps, 1977-82, was born on April 4, 1926. She died on June 25, 2011, aged 85*

—*w*—

AMY WINEHOUSE

SINGER AND SONGWRITER WITH AN ASTONISHING VOICE AND TALENT, WHOSE CAREER WAS TARNISHED BY DRUGS, ALCOHOL AND SCANDAL

JULY 25, 2011

Out of the chaos of a deeply troubled personal life and an unhealthy predilection for self-destruction, Amy Winehouse fashioned a rare artistry to become the most talented British female singer of her generation.

When she burst on to the scene in 2003, pop music was dominated by girl-next-door types such as Dido and Katie Melua. It was immediately evident that Winehouse came from a quite different tradition and her whisky-breathed, nicotine-stained bad-girl attitude, allied to a powerful and lived-in voice, revived the lusty, man-eating spirit of ball-busting but troubled divas of earlier eras such as Billie Holiday and Janis Joplin.

The image could have been contrived but sadly it was all too dangerously real. Almost from the outset, she cut a doomed figure who lived on the edge. Yet along with the impression that she was never far away from self-destruction came real talent. She was just 20 when she made her breakthrough but her artistic maturity was remarkable as she married a thrilling jazz-soul voice of compelling conviction to a precocious songwriting talent.

Success was almost instant. Within three years of her debut she had become the biggest female singer in Britain, showered with Ivor Novello and Brit awards and half a dozen Grammy awards for her two critically acclaimed multimillion selling albums. But she was also living up to her bad-girl image and was regularly photographed by the paparazzi falling out of her high heels as she left clubs considerably the worse for wear in the early hours.

As it became increasingly obvious that she was finding it difficult to cope with fame, fears about her health spread. She shed her original, voluptuously full figure and became stick-insect thin, leading to much tabloid speculation. She later admitted that she was a manic depressive and suffered from eating disorders. Performances were abandoned when she appeared on stage intoxicated or concerts were cancelled at short notice with the singer pleading "exhaustion", although on at least one occasion when she should have been on stage, she was then photographed drinking in a bar.

Her notoriety was such that bookmakers began offering odds on whether she would turn up for her next gig. Instead of destroying her career, for a while her unreliability and much-publicised troubles only seemed to enhance her appeal. On her biggest hit *Rehab* she boasted of her refusal to seek help for her drinking. It appeared that much of her audience not only accepted her "unpredictability" as the by-product of a genuine artistry but indulgently admired her wildness as a not-unwelcome antidote to the cold calculation and manipulative spin of much of the rest of the pop world.

But as the years rolled by without any sign of her getting her act together, the patience of even her most dedicated fans began to wear thin. Her sporadic concerts were often booed when audiences realised she was too drunk to deliver a professional performance. Her record company grew increasingly frustrated by her failure to follow up her triumphant 2006 album *Back To Black*, which won six Grammy awards.

Amy Jade Winehouse was born in 1983 into a Jewish family in Southgate, North London. Her father Mitch was a taxi driver and her mother Janis a pharmacist, but there were several jazz musicians in the family and she grew up listening to such singers as Sarah Vaughan, Dinah Washington and Ella Fitzgerald as well as to the pop music of the time. She also showed a precocious interest in performing herself.

At the age of 10 she formed a rap duo with a schoolfriend called Sweet 'n' Sour, in the style of the black American female duo Salt-n-Pepa. She was Sour and her enthusiasm and precocious talent encouraged her parents to enrol her when she was 12 at the Sylvia Young Theatre School, where other famous former pupils include members of the Spice Girls and All Saints.

However, the rebellious streak that was to become a trademark of her career asserted itself immediately and within a year she had been expelled for "not applying herself" and for defying school rules by piercing her nose.

In 1997 she transferred to the Brit School in Croydon, another performing-arts college but where a more relaxed attitude to the creative process prevailed. While there she took guitar lessons and began writing her own songs. By 1999 she was already singing professionally. After her friend Tyler James, the singer, circulated her demo tape to a number of contacts in the music business, she signed a deal with 19 Management, owned and run by Simon Fuller, whose other clients included the Spice Girls and who went on to launch the *Pop Idol* TV series.

He secured her a contract with Island Records, which in turn teamed her with the producer Salaam Remi to write and record her debut album, *Frank*. Released in October 2003, the album's combination of jazz, funk and r&b received enviable reviews and excited flattering comparisons with everyone from Nina Simone to Erykah Badu. Her husky vocals exuded a

Amy Winehouse outside Westminster Magistrates Court in 2009, where she was on trial
for an alleged assault on a woman at a charity ball

potent sexual charge and her lyrics were wantonly honest and risqué, no more so than on *I Heard Love is Blind*. The song was about infidelity but found her professing no guilt as she explained: "What do you expect?/ You left me here alone/ I drank so much and needed to touch/ Don't overreact/ I pretended he was you/ You wouldn't want me to be lonely."

Yet there was also warmth and a tongue-in-cheek wit alongside the feistiness and it seemed astonishing that she was only 20, for she sounded as if she had been singing the songs in jazz clubs every night for years.

Critical acclaim was swiftly translated into commercial success and in early 2004 the album broke into the British top 20. She was also nominated for Brit Awards as best female solo artist and best urban act. She won neither but later that same year she scooped the prestigious Ivor Novello award for best contemporary song for *Stronger Than Me*, the album's first single, which she co-wrote with Remi. *Frank* also made the shortlist for the 2004 Mercury Music Prize. But despite such accolades, Winehouse later said that she was "only 80 per cent" behind the album and complained that her record label had interfered by demanding the inclusion of certain songs and mixes she disliked.

Back to Black, her second album, appeared in October 2006, exactly three years after her debut. It swiftly dwarfed the success of that earlier record, topping the British album charts and reaching No 7 in the US, at the time the highest debut entry for an album by a British female solo artist (a record soon to be snatched away by Joss Stone, who debuted at No 2 with her first album, *Introducing Joss Stone*).

This time Remi shared the production credits with the New York-based Mark Ronson, while Winehouse's jazz leanings were augmented by a new set of influences derived from a love of the classic "girl groups" of the 1950s and early 1960s. Among the album's most potent songs was *Rehab*, a real-life drama about her own refusal to attend an alcohol rehabilitation centre, and which gave her a top 10 single in both Britain and America. The song was written in response to her management's attempt to force her to attend a clinic and she fired them in protest.

That she had an alcohol problem, though, was all too obvious. While promoting *Back to Black* she appeared intoxicated on Charlotte Church's TV show and on *Never Mind the Buzzcocks* and garnered further lurid tabloid headlines when she drunkenly heckled a speech by Bono at the Q awards. She also got into a fight at her album launch party and later confessed that when she drank she became "an ugly dickhead". Around the time of the release of *Back to Black* she also revealed that she was a manic depressive but refused to take any medication for the condition.

She further confirmed rumours that she suffered from eating disorders, confessing to "a little bit of anorexia and a little bit of bulimia". Photographs of her with scars on her arm, some old and some apparently freshly inflicted, also led to speculation that she was subject to bouts of self-harm.

None of this hindered her success or harmed her record sales. In February 2007 she won a Brit award as best female artist and three months later *Rehab* won her a second Ivor Novello award.

Her growing celebrity, however, only appeared to amplify her problems. During early 2007, she began cancelling concerts at short notice and with increasing regularity. On the day of one cancelled appearance she was photographed buying drink in her local supermarket in the morning and boozing in a Camden bar that night. In Australia, a performance was halted after one song when she vomited on stage.

Part of her unhappiness was attributed to her estrangement from her boyfriend Blake Fielder-Civil, but after a year apart they were reconciled and married in Miami in May 2007. Yet marriage did nothing to stem the chaos and the cancelled shows. Both were drug addicts and their relationship remained turbulent.

"I'll beat up Blake when I'm drunk," she told a TV interviewer a month after they had wed. "I don't think I have ever bruised him, but I do have my way. If he says one thing I don't like then I'll chin him." They were eventually divorced in 2009.

During the last five years of her life there was plenty of tabloid notoriety, legal troubles and numerous paparazzi pictures of her in various states of dishevelment and distress. But there was little new music.

A cover of a Sam Cooke song appeared on a charity album and a version of *It's My Party* was recorded for a Quincy Jones tribute.

But despite repeated claims that she was starting work on the follow-up to 2006's *Back to Black*, nothing appeared. She even announced she was setting up her own record label, Lioness Records, but all that emerged was an album by Dionne Bromfield, Winehouse's 13-year-old god-daughter, on which she sang some backing vocals.

Despite the defiance of the lyrics of her hit song, there were several attempts at rehab, the most recent of them only a few weeks before her death. Her short stay in a clinic was prompted by her need to get in shape for a European tour. In the event, the attempted return to the stage was a disaster; after being booed when she appeared too drunk to sing on the opening night in Belgrade, the remaining dates were cancelled.

Amy Winehouse, singer, was born on September 14, 1983. She was found dead on July 23, 2011, aged 27

—◆◆◆—

WANGARI MAATHAI

SOCIAL ACTIVIST,
ENVIRONMENTAL CAMPAIGNER
AND THE FIRST AFRICAN
WOMAN TO WIN THE NOBEL
PEACE PRIZE

SEPTEMBER 27, 2011

Wangari Maathai was a courageous Kenyan environmentalist and social activist whose fight to preserve her country's fragile forests led her into a battle against corruption and political oppression. She became the first African woman to win the Nobel Peace Prize.

The environmental organisation that she founded, the Green Belt Movement, along with its team of mainly women helpers, planted more than 40 million trees in Kenya, Tanzania, Uganda, Malawi, Ethiopia and Zimbabwe. Maathai's message was simple: one person, one tree, and she worked tirelessly to build a sustainable relationship between human beings and the land. To her the tree was the practical solution to the complex causes of poverty and environmental degradation in rural communities. It also became an emblem of her struggle for peace, democracy and civil liberties, which threw her into direct confrontation with the regime of the Kenyan president Daniel arap Moi.

Wangari Maathai was born in 1940 in Nyeri, a coffee-growing region in the shadow of Mount Kenya in the central highlands. She recalled as a child watching the destruction of wildlife and flora as the forests around her home were cleared to make way for commercial plantations. She was educated by nuns before winning a scholarship to study biology in the United States. She returned to Kenya and the University of Nairobi and became the first woman in the country to earn a doctorate, before being appointed a professor of veterinary anatomy, another first for Kenyan women.

Her interest in the environment grew when she was called upon, as director of a branch of the Red Cross, to set up an environmental centre. In 1975 she became part of a group of women discussing issues to take to a UN conference on women and, having spoken to women struggling to gather enough firewood for fuel or clean drinking water, proposed the idea of planting trees to assist rural communities.

Kenya's delicately balanced ecology is dependent on the survival of its forest, especially for its water supply. However, after more than a century of environmental degradation, under the policies of the colonial British and post-independence governments, Kenya's tree cover had shrunk to less than 2 per cent. Rivers, such as those flowing from the great Mau forest in the Rift Valley, began to dry up.

Maathai, with a small group of women, set about planting trees on the land around schools, churches and their homes. Her idea was initially to provide a simple, cheap method of breaking the chain of poverty and environmental degradation, each exacerbated by the other. "It wasn't something I had given much thought to," she later said. "But it turned out to be a wonderful idea because it is easy, it is do-able, and you could go and tell ordinary women with no education: 'OK, this is the tree. We're going to observe the tree until it produces seeds. When they're ready, we'll harvest them. We'll germinate them. We'll nurture them. We'll plant them in our gardens. If they are fruit trees, within five years we will have fruits. If they're for fodder, our animals will have fodder.' "

In 1977 she founded the Green Belt Movement with the aim of encouraging people, especially women, to plant trees and protect green spaces and forests for their communities. The number of planting groups were soon numbered in their thousands.

However, it soon became clear to Maathai that the survival of the forests could be guaranteed only with a democratic, responsible system of governance. By the 1980s — with Moi in power and tracts of forest being consumed in illegal land grabs by his cronies and by state-backed deforestation — her conservation fight had become part of a much bigger struggle against the power abuses and endemic corruption of Moi's regime.

She was a fearless opponent, organising sit-downs and holding seminars to educate communities on how their land was being destroyed, as well as taking the government to court for illegal land grabs. In 1989 she took on one of Moi's ministers and campaigned against his plans for a high-rise building on the green space of the Uhuru Park in central Nairobi. Her protest was violently broken up but she was successful and foreign investors withdrew their money. Labelled a "crazy woman" by the Moi regime, she was criticised for not behaving like a traditional African woman and interfering in male-dominated affairs. Her husband, with whom she had three children, divorced her, saying she was "too strong willed and educated".

As many of Moi's political opponents simply vanished, Maathai suffered harassment from beatings and whippings to death threats and spells in prison. In 1999, after leading a protest against secret government land allocation deals and planting saplings in Karura forest in Nairobi, Maathai and her followers were beaten by police and Maathai ended up in hospital.

On another occasion in 2001 while mobilising support against an illegal land grab in a village near Mount Kenya, her Land Rover was hijacked by the state police and she was driven to prison and locked in a cell. But by this stage international support for her movement had become so great that Kenya's authorities were overwhelmed with complaints from around the world and released her without charge.

In 1991 she won the Africa Prize, awarded for helping to eradicate hunger. Then in 2004 she won the Nobel Peace Prize. The committee described her as a source of inspiration for those fighting for sustainable development, democracy and peace. Her award also acknowledged the significance of environmental projects in preventing conflict over limited resources, a concept whose importance Maathai had long since argued. "In managing our resources, we plant the seeds of peace," she once said.

After 24 years in power President Moi was ousted in 2002 and replaced by Mwai Kibaki. Maathai was elected an MP, serving until 2007, and appointed deputy minister for the environment. However, having called for a recount of the 2007 elections, in 2008 she took part in a protest in Nairobi against Kibaki's plan to increase the number of ministers in the Cabinet and was teargassed by police.

Maathai became increasingly involved in environmental affairs internationally, including in 2007 managing a fund to save the Congo basin forest, where 6,000 square miles were being destroyed by deforestation and war. She also campaigned for the cancellation of debt for African countries, having become co-chair of the Jubilee 2000 Africa Campaign in 1998.

Remembered fondly by supporters for often sporting muddy knees from showing so many people how to plant trees, Maathai published a biography, *Unbowed: One Woman's Story* in 2006.

She is survived by her three children. *Wangari Maathai, environmentalist and social activist, was born on April 1, 1940. She died of cancer on September 25, 2011, aged 71*

SHIRLEY BECKE

FIRST FEMALE POLICE COMMANDER WHO CAMPAIGNED SUCCESSFULLY TO BROADEN THE ROLE OF WOMEN WITHIN THE FORCE

NOVEMBER 15, 2011

Shirley Becke, the first woman to reach the top British police ranks, never accepted any distinction between male and female police officers and maintained that there were few, if any, places where a woman police officer could not tread.

Becke originally became a police officer during the Second World War, intending to return to civilian life in peacetime. Instead she stayed 33 years, retiring as Scotland Yard's first woman commander, equivalent to an assistant chief constable.

She was a key campaigner in the battle to end the limitations on the work of women police officers and bring them into the forefront of police work. "There is no such thing as a lady policeman," she once declared. "We are police officers who just happen to be women." She had little time for senior male colleagues who were reluctant to deploy female officers, and she was equally impatient at female officers who held back.

Becke, who had herself worked for years in the vice-ridden streets of Soho and Piccadilly, said: "Maybe some of the senior men still feel reluctant to send a woman out on certain jobs. But in fact today there is only one thing a policewoman cannot do — she cannot opt out of a situation; she cannot say, 'Not me. I'm a woman', especially if she's in uniform."

When Becke joined the police, women officers were regarded as limited specialists, reserved for dealing with children and female prisoners. They could not marry, were paid less than men and numbered a few hundred in a London force of thousands.

Seventy years later police and public take the appearance of women in a wide variety of functions, from senior anti-terrorist detective to chief constable, as normal. That progress is due to redoubtable pioneers like Becke. She once said that river patrols were the only duty women were still not doing, and that was purely because the work could be too physical.

Shirley Cameron Becke, née Jennings, was born in 1917 in London. She was the daughter of a gas engineer who encouraged his daughter to believe that she could do whatever she wanted, regardless of her sex. Educated at Ealing Grammar School, Becke followed her father's advice and his profession, training as a gas engineer at Westminster Polytechnic from 1935 to 1939. She was the first woman to pass the Institution of Gas Engineers' higher grade examinations.

When war broke out she decided to join the police as her contribution to the war effort. She went to Scotland Yard in 1941 merely to ask for details on how to apply. Once there she decided on the spot to join and after a rudimentary four weeks' training was posted to West End Central, which covered the fleshpots of Soho and Piccadilly. Years later she still ruefully remembered spending months watching illegal bars.

At the end of the war she became one of a handful of women CID officers in London. In those days the work of policewomen was limited to shoplifting cases, taking statements from victims of sex attacks and theft incidents, provided the offence had taken place in a women's toilet. Working in the West End again Becke and a colleague Barbara Kelley, who later became the first female detective chief superintendent, persuaded their boss to let them take on a broader cross-section of investigations.

It brought unexpected consequences. Becke, promoted to detective sergeant, investigated allegations of theft at a Mayfair oil company. The complainant was Justice Becke, the firm's accountant. The two married in 1954. He later took holy orders and became a vicar in Surrey (luckily the previous incumbent had been a bachelor, so the parish did not have great expectations of Becke's availability to be a traditional vicar's wife).

By the time she moved from CID work in 1959, as a chief inspector, Becke had earned 13 commissioner's commendations and made hundreds of arrests. She admitted that she had been involved in more than one "scuffle" but was never seriously hurt. "There is always an element of physical danger," she said, "but

I tried to get the best possible results with the least possible risk."

Transferred to Scotland Yard, she was appointed chief superintendent in 1966 and was put in charge of A4, which was then a separate department for women officers. She commanded 483 women and launched a vigorous campaign to increase the numbers, declaring that police work was one of those rare jobs where a young woman could "come straight in and do something positive and make her own decisions".

She also tried to broaden the appeal, urging women in their thirties who had already married, had families and still wanted a career, to join up. She launched advertising campaigns for women recruits featuring officers in new, smarter modern uniforms designed by Norman Hartnell and she widely publicised the policewoman's role.

In 1969 Becke was appointed as a commander in the Metropolitan Police. She was not only the Yard's first female commander but also the first woman to join the ranks of the Association of Chief Police Officers and the highest-ranking woman in the country. In 1970 she was included in a volume of biographies of distinguished women including Barbara Cartland, the novelist, and Barbara Hepworth, the sculptor.

Becke herself eventually appeared in print after campaigning for a better deal for children held in custody and was the author of papers printed in a collection by the Institute for the Study and Treatment of Delinquency.

In 1973 A4 was dissolved by Sir Robert Mark, the Met Commissioner. New equal pay legislation and the pressure for change meant a separate women's section was no longer acceptable and women could serve in any police branch. Becke moved to the Yard's internal inspectorate.

By the time she retired in 1974 women police officers had for the first time taken part in public order duties at Trooping the Colour and others were training as dog handlers and police drivers. They were accepted into the river police in 1980.

In retirement Becke was a regional administrator for the London region of the Women's Royal Voluntary Service and a vice-chairman in 1976-83. She was awarded the Queen's Police Medal in 1972 and appointed OBE in 1974. She was predeceased by her husband, the Rev Justice Becke.

Shirley Becke, OBE, QPM, police commander, was born on April 29, 1917. She died on October 25, 2011, aged 94

MARIE COLVIN

RESOURCEFUL AND
COURAGEOUS FOREIGN
CORRESPONDENT RENOWNED
FOR HER INTREPID FORAYS
INTO SOME OF THE MOST
DANGEROUS PLACES ON EARTH

FEBRUARY 23, 2011

In August last year, after a sweltering day covering the gunfire and chaos of the battle for Tripoli, Marie Colvin and a group of Western journalists found themselves outside the high walls of the mansion of Muatassim Gaddafi, son of the fleeing dictator. The other journalists, all much younger but worn out after a long day of intense reporting, said they could not be bothered to scale the wall and sneak inside.

But Colvin, who had been covering wars for more than a quarter of a century, and had lost an eye on the front line of Sri Lanka's civil conflict in 2001, jumped out of the van and threw herself at a ladder that some helpful locals had procured. Indefatigable, unafraid as ever, she was the first over the top, as the other reporters reluctantly clambered after her.

It was a shock then, but no surprise to colleagues, that Colvin, an American reporter for *The Sunday Times* who became a legend on Fleet Street, was killed yesterday in the terrible slaughter of Homs, a city that has been besieged and bombarded by the Syrian Government for more than two weeks. She had filed a moving report from the city just days before her death in the rebel-controlled enclave of Baba Amr, describing the plight of women and children huddling for elusive shelter in the so-called "widows' basement".

One of the most resourceful and courageous foreign correspondents of her generation, Marie Colvin had made her name for her intrepid forays into some of the most dangerous war-torn regions of the world, and through the graphic copy which these perilous forays produced for *The Sunday Times* for which she had worked for the past 25 years. She was killed along with a French photojournalist Remi Ochlik when shells and rockets hit the house in Baba Amr where both were staying.

Since losing the sight in her left eye while covering the fighting between government troops and Tamil rebels in Sri Lanka in April 2001, Colvin had been instantly recognisable for her trademark eye-patch.

It was the result of what appeared to be a deliberate attempt to silence her. Lucky to escape with her life when Sri Lankan government soldiers fired on her and a grenade was lobbed in her direction, she sustained four shrapnel wounds in shoulder, chest, thigh and eye, for which no medical treatment was tendered to her for ten hours after the incident. Given the hostility towards her from government quarters, colleagues took the decision to have her flown out of the country in spite of the seriousness of her injuries.

Colvin's reports were always redolent of the violent atmosphere of life in the front line where, as she was always candidly aware, the dangers that eventually claimed her life were part and parcel of the desperate existence of a population on the ground that simply had nowhere to flee from them. Only recently, while reporting, she had not hesitated to confess herself "more awed than ever by the bravery of civilians who endure far more than I ever will. They must stay where they are. I can come home to London".

One of her last pieces of commentary from the conflict in Syria, whose bloodshed she described as "absolutely sickening", was of a piece with the immediacy she brought to her reporting. "I watched a little baby die today," she told BBC television by phone from Homs. "Absolutely horrific. His little tummy just kept heaving until he died."

The plight of children and women in wartime was among her particular preoccupations as a correspondent. During her career her coverage had ranged over the conflicts in such countries as Syria, where she died, Chechnya, Kosovo, Sri Lanka, and more recently the uprisings of the Arab Spring in Tunisia, Egypt and Libya. She had also covered the Iran-Iraq War, the 1991 Gulf War, and conflict in Sierra Leone and East Timor.

Marie Catherine Colvin was born in 1956 in Oyster Bay, New York State, a small town in Nassau County on Long Island Sound. She was educated at Oyster Bay High School from where she went to Yale University in 1974 and took her bachelor's degree. Beginning her journalistic career in the United States, she came to Europe in 1984 as bureau chief in Paris for the agency United Press International (UPI). In April 1986, just before President Reagan launched airstrikes on Libya and while working as a reporter for UPI, Colvin was awakened at 3am and escorted to her first of many interviews with Muammar Gaddafi at his Bab al-Aziziya compound in the centre of Tripoli. She recalled the Libyan leader as dressed in a red silk shirt, white silk pyjama trousers and lizard skin slip-ons, obsessed with security and living in his bunker (which was garishly decorated) in isolation from world events. In 2011 she was to see the compound looted and in chaos while covering the uprising that overthrew him.

Later in 1986 she joined *The Sunday Times*, working as Middle East correspondent for nine years, after which she became Foreign Affairs correspondent. Her area of specialisation was the politics and culture of the Arab and Persian worlds, but as time went on she came increasingly to be present in countries where conflict was destroying societies, particularly the lives of the weakest members of them.

The human misery left in the break-up of the Soviet Union and then Yugoslavia was a reporting imperative for her. She exposed herself to danger in Chechnya where she was attacked by Russian jets while reporting on the rebels. On one occasion she went missing for several days and there were fears for her safety. In the Balkans she went on patrol with the Kosovo Liberation Army as it took on Serb forces.

Colvin won many awards throughout her career, including Foreign Reporter of the Year in the British Press Awards (2001 and 2010); the International Women's Media Foundation award for Courage in Journalism, 2001; the Foreign Press Association's Journalist of the Year award, 2002; and Woman of the Year (Britain) 2002.

She set out her journalistic credo in a starkly moving address that she gave to the congregation during a service, "Truth at all Costs", which was held at St Bride's Church, London, "Fleet Street's church", in November 2010, to commemorate journalists and media workers who had died this century while on assignment.

To an audience containing many of the most distinguished journalists of the day she said: "Covering a war means going to places torn by chaos, destruction, and death... and trying to bear witness. It means trying to find the truth in a sandstorm of propaganda when armies, tribes or terrorists clash. And yes, it means taking risks, not just for yourself but often for the people who work closely with you.

"Despite all the videos you see from the Ministry of Defence or the Pentagon, and all the sanitised language describing smart bombs and pinpoint strikes... the scene on the ground has remained remarkably the same for hundreds of years. Craters. Burnt houses. Mutilated bodies. Women weeping for children and husbands. Men for their wives, mothers, children."

She concluded: "We always have to ask ourselves whether the level of risk is worth the story. What is bravery, and what is bravado?"

She provided the answer for herself and her audience. "Our mission is to speak the truth to power. We send home that first rough draft of history. We can, and do, make a difference in exposing the horrors of war and especially the atrocities that befall civilians... The real difficulty is having enough faith in humanity to believe that enough people — be they government, military or the man on the street — will care when your file reaches the printed page, the website or the TV screen. We do have that faith because we believe we do make a difference."

It was the credo which led her to expose herself to danger in the pursuit of truth right to the end of her life.

In her periods of relaxation Colvin was a glamorous host at her London house, presiding in a black cocktail dress and a special eye-patch studded with rhinestones, over parties full of actors, politicians, writers and journalists. An expert yacht skipper, she also liked to take time off in the summer to go sailing.

Marie Colvin was three times married. She had no children.

Marie Colvin, journalist, was born on January 12, 1956. She died in an artillery bombardment in Syria on February 22, 2012, aged 56

———w———

BARONESS THATCHER

INDOMITABLE PRIME MINISTER
WHOSE UNSWERVING
BELIEF IN FREE ENTERPRISE
TRANSFORMED THE POLITICAL
AND SOCIAL LANDSCAPE

APRIL 9, 2013

Margaret Thatcher was one of the greatest British politicians of the 20th century. The first woman prime minister in Europe, she held the job for 11 years. In the 20th century no other prime minister had been in office for such a long unbroken period, and no one since Lord Liverpool (1812-27) had had such a long continuous run as Prime Minister.

She led the Conservative Party for 15 years, won three general elections in succession, and never lost a significant vote in the House of Commons. Since Walpole in effect invented the role, only six men have served for longer than her as prime minister: Walpole himself, Pitt, Lord Liverpool, Lord Salisbury, Gladstone and Lord North. She fully earned her place in this company.

Thatcher set out, first as party leader and then as prime minister, to overturn the consensus that had shaped postwar British politics and to replace it with a more competitive ethos of free enterprise.

She wanted to rescue Britain from the debilitated state to which she believed it had been reduced by socialism and, in the words of her last bravura speech as Prime Minister to the House of Commons, to give back "control to people over their own lives and over their livelihood".

It was a paradox of British politics that Thatcher, suspicious of government, made activist government possible again after a decade or more in which it seemed that the abuse of union power had rendered Britain ungovernable. A country that had become resigned to genteel decline was for a time imbued by Thatcher with a confidence in its ability to succeed economically and to take a leading role in the defence of the West.

Thatcher did not succeed in all her objectives. Argument will continue to focus on the extent of the improvement in Britain's underlying economic performance under her premiership, on the marginalisation of Britain within the European Union, and on the divisiveness occasioned by her abrasive approach to social policy and, indeed, to politics as a whole. But the scale and permanence of her impact on British politics can be judged by the move of the Labour Party under three successive leaders — Kinnock, Smith and Blair — back into the centre ground, and by the moderate, market-orientated and fiscally cautious policies of the Blair administration elected in 1997. Her opponents attacked her furiously even while implicitly accepting much of her reshaping of the country's political landscape. It was a tribute she accepted with ironic satisfaction.

Thatcher was immensely hard-working and highly intelligent without being intellectual. In practice her ideological attachments and prescriptions owed more to her gut feelings than to any works of political philosophy, although one aspect of her occasional vulnerability was her determination that what she stood for should always be invested with appropriate academic seriousness. She was familiar with the classics of economic theory, and would often produce from her capacious handbag fragments of philosophy and literature to buttress her arguments. She enjoyed the company of academics and intellectuals, particularly when it offered the prospect of a good row about first principles.

Unlike any of her predecessors, she saw her name become attached to the policies she pursued. "Thatcherism" and "Thatcherite" became terms of bitter abuse or warm approbation. But "Thatcherism" did not encapsulate a wholly coherent political approach that could be passed inviolate to future generations.

Thatcher believed in thrift, hard work, personal responsibility and market forces, but would not push these ideas so far as to weaken her base of middle-class support. She was often radical in language and design, but invariably cautious and suspicious of change when it came to action. Her dislikes — as important as spurs to action as her beliefs — included trade unions, corporatism, the political left,

local government, the BBC and what she regarded as the enfeebling consequences of a welfare state out of touch with its original purposes.

Thatcher had no time for those who espoused a traditional, moderate Toryism. They were in her view "wet", and she often ascribed their concern for the social results of tough economic policies to the guilty feelings of the well-off. In her attitude to foreign and defence policy, she saw herself as a simple patriot, instinctively Atlanticist and suspicious of the European Union. She gained much political credit at home — and opprobrium abroad — for standing up for what she perceived to be Britain's interests, however much offence this might cause to foreigners.

In her early political life, Thatcher undoubtedly felt an outsider in a man's world. The "clubbiness" of parliamentary life meant nothing to her, and while as leader she assiduously cultivated her links with the parliamentary party, she never much liked the Commons as an institution. She had a tendency to be the "odd one out" in any discussion, and once described herself as the rebel in her own Cabinet. She was suspicious of pressures to arrive at a consensus as the basis for making policy; which of the prophets, she used to ask, had sought a consensus before charting the way ahead? In her early days of leadership, men often underestimated her talents, and throughout her career many of her colleagues seemed uncertain how to treat a woman in authority.

Thatcher possessed most of the important political skills. While not a persuasive or emollient public speaker, she had an effective combative style and was rarely worsted in debate inside or outside Parliament. She was one of the best campaigners in modern electoral politics, with a keen awareness of the techniques and requirements of the television age, in which she was schooled by her long-time adviser, Sir Gordon Reece.

But her greatest attributes as a political leader were courage and luck, both shown in full measure during the Falklands War of 1982. At almost every turn in her political career she was braver than her foes — sometimes to a point which seemed reckless — and she rode her good fortune hard. She was lucky in those who opposed her — Galtieri and Scargill, Foot and Kinnock; lucky to lead her party at a time when the political forces against her were split; lucky to be at the helm as the Soviet Union and its European empire began to disintegrate; and lucky to be Prime Minister in a decade when North Sea oil revenues were at their highest.

Public opinion was warmed by her courage and cooled by her obstinacy. Though personally considerate and generous to her friends (sometimes to a political fault), she acquired somewhat unfairly a reputation for being mean-spirited and narrow-minded. She was admired and hated, both (for a democratic politician) in rather alarming measure.

From Thatcher's earliest days as Prime Minister, the Cabinet acquired something of a ceremonial character and real political argument — when there was any — took place in smaller, ad hoc groups. Thatcher towered over her political colleagues, and suffered from being isolated from the rest of the political world by a personal staff who often confused loyalty with servility. Her style of government and her lack of candid friends led directly to the Westland political crisis in 1986 and to the introduction of the hated poll tax, which played a substantial part in her fall.

Thatcher was the first leader of the party for many years who felt instinctively in tune with the simplest views of her supporters. For their part, they responded enthusiastically to a woman who showed such evident contempt for hand-wringing defeatism and who regularly rode out to slaughter the dragons they had learnt to loathe. By the tests of party politics, Thatcher was indisputably a champion.

Margaret Hilda Roberts was the second daughter of Alfred and Beatrice Roberts of Grantham, in the heart of middle England. Like Edward Heath, she came from a modest background; one grandfather was a shoemaker, the other a railway cloakroom attendant. Alfred Roberts kept a corner grocer's shop in which both of his daughters helped out. Margaret was often to cite in later years the lessons she had learnt from this small business background and what her father taught her about responsibility, self-reliance and hard work. "I owe almost everything to my father," she once said. In particular she was grateful for what he had taught her about integrity. "[You] first sort out what you believe in. You then apply it. You don't compromise on things that matter." Her mother appeared to have made no similar impression on her outlook and attitude.

Alfred Roberts was intelligent, energetic and self-educated. He was a Methodist lay preacher, much interested in current affairs. Originally a Liberal, he turned to the Conservatives after the First World War but sat for 25 years as an Independent, Chamber of Trade representative on the borough council. He became Mayor of Grantham and an alderman. He was ambitious for his children and at the age of 10 Margaret lived up to his expectations by winning a scholarship to Kesteven and Grantham Girls' School. She narrowly obtained a place in 1943 at Somerville College, Oxford, to read chemistry, taking coaching in Latin to meet the university's entrance requirements. With the help of bursaries and some last-minute elocution lessons, she went up to Oxford in the autumn of that year.

She threw herself enthusiastically into politics. Though the mood in her college was left-wing, Thatcher was a committed Conservative. In her third year she became president of the University Conservative Association, the first woman elected to the post. It was a tribute to her assiduous political work.

In January 1985, however, after the university's Hebdomadal Council had proposed to grant Thatcher an honorary degree, the Congregation refused it, by 738 votes to 319; although the previous six Oxford-educated postwar Prime Ministers had all been granted the honour, many dons were protesting against a reduction in funding in higher education.

She gained an adequate second-class degree and took a job as a research chemist with J. Lyons and Company and became the prospective Conservative candidate for the Kent industrial seat of Dartford, whose Labour incumbent had a majority of nearly 20,000. She fought the 1950 and 1951 elections with great vigour but no success. At the same time she married Denis Thatcher, a business manager ten years older than herself whose previous wartime marriage had been dissolved before he met her.

The marriage was to prove long and happy, with Denis — a man of bluff, right-wing views — playing a loyal supportive role as his wife's career prospered. Margaret gave birth to twins, Mark and Carol, in August 1953. Mark was to become a businessman, Carol a journalist.

On her marriage, Thatcher gave up her job as an industrial chemist to read for the Bar and to keep house for her new husband. After passing her Bar finals, she specialised in tax law. She continued to pursue her parliamentary interests and missed selection in several constituencies until eventually, in 1959, she was chosen as Conservative candidate in Finchley, North London.

She won the seat at the subsequent general election and retained it for the rest of her parliamentary career. She was a conscientious and popular

constituency member, continuing to devote much time and attention to her constituents' affairs even when Prime Minister. Many Jewish families live in Finchley, and through them she developed her first contacts and friendships with the Jewish community at home and abroad.

Thatcher was not slow to make her mark in the House of Commons, piloting through Parliament a Private Member's Bill to open council meetings to reporters. This was less the result of a passion for press freedom than an attack on those Labour councils which had excluded journalists who worked for papers that had used strike-breaking labour during the newspaper dispute of 1958.

In 1961 Harold Macmillan appointed her Parliamentary Secretary at the Ministry of Pensions and National Insurance, a post which she retained in the Douglas-Home administration.

In the years of Opposition after 1964, she held a wide range of Shadow responsibilities, impressing her colleagues by her rapid mastery of the subjects she was covering and by her competence at the Dispatch Box. When the 1970 election came she was covering education, and after the Conservative victory Edward Heath invited her to run that department because (in his words) she had shadowed it so effectively. Thatcher found the constraints of the department (described by Harold Wilson as "a post box") irksome, and the attitudes of her civil servants and the educational establishment provocatively hostile.

She got off to a bad start with the educational press and with public opinion over the decision to end free school milk for 7 to 11-year-olds at a saving of £8 million a year. The controversy — which earned her the nickname, "Milk Snatcher" — was out of proportion to the size of the issue. She also presided over a policy that she did not like, namely the comprehensivisation of secondary schools.

Despite her difficult start and her distaste for much of what she had to do, she gradually earned the grudging respect of her civil servants and many in the educational world for her hard work and her success in winning resources for her department. Education spending reached 6.5 per cent of gross national product, exceeding for the first time the proportion spent on defence. She was keen to ensure that much of this increase in spending went to develop nursery education.

During her three years as Secretary of State for Education, Thatcher was never a member of Heath's inner group of ministers and was not closely involved in the major policy issues of that period. Her range of government experience was therefore narrow. If she disapproved of the twists and turns of economic policy, she was cautious about demonstrating it. Nevertheless, the Heath Government's record of economic interventionism, and its attempts to run a statutory pay and prices policy, confirmed her growing conviction that Conservatives should put their trust in market economics. She was to draw a direct connection between the shifting policies pursued by the Heath administration and her own later approach as Prime Minister.

The surprising and calamitous defeat of the Conservative Government in the February 1974 "Who Governs Britain?" election (brought on by the miners' strike) called Heath's position into question. Pressure for his replacement was inhibited between the February and October elections by the certainty that the fine balance of the parties in the Commons would sooner or later lead on to a second election. In the event, the Conservative Party fought a surprisingly successful defensive campaign and the Wilson Government was re-elected by only a slender majority. But criticism of Heath mounted, and he was forced to concede an election for the leadership.

Of all the candidates Thatcher seemed at the outset the least likely winner. However, several factors played into her hands and she seized every opportunity with verve and courage. First, she gained prominence in the October election campaign as the party's environment spokesman, promulgating campaign promises to abolish domestic rates and to establish a ceiling for mortgages of 9.5 per cent "by Christmas". The Nuffield study of that campaign suggested that Thatcher gained more sympathetic coverage for these policies (neither of which she much cared for) than had been attracted by any similar electoral initiative since the war.

Secondly, she was then able to demonstrate her talents in the Commons. As number two to Robert Carr in the Shadow Treasury team with special responsibility for financial legislation, she made as much of a mark in this job as Heath himself had in leading the opposition to the 1965 Finance Bill. In particular, she earned much credit from a withering attack on the Labour Chancellor, Denis Healey: "Some Chancellors are micro-economic, some Chancellors are fiscal. This one is just plain cheap. If this Chancellor can be a Chancellor, anyone in the House of Commons could be Chancellor."

Thirdly, the leading intellectual critic of Heath's policies, Sir Keith Joseph, scratched himself from the race after he had attacked the Keynesian consensus in an embarrassingly timed speech at Preston just before the October election. Thatcher was close to Joseph and regarded him as the intellectual standard-bearer of her brand of Conservatism.

In the first ballot Thatcher secured 130 votes to Heath's 119. Heath immediately resigned, and in the second ballot Thatcher easily defeated William Whitelaw, by 146 votes to 79. Her triumph was a tribute to her daring and to her ability to rise to the occasion. She also benefited from the advice of a shrewd campaign manager, Airey Neave, the MP for Abingdon and a former escaper from Colditz. One of many Conservative MPs with personal cause for disliking Heath, he became Thatcher's most trusted lieutenant until his murder by Irish terrorists in March 1979.

Margaret Thatcher acknowledging a five-minute standing ovation after making her "The lady's not for turning" speech at the Tory conference in 1980

Thatcher's first task was to consolidate her position and unite her party. Four of the contestants in the leadership election agreed to serve under her: William Whitelaw, as deputy leader, James Prior, Sir Geoffrey Howe and John Peyton. Former ministers such as Sir Ian Gilmour accepted Shadow appointments in her team. Her exclusion of Peter Walker was rectified when she formed her first administration. Reginald Maudling was brought back as Shadow Foreign Affairs spokesman, though his relationship with Thatcher was never easy and she replaced him the following year. She bowed to advice not to appoint Sir Keith Joseph as Shadow Chancellor, on the ground that his known views would make this too controversial a move. She turned instead to Howe, who was to serve her loyally in and out of government in economic and foreign policy. She also cultivated her contacts with backbench MPs, a job which she was always to regard as important.

Caution also played a part in her political tactics. She steered the party through the parliamentary arguments over the Labour Government's devolution proposals. Despite her instincts, the party did not oppose the Government's rescue of the British Leyland and Chrysler companies; nor did it wage all-out war on the closed shop.

In the development of policy, overall, she was keen to avoid too many specific commitments. This affected even her attitude to the economic argument which raged over the nature and causes of inflation and unemployment. In the academic world, in the media and now at Westminster, there was increasing interest in the relationship between the money supply and inflation, and much scepticism about the economic policies of the past three decades. In the past there had been little political challenge to the idea that when unemployment went up demand should be boosted, and that when inflation rose demand should be curbed. The discrediting in the 1970s of wage and price policies gave added attraction to the views of the monetarists.

There was no doubt where Thatcher stood in this argument; her monetarist sympathies were closely related to her conviction that public spending should be restrained and taxes should be cut as the best means of promoting economic growth and personal choice and liberty. However, she contained the party disputes over these matters within some fairly bland statements. The main policy documents of the period, *The Right Approach* (1976) and *The Right Approach to the Economy* (1977) were primarily aimed at uniting the party and reassuring the public.

In only two areas did Thatcher take obvious risks. First, in January 1978 she courted the populist right-wing vote on race by referring to fears that the country would be "swamped" by Asian and West Indian immigration. Both the criticism and the praise which she elicited were predictable and strident. Secondly, while almost totally inexperienced in defence and foreign affairs, she chose to question more publicly than others the Helsinki agreement with the Soviet Union and the policy of detente. Not for the last time, she abandoned the customary euphemisms of diplomacy and earned Moscow's sobriquet of "the Iron Lady". This did her no harm in her own party.

Following the inflationary storms of 1975 and 1976, and the agreement with the International Monetary Fund in that year, the Labour Government under James Callaghan made a slow but steady recovery in public esteem. Its fragile parliamentary position was temporarily secured by a pact with the Liberal Party in March 1977, and for a while a more orthodox economic policy helped to restore economic stability, albeit at the expense of a rise in unemployment to more than 1 million. By the autumn of 1978, living standards showed an annual advance of 6 per cent, and the political standing of the Government had risen too. At the same time, the Conservative Party still had difficulties in living down its defeat at the hands of the miners in 1974, and in explaining how it would avoid similar difficulties in the future.

Much against expectation, Callaghan announced in September 1978 that there would not be an election that autumn, but committed the Government firmly to a 5 per cent wage limit for the coming year. The initial consequence was a row within the Conservative Party, with Heath bitterly attacking Thatcher's refusal to support this pay policy in the national interest. At the Berwick and East Lothian by-election at the end of October there was a swing to Labour.

However, the Labour Party's pleasure was short-lived. In the first days of 1979 a lorry drivers' strike against the pay policy began and this was followed by a series of strikes in the public sector. A Government which had been thought to have a special relationship with the unions was left looking helpless as union action, sometimes of a deliberately vindictive nature, disrupted the health and local government services. The Conservative Party's main handicap was removed at a stroke, and Thatcher took advantage of the chaos to appeal for an all-party agreement on legislation to prevent this sort of industrial militancy.

Any doubts that the Conservatives might win the forthcoming election disappeared. With the Lib-Lab pact ended, the Government lost a confidence vote in the Commons by one vote. A general election was called for May 3. The polls favoured Thatcher from the start of her campaign, which concentrated more on sophisticated public relations techniques than on the setting out of detailed policies.

She exploited her personality, energy and convictions for the cameras. Simple themes were reiterated in campaign speeches, broadcasts and the advertisements which had been designed by the agency Saatchi & Saatchi. Most damning was the slogan "Labour isn't working", set against a picture of the unemployed.

The Conservative Party won 43.9 per cent of the vote — little more than its postwar average but enough to give it a majority of 43 over all other parties, since Labour's share fell to 36.9 per cent, its lowest since 1931.

In Downing Street, after being asked to form a Government by the Queen, Thatcher quoted the purported words of St Francis of Assisi: "Where there is discord, may we bring harmony. Where there is error, may we bring truth. Where there is doubt, may we bring faith. Where there is despair, may we bring hope." Her years in office were characterised more by faith than harmony.

She saw the main tasks of her Government as lying in the economic field. She wanted to revive private enterprise and initiative, to curb public spending, to reform the tax system, to reduce the size of the Civil Service and to break away from the Keynesian fine-tuning of the economy which had in her view led to ever higher rates of inflation and to an aggrandisement of trade union power. Her Chancellor of the Exchequer, Sir Geoffrey Howe, accordingly took an axe to the controls over pay, prices, dividends, bank lending, hire purchase and foreign exchange. In his first budget he cut taxes on income (particularly the higher rates) and doubled VAT. He also began the attack on the spending plans inherited from Labour, squeezed public borrowing hard and set tough targets for monetary growth.

The initial results were disconcerting. The new Government's first months had been accompanied by a steep rise in the price of oil, and this, taken with the transfer of part of the tax burden from income to spending, helped to push inflation up from 10 per cent to

22 per cent by May 1980. High interest rates at home hurt industry, and the pain was intensified by a soaring exchange rate — a result of sterling's status as a petro-currency and the tight domestic squeeze. Manufacturing industry in particular found it expensive to borrow at home and difficult to sell abroad. The reduction in industrial over-manning, essential to the restoration of Britain's competitiveness, arguably went far further than was necessary.

The result was a sharp contraction in production and output, a rush of bankruptcies and an alarming rise in unemployment. While inflation fell after its peak in May 1980, the jobless figures doubled in the two years after the 1979 election and exceeded three million in January 1982.

Other measures were introduced at home to encourage ownership and an enterprise economy. The first steps were taken in a substantial programme to privatise nationalised industries. Council tenants were allowed to buy their own homes. This was popular and led to a marked increase in home ownership. It was the first of a series of interventions in local government under Thatcher. Her ministers took powers to limit rate rises and to check town hall spending. Under Thatcher, while economic power was devolved, political power was ruthlessly centralised.

Rising unemployment and the recession helped to produce a calmer period on the industrial relations front. There were disputes with steel workers in 1980, civil servants in 1981 and railway workers in 1982. In 1981 a dispute with the miners over pit closures was avoided by a government climbdown. The time was not yet ripe for taking on this most powerful of industrial unions.

Despite this tactical retreat, however, the political and industrial grip which the unions had seemed to exert over the country was steadily weakened. "Beer and sandwiches" at No 10 — political deals between ministers and union leaders — were things of the past. The Government began a reform of union legislation with limitations on secondary picketing and the closed shop.

In its first two years the Government's greatest successes were secured abroad. At the first meeting she attended of the European Council, in Dublin in November 1979, Thatcher raised the question of the UK's high contribution to European Community revenues. She asked in effect for a renegotiation of the terms of the UK membership of the Community. She continued this campaign (more militantly than her European partners and many of her advisers cared for) and at the Venice summit of 1980 she secured much of what she had sought. In a rare example of Cabinet government, her colleagues insisted that enough was enough. It was a bruising but ultimately successful diplomatic episode, and set the pattern for her subsequent treatment of European affairs.

Even more notable was the Government's success in ending the long-running Rhodesian dispute. Prolonged negotiations in London, during which Lord Carrington's formidable diplomatic skills were fully stretched, led to an end to the guerrilla war and agreement on elections and a constitution. Lord Soames as Governor presided over elections in which guerrilla leaders and their supporters were involved, and then over the granting of independence to the new Prime Minister, Robert Mugabe. This ended the Rhodesian whites' 15 years of unilateral independence.

The year 1981 proved to be the most testing for Thatcher's policies. In his spring Budget Howe tightened the squeeze on the economy despite pressure — not least from sections of the Conservative Party — to allow a moderate expansion. Supporters of the Government's strategy later argued that this tough Budget was crucial to the subsequent upturn in the economy. But at the time criticism (including coded comments by members of the Cabinet) was intense. The Government's popularity sank. By the end of the year, support in the polls had fallen to 23 per cent.

Thatcher's own standing fell too, hitting in the autumn the lowest mark ever recorded for a prime minister. Riots in Brixton in April and Toxteth, Liverpool, in July further dented the Government's image.

Thatcher's reaction was to make it clear that she would not change her strategy. Critics who advocated a "U-turn" were reminded of what she had said at the previous year's autumn conference: "The lady's not for turning". She had already made this clear

with a Cabinet reshuffle. Gilmour, Soames and Mark Carlisle, all identified with the moderate left of the party, were ousted, as Norman St John Stevas had been in January. Jim Prior was moved from the Employment Department to the Northern Ireland Office. He was replaced by Norman Tebbit. Cecil Parkinson was made chairman of the party. The ministerial changes were a decisive act of prime ministerial authority. Thatcher had nailed her colours to the mast more firmly than ever before.

The following year saw a transformation of the Government's electoral prospects under surprising circumstances. The apparent electoral liability of Thatcher's obstinacy was transformed into a glittering asset. Since 1979 the UK had been involved in a dispute with Argentina over the Falkland Islands. But any compromise with Argentina over sovereignty had been bitterly resisted by the House of Commons and the Falklanders themselves. Suddenly the Argentine military junta lost patience and invaded the Falklands on April 2, 1982. The political effect was calamitous. Carrington and two other Foreign Office ministers had to resign on the grounds that they had misread Argentinian intentions. (The Franks inquiry into the causes of the war later concluded that the Government could not in fact be blamed for the Argentinian invasion.)

After initial uncertainty, Thatcher moved decisively, in support of the advice she received from the Royal Navy that an expedition to recover the islands could succeed. It was an enterprise fraught with political and military peril. Despite anxious moments, most notably the sinking of HMS *Sheffield* and the loss of two landing ships and 51 men at Fitzroy, the expedition succeeded. South Georgia was recaptured on April 25, and the expedition pressed on to relieve Port Stanley and secure the surrender of the Argentinian forces on June 15. During the campaign 255 British servicemen were killed and four fighting ships were sunk. After the first military success in South Georgia, Thatcher had advised the nation to "Rejoice". Watching the successful campaign unfold on their televisions, the nation did rejoice. There was an upsurge of patriotic feeling, and any criticisms of the Government's handling of the war (most notably, the sinking of an Argentine cruiser, *Belgrano*) were given short shrift.

The Falklands campaign led to a steep rise in the Government's popularity, which was assisted by a fall in inflation and a rise in the living standards of those in work. The pressure to cash in on the change of electoral mood became irresistible and Thatcher eventually accepted the view of her closest advisers and went to the country in June 1983, buoyed up by an unassailable lead in all the polls.

One other factor played decisively into the Conservative Party's hands in the campaign. In October 1980 Callaghan had retired as leader of the Labour Party, to be succeeded by Michael Foot. The choice confirmed the electorate's fears of a leftward

shift in the Labour Party and helped to precipitate the departure of some of its leading members to form the new Social Democratic Party. Foot's unpopularity, combined with the mid-term unpopularity of the Government, helped to launch the SDP in alliance with the Liberal Party on a successful run of by-election campaigns.

By the general election campaign in the summer of 1983 a recovering Conservative Party was well placed to face a split opposition. Labour's avowedly left-wing manifesto and unilateralist defence policy played into Conservative hands. The Conservatives took full advantage in a smooth campaign masterminded by Parkinson and on June 9 it won the largest margin in terms of seats since 1945 and the largest in terms of votes since 1935.

The Conservatives claimed 61 per cent of the 650 seats in the Commons, with 42.4 per cent of the vote. Their majority increased from 43 to 144, even though their vote was lower than in 1979. An indication of the importance of the split in the opposition was that in 1964 the Conservatives had lost an election with a slightly higher proportion of the vote than they secured in 1983.

While the election result was never in doubt, there was more uncertainty about what the Government would do with the fruits of victory. It had played safe in the election campaign and given little hint of a strategy, let alone of any radical proposals, in its manifesto. With no clear guidelines, it stumbled from one banana skin to another. A personal scandal caused the resignation of Parkinson and added to the Government's misery. Much parliamentary time and some political credit were dissipated in bruising battles with Labour local authorities.

The struggle between central and local government played a prominent part in Thatcher's second administration. Exasperation at the antics of left-wing Labour councils (for example in Liverpool) and anxiety that over-spending by local government could jeopardise the Government's economic policies triggered an ill-judged attack on the rights and functions of town and county halls. Eventually this was to lead the Government into its most electorally damaging policy, the poll tax. Legislation was first introduced to protect ratepayers from the consequences of high-spending local authorities. The Greater London Council and the Metropolitan County Council were abolished after a long battle.

Thatcher also pressed ahead with plans to replace rates with what was formally called a community charge, initially in Scotland, where a revaluation of the domestic rates had greatly increased the unpopularity of this local tax.

A long, bitter dispute with the teaching unions over pay and the introduction of a contract of employment brought to a head dissatisfaction about the management of education by local authorities. Thatcher supported moves by her education ministers, Sir Keith Joseph and Kenneth Baker, to transfer more power from local authorities to parents and to central government.

A greater strategic grasp was evident in her Government's programme of privatising state-owned assets. With the sales of British Telecom, British Gas and British Airways in the van, the Government had by the end of the Parliament sold 40 per cent of the state sector that it inherited. This helped to stimulate a threefold increase in share ownership and improved performances in some industries. The Jaguar car company, for example, increased its profits, investment, output and workforce. British Airways became one of the foremost world carriers.

The middle period of the Parliament from 1984 to early 1986 was dominated by the miners' strikes and the Westland affair. These events showed Thatcher at her best and her worst.

During her first administration, the miners had been treated with kid gloves. The threatened walkout over pit closures in 1981 had been bought off, and generous pay settlements in the industry helped to ensure that three subsequent attempts to call strikes were defeated in pithead ballots. But Thatcher was in no doubt that sooner or later the militant leader of the National Union of Mineworkers, Arthur Scargill, would try to engineer an industrial confrontation with her Government, aiming to break it as he had helped to break the Heath Government.

She ensured that the ground was carefully prepared for a battle which she reckoned was inevitable. She moved Peter Walker to the Energy

Department, where his political skills could be deployed in a cause where he shared the Prime Minister's views.

Sir Ian MacGregor was moved from British Steel to the chairmanship of the National Coal Board. Stocks of coal were built up against a possible strike and police preparations were carefully made. The first skirmishes began in the winter of 1983. Through the following year the confrontation was fought out with considerable brutality. There were pitched battles between rioting miners and the police. Mining communities were divided between those who wanted a settlement and those who stuck by Scargill.

The Coal Board, the police and the Government stood firm, and with the more moderate among the miners breaking off from the NUM to form their own union, the militant leadership was eventually routed. While the dispute had provoked as much bitterness as any in Britain's industrial history, it was essential for constitutional as well as economic reasons that it should be resolved in favour of the Government and the National Coal Board. Thatcher saw it through with steely resolve.

The Westland affair blew up out of a clear sky. This Somerset helicopter manufacturer, faced by a tightening market and growing competition, was seeking a foreign company which could take it over and secure its future. This relatively slight issue was inflated into a heated argument about whether the British armaments industry should be associated with European or US technological competitors. The Defence Secretary, Michael Heseltine, championed the European cause, while the Trade and Industry Secretary, Leon Brittan, supported Westland's preference for a deal with the US company Sikorsky.

Instead of restoring order between her warring ministers, Thatcher allowed the affair to boil over into a major political scandal which came close to bringing her down. In a welter of fabrications, leaks and banner headlines, Heseltine quit and Brittan was forced to resign, and the Government's survival in the subsequent parliamentary debates owed more to the inadequacy of the Opposition and the skill of the whips than to the strength of the administration's case.

The affair demonstrated the weakness of Thatcher's style of political management, her difficulty in dealing with strong-minded colleagues, and her excessive reliance on close personal advisers such as her press spokesman, Bernard Ingham, and her Private Secretary, Charles Powell.

On the economic front, in the meantime, Thatcher continued to pursue fiscally cautious policies with what seemed to be growing success. Nigel Lawson, whom she had appointed to the Treasury in 1983, was able to point to steady economic growth, low inflation and public borrowing and growing investment. As the Parliament drew towards its end, the Chancellor was able to offer the prospect of increased public spending in areas such as health and education, reductions in taxation and an easing of interest rates. Moreover, in industrial relations, ministers were able to note that disputes were at their lowest level for 50 years.

Inevitably the longer that Thatcher remained in office, the more she became a significant figure on the world stage. In Europe she continued to battle successfully for reductions in Britain's net contributions to the Community. She presided over an improvement in relations with Spain, which led to an agreement over Gibraltar in 1985, and she brought to a successful conclusion discussions with the Chinese over the future of Hong Kong. The Sino-British Joint Declaration, which was ratified in May 1985, represented the pragmatic side of her foreign policy.

The same could be said of the Anglo-Irish agreement concluded at Hillsborough in the same year with Dr Garret Fitzgerald's Fine Gael-Labour Party Government. On October 12, 1984, at the Conservative Party conference in Brighton, Thatcher had almost been killed by an IRA bomb at the Grand Hotel.

In her autobiography, *The Downing Street Years* (1993), she recalled: "At 2.54am a loud thud shook the room. There were a few seconds' silence and then there was a second slightly different noise, in fact created by falling masonry. I knew immediately that it was a bomb — perhaps two bombs, a large followed by a smaller device — but at this stage I did not know that the explosion had taken place inside the hotel. Glass from the windows of

my sitting room was strewn across the carpet. But I thought that it might be a car bomb outside. (I only realised that the bomb had exploded above us when Penny, John Gummer's wife, appeared a little later from upstairs, still in her night clothes.) The adjoining bathroom was more severely damaged, though the worst I would have suffered had I been in there were minor cuts. Those who had sought to kill me had placed the bomb in the wrong place."

Characteristically, she was determined that the conference should continue and she hastily rewrote the speech that she was due to deliver that day.

"I knew that far more important than what I said was the fact that I, as Prime Minister, was still able to say it. I did not dwell long in the speech on what had happened. But I tried to sum up the feelings of all of us.

"The bomb attack... was an attempt not only to disrupt and terminate our conference. It was an attempt to cripple Her Majesty's democratically elected Government. That is the scale of the outrage in which we have all shared. And the fact that we are gathered here now, shocked but composed and determined, is a sign not only that this attack has failed, but that all attempts to destroy democracy by terrorism will fail."

Five people were killed in the blast and 34 were injured. Among the dead were Sir Anthony Berry, an MP, and Roberta Wakeham, whose husband John was Tory chief whip. Margaret Tebbit, whose husband Norman was a former

Trade and Industry Secretary, was left paralysed and confined to a wheelchair.

The Anglo-Irish agreement of 1985 improved relations between the UK and the Republic of Ireland, increased nationalist acceptance of the institutions of Northern Ireland and enhanced understanding and co-operation over Irish policy — not least in relation to terrorists in the US and elsewhere. However, the agreement was criticised by Unionists who refused to accept that its references to the principle of consent served to confirm the constitutional status of the Province. Thatcher, who had been in many respects the most Unionist of Conservative prime ministers, never much cared for this agreement and was to disavow it in her retirement.

But it was as an influential and outspoken western alliance leader that she played her most prominent international role. She remained a loyal ally of President Reagan and the US, and earned Washington's warm approval for her politically brave decision to allow US military bases in Britain to be used for bombing raids on Libya in 1986. Her loyalty to the alliance earned her the right to express forcefully to the US Administration European concerns about disarmament and the Strategic Defence Initiative before and after Reagan's summit at Reykjavik with the Soviet leader, Mikhail Gorbachev. She journeyed herself to Moscow to meet Gorbachev in March 1987.

In the wake of this visit Thatcher faced the prospect of an imminent election with quiet confidence. She had made a major mark on the international scene and, despite a muddled record of domestic reform, she was seen to have presided over a steady economic recovery. Public spending had been increased in the autumn of 1986, taxes were cut in the spring Budget of 1987, and shortly afterwards the Conservatives did well in the local elections. Thatcher asked for a dissolution of Parliament in May.

With a comfortable lead in the polls, a Conservative victory never seemed in doubt, but the Conservative campaign was not a happy one. Labour fought with a new vigour and confidence, and the Conservative team was divided and mutually suspicious. Thatcher had become increasingly concerned that Tebbit, whom she had made party chairman, was trying to promote himself not her, and she inserted her trusted ally, Lord Young, into Conservative Central Office to keep an eye on its chairman. The result was predictable. Backbiting and indecision exploded into a full-scale row on "wobbly Thursday", a week before polling day, when anxieties about the election's outcome led to unnecessary expenditure on advertising.

On June 11 the Government was returned with a majority of 102 seats over all other parties. Thatcher was the first leader since Lord Liverpool in the 1820s to score three successive general election victories. She was granted a prospect given to no other 20th-century prime minister — a third full term and a clear parliamentary majority. She seemed to be more dominant than ever.

Her fall from this political peak three years later had three principal causes. First, learning from the mistakes of the previous Parliament, the new Government embarked on a sweeping programme of reform; yet the flagship of this programme — the launching of the poll tax — was to prove the single most unpopular domestic policy initiative taken by any postwar government. Secondly, Thatcher's own concerns about developments within the EU, and particularly about moves towards monetary union, put her increasingly at odds with many of her own ministers and MPs. Thirdly, her style of political management brought her into collision with two senior ministers, and after his resignation following illness in 1988 she no longer had her loyal and politically astute deputy Willie Whitelaw to rescue her from the consequences of high-handed rashness in personal dealings.

The new Parliament was remarkable for the radicalism of the Government's domestic programme. There were privatisations of steel (1988), water (1989) and electricity (1990-91), and the ailing Rover car firm was sold to British Aerospace. Of the core utilities only rail and coal remained in public ownership. The privatisation measures were largely responsible for extending share ownership from seven per cent to 21 per cent of adults.

At Education, Kenneth Baker was responsible for a far-reaching Education Reform Act (1988), which introduced a core or national curriculum in schools, permitted schools to opt out of local authority control and provided for the local management of school budgets. Thatcher, as a former Education Secretary, took a close interest in the policy. In higher education the number of students was significantly expanded and student loans were introduced.

Thatcher also headed a working group, based in Downing Street, to explore ways to improve the working of the NHS and contain the constant demands for more public money. The final policy was influenced by Kenneth Clarke, whom she had appointed Health Secretary in July 1988. In spite of the opposition of doctors, he imposed a new contract on them, relating payments to work done, and created an internal health market within the NHS.

The Government fought bitter battles with the professions. Earlier reforms had already produced far-reaching changes in the trade unions and local government; now the universities complained of niggardly public funding, teachers and doctors objected to the changes to their work practices, and barristers protested at the proposals of the Lord Chancellor, Lord Mackay of Clashfern, to extend competition in the legal system and give solicitors the right of audience in higher courts. The culture of the Civil Service was affected by the emphasis on managerial skills, value for money and the Next Steps programme, which transferred much Civil Service work to independent agencies.

In 1990 Thatcher achieved a long-held ambition when household rates were replaced by a community charge or poll tax (which had been introduced in Scotland the previous year). The scheme had been concocted by Kenneth Baker and William Waldegrave in 1986 and she backed it enthusiastically. The original proposal had been to phase in the introduction of this tax, but, spurred by the enthusiasm of a Conservative conference, the new Environment Secretary, Nicholas Ridley, decided to bring it in without any phasing. This "big bang" proved disastrous. The tax had never enjoyed much more than lukewarm support from Cabinet members, and some — notably the Chancellor, Nigel Lawson — strongly opposed it. Lawson set his face against any measures substantial enough to ameliorate its effects, arguing not unreasonably that only huge expenditure could soften its inherent unpopularity.

The principle behind the reform was that every adult should pay something for local services, and that this would produce the sort of democratic accountability which would rein in big-spending local authorities. But the size of the tax made its regressive nature ever more obvious and obliged the Government to cap the amounts that councils could charge. So the link between spending decisions and their political consequences was lost, and the perceived unfairness of the measure meant that the blame for high bills was mostly laid at central government's door.

While Thatcher had always been very careful about the impact of any measures on the household accounts of the average family, her dislike of local government and other preoccupations blinded her to the poll tax's effect on the living standards of many formerly loyal supporters. The political fallout was devastating.

Meanwhile, problems began to occur on the economic front as well. The boost to public spending and the tax cuts before the 1987 election were followed by a further tax-cutting Budget in 1988. Moreover, after the stock-market crash of October 1987 interest rates were also cut. For the moment Lawson was a Conservative hero, but inflationary fears soon began to arise as a serious difference on policy emerged between Thatcher and two of her senior ministers.

In her first two terms she had enjoyed good relations with her Chancellors but during 1989 tensions grew between No 10 and No 11 and the strains became semi-public. Since 1985, in an attempt to stabilise the value of sterling, Lawson (and Howe) had wanted Britain to enter the European exchange-rate mechanism (ERM), something that Thatcher would not entertain. Her vague promise to join "when the time is right" was a cover for "never". As a substitute, Lawson arranged for sterling to shadow the mark, and the Bank of England dipped heavily into its reserves to maintain the target value.

When Thatcher learnt of the scale of the Bank's intervention and of her Chancellor's defiance, she was furious. Her opposition to this policy was supported by her economic adviser, Sir Alan Walters. "There is no way in which you can buck the market," she said in the House of Commons, clearly dissenting from her Chancellor.

The Opposition exploited the split, just as other members of the European Union, encouraged by the President of the Commission, Jacques Delors, tried to speed up moves towards monetary union. On June 25, 1989, before the EC summit at Madrid, Lawson and the Foreign Secretary, Howe, presented what was in effect an ultimatum — backed by the threat of resignation — for Thatcher to agree to set a timetable for Britain to enter the exchange-rate mechanism. They were concerned that without such a commitment Britain would become increasingly isolated within the EU, unable to influence developments.

But Thatcher, who had stated her case for a Europe of nation states, in a controversial speech in Bruges the previous September, dug in her heels. She did not mind being isolated in Europe — indeed, she sometimes appeared to relish the prospect. She feared that any flirtation with monetary union would open the door to federalism and that Britain would lose control of monetary policy and interest rates. Helped by her foreign affairs adviser, Charles Powell, she refused to set a timetable but proposed a set of conditions for membership (including completion of the single market and the convergence of Britain's inflation rate with the average of ERM states). She did not think the terms would be attained.

She resented the pressure put on her by her two colleagues, and as soon as an opportunity arose, in the July ministerial reshuffle, she broke up this dangerous alliance of senior ministers, moving Howe from the Foreign Office and replacing him with John Major. After much undignified argument, Howe was partially placated with the title of Deputy Prime Minister to go alongside his Leadership of the House of Commons, but he was aggrieved by his treatment and further wounded by briefings from Downing Street which suggested that his new title was of no consequence. The lines for the future calamitous Cabinet battles were now drawn.

The new Cabinet line-up did not last long. In October 1989 the publication of criticisms of the European Monetary System by Walters finally snapped the patience of the Chancellor. Although the article had been written many months earlier and said nothing new, Lawson insisted that Walters's position as her adviser was unsettling the markets, and that unless Walters was dismissed he would himself resign. Thatcher made several unsuccessful attempts to keep her Chancellor and seemed genuinely surprised that he was so adamant. She later suggested that he was seeking an excuse to leave before the full inflationary consequences of his policies became apparent.

In place of Lawson as Chancellor, she appointed John Major (who, paradoxically, was also firmly committed to Britain joining the ERM). Walters was obliged to resign. And Douglas Hurd moved from the Home Office to become Foreign Secretary.

The politics of Europe continued to take their toll on Thatcher's Government. In July 1990 she lost perhaps her closest Cabinet colleague, Nicholas Ridley, the Secretary of State for Trade and Industry. In the course of an extraordinarily frank interview in *The Spectator*, he bitterly criticised the European Community, claimed that the ERM and EMU were "a German racket" and compared current German ambitions within the EU to those of Adolf Hitler. What was especially damaging was that his sentiments were widely regarded as an expression of Thatcher's own views.

During 1990 Hurd at the Foreign Office and Major at the Treasury — buoyed by Thatcher's Madrid pledge on the ERM — induced her to take a more pragmatic approach to Europe, and eventually persuaded her to agree to British entry into the ERM that October. In return, she insisted on a 1 per cent cut in interest rates. She was already sensitive to the severity of the recession. Her ability to deny the Chancellor his way was weaker since she had already lost Lawson over this issue, and the rise in inflation and other economic difficulties made membership more attractive as a way of sustaining market confidence.

But Thatcher was half-hearted to the end. Her own view was that the European Community should be nothing more than an open economic market with no real political dimension, and that its members should remain independent states co-operating only in a few areas where this was mutually beneficial. She therefore supported the creation of a single market, but not steps to what she dismissed as federalism, including economic and monetary union, the Social Charter, majority voting on foreign affairs and defence, or any further transfer of power to the European Commission or Parliament. Membership of the ERM would undoubtedly constrain Britain's room for manoeuvre in macroeconomic policy. Thatcher never accepted this, and became increasingly outspoken in her denunciations of it.

Nonetheless she continued to play a commanding role on the international stage. In part this was a consequence of her close relationships with the US Presidents Ronald Reagan and George Bush Sr. She also enjoyed a good relationship with President Gorbachev of the Soviet Union, and took pride in the claim that she had "discovered" him in 1984.

By nature an Atlanticist, suspicious of European entanglements and the ambitions of European "partners", she was at first resistant to the idea of the speedy reunification of East and West Germany. Douglas Hurd persuaded her to acquiesce, however, largely on the ground that there was nothing Britain could do to stop it. The collapse of the Soviet empire in Eastern Europe enhanced her reputation in East European states, which were turning to their own versions of Thatcherism — experiments with markets, economic incentives, and the privatisation of state enterprises. She argued that it was the strong stand taken by herself and Reagan that helped to ensure the breakdown of Soviet hegemony.

Thatcher's warrior qualities were again displayed in August 1990 in the Gulf crisis, occasioned by the Iraqi seizure of Kuwait. She was outraged by this aggression and clear breach of international law. From the outset she wanted strong measures. She helped to stiffen President Bush's resolve to send troops to protect Saudi Arabia and free Kuwait, and Britain contributed to this force. The dilatory response of most other European states only increased her scepticism about their intentions.

Imperious abroad, Thatcher was starting to face stirrings of discontent at home as inflation and unemployment started to rise and the recovery to slow. Talk of Britain's "economic miracle" began to sound hollow. Her own backbenchers became restive, and one, Sir Anthony Meyer, challenged her for the leadership in November 1989. He was seen, and presented himself, as a stalking-horse for the exiled Heseltine, who represented for many Conservatives a more politically acceptable style of charismatic leadership. Thatcher saw off the challenge easily, but her campaign managers told her that it represented a deeper dissatisfaction at Westminster, and the very fact of the challenge encouraged more mutterings about her political mortality. The scene was set for the terminal drama of the following year.

Once more Britain's relations with the European Community and Thatcher's tendency to stand apart from her own Government were at the root of the immediate problem. At the Rome meeting of the European Council in October 1990, Britain and the Prime Minister were isolated yet again, this time over the content and timing for stages two and three of the proposed economic and monetary union. Thatcher reacted with angry brio, declaring that she would simply veto any future EMU treaty. She accused foreign heads of government of living in "cloud-cuckoo-land". Her anger boiled over in the House of Commons on October 30, when she went beyond the parliamentary statement agreed with her Foreign Secretary and Chancellor of the Exchequer and made a wide-ranging attack on the European Community, accusing its Commission of trying to "extinguish democracy" in Britain. Some Cabinet colleagues were appalled. The Conservative Party (particularly at Cabinet level) was still basically pro-European, although it contained a vociferous minority opposed to any further strengthening of links with the EU. Thatcher's passionate attachment to sovereignty was proving increasingly unacceptable to many ministers and was clearly destabilising the Cabinet. Her senior colleagues were agreed that good relations with the EU were crucial to Britain's foreign and economic policy.

Two days later, on November 1, Sir Geoffrey Howe, the Deputy Prime Minister and Leader of the House of

Commons, resigned. His letter of resignation referred to growing differences from Thatcher over the EU. This move shook the party, leading to speculation about a possible leadership bid. More devastating than his resignation itself was his subsequent resignation speech in the House of Commons on November 13. It was such a spirited personal attack — and from one who was generally so mild-mannered — that it stunned Thatcher. He said that her attitude to Europe, especially on EMU, was straining Cabinet government and risked damaging the national interest. The speech left Thatcher increasingly beleaguered, and made inevitable a more serious challenge to her leadership in the annual election. This time there was to be no "stalking-horse", but a beast of real pedigree. Heseltine was catapulted into the contest by the exuberance of Howe's parliamentary attack.

The election was held on November 20, when Thatcher was in Paris, at a summit meeting of the Conference on Security and Co-operation in Europe to discuss the post-Communist future of Eastern Europe. The Prime Minister won the ballot by 204 votes to 152, but was four votes short of the necessary 15 per cent majority that would have settled the matter. Her supporters pointed out that in the second ballot she would need a simple majority of the 372 MPs — only 187 votes, or 17 fewer than she had just won. She had no doubts about fighting on and promised to campaign more vigorously. But Heseltine's vote plus abstentions significantly exceeded expectations.

It was clear that at least 40 per cent of MPs wanted a change. Heseltine's promises to alter the style of government, review the poll tax (which was already taking its toll on Conservative prospects) and adopt a more positive approach to Europe attacked Thatcher at her weakest points. Her campaign had been poor, although she felt that her prime ministerial duties and the need to appear confident limited the extent to which she could campaign.

In addition her advisers took too much for granted or were too abrasive in their approach. But in any circumstances it would have been uphill work. Many MPs, including those passed over or dismissed over the years, had reason to feel aggrieved about her. Above all, many also felt that they simply could not win another election under her leadership. For them, if not for her, it was clear that the Iron Lady was showing metal fatigue.

More significantly, many Cabinet ministers quickly decided that she would lose in the second ballot to be held a week later, or would win so narrowly that her authority would be fatally undermined and that she would still have to step down. Some of these were alarmed at the prospect of a Heseltine succession and wanted to have a wider choice in the ballot. But Hurd and Major still refused to enter the race and again signed her nomination papers.

Thatcher's support was weakening the whole time. She consulted her Cabinet individually; most expressed doubts about whether she could win, and some argued that she should throw in the towel straight away. Though the party in the country unsurprisingly remained loyal, she decided that without the strong support of the Cabinet she could not fight on.

It was time to depart, and she announced this to a meeting of the Cabinet on November 22. With typical courage she then went to the House of Commons to speak in a confidence debate. It was a rousing performance, a reminder of her gallantry, flair and conviction. She had not tired of her mission, but those whom she had led had tired of her.

Thatcher resigned as Prime Minister on November 28, leaving Downing Street, a little tearfully, though with the partial satisfaction of knowing that she was not to be succeeded by Heseltine but by her own favourite, Major, who had defeated Heseltine and Hurd in the parliamentary ballot to follow her.

Life out of office was initially miserable. Like her predecessor, Heath, she seemed disorientated by the loss of power. But with typical gumption she threw herself into establishing a foundation (named after her) to support business training projects in Eastern Europe and the former Soviet Union and the establishment of a chair of Enterprise Studies at Cambridge University. She toured the world, speaking for large fees in the foundation's name and to its great financial benefit. She remained immensely popular in several countries, particularly the US, Japan and Eastern Europe. She was the symbol of the defeat of communism and the triumph in the 1980s of market economics.

She returned sporadically, and not always helpfully, to the political fray. Her support for Major waned as he set out on a more pragmatic European policy than her own. She allowed her own more nationalist opinions to seep out into the public domain, and became ever more forceful, outspoken and extreme in her denunciations of the moves towards political and monetary union in Europe.

The division over Europe that had helped to end her years in office yawned ever wider within the Conservative Party, which had once regarded itself as the pro-Europe party.

Thatcher plainly admired the style and determination of Tony Blair, who crushed John Major's Conservatives in the 1997 election, and he for his part seemed content from time to time to be compared with her as a strong leader. She regularly revisited some of the issues that had dominated her years in office; for example she gave strong support to the development of democracy and the protection of the rule of law in Hong Kong as promised in the treaty she had signed with China. In 1999, in her first conference speech since her resignation as leader, she defended General Augusto Pinochet, the former dictator of Chile, who was held in Britain after his arrest in 1998.

When Thatcher joined the campaign trail for the 2001 general election, she was followed closely by the media. After several minor strokes, however, it was announced in 2002 that she would cut back her heavy schedule.

By this time she was set to have a permanent place in the House of Commons, after a rule change meant that an 8ft marble statue, for which she posed with her familiar handbag, could be placed there during her lifetime. When on display at Guildhall, however, it was decapitated by a man with a cricket bat, and so was withdrawn from public view. It was to be placed outside the House of Commons chamber, opposite Winston Churchill.

Thatcher received all the greatest honours that her country could bestow. She became a Fellow of the Royal Society in 1983, received the Order of Merit in 1990, was made a Baroness in 1992 and joined the Garter as a Lady of that Order in 1995.

She remained a political star until deep into her retirement from full-time politics. Like the greatest divas she could be temperamental and difficult but she was always able to rise to the great occasions, not because of her ability as an orator but because of the passionate strength of her convictions.

She was driven by those beliefs to tackle the task of halting and reversing her country's decline and to ensure that it played its full part in defending the freedoms of the democratic West. Her record and her personality will be the subject of continuing controversy. But no one will ever doubt her sincerity and her courage, and most will concede that the far-reaching changes she made would have been impossible without her.

Her husband predeceased her. She is survived by their twin children, her daughter Carol and her son Mark, who has inherited his father's baronetcy.

Baroness Thatcher, LG, OM, FRS, Prime Minister, 1979-90, was born on October 13, 1925. She died on April 8, 2013, aged 87

—◆—

MAVIS BATEY

GARDEN HISTORIAN WHO FOR
DECADES KEPT SECRET HER
DRAMATIC WARTIME ROLE
IN DECODING THE GERMAN
ENIGMA CIPHERS
AT BLETCHLEY PARK

NOVEMBER 15, 2013
In 1999, acquaintances of the garden historian Mavis Batey — then 77 — were astounded to see her on Channel 4's series *Station X*, describing the vital work that she and the other Enigma codebreakers did at Bletchley Park in Buckinghamshire during the Second World War. All those years later, it was astonishing to learn that this grey-haired Englishwoman, whose interests were garden history, walking, birdwatching and the works of Jane Austen, had played a key role in cracking the Enigma ciphers that were vital to Britain's victory in the Battle of Matapan in 1941 and in the Double Cross deception plan for the D-Day landings in 1944.

Bletchley Park's codebreakers had all been sworn to secrecy at the time. Impressively, no hint of the true nature of their work had leaked out until, in 1974, Group Captain Frederick Winterbotham was allowed to publish his account of their activities in his book *The Ultra Secret*. Other authors followed suit, and Batey's role began to be known. It was not until Batey's 1999 television appearance, however, that many of her colleagues in the garden history world became aware of her remarkable past.

It was as Mavis Lever, a teenager not long out of convent school, that Batey had been recruited at the outbreak of war in 1939 to work for the Government Code and Cypher School in London.

There she began by checking the personal columns of *The Times* for messages that might have been placed by spies. At the time she had been midway through a German degree at University College London, which she was doing not from any inkling of what was to come but because of love of the German Romantics nurtured at school and on holiday in the Rhineland.

The notion that her German might after all be useful in the world of wartime intelligence at first somewhat excited her, as she admitted later, and she had momentary visions of a Mata Hari-like existence. The realities of what she was called to do had none of that kind of febrile glamour, but were of fundamental importance to the winning of the war by the Allies. Her German was a valuable asset for the job to which she was transferred in April 1940: deciphering enemy radio messages at the school's top-secret codebreaking establishment, Bletchley Park.

The Germans' confidence in the impenetrability of their wartime code-making was understandable because the Enigma machines which encoded their radio messages could each be set in as many as 159,000,000,000,000,000,000 ways. Reasonably, they believed that only the destination machine, similarly set, would be able to unscramble each communication. They were proved wrong by the ingenuity and dedication of a remarkable band of mathematicians, crossword enthusiasts, chess players and linguists who would pore over the intercepted radio messages looking for patterns, such as repetitions, that might provide a clue to the way each individual machine had been set.

Batey was assigned to Dillwyn Knox's research unit, later to be known as the ISK (Intelligence Section Knox), which operated from a cottage on the Bletchley Park site. Her efforts there were unrelenting. "You would have to work at it very, very hard," she recalled years later, "and after you had done it for a few hours you wondered whether you would see anything when it was before your eyes because you were so snarled up in it. But then, of course, the magic moment comes when it really works and there it all is, the Italian or the German, or whatever it is. There is nothing like seeing a code broken. That is really the absolute tops."

Dramatically, she played a major role in the first big success of Knox's team when, in March 1941, they decoded the ominous message, "Today's the day minus three", which told them the Italian Navy was up to something.

Batey and her colleagues worked frantically for the next three days and nights, decoding with more than usual urgency every Italian Navy intercept that came in. Sleep was a secondary concern, and it was at 11pm on the last evening that Batey finally decoded an exceptionally long message, detailing the Italians' plan to intercept a British convoy en route from Egypt to Greece. Helpfully, the Italians had even included the positions of all their ships.

Elated, Batey sped out into the pouring rain to get the message sent to the Royal Navy's Mediterranean Fleet, under Admiral Sir Andrew Cunningham. Forewarned at his HQ in Alexandria, Cunningham threw enemy agents off the scent by ostentatiously going ashore with his overnight case and golf clubs. He then nipped back to his fleet, which consisted of three battleships, four cruisers and an aircraft carrier, under cover of darkness, and took the Italians by surprise. After slowing down Admiral Riccardi's ships with air attacks, Cunningham's fleet closed with them, opening fire at 10.25 pm on March 28. The damaged Italian battleship *Vittorio Veneto* managed to escape, but Cunningham's force sank three heavy cruisers, two light cruisers and two destroyers in what became known as the Battle of Matapan.

Admiral Cunningham later visited Bletchley Park to congratulate Batey and her colleagues and to see the original intercept. Years later, an embarrassed Batey recalled that, while there, he fell victim to the young codebreakers' high spirits, going away with his uniform besmirched with whitewash.

Perhaps the Bletchley operation's biggest single coup, though, was to break into the Enigma cipher used by the Abwehr (German Secret Service). For this, again, Batey was part of Knox's team, and worked with another colleague, Margaret Rock. The British Secret Intelligence and Security Services MI6 and MI5 had identified most of Germany's spies in Britain and in neutral capitals. Most of them were thought to have been turned, and were successfully being fed with false information about D-Day, namely that the main landings would be in the Pas-de-Calais, not in Normandy. It was vital to know whether the Abwehr had swallowed this information as the truth.

The cracking of the Abwehr Enigma by Knox and his team enabled a stream of scraps of information to be fed to the German High Command which convinced Hitler that the Pas de Calais was the intended destination of the Allied invasion. As a result he retained two divisions to reinforce this area.

It was not until the 1970s that Batey was able to tell her own children about her codebreaking. She was luckier than some in that she could discuss those wartime days with her husband, the mathematician Keith Batey, because he, too, had been a member of Knox's team. They were married in 1942. At the end of the war, Batey was still only 24, but her husband's diplomatic career and her role as a wife and mother left her no time to complete her degree. By the 1960s, however, Keith Batey was based in Oxford and his wife was making good use of the Bodleian Library. As in the war years, she was still busily making connections, this time historical ones, researching landscape and garden history and identifying Nuneham Courtenay, where the Bateys lived, with the 18th-century *Deserted Village* of Oliver Goldsmith's poem.

Articles for *Country Life* and *Garden History* followed, as did many books: most recently, in the autumn of her 80th year, *Indignation! The Campaign for Conservation*, a study of the past and future of the conservation movement, written with David Lambert and Kim Wilkie for Kit-Cat Books.

By 1970 Batey was a part-time tutor with Oxford's department of external studies, teaching landscape and garden history to summer school students. She became honorary secretary of the Garden History Society in 1971, and, nearly 30 years later, was still helping to organise, and speaking at, its annual joint conference on landscape history with what by then had become Oxford's department for continuing education.

Despite her painstaking archival research, she was no dry academic, but an eloquent public speaker, charming and warm-hearted whether on or off the lecture platform, and with a mischievous sense of humour. Called in by the BBC to provide a list of historically correct plants for the 1995 television dramatisation of *Pride and Prejudice*, she recommended shrubberies of robinia, dogwood, guelder rose, euonymus, philadelphus and sweetbriar roses, but then chortled over the BBC's mistake in giving Darcy's house, Pemberley, a great expanse of artificial water where Jane Austen had described a feature of tastefully natural appearance. In 1996 Barn Elms published her definitive study *Jane Austen and the English Landscape*. For the feature film released in 2001 that was based on Robert Harris's book *Enigma*, she advised the actress Kate Winslet on what it was like to be a female codebreaker at Bletchley.

Batey created a new garden trail at Bletchley Park in 2004 to mark Britain's special relationship with America; each of the US state emblems was included in the trail, from California's sequoiadendron to Kansas's sunflower and West Virginia's sugar maple.

She was awarded the Royal Horticultural Society's Veitch Memorial Medal in 1985, and appointed MBE in 1986.

Her husband died in 2010. They had a son and two daughters.

Mavis Batey, MBE, garden historian and Second World War codebreaker, was born on May 5, 1921. She died on November 12, 2013, aged 92

DORIS LESSING

NOBEL PRIZE-WINNING
WRITER WHOSE RADICAL
BELIEFS AND PASSION AGAINST
INJUSTICE WERE AMPLY
MANIFESTED IN HER OFTEN
EXPERIMENTAL NOVELS

NOVEMBER 19, 2013

One of the great writers of our time, Doris Lessing was a pioneering individualist, a woman chronicling the pains and pleasures of her sex long before the flourishing of feminism, attracted by difficult, sensitive subjects, and highly imaginative in her sympathies. With her zest for experiment, she often foreshadowed the shape of things to come in fiction and in society. Perhaps this was why she seemed perennially youthful and attractive, a writer who had loving friends as well as admirers all over the world.

Her radicalism ensured that she was regarded with caution by the literary establishment, for which, it should be said, she had little respect. In 2007, however, when she was 88, she was awarded the Nobel Prize for Literature. If she sometimes lost direction, it was because she remained ready to shock, was often carried away by rage or hope, and wrote with an implacable, heroic thoroughness which some found unwieldy. She referred caustically but without rancour to the categories "that every established writer has to learn to live inside. Mine were... communism, feminism, mysticism".

She outgrew categories, however, and later she came to distrust and even despise the kind of crutch that they had offered: "Oh, I do loathe groups, clans, families, the human 'we'. How I do dread them, fear them, try to keep them well away. Prides of lions or packs of wild dogs are kindly enemies in comparison." She was sui generis. Yet she was always generous with her time and her compassion, and she had friends all over the world.

Doris May Taylor was born in Iran in 1919, the daughter of Captain Alfred Taylor, who shortly afterwards bought a farm in what was then Southern Rhodesia. Money was always tight, her father had lost a leg in the First World War, and her mother had been denied the social life she felt was her due. For the child the freedom of the bush and the companionship of animals was some compensation.

She remembered the closeness to nature in intimate detail — "mud squishing through my toes" — and years later she would write a diary of a year's close observation of Regent's Park.

Necessarily she became self-reliant at an early age and adept at every practical skill, and from then on nothing could daunt her. "I was equipped with a fine organ of self-preservation," she remarked. Yet her greatest adventure was reading, which she did voraciously, with few of the modern distractions (she was old enough to remember the coming of the talkies in Africa).

Many of her stories and her first novel, *The Grass is Singing* (1950), describe growing up with parents who never doubted their right to employ black people in slave-like conditions. The young girl, all energy and observation, thought very differently. "I wandered about the bush or sat on an antheap, angry to the point of being crazy myself, seeing my parents as they were now and what they ought to have been — and from here it is only a step to the thought, If we make war impossible the world will be full of whole and healthy and sane and marvellous people... In my mind I lived in utopias, part from literature and part the obverse of what I actually lived in. Into these lovely and loving societies I had begun to fit black people, particularly black children. Kindly, generous, happy people in cities where no one went to war, black, brown, white people, all together..."

She was in a hurry to do it all: to escape, to write, to travel, to marry, to have children, to change the world. She struck out on the first stage of her journey by moving to Cape Town University, and married at 19, just before war broke out.

With two children promptly born, she tried the bourgeois life with Frank Wisdom, but war and a political conscience led her into a communist cell among other dissidents and refugees. Though always an individualist, she was drawn to ideals of co-operation. "The fact that human beings, given half a chance, start seeing each other's point of view seems to me the only ray of hope."

These experiences of revolutionary spirit, and her second marriage, in 1943 to one of the refugees, Gottfried Lessing, appear thinly disguised in the middle volumes of her great fictional memoir *Children of Violence*, the story of Martha Quest — and it was as Martha Quest that Doris Lessing became famous.

Characteristically honest, the five-volume sequence depicts an egotistical, independent and stubborn young woman prone to be the victim in passionate entanglements. One of her most remarkable achievements, the sequence took Lessing 17 years, from *Martha Quest* (1952) through *A Proper Marriage* (1954), *A Ripple from the Storm* (1958) and *Landlocked* (1965), to *The Four-Gated City* (1969). As well as colourfully evoking the period and place, it gives a thorough and complex analysis of the individual conscience at odds with the collective, as Lessing so often was. Yet she understood supremely well how to write about people behaving politically without herself trying to make political arguments.

The marriage to Lessing was a temporary arrangement from the beginning. "We knew we were not well suited. We said, It doesn't matter, we will just get divorced when the war is over." They did, and her former husband went on to become president of the Board of Trade in East Germany. In the meantime their casualness about the marriage did not prevent them from having a child, informing their friends: "We're going to fit in a baby now, because we've got nothing better to do." In retrospect she may have agreed with her mother that this insouciance was negligent and selfish — most probably she did — but her autobiography offers no judgment, recording only her impulses of the time. What she did concede was that she was "deeply in the wrong" to allow her first two children to be utterly confused by seeing her at this time with her new husband and baby.

Separating once again, and arriving with a small son and no money in the frugal London of 1949, she earned a precarious living by odd pieces of journalism and by publishing stories. She described the cheerful, generous expatriates' bedsit world in a documentary, *In Pursuit of the English*, in 1960. A lifelong devotion to cats, about which she often wrote, first surfaced in that charming book.

In 1953 she won the Somerset Maugham Award with *Five*, a volume of stories, and in 1957 *The Habit of Loving* confirmed that the short story was one of her most effective forms. Some might say that the discipline of brevity and singularity were just what her untidy fictional style most needed. She continued writing short stories, often about eccentrics, well into her seventies.

The arrival of Clancy Sigal, a "lonely cowboy" American and her lover for three years, caused, she wrote, "as severe a dislocation of my picture of myself as ever in my life. I had always been seen as a maverick — tactless, intransigent, 'difficult' — and now, all at once, I was accused of being an English lady." A Trotskyite from a poor family, he taught her about jazz and the blues, but could not prevent her growing doubts about the dangerous sentimentalism of the Left.

Hers was, in Samuel Beckett's phrase, "a mind on the alert against itself": "Sometimes I survey my current thoughts," she wrote, "and wonder which of them — some of them new, with the overemphasis of outline that befits an untried idea, not worn into shape by events, some astounded at their own effrontery — will turn out to have been the ones I should have been listening to, developing. Which of them will seem absurd, and even pathetic, in a decade or so?" With her emotional acuteness enhanced by such conscientiousness, she was a reporter not only of experience, but from inside experience. As well as investigating the life around her — pacing the streets at night, for instance — she experimented with experience, as when she tried living without sleep or enough to eat.

In 1956, by now established as a politically influential writer, Lessing paid a brief visit to South Africa and Rhodesia, reported in *Going Home*, which led to a permanent ban on entry. When Hungary was invaded by the Soviet Union that year, she left the Communist Party.

The invasion was one of many signs that the revolutionary doctrine in which she had invested so much was not worthy of her faith. In retrospect, there were many reasons to escape from what she called "a mass social psychosis", but it was an enormous emotional effort to do so, and she often felt that she was caught with only a choice of betrayals.

She remained politically active, however, going on the Aldermaston marches and being present with Bertrand Russell and Canon Collins at the meeting which brought into being the Campaign for Nuclear Disarmament.

Her first proto-family in London, who appear in the Quest series as the Coldridges, prefigure much of what came later to be Sixties culture. Drugs, divorces, dabbling in extrasensory perception, left-wing politics and ecology had by now been replaced for her by the more solitary — and liberated — life that appears in the mammoth novel *The Golden Notebook* (1962), which was perhaps her greatest success and which associated her forever with the feminist movement.

Anna shares her one-parent world with a series of lodger-lovers, and longs for freedom to write. Her experience, in five overlapping notebooks running to nearly 600 pages, is related in kaleidoscopic detail. As she struggles with stormy private problems (and tries to become a good novelist along the way), dreams are roughly destroyed, lovers and friends prove broken reeds, and money and time run out.

This theme, and some characters, re-emerge in one of her dramatic pieces, *Play with a Tiger* (1962), which disappointed the critics and was described by one as "the epitaph of a generation which expected to die at 30". Being part of the circle of young writers associated with the Royal Court and Tony Richardson in the 1950s and 1960s, Lessing wrote several other plays, but one way and another all were dogged by bad luck and she gave up the theatre.

Lessing remembered the 1960s differently from most commentators. The things that were often thought to be new, she wrote, such as free sex, idealism and popular political activism, had mostly been features of the 1950s.

"But there was one thing that did start in the Sixties: drugs." And, having acted as a housemother for six years, looking after adolescents and young adults who were in trouble or disturbed, she remembered much about the decade that was grim — suicides, madness, the imprisonment of friends — as well as the optimism and the anthems.

In 1976 a French translation of *The Golden Notebook* won the Prix Médicis. The remainder of that decade was productive for Lessing, but it ended in a breakdown which she preferred to call a rebirth. Strongly influenced by the work of the psychiatrist R. D. Laing, she published *Briefing for a Descent into Hell* in 1971. In it, an amnesiac describes his visionary adventures before being reduced, with electro-convulsive therapy, to limp apathy. Rage against such treatment blazes on every page.

This was followed in 1973 by *The Summer Before the Dark*, in which a middle-aged, middle-class woman abruptly abandons security for freedom. In a kind of sequel, *Memoirs of a Survivor* (1974), the narrator identifies with a simple girl and both regress through a mystical infancy. As well as giving a memorable account of her suffering, Lessing looked ahead to a fearful Armageddon; our universal imagined future was to preoccupy her for a decade.

Shikasta (1979), *The Marriages between Zones Three Four and Five* (1980), *The Sirian Experiments* (1981), *The Making of the Representative for Planet 8* (1982) and *The Sentimental Agents in the Volyen Empire* (1983) were ambitious science fiction experiments, with galactic empires dominated by Queen Vashti and the devilish Shamat, and Johor (who sometimes becomes George Sherman) as an explorer examining the morality of human society. Some readers felt the ingenuity of these books was more apparent than the purpose, but Lessing was obviously happy writing in this form, and there was the bonus of teasing her usual public. This series of cosmic novels was a serious attempt to look at the grand questions of life from an original standpoint. It also enabled Lessing to escape the categorisation of "radical" and "campaigner". Her dislike of conformism extended to the kind of conformism even of her own social circle, which she diagnosed in the story *The Temptation of Jack Orkney*:

"They were journalists and editors, actors and writers, film-makers and trade unionists. They wrote books on subjects like Unemployment in the Highlands and The Future of Technology. They sat on councils and committees and the boards of semi-charitable organisations, they were Town Councillors, Members of Parliament, creators of documentary film programmes. They had taken the same stands on Korea and Kenya, on Cyprus and Suez, on Hungary and the Congo, on Nigeria, the Deep South and Brazil, on South Africa and Rhodesia and Ireland and Vietnam and... and now they were sharing opinions and emotions on the nine million refugees from Bangladesh."

Their names, she wrote, "appeared continually together on dozens, hundreds of letterheads, appeals, protests, petitions: if you saw one name you could assume the others", but Lessing did not like to be assumed. And furthermore, they were finding more and more often "that their views were identical with the conventional views put forward by majorities everywhere". Lessing's liberalism was winning, and she was not sure it was having the effects she had hoped for. She wrote in 1994 that her lifetime had seen "a general worsening of conditions".

Although she claimed to be a writer before anything else, she did not move mainly among writers, and although widely read was not a very good judge of writing itself, for she was always distracted from it by questions of personality. Surprisingly, she had no sense of poetry, and when she misquoted Larkin ("Sex began in 1963") she referred to him as "the poet Philip Larkin", as if reminding herself who he was.

Disrespect for authority led Lessing to play a famous practical joke on publishers and critics in the early 1980s by submitting a novel, *The Diary of a Good Neighbour* under the pseudonym Jane Somers to test the power of literary reputations. The novel — and its sequel *If the Old Could...* (1984) — dealing with the relationship between an old derelict and the menopausal editor of a chic magazine, did not approach Lessing's sales.

The critics were not amused by her ploy. She refused ever to join their ranks, delighted schoolchildren by telling them to avoid studying English literature, and thought literary prizes were "just part of the selling mechanism". But the WH Smith Award in 1985 for *The Good Terrorist* was a sign of the literary establishment's regard for her, and in the same year she was shortlisted for the Booker and Whitbread prizes. The novel describes a terrorist cell in London deciding how to blow up a large store, and was almost uncannily prescient: the Harrods IRA bombing happened shortly before the book was completed.

In matter-of-fact style, Lessing demonstrates how Alice, middle-class and lonely, gravitates to the IRA, where she finds that her domestic drudgery is only just redeemed by the feeling of self-importance arising from the risk and dedication. Horror, inadequacy, farce and satire make a strange but convincing compound, a telling and all too believable assessment of the way disillusion can slip into moral dissolution.

Lessing's interest in the macabre appeared again in another exceptionally fine novel, *The Fifth Child* (1988), in which a decent, kindly mother finds she has given birth to a monster over whom she has no control. The child is eventually dispatched to a containment institution, which Lessing describes in horrifying detail. Writing powerfully about deformity, exhaustion, threat,

resentment and siege, she was asking urgent questions about how society deals with its misfits.

In 1994 Lessing published the first volume of a magnificent autobiography, *Under My Skin*, pre-empting, she claimed, five rival biographers. It was one of her finest books, setting a standard that its sequel, *Walking in the Shade* (1997), taking the story to 1962, could not maintain, bogged down as it was, as her life had been, in the endless wrangles of communist correctness.

Further novels included *Mara and Dann* (1999), *Ben, in the World* (2000), *The Sweetest Dream* (2001), *The Story of General Dann and Mara's Daughter, Griot and the Snow Dog* (2005), *The Cleft* (2007) and *Alfred and Emily* (2008).

Lessing never condescended to those who believed in ideals, though her own subscriptions may have lapsed. She sided with the down-and-out against the do-gooder, but remained loyal to the older socialist tenets (including the State of Israel) rather than the tough pragmatic Left. She hated publicity and remained quite unspoilt by success, joining polytechnic students to learn Russian in her late sixties "to keep my brain busy".

She had friends of all ages, who enjoyed the warm, gentle voice and sense of humour that lit up a somewhat solemn and austere countenance, which was made the more severe in later life by a geometrically central parting.

Flaws in her writing matter little beside the grand attempt; the occasional clumsiness is forgotten amid the accuracy of her observation. If ever a novelist was committed, not just to ideas and moral truths, but to the refractory business of communicating everyday concerns in the light of passionate involvement, that novelist was Doris Lessing.

She was made a Companion of Honour in 2000 and a Companion of Literature (the Royal Society of Literature Award) in 2001.

She is survived by a daughter.

Doris Lessing, CH, novelist, was born on October 22, 1919. She died on November 17, 2013, aged 94

SHIRLEY TEMPLE

ANGELIC CHILD STAR WHO BECAME A US DIPLOMAT AFTER HER SCREEN POPULARITY WANED

FEBRUARY 12, 2014

"When the spirit of the people is lower than at any other time during this Depression," said President Franklin D. Roosevelt in the 1930s, "it is a splendid thing that for just 15 cents an American can go to a movie and look at the smiling face of a baby and forget his troubles."

Shirley Temple in her prime was a bit bigger than a baby and considerably more than a smiling face. With her dimples, golden curls and winning smile she was undeniably cute, but with a knowingness that cut across the sentimentality of her films, and she had a precocious natural talent as actor, singer and dancer that could make seasoned professionals look awkward beside her.

For millions of American cinemagoers during a bleak period in their history, she offered optimism and reassurance. Not for nothing did the plots of her most successful films cast her as a saviour and a healer, softening the hearts of grouchy grandpas, comforting the luckless and persuading divided families to set aside their feuds. For four years running during the 1930s she was the most popular film star in America.

Temple's time at the top was brief. She did not have the same appeal as a teenager that she had had as a toddler and was finished with films by the age of 21. However, she made a happy second marriage and spent contented years bringing up her children before returning to public life in Republican politics.

Although her attempt to win a seat in Congress failed, she was given important diplomatic jobs by Presidents Nixon, Ford and Bush, culminating in three years as US Ambassador to Czechoslovakia during the post-Cold War turmoil in Eastern Europe.

She was born in Santa Monica, California in 1928, and like many young stars she owed her early start to a fiercely ambitious mother. The motive was not financial. Temple's father, George, was a banker, and although he had to take a pay cut during the Depression the family was comfortably off, with its own house and car.

Her mother, Gertrude, had been frustrated in her own ambition to become a dancer and was determined that her daughter should not miss out. Her sons showed neither the talent nor the inclination to become performers, but Shirley, who was born when her brothers were 13 and 9, did.

She was enrolled for dancing classes at the age of 2, and at 3 was spotted by a scout for the Educational Film Corporation, which was about to launch a series called *Baby Burlesks* to rival the *Our Gang* comedy shorts. The *Baby Burlesks* were ten-minute films in which children parodied the film stars of the day — Temple took easily to the idea, not least with a character called Morelegs Sweet Trick, alias Marlene Dietrich. When any of the children starring in the *Baby Burlesks* misbehaved, they were locked in a windowless sound box with only a block of ice on which to sit. "So far as I can tell, the black box did no lasting damage to my psyche," Temple wrote in her 1988 autobiography *Child Star*.

The *Baby Burlesks* were a start but it took the persistence of her mother to ensure that she made the transition to feature films. Gertrude Temple became her daughter's coach — teaching her how to project herself physically and through her voice — as well as her agent, scouring casting offices to find her work. She would always instruct her daughter to "Sparkle, Shirley!" before she appeared before an audience.

After a series of small parts Shirley was recommended to the Fox studio, which put her in *Stand Up and Cheer* (1934), a film designed to counter the Depression blues. Temple sang a song, *Baby Take a Bow*, and although she was well down the cast list she impressed Fox enough to put her under contract. Her first starring role came in *Little Miss Marker*, a Damon Runyon story in which she did the first of many celluloid good deeds by reforming Adolphe Menjou's renegade gambler. She proved so intimidating, with her 56 perfect blonde ringlets, unshakeable optimism and boundless self-confidence, that Menjou said that Temple was "making a stooge out of me".

After supporting Gary Cooper and Carole Lombard in *Now and Forever* she confirmed her stardom on *Bright Eyes*, in which she performed her most famous song, *On the Good Ship Lollipop*, which sold half a million copies in sheet music. During 1934 she made nine films and the year's work brought her a special miniature Oscar.

By the end of 1935 she was America's most popular star, thanks to well-chosen vehicles such as *The Little Colonel*, which saw the first of several appearances with the black dancer, Bill "Bojangles" Robinson, and *The Littlest Rebel*, in which she sat on President Lincoln's knee to plead for her imprisoned father.

In 1935 she was taken by her parents to Washington to meet President Roosevelt and his wife, Eleanor. The President invited the Temples to a barbecue at the Roosevelt home in

Hyde Park, New York, where Eleanor, bending over a grill, proved too much of a temptation for the impish child star. Temple unleashed a pebble from the catapult she carried in her lace purse and hit the First Lady smartly on the rear.

Temple herself proved such a money-maker that her mother and studio officials colluded to shave a year off her age to maintain her child image. At her peak she earned huge sums and an industry grew up around her, of dolls, toys, clothes, books, and soap. As a result of her father's banking expertise her money was sensibly handled and led to none of the acrimony which blighted the adult lives of other child actors. The price of wealth and fame, however, was vulnerability to kidnap and the studio was forced to provide Temple with a bodyguard.

While films such as *Curly Top* and *Dimples* were created around Temple's natural assets, others were specially tailored versions of well-known children's stories. *Wee Willie Winkie* (1937), her most expensive picture and the first with a frontline Hollywood director, John Ford, came from a Kipling story in which the child who becomes a mascot to a British regiment in India was a boy.

Wee Willie Winkle sparked a famous London court case in 1938 in which Temple and 20th Century Fox sued Graham Greene, then a leading film critic, for libel. In his review in the magazine *Night and Day*, Greene suggested that Temple was an adult masquerading as a child and wrote of her "dimpled depravity" and "dubious coquetry". Greene lost, and *Night and Day* was closed down.

Temple was awarded £2,000 in damages — later used to build a youth centre in England — and the film companies were awarded £1,500 for the "beastly libel".

Johanna Spyri's *Heidi* was another children's classic accorded the Temple treatment; yet another was Frances Hodgson Burnett's *The Little Princess* (1939), her first Technicolor feature. By now Temple's popularity was slipping fast. She was a candidate to play Dorothy in *The Wizard of Oz* but the part went to Judy Garland, and at the age of 11 Temple's career as a child star was over.

Her contract with Fox was cancelled and she moved to MGM — which let her go after one film. From then on she made her way in character parts, and apart from John Ford's *Fort Apache* her later films were undistinguished. Ford, though, still thought enough of Temple's pulling power in his 1948 western to pay her the same as his lead actors, John Wayne and Henry Fonda. In *Fort Apache* Temple played opposite her husband, John Agar, the former Army Air Corps sergeant turned actor, whom she had married in 1945 when she was 17. The marriage, which produced a daughter, Linda, was short-lived: Temple filed for divorce in 1949.

In January 1950, at a cocktail party in Hawaii, where she was taking a holiday after her divorce, she met the man who was to become her second husband, Charles Alden Black, a decorated war veteran and businessman from a wealthy Californian family. "We were introduced," Temple later recalled, "and he said 'What do you do, are you a secretary?' I said, 'I can't even type. I make films.' He wasn't too sure what I did. It was very refreshing to me — a handsome guy who wasn't interested in Hollywood or anything about it."

After a whirlwind romance — Black wooed her with a Tahitian love song and proposed after 12 days — they were married in December of that year, and she announced her retirement from films. The couple subsequently had a son, Charles Jr, and a daughter, Lori, and Black adopted Linda, Temple's daughter with Agar.

In the late 1950s, having given up her acting career to be a mother and homemaker, she made a comeback on television. *Shirley Temple's Storybook* was a series of dramatised fairytales which she introduced and appeared in, along with star names including Charlton Heston, Claire Bloom and Elsa Lanchester. *Shirley Temple Theater*, a similar concept, followed two years later, but the show lasted only one season and her screen career fizzled out.

The Temple family had always been Republicans and in 1966 Shirley worked for a fellow screen actor, Ronald Reagan, during his successful campaign for Governor of California. When a congressional seat became vacant the next year, Temple declared herself a candidate. Her political inexperience showed, however, and she failed to get beyond the primary. It probably did not help that *On the Good Ship Lollipop* was repeatedly played at rallies during her campaign.

There was compensation when President Nixon appointed her as a US delegate to the United Nations in 1969. She performed well in the role, speaking out about the problems of the aged, the plight of refugees and, especially, environmental problems.

When President Ford made her Ambassador to Ghana in 1974, it caused an outcry in some quarters. She said after her appointment: "I have no trouble being taken seriously as a woman and a diplomat here [in Ghana]. My only problems have been with Americans who, in the beginning, refused to believe I had grown up since my movies."

She later became the first woman to hold the post of Chief of Protocol of the United States, responsible for organising President Carter's inauguration in January 1977. One of her duties was leading a one-week training programme for new government envoys, she said: "We teach them how to get used to being called Ambassador and having Marines saluting. Then, on Day 3, we tell them what to do if they're taken hostage."

Although no worthwhile job resulted from the Reagan Presidency, George Bush chose her to run the US Embassy in Prague when he succeeded Reagan in 1989; her time in office thus coincided with the fall of Communism in Eastern Europe. The post would normally have been expected to have been awarded to a career diplomat, but Temple served for nearly four years in the post, earning widespread admiration in the process

— Henry Kissinger, for one, called her "very intelligent, very tough-minded, very disciplined". While in Prague she also learnt that there had been a Shirley Temple fan club in the city 50 years previously; people with long memories brought old "Shirleyka" membership cards for her to autograph.

She was disappointed that her political appointments did not lead to bigger things. Her film career, however, was recognised: in 1985 the Academy of Motion Picture Arts and Sciences presented her with a full-size Oscar to replace the miniature one given 50 years earlier.

In 1972 she had breast cancer diagnosed and underwent a radical modified mastectomy. In going public about it, she was one of the first Hollywood stars to highlight the disease, which brought her 50,000 letters of support. She held a news conference from her hospital bed to urge women who found lumps not to "sit home and be afraid".

When her second husband died of bone marrow disease in 2005, she kept his voice on their answering machine, saying: "I don't ever want to erase it." As he lay dying she sang him the same Tahitian love song that he had sung to her during their courtship.

She is survived by her three children: Lori played bass guitar for various bands before becoming a photographer, Charles Jr became a businessman and Linda a high-school librarian.

Shirley Temple, actress and diplomat, was born on April 23, 1928. She died on February 10, 2014, aged 85

ALICE HERZ-SOMMER

CONCERT PIANIST WHOSE MUSICAL TALENT SAVED HER LIFE IN A NAZI DEATH CAMP AND WHO BECAME THE WORLD'S OLDEST HOLOCAUST SURVIVOR

FEBRUARY 24, 2014

Amid the glitz and glamour of the Oscar ceremony in Los Angeles next month, there will be a celebration of a life more extraordinary than any created by Hollywood. *The Lady in No 6* has been nominated in the category of best short documentary and its subject is Alice Herz-Sommer, the oldest survivor of the Holocaust.

During the film, Herz-Sommer plays the piano in her one-roomed flat in Belsize Park, North London. She still played every day, spending many hours practising Bach and Beethoven, and it was her consummate gifts as a concert pianist that enabled her to survive two years in the Theresienstadt ghetto, a Nazi concentration camp in Terezín in her homeland of Czechoslovakia.

Herz-Sommer reckoned to have given more than 100 performances at the behest of the Nazis. Music saved her life and that of her son but it could not spare her husband, who was sent to

Dachau and died of typhus in the final days of the war.

Alice Herz was born one of twin sisters in Prague in 1903. Her life came to typify the fate of so many assimilated Central European Jews in the 20th century: she strove to become part of a German cultural world in the final years of the Austro-Hungarian empire; was rejected by the Czechs after the creation of Czechoslovakia; persecuted by the Germans who occupied Prague in 1939; and then shunned and tormented by the Czechs after May 1945. She found refuge only in the new state of Israel, and latterly in retirement in London.

Her father, Friedrich, owned a factory making precision scales and had customers throughout the Austro-Hungarian empire. Her mother Sofie (née Schulz) was from Iglau (Jilava), a former German-speaking pocket south west of Prague. Gustav Mahler came from Iglau, and the Schulz and Mahler families had been acquainted.

In Prague the Herz family belonged to a world of German-speaking Jews that would later achieve world fame through Franz Kafka and Max Brod. Alice knew both men well.

She grew up as an assimilated Jew. There were more than a hundred thousand Jews in the city, and of these a little under half gravitated towards the small, but powerful German community based around the garrison and the university. They tended to be professional and middle-class. Religious observance was limited.

At the age of six Alice began to learn the piano. She would perform duets with her brother Paul, a talented violinist. Her elder sister Irma, also a pianist, introduced her to a teacher who fostered a love of modern Czech music that formed part of her repertoire all her life.

The Herz family was dealt a blow when Austria-Hungary sued for peace in 1918 and Tomas Masaryk called the Czechoslovak Republic into being. Masaryk was himself anxious to make a multi-ethnic Czechoslovakia work, but many Czechs were not keen, and shortly after the end of the war there were riots directed at the Prague Jews.

Herz-Sommer remained firmly implanted in the embattled German world. At 16 she gained a place in the piano master-class at the new German Academy of Music. Her master was Liszt's pupil Conrad Ansorge. She graduated with distinction and she was soon dividing her life between the concert stage and private teaching. Immediately after leaving the Academy in 1924, she made her debut performance with the Czech Philharmonic and from then she gave two or three solo recitals a year. She continued to take lessons and for a while was taught by Eduard Steuermann, but she was unhappy with his teaching as she thought he was interested only in money. She auditioned for Arthur Schnabel in Berlin, who told her he could not teach her anything she did not know already.

In 1931 she married the businessman Leopold Sommer. Their only child, Stephan, was born in 1937. When Hitler's armies marched into

Prague in March 1939 many members of her family left, but Herz-Sommer decided that she could not abandon her mother, and that Stephan was too young to move.

As a Jew, Leopold lost his job and briefly worked in Belgium but when the Nazis occupied Brussels he returned home. Bit by bit everything they valued was taken from them, but they clung on to music, and Alice and her fellow Jewish musicians held illegal concerts in their flats using instruments they had kept hidden from the Nazis.

Leopold worked for the Jewish community organisation and was involved in drawing up the lists of those to be deported to the "model ghetto" of Theresienstadt, north of Prague. One by one the family's friends and relations were deported there or to other camps. Alice's beloved mother, in her seventies, was sent on a "work detail"; after six months in Theresienstadt she was taken to Treblinka where she died.

The Herz-Sommer family were summoned to assemble for transportation on July 5, 1943. At Theresienstadt the Nazis had used the idea of creating a modern ghetto in an 18th century fort to fool the outside world into believing they had no evil intentions towards the Jews. Although the camp was hopelessly overcrowded and lethally unhealthy, it was not the policy to exterminate Jews there. On the other hand there were sickeningly frequent transports towards the ghettos and extermination camps in the east.

As a well-known concert pianist, Herz-Sommer was "protected" from transport while she could put on concerts that would help to maintain the deception. Operas were performed with the blessing of the commandant and a propaganda film was made to show off life inside the walls. Stephan performed in the children's opera *Brundibar* and slept at his mother's side. Years later he recalled: "She did everything to hide the atrocities from me, and to create a kind of normality."

He shared her protection but her husband was shipped off to Auschwitz in September 1944 and from there to Dachau.

Herz-Sommer performed her concert repertoire many times, ending up with her fourth programme: a rendition of the fabulously difficult Chopin Études. Her music gave solace to her fellow prisoners but many of them were sent to Auschwitz as soon as they had outlived their usefulness.

By the beginning of 1945 the camp was half empty. It began to fill up again with "protected" Jews who were married to Aryans. They were followed by half-dead, plague-ridden prisoners who had been evacuated from other camps before the Russian advance. Herz-Sommer stayed in her room but her son fell ill and when the Red Army liberated Theresienstadt, she could not leave. A month passed before she returned to Prague.

She soon learnt that she was not welcome in her home town. The native Germans had already gone: they had been beaten (and often killed), dispossessed and shoved into transit camps awaiting expulsion. For

Jews, the right to reintegration was based on "orientation". If they were "German-orientated" they were liable to expulsion. Herz-Sommer was compelled to lie; she told the civil servant that she had spoken Czech at home, read Czech newspapers and had Czech-speaking friends.

She was allowed to stay but could not move back to her home or retrieve her belongings. Everywhere she encountered flagrant anti-Semitism. She decided to begin a new life in Palestine. At first the Czech authorities would not countenance her taking her newly acquired piano. It was only with the help of Max Brod that the president Klement Gottwald allowed her to ship her concert grand. When she finally took delivery of the piano in Jerusalem, however, she found it had been left out in the rain and the hammers had rusted.

In the newly created state of Israel in 1949 Herz-Sommer found work as a piano teacher at the Jerusalem Conservatory. She had made a decision in Prague not to talk about Theresienstadt and found that this was in keeping with Israeli thinking at the time. It was only with the trial of Adolf Eichmann that the silence was broken. She was allowed to attend the trial. A lifelong optimist, she still found she could not hate the man responsible for the deaths of her husband and mother.

Her son adopted the name of Raphael in Israel and later studied cello, becoming an international virtuoso. In 1986, after her retirement, Herz-Sommer moved to London where her son and his family had settled. Raphael Sommer died suddenly of a heart attack during a concert tour of Israel in 2001. She was 99 and the grief nearly killed her.

In her declining years she liked to receive visitors in the afternoon. To leave herself more time for the important things in life, she had reduced her diet to a daily bowl of chicken soup prepared fresh once a week.

She is survived by her grandsons, David Sommer and Ariel Sommer, and her son Raphael's widow Genevieve. *Alice Herz-Sommer, Holocaust survivor and concert pianist, was born on November 26, 1903. She died on February 23, 2014, aged 110*